Leadership and Management Development

PEARSON

We work with leading authors to develop the strongest educational materials in management, bringing cutting-edge thinking and best learning practice to a global market.

Under a range of well-known imprints, including Financial Times Prentice Hall, we craft high quality print and electronic publications which help readers to understand and apply their content, whether studying or at work.

To find out more about the complete range of our publishing, please visit us on the World Wide Web at:
www.pearsoned.co.uk

Leadership and Management Development

Developing Tomorrow's Managers

Kevin Dalton

Financial Times Prentice Hall
is an imprint of

PEARSON

Harlow, England • London • New York • Boston • San Francisco • Toronto
Sydney • Tokyo • Singapore • Hong Kong • Seoul • Taipei • New Delhi
Cape Town • Madrid • Mexico City • Amsterdam • Munich • Paris • Milan

Pearson Education Limited
Edinburgh Gate
Harlow
Essex CM20 2JE
England

and Associated Companies throughout the world

Visit us on the World Wide Web at:
www.pearsoned.co.uk

First published 2010

© Pearson Education Limited 2010

The right of Kevin Dalton to be identified as author of this work has been asserted by him in accordance with the Copyright, Designs and Patents Act 1988.

All rights reserved. No part of this publication may be reproduced, stored in a retrieval system, or transmitted in any form or by any means, electronic, mechanical, photocopying, recording or otherwise, without either the prior written permission of the publisher or a licence permitting restricted copying in the United Kingdom issued by the Copyright Licensing Agency Ltd, Saffron House, 6–10 Kirby Street, London EC1N 8TS.

Pearson Education is not responsible for the content of third party internet sites.

ISBN: 978-0-273-70470-6

British Library Cataloguing-in-Publication Data
A catalogue record for this book is available from the British Library

Library of Congress Cataloging-in-Publication Data
Dalton, Kevin.
   Leadership and management development : developing tomorrow's managers / Kevin Dalton.
       p. cm.
   Includes bibliographical references and index.
   ISBN 978-0-273-70470-6 (pbk. : alk. paper)   1. Executives—Training of.
2. Career development.   3. Organizational learning.   4. Management.   I. Title.
   HD30.4.D354 2010
   658.4'07124—dc22
                                                                 2010010960

10 9 8 7 6 5 4 3 2 1
13 12 11 10

Typeset in *9/12 Stone Serif* by *73*
Printed by Ashford Colour Press Ltd., Gosport

Contents

Preface	xi
Acknowledgements	xii

1 Introduction to management development — 1

Learning outcomes	1
1.1 Introduction	1
1.2 Definitions	3
1.3 Debates	4
1.4 Taking MD seriously	11
1.5 Overview of the book	11
Review questions	14
Web links	14
DVDs/Videos	14
Recommendations for further reading	14
Bibliography	15

2 Management process, roles, behaviour and skills — 16

Learning outcomes	16
2.1 Introduction	16
2.2 The meaning of management	17
2.3 Is management leadership?	22
2.4 The skills and qualities of the manager	27
2.5 Conclusion	44
Review questions	44
Web links	45
DVDs/Videos	45
Recommendations for further reading	46
Bibliography	46

3 The models and theories of management development — 48

Learning outcomes — 48
3.1 Introduction — 48
3.2 The nature and value of theory in MD — 49
3.3 Typologies of MD — 52
3.4 Systems theory and MD — 56
3.5 Radical pluralistic models — 61
3.6 The emergent paradigm of management learning — 62
3.7 Critical theory and MD — 64
3.8 Conclusion — 67
Review questions — 67
Web links — 68
Recommendations for further reading — 68
Bibliography — 68

4 Strategy and the organisation of MD — 70

Learning outcomes — 70
4.1 Introduction — 70
4.2 MD and strategy — 71
4.3 Theoretical modelling of MD as a strategic link — 72
4.4 Obstacles to strategic management — 74
4.5 Elements of a strategic approach — 79
4.6 Processes in developing MD strategy — 89
4.7 Strategy reconsidered — 95
4.8 The organisation of the MD function — 97
4.9 Conclusion — 102
Review questions — 102
Web links — 102
Recommendations for further reading — 103
Bibliography — 103

5 Assessing development need and development planning — 105

Learning outcomes — 105
5.1 Introduction — 105
5.2 MD as a development system — 106
5.3 Performance management and review — 107
5.4 Competency frameworks — 109
5.5 Appraisal systems — 120
5.6 Assessment of development need — 125
5.7 Personal development plans — 137
5.8 Conclusion — 138
Review questions — 139
Web links — 139
Recommendations for further reading — 140
Bibliography — 140

6 Management learning: individual and collective learning theory — 142

Learning outcomes — 142
6.1 Introduction — 142
6.2 Some general theories of individual learning — 143
6.3 Organisational learning and the learning organisation — 160
6.4 Knowledge management — 166
6.5 The learning organisation — 168
6.6 Conclusion — 175
Review questions — 175
Web links — 176
Recommendations for further reading — 176
Bibliography — 176

7 Informal management learning — 179

Learning outcomes — 179
7.1 Introduction — 179
7.2 The irresistible rise of experiential learning — 180
7.3 Experiential learning: only two cheers? — 182
7.4 The nature of experiential learning — 184
7.5 Conditions of experiential learning — 189
7.6 Self-development — 192
7.7 Methods of experiential learning — 202
7.8 Conclusion — 217
Review questions — 217
Web links — 218
DVDs/Videos — 218
Recommendations for further reading — 218
Bibliography — 219

8 Formal management development: management training — 221

Learning outcomes — 221
8.1 Introduction — 221
8.2 The 'informal' v 'formal' debate — 222
8.3 Patterns of formal management development — 224
8.4 Designing management training — 227
8.5 Management training courses — 233
8.6 Off-the-job MD methods — 241
8.7 Conclusion — 255
Review questions — 255
Web links — 256
Recommendations for further reading — 256
Bibliography — 256

9 Formal management development: management education — 258

Learning outcomes — 258
9.1 Introduction — 258
9.2 Management education: the British case — 260
9.3 Is management a profession? — 264
9.4 An overview of management education — 265
9.5 The Master's in business administration — 269
9.6 Trends in the MBA — 274
9.7 Are business schools doing a good job? — 280
9.8 Prospects for management education in the future — 286
9.9 Conclusion — 291
Review questions — 291
Web links — 292
Recommendations for further reading — 292
Bibliography — 293

10 Management careers, succession and talent management — 295

Learning outcomes — 295
10.1 Introduction — 295
10.2 Trends in management careers — 296
10.3 Career management and development — 302
10.4 Succession planning and management — 315
10.5 Conclusion — 329
Review questions — 330
Web links — 330
DVDs/Videos — 330
Recommendations for further reading — 331
Bibliography — 331

11 Cross-cultural management development — 334

Learning outcomes — 334
11.1 Introduction — 334
11.2 Variations in national management culture — 335
11.3 National systems of management development — 339
11.4 Comparative MD approaches — 360
11.5 Conclusion — 364
Review questions — 365
Web links — 365
Recommendations for further reading — 365
Bibliography — 366

12 International management development — 367

Learning outcomes — 367
12.1 Introduction — 367
12.2 The globalisation of business: modelling the process — 368
12.3 Managers and transnationals — 371
12.4 What makes an international manager? — 373
12.5 Who are the international managers? — 375
12.6 Developing the international manager — 376
12.7 International MD and organisational learning — 388
12.8 Conclusion — 388
Review questions — 389
Web links — 389
DVDs/Videos — 390
Recommendations for further reading — 390
Bibliography — 390

13 Management development and organisational development — 392

Learning outcomes — 392
13.1 Introduction — 392
13.2 The relationship between MD and OD — 393
13.3 The nature of organisational development — 394
13.4 The techniques of OD — 399
13.5 Power, politics and OD — 406
13.6 The skills of the OD practitioner — 407
13.7 A critique of OD and its future — 410
13.8 Conclusion — 413
Review questions — 413
Web links — 414
DVDs/Videos — 414
Recommendations for further reading — 414
Bibliography — 415

14 Evaluating management development — 417

Learning outcomes — 417
14.1 Introduction — 417
14.2 Why evaluation is often not done — 419
14.3 Why evaluate? — 421
14.4 Models and frameworks for evaluating MD — 425
14.5 The special problems of evaluating MD — 431
14.6 Design issues in the evaluation of MD — 434
14.7 Methodology and evaluation in MD — 436

14.8 MD and the politics of evaluation	444
14.9 Conclusion	447
Review questions	447
Web links	448
Recommendations for further reading	448
Bibliography	449

15 The future direction of management and leadership development 451

Learning outcomes	451
15.1 Introduction	451
15.2 The changing nature of management and the context of MD	451
15.3 Leadership and leadership development	462
15.4 The future for management and leadership development	475
15.5 Conclusion	483
Review questions	484
Web links	484
DVDs/Videos	485
Recommendations for further reading	485
Bibliography	486

Index 489

Supporting resources

Visit **www.pearsoned.co.uk/dalton** to find valuable online resources

For instructors
- Complete Instructor's Manual
- PowerPoint slides that can be downloaded and used for presentations

For more information please contact your local Pearson Education sales representative or visit **www.pearsoned.co.uk/dalton**

Preface

Leadership and Management Development aims to describe, analyse and synthesise a wide range of themes from management development, leadership development, organisational development and organisational learning. It attempts to provide a balanced introduction to this broad-ranging and developing field by discussing the key debates, the main schools of thought, the findings of academic research and the stories of organisational experience. Contemporary trends are analysed, including current fashions which are critiqued, but older relevant literature is not ignored where its contribution remains evergreen. While 'leading edge' examples are included from Western and international business there is also an attempt to include examples of managing and development from many parts of the world and from the public and 'not-for-profit' sectors.

This is not a book that offers 'instant solutions' or prescriptions for 'good practices' which are supposed to hold good in all times and places. But neither is it densely academic or theoretical. It does not patronise the reader with over-simplification but neither does it mystify him or her with over-complexity. It is mostly concerned to help managers to reflect, to value their own experience and draw critically on the insights of Social Science in making sense of that experience as part of the never-ending process of becoming a *wise* practitioner in the art of managing.

The book is intended for students in higher educational programmes, professional programmes and managers engaged in their own personal development. As we explain in chapter one, this book is explicitly aligned with the CIPD's latest professional standards and revised syllabus for specialist programmes in management development, human resource development, learning and development, organisational design and development. It will also be of value to other postgraduate students on management courses, including the MBA, where there is a focus on people issues, learning and development and organisational analysis.

Undergraduates in business and management doing specialist modules in HRM, industrial sociology, organisational psychology, learning and development will find much of interest here. So too will managers on corporate development programmes, OD and MD advisors and consultants, those with responsibility for growing their own staff and those thinking managers who take self-development seriously and want to improve their game.

A distinguishing feature of the book is that it deliberately embeds MD within a *social context* and considers MD in terms of organisational behaviour and organisational development. It does this without neglecting the professional learning and individual development aspects. The study features have been specially designed to appeal to quite diverse groups-those who are studying to become managers, those who are in work and aspiring to go into management and those who are established in their management careers. All the questions, case studies and 'pause for thought' exercises, web links, annotated bibliographic notes and DVD/video recommendations are intended to build the psychology of the self–developing, thoughtful manager who understands the practical value of ideas.

Acknowledgements

When I was given the opportunity to write a textbook by Pearson Education I was truly elated, little understanding the amount of time it would take in reading, note taking, organising, drafting, revising, editing and proof reading. Over the years I grew tired of the standard question by friends and colleagues, 'Is the book done yet?' and developed standard formula for replying. However, it has been rewarding to finish such a Herculean task which hopefully contributes something to the study of the area, if only to draw together a lot of disparate material in one place and make some of the existing texts more accessible to students of management, leadership and development. It would not have been completed without the assistance of many people along the way whose help I wish to acknowledge.

Firstly, Charles Handy, John Burgoyne and Alan Mumford. Although I have never met these authors their books provided me with a lifeline when I was unexpectedly made Director of a Management Development Institute in the Seychelles Islands, with no local expert to turn to and, in the tradition of 'stretch assignments', had to learn MD whilst doing it. Then, in terms of intellectual debt, I should mention Jean Woodall whose work guided me long before she became the Dean of the Business School where I now teach. I would also like to thank, very warmly, other luminaries in the MD field who have personally supported and encouraged me at various stages in my career. John Hunt, David Sims and the late Iain Mangham all helped me to cultivate the 'ways of seeing' of a developer long before I had defined myself in these terms. The writings of all these people are liberally referenced throughout this text.

I must mention too the people who gave me a chance to become professionally established, not least the many politicians, officials, managers and international consultants, members of the Seychelles Long Term Vision Task Group and the international cast at the Seychelles Institute of MD, with whom I worked. Thanks also to Zoe Van Zwanenberg, Annette Monaghan and the other OD consultants at the Strategic Change Unit, NHS Scottish Executive for helping an academic become more practitioner-oriented.

At Westminster Business School, I would like to mention my boss, Christine Porter, and colleagues, Robin Theobald, Alex Weich and John Bowden for giving me constructive feedback on earlier versions of the text. Also Sue Miller, Carol Wood, Keith Porter, Liz Kennedy and David Simmonds, all well known professionals in the Learning and Development field, for giving peer support, colleague advice and friendly encouragement to persist when the going seemed tough.

Thanks too for some of my former students, not least Tim Morrell and Azeema Pardiwalla for reviewing and commenting on earlier drafts. I am also grateful to the staff and management of various cafes, coffee shops, restaurants and bars in the Orpington, Petts Wood and Bromley areas to which I often retreated when my office was too noisy or my study seemed too oppressive. Gerry Boyle, Steve, Lynne and the others who knew I was writing a book and have long tolerated the shadowy presence of an informal 'writer in residence' who made a single drink last a long time.

However, my main thanks goes to my friends and family. My former girlfriend, Wan Huei, inspired me to write a textbook in the first place as a way of making sense of the 'stuff' I was teaching and feel more ownership of it. This was a wise challenge which I commend to any teacher or practitioner. Other friends, Tina and Louise, also gave their quiet support. But it is to my family that I owe most. My mother, Patricia, stepfather, Chas, and sister, Lynne gave me the continuous unconditional emotional encouragement during the long and difficult journey this book has proven to be, and my debt of gratitude to them can never be repaid.

Finally, of course, acknowledgments to my patient publisher, Pearson Education and the various editors I have worked with, who showed commendable tolerance in allowing this Odyssey to run its course. I hope the final result repays their patience.

Publisher's acknowledgements

We are grateful to the following for permission to reproduce copyright material:

Figures

Figure 3.1 from Organisational transformation and renewal, *Personnel Review*, Vol 24, No 6 (Doyle, M. 1995); Figure 3.2 from *Journal of Management Development*, Vol 19, No 7 (Doyle, M. 2000); Figure 3.3 from *Changing Patterns of Management Development*, Blackwell (Thomson, A., Mabey, C., Storey, J. et al 2001); Figures 4.2 and 14.1 adapted from *Employee Development Practice*, Pearson Education (Stewart, J. 1999); Figure 4.3 adapted from A unified management development programme, *Journal of Management Development*, Vol 6 No 1 (Hitt, W. 1987); Figure 6.2 adapted from *Experiential Learning*, Pearson Education (Kolb, D. 1984), Prentice Hall, KOLB, DAVID A., EXPERIENTIAL LEARNING: EXPERIENCE AS A SOURCE OF LEARNING & DEVELOPMENT, 1st, ©1984. Electronically reproduced by permission of Pearson Education, Inc., Upper Saddle River, New Jersey.; Figure 6.3 adapted from *The Organisational Learning Cycle*, McGraw Hill (Dixon, N. 1994); Figure 6.4 adapted from *The Learning Company*, McGraw Hill (Pedlar, M. and Burgoyne, J. et al 1991), Reproduced with the kind permission of The McGraw-Hill Companies. All rights reserved; Figure 10.1 from *Management Development: Strategy and Practice*, Routledge (Woodall, J. and Winstanley, D. 1999) p. 10; Figure 14.2 from The EFQM Excellence Model, European Foundation for Quality Management, 1999.

Tables

Table 2.1 from Political Management: developing the management portfolio, *Journal of Management Development*, Vol 9 No 3, p. 42–59 (Baddeley, S and James, K 1990); Table 8.1 adapted from Learning in Management Education, *Journal of European Training*, Vol. 3 no. 3 (Pedlar, M. 1974); Table 8.2 adapted from *Facilitation Skills*, CIPD (Bee, F. and Bee, R. 1999)

Text

Article on page 328 from Talent Management: Make sure the cream rises to the top, *Financial Times*, 18/10/2004 (Donkin, R.), Financial Times, 18 October 2004 (Donkin, R.); Article on page 387 adapted from Cross Cultural training: Learning to make the most of increasing internationalism, *Financial Times*, 11/05/2005 (Murray, S.), Financial Times, 11 May 2005 (Murray, S.); Article on page 458 adapted from People skills still rule in the virtual company, *Financial Times*, 26/08/2005 (Conger, J. and Lawler, J.), Financial Times, 26 Aug 2005; Article on page 481 adapted from Risky lessons from judo and fast cars, *Financial Times*, 11/08/2003 (Murray, S.), Financial times, 11 August 2003 (Murray, S.); Activity on page 136 adapted from Appointments: patterns can show if you are up to the job, *Financial Times*, 29/01/2004 (Donkin, R.), Financial Times, Jan 29 2004 (Donkin, R.) Box on page 251 from *Six Thinking Hats™*, The McQuaig Group (de Bono, E. 1986).

The Financial Times

Article on page 350 adapted from Teaching Shop Floor Principles to the Executive Suite, *Financial Times*, 13/08/2002 (Witzel, M.); Article on page 380 adapted from GE's corporate boot camp cum talent spotting venue, *Financial Times*, 20/03/2006 (Knight, R.); Article on page 252 adapted from I will never again pour cold water on corporate firewalking, *Financial Times*, 17/03/2006 (Sathnam, S.); Article on page 273 adapted from From chaos comes order and composure, *Financial Times*, 30/05/2005 (Huang, L.); Article on page 279 adapted from FT Report: Business Education: An ever more exclusive degree, *Financial Times*, 9/09/2002 (Matthews, V.); Article on page 285 adapted from Building the Global Corporate University, *Financial Times*, 5/09/2002 (Dzinkowski, R), Financial Times, 5 September 2002 (Dzinkowski, R)

In some instances we have been unable to trace the owners of copyright material, and we would appreciate any information that would enable us to do so.

1 Introduction to management development

Learning outcomes

After studying the chapter you should be able to understand, analyse and explain:
- the management development process as a whole;
- the contested definitions of MD;
- the key debates in management development;
- emergent themes and concerns within the field of MD;
- the nature and form of this book.

1.1 Introduction

This is deliberately a short chapter, a set of signposts and a laying-out of agendas for the rest of the book.

There is a growing awareness that the managerial role has become essential to business success. Organisations are run by managers striving to meet strategic goals, so their quality is increasingly recognised as vital to the performance of the organisation. Not only are managers now seen as a critical resource for unlocking the potential of an organisation but also more is expected of them. Modern business conditions mean that they have to be more strategic, more entrepreneurial, more innovative and more change-centred. This realisation is leading organisations to look more carefully at their management cohorts – their numbers, their deployment and also how they might be helped to learn effectively.

Although old attitudes die hard, there is now a broad consensus that managers are neither born nor made but 'grow' themselves if the organisation provides a nurturing climate. There is also an emerging appreciation that management development is fundamental to organisational renewal and the management of change – key driving forces for any organisation seeking to survive in the white-water conditions of modern business. These concerns merge with new-wave humanistic issues such as lifelong learning, the learning organisation, knowledge management, creativity and empowerment, to provide an arena in which MD can establish itself as a core business process and a stimulus to continuous professional growth.

Indeed, as organisations begin to realise that MD can be a key process for organisational change and the achievement of business strategy, it is becoming a major growth industry. About thirty years ago there were perhaps just half a dozen business schools in Britain; now there are more than a hundred. Other university departments are jumping on the bandwagon, all the big accountancy firms have management and leadership development arms and so do most sizeable companies (many have corporate universities) and there are innumerable small 'boutique' consultancies specialising in instant management improvement (Beardwell and Holden 2001). Management and leadership development is big business and getting bigger.

However, despite this surge of interest in MD as a vehicle for delivering the skills and knowledge needed for the new managerial agenda and as a transformative tool, there are many criticisms of its effectiveness. As John Burgoyne (Pickard 2001), one of the gurus in the field, likes to say:

> There is no human endeavour to which MD has not been applied. So, we have walking on hot coals, role plays, business, outdoor adventure and even the pruning of bonsai trees presented as ways of building the manager of the future.

However, the startling point about all this activity is that there is no certainty that any of it works. As we will see, very often MD is the focus for management fads and fashions, impression management, political games and the posturing of sectional interests. There is also the issue that the tendency of organisations to view MD as a set of discrete and isolated learning events can mean that it becomes uncoupled from the strategic development of the organisation and therefore risks accusations of 'marginality'. How can we make MD strategically aligned, politically and culturally aware and appropriate to ordinary managers by providing evidence-based, evaluated approaches that are known to work?

Creativity or charlatanism?

Below are some of the more unusual techniques used by developers to stimulate their learners to think about managing and leading.

- As a problem-solving exercise, a group of managers are asked to use Japanese haiku, a form of simple, cryptic poetry, to open up their awareness of self and language as a means of conveying and receiving meaning (Fee 2001).
- As an exercise in leadership and team working, managers are brought into a darkened warehouse that is internally configured into a sort of maze. Managers have to link up and then work as a team to capture a large python somewhere in the labyrinth.

- As an exercise in communication and interpersonal sensitivity, managers are shown a videotaped scene from a soap opera with the sound turned down. Managers are asked to script it, based on their observations of the action and actors' body language, gestures, expressions, etc. (Fee 2001).
- As the 'experiential' element of an innovative MBA, students choose projects from which they grow as people. Examples include membership of a climbing party scaling Mont Blanc; spending six weeks as a novice monk in a remote monastery; running a soup kitchen for the homeless (Aspen 1994).
- Samba drumming is used on some senior management courses to teach leadership qualities e.g.: learning through doing, learning on your feet, learning from mistakes, using others as a learning resource.
- Japanese managers on a development course do a period of guided reflection at a mountain retreat to learn the precise art of tea making and observing the movement of carp in a pond. Part of a course to develop aesthetic sensibilities for business (Matsushita Corporation).

When considering MD and the forms it takes, it is important to resist cynicism. That is the easy, knee-jerk reaction, but it is useful to defer judgement; after all, difficult things are being attempted here – helping people to become persuasive with others, to think creatively and act with judgement – among many other qualities of managing and leading which we still do not fully understand, let alone know how to inculcate.

1.2 Definitions

But there might be a danger here of jumping too far ahead. Perhaps we first need to map the terrain and then define the boundaries of MD. MD is a broad-ranging field. It is also a new field. Despite the recent enthusiasm for MD, it is actually a neglected subject. Of the many books published each year on management only a few directly engage with this subject. As Fee (2001) suggests:

> Many, perhaps most, business thinkers see MD as a sub-set of HRD, itself a sub-set of HRM, which in turn is often seen as a support function, peripheral to the core disciplines of business.

This is a strange paradox: as we have said, managers are vital to business success, yet only recently has MD been recognised as a key tool for developing their potential and it is still establishing itself as a driving force in business strategy. As a discipline, MD is still defining its scope, refining its core concepts and setting out its stall. However, in the ambiguity and emergence of a 'frontier subject' also lies vibrancy and excitement. It means that the ideas and experiences of reflective managers, and that includes students of management like many of you reading this, can contribute to new thinking about professional practice and its application.

In a field which is still evolving there is much room for controversy about purpose and process. Some of this is apparent from the jarring descriptions of the nature of MD offered by academics and practitioners.

Molander (1986) says that MD is

> A conscious and systematic decision-action process to control the development of managerial resources in the organisation for the achievement of organisational goals and strategies.

Mumford (1987) agreed:

> Management Development is an attempt to improve managerial effectiveness through a planned and deliberate learning process.

However, Mumford (1997) later changed his mind to the belief that

> Management Development is a continuous, ever-changing process where managers often learn through informal, unplanned experience.

You will probably notice here the subtle shift from a formalised process to a 'total learning process' which admits the value of informal processes by which managers grow and improve their abilities to perform ever more complex managerial tasks. This is consistent with other recent definitions of MD, for example, Lees (1992):

> MD is a term which embraces much more than simple education or training. It is the entire system of corporate activities with the espoused goal of improving the performance of the managerial stock in the context of organisational and environmental change.

And to bring the story up to date, Espedal (2005):

> We may define appropriate MD as a dynamic capability through which the organisation systematically generates and modifies its processes for efficiency and effectiveness.

What emerges is that MD must be one of the most notoriously ill-defined and variously interpreted concepts in management. Until recently the thrust seems to have been towards organisational processes and satisfying corporate needs; only in recent times do we hear much about the learning of individuals and groups. The latest turn is towards helping the learning of both individual *and* organisation.

Overall, the trend seems to be towards more generic definitions of the scope of MD, to incorporate highly structured processes like forecasting skill needs at one end and highly unstructured processes like self-managed learning on the other, and to be increasingly aligned to the effective development of the individual as well as the organisation. However, as we will see, whatever the thinkers may claim, this is not always how MD is seen or practised 'on the ground'.

1.3 Debates

As these quotes indicate, there is no single and agreed definition of what MD is or how it should be practised. In fact, these perspectives suggest that MD is riven with many contrasts and contradictions. The lack of a consensus about this area gives rise to many debates.

At the *micro-level,* MD is often concerned to improve the performance and potential of individual managers, to identify learning gaps and help to prepare them for future responsibilities. In particular, MD is sometimes used to help managers to adapt to downsizing and delayering and to find ways of coping with a widened and more complex role as the traditional career ladders disappear. MD enables managers to acquire the right competencies to survive in a changing environment. At this level Harrison (2001) suggests that 'management development' is really 'manager development', that is, developing the qualities needed to manage self and others.

However, taking a *macro-view,* some would say that MD must go beyond individual learning and development. It should also be a vehicle for change. So Lippitt (1982) talks of MD as a means for organisational renewal, for engaging people in continuous collective learning. At its most sophisticated, MD can act as a means of building common management culture across the whole management group based on shared values and a consistent management style. Margerison (1991) believes it is a process by which an organisation maintains its vigour, creates a competitive edge and properly harnesses its talent. This leads on naturally to the implementation of larger approaches to MD such as strategic management, OD (organisational development) and the Learning Organisation.

Another debate is about *where MD should be located intellectually*. We will examine this a little later, but it is important to register here that MD straddles two very different historical traditions. MD can trace its roots as an instrumental, work-oriented, performance-driven management practice. This logic subsumes MD within HRD and training and development. This is a functionalist, means–ends definition of the subject area which owes much to 'scientific management', skills analysis and development. However, an alternative perspective is to see MD as a much wider, holistic, subject which is multidisciplinary and humanistic in character. By this definition, MD is ultimately about developing the whole person not just particular competencies. It attempts to build human potential, especially as this relates to leadership, as part of a wider learning process which involves developing the manager by developing the culture of the organisation of which s/he is a part.

These intellectual forces coexist uneasily within MD, creating cleavages of philosophy, vocabulary and practice which are a long way from being reconciled.

Then there are the *clashing agendas* which form around MD programmes. Some elements of the organisation will be mainly concerned that the group of employees who most 'add value' (the managers) have the skills and experience available to meet the organisation's overall objectives. Stocktaking of existing strengths and weaknesses among the existing group of managers and deciding how they can be developed to help corporate issues, e.g. quality, cost and profitability, is central to a strategic conception of MD. However, managers themselves have their expectations. They may be concerned that MD addresses personal development needs, giving them marketable skill, useful knowledge and support to fulfilling their career aspirations.

A further axis of debate is between those who believe that MD should be mainly concerned with *planned, formalised developments* (e.g. courses, secondments, special postings and projects) and those who believe that the 'best' MD is really more *informal, experiential and processual* (as the second of the quotations from Mumford above suggests). We will consider this issue further later on. However, it is useful to note here that the design of MD has often been very systematic, that is, in institutionalised blocks of instruction to 'teach' managers their roles and functional skills in an orderly fashion. The 'new turn' is to work-based experiential learning in which management is seen as a complex web of social and political interaction and managers are encouraged to learn through doing, reflecting and trying again.

In reality a well-designed and focused MD programme will probably provide a blend of both formal and informal processes, 'on and off' the job interventions, skills, behavioural and cognitive development. However, the crucial judgement for those tasked with difficult design decisions will be how to find the most 'appropriate' balancing point in existing circumstances.

Then there is the age-old debate of whether *MD represents a universalistic set of principles or has to be contextualised* within the local culture to be helpful to local managers. Traditional, often Western, concepts of management define it as technocratic and value-neutral, a set of 'truths' universally and timelessly appropriate to all places at all times. This creates a 'one size fits all' approach to developing managers (what works to develop managers at an American business school should work in an Indian factory) and implies a prescriptive approach to doing management which has come under attack in recent years. Cultural relativism in the design of management learning is a growing force and set fair to become the new spirit of the age.

Another cleavage is the tension between two forces inherent in MD, that is, its potential to promote *diversity, creativity and individual difference* and its equal and opposed potential to build *common corporate values and culture*. One view is that MD is about encouraging managers to be independent thinkers, to be critical, sceptical, conceptual and creative, providing an education for the 'movers and shakers' of corporate society. But perhaps it is also about building common attitudes and behaviours? If the latter, then the emphasis will be less on reflective self learning and experimentation, more on understanding the 'company way' and finding ways to express this in everyday organisational behaviour.

Then there is the very modern debate about *leadership*. Is this yesterday's debate about how to develop better managers for corporate responsibility with new nomenclature or does the 'new economy' really require a different skill set for which the instruments of MD are inadequate? This is one of the key themes of this book.

Finally, there is controversy and ambiguity around the *sub-processes which make up the larger field of management development*. Here a number of definitions of these sub-processes are offered. These will be further clarified as the book develops.

Historically, *management education (Med)* has been described as those techniques concerned to improve the learning and knowledge of managers. Med has always been about the 'professionalisation' of management, giving managers expertise, abstract knowledge and techniques to conduct their work more effectively. Typically, the content has been technical, functional and academic, helping managers to improve their understanding of the organisational/professional world which they occupy. However, increasingly it is about helping managers to think independently and critically and to conceptualise the lessons of personal experience.

Management training (MT) is a little different. It is more specific and short-term, concerned with teaching managers the skills they need to perform their jobs more effectively, for example, short courses and seminars in specific subjects such as financial planning, communications, HRM, decision-making and so on. Training tends to be technocratic–pragmatic, problem-solving, vocational and skills-based rather than conceptual/theoretical.

Management learning (ML) is at the very heart of MD, that is, experiential learning and self-reflection supported by coaching, mentoring, learning sets, reflective feedback to help the manager develop the 'whole person' (not just some particular skills) and become a master of the 'craft' of managing (or leading). Fox (1997) makes the useful distinction between 'knowing what' and 'knowing why' which can come from management training and management education, as opposed to 'knowing how' which comes only from reflective understanding or 'management learning'. How management learning intersects with the other categories – whether ML is just another 'field' or subsumes the others (Med, MT and even MD) is one of those vexed questions which will resonate throughout the book.

Leadership development (LD) is another problematical piece on the board. As the search for good managers turns into the search for good leaders, a 'Pandora's box' of new questions emerges about the real differences between managing and leading and whether the issues are those of semantics or are substantive. If real, are managers and leaders on a continuum and can be developed in similar ways or are they separate groups with different learning needs?

Career development (CD) is concerned with the question of who 'owns' a manager's career: the organisation or the individual? How can talent management, succession planning and career management be reconciled with the preferences and aspirations of individual managers?

Organisational development (OD) is concerned with the improvement of organisational structures, culture and systems to help the achievement of organisational objectives. Often OD is led by action research, focuses particularly on team-based solutions to problems and is led by models in the management of change. It is also increasingly involved with *Organisational learning (OL)*.

Inevitably the boundaries between these sub-processes are quite fluid. For example, a manager may take a part-time MBA at a university (*management education*) which will also require a lot of project work in learning sets (*management learning*) and learning specific skills (*management training*). This will be linked to improving practices within the organisation (*organisational development/organisational learning*) and the development of self-awareness as an effective manager (*self-development and career development*). Some of the work requires strategy, envisioning and persuading people (*leadership development*).

Of course, this silly analogy hardly does justice to the subtle issues involved but it does make the point that, in the end, MD is really a total process, a confluence of varied strands of development at different levels of generality. Each interlinks with the others and, where the system is strategically organised and directed, each part is mutually reinforcing in support of personal and organisational goals.

All the shiny pieces: how are the elements of MD connected?

Figure 1.1 on the next page represents the author's view of the relationship between the categories considered above and in terms of shaping a community of managers and an individual manager.

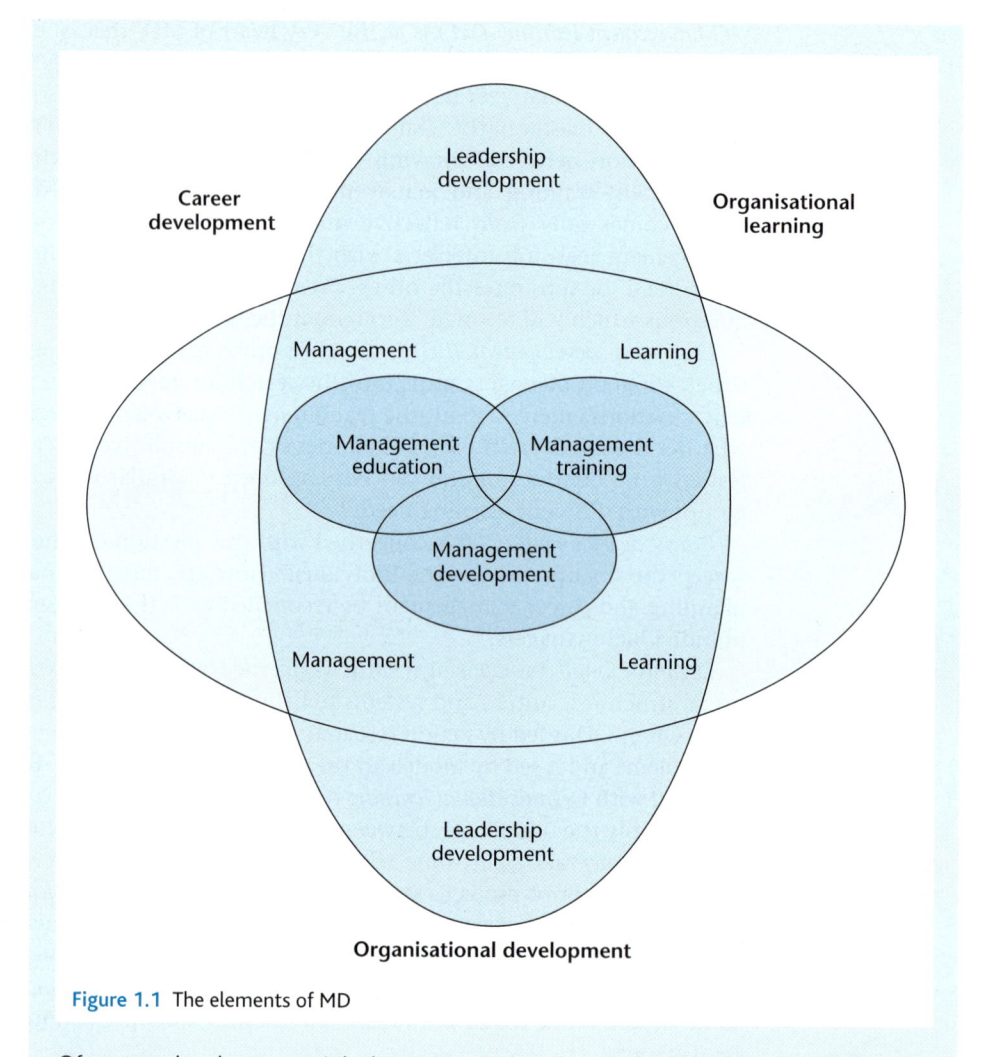

Figure 1.1 The elements of MD

Diagram shows overlapping ellipses labeled: Career development, Leadership development, Organisational learning, Organisational development, with inner regions labeled Management, Learning, Management education, Management training, and Management development.

Of course, the elements might be rearranged, with equal justification, into a different pattern.

Questions
Why not have a go at arranging the elements into a pattern which makes intuitive sense to you now. When you have finished reading the book why not try arranging the elements again. Is the pattern different?

We will be returning to all of these debates as the book progresses.

Do you trust the organisation with your development?

In many organisations development is something 'done to' people because it is seen as good for them or good for the organisation as a whole.

> This is a personal experience. Sitting in a room in the Regional Health Authority, as a twenty-one-year-old trainee manager back in the 1980s, I was waiting for the Regional Training Director who would tell me where I would be despatched next as part of the rotation training programme to develop my basic management skills.
>
> A big, ruddy-faced man put his head round the door and asked me where some meeting was to take place. 'Oh I must have the wrong room', he exclaimed. He then asked me what I was doing there and what meeting I was early for. I replied that I was on the management training scheme, waiting to be told how I was to be further developed.
>
> > Ho, ho, stuff and nonsense, develop yourself, young man! Be your own developer, matey. Remember, despite all that planned development guff, no one else really cares about your career apart from you, and to the system you are just an interchangeable part . . . But perhaps I'm just an old cynic. Best of luck.
>
> I never saw him again but I never forgot his words.
>
> ### Questions
> *What do you think of this advice? Do you think there are inevitable tensions between the views of the organisation on how you should be developed and your own views about what you need?*

These paradoxes are the first taste of debates which will echo throughout the book. What surely emerges is that MD is not easily defined even by those who practise in the area. Talbot (1997) believes this is because 'MD combines a disputed process (development) with a contested object of the process (management)'. The ambiguity of these terms guarantees that MD will always be blurred and a little vague in focus and be interpreted in different ways by different people. Its proper realm of concern will always be contested. While some will place emphasis on discrete activities, specific skills and formalised processes, others will define MD as a more informal force for personal growth and contextualise it within a wider social, political and cultural context.

At the moment, definitions of MD as broad and generic, rather than technocratic and particular, are gaining ground. Some place MD within the context of multiple streams of learning (personal, experiential, situated, formal, organisational learning) coming together to bring forth 'step change' (Fox 1997). Others, like Thomson et al. (2001) Mabey and Finch-Lees (2008) and Storey (1989), see MD as a multifaceted system of corporate and individual activities (holistic, systematic and integrated) to improve organisational performance as a whole. Burgoyne (1988) echoes this by suggesting that MD is a meeting point between two key spheres of activity, that is, structural activity (succession planning, appraisal systems, etc.) and developmental activity (mentoring, self-development, etc.) mediated by MD policy which harmonises these strands into corporate strategy. Finally, in what may be arguably the most radical perspective, cultural theorists such as Brown (1998) suggest that MD is ultimately about disseminating values, symbols and meanings within the culture. MD is part of the learning processes which help managers with their sense-making of how the organisation goes and with building a shared culture of learning.

These definitions are encouraging for anyone who hopes that MD will play a more ambitious role linked to emergent forces such as lifelong learning, the learning organisation and knowledge management, acting as a central discipline within organisational development and strategic management, but the future role of management development (or is that leadership development?) is currently uncertain.

Glancing backwards and peering forwards

Historically, it is interesting to note that MD was largely concerned with individual manager development until the 1980s. There was little development for top managers (who were largely assumed to not need further developing), personal development was given quite low priority and there was little linkage between development and organisational objectives. During the 1980s, MD took off as a practical activity. There was far more development for the top of an increasingly sophisticated kind; development came to be seen as continuous professional development; development became planned and focused and integrated into corporate planning. The coverage of MD expanded from its original focus on training and development to strategic and organisational development. This brings us to the present phase which might be dated from the early 1990s in which the following themes seem apparent.

- *MD is increasingly aligned to corporate strategy* – this involves the positioning of management learning as a strategic force, integrating learning with performance and innovation.
- *MD is increasingly seen as a tool for achieving the strategic concerns of the organisation* – building management capability for cost reduction, quality improvement, productivity and profitability.
- *MD as self-development* – managers are increasingly seen as taking responsibility for their own learning. The individual drives his or her own personal development agenda but within a supportive MD framework.
- *MD is increasingly about building the 'whole person' and not just specific skills or behaviours* – orientation, social and emotional skills and 'character' are the focus of development.
- *MD is increasingly about building the 'psychological contract' at work* – helping managers with identity and commitment issues at a time of constant restructuring and changing employment expectations.
- *MD extends into team learning* – the new emphasis on the workplace team/ management decision-making means that team building is now an important element in MD.
- *MD is turning into leadership development* – this goes beyond executive development to engage wider circles of people many of whom are not managers; MD/LD can act as a form of empowerment.
- *MD incorporates OD* – increasingly MD blends into OD as MD practitioners are becoming drawn on as change consultants to change beliefs, attitudes, values within management and the wider organisation.

- *MD is increasingly concerned with organisational learning* – MD seems to be taking on a leading role as facilitator of the organisation's learning climate and an architect of knowledge management as strategic learning.

These and other trends in MD promise to change the landscape of MD and transform it as a professional practice. We will examine all of these elements and others in detail at different points in the book. In the final chapter there is an attempt to link emergent themes with developments in management and the role of the manager and leader and attempt some predictions for the future.

1.4 Taking MD seriously

These are significant themes and trends of concern to any organisation. Indeed, they will increasingly become vital in determining whether the organisation survives or not. The case for taking MD seriously, becoming aware of its concepts ideas, knowledge base and controversies seems to write itself, at least for this author. Whether you are a young management student or a seasoned veteran of management, the questions in MD claim your attention.

For example, how can we identify and develop 'managers' and 'leaders' in the future? Are we clear about the differences between them or are they more rhetorical than real? How can we define the capabilities we want from these powerful groups within the organisation? How can we assess the capabilities of our existing cadre of managerial leaders against benchmarks and criteria for competencies in facing the inevitably more challenging times to come? How should we use our precious resources for development? Cultivating leadership talent is difficult and takes a long time; the outcome is always uncertain. There are costs to individuals as well as organisations, so how do we know if an investment in an expensive corporate programme or facilitated self-development is likely to give the better return?

But it is not just the business aspects of MD that command attention. MD is a vehicle for giving people a hand up in career terms, conferring identities and socialising people in their role and their organisational culture. MD transmits messages, sets the terms by which agendas are prosecuted, ideologies are promulgated, ethical positions are either taken or undermined. This book is concerned with the social and behavioural aspects of management and leadership quite as much as with institutional processes, with the individual experience of the manager wrestling with career dilemmas as with the organisation developing its succession plan.

1.5 Overview of the book

As we have suggested, MD is a relatively new discipline searching for direction. This book hopes to make a modest contribution to setting its compass points. It seeks to provide an overview of existing theory, research, practice and experience within MD and relate this to contemporary themes and trends in this area.

Despite some excellent recent books on MD, there seems to be a gap for a book which provides an introduction to the field, that is easy to read, tries to be clearly presented and evocative, yet analytical in blending theory with contemporary issues in the 'doing of management' and its development. Most of all, there seems to be a need for an introductory book which provides a genuine starting point for study for the aware but inexperienced HR practitioner and the young, but inquiring and ambitious manager.

Whether this is that book only time will tell, but it certainly sets out to be introductory without being elementary, or 'simplistic' or 'dumbing down'. Some chapters place real demands on the reader who is new to the field and the temptation to reduce to 'bullet points' has been largely resisted. This is certainly not a primer or a 'how to do it in 10 easy lessons'. However, it also steers away from being too densely theoretical and conceptually daunting.

This is a 'middle way' book. It aims to balance academic knowledge and practitioner application. It celebrates ideas, concepts and evidence-based research (often summarising and critically reviewing this work) because these are tools for diagnosis and considered action by the 'reflective practitioner' (who is assumed to be the reader of this book). However, it also tries to be of practical help to managers or people aspiring to become managers with an orientation to principles of professional practice, critique of that practice and real examples from real organisations.

An important feature of the book is that it sets MD within a broader frame than the professional discipline of 'learning and development'. We see MD as more than just a subset of HRD; it is located within the much broader context of interpretive social science, for example, social psychology, organisational behaviour, culture and language. In particular, MD is seen as part of the larger sphere of organisational development (i.e. social processes, leadership, organisational design, change and learning) which may be the future of the discipline. This means that the references, case studies and stories are drawn from a wider field than in other texts. An interwoven theme here is that 'managing', 'leading' and 'developing' are very human experiences, happening all the time, and require many of the political, social, interpretive and interactive skills which we take for granted and use in many aspects of our lives.

Another feature of the book, which hopefully sets it apart a little, is that it does not attempt to offer simple definitions or ready solutions to the issues within MD. While current best practice is described, the text is careful to emphasise that there are no statements about management or development which apply universally and no magical 'touchstone' of success. Instead, the reader is encouraged to develop an attitude of 'reflective sensitivity' to arguments, evidence and rhetoric, not least to the form which ideas are presented in this text.

In terms of scope, this book has been designed to meet the needs of a range of readers – full-time postgraduate students, practitioner students who are studying at Master's level in HRM or general management and business (e.g. a Master's in management or MBA) but also final-year undergraduates who are studying business with a bias to HRM and organisational behaviour. It is completely aligned with the CIPD national professional standards for MD as a subject for study and is entirely consistent with the CIPD's new emphasis on OD and change management in its revised curriculum.

The 15 chapters also cover the main features of the curricula for MD on Master's and professional courses on programmes in many parts of the world (including corporate programmes). While this will inevitably be defined as a 'student text', there is much in it that will be of interest to practitioners, even those with considerable experience.

The framework chosen to represent the field follows a logical schema. Management development is introduced as an area of study, theory and practice in Chapter 1. The nature of managing and leading (and the conceptual distinctions between these approaches) is then discussed in Chapter 2 with the emphasis on individual experience. The theoretical background of the subject is discussed in Chapter 3. Then the focus broadens to take in the strategic dimensions of the subject and the organisational definitions of MD (Chapter 4). The development planning cycle, at the nucleus of the institutional processes of MD, is considered in Chapter 5 and forms the lynchpin between strategy, development, career planning and evaluation which form subsequent chapters. Chapter 6 looks at theories of learning and development and their relevance to development design. The next Chapters (7, 8, 9) form a critical appraisal of forms of development concentrating particularly on the dynamic tension between formal and informal methods of development. Later chapters are concerned with the international aspects of MD (Chapters 11 and 12), and point up the cultural relativity of all forms of MD. Chapter 13 considers the increasingly important themes of organisational learning and development (Chapter 13). Chapter 14 looks at the considerable methodological problems of evaluating something as nebulous as MD. The book ends with a stocktaking of management trends and attempts some 'futurology', by anticipating future trends and prospects for MD with the rise of 'leadership' as the dominant concept in the field (Chapter 15).

Perhaps a note about pedagogy is in order. The book does not flinch from theory because it does not recognise a neat division between theory and practice. Both are needed. Theory is presented with illustrative insights and stories where the material lends itself to this. Throughout, the style is hopefully critical and discursive and prescriptive writing is avoided, although on occasions a strong steer is given on approaches and practices where there is a large measure of professional consensus at the point of writing.

The text makes use of various pedagogical features such as reflective boxes, review and discussion questions, anecdotes, case studies, annotated reading, even references to popular and documentary film, to hopefully engage students with the text, encourage further reading and help them make links to their own organisational experience.

Finally, a cross-cultural point. Those students who come to this subject from outside Europe and the USA will probably notice that most of the models, theories and discussions of management practice are very oriented to Western behaviour. This ethnocentrism represents the balance in the literature of this young subject at this particular point in history. Most of the thinking has been done by Westerners (especially Anglo-Americans) about Western experience and this raises questions about the relevance of much of this corpus of knowledge to those who are from the rest of the world. More generally, it raises the question of whether MD offers universal principles of learning practice or whether learning to be a manager is always a culturalised, contextualised experience.

We return to these conceptual questions in Chapter 11. On the more practical issue of cross-cultural relevance, this book makes an attempt to counterbalance the inherent ethnocentrism with examples that are not Anglo-American and references other cultural experience where material is available. In future, as world economic forces realign, it is likely that research on managers outside the West will increasingly redress the imbalance of evidence that currently exists. This is good news for readers from outside the Western mainstream; there is much virgin soil to be upturned here and writing up your managerial experience for publication will add to the knowledge base and sophistication of this emergent and increasingly important subject.

Review questions

1. Do you think that tensions between the needs of the individual and the needs of the organisation are inevitable in the design of any MD system?

2. Kenneth Fee (2001) thinks that MD is in the same 'Cinderella' situation as marketing was before 'Philip Kotler made the case for it to become a central discipline of business, bringing it out from under the shadow of the sales function. MD lacks coherence as a discipline, a compelling message and strong champions'. Do you agree with him? Discuss.

3. How far would you agree that the central dilemma for MD is that the things that cannot be taught in a rigorous way to managers are precisely those things they most need to know?

Web links

The Academy of Management (AOM) fosters a thinking approach to managing and leading. Try its website:
http://www.aomonline.org/

The European Foundation for Management Development (EFMD) is also well known for its thinking about the future of MD as a discipline. Its website is:
http://www.efmd.be

Or try:
http://www.efmd.org/html/home.asp

DVDs/Videos

The Brittas Empire (TV series in the 1980s/90s) ITV
A satirical look at management, its obsessions, fads and fantasies. The focus is particularly on Mr Brittas, a manager who has been on the courses, knows the words but not the music.

The Devil Wears Prada (2002) Director Wendy Finerman; starring Meryl Streep, Ann Hathaway
An interesting psychological portrait of a boss who definitely needs some management development.

Recommendations for further reading

Those texts marked with an asterisk in the bibliography are recommended for further reading, especially the books below.

There are a number of good textbooks in the field that have helped bring this author into the field of study and have been heavily cited in the text. They may be the best entry point, along with this book, to survey the field as a whole.

Burgoyne, J. and Reynolds, M. (1997) *Management Learning: Integrating Perspectives in Theory and Practice.* A collection of papers by some of the most insightful writers in the field. Some contributions are pitched at quite a high conceptual level but they repay the effort involved in seeking to understand them.

Mabey, C. and Finch-Lees, T. (2008) *Management and Leadership Development.* A radically different book, only recently published, which challenges many of the assumptions within this field. Philosophical and theoretical, it is heavy going for the newcomer but will probably be seen as a 'path breaking' book in the years to come.

Mumford, A. (1989) *Management Development: Strategies in Action* Mumford's classic work which was very influential. Although aimed at the higher level practitioner, it is full of excellent insights for anyone interested in MD. A landmark book.

Mumford, A. and Gold, J. (2004) *Management Development: Strategies for Action.* A dramatic reworking of the earlier book by Mumford to make the ideas in this field more accessible.

Thomson, A., Mabey, C., Storey, J., Grey, C. and Iles, P. (2001) *Changing Patterns of Management Development.* A report on a survey carried out at the beginning of the millennium, it touches all the main areas of MD. Combines empirical work with good analysis and coverage.

Woodall, J. and Winstanley, D. (1999) *Management Development: Strategy and Practice.* A good starting point, it provides an overview of the subject as a whole and a framework for appreciating the core concepts involved.

Bibliography

Aspen, P. (1994) 'New themes in management education', *THES* April.

Beardwell, I. and Claydon, L. (2007) *Human Resource Management: A Contemporary Approach*, Prentice Hall, Ch. 9.

Beardwell, I. and Holden, L. (2001) *Human Resource Management: A Contemporary Approach*, Prentice Hall, Ch. 9.

Brown, A. (1998) *Organisational Culture*, Prentice Hall.

Burgoyne, J. (1988) 'Management development for the individual and the organisation', *Personnel Management*, June.

Espedal, B. (2005) 'Management development: using internal and external resources in developing core competencies', *Human Resource Development Review*, Vol. 4.

Fee, K. (2001) *A Guide to Management Development Techniques*, Kogan Page.

*Fox, S. (1997) 'From management education and development to management learning, in Burgoyne, J. and Reynolds, P. (1997) *Management Learning*, Sage.

Harrison, R. (2001) *Learning and Development,* CIPD.

*Lees, S. (1992) 'Ten faces of management development', *Management Education and Development*, Vol. 23, No. 2.

Lippitt, G. (1982) 'Management development as the key to organisational renewal', *Journal of Management Development*, Vol. I, No. 2.

*Mabey, C. and Finch-Lees, T. (2008) *Management and Leadership Development*, Sage.

*Margerison, C. (1991) *Making Management Development Work*, McGraw Hill.

Molander, C. (1986) *Management Development*, Bromley.

*Mumford, A. (1989) *Management Development: Strategies for Action*, CIPD.

*Mumford, A. (1997) *Management Development: Strategies for Action*, CIPD.

*Mumford, A. and Gold, J. (2004) *Management Development: Strategies for Action*, CIPD.

*Pedler, M., Burgoyne, J. and Boydell, T. (1994) *A Manager's Guide to Self Development*, McGraw Hill.

Pickard, J. (2001) 'Tester of faith', *People Management*, February.

Storey, J. (1989) 'Management development: a literature review and implications for future research, *Personnel Review*, Vol. 18, No. 6.

Storey, J. and Tate, W. (2000) 'Management development', in Bach, S. and Sisson, K. (2000) *Personnel Management*, Blackwell.

*Talbot, C. (1997) 'Paradoxes of management development', *Career Development International*, Vol. 2, No. 3.

*Thomson, A., Mabey, C., Storey, J. et al. (2001) *Changing Patterns of Management Development*, Blackwell.

2 Management process, roles, behaviour and skills

Learning outcomes

After studying this chapter you should be able to understand, analyse and explain:

- different models and approaches for defining management behaviour;
- the nature of the management process;
- the extent to which leadership and management should be regarded as synonyms or alternative concepts;
- perspectives on the skills and qualities needed by the effective manager, e.g. technical, personal, social, cognitive, political, etc.

2.1 Introduction

A criticism often applied to MD programmes is that they can seem remote from what managers actually do. MD processes can seem to be disconnected from the realities of 'doing management'. Secondments, job rotation and training can appear over-planned and programmed, distant from managers' everyday lives. As a result, MD solutions can seem too abstract, neat and logical, removed from the confusing and fragmented nature of management as 'lived experience'. MD programmes can also seem very prescriptive, implying that managers need to behave in particular ways if they want to be effective and that there are universalistic 'best practices' in the conduct of management (Mumford 1993).

A major thrust of these criticisms is that MD needs to be located in what managers define as their organisational reality if they are to 'own' the learning processes and really grow from them. From this it follows that sensitivity in the design of MD and concern for its effectiveness is intertwined with thinking about management as an activity. Unless we have a conceptualisation of the management process, how can we decide on strategies to develop the manager?

2.2 The meaning of management

Bertrand Russell (1962) once distinguished between two types of work:

> The first, altering the position of matter near or at the earth's surface relative to other matter. The second, telling other people to do so. The first is unpleasant and ill paid; the second is pleasant and highly paid. The second kind is capable of indefinite extension; there are not only those who give orders but those who give advice as to what orders should be given.

Managers definitely fall into the second category of work (and MD practitioners might be part of the 'indefinite extension').

The rise of 'management' and 'managerial values' is part of the spirit of the age. 'Management' forms much of the vocabulary, the criteria of judgement and 'world view' of post-industrial society in the early millennium. However, 'management' only really emerged as a separate discipline with the ascendancy of nineteenth-century capitalism. Since then it has gone on apace to become one of the basic institutions and key forces permeating all aspects of society (Mullins 2001). However, although 'management' is universally acknowledged as a major ideology underpinning the modern world, and part of the global paradigm shift to business values, there is no general agreement on what it is.

In the early days, management was largely seen as a mechanistic, functional and technical activity concerned with rational organisation of resources for efficiency and performance. In more recent times, it has come to be defined less as a discrete activity, the preserve of a single discipline (accountancy, engineering, HRM, etc.) and more as a process which cross-cuts all organisational functions, an integrating force for relating the myriad activities within an organisation to serve overall goals. But although synthesising and coordinating, contemporary views of management insist that it is not homogenising.

Management work varies so much. It takes different forms in different places and is practised in varying ways at various levels. There are big variations between managers in the degree of independence they are allowed and the demands placed upon them and then there are the subjective factors, differences between managers in how they *interpret* the demands and constraints placed upon them (Stewart 1985).

On top of this there is a cultural overlay which implies other differences. As Chapter 11 on cross-cultural patterns of management and development suggests, there are national variations in how management is defined and practised and, by implication, the skills and development involved.

Hales (1986) summarises the diversity and complexity within the structure of management work by suggesting four broad observations.

1. Managerial work is contingent on management function, level, organisation (type, structure, industry, size) and environment (including national culture).
2. Managerial jobs usually have an element of flexibility within them. There is usually room for choice on the basis of personal values and style and interpretation of strategy and organisational purpose.
3. Managerial work does not fall into neat sequences of tasks. Often these are contradictory, competing and ambiguous in form.

4. Managerial work is constantly being negotiated and renegotiated as circumstances change. Two managers with the same job title may be performing very different kinds of work.

Heller (1985, 1995), who has written so much that is pithy and memorable about managing, likes to claim that management is not one but a number of occupations and the skills involved are very context-dependent. He also implies that management is not something grand. In fact, it is quite a homely occupation, even if it is complex and problematic. It is as much art as science and learnt as much through homilies, maxims, stories and aphorisms as techniques and principles. Even allowing for some dramatic licence, this seems very plausible.

Mark Easterby-Smith (1986) adds to our understanding of management by suggesting that:

- management work is complex and variable; it seems far more easy to do than it is;
- managing involves ordering and coordinating the work of others, but to do this managers first have to create similar order within themselves;
- managers deal with the unprogrammed and complex problems, that is, those which cannot be routinised through ordinary organisational process;
- managers need to be able to move between technical, functional and cultural boundaries, to build order from fragmentation.

These models present very different, but not at all contradictory perspectives on the managerial project.

2.2.1 Doing management

Management has always been based on myths. One of the oldest approaches to describing management is to attempt to group management activities by type and provide a framework to explain their activity. Many classical writers have made contributions on these lines – Fayol, Brecht and Urwick, among others (Mullins 2001).

The classifications of this 'classical' school involve abstractions which attempt to capture the 'essence' of managing. Often they involve lists of what managers are supposed to do all day:

- planning/forecasting;
- organising;
- motivating;
- controlling;
- developing, etc., etc.

There are several drawbacks to these definitions. Firstly, there is the lack of clarity in the concepts. Arguably they are over-abstract and thin and pretend to an understanding of issues which are actually far more complex when they are taken apart and examined closely. They also suggest that management is a rationalistic 'step by step' process. However, this flies in the face of much recent evidence that management is really holistic and disjointed, emergent and disordered. In particular, there are important results from the work of Stewart (1985, 1994), Mintzberg (1973), Kotter (1982) and Mangham and Pye (1991) which have added immeasurably to our understanding of the processual nature of management by dissecting the reality of how managers perform their jobs, using detailed ethnographic observation. All these studies agree that while management does have elements of technicism and some of it can be systematised around agreed principles of 'good practice', it also retains many elements of art – sensitivity, personal judgement, sense-making, having a feel for situations and the flow of events.

One theme to emerge from the empirical studies is that management can be described as a cluster of roles. Mintzberg (1973) in ground-breaking research suggests that managers typically perform ten roles, which he subsumes under key headings: interpersonal, information-handling and decisional roles. While proposing that all managers at some time exercise each of these roles, Mintzberg also recognises that individual managers will give different priorities to them. This will be an expression of their personal style and interpretation but also situational factors in the job, the organisation, the industry and the environment. Other research on management roles by Rosemary Stewart (1985) has suggested that management jobs are always a synthesis of objective and subjective factors, that is, contextual demands, the constraints which limit what the manager can do but also the choices s/he makes about what s/he will do. Nothing is determined, even if contexts set limits. It is interpretive meaning – how the manager makes sense of his or her situation – which ultimately shapes behaviour. This is the counterbalance to any claim that management is homogeneous and universal principles of good practice apply everywhere. All the evidence suggests that management can be conducted in different ways in different situations, yet with equal success.

2.2.2 Management process

The empirical studies have also provided us with vivid pictures of the experiential processes of general management. One of their undoubted effects has been to challenge some of the common assumptions about management on which traditional MD has been based. For example, Wrapp (1967) talks about the 'sacred cows', the myths which senior managers want to believe about themselves, for example:

- that general managers have a helicopter view of the organisation and know everything of importance that is going on within it;
- that general management is proactive, anticipating problems and taking opportune action to steer the course of events;
- that general management is about formulating precise objectives, conceptualising problems, reflecting on trends, developing the organisation, that is, it is very high-level strategic and change-led activity.

However, observation of managers in action suggests that actual behaviour rarely reflects these presumptions. Kotter (1982) found that compared with how the textbook said they should behave, real managers were not well organised, not systematic nor strategic. Goals were often set in conditions of uncertainty or only arose retrospectively as the direction of the organisation became clear. Resources were often allocated on political grounds, problem-solving was more about firefighting not reasoned thinking and the construction of problems presumed their solution.

Looking at daily behaviour, Kotter found the following patterns.

- Managers spend a lot of time with others in face-to-face contact, especially those at their level and external stakeholders (e.g. customers, suppliers, consultants, etc.).
- Discussions are not just focused on business decisions, but also involve a lot of general 'ad hoc' talk (e.g. asides, anecdotes, gossip).
- During these informal discussions managers ask a lot of questions during which they are probing the underside of issues, piecing together bits of data and assessing the credibility of stories to get a full picture of a developing situation.
- Managers rarely give orders but spend a lot of effort trying to influence others obliquely through cajoling, persuading, requesting, suggesting and coaxing.
- Much of the work seems to require skill in the use of language (rhetoric, imagery, use of symbols), sensitivity to personal differences and political understanding of various actors and the opportunities inherent in situations as they emerge.

In this whirl of disjointed activity it is hard to see any underlying order, certainly not the working out of rational management principles. However, what emerges from Kotter's work is that the apparently casual and accidental way in which managers use their time, set priorities and handle a network of problems and relationships is actually an efficient strategy for dealing with ambiguity and complexity. He calls this, dramatically, 'the efficiency of apparently inefficient behaviour'.

In fact, Kotter claims that if you look closer with an analytical eye, it is possible to discover some consistencies in the work of managers widely regarded by their peers as very effective. These 'consistencies' appear to go beyond the limited, rationalistic models of the classicists. In particular, managers seem to perform two key activities.

Firstly, managers build agendas during the first six months or year on the job. Typically the agenda is composed of loosely connected goals and plans. These are not formal plans but checklists to action which involve personal as well as organisational goals. Agendas help the manager to decide what to do despite uncertainty, conflicting demands and the vast amount of information which is available. Agendas help the manager in focusing time and energy.

Secondly, good managers tend to have well-established networks of cooperative relationships with people both inside and outside the organisational structure. The network helps the manager keep informed about issues at different levels. The cultivation of varied sources of information (on shifting relationships, perceptions, organisational issues) means that the manager can view any situation from a variety of perspectives. Effective managers know how to play this network – who to contact to bring together a team of balanced talents, how to create cooperative relationships between organisations, how to build alliances between different interests and how to mobilise knowledge/skills within the political community of the workplace.

Pause for thought

Talk is the work

If you are a manager, do you recognise you own 'crazy days' in the office in the following quotation? If you work with managers, perhaps you're in a position to observe how they work.

> This is an extract from my field notes, the comments of a general manager running a busy clinical unit in the NHS. I asked her what she did at work.
>
> > Meeting and talking with people mainly . . . Talking seems to be what I'm paid to do. So talking on the phone, in boardroom meetings, in the car going to a meeting, in the canteen, in the corridor, walking across the car park . . . and when I'm talking I'm gathering data, so a lot of listening – mostly to other peoples' ideas and opinions; but also a lot of persuading, arm twisting, asking 'what if' hypothetical questions . . . agreeing a line. There's also some swapping of gossip and joking mixed in with negotiating and deciding how to handle something . . . most of it involves social process; there's not much time for reflective thinking. You get distracted so often . . .
>
> Source: Personal field notes.

Other writers have added to Kotter's conclusions about the nature of management by emphasising that it is less about systems, practices and procedures, far more about organisational patterns, built up and maintained through constant social interaction. Watson (2001) talks of management as a very messy, very human experience.

- *Being part of the process* – Successful managers are said to be sensitive to the organisation's social process. They can 'tack and trim' their management style. Sometimes they are more of a boss and sometimes they are less of a boss. This 'Janus-headed' style also extends to the political arena – knowing when to conciliate and when to confront.
- *Having a political sense* – Managers who are effective often seem to be involved in political activity – bargaining, sweet-talking, compromising, persuasion, arm-twisting, being able to influence others and enlist their support, manoeuvre and shape the system to achieve a purpose.
- *Practising the art of imprecision* – Successful managers know how to make the organisation feel a sense of direction without publicly committing themselves to a precise set of objectives. Instead they set a general compass point as a steer for their overall purpose and strategy.
- *Muddling with a purpose* – Managers who achieve results often see the futility of trying to push through with a comprehensive programme. They are willing to compromise to achieve modest progress. They also understand the interconnectedness of problems and the need to remain focused on underlying issues and ultimate goals whatever the localised issues.

Managing as a 'blur of activity'

Consider this piece of dialogue between a researcher and the manager of a charity.

Tony (researcher): So Peter, can we take a few minutes to review what you have done today? I feel pretty exhausted just trying to keep up with you.

Peter (manager): Yes, it's usually like that . . . one thing after another. . . . A lot of my work is winning people over to dealing with the difficult things we get involved in as a charity. Do you remember this morning? The first thing I do every day is wander round the staff in the office, passing the time of day and all that . . . it's having a word, seeing how they are getting on, letting them ask me things. . . .

Tony: So it's about building relationships . . . trust?

Peter: That's part of it, but it's also smoothing the way, even smooching with the power holders, doing a lot of fixing . . . rushing around and keeping things going. You start a conversation and then you're interrupted. There's a lot of persuading, encouraging . . . keeping this person right, then that person. . . . It's difficult to keep tabs on just what I'm doing from one moment to another but at the end of the day I try to add up the bits and paint myself a picture of what's going on and how I am shaping things to achieve my goals.

Question

Consider the social, cultural and political processes involved. Would you discern any strategic purpose in all this micro-dot activity?

Source: Adapted from Watson, T. Conference presentation papers Judge Institute (2002a); Watson, T. (2001) *In Search of Management*; Watson, T. (2002b) *Organising and Managing Work*.

Considered together, these observations are very useful in demonstrating that the traditional image of the manager who sits at a clear desk, quietly planning and controlling in an ordered way, is no more than a self-serving myth adopted by managers who want to believe that they are in control but know that they are not. Perhaps managers are more jugglers of human affairs than the brainy controllers of a smoothly functioning machine (Wrapp 1967). Perhaps a more realistic way of seeing managerial reality is as a 'negotiated order'(Strauss 1978) in which the manager sits at the centre of a net of interests, ideas, projects, groups and issues, constantly pulling one thread and then another, trying to maintain a precarious sense of balance through diplomacy, judgement and talk. It is through clever juggling, skilful diplomacy and astute coordination of people, budgets, issues and agendas that policy emerges and objectives are achieved.

As we will see, this new picture of what management is has important implications for how MD should be defined and how it should be conducted.

2.3 Is management leadership?

In recent years the focus of those who run organisations has shifted and shifted again. Concern to develop good administrators in the 1970s became the search for 'entrepreneurial' managers and then 'managers of excellence'. Since the 1990s the new obsession is with recognising and developing leaders. However, we should recognise that there is a cross-cultural dimension here. The modern concern with leadership is predominantly an Anglo-American phenomenon. There is not the same obsession with it in Japan, China, Germany or France (see Chapter 11).

In the West, 'leadership' is one of the great slogans of our time. We will examine the reasons behind the new priority to develop leadership capability among managers in the final chapter. However, at this point our main concern is to examine the value of attempting to distinguish between 'management' and 'leadership' as different roles requiring different behaviours.

The issues here are tangled and difficult. Certainly in most of the literature of social psychology, OA and development, 'leadership' and 'management' are terms used interchangeably (Brotherton 1999). It is not clear how the roles of manager and leader differ and how behaviours are distinct. Until the mid-1990s, people in authority, certainly higher management, were largely assumed to have a leadership role. It is a break with previous assumptions to attempt to differentiate 'managing' from 'leading'. Could it be that in the past the overlap between them was exaggerated or are we witnessing a false distinction largely based on misunderstanding of what the senior, general management role involves? In short, has the 'sine qua non' of effective senior management always been leadership?

One way of conceptualising the spheres of 'managing' and 'leading'

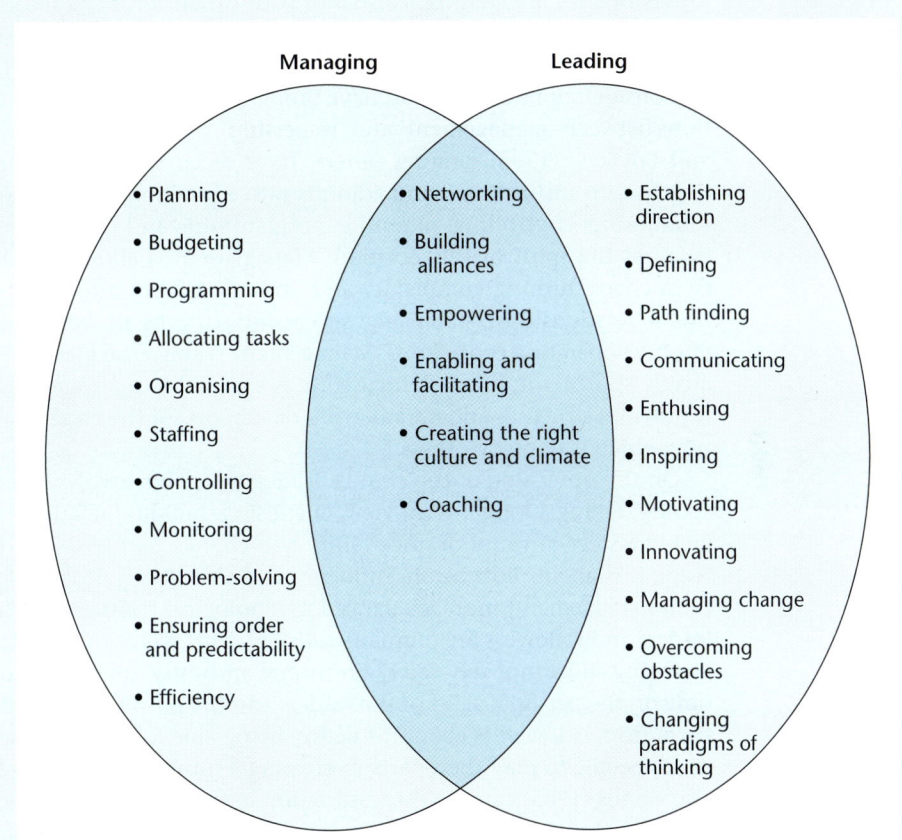

Managing

- Planning
- Budgeting
- Programming
- Allocating tasks
- Organising
- Staffing
- Controlling
- Monitoring
- Problem-solving
- Ensuring order and predictability
- Efficiency

Overlap:
- Networking
- Building alliances
- Empowering
- Enabling and facilitating
- Creating the right culture and climate
- Coaching

Leading

- Establishing direction
- Defining
- Path finding
- Communicating
- Enthusing
- Inspiring
- Motivating
- Innovating
- Managing change
- Overcoming obstacles
- Changing paradigms of thinking

Figure 2.1 One way of conceptualising the spheres of 'managing' and 'leading'

Question
Do you think that management blurs into leadership or are these categories sharply distinguished?

There can be no dispute that managers like to see themselves as leaders because that legitimates their position as people well suited to command. However, when you look at managerial leadership close up, you find that 'leadership' here involves the use of formal authority (i.e. controlling, coordinating, directing). A cynic might observe that without the backstop of that authority managers might be unable to achieve their objectives. In these circumstances, are we observing leadership behaviour or merely the exercise of management prerogative? Rollinson (2002) takes this line further by suggesting an analytical distinction between 'headship' and 'leadership'. If managers rely on their formal position and the authority it confers, they are practising 'headship'; 'leadership' requires the authority freely given by followers who allow them to exercise their influence. 'Headship' may get the job done but it only secures compliance, not the enthusiasm and identification of people with a strategy which brings the highest levels of performance. Managerial 'headship' may be disappearing with delayering, decentralisation, the dispersal of authority and empowered teams; heads are becoming leaders using interpersonal skills and building a psychological contract with their followers or they are sharing leadership with others with the informal authority which comes from charisma, ideas and knowledge (Rollinson 2002). 'Heads' who only rely on their position power are a vanishing breed.

Considerations of this kind have brought a number of writers to draw clear distinctions between 'management' and 'leadership'. Bennis and Nanus (1985), Kotter (1982) and Boyatzis (1993), among others, have recently defined managers as concerned largely with institutional and administrative functions, for example, with organising, monitoring, controlling, planning, programming and problem-solving. Barker (1997) captures the spirit of this position. Management is about rationality, building order from chaos, turning complexity and unpredictability into routine, handling transactional relationships, stabilising successful patterns of behaviour and maintaining effective operating procedures. Management is concerned largely with 'doing'; it is relatively short term; it is task focused; it is external to teams and professional activities; it provides structure and a framework of support for the creative work of the organisation which is done by others.

On the other side of the coin is 'leadership'. This involves thinking, visioning, inspiring, taking a longer-term view, energising, building relationships, networking and giving a steer in times of uncertainty and change. Leadership is more internal to the team; it is about motivation, influence and persuasion. It is less of a one-way process than management, more a balanced psychological contract in which the needs of the leaders and followers are mutually satisfied. This relationship is fragile and constantly changing. It cannot rely solely on formal authority, on power conferred from above, only on the personal skills of the leaders and the power which followers will confer on them from below. It is about influence, being able to instil a sense of mission and persuade people to play their parts in creating a future order (Sadler-Smith 2006). Bennis and Nanus (1985) capture this distinction in their now well-known mantra that 'managers do things right; leaders do the right thing'. The contrasts in style which are involved are captured in the stories below.

Management or leadership?

Consider these two stories of management style. Do they illustrate the essential differences between managing and leading?

Harold Geneen, head of ITT, one of the largest multinationals in the world in the 1970s, presides over yet another management review meeting. We have to imagine 100 very senior international managers seated around a huge U-shaped table in a darkened room. A screen displays the performance results for each division. Each manager, representing different regions of the ITT empire, is called to the stage to give a presentation. There is a crackling atmosphere of anxiety. An illuminated green arrow moves up and down lists of figures on the screen, pausing at key stages, which usually represent an operating loss or failed profit target. The corporate managers from HQ then interrogate the manager about this issue in front of his peers.

Through the interrogations, Geneen sits there looking over his horn-rimmed spectacles, cold and impassive. He fires questions in a machine-gun manner: Why was that profit so low? Why is that project behind schedule? Why the overspend? Strong managers were known to break.

The style here seems to be that of tough-minded management planning, control, performance monitoring and evaluation – the essential stuff of managing.

However, the scene now shifts to Sweden in the 1980s, Jan Carlzon, aged just 36, has been appointed as head of Scandinavian Air Services. On his first day in office he calls a meeting of all the staff of the company – in a deserted aircraft hangar outside Stockholm. Carlzon addresses the crowd from the top of a 30-foot ladder. He does not harangue them or offer the one true vision of the future. Instead, he speaks directly and evocatively about where the company was and what it might become. He asked for help in overcoming the obstacles. It would be a long journey. He would welcome contributions from all parts of the company in developing the strategy.

Later, when SAS had gone on to great success, Jan Carlzon's speech would be remembered by staff as a defining moment in the company's history and as an inspiring starting point in the change process.

Is the style here that of leadership, of building identification with followers, engaging emotionally as well as cerebrally with people to enlist their support for change?

Source: Adapted from: Carlzon, J. (1987) *Moments of Truth*; Sampson, A. (1973) *The Sovereign State*

Brotherton (1999) believes that managerial leadership in the past was based on an impoverished model of 'leadership' (top–down direction) which ultimately rested on management prerogatives. Even the much vaunted social skills of participative leadership, fashionable in management thought since the 1960s, were no more than manipulation ultimately legitimated by formal authority. Only now with the appearance of more complex, democratic organisations, are new patterns of leadership emerging which go beyond managerialism and draw on leadership wherever that is found within the organisation. Innovative organisations require visionary, transformational leadership on which management does not have a monopoly. The future of management may be far less heroic than in the past, providing a nurturing environment for the exercise of leadership distributed throughout the organisation.

However, while there is consensus on the importance of leadership as the dynamic force within organisations, voices are now being raised against the implied subordination of managing. For example, Mumford (1999) believes that assigning the enabling, supporting and boring parts of the organisational process to the manager while attributing the visionary, dynamic and exciting parts to the leader risks demeaning the complexity of the management process and underestimating the subtle skills of individuals engaged in the difficult art of managing. Raelin (2004) builds on this by suggesting that one-dimensional categories underpinned the differentiation of leadership from management, which were misleading. Managers had always been more than administrators and to view leaders as 'saviours' was to risk the same heroic thinking (and the same eventual disappointment) which once marked the rise of managerialism. A little TV watching of the 1960s soap opera *The Power Game* which captures the messianic hopes invested in the new men of management as agents of change, hopes destined to disappointment, should give even the most enthusiastic advocates of 'leadership' a sense of déjà vu.

Although managers were not always leaders and many management functions did not require outstanding leadership capabilities, senior managers, corporate managers, general and strategic managers had always needed to be leaders if they wanted to be effective. For decades (probably since the Hawthorne experiments of the 1930s) it had been recognised within the management community that sophisticated managers needed the ability to motivate, persuade, to form effective teams, to mobilise power through networks and build strong cultures, all of which required the sophisticated socio-political skills and the use of informal processes which went well beyond the exercise of formal authority. These capabilities amounted to a leadership role which would be essential for managers in the flattened organisations post-millennium.

Yukl (2002) takes up this theme by suggesting that successful managers in senior roles typically perform two leadership functions. One involves the formal leadership arising from their organisational positions. However, effective managers also need to perform a broader leadership role which draws on informal power bases and demonstrates persuasive influence across a much wider span of issues than non-managerial leaders are ever called on to consider. Yukl believes that these two leadership roles are mutually supportive; formal authority provides legitimation for informal leadership, and informal leadership (e.g. networking, building a reputation) augments the formal leadership role (e.g. more leverage with other management leaders).

The latest turn in thinking seeks to redress what is seen as a false subordination of management to leadership. The revisionist argument has it that leadership and management are not opposing ends of a spectrum, rather they are equal and complementary. All managers, but especially those at the top, need both qualities. Without good leadership, organisations are likely to concentrate on doing current things better and better without building a future which may require an entirely different approach (e.g. continuing to improve buggy whips for horse-drawn transport and ignoring the revolution which the motor car would bring). Without good management, leadership can be little more than hot air and dramatic postures which don't provide day-to-day direction (e.g. Bill Gates would not have been successful if his dream of 'a computer on every desk' was not matched by good management skill).

Part of this revisionist thinking also provides a counterweight to an overbalanced preoccupation with leadership by suggesting that while 'leader' may be a function within a role (few people are appointed just as leaders), 'manager' is a role definition (Bass 1995). Management is a broader field of activity than leadership. So, in Mintzberg's (1973) 11 classic management roles, roles which have a leadership element are in a definite minority. Leadership may be seen as subsumed in management, as only one part of it and relatively powerless without the exercise of other aspects of the management process. The mystique which surrounds leadership in modern writing may have caused us to exaggerate both its singularity and its importance.

The implications of this debate are important for the primary focus of this book – a consideration of development theory and practice. Our position here is that despite the contemporary fashion for re-branding learning interventions in 'management development' as 'leadership development', we resist this trend. We believe that much of the corpus of knowledge and technique within MD remains equally valuable for leadership development. This is because much progressive MD has always attempted to develop managers as leaders who demonstrated their effectiveness through their personal qualities rather than the authority vested in their rank.

In truth, leadership and management development theories and methods seem to overlap. At this stage there does not seem to be a different set of learning approaches to developing leaders to those used for developing managers and it is not helpful to separate them out. However, in future, if leadership continues to be seen as a 'distributed activity' empowering many non-managers, then 'learning for leadership' may develop its own unique identity, probably becoming a subset of HRD. In this book we will largely consider leadership development as subsumed within management development while remaining open to insights from the burgeoning area of leadership studies and leadership development to the extent that they form a new body of knowledge and practice in learning.

2.4 The skills and qualities of the manager

Management developers need working models of managing which reflect what managers actually do. Without them management development processes become distant from the 'lived experience' of managing and lack credibility with those who are supposed to be developed by them. This can mean that managers become disengaged, even alienated from MD as a set of tools which are irrelevant and ineffective. MD will be perceived as something 'done to them' not something they 'own' because it helps them at work. MD of this kind can also perpetuate myths about managing which are misleading and counter-productive.

The value of the empirical studies which we have considered is that they prick the pomposity of management and reveal that in essence it is not some grand thing described by a term like 'strategic management' or 'developing the organisation'. Instead it emerges that managing is far more mundane and also chaotic and complex than the abstract categories suggest. The process of 'doing managing' (Mangham and Pye 1991) emerges as something quite commonplace – a series of small choices, actions and reactions, for example, writing some e-mails; scanning someone's report; talking to a group of staff; having conversations with people who come into the office and so on, which over time come together to form a line of development (which we might call a policy) for the organisation.

As well as clear pictures of managing, management developers also need a clear view of the qualities, skills, attributes and competencies (are these synonyms or do they differ in meaning?) displayed by effective managers. Here again there are issues of definition and meaning which are rarely acknowledged by writers in the field, let alone professional developers. However, as Mangham (1988) has perceptively suggested, management vocabulary is full of terms which purport to describe the qualities of managers, for example, 'an empowering leadership style'; 'ability to motivate others'; 'a strategic understanding', yet are imprecise in meaning and are often interpreted very differently by those who use the same phrases. Mangham suggests that these descriptors of management capability are too vague to be operationalised and there is very little professional consensus on the features of behaviour by which they can be recognised. The reason lies in our lack of understanding of the management process (especially at the higher levels) and what is involved in distinguishing between ordinary and outstanding performance. This is partly because executive work is usually shrouded in secrecy and because higher managers themselves have difficulty in articulating in a coherent way what they do and how they do it. However, it is also a function of the very subtle socio-psychological-political processes involved which require delicate judgements disguised by the big, conventional labels (e.g. 'clear communicator', 'creative decision maker', 'dynamic leader', etc.)

Mangham argues that this is a dangerous situation for both managers and developers. The lack of a shared definitions or criteria for measuring these abstractions, or even a sensitive language to talk about a process about which we still know relatively little, means that managers are in danger of being seduced by management 'fads' and fashionable nostrums which promise easy solutions (e.g. 'transformational leadership', 'excellence', etc.). They are also in danger of being persuaded by self-serving fantasy images of management as a value-neutral, step-like process carried out by rational 'technicians' concerned to find the 'best' solution for all stakeholders to the business.

Lack of understanding of what makes a good manager means that developers are particularly 'at risk' of designing development programmes for qualities which they do not fully understand. If the diagnosis is flawed then it is little wonder that MD programmes are often challenged to demonstrate real improvement in performance and are found lacking.

Mangham was writing in the late 1980s, but the provocative issues he raises have not been resolved, despite the rise of the 'competency movement' which we consider later on. There is a need for much deeper ethnographic research into the management process at the policy levels of the organisation to describe the behaviours involved. In the meantime, bear in mind Mangham's analysis as we turn to a consideration of the literature on management skills and apply it critically to this body of knowledge.

So what are the skills which the effective manager needs to have? What is offered here is an amalgam of the insights from a number of researchers on management in recent years, for example, Pedler et al. (1994), Burgoyne (1988) Kotter (1982) Hales (1986) and so on. Most of these researchers have taken a social constructionist or symbolic interactionist approach. They try to 'take the role of the other', that is, to see the world of managing from the viewpoint of the managers themselves to understand how they make sense of their experiences. This seems like a promising line of approach if developers are to understand enough of the inside experience of managing at different levels and in different conditions to design interventions which capture the imagination of managers.

The consensus of these studies is that the modern manager is not so much a controller or director of tasks and resources as a facilitator and an enabler of diverse constituencies of interests. Management is an interactive, interpersonal and sensing process concerned with building and maintaining a precarious micro-social order so that practical tasks can be accomplished (Barnard 1938). This is echoed by Heller (1995), who claims that doing management well requires the same skills you bring to doing life, but played to the highest standard of social accomplishment.

There is broad agreement that the effective manager, everywhere and at all times, combines a number of skill clusters as shown in Figure 2.2.

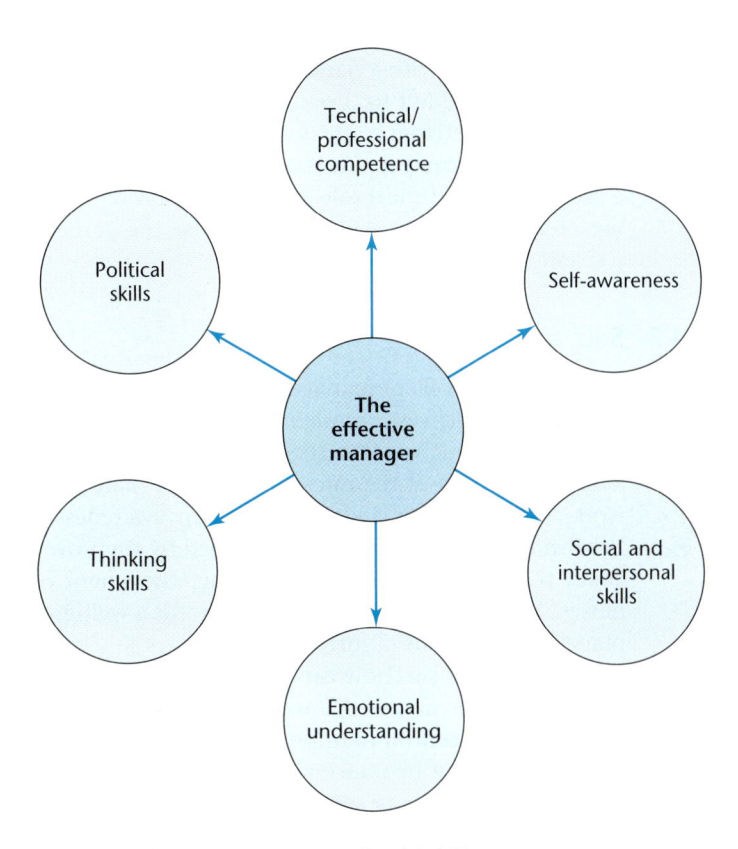

Figure 2.2 The manager: a master of multi-skilling

2.4.1 Technical competence

Management is a practical subject which aims to have an impact on the real world, so it requires functional knowledge and skill in applying a body of professional practice. Here we are talking about knowledge of product technology, marketing techniques, engineering, accountancy, knowledge of relevant legislation, knowledge of basic management principles and theories which purport to help the practitioner with 'best practice' in planning, organising and controlling (Pedler et al. 2001).

Although all levels of management require a technical base, one of the unique aspects of management is that the further you ascend the hierarchy of management, the less direct use is made of techniques and the more emphasis is placed on the social, cognitive and political skills of managing. A major problem for developers is that managers often get promoted to a high level of authority because of their mastery of technical skills. Although they may be highly professional specialists, they may not have had much opportunity on the way up to develop their people skills or to gain a broad appreciation of the organisation as a whole. Once installed in a generalist role, they often find that performance requires strategic and political skills for which their former experience has not adequately prepared them (Garratt 1994).

Typically, these managers find that their technical skills are not much use but they are not sure how they should behave. This role ambiguity can cause not only great anxiety but also behaviour which may be dysfunctional for the organisation as a whole. It is tempting for them to emphasise what they know best and act as higher-level technicians with a narrow problem-solving view of their job, interfering in issues which should be left to those lower down. This is often the situation for directors in medium-sized private companies who are rarely trained for their role. The beginnings of wisdom in management is often knowing when you are no longer paid to perform a professional-technical role and the job now requires a strategic appreciation and the use of social-political skills to harmonise the parts in the service of a greater whole (Garratt 1994).

2.4.2 Self-awareness

At the higher levels of management, technical skills are assumed and effectiveness in management seems very much linked to social and interpersonal skills.

Researchers such as Mangham and Pye (1991) and Watson (2001) have tried to give a detailed picture of the micro-processes of management. The ability to do executive work, Mangham concludes, requires an awareness of self interacting with others. What managers do is very much shaped by their own perceptions of their role, their goals, their values, their feelings, their assessment of personal strengths and weaknesses. To act effectively the manager needs a well-grounded awareness of the self; the manager needs skills of introspection.

This makes sense. How can anyone manage others unless they have first mastered themselves? The knowledge we have acquired about ourselves, which makes up our self-concept, is central to improving our management skills. Knowing ourselves helps us understand our own taken-for-granted assumptions, our categories for defining situations and people, our sensitivities, strengths and weaknesses. This knowledge is self-empowering. It allows us to capitalise on our talents. It is the first step in making any changes to ourselves which are needed to develop the skills we think we need.

Self-reflection is also important because it helps us make our interactions with others more effective and insightful. By understanding ourselves we become more sensitive to the differences and also the similarities between people; it makes us more empathic and more skilful in our repertoire of behaviours. From this 'self/other' awareness, the manager is in a position to look in on his/her own behaviour from the perspective of others. We come to 'objectivise' ourselves as others see us by internalising their perceptions.

This is what the developers mean by 'managing the self so that we can manage others'. By developing a sense of self in the world which is consistent with how we are seen, we have the self-knowledge to present ourselves well – to use the words and take the actions which will influence others through quiet skills of persuasion and coordination.

Managing as a 'Performing art'

An interesting model from micro-sociology, that of dramaturgy, examines some of the processes of 'self making'. Dramaturgy sees the world as a stage and, like actors, we are constantly involved in constructing ourselves in front of others in expressive and symbolic ways so that they will accept our claims to identity.

Erving Goffman (1960) is the theorist most associated with this way of seeing things. He claimed that we are all managing impression with others by manipulating 'sign activity' (verbal and non-verbal behaviour) and 'sign equipment' (props such as clothes, cars, offices, etc.) to convince people to define and relate to us in a certain way.

Goffman believes that we all do this but some more deliberately than others. We lay claim to an identity, for example, a 'shrewd operator', a 'caring supporter', a 'courageous manager' and so on, and dramatise ourselves so that others will accept our claims. This dramatic performance involves 'masks', for example, gestures, voice, rhetoric, the stories we use, which compose our 'personal front' and 'mirrors' in which we reflect on how people are reacting to our self presentation. Sometimes we deliberately rehearse this front, 'backstage', so that it seems as natural as possible when we are 'on stage' in social interaction.

It doesn't take much imagination to see how this work applies to management. Studies by Mangham (1986) and Hunt (1992) have suggested that effective managers are particularly good at understanding how they are seen and can predict others' responses to them. They use their self-awareness and interpretive understanding of others to construct themselves in ways that will win approval and allow them to progress their agendas. This has caused some writers to talk of managing as a 'performing art'.

Although Goffman's work has been criticised as suggesting a cynical view of behaviour and advocating manipulation, this is probably misreading. Goffman seems to be merely holding up a mirror to reflect the tactics people use to manage situations and the social rules of life so that they can be bent to their advantage.

Question
Do you think that one of the great secrets of successful managers is that they are very subtle and accomplished in their dramatic performances?

There seem to be a number of areas of self-awareness (Whetton and Cameron 2002). However, it seems that self-understanding in about *four* of these may be particularly linked to management success.

1. *Personal values* – what are the fundamental things you stand for? What are your core values and what would you be prepared to give up if required to compromise? How are your values related to ethical principles?
2. *Learning and thinking styles* – do you know how you think and learn? Under what conditions are you most creative? What is your preferred learning style? What type of thinker are you? Are you able to take an holistic view of things? Are you a conceptual thinker?
3. *Orientation to change* – do you feel comfortable in ambiguous situations? How flexible are you in accommodating the unexpected? Are you confident of your ability to handle complexity and diversity?

4. *Interpersonal orientation* – are you aware of any patterns in how you interact with people, for example, are you open or closed; assertive or retiring; controlling or dependent, etc? What are the consistencies and do they help or hinder you in achieving what you want?

Becoming self-aware is not easy. We are often resistant to self-knowing because we believe that information will surface which threatens our self-image. We avoid personal growth because we fear finding out that we are not what we want to be. There is also the problem that we can only go so far in understanding ourselves through introspection. We also need other people to reflect back to us how they see our actions. Self disclosure is the best strategy for building the trust which allows others to be honest with us. They mirror back to us their perceptions of our behaviour and we come to form opinions about ourselves (often radically revised opinions about ourselves) by interpreting this mirroring.

Do you know yourself?

- People think they know themselves.
- They may know a lot of who they are, but not all.
- There are likely to be areas of the self which are obvious to others but not us.

The amount of knowledge we can acquire about ourselves will depend on the extent to which we open ourselves to self-understanding.

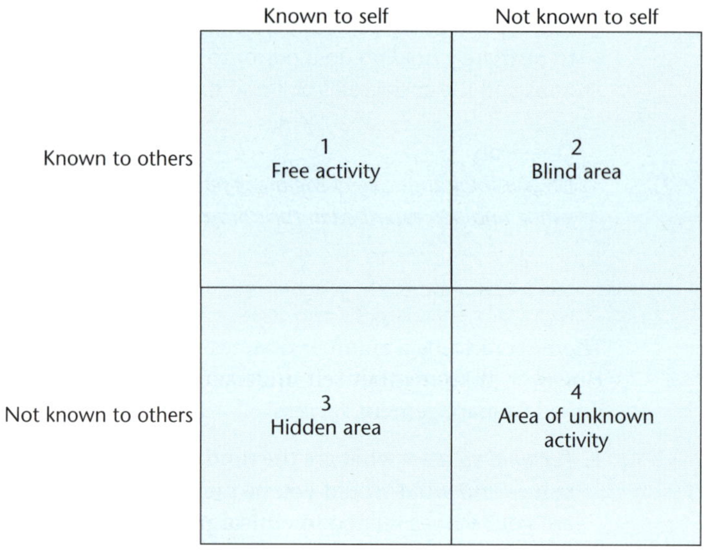

	Known to self	Not known to self
Known to others	1 Free activity	2 Blind area
Not known to others	3 Hidden area	4 Area of unknown activity

Figure 2.3 The Johari Window

Area 1: This is the 'public self' which we know and the world knows.
Area 2: This is the blind area. Includes habits, gestures, tone of voice, etc. which the world sees but of which we are unaware.

> Area 3: This is the hidden area. It is what the individual wishes to conceal from others. It is the undisclosed self.
>
> Area 4: This area is not known to oneself or to others and may come to the surface only in dreams or at a time of considerable emotional pressure.
>
> Self-awareness involves trying to extend the areas of knowledge of ourselves to incorporate more and more of those areas where there is little or no personal knowledge. As we become more honest with ourselves, we move some feelings from the hidden area into the open area. Others notice our greater openness and become more frank and reveal to us observations which had been in the blind area. This takes us into another cycle of self-discovery.
>
> With greater self-awareness we are able to talk to ourselves with greater authenticity, to understand the situations we are in with greater clarity and engage in organisational sense-making with a much greater chance of success.
>
> Source: Adapted from Mullins, A. (2001) *Management and Organisational Behaviour* p. 506

2.4.3 Interpersonal and social skills

These skills are hard to define but they largely mean working with and through other people and using careful judgement. They imply sensitivity to people and situations and skill in persuading people to achieve a common goal.

A lot of management is watching, sensing, doing readings of others' behaviour. In a sense, managers are doing what we all do in social situations, but they are doing it with purpose and through complex webs of relationships within very diverse role sets (e.g. balancing the often conflicting expectations of customers, suppliers, employees, superiors, etc.). From ideas they have of themselves and their own experience managers try to infer what is going on in the heads of others. Mangham (1986) talks of this as 'the theatre of the skull'. Managers engage in a form of 'internal dialogue' to decide on the best line of action. This is really a form of 'role taking': that is, it requires social empathy in which they imaginatively and sympathetically put themselves in the minds of others, anticipating their reactions to the flow of events. By accurately modelling others' behaviour and correctly attributing intention we are well placed to act thoughtfully and appropriately.

Ethnographers of management (Watson, Hales, etc.) have found that as we interact with others in management we are judging others in terms of their significance for our plans. What are their assumptions? What values guide their management? What do they hope to achieve here? Where do they stand on various issues? Is there a difference between what they claim and what they really want? Through these 'readings', managers develop a sense of the strategy best suited to the circumstances and most likely to allow their agenda to be implemented.

The same empathy, feeling and judging are involved in other aspects of the social process. For example, the senior manager needs to have a 'sense of how things are going as a whole'. That means having a 'feel' for how things are interconnected that is, how a micro-situation has implications for the strategy as a whole; how changing the technical system will have a 'knock on' effect for the social system, for example, motivation, morale, culture and the informal relations between groups. Social skills are needed for defining the situation in a way which encourages people to consider an alternative categorisation of experience and to persuade them to have a sense of ownership of it.

For example, senior managers, acting out their corporate role, need the communication and facilitation skills of the change manager. This means working with groups, explaining what the abstractions of the plan imply for practical action, encouraging people to reflect on their habitual scripts', recognise their limitations and disengage from them. It also means acting as a catalyst, helping people to find the confidence to look at things anew and experiment with new ways of behaving.

The social skills involved here are many and need to be employed with great subtlety, for example, 'playing devil's advocate', asking wise questions, summarising, surfacing understandings, ventilating fears, persuading, influencing and building a 'negotiated order' (Strauss 1978) around new behaviours. Ultimately this involves the manager defining the situation in terms which commands the broadest possible consensus.

Sense-making and managing

Researchers such as Weick (1979, 1995) and Pye (2005) suggest that the essence of leadership is 'sense-making'. This means making sense of organisational behaviour through talk and reflection. How do we make the complex, fragmented, behavioural, social and political processes of managing coherent and give them meaning?

This approach attempts to penetrate the constructed world of the manager. How do managers make plausible sense of their experience? How do they construct identity? How do they retrospectively review a number of events and happenings and give them meaning? How do they draw on ideologies ad models to define what is happening and what they should do (e.g. scientific management; markets; flexible form organisation, etc.)? This sense-making is interactive, is mediated by language and is constantly developing (e.g. Fisher 1996, talks of us assuming different 'managerial stances' in our careers as we slowly change our assumptions about the reality of managing).

This may be a productive 'turn' of research which provides insights into how managers make meaning through ideas, constructs, metaphors and images. A sense-making perspective seems particularly useful for explaining how the issues in management remain remarkably similar from one decade to another even though the vocabulary used to define them shifts (e.g. 'managing change' in the 1980s became 'corporate governance' in the millennium; 'empowerment' became 'social capital'; 'innovation' became 'knowledge management). It is through sense-making and its discourses that the issues of management are reframed with new vocabulary even if the basic processes remain largely timeless.

2.4.4 Managing emotion

The 'management of emotion' is also an important social skill for the manager. The manager's job requires a high level of emotional strain, a result of working in situations of endless demands, conflicting pressures, lack of time, lack of resources and lack of clarity in knowing what is expected and how to achieve it.

Managers need to be emotionally resilient to cope with this. According to Howard Gardner (1993), managing requires 'emotional intelligence'. Gardner suggests that people have multiple intelligences – verbal, mathematical, musical, spatial and interpersonal . . . and emotional. While cognitive intelligence may be inherited, fixed and beyond our control, EQ seems to be something we can develop. Good EQ seems to have a strong positive relationship with success in handling difficult social situations and relationships.

So what is EQ? It seems to be the ability to recognise the importance of emotions in everyday life, to be able to monitor your reactions, know your strengths and weaknesses and play to your strengths. Emotional understanding and emotional qualities play a vital part in the use of intelligence in everyday life. Distilling the features of several models and perspectives (e.g. Pedler et al. 2007, Lindenfield 2000, Boyatzis et al. 2002, Goleman 1996, etc.), EQ seems to consist of several dimensions.

- *Self knowledge* – the ability to monitor, recognise and understand your emotions from moment to moment.

- *Self control* – being able to control your moods; keeping in check negative emotions and channelling positive emotions like joy, satisfaction, excitement, passion, etc. into achieving your goals.

- *Self motivation* – the robustness and emotional determination to delay immediate satisfaction for greater future benefit; being able to persist in the face of frustration, disappointment and setbacks to achieve your goals.

- *Self resilience* – means having strategies for coping with stress; not allowing stress to swamp your ability to think clearly; not succumbing to knee jerk reactions or following rigid protocols as a self-defensive means of dealing with stress.

- *Self and interpersonal awareness* – involves the ability to recognise emotion in others by 'reading' the gestures they display, sensitively interpreting tone of voice, etc.; being able to influence others by using language in a way which moves people.

According to Goleman (1996), who has written a best-seller in the field, people with high EQ are sensitive to their own feelings and the feelings of others. They also have the ability to handle emotions in a way which is productive for everyone. People with high EQ show skills in listening to others, reading the emotional currents in a group and appreciating the habitual styles which others use and allowing for them. They are sensitive to others' motivations and moods and can build and sustain deep trust relationships. Goleman went on to claim that EQ is *the* essential quality for senior management. Having it, he said, is a predictor of potential for higher level work and accounts for 85 per cent of all performance in management jobs.

Goleman's claims have been supported by psychometric studies carried out on managers by Vic Dulewicz (2000) at Henley College. He found that EQ managers were successful because of their style. Among other things, they were warm and open; showed respect to others; were 'straightforward' and didn't play games; showed a genuine interest in people and remembered small details about those they met; challenged without spoiling a relationship and had the self-confidence to pursue their ultimate goals despite mistakes and wrong turnings.

It may be that people who have high EQ often had secure and supportive childhoods – they felt safe, understood, appreciated and were helped to value their own goals and to be open to new ideas. From an early age they felt valued, had a good sense of self-worth and were guided by parents to work through their problems. If this research is correct then the 'child is very much father to the man'. Future managers have already developed their essential personal and interpersonal skills for management in the infant's playground. A future society searching for the managers of tomorrow might start with personality profiling of young children; it might also do more to shape the social conditions which help more people to develop the fine balance of emotional robustness and sensitivity which will be needed. Is this sensible social engineering or the glimpse of a new elitist nightmare?

As you may expect for such a new development in thinking about management skills, EQ is not without its critics. Some claim that it is little more than 'psychobabble', others that it is common sense dressed in new language which insightful managers have always practised. Some of this may well be true. Many philosophers down the ages have made very similar observations about the qualities of 'personality' needed for good leadership (Plato's criteria of 'nobility', see Grint 2001). But none of this is to deny the potential value of an approach such as EQ which helps managers to understand the power of emotions in influencing their behaviour and the need for social insight and social skill to marshal the power of emotion for the good of the organisation. Qualities of personality are important in management, and emotional drive can be as important as rational calculation in determining what gets done and how (Davies 2003).

Sadler-Smith (2007) talks about the importance of emotional sensitivity to transformational leadership – the ability of leaders to regulate and use their emotional range for public expression and the importance of self-reflexivity as a key feature of leadership capability. The integration of emotion into MD is a new development, but is consistent with the holistic appreciation of management skill and a major theme in new forms of mentoring, drama and ethical workshops which we discuss later.

2.4.5 Thinking skills

Cognitive skills are another essential attribute of the effective manager. Managers need the ability to think. That does not mean that they have to be original conceptual thinkers, but they do need to have good, clear minds and to be able to see the whole picture.

Many managers like to believe that their cognitive skills define them, that is, that they are sharp decision makers and smooth problem solvers. Management science models emphasise rigorous thinking and hard strategic analysis. However, all the observational studies of managers agree that in reality management involves a lot of improvising and fudging towards a solution which is good enough in the circumstances. Lindblom (1959) has called this style 'disjointed incrementalism'. Many studies of managers as decision makers show that managers typically do not search for the best possible solution to a problem because that would be too time-consuming. Instead they search for a temporary expedient to the problems involved and usually within the boundaries of previous decisions.

Herbert Simon (1957) Nobel Prize winner for work on decision-making, thinks that 'Managers do not seek the sharpest needle in the haystack, just one that is sharp enough to sew with.' By and large, managers need to be masters in making decisions which are 'good enough' in the circumstances, rather than masters of fundamental decision-making which addresses the complexity of a situation and the underlying forces involved. This is what we meant earlier by 'muddling with a purpose'.

Mintzberg (1976) helps us to understand management decision-making by drawing a distinction between *left brain thinking* which he characterises as linear, ordered, sequential and analytical and *right brain thinking* which is holistic, synthetic and intuitive. Mintzberg claims that when you look at management decision-making closely it turns out not to be a regular, planned and systematic process. This is true of strategy as well as more operational decision-making. In fact, it seems discontinuous and proceeds in 'fits and starts'. Despite the obsession with measurement, quantification and sophisticated modelling in management, Richard Heller (1995) stresses that most business decision-making involves thinking with incomplete information, 'back of the envelope' calculations and common-sense constructs which we subsume under the label of 'judgement' because we are not fully aware of what is involved.

Mintzberg thinks that right brain thinking dominates in management. It is the ability to synthesise bits of information into a whole using robust categories of definition and classification which we have built up from the past. It is the ability to conceptualise and create a picture from pieces of evidence which is most needed in management. Continuing his metaphor of left and right brain thinking, in Mintzberg's view really outstanding managers can think in the right (conceptual) hemisphere and develop a whole picture of the organisation and its future but then programme and carry out plans of action with the left (rationalist) hemisphere.

Thinking styles

McKenny and Keen (1976) have suggested that managers exhibit different cognitive styles. Among the various categories they define are the following.

Systematic thinkers – These are the 'methods' people. They define the problem early on in their thinking process, then they search for solutions in a very orderly way. They give a lot of attention to making the implicit explicit and quantifying variables where they can. They are *deductive* thinkers who try to calculate the consequences of different approaches and choose the line which seems most likely to optimise value.

Intuitive thinkers – These managers are particularly sensitive to problem recognition. They are aware that if the problem is wrongly defined, thorough logical analysis will be misdirected and futile. Typically they fend off pressure for an early definition of the problem, instead throwing themselves into the data and thinking *inductively*, often reframing issues several times before coming to a final definition. Choosing a plan of action can also be intuitive, based on grasping a general idea and improvising actions which may make it work. Rational search protocols are sometimes used to justify decisions which might be ultimately described as 'instinctual' (although practitioners of this style may prefer 'calculated risk-taking' as a description). Although management is obsessed with precision in objectives, systems and procedures, the truth is that many decisions in management arise from rough calculations which are more based on vague surmise and a 'nose' for a business opportunity than a careful option appraisal.

Perceptive thinkers – These managers seem to use a thinking style which falls between the two previous extremes. It is essentially a 'mixed scanning' approach which involves building a broad picture of the issues within a context then attending to some 'trigger' factors to focus on certain things in greater depth. Switching alternately between the broad and the detailed they begin to develop explanatory concepts of the relationship between factors which leads to a definition of a problem and the generation of alternative approaches. Standard analytical processes are then often used to choose a final solution.

Other writers on management have suggested a range of typologies to contrast thinking styles, for example, convergent (logical, rational, linear) and divergent (intuitive, expressive, ideational) thinking (Guilford and Hoepfner 1971); romantic and classical thinking; spiral, linear and lateral thinking, etc. There is also the concept of different languages of thinking, for example, spatial, linguistic, mathematical, social thinking (Leavitt and Bahrani 1988). These typifications have their limitations because they seek to capture something fluid and mercurial like thinking with static constructs. However, one consistent finding seems to be that the most effective managers have a broad repertoire of thinking styles, are fluent in various forms of thinking and can adapt their thinking to the needs of the situation. More particularly, they are holistic as well as pragmatic thinkers, they think for themselves, are critically evaluative of orthodoxy, try to learn from experience and avoid the narrow grooves of popular formulae (e.g. 'The One Minute Manager') or the magical appeal of panacea ('excellence', 'business re-engineering', etc.).

A recent, and engaging, attempt to categorise management thinking is an article by Gosling and Mintzberg (2004) which suggests that there are five 'management minds'. Complex organisations of the future need a 'reflective mindset'. They also need people who can probe beneath the surface and understand how things relate together, an 'analytical mindset'. They need managers who have a sense of how things go, a 'worldly mindset'. The diversity and boundary-spanning nature of great organisations requires a culturally sensitive or 'collaborative mindset'. Finally, managers need an 'action mindset' which means creating a sense of shared direction. Managers will be stronger using 'some minds' rather than others. But all managers need to be able to move seamlessly between mindsets as changing circumstances require.

Model building

A distinguishing attribute of effective managers which seems to set them apart is their ability to do accurate 'readings' on situations. They seem to be able to discern patterns in the swirl of events. They recognise 'old friend' patterns because they have been in the loop before. They understand the context, see linkages of cause and effect and how issues interlock.

They can also see new patterns. They can see trends and themes behind the figures. By constantly scanning their environment and focusing on anomalies they notice slight changes from the familiar which sensitise them to the possibility of new trends which may require a timely response.

This is how Harold Geneen (1985) who ran the famous multinational ITT for over 20 years, described his management thinking:

> You're processing a lot of data and then you see something in the figures which stands out. Perhaps something is a little out of gear, perhaps the beginning of a new trend. The figures won't tell you what to do but they get you thinking. You collect other data. Sometimes you begin to see a new pattern, although often it isn't new, it was there all the time . . . you just hadn't seen it.

This cognitive skill seems similar to the idea of 'experiential knowing' or 'tacit understanding' developed by Michael Polyani (1966). This seems to involve an ability to see the underlying form of things through immersion in them. Typically managers work closely with the grain of an emerging situation. By being close to it they come to discriminate more closely between the factors, to see how fragments join together to make larger wholes and how presenting problems become symptoms of other larger issues. This allows them to develop provisional models of what is happening, drawing on accumulated business experience of 'situations like that' or reframing things so that they can be considered from a new angle.

Often thinking unfolds in the context of action. Karl Weick (1983) claims that despite popular myths, managers do not typically think and then do. They are more likely to think through acting. Typically they act with some vague goals, half-thought-out hypotheses and provisional models of the situation. These get them started. They do things and this generates outcomes which can then be examined. By having something tangible to look at means that they can build on earlier lines of action. They are understanding a situation whilst acting within it.

This iterative process may sound inefficient because the thinking is ad hoc and mistakes will be made as people improvise to get it right. But Weick thinks that this is an effective strategy for managers struggling to cope with the chaos of organisational life, such as Kotter, Watson and the ethnographers have described. It allows mental models of the situation to become more and more refined and action more focused as the contours of the problem emerge more clearly.

Weick concludes that managers cannot be reflective thinkers, planning everything out in detail before acting. Instead, they need to be practical thinkers who engage incrementally with the muddle of the organisational process. They should beware of thinking in formulae, avoid the myth of step-by-step logical action and instead operate with clear values and intentions, a few concepts, some simple models and boundless energy and flexibility.

Creativity

Despite the obsession of many managers with the 'one right way', with systems and with 'best practice', successful managers value ideas and creativity (Heller 1995). The capacity to think freshly and to recognise the value of new thinking as it emerges are important cognitive skills for the manager.

Creativity is a special form of thinking where reason, sensitivity and judgement come together. It involves gut feeling and calculated risk-taking, having ideas and knowing how to apply them. Creativity in management often means 'going against the grain' and doing something different. Often it involves an entrepreneurial approach to managing which combines innovation with flair (e.g. Anita Roddick or Richard Branson would be celebrated models).

The literature on creativity is vast and there are many conflicting views on what it is and how it can be encouraged. However, there is a good deal of consensus (e.g. Adams 1988, Weisberg 1986, etc.) that creative managers have the following qualities:

- *Observant of the processes around them.* They give attention to things and are therefore aware of small changes which may be the precursors of new trends.
- *Independent in thought.* They avoid thinking in conventional categories and in stereotypes. They try to reason things out for themselves.
- *Interested in the connections between things.* They have a synthesising ability to relate disconnected things together to form new ways of seeing.

- *Aware of ideas in different areas of knowledge and have an appreciation of how these elements can be combined.* Arthur Koestler, who has written a lot on creative thinking, calls this 'bi-sociation', that is, it is the ability to make connections between previously unrelated areas of thinking.
- *Good at seeing the whole picture because they have a 'helicopter' view of things.*
- *Able to see something new and strange in the familiar and the ordinary.* They can make the familiar strange by looking at it from another angle.
- *Improvisational in approach.* Many researchers on the creative process (like Weisberg), have found that 'leaps of imagination' and 'creative breakthroughs' are a lot less common than trial and error, constant 'worrying' at a problem and continual improvement on what has been tried before until something unusual, fresh and workable emerges.
- *Able to overcome emotional blocks to creativity of which there are many*, for example, fear of taking risks; fear of making mistakes; fear of being judged; fear of standing out.
- *Driven by an obsessive commitment to their work mediated by a spirit of play, fun and adventure.*

Of course, this a tall order and it is not given to all of us to be as original and groundbreaking as we would like. But even if managers cannot always have the ideas themselves, they can at least demonstrate the qualities of empathy and understanding which build an environment in which creative energy is encouraged within the organisation they manage.

Pause for thought

How to disable your creative manager

All too often organisations engage in 'double talk' in which rhetoric about supporting creativity is subverted by the day-to-day processes based on immediate tasks and deadlines. Take this quote from the CEO of a Fortune 200 company:

> We're always on the look out for someone broad gauge. We're especially impressed by good 'all rounders', people with a broad portfolio of talents, interests and achievements. They've done something interesting with their lives and may do something interesting for us. We look at a CV and say 'This man seems different, there's evidence of a creative mind here. He will be an asset to us'. But then, soon after he's appointed, we're groaning that he won't stay late or is reluctant to make the 'stop over' in Scunthorpe because of his poetry class.'

Question
Have you ever been on the receiving end of this sort of 'double bind'?

2.4.6 Political skills

Finally, successful managers display political skills. Organisations are ultimately political systems. All organisations have limited resources. Groups within the organisation all want a share of these resources to further their projects. This means that bargaining, conflict and the selective mobilisation of power are essential to control the process by which the cake is divided. Winners in this organisational game are often those who are politically saavy and know how to make a good case and manage organisational rules in their own favour.

As John Hunt (1992) says, senior managers are not in a position to claim that they are above the dirty business of politics. If they don't play the political game then they are abandoning the ground for others to skew the system in their own interests.

Organisational politics involves:

- senior managers building up their departments by fighting for additional resources and authority;
- senior managers engaging in debate over the 'meaning' of the strategic plan so that definitions favourable to their interests prevail;
- conflict between cliques over equipment, space, budgets, staff, etc.;
- individuals jockeying for position to advance their careers.

Organisational politics is the 'backstage' of the organisation where the empire building, log rolling, careerism, interest-group lobbying and patronage relationships take place. The skills which are needed here involve all the qualities we have considered before and some other, more specific ones.

(a) *Diagnostic skills* – The best political operators seem to be effective in mapping the political terrain. They have a sense of the distribution of power within an organisation, the perspectives and cultures of different groups, who are the prime movers of events, the agendas of different actors and who has to be won over to build a winning coalition behind an initiative (Hunt 1992, Pfeffer 1981).

(b) *Tactical skills* – Managers with political skill seem to know how to switch between methods of influence. They know how to test the water for a proposal while avoiding a commitment on which it is difficult to renege. They use formal authority sparingly because they know that the overt use of power demonstrates not strength but weakness. They prefer to achieve their objectives through more indirect means. The skills here involve 'fixing' meetings in advance by getting the powerful 'on side' before they go into committee; cutting deals with the most powerful players; engaging in social exchange relationships (e.g. support in return for patronage) to construct critical alliances around core issues; controlling the timing and presentation of issues; using outsiders to legitimate activity; using networks to plant and collect confidential information (Kakabadse 1983).

(c) *Shaping skills* – Sophisticated players seem to be good at shaping the political process so that they can achieve their goals indirectly, through influence and persuasion. Accurately attuned to what is at stake for each of the participants in events, the politician-manager concentrates on areas of common interest to build consensus while subtly moving perceptions so that change becomes possible. This involves the ability to read signals, develop rapport and sell ideas in terms of the other's interests. Language skills are important here. Political managers know how to manoeuvre to promote sectional advantage while claiming to speak for the organisation as a whole and justifying what is done in terms of the rallying symbol of the 'greater good of the company'. They use language to 'manage attention' and to 'manage meaning' (Bennis and Nanus 1985). They are adept at presenting arguments, anticipating objections and counter-arguments; using language with a sense of its emotional associations to convince others of their definition of the situation. Here politics shades into 'impression management', conveying messages through personal performances so that others are influenced to endorse values, beliefs and actions (Mangham 1986).

What kind of political animal are you?

All effective managers play the political game but some are more skilful than others. Here is a satirical model of political behaviour which uses animal stereotypes. In terms of these analogies how would you define yourself?

Foxes (clever)
- interested in power
- somewhat unprincipled
- calculating
- simulate feelings
- close to grapevine
- get support through bargaining
- manipulate procedures
- will exploit others' weaknesses
- cunning, manipulative

Owls (wise)
- aware of purpose
- clear principles
- have personal ethics
- tactful/emotionally literate
- good listeners
- learn from mistakes
- use rules for higher ends
- sense of loyalty
- look for win/win
- wise statesman

Donkeys (inept)
- not skilled interpersonally
- play psychological games (badly)
- self-obsessed
- emotionally illiterate
- judgements based on feelings
- inept at building alliances
- not listening
- see black/white
- not tuned to grapevine
- think in formulae

Lambs (innocent)
- ethical
- rely on formal systems
- don't appreciate politics
- believe in authority
- believe in position power
- respect for rationality
- believe ideology
- open/share information
- loyalty
- naivety

Table 2.1 What kind of political animal are you?

Source: 'Political management: developing the management portfolio', *Journal of Management Development*, Vol. 9, No. 3, pp. 42–59 (Baddeley, S. and James, K. 1990)

2.4.7 Managerial wisdom

The genuinely self-developing manager seeking to master his or her craft and become a sophisticated 'master manager' is in search of wisdom to become an organisational owl. Watson (2001) talks of the frustrations of managers trying to articulate deeper processes of thinking, judging and acting which are often 'glossed' as either 'experience' or reduced to a few abstract formulae. Resisting this temptation but continuing to seek your own personal ordering and articulation of meaning within the chaos of organising is the mark of wise practice.

Isaiah Berlin (1979) in a famous essay suggested that wisdom among wo(men) of power starts with an understanding that the strategies are always bound to fail because they can never account for the infinite complexities and variety of human behaviour. The abstractions and formulae of those who claim to plan and control are always at odds with the 'intractable and infinitely complex relationships between men and events'. Instead of trying to rationalise and pretend that their resolutions, decisions and memos can shape the chaos of business and organisational environments, Berlin recommends the cultivation of sensitivity to the deeper structures of experiences. By this he seems to mean the development of a fine-tuned awareness of the way things are going, the flow of events, the boundaries of the possible. Among other qualities it requires an ability to discriminate sensibly between the real and the sham, an appreciation of how issues are interlinked, how change in one sphere will have consequences in another, and things are not always as they seem.

Although this may sound obscurantist and mystificatory to some, others such as Ericisson and Smith (1991) are obviously following a similar track when they say that wise decisions often do not require vast amounts of information or massive expertise, more a different way of seeing which offers a possible way out. Seeing the familiar in a new way is part of wisdom, as are the following.

- Tolerating contradictions between alternative points of view, both of which may have part of the truth and staying with paradox until some resolution can be found.
- Appreciating that the working out of a dialectic is fundamental to the frictional medium in which management must be conducted.
- Recognising that all organisational knowledge is partial, a representation filtered through ideologies, perspectives and expectations.
- Acknowledging that your understanding will be conditioned by your subjectivity. Wise practitioners are fully aware of themselves – their prejudices, values and perspectives (having deliberately made these explicit to themselves through reflection) and understand how these will influence them.
- Appreciating that issues need to be understood in terms of underlying tendencies, not just surface phenomena. Looking beyond facades of coherence and falsely rational appearances.
- Seeking to make critical inquiry an everyday reflex, that is, constant self-questioning, seeing things from the viewpoint of others, accepting that everything cannot be classified into defined categories or clear patterns.

It is likely that the reader will be able to add to this list of 'wise' behaviours. Ericsson and Smith stress that these skills take years to build up through exposure to a variety of experience, observation, reflection, listening to others (and the voice within), mediated by humility and an intrinsic desire to improve.

Grint (2001) concludes that Aristotle's belief that leading (and managing) requires *techne* (skills), *episteme* (knowledge) and *phronesis* (wisdom) is still relevant. While the first two can be taught directly, the third, and most important to managing, may only be acquired through reflection on experience which is ultimately the responsibility of the individual. It is ironic that wisdom, arguably the most important quality in using managerial power with principled purpose, is that very quality which we seem to know least about developing.

> **Pause for thought**
>
> ### Emergent being
>
> Marcel Proust, the great writer, had something to say about becoming wise which applies to being a managerial leader quite as much as being a thoughtful practitioner of life:
>
> > 'We do not receive wisdom, we must discover it for ourselves, after a journey through the wilderness which no one can make for us, which no one can spare us, for our wisdom is the point of view from which we come at last to regard the world'
>
> The beginning of wisdom in management is knowing that you need to make the journey and that you will largely be alone in doing so. Are you ready for that? Do you have some sort of strategy of self reflection and learning so that you can proceed?
>
> Source: Marcel Proust (1927) Remembrance of Things Past, Chatto and Windus

2.5 Conclusion

Management is a complex activity. It requires highly developed cognitive, interpersonal, presentational and political skills. Various empirical studies have found that managerial behaviour defies easy categorisation. Managing is a disjointed activity in which the significant and the trivial are interspersed. The qualities which make up a successful manager are numerous and varied (technical, social, emotional, cognitive and political skills). Despite the many changes in organisations and management that have occurred in recent times, is continuity in the management process and the skills required to perform it more pronounced than discontinuity in the daily experience of managing? Would the manager from the 1940s transported to an office in the early years of the new century still recognise the same deep processes of managing? Perhaps the processes of sense-making, of constructing meaning from the complexity of events and the skills of coordinating and persuading others have a timeless quality to them. Equally, despite the fads and fashions, how quickly do the processes of learning for those who are to be groomed for the use of authority really change from epoch to epoch? These are themes which will thread through this book and are questions to which we will return.

Review questions

1. Can you see a clear linkage between formal, classical definitions of management and what managers do? Explain.

2. Do you think that the practice of management, in its essentials, has really changed over the past 50 years? Discuss.

3. Fashions in training, learning and development come and go and terminology changes. However, the fundamental means by which people are developed to exercise (managerial) power are relatively unchanging. How far would you agree with this statement?

4 'The soft skills in management are the most vital and also the most unteachable. People either learn them for themselves or they don't. Despite its claims, MD is almost irrelevant to building these higher level skills. If you don't have the self insight you won't go far'. How would you react to this comment by a senior manager?

5 How far would you agree with the view that general management requires skills which are not so different from those required in ordinary social life?

6 'At higher levels of management you need to be a lay politician'. Do you agree?

Web links

A website which examines the traits and qualities of managers and leaders:
http://www.mapnp.org/library/ldership/traits.htm

The website of the Chartered Management Institute which has led much recent debate on the qualities needed in management and the role of MD:
www.managers.org.uk

A website on Emotional Intelligence which you might try:
www.myskillsprofile.com

A useful website on leadership issues:
http://leadertoleader.org

DVDs/Videos

Three DVDs, one a soap opera, one a Hollywood film and one a fly-on-the-wall documentary, are worth watching because they give a sense of 'being there' as managers conduct their business. However, with the two dramatisations you have to allow for exaggeration.

The Power Game, Parts 1 and 2, ITV (1964–68)
Gives a sense of managers doing their stuff. Highly popular with the British management community at the time and still relevant today.

Executive Suite (1953) Director: Robert Wise
A believable glimpse of power and politics in the boardroom.

Startup.com (2001) Director: Chris Hegedus and Jehane Noujaim
A documentary which shadows two dot.com entrepreneurs as they try to make their business work. Again, a feeling of watching over the shoulders of directors 'doing management'.

There are innumerable films on leadership, although not many set within business organisations. Try:

Dead Poet's Society (1989) Director: Peter Weir
Gandhi (1982) Director: Richard Attenborough
Thirteen Days (2000) Director: Roger Donaldson
Twelve Angry Men (1957) Director: Sidney Lumet

If you 'read' these films and others cited in forthcoming chapters as 'text', there are many lessons to be had.

Recommendations for further reading

Those texts marked with an asterisk in the bibliography (below) are recommended for further reading, especially the following:

Dalton, M. (1959) *Men Who Manage.* A classic which some readers will question as recommended reading because of its age, but it provides a sense of the day-to-day processes of management and the tactics involved, which has not been bettered.

Kotter, J. (1982) *The General Managers.* Another excellent ethnography of how managers perform their craft with 'evergreen' lessons.

Raelin, J. (2003) *Leaderful Organisations.* Breaks the paradigm by suggesting that building leadership is not just, or even mainly, about developing individuals but more about building teams and building organisations, one of the key themes of this book.

Bibliography

Adams, J. (1988) *The Care and Feeding of Ideas,* Penguin.

*Baddeley, S. and James, K. (1990) 'Political management: developing the management portfolio', *Journal of Management Development,* Vol. 9, No. 3.

*Barker, R. (1997) 'How can we train leaders if we do not know what leadership is?', *Human Relations,* Vol. 50, No. 4.

Barnard, C. (1938) *The Functions of the Executive,* Blackwell.

Bass, B. (1990) *Bass and Sodgill's Handbook of Leadership,* Free Press.

Bass, B. (1995) 'The meaning of leadership', in Wren, J. *The Leader Companion: Insights on Leadership through the Ages,* Free Press.

Beardwell, I. and Holden, L. (2001) *Human Resource Management: A Contemporary Approach,* Ch. 9, Prentice Hall.

*Bennis, W. and Nanus, B. (1985) *Leaders: Strategies for Taking Charge,* Harper and Row.

Berlin, I. (1979) *Russian Thinkers,* Penguin.

Boyatzis, R. (1982) *The Competent Manager,* Wiley.

*Boyatzis, R. (1993) 'Beyond competence: the choice to be a leader', *Human Resource Management Review,* Vol. 3, No. 1.

Boyatzis, R., Stubs, E. et. al. (2002) 'Learning cognitive and emotional intelligence competencies through graduate management education', *Academy of Management Learning and Education,* Vol. 1, No. 2.

Brotherton, C. (1999) *The Social Psychology of Management,* OUP.

Burgoyne, J. (1988) 'Management development for the individual and the organisation', in *Personnel Management,* June.

*Carlzon, J. (1987) *Moments of Truth,* Harper and Row.

Cooper, C. (2005) *Leadership and Management in the 21st Century,* OUP.

*Dalton, M. (1959) *Men Who Manage,* Wiley.

Davies, G. (2003) 'The softer face of the front office', *The Sunday Times,* 9 Feb.

Dulewicz, V. (2000) 'Emotional Intelligence: the key to future successful corporate leadership', *Journal of General Management,* Vol. 25, No. 3.

Easterby-Smith, M. (1986) *Evaluation of Management Education,* Gower.

Ericsson, K. and Smith, J. (1991) *Towards a General Theory of Expertise,* Cambridge University Press.

*Fineman, S. (1994) 'Organising and emotion', in Hassard, J. and Parker, M. (1994) *Towards a New Organisation Theory,* Routledge.

*Fisher, C. (1996) 'Management stances: perspectives on management development', in Stewart, J. and McGoldrick, J. (1996) *Human Resource Development: Perspectives, Strategies and Practices,* Prentice Hall.

Gardner, H. (1993) *Multiple Intelligences,* Basic Books.

Garratt, B. (1994) *The Learning Organisation,* Harper Collins.

Geneen, H. (1985) *Managing,* Grafton.

*Goffman, E. (1960) *The Presentation of Self in Everyday Life*. Penguin.
Goleman, D. (1996) *Emotional Intelligence*, Bloomsbury.
Gosling, J. and Mintzberg, H. (2004) 'The education of practising managers', *MIT Sloan Management Review*, Summer.
Grint, K. (2001) *The Arts of Leadership*, OUP.
Guilford, J. and Hoepfner, R. (1971) *The Analysis of Intelligence*, McGraw Hill.
*Hales, C. (1986) 'What do managers do? A critical review of the evidence', *Journal of Management Studies* 23, 88–115.
*Hassard, J. and Parker, M. (1994) *Towards a New Organisation Theory*, Routledge.
*Heller, R. (1985) *The New Naked Manager*, Coronet Books.
Heller, R. (1995) *The Naked Manager for the 90s*, Little, Brown and Company.
Hunt, J. (1992) *Managing People at Work*, McGraw Hill.
Kakabadse, A. (1983) *The Politics of Management*, Gower.
*Kotter, J. (1982) *The General Managers*, Free Press.
Leavitt, H. and Bahrani, H. (1988) *Managerial Psychology*, Ch. 4, University of Chicago Press.
Lindblom, C. (1959) 'The science of muddling through', *Public Administration Review*, Vol. 2.
*Lindenfield, G. (2000) *Emotional Confidence: Simple Steps to Manage your Feelings*, Harper Collins.
*Mangham, I. (1986) *Power and Performance in Organisations*, Blackwell.
Mangham, I. (1988) 'Managing the executive process', in Pettigrew, A. (1988) *Competitiveness and the Management Process*, Blackwell.
*Mangham, I. and Pye, A. (1991) *The Doing of Managing*, Blackwell.
*McKenny, J. and Keen, P. (1976) 'How managers' minds work', *Harvard Business Review*, May.
Mintzberg, H. (1973) *The Nature of Managerial Work*, Harper and Row.
Mintzberg, H. (1976) 'Planning on the left side and managing on the right', *Harvard Business Review*, July.
Mullins, L. (2001) *Management and Organisational Behaviour*, Ch. 6, Prentice Hall.
Mumford, A. (1993) *Management Development: Strategies for Action*, CIPD.
Mumford, A. (1999) 'What managers really do', *Management Education and Development*, Vol. 18, No. 3.
Mumford, A. and Gold, J. (2004) *Management Development: Strategies for Action*, CIPD.
Pedler, M., Burgoyne, J. and Boydell, T. (1994, 2001, 2007 editions) *A Manager's Guide to Self Development*, McGraw Hill.
Pettigrew, A. (1988) *Competitiveness and the Management Process*, Blackwell.
Pfeffer, J. (1981) *Power in Organisations*, Pitman Publishing.
Polyani, M. (1966) *The Tacit Dimension*, Routledge.
Pye, A. (2005) 'Leadership and organising: sense making in action', *Leadership*, 1(1).
*Raelin, J. (2003) *Leaderful Organisations: How to Bring Out Leadership in Everyone*, Barrett-Koehler.
*Raelin, J. (2004) 'Don't bother putting leadership into people', *Academy of Management Executive*, Vol. 18, No. 3.
Rollinson, D. (2002) *Organisational Behaviour and Analysis*, Prentice Hall.
Russell, B. (1962) *In Praise of Idleness*, Unwin.
Sadler-Smith, E. (2006) *Learning and Development for Managers*, Blackwell.
Salaman, G. and Mabey, C. (1995) *Strategic Human Resource Management*, Blackwell.
Sampson, A. (1973) *ITT: The Sovereign State*, Coronet.
Simon, H. (1957) *Models of Man*, Wiley.
*Srivasta, S. (1983) *The Executive Mind*, Jossey-Bass.
Stewart, R. (1985) *The Reality of Management*, Pan.
Stewart, R. (1994) *Managing Today and Tomorrow*, MacMillan.
Strauss, A. (1978) *Negotiations*, Jossey-Bass.
*Watson, T. (2001) *In Search of Management*, Thomson.
Watson, T. (2002a) *Conference presentation papers*, Judge Institute.
Watson, T. (2002b) *Organising and Managing Work*, Prentice Hall.
*Weick, K. (1979) *The Social Psychology of Organising*, Addison-Wesley.
*Weick, K. (1983) 'Managerial thought in the context of action', in Srivasta, S. et al. (1983) *The Executive Mind*, Jossey – Bass.
Weick, K. (1995) *Sense making in Organisations*. Addison-Wesley.
Weisberg, R. (1986) *Creativity: Genius and other Myths*, Freeman and Co.
Whetton, D. and Cameron, K. (2002) *Developing Management Skills*, Pearson Education.
*Wrapp, E. (1967) 'Good managers don't make policy decisions', *Harvard Business Review*, Sept.
Yukl, G. (2002) *Leadership in Organisations*, Prentice Hall.

3 The models and theories of management development

Learning outcomes

After reading the chapter you should be able to understand, analyse and explain:

- the value and relevance of theory to the modelling of MD processes;
- the contribution of various typologies, frameworks, theories and models to conceptualising MD;
- the dimensions of systems, relational models, radical pluralist and critical perspectives to understanding MD as a total process;
- the value of critical theory as an alternative to mainstream theories;
- the turn to management learning as a new paradigm for critical understanding.

3.1 Introduction

In this deliberately brief chapter we will look at the theoretical literature on MD. Can we map the field of the territory for the newcomer and provide an overview of the main theoretical approaches which make up this subject? A critical review of MD theory at this stage may help orientation to this complex area of thinking and practice. The value of theory to the practitioner is that it gives you a framework of analysis and holistic understanding to help diagnosis and modelling the learning processes in real-world experience.

Of course, there is a danger of scaring off the unwary reader with the complexity of some of the thinking, but the reader is encouraged to stay with it and master the overall construction of reality which is being proposed. Effective and appropriate action in MD arises from clear thinking and from having a strategic sense of the whole. Reflect on these models for developing your own organising frameworks to make sense of the paradoxes and contradictions which are evident in MD.

3.2 The nature and value of theory in MD

During the course of this book various theories of social science will be considered in areas as diverse as learning theory, theories of the learning organisation, psychological theories of creativity, thinking and team process, theories of organisation behaviour, HRM, labour market and human capital, as they impact on MD. This field of study and practice seems to delight in eclecticism. The strands of conceptualisation from which MD, as an applied social science, is woven are represented in the box below. Some particular concepts drawn from these broad areas of knowledge have become central to the thinking and doing of MD (that is, its applied knowledge or 'praxis'). So, ideas in cognitive psychology underpin the psychometrics and 'learning styles' approach used on thousands of management training courses; humanistic psychology informs techniques in team building and OD; famous theories in learning theory such as Argyris's (1992) 'single and double loop learning' and Nonaka's (1996) 'tacit knowing' models have been used by legions of developers to guide learning and justify a commitment to experiential learning.

However, there are few theories of MD as an intellectual approach *in its own right and as a 'total process'*. This is because this field of study is still in the process of crystallising. It is still in the process of defining its knowledge base, its boundaries and its core concepts. At present, MD is an inclusive term for very practical and prescriptive contributions designed to help busy managers and very theoretical and philosophical contributions intended to encourage new thinking. It sets the terrain on which a diverse range of people – consultants, trainers, change agents, HR practitioners, line managers and academics – come together with their different ideologies and concerns. This diversity can make for rich debate, but it is also evidence that MD is a highly fragmented discipline with little philosophical grounding for good practice, little tested practice or agreement on what it can do.

People tend to come to MD with cultural baggage, derived from the world-views inherent in their professional ideologies. The manager with a training background and an interest in vocational NVQs will have a different perception of the value of MD to the CEO concerned with change management, building knowledge management and the learning organisation; the academic with a background in organisational sociology and concerned with processes of professionalisation in management will have another perspective; so too will the OD consultant concerned to develop the whole system. All will have equally legitimate constructions of MD but their different mental sets will influence what they select as important, their definitions, values and vocabularies.

An eclectic subject: interdisciplinary contributions to the knowledge base of MD

Discipline	Contribution to thinking in MD
Cognitive Psychology	– Personality dimensions and management
	– Motivation
	– Decision-making
	– Job design

Social Psychology	– Leadership and followership
	– Satisfaction at work
	– Psychological contract at work
	– Group/team processes
	– Communication theory
Humanistic Psychology	– Emotional intelligence
	– Personal growth
	– Work and identity
	– Counselling and mentoring
Learning Theory	– Adult learning
	– Learning styles
	– Learning strategies
	– Organisational learning
Sociology	– Organisational structures and managing
	– Systems and organisations
	– Management roles
	– Management authority
	– Power and status
	– Organisational conflict
	– Management of change
Anthropology	– Comparative management cultures/practices
	– Culture and behaviour
	– Cross-cultural patterns
	– Culture, myths and symbols
Politics	– Organisational conflict
	– Inter/intra-organisational politics
	– Networks
	– Power and organisation/management strategies
	– Organisations as 'arenas'
Economics	– Labour markets
	– National competitive performance
	– Government skills, policies
	– Corporate strategy
	– Planning systems

Table 3.1 An eclectic subject: interdisciplinary contributions to the knowledge base of MD

Of course, this is not a complete tabulation of *all* the influences on MD and many of the terms could be placed under different headings. However, it does indicate the 'rainbow' of disciplines and subject areas that make up this field of study and practice.

At present, MD lacks a unifying logic which cements the different disciplinary building blocks into a foundation on which to conceptualise MD as a whole and provide a theoretical underpinning for good practice. A range of authors (Burgoyne and Reynolds 1997, Thomson et al. 2001, Storey 1989) have commented on the meagre state of theory in MD, the lack of a coherent overarching theory or 'meta-narrative' of MD or even a careful 'mapping' of the field so that the nexus of variables influencing the nature and effectiveness of MD is carefully delineated.

Some readers may hesitate here and wonder why models maps or theories are necessary when they pride themselves on their pragmatism. The answer is that we surely need an explicit philosophy of practice if we are not to be in thrall to the assumptions of long-discredited ideas which we have absorbed as common sense (e.g. Keynes's (1936) famous observation on the much vaunted pragmatism of the practical man of business, which turns out, when analysed, to be based on defunct thinking). Unreflective practice gives rise to faddism and constant search for novelty which has always plagued this area of development. Peter Aspen (1994) writes, tongue-in-cheek but with acuity, about:

> The new MD gurus who come across like 'Proz-acked' Nietzsches who have been locked up in a New Age bookshop all weekend . . . Creativity and flux are the buzzwords; the ability to respond to rapid change with imaginative leaps . . . Borrowing from 'the end of history'; new science (chaos theory and fuzzy logic) and philosophy (soft intuition over intractable logic) and Eastern religion . . . Forget management science, management education has gone postmodern.

This quotation is provocative but also illuminating. A professional area so uncertain of its core knowledge and techniques that it feels the need, like a jackdaw, to steal glittery ideas from other disciplines, seems greatly in need of its own body of research, evaluated practice and applied theory to direct professional practice. This could be the basis for the reflective theory and practice *(praxis)* which Burgoyne and Reynolds (1997) advocate. But what exactly does theory offer to the professional management developer?

According to Stewart (1999) professional theories and models (and for convenience they are here assumed to be the same) are important because they:

- abstract reality by identifying the essential variables in a situation so that this reality can be understood 'in the round';
- represent reality by suggesting relationships between the variables, that is, connections and even 'cause and effect';
- explain the structured nature of the relationship between variables;
- suggest other possible relationships to be tested further;
- take you beyond the confusion of current reality by suggesting an ideal or pure state of reality by which to judge an action or outcome;
- allow some degree of prediction using different scenarios.

Some models in MD are more descriptive than analytical and go little beyond categorisation or typology; others try to conceptualise in order to offer deeper explanation; a few attempt analysis to help the decision maker form better judgements and predictions. Models are usually judged by criteria of utility and validity. With this in mind, let us look at some of the recent attempts to provide integrated conceptualisation of this field which may be of value to genuinely reflective practitioners concerned to find a conceptual basis for their practice.

> **Pause for thought**
>
> ### 'Theories in use' and reflective practice
>
> Argyris (1992) talks about 'theories in use' which are the tacit models guiding the judgements of professionals, often different from their 'espoused theories', a more public rhetoric by which they may justify their actions. Sophisticated learning professionals are conscious of their working theories which have often evolved over time by critically engaging with received knowledge tested against their own experience. They try to avoid any major disjuncture between their rhetoric and practice.
>
> #### Question
> *If you were asked to articulate your 'theories in use' and define the core concepts which guide your behaviour as a manager, a developer or a student of management, what would you say?*

3.3 Typologies of MD

Perhaps the simplest models are the categorisations of behaviour into 'types'. There are a large number of these typologies in MD, for example, Mumford's (1993) 'Three types of MD' (informal/accidental, integrated/opportunistic, formalised/planned); Burgoyne's (1988) '6 levels of maturity of organisational management development'; Honey and Mumford's (1992) and Kolb's (1984)) variations of the 'learning cycle' model. We will consider these in detail in those sections of the book where they seem to have a natural place.

At least in the opinion of this writer, these typologies represent the small change of thinking about MD. They are simple formulations which provide practitioners with a reductionist schema and a vocabulary for talking about complex issues. These models may be teleological (evolutionary, moving to an ideal end state) and normative, suggesting progressive movement through a hierarchy of stages (e.g. Burgoyne 1988) or static and descriptive (e.g. Kolb 1984). While providing a 'way of thinking' the danger of these formulations is that the categories are far too abstract and distanced from real-world complexity to be convincing and the classification systems which they represent can easily become ideological labels, inhibiting developers and managers from thinking for themselves. Here the model is used to short-circuit thinking and justify action rather than guide it reflectively, for example, as in the intellectual reflex implied by the statement: 'I'm going to design a short course for supervisors which will satisfy all styles of learning using the Honey and Mumford model'. Notice the ideological knee-jerk here.

Other criticisms of these institutional models are that they tend to suggest universalistic principles which ignore context and they are prescriptive in tone. They also tend to be over-formalised, objectivised and narrowly rationalistic. Based on functionalist or behavioural assumptions, they focus on the impersonal, formal aspects of organisations and present a very one-dimensional picture of organisational process which some critics believe is based on myths (i.e. imply idealised images of management control, organisational integration and unity).

Ashton's MD steps

In some ways, Ashton's model typifies some of the criticisms made above. He defines MD in very institutional and formalistic terms which assume the primacy of managerial interests: 'a conscious and systematic decision making process to control the development of managerial resources and achieve organisational goals and strategies'. However, he does avoid prescription and considers the contingency of MD patterns, seeking to link levels of MD activity and levels of commitment of line managers to MD as the vital relationship in determining how seriously MD is taken in the organisation. He defines three patterns.

- *Pattern 1*: Little or no genuine commitment to MD from line managers. Developing people is not seen as a vital line responsibility and the MD plan is largely ignored or given perfunctory attention. This is reflected in low levels of MD activity.
- *Pattern 2*: Line managers are uncertain about the merits of development and participate with only shallow commitment. The *amount* of MD activity increases over Pattern 1, because line managers feel they have to 'go along', but not necessarily the *quality*.
- *Pattern 3*: A more balanced and integrated situation in which line managers embrace the development concept, to establish a climate of learning in partnership with MD. Development is integrated with normal activities. Ashton believes that MD activity may here be more difficult to detect because it is embedded in the organisational process, but the effectiveness of what is done is better.

This simple model is useful in emphasising that contextual elements, especially climate (e.g. the goodwill and motivation of key stakeholders), may be essential in determining the nature of MD in an organisation. As Storey suggests, it also indicates that 'busy-ness' in MD may not be a reliable guide to the quality of MD which is going on and that formal indicators of activity may be less important than the enthusiasm of key actors. These could be important factors for MD practitioners to bear in mind in making their plans.

Source: Adapted from Ashton, D. (1975) in Ashton, D., Easterby-Smith, M. and Irvine, C., *Management Development, Theory and Practice*

A more recent schema (Barham et al. 1987) conceptualises HRD (and MD) as a progressive movement between levels of strategic sophistication. Again the step-by-step organising logic is dominant. The 4F model has been highly influential in helping MD managers plot their organisation on a continuum of developmental sophistication and its categories have entered into the professional vocabulary of strategic MD (see Chapter 4).

The Ashridge 4F model: stages in the development of MD

The model identifies four phases in the changing development of MD.

- *The fragmented approach*: Here MD is ad hoc and unplanned. There is little connection between the development of organisational goals and the MD.

MD activities cannot be easily justified in terms of the business. MD of this kind puts it outside the loop of corporate strategic development.

- *The formalised approach*: Here MD is systematic, planned and integrated with other HRM functions. However, the downside may be that the MD programme is based on over-formalised analysis and practice which only tangentially links the realities of managers with their own needs for learning. The rationalistic focus, technically discrete and logical in itself, may also fail to connect with larger business concerns and objectives. This is MD which has its own strategies worked out but these are uncoupled from corporate strategy.

- *Focused approach*: At this stage, MD is based on continuous learning. There are clear links between organisational goals and development plans. A blend of development activities is available, contextualised in terms of the realities of managers and their preferences for learning. MD is visionary and open to wider influences (e.g. environment, community, ethics, cross-cultural working, etc.) and enlists the commitment of the line. MD is seen as working for the benefit of the individual and the organisation.

- *Fully integrated model*: Management learning of all kinds is integrated in the everyday work of the organisation and reflection on lessons for development (individual, group and organisational) is part of the common sense of organising. MD is closely tied to all aspects of HRM, close to the centre of corporate policy-making and recognised as a key driver of overall strategic performance.

The Ashridge model holds out the prospect of steady movement to higher levels of MD sophistication, strategic integration and purpose. However, the model is open to criticism, as with all the taxonomies, for its simplistic definition of stages and the teleological assumptions.

Source: Adapted from Stewart, J. (1999) *Employee Development*, Prentice Hall, p. 129. Original: Barham, K., Fraser, J. et al. (1987) *Management for the Future*, Ashridge College

While acknowledging their limitations, some taxonomies which try to take a big broad view suggest the possibility of a new way of looking at familiar phenomena. They can jar us sufficiently to reflect on and revise our assumptions (see box below).

Rationales for organisations investing in MD

Lees (1992) argues that MD can only be understood as a 'negotiated order' built from the confluence of three influences ie: individual career ambitions; organisation succession plans; organisational performance management. (Perhaps in more recent years we might want to add another: 'personal development plans'). Lees believed that the '10 faces' of MD, or the 10 agendas, which she identified, were a consequence of the interplay between these influences.

- *Functional performance*: these are mainstream managerial assumptions about MD. MD is driven by strategic objectives and the corporate needs (eg the right mix of talents for competitive positioning) and is rational and planned.

- *Agricultural rationale*: perceives the need to 'cultivate' managers so that they grow into their jobs. Unlike the functionalist perspective this 'agricultural' metaphor defines MD as befittingly 'organic', rather haphazard and mostly based on natural learning.
- *Functional–defensive*: conceives of MD as a process of building a talent pool of skills for the future; this often happens in an informal way, however planned the process.
- *Socialisation rationale*: sees MD as mainly about culture building; diffusing company values so that managers have shared values. MD is associated here with maintaining order.
- *Political reinforcement*: here MD is regarded as propaganda. It is a means of building the political credibility of those leading the change process and ensuring loyalty among managers.
- *Organisational inheritance*: MD is defined as the key to management succession and career success; MD rituals anoint the 'chosen ones' and help them with the 'dramaturgical' skills which successful use of power requires.
- *Environmental legitimacy*: sees MD as mainly about public relations, shows outside stakeholders that the organisation is living out its own myths (eg: '*in this organisation we invest in professional management*').
- *Compensation*: suggests that MD is offered, and may be seen as offering, some compensation for failures, disappointments and frustrations at work.
- *Psychic defence*: regards MD as a means of creating a sense of belonging in the community of managers (eg: the rituals of MD act as an antidote to anxiety and give people a sense of place within a community).
- *Ceremonial*: defines MD as part of the symbolism of organisation eg: as a 'rite of passage' at different stages of a managerial career and as an emblem of the culture building and strategic impact which the top promotes.

Source: Adapted from Lees, S. (1992) 'Ten faces of management development', *Management Education and Development*, Vol. 23, No. 2

Reflecting on the agendas, you may believe that some are rather cynical or far fetched. However, the value of a simple model like this, which is really no more than a list of categories, is that it opens you up to a different view of the organisation ie: as a locus of competing values and conflicting tensions around MD. This is a useful corrective to orthodox, functionalist thinking which suggests that organisations are balanced harmonies of interests. The model is valuable because it reminds us that there are a number of stakeholders with an interest in the MD of an organisation and shows us that the official agendas of the organisation and personal agendas will differ. This may encourage us to be wary of prescriptive models which define MD ends as if they are uncontroversial and accomplished by neutral technical means. After all, one group's 'rational plan to build management culture' may be another's 'ideological control'.

3.4 Systems theory and MD

Another theoretical perspective on MD is that of systems theory. The word 'system' implies a set of interdependent, interacting elements, combined together in an organised form so that change in any one part will influence change in all the others. This is a concept which derives from an eclectic range of sources, especially the biological and physical sciences.

Mike Doyle (2000, 2001) is the main name associated with systems thinking in MD. His 'open systems' model is reproduced below. He sees it as offering an approach which moves thinking about MD away from what he calls the 'processual and discrete view of MD' to a more strategic focus. Simplistic models of MD based on universalistic claims of 'one solution fits all' (e.g. competency) have encouraged 'canned' unsystemic solutions and disconnected MD from strategic purpose. Doyle (2000, 2001) believes this piecemeal and fragmented pattern of MD can be addressed with a 'full throttle' systems perspective.

Doyle reminds us that the 'systems' approach is just one of the metaphors we can use to imagine the organisation (other metaphors include cultures, theatres, psychic prisons, etc. (see Morgan 1990). 'Systems' represent a useful way of seeing because they help us to think holistically about the 'totality of causal and interdependent patterns' (Doyle 2000, 2001) through which the organisation conducts its business. Using a 'systems' approach MD directs attention away from looking at MD in isolation. Instead it is defined as part of the larger organisational process, linked to the local context of managerial work. This makes it more relevant to those it seeks to help.

Taking a systems approach, MD is defined as an assemblage of elements interrelated to a common goal. As shown in Figure 3.1, inputs are received from beyond the organisation and then transformed by the MD process into outputs. Outputs may be

The management-development process

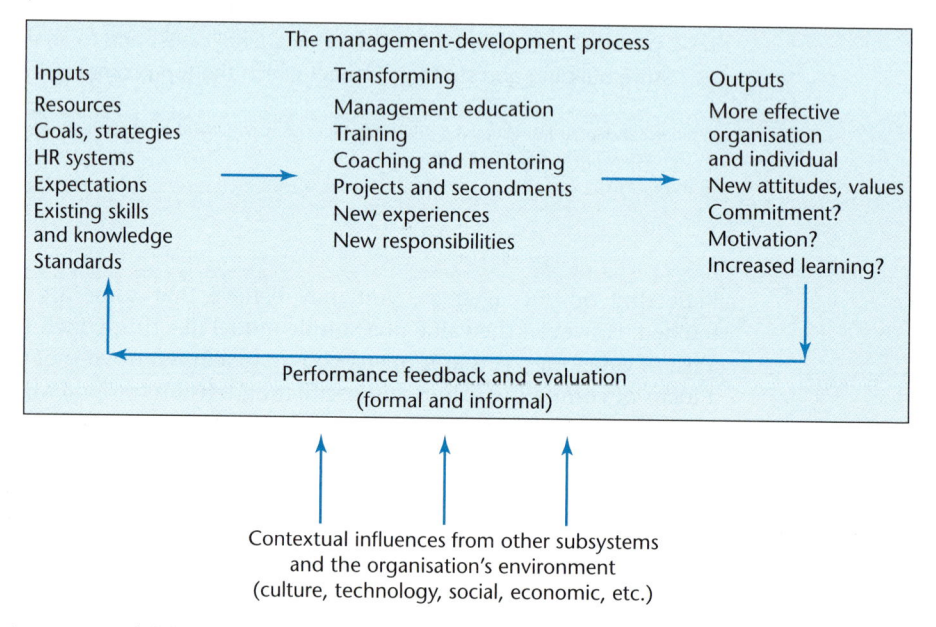

Inputs	Transforming	Outputs
Resources	Management education	More effective
Goals, strategies	Training	organisation
HR systems	Coaching and mentoring	and individual
Expectations	Projects and secondments	New attitudes, values
Existing skills	New experiences	Commitment?
and knowledge	New responsibilities	Motivation?
Standards		Increased learning?

Performance feedback and evaluation
(formal and informal)

Contextual influences from other subsystems
and the organisation's environment
(culture, technology, social, economic, etc.)

Figure 3.1 Doyle's 'open systems' view on MD

Source: Organisational transformation and renewal, *Personnel Review*, Vol. 24, No. 6 (Doyle, M. 1995)

increased competency of the managerial workforce, new attitudes and behaviours and better performance in the organisation as a whole. As an open system, the MD subsystem will interact with and be influenced by variables from other organisational and external subsystems (structural, political, cultural, technological, etc.).

Concentrating on the interrelationships and interdependencies between the influences helps policy makers in MD understand more clearly the field of organisational variables within which MD takes place. So, in considering the cultural variables, MD can be used to reinforce *existing* values or as a catalyst for creating counter-cultures of *alternative* values. In terms of the technological and structural factors, attention may need to be given to identifying the resistances to management learning and the transfer of learning to the workplace and find ways of overcoming these blocks (e.g. developing new skills to accommodate technology, new career systems to keep managers motivated in flattened organisations). Doyle (2000, 2001) claims that a holistic framework helps kindle sensitivity to the strategic needs of the system and the network of connections between parts and the whole. In particular, it encourages an appreciation that the development of the whole is contingent on aligning the parts to create synergies and positively reinforcing loops. In Figure 3.2 below, Doyle's (2000, 2001) key variables impacting on the MD subsystem are brought into sharper relief.

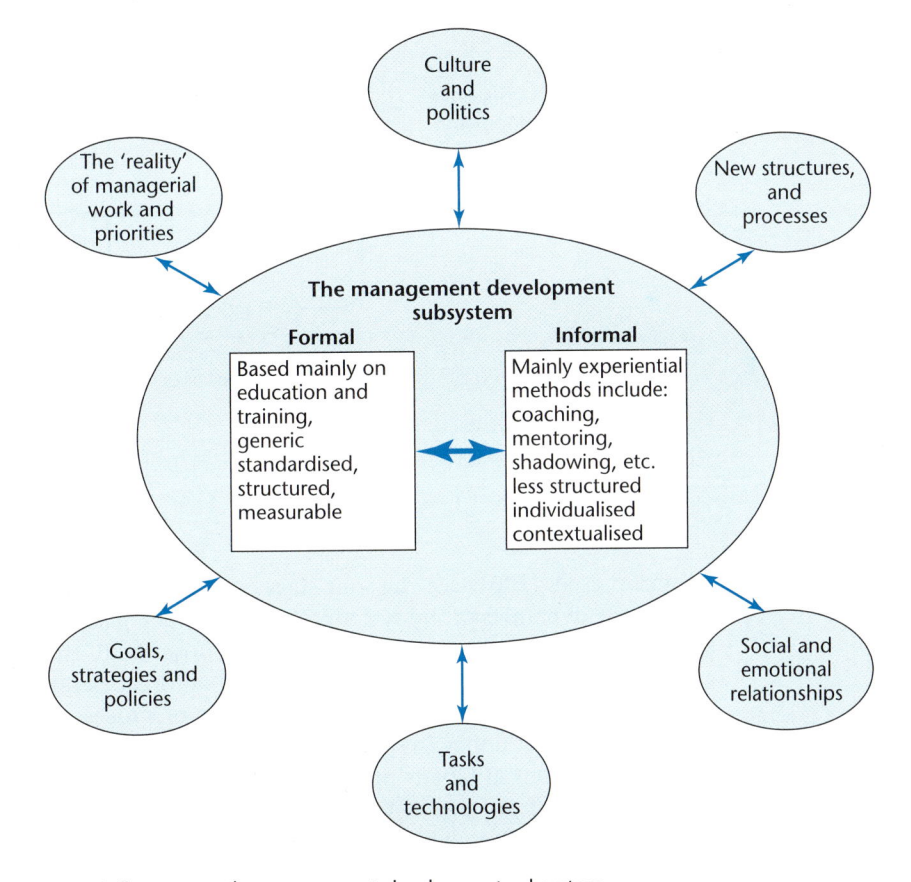

Figure 3.2 Influences on the management-development subsystem
Source: *Journal of Management Development*, Vol. 19, No. 7 (Doyle, M. 2000)

Thomson et al. (2001) have also attempted a holistic model for conceptualising MD in the round, as a totality at the level of the organisation as a whole. What they propose is a framework in which a cycle of four stages set the context for MD processes. The model is clearly influenced by systems thinking and is presented as a format for diagnosing the influences on MD in any particular organisation.

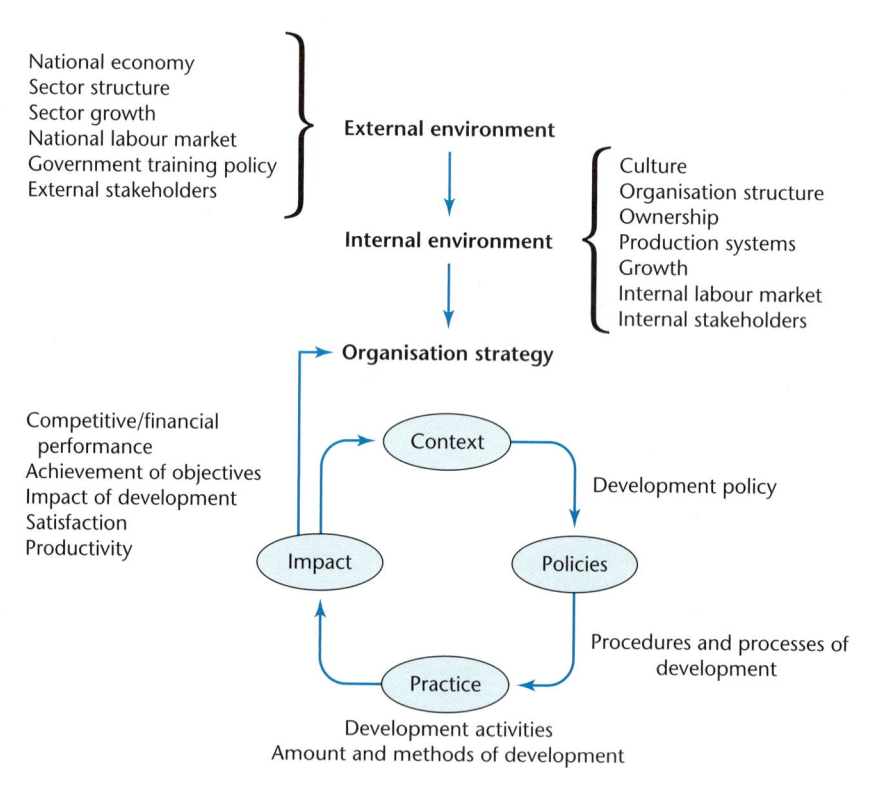

Figure 3.3 Thomson and Mabey's 'new model'
Source: *Changing Patterns of Management Development*, Blackwell (Thomson, A., Mabey, C., Storey, J. et al 2001)

Thomson et al. (2001) see the four stages of the model as interdependent variables driving the dynamics of the system. The *context (or inputs)* are aspects of the external and internal environment influencing organisational strategy to which MD is aligned. Important factors here may be external (organisational size, sector, market); internal (organisational growth, centralisation of processes, responsibility for MD) and labour market policy (in particular the nature of career structures and the degree to which an internal labour market for managers prevails). The context conditions the next element or stage in the cycle: *policies or processes* of MD. MD policy is a reflection of wider HR policy and is taken as an indicator of the degree of institutionalisation and priority given to MD in the system. The implementation of policy will give rise to *practices or outputs*. Outputs will be competency frameworks closely aligned to the organisational needs and managers with more sophisticated skills; they might also be more OD in nature, such as creating a more innovative managerial culture. The effect of these results may have an *impact or outcome* for the organisation as a whole. This is always the most difficult part of MD, to show that all the activity has some larger impact, perhaps on business performance (e.g. productivity, quality of service, management of change, etc.) or on softer indicators (e.g. job satisfaction or organisational commitment). Keeping these stages or elements in the cycle in balanced and smooth synchronisation is seen by the authors as the key to an effective MD system.

Perhaps this is an opportunity to summarise the claimed *benefits* to the organisation of adopting an 'open systems' perspective as a general approach to MD.

- It is a break with institutionalised and over-formalised pictures of MD (some of which we have considered) that lead to ad-hoc, pragmatic palliatives or over-simplified, generic models which are not contextualised or strategic and seem to imply a straightforward, scientific (or is that pseudoscientific?) approach to designing and implementing MD.

- Seeing MD in systems terms means focusing on the organisation's fundamental philosophy, mission and goals and relating MD to its particular circumstances and its managerial needs. By mapping the complex nexus of influences working on the organisation as a whole, MD programmes have the potential to become more strategically directed, more integrated, proactive and appropriate to the complex discontinuous change processes of modern times.

- With a systems view, Doyle (2001) and others believe MD is reframed. Interdependencies and learning loops (negative and positive reinforcing) become apparent (e.g. 'If you develop the organisation you develop the manager; if you develop the organisational culture you develop new managerial behaviour.'). The MD specialist comes to understand the interlocked, interlinked and interdependent nature of organisational life. A leadership development programme, for example, will have consequences for roles, behaviours, managerial ideologies and teamworking which ripple across the organisation. Systems thinking reveals the potential of MD as a change catalyst.

- With a systems perspective, the MD practitioner is likely to be radicalised and to push for involvement in a wider range of activities, developments and strategies. MD emerges from the shadows of HRD and becomes a genuinely transformative organisational learning and development strategy.

It is not hard to criticise this systems model. While it calls to attention a wide range of social, economic and organisational forces operating on and within an organisation which interact to shape the nature of the MD system in any organisation, it could be said that it is over-abstract. The concern to provide a totalising and holistic view seems to overlook human interaction. The focus on interrelationships between 'variables,' and the functions of these relations in strategic terms also presents a picture of organisation as a reified nexus of forces which ignores the 'messy reality' of human choices and actions.

Despite Doyle's (2001) critique of the 'institutional' models, systems approaches share many of the same 'rationalistic', impersonal and fact-like qualities of these earlier representations of MD process. Pitching analysis at the level of the organisation also serves to ignore the perspectives of individual managers who have a big stake in, and influence over MD processes. There is also a sense of *deterministic* behaviour, of 'causal links', 'reinforcing loops' and an 'interconnectedness of parts' which are just a little too contrived as a convincing explanation of organisational process. Biological systems may be part of a vast system of interconnected change, but human interaction seems far less predictable.

Finally, there is the criticism which we return to below, that Doyle's 'open system' model is essentially unitarist in its assumptions. Systems thinking implies that organisations are seen as integrated wholes in which the interests of individuals and even the larger organisation groups are assumed to be largely the same and, through systems engineering, common objectives and shared benefits prevail (or can be 'engineered to do so'). Many critics see this as an unrealistic, even naive picture of human organisation.

Doyle has responded to some of these criticisms by adapting his model to include a 'relational perspective' (Doyle 2000, 2001). He seems to claim that a systems approach can incorporate a model of organisation that is pluralistic and political, even chaotic and disordered. He suggests that the systems framework is not ultimately reducible to a rational-functionalist world-view, that it can be flexed to accommodate a perception of organisations as 'processes' rather than 'things', while preserving the advantages of an holistic focus which maintains a strategic perspective. The consequence of adopting the 'relational perspective' in MD, according to Doyle, is to strongly emphasise its role as a vehicle for OD and the management of strategic change.

Doyle's 'relational perspective'

The following principles underpin Doyle's 'relational perspective':

- Acceptance of organisation as a pluralistic arena. Diversity is acknowledged and managed. The form which MD takes represents the outcome of bargaining between competing interests.
- Recognition that MD is not, and cannot be, based on rational functional processes. Social, political and emotional issues determine the form of development.
- Within this context, MD is part of change management and requires wider change expertise.
- Developers have to build social and political relationships between stakeholders around systemic relationships.
- Ownership of MD is dispersed between stakeholders; MD professionals act as internal consultants reconciling interests in terms of the overall system.
- Criteria and measurement are broadened to include not just outcomes of the immediate programme but 'softer' systems variables and the management of the MD subsystem in terms of the organisational system as a whole (e.g. climate, management style, strategic intent, etc.).

Source: Adapted from Doyle (2000) 'Management development in an era of radical change: evolving a relational perspective', *Journal of Management Development*, Vol. 19, No. 7

3.5 Radical pluralistic models

Burgoyne and Jackson (1997) have taken the shift away from institutional formalised models even further. They see MD as a field of study dominated by functionalist and behavioural thinking. Previous models, including systems, have been too tied to advancing the organisation's instrumental purposes and are allegedly based on an idealised, over-rational analysis of the how things 'should' be working to build learning capabilities rather than how they actually work. This causes analysts to be led by positivist assumptions about the formal aspects of organisation and to seek simple 'cause and effect' relationships (e.g. MD, organisational strategy and performance) which may mystify experience and distort reality.

The *unitarist* model also predominates. Implicitly organisations are seen as based on common interests and all parties are ultimately united in advancing an idealised 'organisational goal' of higher performance through improved learning and cooperative action. The obstacles to achieving this are *institutional* (e.g. lack of 'positive reinforcing links'), rather than *behavioural*. The great weakness of 'unitarism', Burgoyne and Jackson claim, is that it ignores the political dimension of organisations and the cognitive and symbolic behaviour of organisational actors. As a counterpoise to 'unitarism', they posit a 'pluralistic' model as a more realistic frame for understanding management learning in organisations. This recognises diversity of interests within organisations, that conflict between them is an inevitable feature of organisational life, with groups vying for power to realise their projects.

The authors suggest that the image of the organisation as an 'arena' in which various stakeholders come together to define situations in their own interests, bargain and make temporary agreements, is a more useful metaphor for understanding organisational process than that of the 'system'. In this, Burgoyne and Jackson were not original: they were drawing heavily on Silverman's (1970) 'action frame of reference' and Strauss's (1978) 'negotiated order' which have long been established models in interpretive social science. However, putting the concept of the 'arena' within the context of management learning was new.

The 'arena thesis' suggests that management learning activities act as a locus in which the divergent philosophies, purposes, values and agendas of various management departments meet, are contested and differences eventually reconciled. So, for example, a new competency framework or coaching programme may bear the imprimateur of the top management group, but establishing its legitimacy and the form it will take is a matter of political negotiation. Some might say that this is the condition of all management process. However, Burgoyne and Jackson (1997) argue that management learning is a particularly important arena for multiple stakeholder dialogue – questioning, debating, challenging, selling, negotiating and reaching a rough consensus on the purpose and form of a programme – because of the inherent ambiguity of MD (an issue we return to many times in this book) and the multiplicity of interests at stake in shaping management learning (e.g. ideological beliefs about learning, professional 'turfs', diverse perceptions of organisational future, etc.). What emerges from the 'meeting point' of organisational debate are temporary agreements between stakeholders on the meaning and practice of management learning, the form this will take and how it will be implemented.

As Burgoyne and Jackson (1997) wryly comment, institutional theory may actually be disabling to MD practitioners if, in seeking to legitimise their role and authority with the formal techniques of development practice, they ignore the cultivation of political sensitivity and political skills which the MD arena requires to be effective.

3.6 The emergent paradigm of management learning

To recap briefly what has been discussed, the degree of conceptualisation of MD as a dedicated process is scanty. Overall, MD largely remains a meta-field which has generated little theory on its own. However, in terms of the eclectic, interdisciplinary base of this field, MD now encompasses a vast spectrum of applied theory, which has extended far beyond the relatively narrow, professionalised 'learning and development' literature from which it was born, to include sophisticated insights from psychology, sociology, communications theory, philosophy, organisational analysis and many other primary disciplines (Cullen and Turnbull 2005).

Within these areas it may be possible to detect some trends as they apply to MD. One theme seems to be a shift away from positivistic science and functional disciplines which claim 'predictability' to ideas which admit ambiguity and uncertainty. For example, in the field of learning theory, over-rationalistic cognitive and information-processing models are giving way to those involving social and situated learning. Learning models which recognise sociocultural processes, participation, emotion and 'social constructionism' are having a growing influence on the practice of MD (Storey 1989). Functionalist models which assume a simple relationship between learning practices and performance are being replaced with more complex 'process models'. Increasingly too, concepts in social science which move the focus from individuals to the organisation itself as the primary basis for management learning (e.g. knowledge management, communities of learning, the learning organisation, etc.) are gaining ground. Wider frameworks for understanding networks of knowledge, learning and behaviour (e.g. interactive models of leadership and persuasive behaviours) are also in the ascendancy. Then again, theories which emphasise an 'internal frame of reference' in learning and place professional practice in a political context are coming to the fore (e.g. 'tacit knowing', ideologies of managing, managing as a 'performing art', etc.).

It would be an impossibly complex task to trace intellectual developments in all the cognate sources of knowledge which compose this multidisciplinary field or examine their epistemological influence. However, as a measure of the paradigm shift away from the functional and technical (i.e. MD as a subset of HRD) to the political and cultural (i.e. MD as organisational analysis), the term 'management learning', with a more experientially focused, less institutional nuance, is increasingly employed in the literature as a substitute for 'management development' (Burgoyne and Reynolds 1997, Fox 1997). Mumford (1993) for example, defines 'learning' as the central focus of MD, the bridge between theory and practice, a total process which, at its best, integrates learning at every level, from the micro, informal, incidental processes of the individual to the macro, planned and structured processes of organisational learning strategies.

Burgoyne's integrated field of management learning

Burgoyne characterises MD as a field of reflective practice which requires continuous management learning. Reflective practitioners are seen as those who can articulate how they perform. They have a 'theory in action' derived from formal study and self-reflection which goes beyond mere trial and error. The best practitioners are critically reflective in constantly searching for new ideas, concepts and models which they develop from testing ideas from the formal canon against their experience and by drawing their own lessons from 'how things go'.

Burgoyne believes that contribution to 'reflective practice' provides the guiding logic by which the theoretical and pragmatic elements of management learning should be judged. He also believes that the field of management learning is becoming an integrated area of study and practice through the following process.

- *Professional practices*: lessons are derived from practitioner activities such as running learning events, defining competencies, evaluating effectiveness, etc.

- *Multidisciplinary conceptualisation*: theoretical ideas and philosophical approaches are eclectically chosen from a range of disciplines to make sense of practice, for example, learning psychology, sociology of knowledge, political science, etc.

- *Management learning emerges as an integrated area of study*: the tacit and explicit knowledge of practitioners is fused with concepts (as above) to form unified conceptual frameworks (e.g. how concepts in managing, organising, learning and performance can be interlinked).

- *Management learning develops as an applied philosophy*: sophisticated theory emerges which is multidisciplinary in nature but inherent to the problems facing MD (e.g. how do managers learn in the conditions under which managers work? How do we know what is good learning?). As a mature philosophy, MD will address key issues of philosophy – ontology (what can be known), epistemology (how it can be known) and aesthetics (what is desirable). A coherent philosophy helps wise action and is central to the MD agenda.

- *Finally, management learning develops as an applied ideology*: much management learning theory is about emancipating adult leaders by helping them to be independent thinkers and reach their individual potential. It also advocates openness and trust. These values underpin self-development and team learning. However, this humanism can seem utopian in many organisational situations where issues of power and control prevail. The future requires further debate and eventual closure on how MD can act as an emancipatory ideology when management involves the use of power in pursuit of economic agendas.

Burgoyne is hopeful that these perspectives and processes will come together to make MD a more integrated field of thinking and action, more socially and politically contextualised, in the years ahead.

Source: Adapted from Burgoyne, J. and Reynolds, M. (1997) *Management Learning*, Introduction, Sage

3.7 Critical theory and MD

The shift to management learning is part of the new turn in organisational analysis to critical theory as a tool for understanding the social construction of learning. These ideas are gradually infiltrating into mainstream MD and engaging the interest of practitioners (Wilmott 1997). Although critical studies may seem a little too arcane for a mainstream work of this kind, the increasing influence of these ideas on practitioner thinking in the learning field (at the time of writing; see Mabey and Finch-Lees 2008), as academic discourses become popularised, suggests that a few words are needed. Besides, with growing concern over corporate governance, ethical, environmental, diversity and work/life balance issues at work, it is likely that managers will be looking more at the social definitions of management problems which require solutions that go beyond the technocratic (Burgoyne and Reynolds 1997).

Critical theory introduces a spirit of scepticism and questioning of the taken-for-granted assumptions and social and political processes which underpin MD. Critical theory encourages thoughtful reflection on the context of power and ideology within which management developers operate and raises disturbing questions about the nature of management knowledge and the interests it serves (Burgoyne and Reynolds 1997). It covers a wide-ranging field, including insights from Habermas and the Frankfurt School, Gramscian Marxism, Foucault, post-structuralism, postmodernism and the social constructionist tradition in sociology (see French and Grey 1996). These discourses are multiple and diverse but common themes are the cultural contexts in which power is exercised in management and the interests served by ideological processes, including professional management practices in management development and education.

Much of critical thinking is an attempt to expose the political, social and moral nature of management. In particular, it examines claims that management is a neutral and objective force for efficiency and effectiveness: the idea that the 'good of the business is the good of all'. This means showing how organisations may not be unitarist structures of shared interests but pluralistic systems in which sectional interests try to legitimate their values and justify their power ideologically. Critical reflection is brought to bear to deconstruct notions of objectivity and management claims that authority and organising patterns are both natural and fair (e.g. that managers are coordinators of the entire work community, working for the good of all, when in reality they have no recourse but to be agents of capital). Critical insight tries to point up the assumptions on which an implicit social order is based and open up the possibility of alternative perspectives.

A major theme in critical theory is epistemology, how ideas are socially derived and socially interpreted. This often involves critical discourse analysis of how ideology works to justify management power and to disguise unequal power relations between key actors (e.g. the power/knowledge concepts of Foucault 1980). So, for example, critical theorists have looked at appraisal systems as examples of management surveillance and the Panoptican 'critical gaze' (Boje 1996) which help top management maintain its power, yet are presented as rationalistic and commonsense solutions to performance issues. Other analysts have examined the way that the perspectives of different levels of manager are influenced by their structural position in hierarchies of power, but justified by symbols of consensus (Burgoyne and Reynolds 1997). In the same way, critical analysts have looked at multiple discourses in management, the ambivalence involved in a rhetoric of 'participation', 'trust' and 'development' which coexists with an equally powerful rhetoric of 'downward control', 'centralisation of authority' and 'upward accountability'. Is the ideology of 'empowerment' really about encouraging creativity and participative involvement or is it about exposing people to higher performance requirements and increasing management control by shifting performance management to the exacting scrutiny of the omnipresent and all-seeing gaze of the team (Sennett 1998)?

These are the kinds of penetrating questions which critical analysts ask. Often their perceptions have implications for management learning and sometimes their critical lens is specifically applied to MD in its various forms. Critical approaches to learning encourage managers to 'problematise' what they learn at business school or on training courses. They encourage managers to do their own 'critical readings' on the ideological biases of management education and the world-view implicit in, for example, an MBA at an American university. They raise doubts about the taken-for-granted assumptions of management knowledge. Is formal management education often technicist, positivist, functionalist and instrumental? Does it make truth claims on the basis of rationality and objectification which are hard to accept (Grey 2005)? Do the 'neo-engineering' biases of functionalised knowledge in business education encode a perspective of management and business which ignore, even marginalise, other ways of looking at the world? Are the 'breathless and over optimistic discourses' (French and Grey 1996) of Western management and MD really helpful in understanding the gritty and often chaotic conditions of managing and learning how to manage in a real organisation (see Chapter 2)?

Is the Harvard MBA culturally biased?

Here are some extracts from an article by a recent student at Harvard Business School, Philip Delves Broughton.

> Roughly 30% of my class at Harvard was identified as 'international' . . . what I found was an institution that sought to accommodate them in every visible way. There were plenty of classes where we discussed international business problems . . . But this apparent internationalism was little more than a veneer over what remained essentially a parochial institution . . . Experiments with internationalism all too often ended up as cultural stereotyping.

Later Broughton quotes a student on his MBA course from the Middle East who claimed that for all its claims of internationalism, HBS remained east-coast, conservative and assumed American norms of doing business.

> 'It's not really an international school' he told me some time after graduation. 'Internationalism is a fad. If big American companies weren't going big into China, the school wouldn't have been interested in it.' He found the approach to ethics fundamentally puritanical. It put the American spin on every case. If you tried to apply the frameworks we learned in Dubai or Nigeria you would never succeed.

Questions
Would you say that any of the management courses you have studied or are studying are culturally biased? Do they do anything to help you critically examine their knowledge claims?

Source: Adapted from Delves Broughton 'Harvard loses its lustre,' *Prospect* September (2008)

A critical approach to management learning means helping managers to become their own reflective thinkers. It means encouraging them to reason in a philosophical way; challenging ideological assumptions and thinking beyond surface appearances; discerning and balancing the contested discourses which are part of the culture of any organisation. This involves helping managers to become their own practical theorists, starting with their own experience and making sense of them as the basis for building a philosophical foundation for considered action. The ethos that the MD facilitator would hope to encourage is one of critical scepticism. Students are stimulated to challenge and question their own experience and to become independent thinkers, embracing the existential uncertainty of a management role and to consider how it fits within a larger political and social process. How can they escape managerial indoctrination to think through the confusion of organisational process and the contradictions of managerial discourse we have mentioned, valuing their own lived experience and using this as a touchstone for conceptualising a way of being and acting in management? How can they be helped to recognise memorable learning moments and extract them from the stream of experience so that their meaning for self-development can be analysed?

> **Pause for thought**
>
> ### Demystifying texts
>
> As a manager or a student of management, you will have come into contact with many theories of organising and managing. They may have been presented to you as common sense. Have you tried deconstructing these texts to reveal the assumptions on which they are based and their claims to offer neutral, universal, scientific knowledge in management? To do so is to think critically and begin acting as your own practical theorist so that you have your own philosophical grounds for action. This is a useful skill in any management role.
>
> #### Question
> *To what conclusions does your critical thinking lead you?*

Part of the enlightenment that the critical approach implies, is a radical questioning and demystification of management texts within the Western management canon. The spirit of criticality involves the sceptical manager reflecting deeply on the adequacy of conventional thinking in management and recognising the bland 'truth claims' of orthodox management education on the basis of assumptions that management is a 'Newtonian science' (Roberts 1996). That is, it is techno-rational and scientific, both contentious propositions. A critical approach presumes a Socratic technique of sceptical questioning and only accepting theories which can be validated from the individual manager's own experience. In this process sensitive facilitation involving both the MD enabler in the workplace and the tutor in the academy is seen as an emancipating force for creating a dialectic between impersonal theory and personal experience. In this process students translate abstractions into the commonsensical understandings of their own organisational worlds. Students effectively engage in grounded social theorising to produce their own meanings and take control of their own professional lives by building personal philosophies of management practice.

It is claimed that a genuinely critical orientation can be a radicalising force, valorising practical theorising and learning through reflective experience over instrumental technicism as a means for achieving personal emancipation (French and Grey 1996). Skilfully applied, a commitment to criticality might transform mainstream techniques in MD. For example, Wilmott (1997) examines the potential of action learning sets, often vehicles for individualising and psychologising social issues, to become tools for dissecting the obfuscation of ideology, the relativism of perspectives and how power works at the micro-level. So too, in the right hands, projects, peer support and mentoring can all become means for moving discussion of MD away from issues of technique to highlight epistemological issues in management and how the individual can work within a context of contested discourse. Critical thinking may become the means by which managers become genuinely reflective practitioners, always searching for better ways of understanding the social, technical, and political context of which they are part and new ways of improving their practice.

However, it is important to resist romanticism. As Burgoyne and Reynolds (1997) remind us, much of management is 'the use of power on behalf of the powerful' and if managers are not to derail, they must find a way of reconciling ideological insight and personal enlightenment with adjustment to the status quo. It is also the case that while this writer may have betrayed his own enthusiasm for critical theory and its emancipatory potential, it is unclear whether this is the wave of the future in MD or merely the perspective of a minority of academics and thinking managers destined to remain as stinging gadflies to the elephant.

3.8 Conclusion

In this chapter we have argued that MD is not a coherent discipline with generally agreed objectives or defined boundaries. Rather, it can be regarded as a disorganised, meta-field which plunders other disciplines for its insights, making it multivocal and ideologically pluralistic. Cullen and Turnbull (2005) believe that MD is the least defined concept in management. Starkly contrasting definitions and models coexist implying very different approaches to MD practice. Certainly there are signs that MD is becoming defined as a strategic and broadly cultural process, with learning as the rallying point for individual and corporate approaches. However, the forces that would seek to define MD in instrumental, technocratic terms are also strong and the outcome of the battle for the soul of MD is by no means clear. As various schools of thought contend, the dominant form which MD will take in the future will depend on the model of management and managing which gains ideological ascendancy, and it is to this issue that we turn in the next chapter.

Review questions

1 The standard criticisms of systems theory are that it is too abstract and remote from reality to describe and explain MD process effectively. What do you think are the strengths and weaknesses of the systems approach?

2 How far do you believe that MD is largely an underdeveloped discipline, which has generated little theory of its own but relies on the contributions of stronger subjects, or is it a vibrant and eclectic field where many voices contend? Discuss.

3 Do you believe that MD is a field in its own right or is it a sub-field dominated by learning and development and organisational analysis?

4 Do you think the future of MD lies in critical theory? Explain.

5 Do you agree with Keynes that 'there is nothing so practical as a good theory'? Debate.

Web links

Information on theory in HRD/MD, etc. is available on the CIPD website:
http://www.cipd.co.uk

An interesting website that provides ideas about chaos, complexity and systems theory:
http://is.lse.ac.uk/complexity/default.htm

Recommendations for further reading

Those texts with an asterisk in the bibliography are recommended for further reading, especially the following:

Doyle, M. (2000) 'Management development in an era of radical change: evolving a relational perspective', *Journal of Management Development*, Vol. 19, No. 7. A challenging and alternative picture of MD as a complete field of practice, understood in terms of a radical 'systems' perspective.

Fox, S. (1997) 'From management education and development to management learning', in Burogoyne, J. and Reynolds, M. (1997) *Management Learning*. An insightful and influential article which argues for 'management learning' as an organising category and a more holistic, integrative focus for development activity.

Lees, S. (1992) 'Ten faces of management development', *AMED*, Vol. 23, No. 2. A deliberately iconoclastic interpretation of the agendas and purposes of MD which goes beyond the usual functionalist frameworks.

Bibliography

Argyris, C. (1992) *On Organisational Learning*, Blackwell.

Ashton, D. (1975) in Ashton, D., Easterby-Smith, M. and Irvine, C. (1975) *Management Development: Theory and Practice*, MCB, Bradford.

Ashton, D., Easterby-Smith, M. and Irvine, C. (1975) *Management Development: Theory and Practice*, MCB, Bradford.

*Aspen, P. (1994) 'New themes in management education', *THES*, April.

Barham, K., Fraser, J. et al. (1987) *Management for the Future*, Ashridge College.

Beardwell, I. and Clayton, T. (2007) *Human Resource Management*, Prentice Hall.

Beardwell, I. and Holden, L. (2001) *Human Resource Management: A Contemporary Approach*, Ch. 9, Prentice Hall.

*Boje, D. (1996) 'Management education as a panoptican cage', in *Rethinking Management Education*, Sage.

*Burgoyne, J. (1988) 'Management development for the individual and the organisation', *Personnel Management*, June.

*Burgoyne, J. and Jackson, B. (1997) 'The arena thesis: MD as a pluralistic meeting point', in Burgoyne, J. and Reynolds, M. (eds) (1997) *Management Learning*, Sage.

Burgoyne, J. and Reynolds, M. (1997) *Management Learning*, Sage.

*Cullen, J. and Turnbull, S. (2005) 'A meta-review of management development literature', *Human Resource Development Review*, Vol. 4, No. 3.

Delves Broughton, P. (2008) 'Harvard loses its lustre', *Prospect*, Sept.

*Doyle, M. (1995) 'Organisational transformation and renewal', *Personnel Review*, Vol. 24, No. 6.

*Doyle, M. (2000) 'Managing development in an era of radical change: evolving a relational perspective', *Journal of Management Development*, Vol. 19, No. 7.

Doyle, M. (2001) in Mullins, L. (2001) *Management and Organisational Behaviour*, Ch. 23, Prentice Hall.

Doyle, M. (2007) 'Management development', in Beardwell, I. and Claydon, T. (2007) *Human Resource Management*, Prentice Hall.

Foucault, M. (1980) *Power/Knowledge: Selected Interviews and Other Writings* (ed. Gordon, C.), Harvester.

*Fox, S. (1997) 'From management education and development to management learning, in Burgoyne, J. and Reynolds, P. (1997) *Management Learning*, Sage.

*French, R. and Grey, C. (1996) *Rethinking Management Education*, Sage education.

Grey, C. (2005) *A Very Short, Fairly Interesting and Reasonably Cheap Book on Studying Organisations*, Ch. 5, Sage.

Harrison, R. (2001) *Learning and Development*, CIPD.

*Hassard, J. and Parker, M. (1994) *Towards a New Organisation Theory*, Routledge.

Honey, P. and Mumford, A. (1992) *A Manual of Learning Styles*, Honey Publications.

Keynes, J. (1936) *The General Theory of Employment, Interest and Money*, Heinemann.

Kolb, D. (1984) *Experiential Learning*, Prentice Hall.

*Lees, S. (1992) 'Ten faces of management development', *Management Education and Development*, Vol. 23, No. 2.

Lippitt, G. (1982) 'Management development as the key to organisational renewal', *Journal of Management Development*, Vol. 1, No. 2.

*Mabey, C. and Finch-Lees, T. (2008) *Management and Leadership Development*, Sage.

Margerison, C. (1991) *Making Management Development Work*, McGraw Hill.

Molander, C. (1986) *Management Development*, Chartwell-Bratt (Bromley).

Morgan, G. (1990) *Images of Organisation*, Sage.

Mumford, A. (1993) *Management Development: Strategies for Action*, CIPD.

Mumford, A. (1987) *Management Development: Strategies for Action*, CIPD.

Mumford, A. and Gold, J. (2004) *Management Development: Strategies for Action*, CIPD.

Nonaka, I. (1991) 'The knowledge-creating company', *Harvard Business Review*, Dec.

*Pedler, M., Burgoyne, J. and Boydall, T. (1994) *A Manager's Guide to Self Development*, McGraw Hill.

Pettigrew, A. (1988) *Competitiveness and the Management Process*, Blackwell.

*Ready, D. and Conger, J. (2003) 'Why leadership development efforts fail', *Sloan Management Review*, Spring.

Roberts, J. (1996) 'Management education and the limits of technical rationality', in French, R. and Grey, C. (1996) *Rethinking Management education*, Sage.

Salaman, G. and Mabey, C. (1995) *Strategic Human Resource Management*, Blackwell.

Sennett, R. (1998) *The Corrosion of Character*, Norton Books.

Silverman, D. (1970) *A Theory of Organisations*, Heinemann.

Stewart, J. (1999) *Employee Development Practice*, Ch. 7, Pitman Publishers.

Storey, J. (1989) 'Management development: a literature review and implications for future research', *Personnel Review*, Vol. 18, No. 6.

Strauss, A. (1978) *Negotiations*, Jossey-Bass.

Thomson, A., Mabey, C., Storey, J. et al. (2001) *Changing Patterns of Management Development*, Blackwell.

Wille, E. (1990) *People Development and Improved Business Performance*, Ashridge Management Research Group, Ashridge Management College.

*Wilmott, H. (1997) 'Critical management learning', in (1997) Burgoyne, J. and Reynolds, P. (1997) *Management Learning*, Sage.

4 Strategy and the organisation of MD

Learning outcomes

After studying this chapter you should be able to understand, analyse and explain:

- models of MD process and their link to strategy;
- theoretical modelling, MD and the strategic link;
- the obstacles which inhibit MD from becoming a strategic force at corporate level;
- the elements of strategic MD and the variables which shape MD as a strategic system;
- modelling the strategic decision-making and the strategic process;
- new ideas in conceptualising MD as a strategic process;
- organisation issues in managing the MD function.

4.1 Introduction

Recent decades have brought a more turbulent and challenging business environment. Global markets, increased competition, new transformative technologies, flexibility, a more mobile workforce, an increasing rate of mergers and acquisitions and accelerating innovation, are just some of the trends which have combined to make the job of managing far more complex and demanding than ever before. Managers need to have the capabilities to think in strategic whole-systems terms and to act as creative agents of change in conditions of great uncertainty.

Just as managers need to be increasingly strategic, so awareness has grown in recent times that MD should play a strategic role in helping managers to acquire the competencies they need to be sophisticated, far-sighted shapers of the future. Frameworks of MD are also becoming more strategic, gearing systems of management learning and development to explicit objectives and performance outcomes.

Strategic MD is about ensuring that the organisation has the right mix of and range of management competencies which will be needed to retain competitive advantage in future markets. It is about developing a community of managers with appropriate skills and bound together by shared values and ethos to face tomorrow's business challenges. But it is more than this. At its best, strategic MD means building the organisation. It is a catalyst for developing processes of collective learning, cultural and structural change which align the business and learning agendas and help the organisation deliver on its strategic goals.

In this chapter we touch lightly on the strategic dimensions of MD, particularly highlighting the differences between rationalistic schema for strategy-making and the actual reality of interlinked organisational dialogues. For readers who feel the need for more detail on strategic processes and techniques, they are referred to one of the big strategy books in the area (for example, anything by Mintzberg or Johnson and Scholes 1993).

4.2 MD and strategy

Most commentators agree that if MD is to impact on the organisation then it needs to be driven by business strategy. An organisation's strategy is its chosen course over the long term, how it chooses to respond to a changing environment, to meet the needs of customers and fulfil stakeholder expectations (Johnson and Scholes 1993). A recent CIPD survey (2002) suggested that there are two main tracks or purposes for MD.

- Track 1: To develop managers so that they can perform their jobs to ever higher levels of performance and allow the organisation to implement its current plans.
- Track 2: To develop managers' capabilities so that they can be effective in driving business strategy for the future.

What emerges from these two pathways is that MD needs to be able to provide the qualities of management as a response to the strategic analysis and strategic choices of top management in the current business plan (i.e. responsive) and to build capability so that the strength, depth and quality of management can drive future business plans (proactive).

To illustrate, with Track 1 the thrust of activity is responding to weaknesses and issues of poor performance in our current stock of managers, developing managerial skills overall and in line with the business objectives. With Track 2 it is anticipating changes in technology, markets, opportunities and building the profile of management capabilities which our business is likely to need to improve profitability and competitiveness. In Track 2 the strength and appropriateness of the management skill base is a strategic driver. As we will see, Track 1 is rarely achieved; Track 2 is sometimes achieved if the value of MD is recognised at a strategic level.

Where there is strategic coupling, the business strategy will be translated into MD strategy, policy, plans, procedures and practices which are then evaluated providing feedback and adjustment (see Figure 4.1 on next page). The business strategy drives decisions in planning the number and distribution of managers, the competency and performance requirements. This is the simple functionalist picture of strategy-making which, as we will see, is rarely so straightforward in practice.

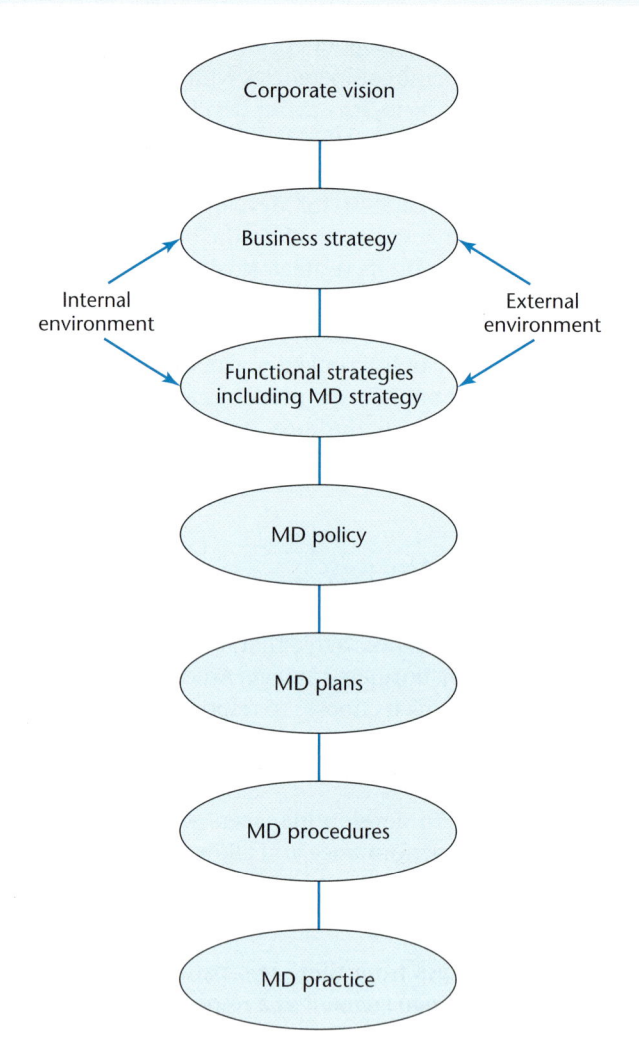

Figure 4.1 The functionalist model of MD strategy

4.3 Theoretical modelling of MD as a strategic link

The search for a good strategic fit between MD and business strategy is the theme of a number of models which attempt to provide a theoretical underpinning for strategy. A well-known model which purports to show the development of MD systems towards greater strategic integration is that proposed by Burgoyne (1988). This model is the result of many years of empirical research and aims to show what is involved in becoming organisationally and strategically sophisticated in using MD.

Burgoyne takes the view that as most organisations grow in scale there is a need to supplement 'natural career learning' (i.e. informal, experiential MD) with 'organisational MD' (i.e. structured and planned MD). Burgoyne talks of levels of 'organisational maturity' in the use of MD (see below).

Burgoyne's model of organisational maturity and MD

Very briefly, Burgoyne speaks of several levels of MD.

- Level 1: Fragmented, uncoordinated MD events. Too much focusing on short, formalised MD courses; lack of awareness of micro-macro linkages.
- Level 2: Isolated, ad hoc tactical MD events.
- Level 3: Integrated, coordinated MD interventions around a plan.
- Level 4: MD strategy plays a part in corporate strategy. A strategic framework for aligning MD with the wider business.
- Level 5: MD contributes to and helps shape the corporate strategy.
- Level 6: MD processes enhance the nature and quality of corporate strategy-making and are integrated in implementation.

Source: Adapted from Burgoyne, J. (1988) 'Management development for the individual and the organisation', *Personnel Management*, June 1988

Burgoyne's model is one of the few attempts to provide an explicit model of MD which is strategically led. Burgoyne offers a recognisable and useable analysis of the formal processes of MD and their relationship to business imperatives. In Burgoyne's view, most organisations are usually at levels 1 and 2. Levels 3 and 4 represent a benchmark standard and Levels 5 and 6 are aspirational, only achieved in some of the largest and most sophisticated organisations and, even then, the position can easily be lost. At these higher levels MD is not just a vehicle of strategy: it can 'lead' corporate strategy by placing learning at the forefront of the change agenda.

Burgoyne helps MD managers to benchmark the MD processes within their own organisation against the hierarchy of progression. In that respect it is a good diagnostic tool for performance measurement. However, the model has flaws, not least that it is over-formalised and is more of a classification than a model that examines dynamic relationships and processes (as with so many of the MD models we examined in Chapter 3).

However, it is theorising in the area of systems theory which offers the most fruitful basis for strategic analysis and development. In this respect, Stewart's holistic integration of the familiar learning/training cycle with the performance review cycle and strategic management cycle offers a useful framework for integrating learning, strategy and performance (see Figure 4.2).

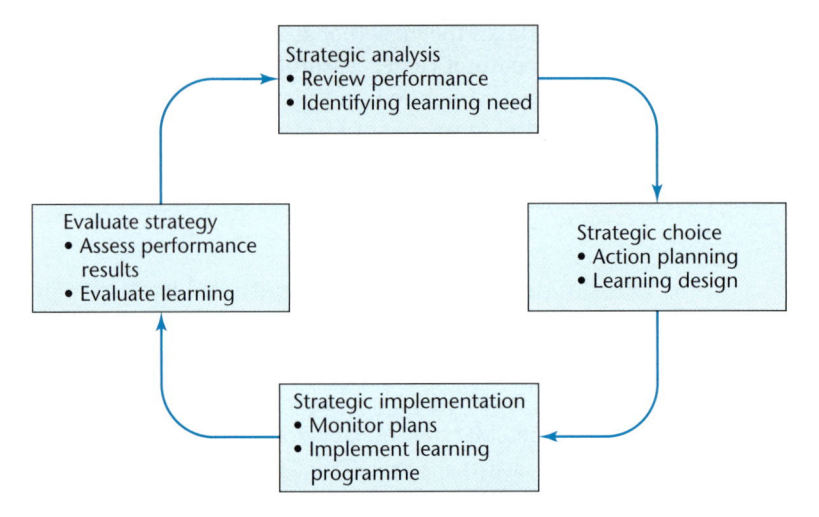

```
              ┌─────────────────────────┐
              │ Strategic analysis      │
              │ • Review performance    │
              │ • Identifying learning  │
              │   need                  │
              └─────────────────────────┘
```

Figure 4.2 The integrated cycle
Source: Adapted from *Employee Development Practice*, Pearson Education (Stewart, 1999).

This approach is a start to thinking holistically, but it is simplistic, highly functionalist and naive. However, it still has an intuitive appeal to busy developers who want a heuristic tool for designing focused and systematic management learning process.

We discussed Doyle's (2001) open systems approach in Chapter 3. He suggests that systems thinking is vital as a counterbalance to instrumental, piecemeal approaches which means that MD is conducted in isolation from the broader organisation. Doyle also suggests that conceptualising MD as a unified system is the key to defining MD as a truly strategic process in which MD is considered as part of the organisational system as a whole, and elements of management learning and management process are brought together in coherent, focused ways to meet corporate and individual goals.

As a simple heuristic, Doyle (2001) offers the unified schema as an open systems model applied to strategic planning in MD (see Figure 4.3).

In the unified model Doyle emphasises that MD can be fully integrated in the organisation's business strategy and business goals. Managing the organisation and developing its managers are activities symbiotically interlinked and all the stages of selecting and developing managers should be geared into the strategic vision and executive processes of the organisation. The model graphically illustrates the strategic stance of MD as a subsystem of the strategy process. It describes an ideal state, not achieved in the real world, but adopting its principles implies that MD is truly part of the business development model and MD practitioners oriented to strategy.

4.4 Obstacles to strategic management

However, there is gulf between strategic modelling and strategy-making in the real world. For decades (at least since the Handy, Constable and McCormick and Mangham reports of the late 1980s; see Thomson et al. 2001), organisations have been exhorted to integrate MD into strategic management.

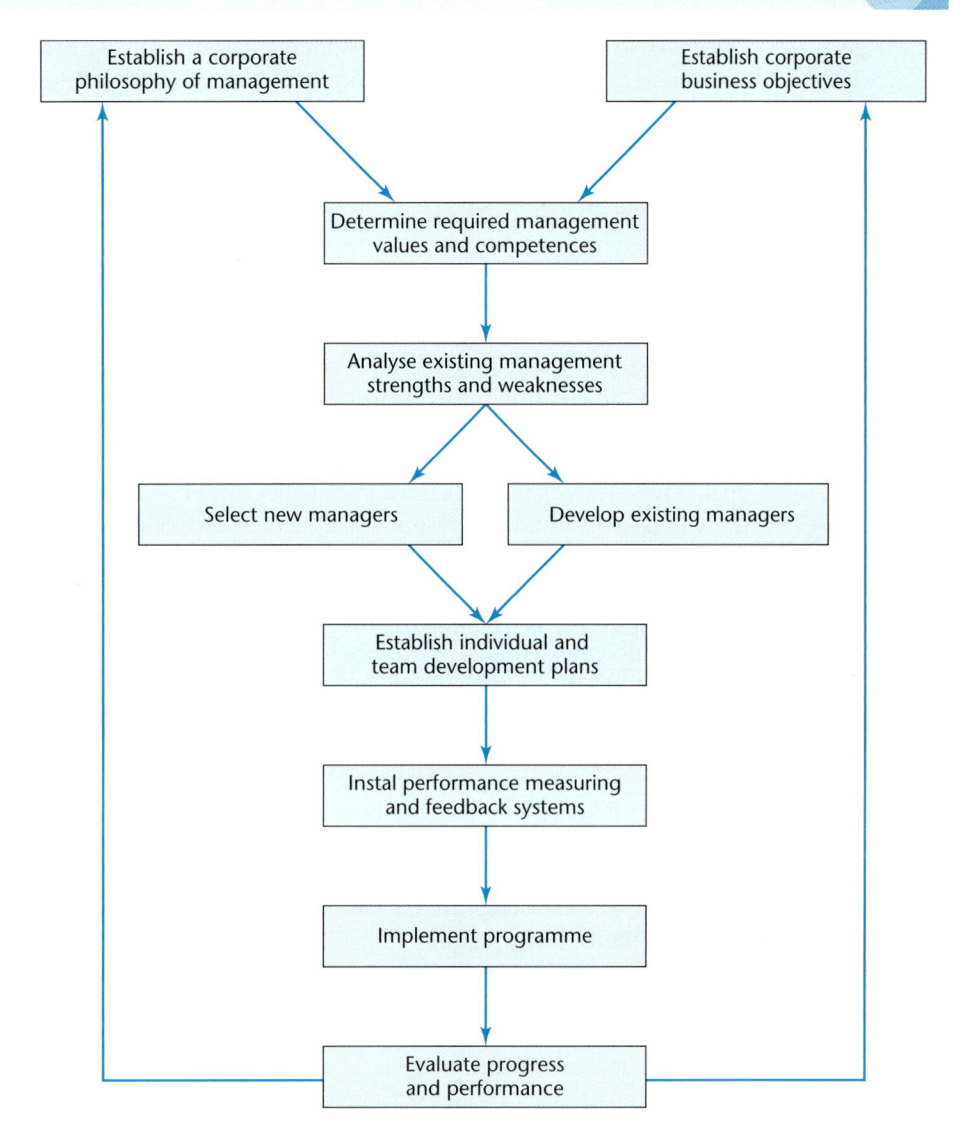

Figure 4.3 A unified management development model

```
┌─────────────────────────┐         ┌─────────────────────────┐
│ Establish a corporate   │         │ Establish corporate     │
│ philosophy of management│         │ business objectives     │
└───────────┬─────────────┘         └───────────┬─────────────┘
            │                                   │
            ▼                                   ▼
            ┌─────────────────────────────────────┐
            │ Determine required management       │
            │ values and competences              │
            └─────────────────┬───────────────────┘
                              ▼
            ┌─────────────────────────────────────┐
            │ Analyse existing management         │
            │ strengths and weaknesses            │
            └──────┬───────────────────────┬──────┘
                   ▼                       ▼
        ┌──────────────────┐    ┌──────────────────────┐
        │ Select new       │    │ Develop existing     │
        │ managers         │    │ managers             │
        └──────────────────┘    └──────────┬───────────┘
                                           ▼
                    ┌─────────────────────────────────┐
                    │ Establish individual and        │
                    │ team development plans          │
                    └────────────────┬────────────────┘
                                     ▼
                    ┌─────────────────────────────────┐
                    │ Instal performance measuring    │
                    │ and feedback systems            │
                    └────────────────┬────────────────┘
                                     ▼
                    ┌─────────────────────────────────┐
                    │ Implement programme             │
                    └────────────────┬────────────────┘
                                     ▼
                    ┌─────────────────────────────────┐
                    │ Evaluate progress               │
                    │ and performance                 │
                    └─────────────────────────────────┘
```

Figure 4.3 A unified management development model
Source: Adapted from A unified management development programme, *Journal of Management Development*, Vol. 6, No. 1. (Hitt, W. 1987)

Yet, despite all the rhetoric around MD as a strategic process and the declared importance of mapping MD to a wide range of organisational processes, Osbaldeston and Barham (1992) and Thomson et al. (2001), in an empirical study of MD practice within a wide range of organisations, found that evidence for a strong linkage between MD and business strategy was often hard to identify. They concluded that, in practice, the relationship between MD and corporate strategy was the weak link in the strategic chain of most British organisations. This was an observation also reported by Seibert et al. (1995) in a comparable study of US firms which found that the link between business strategy and executive development was particularly tenuous. This suggests that despite the claims, MD is often practised in a more traditional way than many of its champions would like to admit.

> The design and implementation of MD interventions may fail to match the needs of corporate strategy for a number of reasons. Let us consider these in turn.

In many places, MD remains a discrete, isolated process largely uncoupled from wider organisational purpose. Piecemeal and fragmented processes typically underpin an ad hoc reactive system of management development. The bias here will be towards narrowly conceived, technique-driven short courses concerned with plugging immediate skills gaps, not anticipating future learning needs. In these circumstances, the appropriateness of MD programmes to the direction of the company and emergent learning needs may be highly questionable. Canned, off-the-shelf solutions almost always prove to be palliatives, leaving larger performance issues unresolved.

Often MD can fail the test of strategic relevance because there is no overall framework of thinking in MD. MD activities are not geared into or led by a guiding philosophy of learning and development. There is no underpinning rationale giving coherence to the learning activities or giving them focus. So, MD interventions can appear unconnected and operationally focused: more the sporadic reactions of local people to locally conceived problems at different levels of the organisation than systematically designed programmes linked to corporate goals. MD uncoupled from corporate strategies risk seeming irrelevant.

MD may often disappoint because it is prescribed as the solution to the wrong problem. Too often MD can come to be seen as a quick fix, a response by senior managers looking to do something about deep-seated strategic problems. Prescribing MD interventions for problems which are really structural or systems based not only invites failure but also risks discrediting MD and distracting attention from its true potential as a tool for change (Brown 2005).

For example, in recent years many organisations have woken up to the need for leadership. However, it is not a panacea for all the woes of an organisation. To ignore close diagnosis of the real issues and to instead send all managers on a sheep-dip style leadership programme is a recipe for disappointment, because the real strategic challenges are likely to be untouched. There is no substitute for having a realistic understanding of what MD can and cannot do, recognising that it will never be a total solution for strategic problems but can only be a part of the solution if used wisely and appropriately with other tools (Berry 1990, Winterton and Winterton 1997).

A related problem here occurs when the architects of MD programmes develop interventions which are based on oversimplified, generic models of organisation (e.g. 'learning organisation' philosophies). At first glance these may appear to satisfy the test of creative strategic vision, but they are arguably based on either overly romantic or excessively rationalistic world-views which use a rhetoric of learning and corporate strategy without delivering any real content. Grand designs can fail in practice to be strategically integrated because the ideas have not been properly thought through and realistically operationalised in relation to the organisation's situation. The result is incoherent thinking and ideological displacement of strategy by theories of managing which have little connection with real-world realities or the conditions under which managers operate (Van der Dikken and Hoeksema 2001).

MD programmes also tend to fail the test of strategic focus and 'integration' when there is poor harmonisation of MD with other aspects of HRM (e.g. recruitment and selection, performance management, HR planning, reward, etc.). This is called 'horizontal integration' in the literature. If MD is not seen to be tightly embedded in strategic HR functions, HR policy or the employment system of the organisation and there is no explicit justification of MD in terms of HR philosophy, then MD may seem to lack both functional and corporate credibility (Harrison 2000).

That at least is one explanation, although Sadler-Smith (2006) raises the question of whether the best interests of MD are really served by close integration with HR strategy. It is well known that the credibility of HR departments varies widely. The status and credibility of MD might suffer if it is seen to be too aligned to a discounted management function. This is why some commentators (e.g. Sadler-Smith 2006; Pettigrew et al. 1982) ask whether the influence of MD might be enhanced by remaining a little distant from the HR agenda, but closely aligned to business strategy, higher policy and the corporate functions of the board. These are issues we will explore more fully later. There is no disputing the reality, widely represented in the literature (Cunningham 2000, Margerison 1991, Mumford 1997), that without top management commitment, MD is unlikely to have much force. Knowing this, it is arguably the responsibility of MD directors to position their function where it will have most influence whatever the HR pundits may say.

The strategic profile of MD requires an evidence-based justification of MD activity. Without a commitment to *evaluation* it is difficult to show a demonstrable relationship between MD resources and performance indicators for the business (Easterby-Smith 1994). Although it may prove hard to provide convincing data of impact at the strategic level, a spirit of inquiry is the best defence against detractors who seek to claim that MD is led by passing fads and fashions and developer concepts of development not owned by management stakeholders and out of kilter with the management culture.

Finally, MD programmes often lose strategic focus because they are hijacked by special interests. MD is usually the focus of competing political programmes and ideological agendas (as we shall see later in the chapter). This can subvert a strategic orientation. Sectionalism and ideological projects (e.g. MD used to promote a particular philosophy of managing or social engineering) do not promote a disinterested diagnosis of need in terms of the organisation as a whole and its vision. Powerful managers may try to bend MD to the service of their own agendas or force an emphasis on today's problems, not tomorrow's. The result can be that MD is distracted from leading strategic cultural change; it is seen to be partisan to certain values and interests and thereby discredited in the eyes of top managers who control future resources.

That said, sometimes the use of MD for ideological purposes (e.g. changing the social mix of senior management and extending diversity) may be in the ultimate interests of the future of the organisation even if it flies in the face of immediate strategies concerned with strictly utilitarian concerns (getting the right managers in the right numbers) or a rhetoric that pretends that organisational need can be assessed objectively.

Pause for thought

Why MD can fail

This is a synthesis of the reasons given by a number of commentators (e.g. Margerison, Mumford, etc.) for the failure of MD strategies and programmes. The presence of these factors is often a sign that MD is not taken seriously in an organisation. Reflect on this list in terms of your own knowledge and experience. Consider if you want to add any reasons of your own.

- Top management shows little interest, enthusiasm or support for MD.
- Resources for MD are limited.
- MD interventions are not driven by the business; MD strategy isn't geared to the business strategy.
- The purpose of MD activities is unclear to the stakeholders.
- The diagnosis of need (individual and collective) is poor.
- The focus is on individual development, not organisational development or collective learning of key groups/the organisation as a whole.
- The dominant form of MD intervention focuses on today's fashion, not tomorrow's problem and special pleading seems to drive the process.
- The form of MD interventions is not appropriate to the corporate culture.
- Career and succession planning/management seem dead.
- Managers are not much involved in diagnosing their own needs.
- Managers do not own the development (e.g. seems unreal, too abstract and general to them; does not reflect their experience or win their engagement, etc.) and they feel little engagement with MD.
- Managers don't accept responsibility for self-analysis, self-appraisal and self-development and self-management of careers.
- Managers don't accept a responsibility to develop their staff.
- The MD providers lack credibility with the line.
- Systems for reviewing the effectiveness of MD activities either do not exist or are poorly done.
- Those managing the MD process are not politically sophisticated or aware.

Questions

If you were offered a job in an organisation where the MD function was so lacking in strategic consciousness and so poorly regarded, you might hesitate to take it on. If you did, how would you set about improving the profile of MD? Would it just be reversing all the dimensions above or is there a vital 'x' which is missing?

Source: A personal commentary drawing on insights by Mullins (2007), Mumford (1997), Cunningham (2000), Harrison (2000) and Margerison (1991)

4.5 Elements of a strategic approach

Despite the many forces which work against the integration of MD with business strategy, some of the largest and most progressive companies are seeking to make it a strategic tool and a lever for transformational change. Thomson et al. (2001) report that 3M and Motorola have deliberately tried to use MD as a business driver, that is, each new business issue is interpreted in terms of MD activity and MD is used as part of a process of encouraging an outward-looking focus in the organisation. Jaguar, BA, Lucas and Courthaulds are also reported as using MD as a tool for organisational renewal and corporate turnaround.

Thomson et al. (2001) give evidence that MD has been employed by blue-chip companies as an instrument for achieving business goals such as total quality management, project and unit performance, building a business culture after a merger and integrating learning and development as a core value of the business. Certainly, aligning MD to business programmes like balanced score card, high performance management systems, improving best practice and so on, can serve to make MD prominent and aligned to big things going on in the organisation, but does that make MD strategic? In these cases, it can be difficult in practice to distinguish between the rhetoric, such as, 'MD is a force for disseminating company values' *or* 'MD is a strategic tool of the learning organisation' and so on, and anything new happening to real behaviour. These declarations will only have real impact if there is a detailed reconfiguring of each programme so that the learning elements are identified and specifically addressed. Thomson et al. (2001) conclude that the forces which influence the profile of MD in any particular organisation and its centrality in organisational strategy remain obscure and they rightly call for more detailed empirical inquiry.

What follows is a critical assessment by this author of the variables which may shape the nature of MD within an organisation and determine how far it has a genuinely strategic impact. It is a distillation of thinking by Mabey et al. (1998), Mabey (2002), Cunningham (2000), Garavan et al. (1999), Osbaldeston and Barham (1992), CEML (2002), Mumford (1997) and many others. This is not meant to be the last word in this undefined area but a contribution to debate in which the reader is asked to participate with his or her thinking and experience.

4.5.1 MD is driven by the top

The single most important factor in determining whether MD will be strategically focused seems to be top management support. Top management which is committed to a strategic MD is likely to have a well-articulated philosophy of learning, culture and change and will put this at the heart of its organisational vision. The outward sign will be a business strategy that contains key phrases about the value of learning and how it contributes to the organisation's sense of purpose; that learning is a 'core competency' of the organisation; that building a skilled management workforce through learning is vital to the company's future; that learning is integrated in everything the company does, and so on.

However, for these to be more than empty words, the board will need to demonstrate its active and close support of management learning. So, perhaps it will be setting its own example of continuous professional development by showing that it is embracing self-managed learning and is abreast of contemporary thinking and skills. Perhaps, too, it will be taking a visible lead in emphasising an organisation-wide commitment to learning by cascading down concepts such as 'learning partnerships', 'learning teams/circles' and asking line managers to create 'meaningful informal learning opportunities' for their reports. A sincere board will be taking a close interest in all MD projects and also in the translation of strategic learning philosophies (e.g. 'building a talent pool of future leaders') into practical programmes of action. This will signal to line managers in the divisions and units that development is a core concern of higher management on which they will be appraised and to which they must give priority.

A wise MD director will probably seek the top management's involvement in the MD strategy from the start, although this is easier said than done. It is often difficult to get a board to focus on issues which are not pressing and immediately task-oriented. Many boards only wake up to the importance of MD when they have introduced a significant project without considering the capability of their managers to introduce it. It can often take a crisis for the board to realise that its managers do not have the skills to manage this order of change and appreciate that they need to invest in MD.

Strategic management development in India

In 2002, the Issam company in India, a large steel manufacturing organisation, decided to align its MD strategy with its corporate strategy.

The starting point was an analysis of MD in terms of the internal and external environments of the company. What were the issues now? What were the challenges that could be anticipated in future? The board had its own view but it also wanted to take soundings from other levels, so a survey of management opinion was conducted.

What emerged was a consensus among the managers that this was a company moving into the new century facing intensified globalised competition and a fast-moving business environment. However, the managers (average age only 33) believed that the culture was rather bureaucratic and slow-moving. Managers said they wanted larger roles with more discretion, more challenge and more reward for performance. However, these managers also recognised their learning needs. They were primarily technical in background and realised that they needed general management knowledge, experience and skills.

In response to this, along with other skills audits and strategic performance information, the MD function was asked by the board to design an appropriate MD plan. The centrepiece of this plan was a development programme designed by the corporate L/D department and a leading Indian business school to create a vital link between MD and strategic objectives to build the strengths of the management workforce into the future. The key criteria of the programme were:

- to be business-focused, cost-effective and reflect corporate values, priorities and objectives;
- to command the *involvement* (not just the support) of senior management;

- to emphasise self-development and learning from each other and through project management and team process;
- to focus on real strategic business issues that the company faced and enhance the managers' ability to understand and respond skilfully to those issues.

The design of the programme put a lot of emphasis on project work, assignments, benchmarking and action learning to tackle real strategic issues, give managers more consciousness of the business challenges and take their skills and new business orientation back to their various workplaces.

Running in tandem with the programme, the MD department also launched some other initiatives which augmented this approach of building business awareness:

- 'Learning rooms' equipped with advanced multimedia and audio-visual systems were established to help a culture of self-learning and continuous learning.
- An audit of the entire management workforce was undertaken to identify priority learning needs in terms of strategic requirement.
- A fast-track executive leadership programme was set up for younger executives to expose high-flyers to wider influences and give them the opportunity to interact socially with top executives as a way of learning the real problems of the business and become socialised into the higher management culture.

The architect for this strategy claims that it has been very popular with younger, able, highly motivated managers because it deepened their managerial competencies and stretched them. As he tells it, the programme has also satisfied top managers' expectations because it has encouraged more proactive behaviour and helped managers to better appreciate the big challenges facing the company. As a strategic management development initiative it was seen to have succeeded.

Question

If you were the MD director here, given the brief to design a 'strategic programme', what might you have done?

Source: Confidential conversation and company papers

4.5.2 MD is integrated with other organisational activities

Where MD is well established within an organisation, well respected and in a position to play a strategic role, it is often tightly interlinked with the organisation's other systems and processes. This is another way for the top management to show its support for management learning as a competitive strategic resource.

Where this is happening, MD will be managed as a deliberate business process and be seen as one of the key drivers for results. MD values and concerns will be deliberately mapped on to all relevant HR processes (e.g. mechanisms for recruiting and selecting managers, appraising and assessing them, motivation and reward systems, HR planning and career development). Care will be given to ensure that learning and HR policies and practices are mutually supportive and linked to performance outcomes.

Business plans will also be analysed in terms of their implications for management learning. Each business plan will be assessed in terms of its implications for learning and MD. For example, the *developmental* potential of an assignment as well as *task* become criteria for allocating managerial work. Procedures and practices are reviewed to remove barriers to learning, development and innovation.

4.5.3 MD management has credibility and status

MD departments and MD directors have historically lacked status and credibility in management decision-making. This may have been due to the reputation MD acquired in the past of adopting 'flavour of the month' initiatives which were not closely aligned with strategic priorities. MD was also seen by many as being out of touch with management experience – formal, often remedial, in nature. While these characteristics are less likely to be true today, MD needs to be held in high respect as a professional function which is expert in what it does and able to add value to the organisation's vital business processes and strategic direction. MD directors need to be sophisticated operators who take a proactive view of learning, can speak the language of business and act as spokesmen capable of putting the MD case to the top management in the bottom-line terms which it understands. Only then will they be treated seriously as strategists.

Although a new generation of MD practitioners is emerging, MD professionals can still suffer a credibility gap with line managers who see them as lightweights in terms of their business impact. However unfair these attributions, while they prevail line managers can remain indifferent to development priorities.

4.5.4 The MD strategy is coherent and relevant

For MD to become part of the corporate strategic process, its own functional strategies need to be coherent. Even if MD has high energy and initiates a lot of activity, if there is a feeling that this energy is dissipated or misdirected, this will reduce its credibility at higher levels and inhibit its corporate influence. In particular MD needs a strategic framework and a binding value system so there is no sense of it lurching in fits and starts from one programme to another or sharply changing strategic direction (e.g. advocating from formal to informal learning, getting people on MBA course to learning sets, etc.). Where the MD strategy is seen as coherent and relevant it is likely to have the following characteristics.

- There is a clear MD mission linked to business objectives.
- All MD activities can be traced to a business objective and be justified in terms of external challenges or major internal issues facing the organisation.
- The MD department can position itself clearly with its own learning values, philosophies and approaches being transparent to all stakeholders.
- Its role in the process of developing managers and facilitating wider processes of organisational learning is robustly delineated and understood by all the key participants. All the key actors understand the role of MD and its priorities.
- Its policies, procedures and plans are clear, internally consistent, mutually supportive and based on consultation with all key stakeholders, especially line managers.

- MD is seen to facilitate a coherent and systematic development process which reaches through the organisation to all levels. This means that there is an integrated framework for identifying learning needs, selection of managers for development, assessing their potential and performance, and managing careers.

- This framework is closely integrated with all other relevant HR processes, especially the HR planning, succession planning, appraisal and performance systems.

As we have seen, MD has to be close to corporate strategy or it won't be effective. However, the prelude to this integration is the capacity of MD to show that it can make management learning become a real force in the ordinary lives of the company's managers. That means having a well-organised and targeted MD function with high-profile presence.

4.5.5 MD embraces partnership

One of the means for building such presence is through business partnership. Where MD is successful it often seems to involve the sharing of ownership for MD between specialist advisers and line managers. Traditionally, the board usually holds responsibility for initiating MD interventions and MD/HRD has the role of implementing them. However, line managers have a gatekeeper role in development. Unless line managers in the business units or divisions feel involved in assessing the managerial potential and learning needs of their employees, their career development and the design of management learning, they are unlikely to feel committed to the outcome.

This was particularly true in the past when MD had a reputation for often being developer-led and MD interventions could be seen as too remote, even irrelevant, to the working lives of managers. This often led to real tensions between *line managers* who were reluctant to give time off for their managers to attend programmes which they regarded as a distraction from the real work of managing and *developers* keen to press forward with their technocratic solutions. Now that MD is more informal and workplace-based this is less of a problem, but real effort needs to be given to ensure that the MD plan is owned by the line and that it takes responsibility for implementing it (Harrison 2000).

The contemporary trend is for the line to be involved at all stages in developing the MD strategy and in the design of constituent programmes, from jointly agreeing learning goals, to assessing need, selecting participants and reviewing action plans (Mabey 2002). This encourages line managers to appreciate that development is not something that happens in specialist settings. As managers they have responsibility to develop their line reports day to day and for creating a climate for development on the job by integrating learning with the task side of work (e.g. coaching, assignments, secondment, project work, etc.). The cooperation of line managers is most important for planned job experience. Traditionally line managers are reluctant to agree to cross boundary moves (job rotation, secondment, etc.) if they believe they will lose good staff. All the diplomatic and persuasive skill of the MD department will be needed to convince the line that some posts should be designated as 'developmental' and they will gain as well as lose talented staff through lateral moves.

Where partnership becomes a living reality, line managers are proactive in pressing the development agenda, are keen to recognise and reward productive learning and look for opportunities to encourage incidental learning by making use of it for innovation. At its best, where strategic MD is most embedded, managers become the guardians and prime movers of continuous professional development (CPD), and the role of the line in encouraging learning is formalised in 'strategic learning agreements' (Walton 1999).

The other main aspect of partnership involves striking a balance between the needs of the organisation and those of the individual. MD strategy can make the mistake of being so oriented to corporate goals that individuals feel no sense of personal identification with them. This can lead to standardised sheep-dip approaches and programmes which appear to be imposed from above on the basis of very generic assessments of need. Alternatively, MD strategy can be so oriented to the needs of individual managers that there is no drive to change the culture and practices of the organisation. The modern trend is towards a blending of interests. Managers are closely involved in defining their own needs and development. In return the individual agrees to remain up to date in skills and ideas which the organisation regards as important. This may be a tacit understanding or formalised in a learning contract (see Chapters 5 and 7 for the forms this can take).

4.5.6 MD is led by clear policy

A number of commentators – Doyle (2001), Thomson et al. (2001), Reid and Barrington (1999), Cunningham (2000) – agree that a linkage tends to exist between the existence of a written, formal MD policy, the amount of MD activity and the strategic maturity of approach within the organisation. Thomson et al. (2001) see explicit policies in MD as a sign that the function is taken seriously by the organisation. They suggest that the top management gives high priority to MD as a strategic tool and it is interwoven with other aspects of organisation currently regarded as good practice in the field (e.g. competency frameworks, development plans, integrated HRM strategies and procedures, etc.). Indeed, Thomson et al. (2001) suggest that of all the factors influencing MD within an organisation (e.g. labour market, organisational size, economic sector, degree of centralisation, etc.), the presence of a written policy shows the clearest link to the volume of MD activity and its impact. However, Thomson et al. (2001) believe that these organisations are in the minority. In their survey only 45 per cent of organisations (predominantly larger companies) had a formal MD policy with explicit declarations and criteria for regulating process.

Since Thomson's survey, there are signs of a growing trend to institutionalise MD, with more small and medium companies adopting written policies on MD. Well-formulated, well-written policies help the professionalisation of MD and act as a counterweight to ad hoc, unregulated policy development which often happens when policy is informal and remains within the heads of senior managers. However, formalisation can be at the expense of flexibility and in this regard it is interesting that some of the largest transnational companies are loosening their policy frameworks and moving away from comprehensive written policies because they see them as insensitive to diversity (Thomson et al. 2001; Doyle 2001; Mayo 1998).

MD policy serves several functions. It articulates the organisation's future intentions for MD. It is through MD that the organisation's strategic goals are conveyed to managers for their commitment. Policy is one of the main conduits by which espoused strategic values are transmitted to the management community (e.g. how cultural policy for organisational change is geared to changes in management behaviour through MD). MD is the framework through which the interests of different internal stakeholders are coordinated in programmes of development. Policy defines the categories of managers who will be supported by MD and the priority categories which will drive MD. Finally, policy defines the roles and responsibilities of providers of development, the standards and processes of evaluation (Mayo 1998).

Typical elements of MD policy

Of course, each MD policy will be different, reflecting the special needs of the organisation. However, there will also be common characteristics reflecting legislation, government requirements and schemes of good practice. Here is a synthesis of the elements of a number of private and public sector MD policies known to the author.

- *Objectives*: Statements of the purpose of MD, for example:
  - the importance of developing a continuous supply of talented and experienced managers to fulfil the strategic needs of the organisation;
  - developing managers with a balance of skills which meet the competency profiles of management effectiveness in the future.

  There may also be statements about MD as a force for cultural change; a mechanism for self development; a tool for equal opportunities, and so on.

- *Values*: Statements (which may overlap somewhat with objectives) defining guiding principles and values, for example:
  - a declaration that the organisation believes in helping all managers to meet their potential;
  - a declared belief in partnership, that is, a shared undertaking by the organisation and the individual;
  - a confirmation of the organisation's belief in teamworking and collective development.

- *Priorities*: Statements of intent regarding organisational groups which have a priority claim on MD resources (e.g. young high-flyers; functional managers acquiring commercial skills; professionals new to management, etc.). What is the nomination process for access to MD resources and how does the criteria favour some claimants above others?

- *Accountabilities*: Statements about who is responsible for development; how MD fits with other aspects of HRM/HRD; the performance criteria by which development activity will be judged; the degree to which the framework of policy balances global and local policy (e.g. in multinationals).

- *Specialist areas*: Statements of clarification and commitment concerning behaviours, processes, conduct and standards, for example:
  - the mechanisms to support MD processes for identifying and developing managers (e.g. audits, assessments, appraisals, PDPs, performance reviews, etc.);

- how processes of development should be conducted (e.g. mentoring, CPD, career counselling, etc.);
- degree of support for personal development (e.g. criteria and conditions of eligibility for sponsoring in taking an external management qualification);
- the operation of the career system (e.g. policies concerning internal promotion as against external hire; degree of progressive, planned career management).

- *Plans*: Finally, policy defines the development plans of different levels of the organisation. These will be outlines of local training needs objectives, targets, budgets and activity, action programmes, timescales and so on, for the staff in various departments, divisions and units.

Within this general framework, company policies can take an almost infinite variety of forms. In all cases there will be an inherent tension between the impulse to provide comprehensive coverage and clarity and the need for flexibility around the merits of individual cases and unforeseen contingencies.

MD policy has the potential to link the abstractions of strategy with the specific forms of desired action. However, despite the symbolic importance accorded to policies as expressions of the organisation's commitment to development, do formalised policies have much effect on real behaviour? Statements of intent can become just aspirations and policy a dead letter if there is no driving force to ensure that the declarations of policy are integrated into plans and practices or its values do not infuse real development programmes. Managers will not necessarily operationalise corporate policies within their areas of responsibility unless they are motivated to do so or persuaded of their value. Broad statements of intent and rules of behaviour only become real and shape what happens when they are translated into concrete terms for each part of the organisation. In the end, policies are only as good as the leadership behind them. In a period of organisational flux, downsizing, delayering and management insecurity, it is understandable if managers often greet MD policy statements with scepticism as either unrealistic aspirations or yet another exhortation from the top management to further effort, not realistic guides to behaviour (Harrison 2000; Jennings 2002). It is leadership which makes policy come alive.

4.5.7 MD is organised to build a culture of learning

MD is truly strategic when it becomes a key driver of the corporate strategy as a whole. Where strategic MD is embedded in the organisation, learning becomes a galvanising force permeating all its parts and directing its processes. Although this is rarely achieved, it is the aspiration level for MD (i.e. level 6 of Burgoyne's schema).

Where MD has come of age in an organisation, management learning (notice management 'learning', perhaps a deeper, more inclusive, concept than 'development') will be part of the larger processes of building a climate of empowerment and continuous learning at all levels of the organisation. A number of commentators (e.g. Walton 1999; Garavan et al. 1999; Mumford and Gold 2004) have suggested the features of a genuinely corporate and integrated approach to management learning. This is a synthesis of contemporary thinking.

- *There is an overall vision of learning as an empowering force.* The board will show its commitment with policy statements about the value of learning as a way of life for the organisation, a source of creativity, value creation and intellectual capital on which the future competitiveness of the organisation depends. These intentions will be matched with commensurate resourcing.

- *There is an explicit learning philosophy driving all learning activities.* At this high level of strategic development there will be a coordinated approach to learning and development which integrates MD with all business strategies. There is a widespread understanding among all the key players that knowledge and skill are the primary forms of competitive advantage, and investing in individuals is the best way of mobilising the creative capacity of the management community as a whole. In some organisations these values may be part of an explicit statement of intent to become a learning organisation (see Chapter 6).

- *MD becomes a force for cultural change.* There is a widespread recognition that MD is more than just building the skills of individuals and groups. It can be a force for developing an ethos of learning throughout the organisation as a whole. This means that MD becomes a tool of OD working to improve performance by developing organisational effectiveness. For example, it brings together structure, strategy and learning so that they are mutually reinforcing; working to make systems of authority more flexible so that managers are more able to experiment and run with new ideas.

- *MD becomes internal consultancy.* As MD becomes more integrated with OD, there is less focus on individual managerial effectiveness, more on the effectiveness of groups and processes. MD acts as a vehicle for changing values, roles, attitudes and style of management. That means building the whole socio-technical system so that it facilitates learning and innovation.

In practical terms, meeting these criteria may involve MD taking on a new facilitating and enabling role, acting more as internal consultants than deliverers of development. In new partnership arrangements MD practitioners might be helping customers of learning to build competencies and processes of learning which are locally relevant to their performance. This could mean helping managers think through the social processes of organisation (e.g. roles, relationships, strategies, etc.) so that they support the development of a culture where managers feel motivated to contribute more of themselves. It might mean MD working with a line manager to design flexible systems which accommodate both individual and organisational needs and build collective intellectual capital. Perhaps it means acting as process consultant with a management team to stimulate it to become more self-reflective and productive. It will certainly mean facilitating deep-learning processes so that CPD becomes more than a slogan and managers are appropriately assisted in staying abreast of professional knowledge (see Chapter 13 on organisational development).

Of course, few organisations are near the stage of employing learning strategy as a truly empowering force. However, where there are deliberate attempts to move to a learning culture (e.g. Texas Instruments, Nissan, Motorola) MD is in the vanguard of these processes.

Case study: MD strategy at Big Energy plc

This is an example of a global company (BE plc) with operations around the world but with its HQ in the Middle East, which rethought its business strategy, structure and culture and designed an MD programme explicitly focused on achieving business results.

Under the old MD system, managers were assessed annually on eight performance criteria (current capabilities and potential) and the rating was used to define their formal development for the year. This was complemented by a system of planned career management under which managers were moved every few years to new assignments and jobs within the organisation to get the breadth of experience they would need for senior management positions. This reflected BE's philosophy of 'growing its own timber' and taking a long-term view of career progression to develop a cadre of managers with global perspective.

This system served the BE well for decades. However, a new corporate strategy which involved entering new markets, new technology and the organisation of work (lean production and radically re-engineered processes) as well as decentralisation to new business units, suggested a new profile of skills for managers and a different MD system for building them.

A new competency framework was formulated based on a set of common criteria for all managers (e.g. 'change agency', 'managing complexity', professional leadership skills, etc.) and specific competencies for specialist roles. The competency framework stemmed from detailed task analysis and panel discussions involving top managers concerning the roles required of managers now and in the future (more business aware, more policy focused, etc.). The competency framework led the talent review process based on 360-degree feedback, scorecard and assessment centres to assess the strengths, weaknesses and potential of the entire management stock. This auditing and assessment provided the top management with a clear overview of leadership capabilities of its managers and the gaps which would have to be filled to reach the strategic goals.

As part of its redesign of the MD system, the company shifted from growing its own managers internally through centrally planned, progressive career moves and structured experience to a more open system based on performance. Under the new system individuals and their line managers agreed the most appropriate development opportunities. This meant that the company was moving from a system of coordinated MD activities (level 3 in Burgoyne's terms) to an integrated framework linked to corporate strategy (level 4). Under this partnership model the organisation provided tools and support for development but the individual had flexibility in using these to progress their careers.

It was anticipated that this open resourcing system based on managers internally competing for assignments and self-selecting development opportunities would allow the best talent to rise to the top. It was considered less paternalistic than the former system and encouraged attitudes of self-reliance, independence and versatility which were needed in higher management within a global arena. It was also compatible with a strongly performance-led system in which promotion would be based on demonstrable effectiveness in increasingly volatile business conditions and with ever exacting demands.

The leadership/management development experience at BE is now believed to be far more strategically aligned, more flexibly organised, more self-managed and owned by the managers themselves.

Overall the new MD system at BE is thought to be successful by its stakeholders. It supports the strategic focus of the business and appears to engage many managers by providing a palette of managerial learning (Van Der Dikken and Hoeksema 2001) that blends individual learning with the performance management process.

Question
This is an account of an MD programme which is strategically aligned. Here MD strategies have been designed which address business priorities, performance, career and development processes. It sounds like a success story. However, as the independent and sceptical thinker which this book encourages you to be, what doubts may linger in your mind which you would want dispelled by the architects of this programme?

Source: Personal fieldwork and communication

4.6 Processes in developing MD strategy

The processes for developing a coherent MD strategy are similar to the processes of organisational-strategy-making in general. This is not a textbook in corporate strategy so we will only outline the process. The reader who is interested in sophistication and detail may want to consult one of the many textbooks in this area.

For convenience, the strategy process is presented as a series of stages. In the real world, strategy is far more disjointed and incremental as we will consider later, but this abstraction helps us to get started using a basic scaffolding inspired by the Council for Excellence in Management (CEML 2002) as a proposed model of strategic development in learning.

The strategy development process: management development

Step one	Analysing the current situation for MD: where we are now.	Strategic analysis
Step two	Developing future scenarios: where we want to be.	
Step three	Analysing the gap: where we fall short.	
Step four	Closing the gaps: plans and programmes.	Strategic choice and implementation
Step five	Evaluation.	

Strategic analysis overlaps with strategic choice as programmes are interpreted and revised. Here we examine the first four steps and the fifth, evaluation, is considered in Chapter 14.

Source: Adapted from CEML schema

4.6.1 Analysing the current situation

MD strategy-making usually starts with a modelling of the organisation's position in the world and the variables which may impact on issues of management learning and developing human potential. This is the external environmental analysis which needs to be harmonised with an internal analysis of business goals, competencies, corporate strengths and weaknesses and their implications for learning process.

Mayo (1998) speaks of 'general strategic drivers'. These are the facts of life for the organisation and define its position in the world. They set the context for the general business strategy and signal the key issues with which the MD director must engage in developing specific learning programmes which are strategically relevant. Some of the challenges will emerge from 'environmental scanning'. What are the changes in technology which concern the business? How do we see current and likely competition within the marketplace? Can we see any patterns in consumer demand or make any informed predictions for the future? Shifts in government policy, requirements of professional and other regulatory bodies, industry standards and so on will also impinge on the organisation and signal learning and development needs.

Other challenges will emerge from an appraisal of internal processes inter alia: the managerial work which will be needed to be competitive (e.g. reducing costs, increasing sales revenue, improving productivity whatever); shifts in the beliefs and values of management culture; the suitability of organisational structures and whether they continue to be enabling; the distribution of talent as it relates to future business; the core competencies of the organisation and their relevance to the environment; the existing profile of skills and dominant leadership styles and their continuing relevance are just some of the likely variables involved.

The first stages of review will probably involve some form of SWOT/PEST analysis, 'force field analysis' and modelling of *external* factors. Stakeholder analysis, core competency analysis, cultural inventory, benchmarking and so on will be used for the *internal* factors. These exercises may be undertaken for the corporate business as a whole but the MD department, if it aspires to strategic linkage, will be teasing out the implications of strategic data for MD activities and commissioning its own fact-finding to help the development of the MD strategy.

4.6.2 Developing future scenarios

This is the reflective stage. In practice it is likely to run in parallel with review as information-collecting, analysis and reflection become joined together in a number of iterative cycles. This is also the part where the MD director really needs time with the board. As we have seen, the extent to which any MD programme is truly strategically driven will depend on the perspectives of top management and the importance they give to management learning.

An essential early stage in the development of an authentically strategic MD approach is facilitating the board's thinking and clarifying assumptions concerning learning development and management culture. The task here is for the MD director to help the board think, to conceptualise the big questions, articulate a philosophy of learning which is consistent with the strategic drivers of the business context with corporate vision and with the main items of the development agenda.

If MD has credibility in the organisation, MD directors may have already played an important role in fashioning the overarching corporate and unit business strategies within which the MD strategy is framed. They will have used their influence to assert learning and development values, for example, learning and higher performance, organisational learning and the self-renewing organisation, learning and the development of human capital. In the most favourable circumstances, the board will have already signed up to learning and development as a source of creativity and business advantage. However, this is often not the case and MD directors are usually faced with the hard task of encouraging top management to translate the abstractions of the business plan into concrete learning strategies (Doyle 2001).

This requires the skills of a process consultant. It means managing a process of questioning and discussion, drawing out the implications of each strategic business driver and corporate goal for learning strategy. What do the words of the corporate vision mean for MD? Are the board's intentions for learning incorporated within its corporate thinking? The MD director as facilitator of the strategic discourse will be gently provoking the board to make its position clear on key questions. Often clarity in deconstructing terms and defining intentions and expectations will give rise naturally to other related questions. Here are some hypothetical questions which the director-facilitator may be putting.

- *Does the board have a clear idea of what it wants from its managers in the future?* It is important to go beyond slogans. So if the board says that it wants skills of 'good decision-making' in its managers, does that mean it wants 'calculative risk-taking' or does a 'good' decision mean 'minimising the commercial risk to the organisation'?
- *The Board talks of more 'entrepreneurial leadership': can it be more specific in defining what this might involve?* Consensus on the answer to this question may suggest a different organisational structure, perhaps less formalised, more based on project teams and networked relationships. To the alert MD director this may imply OD intervention: organisational redesign, redefining management roles, changes in organisational culture and an agenda for enhancing the capabilities of the organisation as a whole which require greater emphasis on collective learning. The director has a responsibility to tease out wider implications and mirror them back.
- *Where does the board see the main gaps in management performance?* The board's consensus on this question may tell the MD director a lot about its perceptions of the strengths and weaknesses of its stock of managers and, by implication, its assumptions about effective leadership. This is good 'prima facie' information on which to construct competency frameworks, performance criteria, undertake auditing and learning-need analysis.
- *Does the board believe that leadership is needed at all levels or only at senior management and above?* An answer to a question like this might reveal a lot about the board's concepts of leadership and their interest in moving to a more empowered framework with radically decentralised authority and freedom granted to people to be creative.
- *Does the Board recognise the links between its policy of devolving authority to the new business units for budgets and product innovation and the new profile of management competencies which will be required?* Just raising a question like this may be enough to challenge the board to think in a more joined-up and coherent way. Does it recognise that business and organisational restructuring decisions have learning implications and to ignore them risks creating dislocations which may undermine business processes?

Pause for thought

Questioning the board

Questions
Imagine you are the MD director helping the board think strategically about MD. What would you ask? What questions would you add to this list?

Of course, the range of possible questions you might address to the board as a facilitator is vast. The quality of MD will be proportionate to the quality of thinking and facilitated discussion that goes into it. Where the board is really committed to thinking in learning terms, it will be explicitly reviewing each of its business goals and strategic intentions in terms of learning activities and outcomes. Through a careful mapping and linking exercise, hidden assumptions and unarticulated values come to the fore. The MD director will gain a clearer picture of top managers' objectives, be better placed to make the business and learning agendas explicitly aligned and design MD programmes which embody a coherent message from the board. Unfortunately, the time and goodwill of busy boards are never infinite and it is only too common for this vital stage to be rushed.

Armed with the results of the board consultation, the shrewd MD director may then seek to widen the circles of dialogue, drawing in senior management, specialists and line managers to discuss the relevance of the board's expectations for management learning. The director will certainly want to bring the debate back into the MD department as a way of building agreement on core values, priorities and approaches in the MD strategy. As with so much of strategy, it is the flow and openness of the cycles of debate (and here there may be several cycles of iteration) which will have a crucial bearing on the quality of the policy outcome (Mayo 1998).

4.6.3 Analysing gaps and auditing

The strategic review and strategic discussions may have signalled 'prima facie' where the gaps exist between existing capacity and a future desired state. However, it is likely that more information will need to be gathered to diagnose the exact situation on the ground and to feed into processes of reflection, questioning and strategic choice. It is at this point that strategic loops overlap with the performance development cycle (discussed in Chapter 5).

Establishing the nature of the gap requires research. The first step is often to interpret the implications of strategic goals for expected performance. Is the performance gap a development gap which can be closed by development methods or do the issues require other approaches? If development is misapplied to the wrong problems, then not only will the development resource be wasted but also the development function may be discredited because it will not deliver the results expected (Stewart 1999).

Research is needed on the precise nature and dimensions of the performance gap and its development implications. This usually involves synthesising data from objective indicators, (for example, productivity, sales, financial results, quality assessment data and so on) and more qualitative data such as survey information on attitudes, culture, climate, critical incidents. Benchmark data may also be collected and comparisons made with other organisations (industry standards, best-practice indicators, etc.). The patterns which emerge from these diverse data sets then need to be weighted against standards and objectives which the board has committed the organisation to achieving. Reflection on the data will begin to show where performance issues may exist and this should lead on naturally to a discussion of the management learning they imply. At this problem-formulation stage decision makers may feel the need for more detailed information.

Organisations vary widely in the mix of methods they use for auditing and learning-needs assessment and the thoroughness with which they analyse data. Most use HR planning and succession data, appraisal data aggregated to show trends and performance outcome indicators. However, some complement this with specifically targeted data collection in relation to strategic learning issues. Data for assessing learning need is often collected at a number of levels and brought together in an overall framework of diagnosis.

Auditing and analysis at the organisational level

A macro-level analysis is often an early part of learning-needs assessment. This may involve analysis of the learning implications of corporate objectives, new product mix, technology and organisational developments (e.g. what does the board's target of increasing productivity by 15 per cent mean for development?). It may also mean considering the themes from surveys of culture, structure and the working of the organisational system as a whole. Where are the blocks which inhibit individual and collective learning? Behavioural analysis may surface generic needs of key groups of managers (e.g. perhaps there are consistent indicators that specialist managers lack social/interactive skills) and learning needs which cut across groups (e.g. a broad swathe of managers need instruction in efficient use of the company's new intranet and responsibilities under equal opportunities). Socio-technical data may reveal areas where the system prevents learning (e.g. the inflexible rules on budgets deny managers real learning opportunities for the exercise of authority). Summaries of appraisal themes and 360-degree feedback help mapping of learning gaps within the overall performance framework. The value of this high-level analysis is that it provides a matrix of forces encouraging and preventing learning and suggests areas where OD and learning resources need to be directed.

Auditing and analysis at the job level

Job analysis is an important element in learning-needs assessment. It involves breaking the job down into component parts, constituent tasks and defining the skills and knowledge required to meet performance criteria derived from the strategy. Job analysis is complex and time-consuming but it provides valuable data on the skills, knowledge, attitudes and so on needed to do the job, the problematical areas where further development is needed and possible changes in tasks and skills in response to strategic priorities.

A hallmark of this approach is the systematic analysis of all parts of the job. Typically, objective methods such as analysis of job specifications and descriptions, structured observation and measurement of behaviour are used to define job requirements and the skill needed for effectiveness (we discuss these elements in Chapters 5 and 8 in the context of NVQs). Depending on the methodology adopted, sometimes more subjective analysis supplements this hard data and provides insight into the human dimension. Self-report diaries, critical-incident analysis, mind-mapping, repertory grid, scenario appraisal and protocol reflection (techniques considered in other parts of the book) can all help in identifying behaviours which may be effective within the context of the organisation and pinpoint where the real learning priorities lie.

Auditing and analysis at the individual level

We deal with individual assessment of capability in detail in Chapter 5 we also consider techniques for auditing individual management skills and potential when we look at succession planning in Chapter 10. The value of individualised appraisal and assessment for strategists is that it provides developers with fine detail on the capabilities of managers. Summaries and aggregations of results from these sources give a humanised dimension to trend analysis. Bringing together data from personnel files, appraisal interviews, development centre results help to recreate the realities of management experience which high-level audits of capabilities and surveys of learning need may miss. It also provides a much needed counterpoise to over-self-confident and over-generalised, top–down development planning which can overlook the individual manager (with all the risks of breaching the psychological contract at work which we have considered) in seeking to plan for management cadres as a whole.

Assessing the learning gap is always a difficult judgemental process involving different interpretations of the nature of the gap and how to fill it. Assessment is needed so that higher-level diagnosis is not too remote and lower-level assessment is not too steeped in a scatter of distracting detail. Both soft and hard data are needed to build as comprehensive a picture of existing capabilities and learning priorities as is possible and give the best chance of focusing effort where it will most help strategic performance. This is never a one-off task and will involve concurrent streams of data from successive cycles of needs assessment, evaluation and performance planning (see next chapter).

4.6.4 Closing the gaps

Having assembled diagnostic data from various sources, the MD director and his or her team then need to choose a route of development which promises most success in achieving learning objectives derived for each business goal and satisfying measures of organisational performance. In the best crafted strategic process (e.g. at 3M and Motorola), business initiatives and learning implications are interwoven in a mutually reinforcing, virtuous cycle.

Typically this strategic reflection and choice phase will involve a further round (or series of rounds) of questioning, dialogue and discussion with key players. The data might be used to ask soul-searching questions of key actors, for example, the board, strategic and general mangers, specialists, and so on.

- Given the hard evidence we now have, is it realistic to expect your managers to be more proactive strategic leaders?
- Does the data confirm our initial assumptions about the profile of our management staff?
- Should MD be focusing on changing existing managerial behaviour to reflect new expectations or building their professionalism and technical skills?
- With our data, do you have a clear view about the number and distribution of managers, by grade, function and expertise, which will be needed in the future to achieve the strategic objectives?
- Are we developing for the longer-term supply of managers to fit the profile or to satisfy more specific strategic requirements?
- Can the talent we need be developed from within our existing pool or do good people need to be brought in from outside?

It is only when questions of this kind have been debated with all key stakeholders in terms of vision and available diagnostic data that the organisation can form a coherent, shared view about the objectives of its development activities, the priority ordering of its needs and the programmes which will promise the best chance of success. These are the questions which help the framing of succession management and talent management plans. A politically conscious MD director will extend the circles of discourse and debate to divisional, business unit and functional levels to ensure that the MD strategy is developed as a collaborative process, and larger goals are aligned as far as possible with lower-level goals, plans and the self-defined needs, even aspirations, of managers. Only by extending the orbit of involvement will there be wide ownership of the strategy.

The draft MD strategy which emerges from this interactive process will show the signs of adaptation, adjustment, compromise and even fudge, which building agreement among such diverse constituencies inevitably brings. However, if the MD director has piloted his ship well the outcome will still retain its strategic integrity. It will then need to be signed off by the board as vertically and horizontally integrated with the corporate process and compatible with other HR plans and systems.

Then the strategy is implemented as a series of plans and programmes, the design of which will require further negotiation of values and the feasibility of different approaches (it is never just 'rolled out'). The MD department will still have to resolve difficult, more operational, questions with its stakeholders.

- Should development be off-the-job or on-the-job?
- Although managers may prefer on-the-job, experiential learning, do we have line managers who are motivated and effective in providing the necessary support?
- How should development responsibilities be shared with the line in a way that guarantees that they are performed professionally?
- How far can we accommodate the self-defined needs and preferences of individuals for learning in addressing organisational needs?

It is at this point that the corporate MD strategy is reconciled with unit business and MD plans and local-level audit or HR planning data on skills gaps, needs and expectations of different categories of managers. The implementation can be the trickiest part of the whole process because it requires careful management of complex organisational relationships with a wide net of stakeholders including: power holders such as unit managers and individual managers who may have different priorities to those at the top and apply varied interpretations to higher-level direction. A good result would be a consensus on current learning goals, local capability gaps and unit plans, with milestones on how to achieve them. How this is achieved – horse-trading and bargaining, managed debate, *force majeure* – is very much an expression of the relationship of MD and its business partners.

Good evaluation and feedback will keep the MD director informed of how far results are being achieved and where the strategy needs to be amended in further cycles.

4.7 Strategy reconsidered

Much of the above assumes a direct and unproblematic relationship between MD and business goals and their achievement. The orthodox view suggests that MD cleanly, clearly and appropriately delivered, in agreed terms, and with a strategic focus, should then provide the learning outcomes that lead to competitive market advantage. In an ideal world, all MD activity would be linked to core values and there would be clear line of sight between objectives and implementation.

However, the trouble with so much strategy is that it fails to represent the complexity of the organisation, the ambiguity of the environment, constant change and the multiple expectations of different constituencies. It uses the metaphor of 'rolling out' when the reality is a complex dialogic process of negotiating and iterative adjustment which satisfies the expectations of multiple stakeholders (A new book by Mabey and Finch-Lees 2008 tries to capture the complex discourses involved.)

So much of management assumes a structural-functionalist and rational approach. Strategy is seen to follow a linear path from diagnosis through objective setting, diagnosis, rational choice between alternative paths and implementation. Planned learning is regarded as a part of planned business management. But many theorists would take issue with this model (e.g. Stewart and McGoldrick 1996; Stewart (1999); Lundy and Cowling (1996); Johnson and Scholes 1993). In truth, MD strategy seems to progress as a far more emergent, interpretive and iterative process.

For example, despite the rhetoric that MD should interweave with the business agenda and support its objectives, in practice this is often difficult to achieve. For example, the multiple forms of organisation which now exist in the business world – matrix; divisional; project team based, etc. – often coexisting in the same organisational space, impose structural obstacles to a close linkage between MD and business strategy. This is especially true where responsibility for learning has been decentralised. Flexible networked organisation, which may even involve outsourcing of functions to complementary organisations, does not sit easily with the development of coherent and common MD strategies which purport to bind all parts of the modern organisation. The shift from long-range planning to strategic management based on the leadership of line management, rather than detailed programmes of planned action, is another structural trend making it difficult for the MD specialist to interpret and implement business strategy in learning terms (Mabey and Finch-Lees 2008).

Many commentators (e.g. Mabey 2002; Stewart 1999; Mumford and Gold 2004) talk of the vagueness and lack of clarity within modern strategy. The complexity and uncertainty of the current business environment has led most organisations to step away from processes which are structured and formalised. This helps the organisation to flex and adapt but it often creates problems for those responsible for aligning functional strategies (like MD strategy) to the corporate goals. Typically, the links between unit and corporate strategies and strategic and operational plans can be indistinct. It is also often uncertain where real power lies. Is the organisational ethos (usually implied not stated) top/down, bottom/up or loose/tight? As always, the situation on the ground may be very different from the corporate rhetoric (e.g. 'We empower our managers' may be an *intention* of those at the top but not the *experience* of those in the units). For MD practitioners it is often difficult to distinguish formal policy from the myth that surrounds it and to know what weighting to give to the different factors in developing an MD strategy. In the circumstances, it is perhaps not surprising that many MD managers have only a vague understanding of corporate strategy and how it relates to what they do. The link is celebrated more in oratorical declaration than in operational practice (Thomson et al. 2001).

This suggests that MD strategy-making is 'political' because the management process *is* political (Easterby-Smith 1994; Doyle 2001). Strategic imperatives are often unclear. Their meaning and how they are to be achieved needs to be negotiated between different stakeholders (senior managers of different functions, HR managers, individuals, external bodies and the board). Strategy becomes a discursive process of surfacing the assumptions of different groups, agreeing shared understandings (e.g. what does it mean to be 'leading edge' or to want 'entrepreneurial managers'?) and building enough consensus around value and beliefs for action to go forward. In this process the main drivers will be sectional interest and the world-views of different groups and career development quite as much as strategic development.

As Stewart and McGoldrick (1996) say, it is misleading to think of organisations as 'discrete and tangible entities'; they are more like 'bundles of people making decisions and working out complex relationships in terms of the contradictions between them'. Strategy-making involves both 'emergence' as the strategy takes shape in the process of doing and 'enactment' (Weick 1995), as the vague intentions of top managements' documents are interpreted and made real in detailed plans. In this chaotic and interactive process, the definitions of key actors and their ability to get agreement on them are all important. As Stewart and McGoldrick (1996) suggest, what emerges in strategy may be different from what is planned, but something usually emerges which, at best, represents the spirit of the board's intention and a reasonable fit between demands, constraints and opportunities at that moment in the organisation's history (Doyle 2001).

We will return to the politics of MD when we look at evaluation in Chapter 14.

4.8 The organisation of the MD function

We move away from strategy to a related issue: How should MD be organised for greatest impact? *And* does the overall structure of the organisation help or hinder strategic MD?

4.8.1 Centralisation *v* decentralisation

In their important survey of MD provision, Thomson et al. (2001) found that the vast majority of organisations retain the MD function as a HQ activity at the centre. While larger organisations were more likely to decentralise than smaller ones, most organisations kept MD as a function directly accountable to the CEO, the board or an executive committee of the board. In the survey (2001) only 7 per cent of organisations had decentralised their MD responsibilities to the business units. Even where decentralisation had happened, almost invariably there was a senior residual MD function retained at the corporate level.

At first sight this may seem strange. It may seem to buck the trend of contemporary ideology in favour of devolution to the business units or divisions. But there are a number of advantages to the board of keeping MD centralised. MD is often one of those functions which can act as a vehicle for communicating core strategies and building a culture of shared values. MD can be used to cement the organisation with a common experience and as a means of improving organisational effectiveness as a whole. Linked to other HR frameworks like competencies and performance management systems, centrally directed MD can be a mechanism for ensuring compliance with agreed standards and providing a stimulus for unified practice throughout the organisation. Corporately driven MD can also offer the opportunity to build a cadre of senior managers with a common profile of skills and attitudes which encourages *esprit de corps* and a strong culture in the management group, although a cynic might see this as the top management wanting to develop the next generation of managers in its own image. All the same, those organisations which have a centralised MD function seem most likely to take MD seriously and disseminate the professional values and practices of MD throughout the organisation (Harrison 2000).

But there are disadvantages to the centralised organisation of MD. While it may offer the conditions for a systematic, planned and strategically focused approach to MD, this may be achieved at the cost of remoteness and lack of ownership by divisional managers as well as imposing a deadening sense of conformity in MD policy and practice, at odds with modern beliefs about celebrating diversity and difference (Sadler-Smith 2006).

Despite the tendency of top management to hold MD tight to them, MD has not been immune to the wider trend in recent years to break up central HRD departments and devolve responsibilities to business units. The logic behind decentralisation is to make HRD (and MD within it) more business-focused and customer-led and to share responsibility (and therefore ownership) for MD with the line. The advantages of decentralising MD are held to be greater flexibility, greater local involvement and greater responsiveness (Wilson 1999). Business units, with their own devolved budgets and specialist staff, can design MD programmes which are based on local diagnosis of development needs. But there is a well-established downside to decentralisation. Devolution of MD to operational units can lead to the fragmentation of MD policy. Units can become cut off from one another; MD becomes localised and loses its strategic coupling with the corporate business. Decentralisation may also lead to a loss of cohesion within the MD function because of the professional isolation and localised allegiance of outposted MD staff. This will only be offset by a strong MD director who is able to act to unite the dispersed function within a strong framework of teamworking and professional community (Stredl and Rothwell 1987).

4.8.2 Outsourcing MD

In a few places MD, along with other HRD functions, has been extensively or completely outsourced. Harrison (2000) suggests the following advantages to this policy.

With outsourcing there can be an improvement in cost efficiency, effectiveness and added value. There is more choice; flexible contracts can be negotiated to take account of the changing needs of the organisation. External consultants may offer greater professionalism and specialised knowledge. They will certainly bring to bear an independent perspective. Often they act as catalysts helping to raise standards among internal providers. Outsourcing the delivery functions may also help MD to redefine its role. MD can become internal facilitators and internal consultants concerned with identifying learning need, sourcing developers, engaging in OD projects and evaluating effectiveness while the externals do the delivery. With imagination, selective outsourcing of routine development work can support a progressive redefinition of MD as fulfilling a 'strategic change agency'/OD role. Outsourcing works best where this is 'high trust' between contractors and providers, and delivery takes place within a framework of agreed goals, expectations, controls and evaluation.

But 'caveat emptor' (or buyer beware): there are dangers in outsourcing. Although outsourcing helps the MD discipline take on a more proactive role, there are limits. To take outsourcing into the strategic core of MD would be to hollow out the function, neuter its strategic potential and remove it from its hard-won position at the centre of the corporate policy process. Whatever the economic arguments, this would mean a displacement of progressive MD as a strategic driver for organisational learning. There is also the issue that relying on externals can be at the expense of developing in-house capacity, unless a deliberate attempt is made to ensure that skill transfer from external contractors actually occurs (and is not just hot air to get a contract). Finally, outsourcing, especially if it means wholesale dismantling of the MD department, creates many problems of managing people you do not control (Sadler-Smith 2006; Harrison 2000).

4.8.3 Flexible forms of organisation

But there is a middle way. Many organisations have experimented in recent times with quasi-market frameworks in which MD (often HRD services as a whole) are offered to the line on a costed buy-in basis. This serves to redefine MD as internal consultancy, marketing its expertise to managers with the budgets to purchase it. This system provides a stimulus for MD to demonstrate its added value to internal clients and develop its marketing skills in identifying what the customer wants. It encourages collaborative working and a logic of justifying development activity in terms of local need and higher strategy. This negotiated approach may also have the benefit of cementing partnership between managers and developers as a way of working which could lay the foundations of a genuine OD relationship in the future (Thomson et al. 2001; Harrison 2000).

As Thomson et al. (2001) say, recent years have witnessed much oscillation in the organising logic of MD. Many organisations (especially large ones) have experimented with decentralisation and flexibility in good times only to reverse the tendency in recessionary times as part of a policy of consolidating central control. Very often it is difficult to distinguish between a rhetoric of empowerment and partnership and the reality of uniformity and centralism. In this game of gestures MD can become a political football passed backwards and forwards between the key players.

Finding the right point of balance between central direction and local control is always difficult. Loosen controls too much and divisions will develop their own MD strategies. This will result in a diversity of practice and a very chequered pattern of provision. Strong business units will be able to resist corporate MD policies, plans and standards and effectively scupper MD activities which require cross-boundary moves (e.g. CPD, job rotation, etc.). Many organisations (e.g. Courthaulds, Unilever) aim for a strategic balance in which MD at the corporate centre drives initiatives, supervises standards and evaluates outcomes while local units develop plans in dialogue with specialist coordinators. This only works where line managers have a commitment to MD and the skills required (assessing need, coaching, informal on-the-job development, etc.) and hold the corporate MD function in sufficiently high regard to draw on their expertise (Stewart 1999; Storey 1989).

However, whatever the organisational arrangements and the balance of power between centre and periphery and between specialist MD and the line, the modern focus on line involvement in development means that MD has to proceed cautiously. In many cases, the authority of MD is blurred, its organisational status unclear and its role as leader of development sketchy and open to challenge. MD practitioners therefore need to be diplomatic and sensitive in developing and monitoring organisational standards. The sources of tension with powerful line managers are many, for example, local managers not wishing to participate in cross-boundary rotational schemes if it means that they may lose one of their high-performing players; local managers with mental models of development which are at odds with modern ideas in MD; local managers determined to do their own thing even if corporate-wide policies and practices are displaced. MD practitioners need all their facilitating, liaising and persuasive skills to win the trust and commitment of often strongly opinionated line managers to accept the corporate approach (Walton 1999; Thomson et al. 2001).

A final issue here is the question of whether organisational structures influence the *nature* of MD, quite apart from any effects on the management of the MD function. The research seems scanty and inconclusive. However, it is interesting to speculate. Does the modern tendency to decentralise and flatten organisations have implications for the provision of MD? Perhaps so. According to Mabey (2002) multi-divisional structures encourage cross-divisional, cross-functional MD (i.e. organisation-wide MD) based on a dynamic tension between centre and locality. This is MD as a force for corporate unity through (negotiated) common approaches to MD (but with the possible drawback of 'sheep dipping' as the outcome?). With decentralisation, Margerison (1991) suggests that organisations open themselves to more involving MD experiences. Here there is more opportunity for managers to run something significant at an early stage and for stretch assignments to be designed from significant blocks of devolved work. The greater depth of management which localisation often allows provides more opportunity for supervised, mentored and coordinated learning. Joint ventures, commercial partnerships and the involvement of suppliers (sometimes customers) in internal management processes offers opportunities for selecting up-and-coming stars to benefit from the diversity of experience which modern business brings.

Case study: A bigger challenge than she thought

In 2004, Sally Jones was appointed as Director of MD at InCorp, an international white-goods manufacturing company with headquarters in Yorkshire. In her first few weeks on the job Sally discovered that the company had once enjoyed a reputation for being good at management training and development. However, that no longer seemed the case. Downsizing combined with a radical restructuring of the company seemed to have undermined this reputation. As a result of multiple reorganisations, responsibility for all training and development (including MD) had been delegated to the new 'strategic business units'. Corporate MD had been reduced to a 'woman and a dog' as Sally liked to describe her domain. L/D budgets had been much reduced.

In getting to know the organisational culture and the challenges facing the function she now headed, Sally spent her first months meeting key directors of the divisions and units, establishing the presence of MD as a proactive function in touch with the strategic ends of the organisation and building good trust relations. What emerged quite quickly was that the pattern of MD provision was very patchy. Only where the local unit or functional director understood the importance of development for performance was it thriving. However, even in the best cases the nature of the learning seemed rather formal, individualised not collective and a little old-fashioned. In many SBUs, L/D activity of all kinds had dwindled to almost nothing. Moreover, the centre lacked authority and resource to monitor local patterns or press effectively for higher standards.

Sally soon became a familiar figure at the management meetings at all levels. She found that the managers listened politely to what she had to say but the cultures of the SBUs were not supportive of MD initiatives, especially if they took managers away from their tasks at work or diverted SBU resources. From her conversations with managers at all levels Sally came to identify some of the issues facing MD within the company as a whole.

- Many managers had received very little MD of any kind. Where they had, it tended to be short, specific skills courses (e.g. time management, budgetary control, planning skills, etc.).
- There was no real culture of self-development. Self-managed learning was something only a small minority of managers practised and few seemed to be self-initiating in seeking developmental experience or taking formal professional qualifications. PDPs were often very informal, done to satisfy HR and never reviewed.
- There was no competency framework or formal profiling data aside from appraisal reports. However, information from the HR files suggested that the stock of managers was deficient in many competencies which would be needed for the achievement of goals within the corporate strategy (e.g. marketing, entrepreneurial, change-management skills). By and large, managers possessed techno-functional skills and experience rather than general management and leadership capabilities.
- The succession-planning system was poorly organised and sketchy, often ignored in practice when decisions were made about development and promotion. For reasons no doubt related to these conditions, the graduate development scheme, on which such high hopes had been pinned, had a very poor retention rate.
- Although the company was a multinational with many opportunities for providing diverse experience, postings (including interesting foreign assignments) were rarely based on development criteria. Transfers between functions, even divisions were rare; planned job rotation was unsystematic and often blocked by powerful line managers.

Sally realised that she would have to collect more data before she made recommendations to the executive committee of the board to raise the standards of MD. In particular she needed better audit data on the management stock. However, even at this stage her thoughts about change were beginning to crystallise and to frame the new MD strategy she was preparing. On the train between meetings, she scribbled these down as they came to her

- The decentralised structure of the company would make clawing back to the centre the authority for MD difficult and probably ill-advised. Diversity and empowerment of local managers to assess local learning needs and develop their own solutions was to be welcomed. The trouble was: this was not happening. A corporate MD function was needed with the credibility to influence the SBUs to observe company policy on MD, coordinate local activities in terms of strategy and evaluate effectiveness.
- SBUs should be required to construct their own MD strategies but within a corporate framework. There should be a partnership with MD in doing this and plans should be open to monitoring by corporate MD in terms of agreed outcome measures.
- A planned career management programme should be introduced based on cross-triangulated assessments of each manager (e.g. 360-degree, DCs, etc.) and action plans geared to provide focused development appropriate to potential.
- A high-potential group of younger/middle career managers needing challenge and stretch assignments should be identified. Perhaps a sympathetic board director might take a special interest in talent-managing this group.
- MD should take the lead in stimulating a culture of self-development in which partnership concepts of learning became the cornerstone.

However, having set down her first thoughts, Sally remained hesitant. She sensed that a deeper analysis which surfaced cultural norms around learning and careers was needed. She was also not sure that all of her suggestions would work.

Question
In terms of the information you have in this case and what you now know about MD strategy, what advice would you want to give to Sally in resolving her dilemma?

Source: Private conversations and reported data

4.9 Conclusion

The consensus of 'managerialist' literature is that MD fulfils its purpose when it serves as an instrument of corporate strategy. However, what emerges is that the ambiguity at the heart of MD and at the centre of strategy makes that linkage difficult in practice. In the turbulent world of the organisation many factors, not least careers, the ideologies of various groups of managers, cultural beliefs about managers and how they acquire their skills and the rough and tumble of organisational process are at least as important in determining what goes into an MD programme as the dictates of strategy. MD has to work hard to remain relevant to the strategic business agenda and strategically coherent in its own processes. In the next chapter, we look at development planning which is both defined by the strategic context and also interacts with and shapes that context through an iterative process of mutual influence.

Review questions

1. How far would you agree with the proposition that an important part of the MD director's role is to help the board think?

2. If you were an MD director what steps would you take to ensure that the MD strategy was owned by the management community of the organisation?

3. How would you respond to the proposition that MD strategy will only work if it is in harmony with the organisational culture?

4. 'Learning partnerships sound good but they are honoured more in the breach than the observance'. Do you agree?

5. Do you agree that MD is more important in large organisations than smaller ones? Justify your answer.

6. How would you respond to the idea that 'many MD interventions are actually about unlearning previous patterns of working which are now inappropriate and the job of MD strategy is to facilitate this'?

Web links

We looked at the Council for Excellence in Management and Leadership's frameworks and guides to MD strategy earlier in the text. Many of its reports are available on this web link:
http://www.skillsbase.dfes.gov.uk

A link which gives examples of MD strategic documents (although inevitably in a American context), the website of the American Assembly of Collegiate Schools of Business (AACSB):
http://www.aacsb.edu

A website which brings you up to date with new thinking on emergent strategy and strategy-making in conditions of complexity. Some of it relates to HR/HRD strategy:
http://www.santafeassociates.com

Recommendations for further reading

Those texts marked with an asterisk in the bibliography are recommended for further reading, especially the following:

Broussine, M. and Gray, M. (1998) 'The best and worst time for MD', *Journal of Management Development,* Vol. 17, No. 1. Useful case study of a strategic management programme and its impact.

Sadler-Smith, E. (2006) *Learning and Developing for Managers: Perspectives for Research and Practice.* Especially Chapter 2. Has the distinction of relating the commentary to published research studies which are described at length.

Thomson, A., Mabey, C. et al. (2001) *Changing Patterns of Management Development.* Especially Chapters 6,7,9. A very good starting point for examining the vital interface between business strategy and MD strategy and issues of organisation of the function.

Bibliography

Berry, J. (1990) 'Linking MD to business strategy', *Training and Development Journal*, Vol. 44, No. 8.

Boxall, P. and Purcell J. (2006) *Strategy and HRM*, Ch. 10, Routledge.

*Broussine, M. and Gray, M. (1998) 'The best and worst time for MD', *Journal of Management Development*, Vol. 17, No. 1.

*Brown, P. (2005) 'The evolving role of strategic management development', *Journal of Management Development*, Vol. 24, No. 3.

Burgoyne, J. (1988) 'Management development for the individual and the organisation', *Personnel Management*, June.

Burgoyne, J. and Reynolds, M. (1997) 'Introduction', in Burgoyne, J. and Reynolds, M. (eds) *Management Learning*, Sage.

Cacioppe, R. (1998) 'An integrated model and approach for the design of effective leadership development programmes', *Leadership and Organisational Development Journal*, Vol. 19, No. 1.

CEML (2002) *Principles of Leadership Development: A Best Practice Guide*, CEML.

CIPD (2002) *Developing Managers for Business Performance*, CIPD.

Cunningham, I. (2000) 'Single track minds', *People Management*, 28 Dec.

Doyle, M. (2000) 'Management development in an era of radical change: evolving a relational perspective', *Journal of Management Development*, Vol. 19, No. 7.

Doyle, M. (2001) in Beardwell, I. and Holden, L. (2001) (eds) *Human Resource Management: A Contemporary Approach*, Ch. 9, Prentice Hall.

Easterby-Smith, M. (1994) *Evaluating Management Development, Training and Education*, Gower.

*Garavan, T., Barnicle, B. and O'Suilleabhain, F. (1999) 'Management development: contemporary trends, issues and strategies', *Journal of European Industrial Training*, Vol. 23, No. 4.

Harrison, R. (2000) Learning and Development, chs 5, 6, 10, 18, CIPD.

Heller, R. (1986) *The New Naked Manager*, Coronet Books.

Hitt, W. (1987) 'A unified management development programme', *Journal of Management Development*, Vol. 6, No. 1.

Jennings, D. (2002) 'Strategic management: an evaluation of the use of three learning methods', *Journal of Management Development*, Vol. 21, No. 9.

*Johnson, G. and Scholes, K. (1993) *Exploring Corporate Strategy*, Prentice Hall.

Lundy, O. and Cowling, A. (1996) *Strategic Human Resource Management*, Ch. 8, Routledge.

*Mabey, C. (2002) 'Mapping management development practice', *Journal of Management Studies*, Vol. 39, No. 8.

*Mabey, C. and Finch-Lees, T. (2008) *Management and Leadership Development*, Sage.

Mabey, C., Salaman, G. et al. (1998) *Human Resource Management: A Strategic Introduction*, Blackwell.

Margerison, C. (1991) *Making Management Development Work*, McGraw Hill Training.

*Mayo, A. (1998) *Creating a Training and Development Strategy*, CIPD.

McClell, S. (1994) 'Gaining competitive advantage through strategic management development (SMD)', *Journal of Management Development*, Vol. 13, No. 5.

Mullins, L. (2007) *Management and Organisational Behaviour*, Prentice Hall.

Mumford, A. (1986) *Handbook of Management Development*, Gower.

Mumford, A. (1997) *Management Development: Strategies for Action*, Chs 2, 5.

*Mumford, A. and Gold, J. (2004) *Management Development: Strategies for Action*, Ch. 2, CIPD.

Osbaldeston, M. and Barham, K. (1992) 'Using MD for competitive advantage', *Long Range Planning*, 25 (6).

Pettigrew, A., Jones, E. et al. (1982) *Training and Development Roles in their Organisational Setting*, MSC.

Reid, M. and Barrington, H. (1999) *Training Interventions*, CIPD.

*Sadler-Smith, E. (2006) *Learning and Development for Managers: Perspectives from Research and Practice*, Ch. 2, Blackwell.

*Seibert, K., Hall, T. et al. (1995) 'Strengthening the weak link in strategic executive development', *Human Resource Management*, Vol. 34, No. 4.

Sparrow, P. and Hiltrop, M. (1995) *European Human Resource Management in Transition*, Prentice Hall.

Stewart, J. (1999) *Employee Development*, Chs 5, 13, Prentice Hall.

Stewart, J. and McGoldrick, J. (1996) *Human Resource Development: perspectives, resources and practice*, Ch. 5, Prentice Hall.

*Storey, J. (1989) 'Management development: a literature review and implications for future research', *Personnel Review*, Vol. 18, No. 6.

Stredl, H. and Rothwell, W. (1987) *The ASTD Reference Guide to Professional Training Roles and Competencies*, HRD Press Inc.

Syrett, M. and Lammiman, J. (1999) *Management Development: Making the Investment Count*, Economist Books.

*Thomson, A., Mabey, C. et al. (2001) *Changing Patterns of Management Development*, Chs 2, 6, Blackwell.

Van der Dikken, L. and Hoeksema, L. (2001) 'The palette of management development', *Journal of Management Development*, Vol. 20, No. 2.

Walton, J. (1999) *Strategic Human Resource Development*, Ch. 4, Prentice Hall.

Weick, K. (1995) *Sensemaking in Organisations*, Sage.

Wilson, P. (1999) *Human Resource Development*, Ch. 18, Kogan Page.

*Winterton, J. and Winterton, R. (1997) 'Does MD add value?', *British Journal of Management*, Vol. 8 (Special Issue on MD).

Woodall, J. and Winstanley, B. (1998) *Management Development: Strategy and Practice*, Ch. 2, Blackwell.

5 Assessing development need and development planning

Learning outcomes

After studying this chapter you should be able to understand, analyse and explain:

- the development planning process as a holistic system;
- the performance management review system as the context for the management development planning process;
- the purpose and philosophy of competency;
- the main approaches and models of competency, their strengths and weaknesses;
- appraisal systems as assessment and development tools;
- assessment systems and practices, that is, 360-degree; psychometric testing; development centres;
- the role and importance of personal development plans for focusing development activity.

5.1 Introduction

As we turn to the development planning system we are moving to consider the institutionalised and formal aspects of organising MD. If strategy forms the framework of a planned and coordinated approach to MD, then it is through the development process that strategic questions about who to develop and how will be addressed. As Thomson et al. (2001) suggest, these are the MD processes and procedures which are vital for turning the objectives of the business strategy and the priorities of the MD strategy into practical reality. While the previous chapter considered the larger context in which MD is positioned strategically in terms of the business goals, in this chapter we look at the procedures for diagnosing learning needs at different levels, defining learning in terms of strategic goals and the larger performance management process and then subsequently reviewing and evaluating the effectiveness of the development process.

5.2 MD as a development system

For convenience, we call this nexus of interlocking systems of data gathering, assessment, decision-making and review, the 'development planning process'. Figure 5.1 below tries to capture what this involves. It depicts the MD system as a net of sub-processes (competency frameworks, performance review, assessment systems) that serve as nodal points feeding data into core decision-making processes at the centre. The diagram suggests that embedded within the MD system is a virtuous cycle of information and action; inputs of information feed into the system that are interlinked with judgements and decisions brought together in plans and programmes which are themselves subject to review. The system is dynamic and moves forward through constant iteration between cycles of thinking and experimentation.

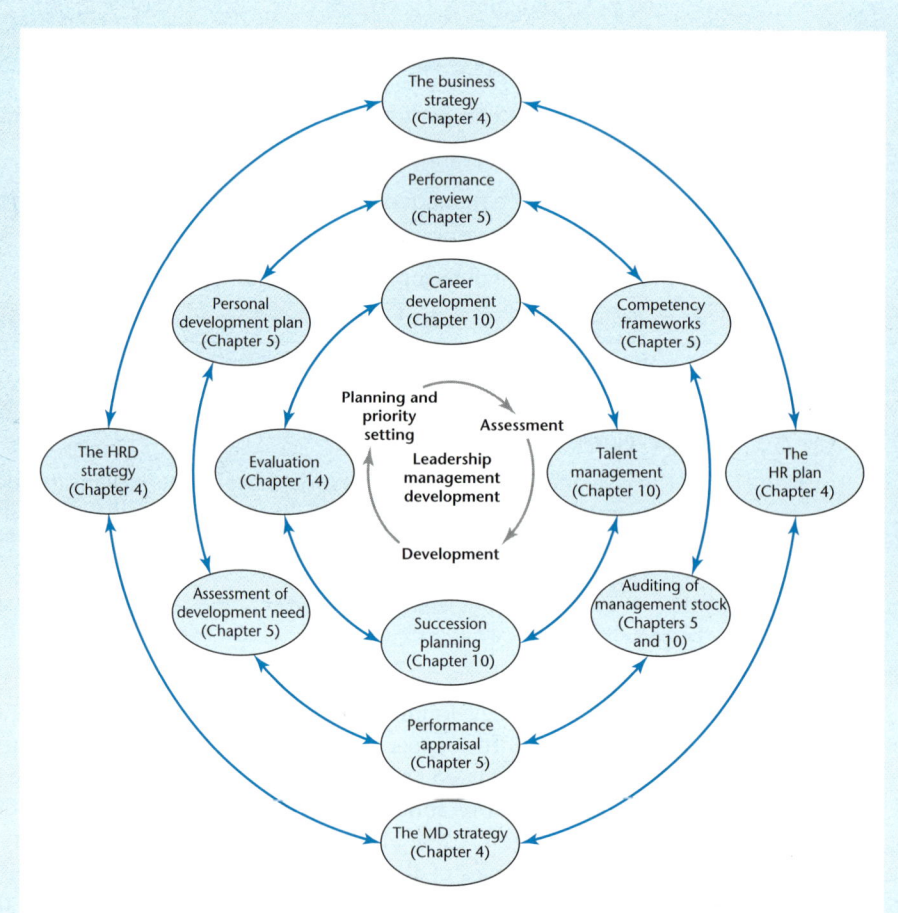

Figure 5.1 The management development planning system

This is a depiction of the development planning system as a set of concentric layers of permeable membranes through which data flows and decision-making happens in an interactive, interconnected way.

Of course, this diagram is a massive idealisation of the complex processes of development planning. The processes are not really as linear, as systematic or as clear-cut as suggested here (e.g. there should be arrows connecting all the subsystems, omitted for clarity). In reality, there is a membrane of mutual interaction between the priorities, definitions and values flowing in from the strategic level and data generated and assessed within the sub-processes and the internal cycle of assessment and planning. Decisions do not emerge in a strictly sequential way. Flows of data and judgements about data lead to a search for new data and assessments. The system is highly interactive between all of its parts and is in constant flux. Politics and intra-organisational bargaining also play a part in the real world. In truth, there are as many ways of reconciling the different processes into a coherent MD system as there are organisations which take MD seriously. However, the simplification which this model represents does at least have the virtue of keeping us focused on its dynamic nature (i.e. a cycle of decision-making within a field of data flows) and helping us to concentrate on the core elements of assessing managers and designing programmes for their development.

There is one other thing to note. Because the development planning cycle is so complex and interwoven, it has been decided to map it through various chapters in this book, on the following schema.

- Business, HRD and MD strategy systems and processes have been considered in Chapter 4.
- Succession and career planning are examined in Chapter 10.
- Evaluation processes are considered in Chapter 14.
- This chapter concentrates on what may be the core processes of the development cycle, that is, performance management and review; competency frameworks; appraisal; assessment of development need; personal development planning.

The reader should try to bear in mind that this is an artificial way of segmentalising episodes in the overall cycle and separating out parts from the whole. Separating the elements also tends to ignore some subtle linkages and feedback processes, for example: developing competency frameworks can help the organisation understand its business objectives more clearly; performance review can have major implications for all parts of the system; appraisal can have an important impact on future recruitment decisions and personal development plans (PDPs) can help build reinforcing loops at all levels of the organisation. However, the positives of using a simple model, considered in terms of its constituent elements, seem to outweigh the negatives which must inevitably occur. All the same, while reading this account readers may feel challenged to redesign the MD system in their own mind in a way which may seem both more elegant and more revealing for them of the essential processes involved.

In the next sections the core elements of the MD system are considered in terms of their relationship to management development as a whole.

5.3 Performance management and review

An organisation with a formal and systematic MD process is likely to have a framework of performance review. The PMS provides the institutional framework for objective setting, outcome measurement, feedback and review of results, monitoring and control. In the most sophisticated systems there is a clear line of sight between objectives at all levels. A corporate vision guides common goals which are cascaded down the organisation to progressively lower levels. Mission and corporate goals are linked with departmental, team and, ultimately, individual objectives. A framework of integration aligns business strategy with the HR and MD strategies. Yardsticks, competencies and critical success factors define the dimensions of good performance, set standards and identify gaps between expectations and results (Armstrong 2004; Armstrong and Baron 1998).

In the best organised systems like management by objectives (MBO) (Armstrong 2004), framework objectives are linked in a continuous chain from strategic to individual levels. The objectives of MD (and other HR functions) and those of the manager unfold logically within a hierarchy of goals, and control measures are agreed upon at each level which become the basis of performance measurement, assessment and action programming (see Cummings and Worley 1997 for an account of MBO when it is working well). For each function (like MD) senior managers meet to go carefully through the business plan and systematically define lower order objectives within higher order goals and the meaning of the business vision for all parts of the organisation (e.g. what exactly will it mean for MD that the organisational strategy is becoming international, with greater priority given to marketing?). In this way, strategy becomes behavioural. Levels of managers agree on performance goals, standards and the types of behaviour which are values and should be promoted (Armstrong and Baron 1998, Gibb 2002).

Cumming and Worsley (1997) emphasise that performance review which really works seems to combine a number of factors. First and foremost, top management recognises the importance of PMS as the crucial, baseline management process from which all else stems. They commit time and energy to integrating performance with the corporate strategic process and interpreting strategic priorities in terms of performance for each of the specialist components of management (e.g. divisions of management, service functions like MD, etc.). It seems too that the best PMS tend to be custom-designed in relation to local culture (Fee 2001) and based on performance measures which go beyond narrow accountancy-led criteria to incorporate learning, quality and creativity factors. Realising that getting the measures right is crucial to determining what gets done, management avoids the trap of requiring too many detailed behaviours as criteria, which will create a cumbrous system and undermines commitment. Instead, it aims for clusters of essential performance indicators which measure key elements and command the commitment of those at the receiving end (Graham and Bennett 1995).

According to Holbeche (2001), PMS are increasingly based on participative decision-making. The organisation as a community defines its own performance ratings. There is a move away from heavily rationalistic and directive systems and narrow measures to performance indicators which involve quality indicators (trust, creativity, diversity, continuous personal development), even if these are more difficult to measure. However, the litmus test of any PMS is whether management define it as the key process for driving forward a corporate agenda and it is seen as just and workable at all organisational levels. So often, PMS fall apart because of management indifference and employee suspicion (Armstrong 2004).

The design of corporate PMS involves issues which are far broader than MD, or indeed HRM as a management function. However, the overall system of aligning objectives, performance and measurement (often linked to reward through performance related pay) can be an important vehicle for emphasising the value of learning and development as well as task achievement, as indicators of performance. PMS can also provide a framework for integrating HRM activities and a logical starting point for identifying MD priorities through an assessment of learning need. It is to this that we now turn.

5.4 Competency frameworks

Competency frameworks are a vital link in the development process. They form the interface between the strategic and development planning spheres. Robust competency frameworks can make management development strategic. Defining corporate competencies for the organisation as a whole (i.e. the business we are in, our core goals and corporate concerns) leads on to interpreting their implications for different occupational groups and ultimately to definitions of knowledge, understanding, skills, attitudes and behaviour (KUSAB) needed by individuals themselves. Done well, this interlocking of strategic imperatives (corporate business competencies) with skills profiles (individual and team competencies) can ensure that the whole organisation is geared to the behaviours needed for high performance and can coordinate its activities to ensure that this happens. This, at least, is what the proponents of competency frameworks proclaim (e.g. Perren and Burgoyne 2002).

5.4.1 The meaning of competencies

Disaggregating the business core competencies of the organisation into team and individual competencies challenges the analytical and interpretive resources of senior managers. Can they define the strategic goals of the organisation in terms of required managerial skills and behaviours? Well done, competency frameworks identify the abilities, traits, skills, knowledge, attitudes, motives and styles that should form the profile of successful managers in the organisation for the future.

So what exactly are competency frameworks? The consensus of the literature is that they are not a panacea for the problem of selecting and developing the right managers to do the right things but an important contribution to a portfolio of methods for defining management jobs and the skills they need (Currie and Darby 1995) Competencies are templates of performance criteria relevant to the organisation against which managers, in teams and as individuals, can be assessed. The idea is that well-designed competency frameworks define the constituent features of desirable management capabilities and the explicit behaviour believed to correlate with high performance (i.e. the conceptual, human and technical skills of managers). Ideally, these criteria will define what the manager needs to bring to his or her role and offer a means of discriminating between performance at different levels of sophistication and effectiveness (Holman and Hunt 1996, Harris and Hogan 1992).

Pause for thought

The ethics of using competency tools

A management consultant from a major firm recently defended competency frameworks as a performance management system on the grounds that 'You can teach a turkey to climb a tree but surely it is easier to hire a squirrel.' What he meant was that while it may be feasible to build a cadre of effective managers from your existing stock, who with time and support would go on to achieve results which the organisation expected, it was more cost-effective to use competency criteria to identify the squirrel and then give it intensive support (development) to become faster at finding nuts and climbing trees than your competitors' squirrels. But where does that leave the 'turkeys', or translated, the solid citizens of the management community?

Tools like competency frameworks to improve the management stock are as good as the values which direct them.

Questions

Competency frameworks can be used to build a strong management community and to target the available resource for building consistent standards and a common management culture. They can also be used (think Enron) to create a neo-Darwinist organisational world in which only the best adapted are helped to prosper or allowed to survive. Do you agree with this? Have you worked out your own principled position regarding these techniques?

The idea of 'competency' seems to originate from Boyatzis's (1982) book *The Competent Manager*. As Woodruffe (1993) suggests, from the beginning there has never been agreement on what competencies are or how to compose competency lists. Boyatzis (1982) defines competency as 'the underlying characteristics' of the person, a broad concept which could include 'a motive, a trait, a skill, aspect of one's self image or a body of knowledge which he or she uses'.

This definition covers a wide range, arguably without getting to the heart of what may distinguish between good and inadequate managerial performance. Dulewicz (1991) explains the confusion that can result in a development centre if there is lack of clarity about what is being measured:

> Without a clear model of competency, a long list of competencies might include behaviours (e.g. behaving with sensitivity), their presumed cause (e.g. emotional stability) and their consequences (good EQ with staff).

Without a clear focus, the analyst will not be sure exactly what is being examined and how to value and rate the information collected. In the end, as we will see, competency only seems to have definition and meaning in terms of the methodology which is adopted.

In the UK, competence-based development (CBD) probably had its origins in the movement to create national standards of management competence and behaviour as a response to the severe criticism of management and the quality of MD in Britain following the Constable and McCormick report (1987) (see Chapter 9). As Doyle (2007) and Cowling and Lundy (1996) emphasise, the Management Charter Initiative was a body set up in the early 1990s to agree national standards of management competency. Their work was to become the basis of the NVQ system of management qualifications which we consider (in passing) in Chapters 8 and 9.

The original standards followed a logic of defining elements of competency which were clustered into complex 'units of competency' which came together to define the managerial role. Defining the units of competency involved an analysis of employment functions, benchmarking of achievement at specified levels, and constructing criteria by which to recognise competent behaviour when it is displayed. This became the basis for the national NVQ system of management qualifications. Responsibility for designing, maintaining and policing the standards has now shifted to the Management Standards Centre (MSC) and the Chartered Management Institute(CMI) (Doyle 2007).

It is probably of more interest to British readers than others to know (although, in a globalised world, models now circulate quickly and become rapidly disseminated) that the original MCI standards have been reviewed and revised over the past 15 years to make them more flexible, more indicative (rather than mandatory), more streamlined and with more emphasis on softer skills. As the British experience suggests, designing competencies so that they sensitively reflect reality is not a one-shot exercise, it requires constant readjustment. Competencies can easily become out of date. Another lesson may be that ambitious national, generic frameworks which aim for universal application are too crude to reflect the diversity and variability of real organisations in the real world.

5.4.2 The value of competencies

Many organisations have adopted a competency-based approach in recent years. The benefits are said to be considerable.

One of the advantages claimed for competencies is that they focus the organisation strategically. Through competencies it is said that the organisation has a methodology for translating corporate concerns about innovation and competitiveness directly into expectations of individual behaviour. Competency is seen as particularly useful as part of a strategy for radically changing the positioning, culture and performance of the organisation because it ensures a mutually reinforcing approach. Well-designed competency frameworks can drive recruitment, appraisal, assessment for development, promotion, job redesign and even (and this is controversial) redundancy decisions. They become the fixed point of a compass by which the organisation orients itself and embeds its corporate strategy in the fabric of ordinary organisational life so it has a living presence.

Well-constructed competencies can have an influence throughout the organisation. In recruitment they are often seen as better indicators than qualifications or formal experience for assessing suitability for a job or promotion. Competencies provide the contextual logic for designing and applying a range of selection techniques to obtain reliable data on the capabilities of people. In performance management terms, competencies are often regarded as 'objective' measures (i.e. stripped of cultural biases) to predict levels of performance in a job (Harrison 2000). The information obtained can feed into appraisal, feedback, development plans and reward systems.

Robust competency frameworks are seen as a key to focusing organisational consciousness on key areas of performance. Applied skilfully they can link performance assessment with performance outcomes. If senior management are clear about the qualities that it wants from its future managers, the competencies can provide the framework for defining and encouraging high performance.

In the end, the great value of competency frameworks, at least as senior managers report their experience of using them, is that they allow reliable discrimination between levels and dimensions of achievement which no other assessment tools seem to provide. For example, Sparrow and Bognanno (1994) have introduced a useful distinction between three categories of performance.

- *Emerging competencies*: are the competencies which will be needed in the organisation of the future. It is top management's responsibility to define what they may be.
- *Maturing competencies*: are the competencies of the present; some will become even more relevant in the future, others will decline.
- *Transitional competencies*: are the competencies that may be needed for the change period but may be superseded in the future as the organisation enters another phase of development.

This ordering of competencies in ascending and descending trajectories aligned to the life cycle of the organisation helps the top management in focusing on leading-edge competencies and disengaging from others which may have outlived their usefulness. Using the model may also raise some issues for MD. Should MD be concerned to develop cadres of managers for all seasons or emphasise more the recruitment of interim managers on time-limited contracts who have the profiles needed at one stage in an organisation's journey but not at another?

Other writers have developed typologies of competency which they believe are linked to superior performance. So, for example, Schroder (1989) claims that a coherent competency framework will bring together these dimensions in an index which distinguishes between average and superior performance:

- cognitive competencies (thinking, judging, reasoning, etc.);
- motivational competencies (the will to achieve);
- directional competencies (leadership skills);
- achievement competencies (social, emotional, people skills).

5.4.3 The methodologies of competency

In recent years, competency frameworks have been adopted by many organisations around the world. As a result, they are becoming more diverse and differentiated, more adapted to the local circumstances of specific organisations. All the same, as we shall see, all competency models used today in modern organisations stem from a few core methodologies.

The functionalist–behaviourist model

This is the approach of the Management Standards Centre (MSC) (see above). It is a job-analysis approach that breaks down management tasks within a job into basic units of competency aligned with performance outcomes.

This task-oriented methodology implies a set of universal management competency attributes based on a scientific analysis of the tasks of managing and the knowledge, skills and attitudes involved, as expressed in outcomes. It is painstaking in its methods and claims to be rigorous in expressing competency in terms of measurable results. A practitioner is deemed to be either 'competent' in terms of demonstrable evidence of performance standards or not. Competency is assessed on a sliding scale of increasing levels of complexity, variety, autonomy, responsibility and breadth of control within the management role.

Those readers who are interested in the detailed methods by which MCI/MSC technologies break down jobs and build bottom–up performance criteria are referred to Harrison (2000) and Reid and Barrington (2000). However, it may be useful here to mention Woodruffe's (1992) suggestions of a protocol for any organisation doing its own competency-based analysis which is based on the task approach.

- Develop a statement of the role or purpose of the job.
- Do a breakdown of the role into discrete areas of competency.
- Define the competencies needed to perform effectively in each area.
- Agree criteria for judging if performance has been achieved in each area.

The functionalist approach has, until very recently, occupied the intellectual and ideological high ground of debate about competency in UK. Its strength is that it offers a clear logic, a common spine for assessing the qualities of all managers as they progress through gradations of mastery and sophistication to higher levels of performance and seniority.

The functionalist approach has not lacked critics. Some have criticised the utilitarian reductionism implicit in this methodology which is perceived to ignore the moral, social, political and ideological aspects of management work. Its categories have been seen as just too crude to capture these subtle processes. Others believe categories based on universalism are socially naive and deny cultural heterodoxy. The claims to generalisation are thin and insubstantial, as Kilcourse (1994) says: 'Competencies thought to have general application will fit where they touch when it comes to specific organisations'. A manager who is defined as 'competent' in one context under a particular competency framework may be seen as 'incompetent' under another (Doyle 2007).

Also, because the templates are superficial and one-dimensional, the critics claim, there is a danger that functionalist schema only legitimate the most obvious dimensions of behaviour and ignore the complex cognitive, social and emotional processes behind them merely because they are difficult to define and measure.

Functional methodologies are therefore in danger of becoming a force for homogenising managerial behaviour, cloning the next generation of managers within straitjacketed criteria. There is also the danger that they provide a means by which upper levels of managers can manipulate assessment criteria so that the next wave of managers are developed in their own image (i.e. maintaining their legacy).

Then there is the critique that the functionalist approach can be seen as mechanistic, reductionist and behaviourist, at odds with the new spirit of creativity, diversity and celebration of the nebulous and 'romantic' (e.g. emotional intelligence, wisdom, intuition, empathy, etc. at work) in the early millennium. Doyle (2007) suggests that competency grew from the social engineering tradition of US management and still retains a residue of its controlling and prescriptive nature, now out of joint with the times.

The person-centred or social model of competency

The behavioural model approaches the concept and application of competency from a very different angle. Instead of defining the tasks in which a practitioner needs to perform and the standards, the social approach, as its name suggests, tries to assess the characteristics of the person (i.e. traits, skills, motives, self-mage, knowledge, etc.) which s/he brings to the role. The focus then is less on the demands of the task, more on the attributes of successful performers.

The researcher associated with this approach is Boyatzis (1982) who has developed a holistic methodology for understanding the behavioural patterns by which general managers achieve results. He sees competencies as far more than mere skills, they are the deeply rooted characteristics of the individual – a mix of aptitudes, attitudes, emotions and orientations – which make up the whole person as a manager. Boyatzis (1982) talks of a set of 18 descriptors of personal dimensions which can be linked (purportedly) to success in general management. This detailed list is grouped into five key clusters (i.e. goal and action management; directing subordinates; human resourcing; managing the social process, and leadership).

Another aspect of the Boyatzis scheme is that he attempts to distinguish between core competencies which represent the 'sine qua non' of managing and may be intrinsic to the person and 'surface competencies' which may be developed with conventional training methods. He also tries to distinguish between 'threshold' and 'superior' or 'high performance' competencies. 'Threshold competencies' are combinations of related behaviours which are commonly associated with managerial performance. In a sense, they describe average performance and research has not linked them to superior management effectiveness. 'High performance' competencies are mutually reinforcing behaviours that distinguish ordinary performers from superlative performers. Using these criteria, higher levels of management can focus on the behaviours which are most in need of development among their cadres of managers if the organisation is to aspire higher, and the schema provides tangible evidence to recognise superior qualities in management when they are demonstrated (Garavan and McGuire 2001).

The Boyatzis definition of competencies associated with high performance

- Use of unilateral power (i.e. being able to take initiative without relying on formal authority).
- Accurate self-understanding (including a sensitive understanding of how people see you).
- Positive self-regard (or self-confidence).
- Spontaneity (an ability to operate outside formal systems).
- Good capacity for logical thought (which also includes conceptual ability, seeing the big picture).
- Emotional intelligence (empathy with others; maturity).
- Specialised knowledge in management.
- The ability and commitment to develop others.

Source: Adapted from Boyatzis, R. (1982) *The Competent Manager*, Wiley

For a more detailed examination of the Boyatzis model, the interested reader is referred to Sadler-Smith (2006), Storey (1989) and Thomson et al. (2001). The great advantage of the Boyatzis framework is that it is based on a large research sample (over 2,000 managers in 41 different management jobs). The Boyatzis model is also attractive because it implies quite a subtle definition of 'competency', not the mere manifestation of behaviours which might correlate with performance, but underlying characteristics that a manager brings to a job. This legitimates the consideration of the softer, less tangible management skills which sophisticated players claim make all the difference.

Many organisations have used Boyatzis, or a modified version of it, as the logical foundation for their management development programmes. However, the model has also been roundly criticised. First of all, like functionalist analysis, the Boyatzis schema is generic; it seems to accept uncritically the premise that it is possible to draw up lists which are predictors of universal competency in management. This downplays the importance of context, climate and culture in identifying the attributes of managing. There is also the issue that Boyatzis's neat categories of definition may be too crude to capture the fragmented processes of management and are really no more than proxies for accurate measurement (Sadler-Smith 2006).

Other methodologies of competency

The concept of competency has established itself as a strategic tool within MD and, indeed, is often seen as the driving force of many MD systems (development centres; assessment; design; evaluation, etc.). For organisations geared up to performance management, competencies are often the lynchpin integrating all parts of the HR function.

By the early years of the millennium most large companies were using some form of competency as a connecting logic for HRD. However, in most organisations there has been a shift away from generic competencies and standardised national schemes because they are seen to fail in capturing the diversity of management or its contextualised nature. Most organisations either customise the Boytazis or MCI schema to suit their needs or develop their own competency frameworks.

The literature is not short on advice for the organisation which decides to design its own framework. Woodruffe (1993, 2003) suggests that a starting point for thinking about competencies is to distinguish between 'areas of competency' and 'dimensions of competency'. Mumford and Gold (2004) use different terminology but make essentially the same point when they differentiate a 'means focus' from an 'end focus'. All commentators emphasise the importance of undertaking an analysis of the work where the practitioner will need to be effective ('area of competency') and an analysis of the traits, skills and characteristics of the person needed for effectiveness ('dimensions of competency').

It is suggested in the literature that defining the 'areas of competency' require some form of functional analysis, breaking down roles into detailed components and then seeking to define the behaviours required. This may involve 'activity analysis'; 'critical incident analysis' and structured observation of behaviour in the role. In the most progressive organisations, concerned to legitimate their competency tools through popular ownership, there is often an attempt to build a broad consensus on the purpose of the role, how it relates to other roles, the expected outcomes and conditions of performance.

Commentators (Woodruffe (1993, 2003) Sadler-Smith (2006)) suggest that 'dimensions of competency', the 'person centred' aspects of competency, require a different methodology and approach. This will be multilateral, and, at its best, richly interwoven. It may involve 360-degree assessment and repertory grid analysis (see later in this chapter), drawing on the reports of those strategically located to assess the talents which are needed.

Other methods used in 'person centred' competency analysis include management 'self reports'; 'depth interviews' with managers who are 'peer referred' as excellent performers (i.e. to identify the essence of their capability); 'shadowing' of 'stars' and 'focus group' discussions about the constituent elements of performance. Finally, many organisations also use 'panel evaluations' in which senior managers, well respected in the organisation, bring their wisdom and experience to bear in defining the skills which will be needed for managing in the future (Thomson et al. 2001).

Ultimately the streams of data from these different sources are brought together in a framework of competency which sets standards and criteria of assessment. In practice competency frameworks are almost always a synthesis of methodologies. The instrument which emerges from the data collection and discussion can provide the galvanising logic for integrating HR systems with performance and providing a vocabulary for monitoring, measurement and motivation.

The role of top management in this process is often overlooked. The top needs to be involved at every stage of the design. In the beginning they are responsible for defining what the organisation does well, what it needs to improve and the issues which will face the organisation in the future. They may also be called on to define the philosophy of management and its expectations of managers in terms of the strategic plan. It is these values and this thinking which must shape and direct the competency framework if is to serve a strategic rather than a technocratic purpose (Margerison 1991). Indeed, the degree to which the competency model permeates the management process will be directly proportionate to the interest that the top takes in it. Where it drives competency and is heavily involved in design decisions there is a good chance that it will become a genuine tool for strategic repositioning and organisational development.

Cockerill and Hunt (1995) make the essential point that the value of any competency mechanism is only as good as the methodology which is used. They identify three groups who can be defined in their orientations to methodology:

The *traditionalists* develop competencies by identifying the most successful managers in an organisation and distilling the characteristics which seem to distinguish between high-flyers and ordinary managers. These factors become the measuring rod for performance management and development. However, rapid promotion within an organisation does not necessarily equate to effectiveness. Successful managers may just be good at playing the political game and impression management (see Chapter 2). There is also the issue that using the qualities of today's heroes as the benchmark for the future runs the risk of reproducing a mode of management from the past when the objective conditions of the times requires new heroes with new qualities.

The second group in Cockerill et al.'s (1995) typology are the *inventors*. Inventors, who are often commercial consultants with their own proprietorial brand of competency, have little interest in the methodological underpinning of the frameworks they propose. Their main concern is to persuade managers to adopt a rhetoric which appears to measure performance, but may in fact be a list of generic or blended characteristics without scientific foundation.

The third group, the *scientists,* understand the linkage between the methodology of competency and demonstrable performance. They seek to develop indices which are predictive. They use empirically validated techniques to derive the standards and criteria and are conscious of the need to set conditions for their use.

Cockerill et al. (1995) believe that scientific competency criteria based on local empirical assessment of the skills needed in changing conditions are quite rare. Most competencies used by organisations are either blended from universal lists or based on assumptions about what good managers do rather than actual observation of them. As such, competencies trade on the illusion of a scientific method, which gives legitimation, while practising a form of manipulative pseudoscience. The authors believe that as a performance-enhancing instrument, competency is as good as the methodology that informs it. If the thinking behind competency is flawed then the outcomes will be flawed. Most competency frameworks, they believe, are deficient in logic and inexpert in methodology; hype typically substitutes for empirical observation or rigorous validation. However, if Cockerill et al. (1995) believe that competencies fail the test of acknowledged scientific method, others, more radical, believe they also fail the larger test of fitness for purpose.

5.4.4 Final thoughts on competency frameworks

The arguments supporting competency as part of a planned development system are well known. The popularity of competency with the big battalions of business suggest that they fully accept its rationale.

However, what we may now be seeing are the beginnings of a counter movement away from competency as a method of assessment which may have been adopted too quickly and too uncritically. There is a growing realisation that the legitimation of competencies resides mostly in the readiness of consultancies to market them and in top managers to adopt them, almost as a magic-bullet solution to the problem of performance development.

One of the most fundamental criticisms of competency frameworks is that they lack precision. What exactly is being measured and how can we be sure that the dimensions which are chosen accurately reflect the realities of managing? Mangham (1986) makes the point that management is too in love with 'portmanteaux' ('big bag') words like 'motivation', 'leadership', 'drive', etc. Designers of competency criteria tend to use these terms very liberally without effectively defining or operationalising them in terms of lived, real experience. So, for example, slogans like 'excellent communication skills' are often cited as a required competency of top management. However, when we deconstruct a term like this so that it becomes measurable, we find that it contains a complex amalgam of attributes, that is, rhetorical skills; fluency; smoothness of presentation; empathy; conceptual understanding; political insight and self-confidence. All these and other qualities become subsumed under a big word like 'communication', as if that alone captures the meaning.

Mangham (1986, 1990) believes that there is too much 'shorthand thinking' in competency descriptors, too much pretending to understand subtle qualities with labels that miss the experience. At our present stage of knowledge we just don't have a clear enough picture of what good management performers do and we lack a vocabulary for realistically describing behaviour. The result is that managers are assessed on the basis of unexamined assumptions and stereotypes, not how they really behave.

Other writers have echoed and developed these themes. They suggest that identifying desirable managerial behaviour is actually very difficult because the role of the manager varies so much; different styles seem to be equally successful and there is, anyway, little consensus on what constitutes good management performance. If precise definition of the qualities which make up competency defy ready analysis, what exactly is being measured? Jubb and Robotham (1997) suggest that many competency systems are actually very static lists which go little further than bland description. As generic tick boxes, they fail to capture the complexity of management. Nor do they address the issue of how managerial action and outcomes are linked, let alone measured.

A related point is the alleged failure of many formulations of competency to engage with the ethnographic data on management process (Watson 1999; Kotter 1982) which we have mentioned before (see Chapter 2). Do competency criteria really do justice to the qualities involved in handling the typical management experience of ambiguity, contradiction, variety and fragmentation of work and the need to create the future while maintaining the existing process? Do they really represent the reflective thinking, empathic understanding, wise appreciation and measured action which compose effective management? Do they reflect the skein of moral, political, cultural and social relationships by which management is conducted?

Any researcher who has looked closely at how managers behave (like this author) will be struck by the degree of choice that is involved in defining situations and choosing from an armoury of approaches (Watson 1999). Typically, management is about navigating between clashing rocks; reconciling contradictory processes; building agreement among diverse constituencies; acting with inadequate information and making constant adjustments to behaviour as the situation becomes clearer through immersion. This requires a wide range of sense-making and execution skills which we still do not understand. For example, as this author has suggested (Dalton 1993), 'naturals' at management seem also to be 'naturals' at social life, for example, they often tell good stories to disseminate a vision, they talk in images which make their points memorable and can tell good jokes which bring people onside. Likewise, the capacity to hold about three opposing ideas in the mind while sifting between them and still acting coherently seems to be related to higher-order management skill.

It would be a rare competency framework which accommodated these things. Indeed, in their preference for the explicit, measurable and convenient over the implicit, intangible and thoughtful, competencies are in danger of offering only a thin and insubstantial caricature of what management involves, especially in a period of rapid change which puts high value on the less easily defined, softer, interactive skills of management (Garavan and McGuire 2001).

Another concern relates to the holistic nature of modern management process. Increasingly management is about sharing power, facilitating through others and empowering teams. The individualistic bias of competency signally fails to reflect the increasingly interconnected nature of the organisational process. To focus too much on individual contributions to performance, especially if competency measurement is related to pay, may be to contradict organisational strategies for building creativity through groups (Sadler-Smith 2006). In future we may see more emphasis on designing *team* competencies.

So much of the accumulating evidence suggests that the advocates of competency should recognise the limits of their method and be more humble in their claims. Monica Lee (2004) rightly mentions the fear of many that the increasing adoption of competency models threatens to create an ethos of standardisation, compliance and control when a more complex business environment requires diversity, flexibility and experimentation with new ways of managing. Many competency schemes threaten to bureaucratise the process of assessment with narrow and technicist measures which may be administratively convenient but lack analytical depth. The unreflective adoption of competency implies the search for an identikit, interchangeable manager (Mangham 1990) based on generic skills (even if the framework is customised to a single organisation) which may be to pursue a myth. Only richly textured and carefully validated measures, well contextualised with sensitive understanding of cultural fit, will ever do justice to the variety of effective managerial behaviour. We are a long way from developing such tools (Antonacopoulou and Fitzgerald 1996).

Finally, it is relevant here to mention an interesting insight made by Mumford and Gold (2004). They suggest that the competency movement is mainly important for its ideological power. The language of competencies has become so embedded in management psychology that it has become accepted as unremarkable commonsense in defining management performance and development needs. Managers everywhere now construct management performance in the terms handed down by competency. In Foucault's (1980) interpretation this is an expression of the power of an idea and language to define reality. Managers themselves now talk of their managerial identities in terms of competency and it has arguably become a useful rhetorical device to justify the endless restructurings and intensification of work which all managers have experienced in recent years. However, time marches on and the age of the competency framework may be coming to an end.

If competency is to survive as a concept and an approach it will need to engage with the points made above. In particular, it will need to find closure in the debate on whether there are universal competencies in management and how these can be designed. It needs to focus on team competencies as well as individual competencies and go beyond skill-based competency to find ways of defining and operationalising 'aspects of character' and/or 'affective competencies' for the organisations of the future (Mangham 2005).

Case study — Competency-based development at a Regional Health Authority

In 2002 a large northern Regional Health Authority decided to 'renew and refresh' its leadership profile. The purpose of the review was to develop a competency model that could be used as a diagnostic tool for recruiting and developing leaders in the future. This was particularly timely and important because of the increased emphasis placed on clinical leadership and the need to decide whether the new imperative to deliver the modernisation agenda required a shift in competency profiles.

The Health Authority defined 'competency' as the characteristics which a person brings to a role which are likely to create superior performance. Such characteristics were defined not simply as skills and knowledge but also included values, sources of motivation and aspects of character.

A top team of senior managers with academic advisers were charged with developing a competency framework for top management. These are the steps they took.

1. Clarification of the roles being studied. This involved judgement in determining whether professional roles had a leadership element and how roles might be different in the future. Past expectations of a role and behaviour within it were not necessarily a guide to future behaviour.

2. Developing prima facie criteria for identifying people as 'good performers'. The attributes seen as most highly rated as indicators of good performance were:
   - making good progress in leading change on the new NHS agenda;
   - delivering must-be-done performance targets;
   - developing a healthy organisation.

3. Chief executives of health trusts and other top managers at regional level were asked to nominate people who they thought substantially met these criteria. In the event, 40 people – clinicians and general managers – were identified who were asked to attend focus groups. The focus groups were asked to act as 'expert panels' and take part in a number of exercises.

4. The first exercise was 'repertory grid'. Individuals wrote down a sample of good, average and struggling leaders they knew, then identified the skills, knowledge and personal characteristics that differentiated them.

5. The second exercise used was 'critical incident interviewing'. Participants identified a representative sample of critical events from their work as leaders over the past year or so, including at least one successful and one unsuccessful event. They were then interviewed by a colleague about their approach to each event, what specifically they did and the thinking behind it. The colleague noted particular behaviours, skills and personal characteristics displayed by the events.

6. The group then came together and, using repertory grid and critical incident notes, attempted to answer the question 'What are the main competencies that top managers as leaders need to have?'. Where necessary, the facilitator probed for more specific data.

7. The data collected from the sessions were collated and points clustered. The results were compared with other NHS competency studies to ensure consistency and completeness.

8. Finally, 12 board and clinical leaders who were regarded as having particular credibility in the leading change were asked to comment on the competencies and suggest a rank order of importance for them.

The competency framework which emerged was divided into eight clusters of capabilities, each sub-divided into positive indicators and contra-indicators. The framework was used to identify managers for accelerated development, building a pool of talent for succession planning, focused career development and performance review. It was fundamentally revised three years later to take account of the implications of new government initiatives.

Question

What would you regard as the strengths and the weaknesses of this approach to developing a competency framework?

Source: Confidential internal Health Authority documents anonymised for this study

5.5 Appraisal systems

Another link in our representation of MD system is appraisal. Performance appraisals are pivotal to MD. They are the mechanism by which strategy and the priorities of the corporate PMS cycle are translated into the objectives and criteria by which managers will be judged.

5.5.1 The value of appraisal as an assessment tool

Mumford (1993) talks of appraisal interviews as the crucial part of the planned assessment and development process. It is through appraisal that individual objectives are set and performance over the past year is reviewed. It is also the time when development needs are assessed. The appraisal is supposed to provide a stream of valuable management information: on role-set expectations; performance strengths and weaknesses; the reasons for performance shortfalls and priority areas for improvement. This information is useful for allocating reward, succession planning, identifying learning needs and talent-spotting for potential. Used effectively, appraisals are about development as well as control.

In most workplaces, appraisals are still the most used means of defining individual development needs (Mumford 1993) Appraisal systems vary. However, most are conducted by line management as an expression of their authority and appropriate because they usually have power over career progression. However, as we will see, this may raise issues of the commitment of the line to the process and the skill with which it is carried out. Where there is a competency framework it is likely that the appraisal process will be structured around it and be linked explicitly to its criteria. Some appraisal systems can be very complex with a lot of form-filling and assessment against multiple categories; others can be just a simple list of headings like 'performance in the last year', 'achievement of objectives', 'the conditions which explain performance', 'expected improvements' (Mumford 1993). It is not the sophistication of the system which conduces to effectiveness but the climate in which it is conducted and the skills of disclosure and analysis of the people concerned. In most cases, appraisals are tense, especially if pay and promotion are at stake and joint decision-making can easily descend into inquisition.

5.5.2 The problems of using appraisal as assessment

As hinted in the case study above, appraisal is often flawed as a method for assessing development need. There are often design faults which reduce the utility of the system. Performance objectives may not be clearly defined or agreed. The measures of appraisal may not clearly link with the objectives and bear little relation to the reality of doing the work. Then, there can be a conflict between performance and development objectives. A system which is about identifying weaknesses of performance may be at odds with values of development and career counselling. Typically, performance issues will dominate and create a climate of defensiveness and self-protection which will make it difficult for people to admit limitations and ask for help.

For the appraiser, the dual roles of acting as judge on a performance record (which often may have significant effects for promotion chances and bonus) as well as coach facilitating a future development plan, may seem contradictory. In practice, it is likely that the latter role will be subordinated to the former or just ignored (save perhaps for a ritualistic nod in the direction of 'development' at the end of the session). For the appraisee there is a paradox: in 'performance' discussions the aim is to present personal strengths for the best rating, yet when discussing development you are exposing weaknesses (Woodall and Winstanley 1999). Appraisal systems that attempt too much (as our example, below, suggests), are likely to collapse under the strain of these contradictions. As Mumford (1993) rightly observes, it surely beggars belief that proactive managers, rewarded for being dominant and directive, will be able to shift wavelength from being the critic required in performance management to being the reflective listener which is required of the developer. Equally it strains credulity to believe that appraisees, having received the criticism, will then feel sufficient trust to openly discuss their self-perceived faults so that the organisation can help them develop. In view of the power dynamics, it is little wonder that relationships of dominance/submission; aggression/defensiveness, jealousies, suspicion and mistrust often displace real communication and real development.

Finally, the literature is critical of the process of rating performance in the typical appraisal situation. Evaluation studies suggest that even where objective performance criteria exist, people are often assessed in practice by their personal qualities. Articulacy and self-confidence often substitute for objective success. It appears too that the larger, situational factors which may be crucial in shaping performance are often overlooked; the individualistic nature of the process creates an ethos which tends to deny context as an admissible reason for performance failure. The result can be a distorted picture of development need.

For all these reasons, the appraisal interview is often a flawed experience. Managers invariably believe that it is time-consuming and dislike playing god with their subordinates' careers. Often they approach appraisal as a ritual foisted on them by HRM in which they have only a limited sense of ownership. All too often appraisals become little more than formalities with little real use made of the results, especially for development.

5.5.3 Making appraisal work

So what is needed for appraisals to work and, in particular, to be vehicles for development? A distillation of the literature suggests that effective appraisals may have the following characteristics.

- *Ownership*: Line managers need to feel committed to the appraisal process for it to work. This means involving them in the design and persuading them of the benefits of the system.

- *Training for appraisers*: Line managers need to be trained in the social skills involved in successful appraisal, for example, encouraging honesty in discussion; being reflective on the impact of their style; empathising with the appraisee; being able to assess their likely reaction to criticism and suggestion of development; listening actively; asking appropriate questions; making accurate judgements; giving effective feedback.

- *Clear goals, standards and ratings*: Appraisal systems will only work if their purpose is clear; if corporate goals are geared into lower-level goals; standards are defined and people see the ratings systems as transparent. People need to perceive that the system is more than just control and is really a vital hinge in the HRM process as a whole, which can take the organisation to higher levels (from which they benefit).

    Newer systems are going beyond this minimum requirement, finding ways of synthesising judgements into an overarching view of a person's performance and incorporating multiple ratings (360-degree). They are also incorporating elements of upward appraisal which counterbalance the downward imposition of power which traditional systems can imply.

- *Separating performance issues from development issues*: This may be the only way to ensue that performance issues don't always dominate the agenda, crowding out decisions on development which may be of greater long-term importance for performance. Where the central thrust of appraisal is developmental, it should be easier to move towards openness in jointly diagnosing strengths and weaknesses, growth needs, new challenges and how people can be prepared for them.

- *Self-appraisal and development*: Increasingly there is an acceptance that appraisal systems are only legitimate if they involve appraisees making their own self-assessments of performance and development. While cynics may say these will be self-serving they are no more likely to be inaccurate than the traditional appraisal where the manager only has a hazy picture of what his or her subordinates have been doing in the past year (Mabey and Iles 1994). A self-appraisal element helps to shift the balance away from judgemental review by the boss to a more participative approach in which development needs are more easily articulated.

In truly sophisticated organisations, appraisees will have discussed performance and development issues with their mentors and even rehearsed arguments on issues which may come up in the forthcoming appraisal. The actual event then rarely introduces any great surprises. This goes some way to redressing the imbalance of power and helps to put development on the agenda as a priority issue.

So far, we have only considered individual appraisal. However, a growing trend is *team appraisal*. Margerison (1991) suggests a method in which the management team takes time out each year to consider its effectiveness as a team (e.g. people suggest examples of the team when it was 'flying' and the team when it was 'diving'). Then everyone in the team takes a turn in facilitating discussion on their personal contribution to the team's performance. They share with the team their own perception of performance and invite comment from colleagues. Margerison (1991) sees this as a way of bringing openness to team processes. It forces people to be honest about experience, including the sensitive issue of colleague performance which might otherwise not be addressed and remain forever behind the scenes, the subject of gossip, whispering and innuendo, insidiously poisoning team relationships. Out in the open, individuals and the team can move by degrees to a new accommodation to the issues and what needs to be done for improvement. Handled well, this feedback data can take trust to new levels; handled badly it is a ticking bomb which can explode in everyone's face.

Another form of team appraisal involves a higher team (and/or a consultant working on their behalf) appraising a lower team. This may involve the use of Belbin (1993) and other team audit tools and process observation. These are techniques for exposing weaknesses in team behaviour (e.g. perhaps people don't give each other support; perhaps everyone is looking for someone else to take the lead; perhaps people say they want leadership but won't accept any that emerges, etc.). They also provide a framework for team members to discuss in non-threatening ways how they think they are seen and how they could be more effective.

Although appraisal is part of Foucault's (1980) 'panoptican' of surveillance and control in the modern organisation, making all behaviour transparent and accountable to the managerial 'gaze' (Townley 1993), this does not have to be its only function. Suffused with the right values and in the right hands it can also provide individuals with valuable feedback for personal development.

Case study: How organisations conduct appraisals: the case of a large retail chain

In the 1990s a British company in the leisure industry attempted to introduce a new appraisal system for its managers. It was to be based on the following principles.

- *Clear performance requirements*: This was a results-oriented approach led by an MBO philosophy. Goals at the corporate level were to govern goals at the lower levels.
- *Sophisticated achievement*: Using 'job analysis', objectives were broken down into task elements linked to competencies, standards and corporate value statements (i.e. how you did the job was as important as what was achieved). The goals were to be SMART (specific, measurable, achievable, timebound).
- *Frequent feedback*: The reviews were to be conducted every six months, so that each performer would know exactly, at any given point, if s/he was meeting performance requirements.
- *Scientific assessment*: The architects of the system believed that they had devised a fair and impartial system of rating based on six levels of performance, defined in terms not of personal qualities but in relation to the achievement of objectives.
- *A commitment to development*: Managers were required to focus not just on any immediate performance gap and how to close it but also the longer-term development needs of the individual. For this purpose appraisers and appraised would be required to agree a 'personal development portfolio' which clearly defined, as a learning contract, what help they could expect from the organisation and what was expected of them in terms of performance.

On paper, this seemed like a fine system which balanced the needs and interests of employees with those of the employer. Unfortunately, it didn't work in practice. What went wrong?

- From the start, top management seemed lukewarm about the appraisal system. Despite HR's efforts they didn't really buy in. Evidence of this was their reluctance to come to appraiser training.
- Because the top was seen to lack commitment, lower-level managers felt safe in either ignoring it or using it in a perfunctory way.
- In implementation, many managers saw little tangible benefit in the scheme. They disliked the sophisticated scaling systems for rating and tended to use the average 'satisfactory' category throughout. They were reluctant to criticise people they would have to work with in the coming year. Many failed to adopt the participative style which HR had recommended in conducting the appraisals.
- Staff were also dissatisfied. They remained confused about expectations and the key skills which they had to demonstrate and believed that the system had been imposed on them.

After much discussion, a much simpler appraisal system was adopted. It remained results-oriented, but there were fewer objectives and a radically simplified rating system. The five-page booklet was reduced to two sides and the earlier emphasis on quantification in the interests of impartiality was replaced by a system which allowed some descriptive narrative to explain mitigating circumstances in performance. Significantly, a self-appraisal section was introduced so that the appraisees had a chance to add their own voice to the judgement.

Although the appraisal system was perhaps less sophisticated now as a measuring tool, the signs were that it had more general acceptance among those who had to make it work. A recent audit has shown that managers are more committed to it and that it is increasingly being seen as a development as well as an evaluative tool, but the tendency for the appraiser to rate all their staff as 'average' or 'above average' continues.

Questions
What was happening here? Is this an example of good practice undermined or a realistic adaptation to prevailing conditions?

Source: Internal company documents

5.6 Assessment of development need

In our idealised diagram of the development planning process, this is another element. Here we are concerned with assessing need at the individual level. Strategic needs assessment is considered in Chapter 10.

It is clear that appraisals, however well conducted, will only give a partial and incomplete indication of individual development needs in relation to objectives. Precise and pointed diagnosis requires corroborative evidence gained through assessment methods. Data from these sources feed into the development cycle. Let us look at some of the most popularly used assessment methods.

5.6.1 Multi-rater feedback or 360-degree assessment

The 360-degree rating methods (Figure 5.2) take the traditional one-dimensional appraisal process and make it 3-D. With this system of assessment managers receive feedback about their skills and behaviour from a variety of respondents differently situated within their role set. Multiple sources of rating might include feedback from superiors, colleagues, subordinates, external stakeholders such as customers or suppliers and self-assessment. This integrates top–down appraisal with upward, peer and self appraisal to provide as broad an overview as possible (Hind 1999).

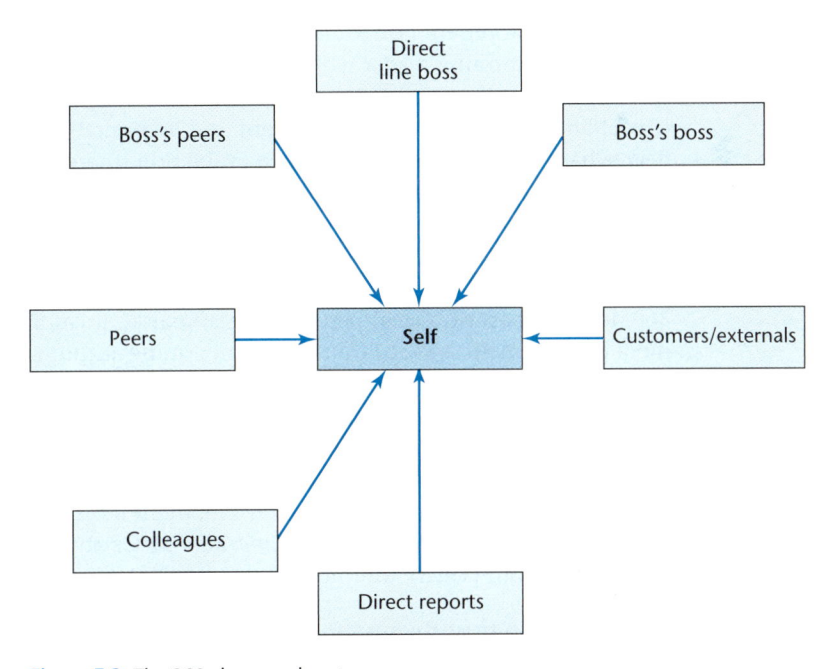

Figure 5.2 The 360-degree role set

The great advantage of 360-degree assessment is that it provides patterns of rating on attitudes, skills and behaviour from a broad cross-section of observers well placed to judge. Consistent feedback from a number of raters is difficult to ignore because it suggests the verdict of a community. Inconsistencies between groups of raters are equally interesting because they may highlight a lopsided profile of skills and suggest priorities for development in particular areas (Mumford 1993). Discrepancies between what individuals think about their own performance and what others say are also interesting. Are the self-ratings lower or higher than the role-set definition? Either way, this data tells MD planners a lot about the manager who is at the focal point of judgement.

Used sensitively this can be a powerful tool for developing self-knowledge of how you are seen by others which, we have stressed, is the ultimate grounding of all self-development. In a sense, the 360-degree acts as a mirror helping managers to see themselves as others see them and offers specific data on personal performance (Yukl 2002) for self monitoring and improvement into the future. When deployed effectively, the 360-degree is not used to expose the deficiencies of people but to help them to understand what is needed for better performance in different contexts.

The technique also brings other benefits. It improves communication between levels and groups. It gives continuous feedback on performance which is more responsive and specific than appraisal data and is arguably more accurate. It can certainly empower both the manager receiving the comment and those who are called on to give it, if it is implemented as a developmental and not an inquisitional tool. Furthermore, the 360-degree can contribute to the building of a climate of constructive criticism within the organisation which may ultimately lead to a culture of creativity and self-reflective development (see Sadler-Smith 2006).

As the questioning reader will understand, 360-degree techniques are only as effective as the spirit in which they are used. For a technique which has been so pushed by consultants as the answer to assessment and accountability, it is strange that the 360-degree has not been subjected to much evaluation (there are parallels here with competencies). We don't know if it has a long-term value. However, what seems clear is that in the wrong hands the 360-degree can be a highly divisive force within the organisation, reinforcing a climate of mistrust and encouraging defensive behaviour from those on the receiving end of assessment. Where the culture is punishment-centred and the 360-degree is part of formal performance appraisal, it can become an intrusive instrument of judgement and control. It can undermine authority, disrupt working relationships, destroy trust and encourage cover-up and 'impression management' responses. As a tool of a blame culture, the 360-degree brings not self-improvement based on feedback but fear and insecurity (Hind 1999; Devine 1997).

So what are the conditions needed for the 360-degree to flourish? It seems that this technique can only work as a tool of development if certain conditions are met. This is a distillation of the current thinking *inter alia:* McCarthy and Garavan (1999); Johnson (2001); Mumford (1993); Mumford and Gold (2004).

- If there is no trust then nothing can be accomplished. All the stakeholders need to sign up to the goals and believe that the process is fair and honest.
- The 360-degree has to be disengaged from the appraisal systems if raters are expected to answer honestly and the assessed are to respond authentically.

- The assessment system needs to be anonymous, probably through questionnaires on-line, if assessors are to give honest feedback.

- Attitudes of openness and responsiveness are needed if managers are going to embrace messages fed to them and accept the need for change. This may require a lot of counselling to help individuals override their defence mechanisms in the face of criticism, hear and accept what is said.

- To succeed, the 360-degree must start at the top and cascade down. Senior managers need the humility to see themselves as others do and to make adjustments to their behaviours. This means follow-up to discuss the meaning of rating and implications for behaviour.

The 360-degree is an ambivalent tool. It has the capacity for greatly raising managerial self-awareness and developing new style and skills. However, there are many issues of measurement, social context, power and the motives for using it. Ultimately, like so many techniques in MD, it is as good as the people who deploy it and the conditions under which it is used.

5.6.2 Psychometric testing

Another important and increasingly fashionable source of assessment data is the use of psychometric testing. This is often justified as a scientific form of assessment to provide objective data on the suitability of people for the job and their development needs. However, this is an area of great controversy and evokes debates which we can only touch on here.

In ability testing, for example, there is controversy over what is actually being measured. Tests are predicated on the belief that there is a *'g' factor* of skill or intelligence which underpins everything we do and can be captured through testing. But is this true? Modern research (e.g. Gardner 1995 and Ornstein 1986, 1988) suggests that we all have multiple intelligences (e.g. verbal, numerical, practical, analytical, even social and musical) and it is questionable if tests are reliable instruments for representing this complexity. There is much discussion about what tests really measure, whether natural abilities can be distinguished from learned, cultural abilities and if tests are predictive of success in the real world. These are fascinating issues which take us a long way from the focus of this book, but readers who are interested in a critique of ability testing are recommended to read Cohen (1999). Certainly in MD, ability or aptitude tests are rarely used beyond the lower levels and, even then, never in isolation, as the section of development centres shows. The management role is so complex and the skills involved so subtle and interrelated that tests of 'management intelligence' are difficult to design and even harder to validate. Where they are used, technical aptitude measures are increasingly likely to be complemented by tests for emotional and social intelligence (see Harris and Hogan 1992; Goleman 1996).

Fit-for-purpose debates are even more intense over personality testing which is used in many forms for establishing development need. Again, there are philosophical issues about whether personality or the self can really be captured. Is the self a fixed entity? Do we have one self or multiple selves? Social dramatists like Goffman (1960) believe that we have as many selves as the social roles we play. We are like actors presenting different faces for shifting audiences. Over time we come to see ourselves as a 'symbolic object' and seek to shape how we present ourselves and how we are seen ('looking glass self' concepts). Social constructionists (Burr 1995) also believe that the self is fluid and emergent. Different people and situations bring out different aspects of ourselves. We are engaged in a constant process of defining ourselves from others' assumed perceptions and playing parts or adopting personas which are contextually relevant. Postmodernists (Harvey 1989) take these ideas further by claiming that the self is fragmented, endlessly reflexive and mutable. It follows that if the self is in constant movement, personality tests, however refined, will not capture this process: they will only provide a snapshot of the self at a frozen moment in time.

Another way of putting this is that if management developers believe that the self is in a 'process of becoming', they will have an *idiographic* view of personality (Hampson and Colman 1996). They will not seek fixed responses to tests scored in terms of a representative population, but use open-ended tests or dispense with testing altogether and rely on therapeutic style self-reporting and self-narrative. Empty-stimuli tests (e.g. Thematic Apperception; Rorschach) in which subject are asked to tell stories around ambiguous images or relate narratives about critical incidents in their lives would fall into this category. However, if management developers have a *nomothetic* view of personality they will believe in the self as a relatively fixed and tangible phenomenon made up of traits which are consistent from situation to situation and can be measured. This will justify the use of psychometric testing (Hampson and Colman 1996; Donkin 2005b).

However, even if we put aside these ontological issues and accept for argument's sake that 'personality' or the 'self' can be defined, how convincing are the instruments available for measuring it? Proponents of personality testing claim they are effective measures because they satisfy the criteria of the scientific method.

- *They are reliable*: because each part of a test measures a definable variable and retesting shows the same result.
- *They are valid*: because the test measures what it claims to do. Its constructs have 'face validity' (i.e. appear meaningful); have 'construct validity' (i.e. offer coherent and defined constructs); have 'predictive validity' (i.e. seem reliable in predicting how people will behave in a variety of situations).
- *They are easy to use*: personality tests are quick, cheap, easy to administer and easy to interpret. As such, they lend themselves readily to electronic, on-line use and provide a convenient administrative means in line with the realities of the organisation.
- *They provide standard measures*: most personality tests assess individual responses against statistical norms of weighted populations. This provides a means of comparative measurement.

However, despite these apparent advantages, in practice personality tests have been subject to many criticisms. First of all, many tests administered by HRM have a low reliability rating. Organisations often use tests which have not been scientifically validated, but aggressively marketed, and are not administered or interpreted by people trained to do so (Furnham 2006; Cohen 1999). Tests which are not linked to statistical norms of population do not correlate with anything except the test administrator's preferences and prejudices.

A miscellany of test instruments

Here are just some of the many tools which are popularly in use for development assessment and appraisal of managers. For more details of these tools the reader is referred to Fee (2001), Hampson and Colman (1996).

- **Margerison and McCann: Management Wheel Diagnostic Test; Belbin Team Roles Inventory.** These are widely used for team appraisal and development, for example, giving feedback on typical behaviour in teams and helping people to develop more versatile styles of group behaviour. They have almost iconic status in MD terms.
- **OPQ (formerly 16 PF Personality Test).** One of the most thorough and best validated tests of personality; associated with R. Cattell (1973). A test that has launched thousands of development programmes and contributed to the recruitment of tens of thousands of managers.
- **Eysenck's Personality Questionnaire (EPQ).** Equally well used by the MD fraternity. A psychometric tool that has been around a long time and used in many contexts. It is based on an assessment of the individual in terms of the 'Big 5' personality traits, that is, tendencies to: extraversion, conscientiousness, independence, agreeableness, anxiety. It is difficult to have a job in management without being exposed to some version of this test.
- **The Minnesota Multiphasic Personality Inventory (MMPI).** A very comprehensive but also unwieldy measurement instrument rarely used in full.
- **The Blake and Mouton Leadership Grid; the Hersey and Blanchard Situational Leadership Matrix.** These measures have also been around for a long time. They purport to classify management style in terms of a complex grid of interlocking dimensions. They are well known to the MD community and have been long tested as assessment tools.
- **The Myers Briggs Test (MBTI).** Said to be the most widely used measure of personality in the world, MBTI is deployed for assessment in selection and development and as a tool to help managers build self-awareness, learning and style with others in groups. Most controversially, it has even been employed as a scientific measure to select people for redundancy.

    It is easy to be critical of this test. Despite its popularity it has never been properly validated (Thorne and Gough 1991) which is not something that seems to worry gung-ho HRM people or MD practitioners. It is a self-report test in which the subject chooses between pairs of preferences which apparently describe personality tendencies. The results are interpreted by a skilled practitioner in consultation with the subject. The advantage of this test is its flexible categorisation which captures gradations of personality and, as such, is far more revealing than the thin classifications associated with many other techniques.
- **Honey and Mumford and Kolb's Learning Styles Inventory.** Equally well known are these self tests of learning style. To complete the inventory in some form is almost a rite of passage in a management career.

- **Goleman's Emotional Competency Inventory.** A personal inventory based on Goleman's famous work on EI which claims to define your socio-emotional competencies. Not yet properly evaluated, it provokes some scepticism that such nebulous properties can be so easily boxed.

- **Repertory Grid and Personal Construct Analysis.** While most of the personality tests mentioned above attempt to provide a profile rating of the subject against predefined categories and a statistical population, repertory grid attempts to model the unique orientations and personal understandings of the individual (see Chapter 6). As such, it is more idiographic than the nomothetic orthodoxy (Franscella 2005).

- **The Thematic Apperception Test; Rorschach Test; House Tree Person Test, etc.** There are a number of tests at the idiographic end of assessment. These are often derived from work in clinical psychology and therefore represent a different tradition from most of the other instruments mentioned here. They claim to plumb the deeper aspects of personality and provide a vehicle for capturing individual complexity using projective techniques. Because the use and interpretation of these tests requires considerable professional skill and experience, they have rarely made the transition from clinical psychology to the applied context of management development. However, their potential remains to be tapped by management developers who want insight rather than easily processed results.

- **Creativity Tests.** On the borderland between ability and personality, there are many well-validated tests of creativity, for example, tests of divergent thinking; tests of holistic and connected thinking; tests of lateral thinking; tests of fluency and flexibility of thought (e.g. 'How many uses can you find for a brick?'). The Edward De Bono (1970) and Weisbord (1986) tests are well known to developers.

The use of tests for assessing potential and likely career success in management is particularly problematical. Evaluation of such instruments has failed to show a clear relationship between traits as assessed by personality inventories and overall management performance and our current state of knowledge encourages caution in their use.

There is also the problem that many personality tests seem to reduce complex individuals to types in terms of pre-established definitions. You don't have to be a social constructionist to believe that there is a danger here of reducing the richness and variety of humanity to a gallery of flat characters or stereotypes. Do the tests really capture subtle but important aspects of management style like 'sensitivity', 'motivation' or 'empathy'? The categories of personality tests seem to many observers to be quite one-dimensional, crude and reductionist, relying on commonsense definitions (e.g. the so-called 'big 5' character traits which are used in a number of tests) (Cohen 1999). At best, they provide some standardised data on tendencies which can be compared with norms within a more general population. However, even at this level there are doubts. Tests are open to fiddling by subjects concerned to give an impression which they think will best serve their interests (Furnham 2006). This raises issues of reliability, as does the common experience of different results from retesting over time. And there is the question of whether the tests really define core characteristics or are merely representing symptoms of much deeper springs of personality? (Dixon 1990).

> **Pause for thought**
>
> ### Personality tests – modern day charlatanism or science?
>
> In medieval times people were defined by their apothecaries as having a character associated with a dominant body humour or fluid within the body (i.e. blood, phlegm, choler, melancholy). These were held to determine a person's physical and mental qualities. Throughout the centuries humans have used astrological signs to understand who they are.
>
> #### Question
> *Are commercial personality tests just the latest in a long line of popular schemes which satisfy our need to distinguish between people?*

Despite these reasonable doubts, anyone who has completed one of the well-known personality tests (e.g. Eysenck 1975; Cattell and Schuerger 1976) will doubtless agree that they do reveal something about you which is recognisable. However, whether we might build more convincing and well-rounded pictures of the individual from depth discussion and self narrative (the psycho-therapy mode) in the restless conditions of the modern organisation remains unresolved. In making decisions about development and potential, prudence dictates a combination of measures in which tests are only one leg of the stool. This is indeed exactly the approach of the development centres to which we turn next.

5.6.3 Development centres

Development and assessment centres are increasingly being used by organisations to measure the current performance of managers and their potential. However, in some organisations, such as the British Civil Service, two or three days in a country house for periodic monitoring and assessment is a long-established part of the corporate culture (Donkin 2005a).

Assessment and development centres are not so much physical locations as multiple methods employed as part of a particular approach to assessment, used to gauge potential, assess for promotability and make informed decisions on development. The methodologies in both *assessment* and *development* centres are similar; the difference between them is that ACs are primarily used for selection, performance review and promotion decisions, while DCs, as the name implies, provide a picture of strengths, weaknesses and potential for development (Woodruffe 2003). Although ACs should be separate from DCs, in practice both strands are intertwined (i.e. feedback and development planning often emerge from assessment for promotability in planned career development systems (e.g. British Civil Service). DCs are usually more relaxed and less competitive in spirit than ACs and more participative. In the best-run DCs there is a sense of involvement and partnership between the organisation and the individual, a sense of 'done with, not done to' (Woodruffe 2003). This means designing DCs which are non-threatening in atmosphere, flexible, open and involving, based on feedback of results and assurances that careers will not be harmed by performance on its exercises.

DCs draw their inspiration from officer selection practices used by the British army in World War One and for the recruitment of German officers since 1923. The British Civil Service was an early convert to the use of a battery of tests for selection and development and Anglo-American blue-chip companies have used them with increasing sophistication ever since (Donkin 2005a).

The purpose of the DCs is to provide a structured setting in which managers can be helped to demonstrate their skills on different competency criteria. The following are other common aims of DCs (e.g. Graham and Bennett 1995; Walton 1999; Woodruffe 2003).

- Through DC exercises, participants come to a greater awareness of what competencies the job requires and the requirements of career development.
- Through DC exercises people display their current competencies in areas which the organisation values.
- From an assessment of strengths and weaknesses, the individual and the organisation can decide on priorities for long-term development (i.e. development planning to help the individual gain the knowledge and experience they will need for a chosen career track).
- With DC data individuals are provided with personal performance data on which to reflect and design their own development plans.

DC results are often used for matching the strategic requirements of the organisation for a distribution of skills with the profile of its stock of managers. Assessments identify, at a generic level, shortfalls and surpluses of skills. This is crucial to career and succession-planning strategies for the organisation as a whole. As such, DCs provide a consistent and reliable instrument for validating assessment criteria as they are aligned to competency frameworks.

From the organisation's perspective, DC results also give a lot of talent-pool data, for example, on those who may be high-flyers, those who are capable of fulfilling management roles following bespoke training and those who need specific help. However, for DCs to elicit truly participative behaviours, any data derived from the tests needs to be treated as provisional and assurances given that results will not be career-limiting need to be made and honoured.

At the level of the individual, DC data encourages self-knowledge and self-definition of potential. It provides evidence for wise choices in continuous personal and professional development. It also gives mentor and mentee confidential information on skills and development needs to confront personal-performance issues. Used flexibly and with imagination, DC results can be truly empowering, but only if the organisation is trusted to use the data sensitively.

So what happens at a DC and are there any generally accepted principles of design?

Development centres involve multiple activities spread over a number of days. Information is collected about the motives, personality, skills and aspirations of the participants. The activities are designed to simulate the behaviours which competency frameworks have identified as essential for effective performance in a target management job (Woodruffe 2003).

The starting point for design is usually a job analysis of the role or generic cluster of the roles which DC participants aspire to reach. Identifying the elements of the job and typical tasks associated with it provides a basis for specifying the competencies needed and for developing exercises which may be predictive of success. Designing simulations is an imaginative process but requires a clear understanding of the typical situations confronted in the target job and the skills which are needed.

Here are the elements you might typically find in a development centre (Woodruffe 2003; Clifford and Thorpe 2007; Woodall and Winstanley 1999).

- *Presentations*. There are often exercises which give participants an opportunity to demonstrate their oral skills. So, for example, participants may be asked to give a 10-minute presentation on their leadership qualities; their vision for the future or the obituary they hope to have at their funeral. This is a way of gauging skills of thinking in the moment and public speaking where there is little time to prepare.
- *Group exercises*. There are many of these, for example, building a tower of bricks; designing a model aircraft, and so on, to test group skills (e.g. chairmanship; assertiveness; social skills; persuasiveness, etc.).
- *Testing*. Aptitude, creativity, personality, motivational and work interest tests may be used. They are usually subsidiary to the other job simulation exercises and intended to provide background data on the candidates.
- *Written work*. Usually there are some written exercises (perhaps an autobiographical essay) designed to reveal analytical and expressive powers and self-perception.
- *Interviews*. Panel and one-to-one interviews provide depth data on motivations, experience, knowledge and attitudes. The whole purpose of the DC is to provide more reliable data than the standard interview but some data may not be easily derived from other sources.
- *Exercises*. These are at the heart of the DC approach. They can be simulations, case studies, in-tray exercises, competitive games, problem-solving exercises, role-plays, time-limited analytical tasks, negotiating exercises, outdoor management events and so on. The box below gives more detail on some of the classical methods. This is an area that gives most scope for creative design of predictive assessments.
- *Self/peer assessment*. In keeping with the collaborative, self-development ethos of DCs, most include an element of self-rating (Schein's career anchors; repertory grid; Myers Briggs, etc.) and peer assessment. For example, in the famous Civil Service assessment centres for selection of high-flyers and in promotion centres, candidates who have spent a week together are asked to rate each other as civil servants and as 'someone with whom they would choose to go on holiday'.

Typical games and exercises at development centres

DC activities take many forms. Many will be designed specifically for the centre but some may be adaptations of standardised formats. Some of these techniques are discussed in more detail in the chapter on management training (chapter 8). The idea of DCs is to use a variety of activities to see how you act as a whole person, how you react to the unexpected and the ambiguous and to tasks which simulate work you might perform on the job.

- **Role-plays**: are well-known exercises for demonstrating behavioural skills. Those who do well have a quick and clear appreciation of expectations in the situation; understand the criteria of assessment; are outgoing and confident with good social skills.
- **In-tray exercises**: are favourites at DCs. The candidates are required to address a number of issues within their in-trays which are similar to the tasks they will undertake in a future job. They decide what action needs to be taken in each case and puts the items in priority order. This tests the skills of the participants and their understanding of future requirements.
- **Management games and simulations**: there are many of these. The best simulate relevant management experience from which some essential personal qualities can be discerned.
    - *The Kite Game*: Tests how people work together to build a kite. The games reveal leadership styles, creativity and how well people interact together.
    - *The Balloon Game*: The group has to pretend that they are in an overloaded balloon and it has to vote on who will be thrown out. People have to imaginative to develop strategies to convince others that they should survive. It is claimed that the game reveals a lot about personality.
    - *Finding the deadly chemical*: This is a sort of detective game involving finding clues. Obstacles and pressures are built in. This is a long executive game which is supposed to test decision-making, teamworking, crisis management and mental stamina.
    - *Smile as you drink yak soup*: This is a negotiating game which tests cultural sensitivity, personal flexibility and the ability to empathise. Some variant of this game is often used to select international managers.
    - *The Whitehall Game*: This is a two-day format set in a hotel or country house. This formula is much beloved by the British Civil Service and blue-chip companies. Usually there are a number of tasks, set-piece scenarios and group activities involved. Performance will be monitored using two-way mirrors and CCTV. The scenarios are supposed to show flexibility and the ability to work effectively with others, often under pressure.

The effectiveness of any simulation is whether it is predictive of managerial effectiveness. It is quite apparent that practice in the games improves your game-playing performance, so they do not test your natural abilities. However, they may reveal more than standard tests and interviews, but this has to be established through evaluation.

A number of writers (Yukl 2002; Fee 2001; Woodruffe 2003) have tried to define the conditions under which DCs operate effectively in identifying talent and development needs. This is a distillation of their views.

Firstly, the atmosphere needs to be open, informal and trusting. Participants need to feel that they have consented willingly to be involved and they fully accept the value of the centre as a source of professional feedback from which they can grow.

They also need to believe the company's promises that although the results may be used for pencilling in peoples' career prospects in the succession plan, they will not alone determine decisions on promotion and reward. Essentially, the collaborative and unthreatening atmosphere needed requires that the DC is not linked with the appraisal process. Without such assurances, DC raters can expect defensiveness, anxiety, withdrawal, impression management and cheating, all of which conspire against the individual being transparent and assessment being reliable.

Successful DCs are careful to choose combinations of methods designed explicitly to provide as fully rounded a picture of the candidate as possible. This involves a detailed understanding of the strengths and limitations of different approaches. It also means aligning the battery of exercises to competency expectations and accepting a commitment to evaluating instruments as predictors of management performance through the rub of experience.

There are other conditions which successful DCs satisfy. For example, attention needs to be given to training the raters who observe participants undertaking exercises and ensuing that the rating is consistent. Arrangements are also needed for ensuring that information from the exercises is synthesised in terms of the competencies which are being assessed. This requires checks that the inferences made from the scores are genuine and impartial in providing an overall picture of the person's competence.

Finally, commentators agree that good practice in DC design and conduct requires a willingness to help participants gain in self-perception. Most DCs incorporate feedback of results to participants and a coaching element. The results are interpreted and there is coaching to focus on key development areas. Sometimes this extends as far as to agree the outline of a PDP with the participant which can then be fleshed out with his manager. Certainly it will involve counselling, or even life coaching, on how s/he might confront key development needs and make sensible career choices in the future. Often the feedback and self-development element are the main lasting benefits of the DC experience. People get a preview through the simulation exercises of work at a higher level, a clearer appreciation of what they need to do to progress and a sense of ownership of their own development (Woodruffe 2003).

DCs are becoming increasingly popular with organisations for assessing their professional and managerial staff. They seem to work best where complex interpersonal, team and social skills are required on the job, or need to be developed. They have also proven very effective for assessing capability where the candidate hopes to make a significant organisational shift into an unfamiliar role (e.g. from, say, clerical work into management; from functional management into general management; divisional to board-level management). They are good too for younger managers still seeking a best fit between their skills and attitudes and the demands of different career pathways.

Some organisations are using DCs as an alternative to appraisal. However, there is a danger here. Although data from DCs/ACs may well improve the quality of data as a complement to the formal appraisal process and help the evolution of more integrated HR systems of assessment/development overall, the blurring of any distinction between testing for appraisal and testing for development will destroy the goodwill on which DCs rely. So too, excessive use of ACs for routine performance monitoring will taint the impartial reputation of DCs as participant–led, development mechanisms.

The overall verdict on DCs is that they are expensive to set up if they are to be truly custom-designed in their processes and they take up a lot of valuable organisational time. However, at their best, they can provide detailed information on competencies and potential of key managers which would not otherwise be available. This is invaluable for succession and development planning. They are also important sources of support for self-development plans informed by critical competency. We can expect to hear more about DCs as a tool of management development in the future. At present there is a dearth of detailed evaluations of these centres and more information would be invaluable to practitioners.

How BT assesses development need

When British Telecommunications wanted to change the way its senior managers looked after sales and marketing, it adopted a psychometrically based system for use in MD. BT wanted to ensure that its senior marketing managers were thinking like mini-chief executives, understanding in deals worth hundreds of millions of pounds that the true value of a sale went well beyond the sale price.

To identify the development needs of these BT managers, BT requires managers to complete an on-line CV and two psychometric questionnaires. The responses are then subjected to computer analysis based on pattern recognition algorithms. The analysis throws up individual issues that can be investigated in workshops with the managers.

The first questionnaire looks at capabilities. The second investigates tolerances – how people react to difficult situations at work. These questions may, for example, look at how someone handles a difficult team member or how the manager would feel about taking the rap for someone else's incompetence.

Then managers are called to a workshop split into three sessions. The first covers the manager's career, the second relates to a recent task the manager found particularly stretching and the third centres on a controversial management policy.

Interviews are carried out by one of BT's divisional managers and two experienced, licensed psychologists. The job of the psychologists is to probe various issues – knowledge, experience, skills and tolerance – that are unlikely to emerge in an ordinary interview. The interviews delve very deep and people tend to open up quickly.

This is a rigorous assessment which can be very revealing. It is also intended as a positive experience. Some managers say that they learn a lot about themselves in just a few hours and come away from the workshops energised.

BT is trying to make rocket boosters for people's careers. The profiling is added to the company database of managers' profiles which HR specialists can search for talent to match to particular projects. Some of the people undergoing this programme will be considered for new posts, some given development to change attitudes or improve their skill mix.

The success of the pilot in auditing sales and marketing talent has encouraged BT to roll out the programme across the board at BT. The intensive use of psychologists in interviewing who can elicit deep insights and the use of pattern recognition on job-specific issues are seen as important features in determining whether someone is likely to perform well on an assignment, posting or project. They have become embedded as permanent features of the assessment system for development planning at BT.

Source: Donkin, R. (2004) 'Appointments: patterns can show if you are up to the job', *Financial Times*, 29 January 2004

5.7 Personal development plans

The result of all this diagnostic work should be a thoughtful set of development targets for each individual and a tailored plan of action which gives practical expression to the MD strategy (Mumford 1993). In our schema of the development planning process, this would be another key element. However, although the PDP does represent a cumulative aggregation of the assessment work we have considered previously, it is important to appreciate that the process is iterative. Reflection on experience gained in implementing the PDP will feedback into the collection of further data for assessment and appraisal. This diagnostic data will also flow into other parts of the MD system such as succession planning; career planning and development and, at a more aggregated level, needs analysis, strategy and evaluation. The point is, PDPs are not the single end result of assessment activity and development planning, which a one-dimensional view of the process might suggest, merely one link in a continuous chain (Sadler-Smith 2006).

The professional literature tells us that PDPs are essentially a learning contract which outlines the actions which individuals should take to develop themselves and how the organisation will help them. Good PDPs are a 'tailored plan of action' (Thomson et al. 2001) derived from a consideration of the strengths, weakness and aspirations of the individual within the context of the priorities of the corporate development plan.

The PDP is intended to help development in the present role and development for future roles. Typically, it defines priority areas for improvement, specifies the skills which need to be enhanced and opportunities for development. The plan is intended to give people a clear picture of what is expected of them and what development will be put into place.

Where a range of diagnostic methods have been used, the results need to be pulled together to show an overall profile of capability which should form the ground on which all personal development planning should be based. From the analysis, in which the individual is involved, a set of clear and appropriate development goals should emerge. These need to reflect not only the personal needs of the individual but also the strategic priorities of MD and the business if they are to serve the vital purpose of corporate performance and organisational development. It is the uncoupling of personal development from corporate goals which is a common fault of these programmes and one of the main reasons why they are ignored or underestimated by senior management (Sadler-Smith 2006).

Parsloe (1999) suggests that PDPs should be agreed between a subordinate and his or her boss, who also monitors tracking against the plan timetable. However, the subordinate's mentor may also be closely involved in interpreting the practical meaning of the plan and helping the mentee to learn the behaviours needed to achieve it. There are other aspects of PDPs which command consensus: they should have SMART goals written in behavioural terms which define what the appraisee will be able to do differently following development interventions; the activities planned (e.g. courses; attachments; self-development processes like learning logs, support groups, etc.) and the timescales for performance and review arrangements defined.

Agreeing a PDP is usually the easy part. More difficult is to make it work so that it becomes a real compass guiding personal behaviour day to day and mobilising learning and development opportunities to support the plan. The chances of the PDP becoming more than just a ritualistic exercise are greatly increased if the individual feels a sense of ownership for it. This means that the PDP should address concerns in professional development (e.g. perhaps transferable skills) and career development (e.g. what the person needs to do to prepare for promotion) as well as continuous improvement in the current job. It must seem to be a contract freely entered into which offers something to individuals as well as the organisation and the organisation is seen to commit itself to their continuing growth (Mumford 1993; Parsloe 1999).

All too often these requirements are not met. Often the PDP is forgotten by both parties as soon as the ink has dried. Ad hoc decisions then determine development, not the plan. Another experience is for the individual to embrace PDP in the spirit of self-managed learning but in the hurly-burly of normal organisational life supervisors fail to discharge their part of the learning contract. The attachments and shadowing activities which were promised somehow fail to materialise and individuals find it difficult to get their managers to keep appointments to review progress on the development plan. Typically motivation drains away and is replaced by a sense of betrayal and disengagement.

However, when the PDP does become a living reality in organisational life the script can be very different. PDPs which have shared commitment keep people focused on performance priorities, raise standards of work and help learning to happen. Commentators (Sadler-Smith 2006; Mumford 1993; Woodall and Winstanley 1999), all speak of PDPs as a mechanism for encouraging individual responsibility for learning, energising people to raise their game, motivating them to use their jobs as platforms for the next promotion and lifting job satisfaction. Where these happy conditions apply, there is often a sense of trust; people feel that the PDP demonstrates management's commitment to them as valued organisational members and both parties have a common stake in development. The key seems to lie in organisations demonstrating that it takes workplace learning seriously and rewarding people for translating new learning into new performance.

5.8 Conclusion

Although this chapter has only just scratched the surface of such a big subject as development planning and assessment, it is hoped that enough has been done to demonstrate its centrality to all aspects of MD. The development cycle is the inclusive process by which corporate performance requirements are interlinked with methodologies of competency, performance measurement and appraisal to assess the strengths and weaknesses of individuals and the management stock as a whole. This is essential auditing against skills profiles for designing, planning and reviewing learning and development programmes. It is also essential for succession, talent and career planning which we consider in another chapter. All the techniques are only as effective as the skill with which they are combined, the logic which directs their use and the analysis which interprets the patterns they yield for development design.

Review questions

1. If you have organisational experience you are likely to have faced an annual or six-monthly appraisal. Did you find that performance evaluation prevailed over discussion of learning needs? Was there more you could have done to shape the event around your needs? Do you think you will approach the experience differently next time?

2. Do you believe that the complexity and ambiguity of managerial work really allows for quantitative measurement of performance? Argue either in favour or against this proposition.

3. 'If executives had to sign off appraisals as they do with financial accounts and could go to jail for phoney appraisals, then managers would take them seriously. At present they are as useless as school reports were to helping you develop' How far would you agree with these sentiments?

4. 'Psychometric testing is based on an obsessive desire to be scientific in assessment and remove the subjective element. This may be an admirable ambition but in truth we are using techniques which are questionable to measure qualities which we don't really understand. This creates another form of unfairness.' Discuss this statement.

5. 'Management competencies may have been sold to the management community as a better way of spotting talent and developing it but they are really about reinforcing top–down control over management performance?' How do you react to this claim?

Web links

A web link on testing instruments often used in management:
http://www.psychnet-uk.com/industrial_psychology/management_personnel_training.htm

A web link which gives more information on the Boyatzis model of competency:
http://www.trainingjournal.co.uk/articles/boyatzis.htm

The CIPD has good coverage of competency frameworks at web link:
http://www.cipd.co.uk

360-degree feedback is covered at web link:
http://www.humanresources.about.com

A web link which deals with a number of performance issues and systems in management:
http://www.managementandleadershipcouncil.org

A website on DC methods:
http://www.shlgroup.com/uk#

Recommendations for further reading

Those texts marked with an asterisk in the bibliography are recommended for further reading, especially the following:

Cockerell, T., Hunt, J. et al. (1995) 'Management competencies: fact or fiction?', *Business Strategy Review, Autumn*. An incisive critique of 'competency' and the differences between 'scientific' and 'consultancy' approaches.

Fee, K. (2001) *A Guide to Management Development*, Kogan Page. A 'no nonsense' account of the techniques used in MD with the practitioner very much in mind. Will appeal to pragmatists.

Mangham, I. (1986) 'In search of competence', *Journal of General Management, Vol. 12, No. 3*. Raises provocative questions about the meaning of the terms which are used without definition in management yet act as criteria for assessing individual managers.

Bibliography

*Antonacopoulou, E. and Fitzgerald, L. (1996) 'Reframing competency in management education', *Human Resource Management Journal*, Vol. 6, No. 1.

*Armstrong, M. (2004) *Performance Management: Key Strategies and Practical Guidelines*, Kogan Page.

Armstrong, M. and Baron, A. (1998) 'Performance management: the new realities', CIPD.

Ashridge Management Reserach Group (1997) *360 degree Feedback: Unguided Missile or Powerful Weapon*, Ashridge Publications.

Belbin, R. (1993) *Team Roles at Work*, Butterworth Heinemann.

Boyatzis, R. (1982) *The Competent Manager*, Wiley.

Burr, V. (1995) An *Introduction to Social Constructionism*, Routledge.

Cattell, R. (1973) *Personality and Mood by Questionnaire*, Jossey-Bass.

Cattell, R. and Schuerger, J. (1976) *The Objective Analysis Test Battery*, Institute for Personality and Ability Testing.

*Clifford, J. and Thorpe, S. (2007) *Workplace Learning and Development*, Kogan Page.

*Cockerill, T., Hunt, J. et al. (1995) 'Managerial competencies: fact or fiction?', *Business Strategy Review, Autumn*.

*Cohen, D. (1999) *How to Succeed in Psychometric Tests*, Sheldon Press.

Constable, J. and McCormick, R. (1987) *The Making of British Managers*, BIM.

Cummings, T. and Worley, C. (1997) *Organisation Development and Change*, Ch. 5, Southwestern.

Currie, G. and Darby, R. (1995) 'Competence-based management development: rhetoric and reality', *Journal of European Industrial Training*, Vol. 19, No. 5.

*Dalton, K. (1993) 'The Performance of Narrative and Self in Organisational Culture', PhD, Bath University, School of Management.

De Bono, E. (1970) *Lateral Thinking: Creativity Step by Step*, Penguin.

Devine, M. (1997) 'Top dogs sit up and take note', *The Times*, 29 May.

Dixon, M. (1990) 'Backing a wrong shot', *Business*, July.

Donkin, R. (2004) 'Appointments: patterns can show if you are up to the job', *Financial Times*, 29 Jan.

*Donkin, R. (2005a) 'Assessment centres: superior tactics in the war for talent', *Financial Times*, 14 Oct.

Donkin, R. (2005b) 'Appointments; the proper place for psychometric tests, *Financial Times*, 24th Feb.

Doyle, M. (2007) 'Management development', in Beardwell, J. and Claydon, T. (2007) *Human Resource Management*, Prentice Hall.

*Dulewicz, V. (1991) 'Improving assessment centres', *Personnel Management*, June, Vol. 50, No. 1.

Eysenck, H. (1975) *The Eysenck Personality Questionnaire*, Hodder and Stoughton.

*Fee, K. (2001) *A Guide to Management Development Techniques*, Kogan Page.

Foucault, M. (1980) *Power/Knowledge: Selected Interviews and Other Writings*, Pantheon.

Franscella, F. (2005) *Skills and Tools for Personal Construct Users*, Wiley.

Furnham, A. (2006) *Management Mumbo Jumbo: A Sceptic's Dictionary*, Palgrave.

*Garavan, T. and McGuire, D. (2001) 'Competencies and workplace learning: some reflections on rhetoric and reality', *Journal of Workplace Learning*, Vol. 13, No. 4.

Gardner, H. (1995) *Leading Minds*, Basic Books.

Gibb, S. (2002) *Learning and Development*, Palgrave Macmillan.

Goffman, E. (1960) *Presentation of Self in Everyday Life*, Penguin.

Goleman, D. (1996) *Emotional Intelligence*, Bloomsbury Publishing.

Graham, H. and Bennett, R. (1995) *Human Resource Management*, M & E Handbooks.

Hampson, S. and Colman, A. (1996) *Individual Differences and Personality*, Longman.

Harris, G. and Hogan, J. (1992) 'Perceptions and personality correlates of managerial effectiveness'. Paper at 13th Annual Psychology in the Defence Symposium, Colorado Springs.

Harrison, R. (2000) *Learning and Development*, Ch. 18, CIPD.

Harvey, D. (1989) *The Condition of Postmodernity*, Blackwell.

Hind, P. (1999) 'Leaderabilities', *Ashridge Journal*, April.

Holbeche, L. (2001) *Aligning Human Resources and Business Strategy*, Butterworth Heinemann.

*Holman, D. and Hunt, L. (1996) 'Competency in MD: rites and wrongs', *British Journal of Management*, Vol. 7, No. 2.

Johnson, R. (2001) 'Doubled entente', *People Management*, 3 May.

*Jubb, R. and Robotham, D. (1997) 'Competencies in management development: challenging the myths', *Journal of European Industrial Training*, Vol. 21, No. 4.

Kilcourse, T. (1994) 'Developing competent managers', *Journal of European Industrial Training*, Vol. 18, No. 2.

Kotter, J. (1982) *The General Managers*, Harvard Business Press.

Kubr, M. (1995) *Management Consulting: A Guide to the Profession*, ILO.

Lee, M. (2004) 'A refusal to define HRD', in Woodall, J., Lee, M. and Stewart, J. (2004) *New Frontiers in HRD*, Routledge.

Lundy, O. and Cowling, A. (1996) *Strategic Human Resource Management*, Routledge.

Mabey, C. and Iles, P. (1994) *Managing Learning*, Open University Press.

*Mangham, I. (1986) 'In search of competence', *Journal of General Management*, Vol. 12, No. 3.

Mangham, I. (1990) 'Managing as a performing art', in *British Journal of Management*, Vol. 1.

Mangham, I. (2005) 'Character and virtue in a era of turbulent capitalism', in Tsoukas, H. and Knudsen, C. (2005) *The Oxford Handbook of Organisation Theory*, Oxford.

Margerison, C. (1991) *Making Management Development Work*, McGraw Hill Training.

*Marsick, V. and Watkins, K. (1997) 'Lessons from informal and incidental learning', in Burgoyne, J. and Reynolds, M. (1997) (ed.) *Management Learning*, Sage.

McCarthy, A. and Garavan, T. (1999) 'Developing self awareness in the MD process: the value of 360 degree feedback and the MBTI', *Journal of European Industrial Training*, Vol. 23, No. 9.

McClelland, D. (1973) 'Testing the competence, rather than the intelligence', *American Psychologist*, Vol. 28.

Mumford, A. (1980) *Making Experience Pay*, Ch. 3, McGraw Hill.

Mumford, A. (1993) *Management Development: Strategies for Action*, CIPD.

Mumford, A. (1997) *Management Development: Strategies for Action*, Chs. 4, 5, 6, CIPD.

Mumford, A. and Gold, J. (2004) *Management Development: Strategies for Action*, Chs. 3, 4, CIPD.

Ornstein, R. (1986) *The Psychology of Consciousness*, Penguin.

Ornstein, R. (1988) *Multimind*, Papermac.

Parsloe, E. (1999) *The Manager as Coach and Mentor*, CIPD.

Perren, L. and Burgoyne, J. (2002) *Management and Leadership Abilities: An Analysis of Texts, Testimony and Practice*, CEML.

Rae, L. (1999) *Using Activities in Training and Development*, Kogan Page.

Reid, M. and Barrington, H. (2000) *Training Interventions*, CIPD.

Sadler-Smith, E. (2006) *Learning and Development for Managers*, Blackwell.

Schroder, M. (1989) *Managerial Competence: The Key to Excellence*, Kendall and Hunt.

Sparrow, P. and Bognanno, M. (1994) 'Competency forecasting issues for international selection and assessment', in Mabey, C. and Iles, P. (eds) *Managing Learning* (1994), Routledge.

Stewart, J. (1999) *Employee Development*, Ch. 8, Prentice Hall.

Storey, J. (1989) 'Management development: a literature review and implications for future research', *Personnel Review*, Vol. 18, No. 6.

Thomson, A., Mabey, et al. (2001) *Changing Patterns of Management Development*, Ch. 7, Blackwell.

Thorne, A. and Gough, H. (1991) *Portraits of Type*, Consulting Psychologists Group.

*Townley, B. (1993) 'Performance appraisal and the emergence of management', *Journal of Management Studies*, Vol. 30, No. 2.

Walton, J. (1999) *Strategic Human Resource Development*, Prentice Hall.

*Weisbord, R. (1986) *Creativity: Genius and Other Myths*, Freeman.

*Whetton, D. and Cameron, K. (2002) *Developing Management Skills*, Pearson Education.

Watson, T. (1999) *In Search of Management*, Thomson Learning.

Wilson, J. (2000) *Human Resource Development*, Ch. 7, Kogan Page.

Woodall, J. and Winstanley, D. (1999) *Management Development: Strategy and Practice*, Chs 4, 5, 6, Blackwell.

*Woodruffe, C. (1992) 'What is meant by competency?', in Boam, R. and Sparrow, P. (eds) *Designing and Achieving Competence*, McGraw Hill.

*Woodruffe, C. (1993, 2003) *Assessment Centres: Identifying and Developing Competence*, CIPD.

Yuki, G. (2002) *Leadership in Organisations*, Prentice Hall.

6 Management learning: individual and collective learning theory

Learning outcomes

After studying the chapter you should be able to understand, analyse and explain:

- the importance of having a philosophy of learning;
- the contribution, strengths and weaknesses of the main theories of individual learning;
- define the practical learning methods/approaches associated with each learning theory;
- the main strands of debate in organisational learning;
- the theories and models of knowledge management;
- theories and practical applications of the learning organisation.

6.1 Introduction

Some students as well as some managers might question the value of a chapter on learning theory. They might say that they are more concerned with the techniques used for developing managers, not with models which explain how people learn. However, theory should inform professional practice. Theories of adult learning help managers to understand how people learn as individuals, the learning styles and strategies they use and the conditions under which they learn best. Theories of organisational learning tell us about learning as it suffuses through the organisation as a whole.

This is important and practical information if the managers and developers of the future are to be effective. Like professionals and knowledge workers everywhere, the astute managers of the future will be continually updating their knowledge, questioning accepted practice and striving for higher standards. This requires an ability to diagnose self-learning needs, identify opportunities for learning and strive for the conditions in which they learn fastest and most effectively. In the same way, developers need to know how to facilitate these enlightened managers and help them to continue learning so that the organisation remains competitive. This means being aware of current thinking about how managers learn, how to design courses and programmes which encourage learning and build cultures in which informal learning is valued and rewarded. Developers particularly need to have conceptual models for understanding how individual learning feeds into organisational learning so that it becomes integrated and mutually reinforcing.

Management developers who design instruments of learning without embedding them in contemporary thinking about the processes of learning are not admirable no-nonsense pragmatists but unwitting prisoners of implicit 'theories in use' which they have not surfaced. The result is often an incoherent design in which the strengths and weaknesses of various methods go unrecognised, techniques are inappropriately applied and there is a failure to appreciate that different organisational conditions require varied approaches and individuals learn in very different ways. It is not possible to act as a management developer without having a philosophy of learning. The choice is between having a clear picture of the theories of learning and operating with implicit assumptions which, when examined, turn out to be the half-absorbed ideas of theorists who may be long dead, long discredited.

However, perhaps the beginning of wisdom in development is a realisation that no one learning theory can explain the complex processes of learning in all organisational situations. Always there is the need for judgement and choice in designing learning processes. Our operating theories of leaning need to be eclectic, based on what works in the real world.

6.2 Some general theories of individual learning

There are many theoretical approaches which purport to explain how people learn. They form a major part of developmental psychology as a field of study. It is impossible to review all of these theories in depth in the short space available. However, a number of theories which seem to have most relevance for MD are briefly described and critically considered here. We also look at how learning theory can be anchored in the choice and justification of methods of MD considered in further depth in later chapters.

6.2.1 Behaviourism and social learning

No review of learning theories could begin without saying a few words about *behaviourism*. Following the work of Watson (1930), behaviourists see people as products of their social and political environment. We learn to be who we are by reacting to stimuli all around us, responding alternately to rewards and punishments so that we learn behaviour which will maximise the chance of rewards and minimise those of punishments.

Behaviourism is often seen as reductionist. It takes no account of thoughts, values, emotions, motives – only the conditioned response which can be observed. It denies the complex sense-making of people and their role as social actors who interpret situations and make choices on how to act. All the same, although this theory of learning is widely regarded as insufficient as an explanation for learning, developers still make use of reinforcement strategies especially in the more formal and structured forms of training. It could be argued that the management trainer who relies heavily on formalised instructional techniques with positive feedback (e.g. high marks/approbation), for approved behaviour and negative feedback (e.g. low marks/attributions of failure, etc.), for behaviour which is not approved, is acting with a behavioural logic. Even if s/he is unaware of the philosophical grounds for his or her choice of learning approach, s/he is acting to shape the learning of others using reward and punishment strategies which might be interpreted as applied behaviourism.

Behaviourism shades into *social learning*. Social learning involves behaviour modelling, and learning through observation and imitation of good examples. The idea is that people can learn from others by observing a role model who is held out to trainees as an exemplar of desired behaviour. By watching and interpreting the behaviours of others, trainees begin to see what works and what does not. They are likely to imitate behaviours they have seen others use successfully and to avoid those by which others seem to fail. This emphasis on reinforcement and the internalisation of *external* reward and punishment feedback if the learned behaviour is then played out in front of a critical audience has obvious parallels with behaviourism (Bandura 1977, 1996).

Imitative learning has been most used for repetitive exercises, procedures and so on and it is the basis of computer-based training and other electronic self learning in which good practice is demonstrated; the trainee watches and reproduces part of the behaviour and then tests his or her learning. Nadler (1979) believes that observational learning is useful for acquiring complex management skills such as negotiating, communicating and motivating. However, he emphasises that the cognitive processes involved are more than just simply observing and mimicking. Interpretive thinking is also involved. Behaviour modelling of higher-order management skills requires successful progression through a number of steps (Bandura 1996).

- *Attention:* the trainee needs to be aware of the skills which s/he is focusing upon; these are fore-grounded for him or her by a role model from the profusion of other behaviours within the setting.
- *Retention:* the trainee retains in his or her mind a picture of the skills needed and what they look like in terms of behaviour.
- *Enactment:* the trainee has the capability to reproduce the behaviour perhaps through experimentation and the supervisor's feedback.
- *Practice:* the trainee is motivated to behave in the way exemplified by the model and by practising certain reproducible aspects of behaviour it becomes 'natural'.

Social learning theory has had an impact on various MD techniques. Aspects of modelling can be found in role-plays, learning through drama and other simulations which we consider in our chapter on management training and are very popular exercises on management courses. Typically trainees are shown some behaviours modelled by an expert (e.g. leadership in a particular situation) and they then act out a scenario themselves with feedback from tutor and/or peers, follow-up coaching and so on. Behavioural modelling is also the intellectual underpinning of the workplace learning method of shadowing of a senior practitioner by one who is learning the role (see Chapter 7 on experiential learning). Here, however, there may be special problems involved in identifying the skills to attend to, building a clear picture of the behaviour which needs to be reproduced and incorporating it within a management style. The vicarious learning derived from observation may need to be supplemented by other learning activities for it to be seamlessly integrated within an individual's management style.

Various critical studies have been conducted on behavioural-modelling approaches derived from social learning. Latham and Frayne (1989) describe it as a valuable supplement for employee motivation and self-development. Nadler (1979, Nadler et al. 2003) found that when observational learning was compared with other learning approaches such as experiential learning, instructional learning and so on, participants using the observational approach showed the largest improvement in performance, although, compared with those relying on a more didactic method, were less able to articulate the constituent elements of success. Nadler concluded that observational learning (by itself) helps people to imitate outward appearances and may give tacit insight but not the deeper understanding or the *rationale* for practice. Others claim that the results from observational learning are variable; the behaviours acquired through modelling may be quickly gained but they disappear equally quickly without reinforcement and transfer from the artificial setting of a role-play exercise to the workplace can be problematic. The lesson for MD may be that observational learning is an effective but not a sufficient means of developing management skills and the contribution of other techniques and other schools of thought is essential.

6.2.2 Cognitive learning

Advocates of behaviourism and social learning are interested mainly in inputs and outputs, with observable social phenomena. What goes on in the black box of the mind – thinking, reasoning, interpreting and so on – are largely ignored because they are not observable or quantifiable. However, *cognitive theory* focuses on what may be happening within the black box. Cognitivists look at the internal mental processes, how people absorb information, categorise it mentally and use it in everyday life.

One strand of thought which combines behaviourist and cognitivist processes is *cybernetics*. This sees human thought processes, especially learning, as analogous to the way mechanical systems work (Wood 1988). It links input and output with an internal processing capability mediated by feedback. Elements of cybernetic thinking can be discerned in the concepts of single and double loop learning which we discuss later in the chapter (Argyris and Schon 1974, 1978); in the systematic approach to training with its rationalistic bias and feedback loops and in the famous learning cycles (e.g. Kolb 1984) which we will discuss later. Cybernetics thinkers raise questions about whether the human computer (brain) processes data one piece at a time or whether it is more like super computers which can do 'parallel processing', that is, rapid scanning and performing several cognitive tasks (e.g. thinking, arguing and also learning) simultaneously. While parallels between human mental processes and machines only work to a degree, cybernetics provide a useful metaphor for conceptualising complex things, encouraging an understanding of the connectedness of the elements in learning and pointing up the limitations of the human mental equipment which all developers have to recognise (Cheetham and Chivers 1996).

Gagne (1970, 1985) has taken the concept of learners as information processors in new directions. In his computer analogy he claims that people do not just respond to stimuli, as the behaviourists would have us believe. Instead, they seem to work on information, coding it in terms of what has previously been learnt, drawing out associations with other data and building cognitive maps as learning is transferred from one situation to another so that the relationship between concepts, ideas and events can be drawn out.

Others have elaborated these ideas (e.g. Sweller and Chandler 1994; Klein 2003; Bartlett 1932) talk of the process by which people build cognitive maps or schema to organise sensory perception of their environment into patterns to make sense of the world. The claim of this school is that people do not so much absorb specific information as create holistic frameworks of understanding through which they interpret their experience. These maps become the filters by which we give meaning to things and we are constantly refining and developing these 'pictures of how the world goes' as we conduct our affairs. It is through our constructs that we learn (Stewart 1999).

This is the approach of *personal construct theory* (PCT) postulated by Kelly (1955) and elaborated by Bannister and Franscella (1971). Personal construct theory is based on the view that people are essentially thinkers and interpreters. They are not the 'stimulus jerked puppet' of the behaviourists or the 'primitive infants' of humanistic psychology. Essentially, this model implies that men and women are not controlled by mysterious unconscious forces or external determinants but act as independent social investigators struggling to make sense of their social worlds.

PCT claims that we all have our sets of personal constructs or mini-theories to discriminate between people and events. We have developed these categories and understandings by forming hypotheses to explain others' behaviour, testing them out and changing them if they don't seem to fit. Our clusters of constructs have been built up throughout our lives and encapsulate our human experience. It is through the lens of our constructs that we view people and situations. When we interact with others we are fitting what is said and what we see into pre-formulated constructs of people and situations. We all have personal constructions of how organisations work; what motivates people 'of that kind'; how people can be categorised and assessed; what words like 'participation', 'charisma' or 'trust' actually mean for us. As a consequence, we select those pieces of our environment which have meaning within our classificatory systems and ignore the rest.

For example, in our 'mental sets' we have personal constructs for discriminating between people in terms which are meaningful to us, for example, we may construct people on an axis of 'friendly/unfriendly'; 'attractive/not attractive' or perhaps 'intelligent/stupid' or 'fun/boring' are more telling personal discriminators. It's the same with situations. You may have constructions of 'dangerous/safe'; 'stressful/manageable' and so on; someone else viewing the same phenomenon may be animated by constructs of 'stimulating/deadening' or 'challenging/undemanding' depending on our values and essential world-view. We act on the basis of our constructs; it is with our constructs that we anticipate others' responses and predict how the future will develop.

Personal construct theorists believe that learning (including management learning) is about refining and developing our constructs so that they become sophisticated and we evolve 'realistic anticipatory schema of what is practical' (Hayes 1997). Rigid and superficial constructs give way to more fluid definitions; black and white turns into subtle gradations of grey. Being able to get inside others' worlds by imputing their constructions of reality is also an essential part of role-taking or imaginative empathy which we suggest is one of the keys to effective management behaviour (see Chapter 2).

How to construct a repertory grid

PC theorists have developed a methodology which is claimed to provide a systematic way of teasing out the dimensions by which people construct their realities. This is called 'repertory grid interviewing' and involves asking people to compare and contrast social categories so that their unique understandings are surfaced.

So, say the interviewer wishes to explore the mental models of leadership within a management community. The starting point would be to ask interviewees to nominate managers they know within the organisation who they believe have outstanding leadership qualities, who were average and who were poor.

Then the interviewees would be asked to say how two of the nominees were similar to each other but different from a third. This triadic discrimination applied consistently across a cohort of nominees (20–30 people) is likely to generate a number of contrasting statements. So it may emerge that two nominees are defined as outstanding at developing the confidence of staff while the third is self-interested. This polarity is then taken to infer one of the core constructs by which the interviewee conceptualises leadership (i.e. on a continuum between an orientation to 'develop staff' and an orientation to 'self-interest'). Consistently triangulating across the cohort and discussing the defintions which emerge is likely to generate a number of related constructs (e.g. another dimension may be 'change orientation' *v* 'content with status quo' and so on). About ten to fifteen constructs will be generated for each participant that are recorded on a matrix which allows analysis of the relationship between constructs (higher and lower order) and between individuals.

The next stage is to find consistent constructs among the cohort of interviewees and ordering them into higher and lower order categories. This requires painstaking work but it does provide a wealth of data on how people make sense of their organisational experience. It is a useful technique for understanding their taken-forgranted meanings rather than categorising people against pre-coded categories (e.g. a psychometric approach) which may miss their definitions. Diagnostic work of this kind can be the prelude to sensitive design and development work in MD.

For more detailed descriptions of this method, the reader is referred to the relevant sections of Hayes (1997) and Woodall and Winstanley (1999).

A whole sub-school of cognitive learning psychology has developed over the years which sees learning as an holistic process – the *Gestalt* approach (e.g. Perls 1973; Gregory 1970). This school focuses on personality as a whole and especially consciousness as a field of organised mental patterns or structures. Theorists suggest that learning should be studied in the round, not broken down into constituent parts (memory, perception, thinking, creativity, understanding, etc.) and the best learning techniques should engage with the whole person as an active learner. Gestalt practitioners try to identify incoherent and undeveloped mental patterns (or mind-sets) and blockages (called 'unfinished business') which prevent people from achieving their true learning potential. People can be helped to move from tension and incompleteness to equilibrium and wholeness, especially by developing richer and more discriminating interpretive constructs (e.g. often through storytelling, visualisation, mind mapping, etc.).

A technique associated with Tony Buzan (1974) which encourages holistic thinking and learning is mind mapping. This is a technique for organising thoughts and material so that it engages your senses and emotions and encourages you to think connectedly. Typically, a mind map starts with a central concept, hypothesis or definition which is placed in the middle on a blank chart. The learner then develops a spider's web of different major themes which branch out as new connections are made. The advantages of this method as a stimulant for thinking and learning is that it helps people to learn synoptically. It challenges them to examine what they know in a way which draws attention to the links between concepts and to understand a field of knowledge as a whole.

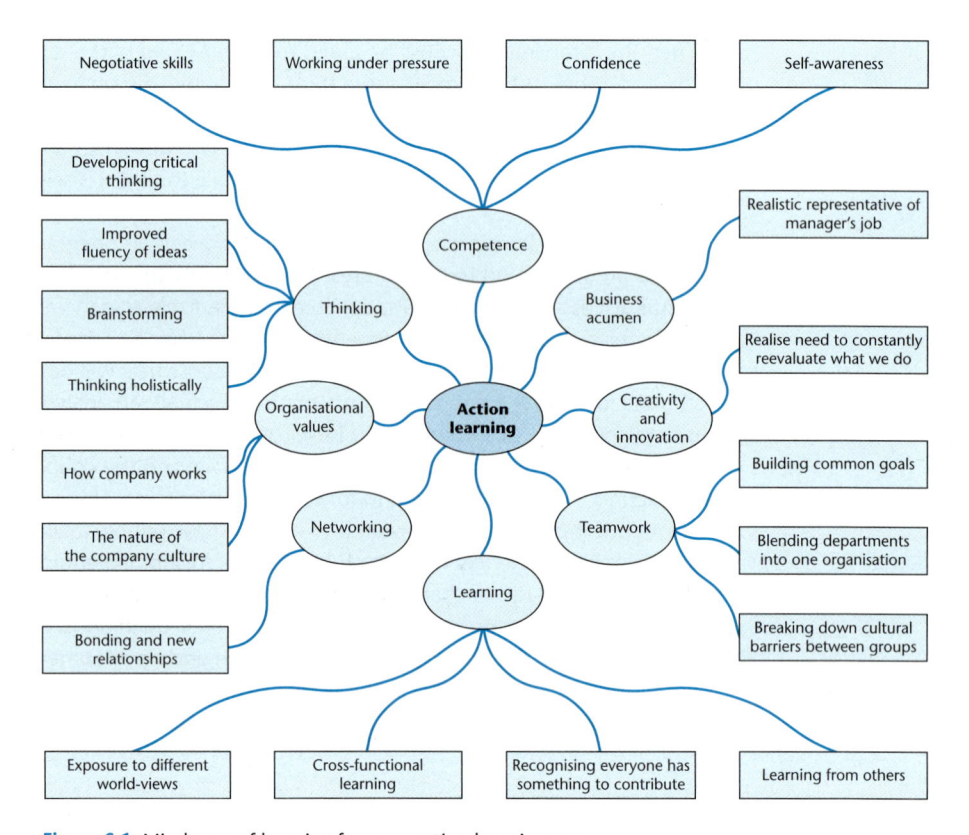

Figure 6.1 Mind map of learning from an action learning set

Storytelling and holistic understanding

There is growing interest in the psychological properties of organisational stories for mapping experience and learning about management. The advantages of stories as vehicles for learning are numerous.

- Stories seem to represent a 'narrative mode of thinking'; they help us think in connected, open, 'whole picture' terms.

- Stories provide us with a holistic, gestalt understanding of human behaviour.
- Stories help us to learn vicariously and increase our experiential range (e.g. listening to how others handled management situations).
- Stories provide us with a vehicle for a group to agree a version of events in a shared story of what has happened in the organisation.
- Stories act as a means of exchanging tacit knowledge and building collective experiential knowledge within a 'community of practice' (see later in the chapter) and act as a means of socialising newcomers into the culture.
- Stories are emotionally arousing; they connect us with eternal themes of the human condition and can both move us and create an aesthetic effect (if well told) which is memorable and potentially influential in defining how we see the world.

For more details on how to design a 'mental map' see Buzan (1974); for more on storytelling see Dalton (1993)

In the view of this author, the cognitive school offers us perceptive insights into how people think and learn and is a welcome counterbalance to behaviourist reductionism. For management developers, cognitivism offers both a diagnostic model for interpreting learning needs and a methodological approach. Many of the informal methods of MD, self-development, cross-cultural, mentoring, feedback, and so on, techniques which we discuss elsewhere, support this learning model. Where the model can be criticised it is in the difficulty of understanding what really happens inside another person's head. People are often not able to give a coherent account of how they think and learn and techniques for helping people to define these nebulous processes (including repertory grid) all have limitations. Cognitive theory can also be criticised for assuming a degree of rationality in our mental processes which may be misplaced and giving too little attention to the role of emotion, intuition, habit and the unconscious in how we orient ourselves to the world.

6.2.3 Constructionist and situated learning

This is the label for a loose grouping of learning theorists who believe that learning takes place within a social framework of involvement. People construct their own meanings as they interact with others and reflect on what they are doing. To understand how people learn, the focus should therefore be on how they frame and reframe their interpretations, how they read situations and develop inferences which can be generalised to a wide range of experience.

Social constructionism believes that learning is active and involves the individual discovering for oneself how one constructs reality. This chimes with informal approaches to development and suggests a role for the MD practitioner as guide, mentor and facilitator of an individual's personal learning. Elkjaer (1999) has suggested some principles of situated/constructionist learning.

- Learning occurs when there is reflection on practice.
- Through reflection, experience is reorganised to produce new meanings.

- Reflection involves an internal dialogue in the head about the lessons of experience and external dialogue with others.
- Focused inquiry of this kind leads individuals to change their mental models. This may mean different behaviours and new learning.

Constructionists believe that learning is most likely to occur in *communities of practice* (COP) where managers with broadly similar values and concerns become engaged in building 'shared ways of knowing' by comparing and contrasting different interpretive understandings.

Fox (1997) and Lave and Wenger (1991) have elaborated these themes into a related concept of *situated learning*. They are concerned to show how people engaged in a work practice learn informally together. Communities of practice are networks of practitioners of different levels of experience. Apprentices learn by copying the master, doing low-risk work but as they gradually become more accomplished take on more complex and demanding work and act independently. This is presented as a natural form of learning from the accumulated wisdom of a professional community. Where the conditions are right, learning is as much from interaction, observing skilled performers and listening to the stories of elders and guided practice as from formal instruction.

Lave and Wenger (1991) argue that learning through the social context of the COP is far superior as a vehicle for professional development to schooling which provides a 'community of discourse' rather than a 'community of practice'. In Western formal education talking and doing are separated and there is a danger of developing people who can *talk* about practice rather than *engage* effectively in practice (one of the reasons why the business schools are said to have lost their way; see Chapter 9).

Fox advocates new forms of situated learning embedded in management communities of discourse *and* practice so that learning happens experientially every day through interaction in the workplace. More experienced managers articulate tacit skills of professional mastery of management to apprentice managers, not through instruction but by guidance, example and feedback. Those new to management learn their craft incrementally by acting as understudies, carrying out tasks of increasing importance, listening to 'war stories' of management behaviour, experimenting and reflecting within a supportive community. Fox calls this 'situated learning'; it is about tapping into the tacit knowing of a management community so that managers learn naturally from the social milieu of which they are part. This may have significant implications for future patterns of MD and, at least to the mind of this author, offers exciting opportunities for the future.

Another important theme for the constructionists and situationalists is the self and learning. The self is considered to be in a state of constant emergence. This is because the self is a social construction which is constantly changing through social interaction, thought and language. Learning is bound up with self-awareness and self-esteem (Freire 1978; Jarvis 1987).

For example, Brundage and Mackeracher (1980) suggest some precepts for understanding adult learning which are said to be correlated with self-image.

- Adults expect to be learning and changing in the direction of their self image.
- Adults with higher esteem learn better than those with lower esteem.

- Our concepts of self are influenced by new roles which we learners take on; these can be blocks or stimulants to learning.
- Adults learn best when they perceive themselves to be learners.

These hypotheses have been supported by empirical work, for example, Lawrence (1985) and Blagg et al. (1993) which show important links between self-confidence, self-learning objectives and success. Learning seems to be easier for those with a good sense of self-worth (which has parallels with the idea of self-efficacy; Locke and Latham 1990). However, it also emerges that this self-confidence can be easily eroded by setbacks or the insensitivity of those in authority. This suggests that close attention to confidence-building should be a key element in all management learning experiences, in both the conducting of management training and the facilitation of workplace learning (e.g. in management styles of mentoring and coaching, etc.).

The constructionist and situated-learning approaches make a valuable contribution by emphasising that individual cognitive processes largely take place within a social context (i.e. within a community setting). This is especially true of management thinking and learning. If learning is 'action in context' then this implies a model for the developer as a facilitator of dialogue within managerial learning communities, which is indeed central to modern experiential approaches to MD (ALS, peer support groups, networks, etc.). The weakness of this school lies in the high philosophical level of the thinking which makes it difficult to translate the concepts into actual professional development practice.

6.2.4 Experiential learning

The last school to be considered is not a coherent model of learning: it is more a collection of related approaches, that is, *humanistic, andragogical and experiential learning theories*. We will look at this body of knowledge in more detail than other schools because it now seems to represent the theoretical orthodoxy of MD practitioners, at least among practitioners steeped in the Anglo-American tradition. Certainly the number of books and MD programmes which pay homage to experientialism and the number of times thinkers like Knowles, Mumford, Kolb and so on are cited suggest that these ideas are most absorbed in the mainstream and influential in framing design and delivery decisions.

Humanistic learning is based on the view that learning is not something confined to the classroom: it is something that people are engaged in all the time. These ideas can be traced back to the work of John Dewey (1938) Kurt Lewin (1935) and Carl Rogers (1980). Carl Rogers, in particular, has had a major impact on thinking in this field. He suggests that all learning comes from insight. People gain insight when the familiar elements of an existing solution are rearranged in a new way. Very often the solution to a problem or the formation of an effective learning strategy does not require new information, merely a new way of seeing and the ability to redefine a long-standing issue in new terms. Learning, Rogers believes, is in the direct control of the learner. It is inner directed learning. The learner controls what s/he learns, when and how.

In this model, the role of the trainer/developer is not so much to impart knowledge as to create a climate in which the person feels free to learn and is motivated to do so. The spur to learning must come from within. This impulse may be the dissatisfaction with present behaviour or an imaginative vision of how to be better (Maslow's (1954) 'self actualisation' drive is deeply rooted in humanism). Whatever the motive, learning implies personal involvement and self-development. Rogers calls this 'person centred learning'. In Rogers's view 'one person cannot teach another anything'. The tutor/facilitator's role is to serve as an enabler, acting with genuineness, acceptance and empathy so that the learner can take risks with his or her learning (Stewart 1999).

Rogers (1980) and other humanists believe that learning is most profound and goes deepest when it is 'discovery learning', which involves individuals or small groups being immersed in difficult problems which they work on with just gentle guidance from a tutor/mentor until they develop insights and find answers or creative solutions which give them a sense of closure and ownership.

Humanistic principles lie at the base of *andragogy,* a term coined by Knowles (1980, 1984) as the study of adult learning. Andragogy is based on the belief that adult learners are self-initiating, self-aware and self-directing. Knowles suggests that the most effective form of learning happens when people assess their own learning needs, create and implement their own learning and evaluate the results. This is the rationale for experiential learning, learning contracts or partnerships and self-development, discussed in the chapter on informal and experiential learning.

The key principles of andragogy

Knowles's work is based on some assumptions about how adults are said to learn which have become famous. Because andragogy is now part of the established ideology of adult education, it is important to engage with its core precepts.

- Adults need to be aware of why they need to learn something.
- Mature adults are self directing and autonomous and feel responsible for their own decisions.
- Adults come to each learning experience with a wealth of life experience.
- Adults are ready to learn when they sense the need to perform more effectively or need more learning to cope with life's demands.
- Adults are quite capable of defining their own learning needs.
- The typical adult orientation to learning is life-centred and problem-centred, that is, they expect learning to pay off in their work or personal life.
- Adults have a need to apply newly acquired knowledge or skills to their immediate circumstances.
- The most potent motivators for the adult learner are internal pressures such as job satisfaction, self-esteem and a better quality of life.

Source: Adapted from Sadler-Smith, E. (2006) *Learning and Development for Managers*, Blackwell; Original source: Knowles, M. (1984) *Andragogy in Action: Applying Modern Principles of Adult Learning*, Jossey-Bass

---

Most of these principles can be found embedded in MD programmes anywhere in the world. The dominance of andragogy explains the modern emphasis on self-managed learning; student-centred learning; the teacher as facilitator (not director) of personal learning; learning through reflection; project-based learning which are discussed elsewhere in this book.

The principles of andragogy seem to have been accepted by the MD establishment as if they were incontestable truths. It is difficult to find a developer who would *not* subscribe to these assumptions about adult (and therefore manager) learning. However, there are grounds for doubt. There is little research to back the assertions, and the claims of universal application are open to challenge. Some have suggested (Woodall and Winstanley 1999), that andragogical assumptions are based on an Anglo-American ideology (e.g. learner autonomy and self directedness is code for the ethic of rugged individualism) and that class and cultural variables have been ignored. For example, Kohn and Slomeczynski (1990) suggests that 'many adults pursue lifestyles in which self directed behaviours are noticeably absent'. For example, middle-class learners appear to be far more flexible and self directed than many working class learners. In a study of British and Chinese managers, Pun (1990) found that the British appeared to adapt well to the open, self-directed approach, the Chinese preferred tutor-directed and more traditionally structured methods. Research which suggests that people vary in their styles of learning raise doubts about the universalist claims of andragogy.

Then there is the issue of Knowles's claim that adult learners can define their own learning needs. Cheetham and Chivers (1996) suggest that in reality the ability to recognise limitations of experience and competence will vary between individuals and in many cases the individual may not be best placed to assess what s/he needs to learn. How do you know what you don't know?

Jarvis (1987) believes that andragogy may perhaps be best understood as a form of mature learning which reflects Western norms of personal autonomy, not as a universal condition of adult behaviour. He suggests the skills of self-empowered learning need to be learned, they cannot be assumed to occur naturally. This observation may be as true for managers and other professionals as for other social groups. All the same, despite the excessive claims made for andragogy, it remains the single most important ideology dominant in management development.

Case study: Andragogy applied: the BigCorp executive programme

In the 1990s, BigCorp of America commissioned a programme for its executives to improve the performance of executives. The plan that was adopted was customised to the company and explicitly led by andragogical/experiential learning principles.

- Participants in the programme were selected for their capacity to be self-developing from experience.
- Participants were able to articulate their own learning needs.
- The organisation entered into a learning partnership to facilitate participants in diagnosing their own learning needs and planning a self-development programme.

The design of the programme involved role modelling – guest speakers, coaching and attachments to senior managers who could exemplify a model of managing and articulate a management philosophy. There were also role-plays, one-to-one and group feedback. A lot of emphasis was placed on individuals assessing their own strengths and weaknesses, bringing live issues at work into the classroom for discussion, learning with and through others in problem-solving sets.

This successful programme satisfied andragogical principles in several respects.

- The programme was bespoke to the needs of 'BigCorp' and tailored to the realities of the managers; they could identify with the learning because it seems experientially relevant to them.
- The learning emphasised learning through doing; learning through others; learning thorough self-reflection; learning through group process.
- It sought to create a sense of ownership among all the stakeholders to the programme.
- Self direction guided the programme. The programme assumed self-initiating learners who were questioning, open to challenge and feedback, self-learning and motivated.

Overall, the results of the programme in terms of more robust and successful managers were seen as a vindication of anadragogical principles applied to the practical design of learning.

Source: Fieldwork notes; confidential discussion

Experiential learning (EL) overlaps with andragogy and these approaches are often seen as synonymous by management developers, but there are some differences. For example, experiential learning theorists do not necessarily support non-directive learning or self-assessment of learning needs. In fact, experiential learning is not a single theory but a cluster of concepts and models of learning. The central tenet of experiential learning is that most of what we learn comes from doing. As we saw in Chapter 2, management ethnographers (e.g. Weick 1995; Watson 2001) talk about 'doing thinkingly'. Typically managers do not think and then do. Instead, they become involved in the action and through activity – doing and reflecting – the problem becomes clearer. Ideas are constantly being formed and reformed through experience. It is through experience that we think and also learn.

Experiential learning tries to explain the processes involved in this 'learning through doing'. The idea of learning through experience as a coherent and holistic process of acting, thinking and reflecting is associated with David Kolb (1984). At the core of this model is the view that 'learning is a process by which knowledge is created through the transformation of experience'. We need to value our experience because it is the medium by which we distil our understanding of organisational process and it is experience which provides us with a guide to reasoned action.

The main elements of Kolb's (1984) philosophy might be summarised here.

- Learning is an holistic process of continual interpretation and adaptation to the world.
- Learning is a process of experience rather than a matter of outcomes.
- Learners learn by constantly exploring, hypothesising, thinking and testing.
- Learning happens through a dialogue with experience, making what is unconscious conscious through reflection.
- Learning involves resolving conflicts of perspective in creating usable knowledge from reflection.

However, Kolb has been most influential in developing his famous 'learning cycle', the centrepiece of a million training programmes. Kolb believes that learning is continuous, cyclical and goal-directed. People grow most from powerful work experiences (e.g. coping with a difficult boss; rising to the demands of challenging experiences where the usual behaviours don't work; responding to the 'jolt' of the new, etc.). He also believes that there is no one best way to develop a manager because people learn in very different ways. Learning is a subjective experience, which most theories of learning fail to recognise.

Kolb suggests a dialectic of learning. The learner is seen as moving from stage to stage in a four-stage cycle. The famous four stages of this dialectic or cycle are these:

- immediate life experience (concrete experience);
- critical observation (reflective observation);
- synthesising reflections and understandings into lessons or 'rules of practice' (abstract conceptualisation);
- actively assessing lessons and concepts against reality (active experimentation).

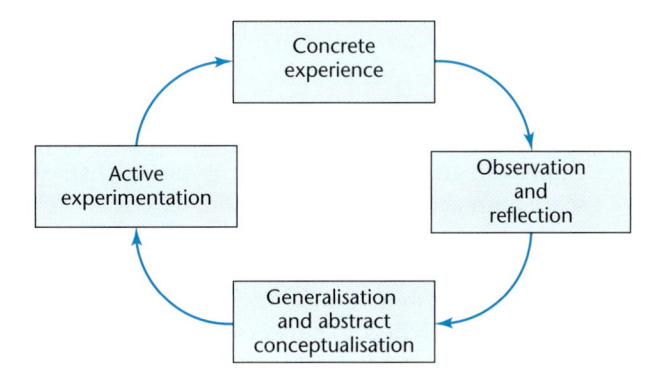

Figure 6.2 The famous Kolb learning cycle

Source: Adapted from *Experiential Learning*, Pearson Education (Kolb, D. 1984), Prentice Hall, KOLB, DAVID A., EXPERIENTIAL LEARNING: EXPERIENCE AS A SOURCE OF LEARNING & DEVELOPMENT, 1st, © 1984. Electronically reproduced by permission of Pearson Education, Inc., Upper Saddle River, New Jersey.

Kolb believes that we are all constantly 'grasping at experience', thinking about its meaning for our lives and transforming experience into knowledge. The learning cycles are continuous interconnected loops of learning connecting at different points which go on until we die.

Kolb has developed a questionnaire to define how strongly an individual identifies with different stages. He posits a set of 'learning types' or styles and preferences for learning associated with each stage of the cycle. This identification characterises our preferred learning mode.

- *The converger* involves himself/herself fully and openly with each new experience and prefers the practical and specific.
- *The diverger* stands back from experience, reflects and observes from different viewpoints.
- *The assimilator* brings observations together in his or her mind so that concepts are integrated into working theories for action; likes concepts and ideas.
- *The accommodator* translates thinking into action and learns mainly from doing.

Real learning requires all stages of the cycle to be completed; all phases need to be synthesised for comprehensive learning and personal growth. However, typically people find themselves blocked at one of the stages. Kolb's 'styles inventory' is intended to help people have a more balanced learning portfolio, resolve conflicts between all the learning modes and integrate their learning for greatest effectiveness.

Honey and Mumford (1986) have elaborated this model into one which is more accessible to managers and developers. They offer four different categories of learning styles which do, however, map closely on to Kolb's schema.

- *The activist* learns through constant and practical involvement.
- *The reflector* stands back, observes and thinks before involvement.
- *The theorist* likes to rationalise and synthesise information into models.
- *The pragmatist* likes to try out ideas and apply them in practice.

Honey and Mumford's learning-styles questionnaire claims to show a person's dominant style. This is potentially a very valuable diagnostic instrument for the learner and the developer alike. Data on learning preferences helps individuals review their approach to learning and seek out or shape conditions so that they can optimise their learning. For developers and managers 'preferred learning type' results may suggest how learning activities could be organised and work redesigned so that people can emphasise and be supported in terms of their strongest suit. So pragmatists need space for practical experimentation; reflectors need very full briefing on any new project and a chance to observe and reflect before offering their views, and so on. Learning styles inventories remind developers that people learn in different ways and counsels them not to making sweeping generalisations about learners. Programme design should reflect that diversity and ensure that it contains a variety of experience from which all can benefit.

Both the inventory and the questionnaire are also useful for diagnosing areas of management weakness. For example, a team composed mainly of managers who are mainly *activists* fixated on 'doing' might need to be rebalanced so that it contains more *reflectors* to improve diagnosis and problem-solving.

The inventory/questionnaire may even help to sensitise developers to deeper learning differences based on personality variables. For example, do extraverts tend to learn through talking while introverts prefer to think things through for themselves? Inventories also help learners in increasing their self-awareness and making better use of learning opportunities as they occur. For the most versatile managers the inventory results are a challenge to build a more diversified repertoire of learning styles by reflecting on a lifetime of learning habits and building up the weaker styles.

Pause for thought

The learning cycle as a game

If you have found the concept of a continuous cycle of learning a little hard to grasp, Margerison (1991) suggests using the analogy of a game in terms of the learning cycle. How would you learn to become effective in playing a game, say squash? As a novice player, anxious to improve your performance you might:

- play a game (action and concrete experience);
- discuss how it went with other players (reflection and review of experience);

- watch other players (observation);
- read about the game (reflection; abstract conceptualisation);
- replay the game in your mind and draw out lessons (generalisation and abstract conceptualisation);
- take a lesson under the supervision of a professional (modelling; concrete experience; instruction);
- shadow a professional (modelling, observation and reflection);
- practise (experimentation);
- think about what you have learnt and what you will do differently next time (generalisation; drawing lessons; abstract conceptualisation).

This list elaborates the learning activities in the learning cycle. The cycle is an ideal. In fact learning in the real world seems to be more chaotic; we jump between stages of the cycle and respond to more diverse influences than Kolb allows. Perhaps this is really several cycles entered at different points. However, the insights that we learn from different experiences, that we all have our preferences for learning and find some ways of learning more difficult than others, provide useful guidance for the self developer.

Questions
Reflect on how you learnt to play a game quite well. Just how did you learn? What activities were easy and what was hard? Does that experience give you any hints about your preferred learning style? What might you do to improve your learning across the board?

Although experiential learning holds the intellectual high ground in MD, it is not without its critics. Some believe that it is romantic to expect learners to find for themselves what is useful in experience and draw coherent lessons from it. Self-directing learners seeking out their own conditions of learning will always be in a minority. In its trumpeting of the 'self organised learner' EL also unduly dismisses the role of the tutor and the value of outsiders to contribute to critical thinking. Brotherton (1991) acknowledges the need for learners to have support in making sense of experience:

> research indicates that the instructor cannot rely upon the instructed person's own ability to discover what is useful through experience . . . positive assistance is required so as to structure experience and draw sound lessons . . .

Sadler-Smith (2006) suggests that EL may be utopian in seeming to imply that learning situations always require a balanced integration of the four stages for effective learning. This may be over-elaborate for many learning situations and may 'over privilege those who can integrate their experiences in constructing knowledge'.

Other criticisms have been made. For example, the claim that learning follows a circle with clearly defined steps seems to some an over-rationalisation of the process of learning, which appears more chaotic and complex than the model allows. Later work by Mumford (1995) suggests that the cycle is more like a learning spiral, with one cycle leading the learner to continuous further cycles and cycles overlapping around learning tasks but still fails to capture the openness and fragmentation of the learning experience for many of EL's critics. It is difficult to escape the view that the MD establishment has adopted the learning cycle model far too uncritically and used it as the theoretical grounding for practical interventions as if it had been fully evaluated and had universal application. This, however, is far from the case; more critical questioning of key assumptions and testing of the model in various contexts is needed.

As a learning model, experiential learning has other limitations which need to be addressed if it is to also be a model of practice. One weakness is that it fails to deal with the emotional aspects of learning. The learning cycle is highly rationalistic; it is about progressing around the cycle in stages using a version of the scientific model of inquiry. However, no account is taken of emotional experience – fears, anxieties, doubts and how people work through the emotions which create blocks to learning (e.g. denial, repression, over-identification, projection, etc.). Emotions may undercut an individual's ability to reflect, observe, experiment and so on and reach closure in the cycle.

The whole area of emotions and learning is an interesting one. Opening up to reflective experience also means opening up to emotional experience (French and Grey 1996). Learning can be a delight and highly pleasurable but also anxiety-provoking. Persistent self questions such as 'Am I competent enough?', 'Can I do it to the right standard?' need to be confronted through experiential learning processes so that managers can be helped to trust their own perceptions, insights and judgements. In the view of this author, this is a major challenge for informal approaches to management development.

There is also the issue that experiential models ignore the political factors of organisation. Far from being places where managers can experiment with learning styles and become deeply reflective practitioners, most organisations are full of pressures and politics (a major theme of this book examined *inter alia* in Chapters 2, 4, 9, 10 and 14). Often the organisation is led by an implicit ideology which privileges one learning style over others and individuals are required to adapt to this (Salaman and Butler 1990). Often the atmosphere in the workplace is just not appropriate to support 'reflective learning from experience'. The ethos is the 'constant now' of immediate problems, not retrospective learning, and management will be particularly prejudiced against EL if it is perceived as 'learning by mistakes' (Sadler-Smith 2006) In these conditions, it is unrealistic to expect managers to use learning styles which do not help their career agendas.

These concerns do not mean that the EL model is discredited. However, it may need to address more robustly the resistances to learning and the blocks which prevent people from achieving their full potential. This may foreground the need to focus less on learning styles and more on the learning strategies people use to reconcile opposing forces in the real world. This will involve an engagement with the organisational context of learning, the theme of the second part of this chapter.

> **Pause for thought**
>
> ## What is your theory of learning?
>
> As we mentioned earlier when we considered personal construct theory, it seems that we all have our theories about how the world is organised, including a theory about how we learn. Argyris and Schon (1978) would call these 'theories in use' (see later on in this chapter).
>
> At this stage you might like to reflect on the different schools of learning outlined above and decide which you regard as the most persuasive. Consider them in terms of your own learning, at work and in social life more generally. Does one capture your experience so well that it gives you a sense of self-recognition and self-enlightenment (the 'aha' effect) or do you want to synthesise the theories into your eclectic working philosophy of learning process?
>
> In developing your own philosophy of learning which will guide you in making design and development decisions, you might like to consider the following questions.
>
> - Consider some memorable incidents recently where you have been successful at work and when you have been unsuccessful. Can you draw any lessons from your behaviour to use in other circumstances?
> - Can you say what you were learning during this experience (values, behaviours, techniques)?
> - Can you say how you were learning (observing; reflecting alone; reflecting with others, etc.)?
> - Did other people help or hinder your learning?
> - What factors overall seemed to help and inhibit your learning?
> - Would you do anything differently next time to make your learning more effective (e.g. learning logs; group discussion; mentoring, etc.)?
> - How generalisable do you think your own experiences in learning might be?
>
> These are only the first steps in developing a personal learning philosophy which will take many years to articulate.
>
> If you enjoy these 'learning how to learn' exercises, try Pedler, Burgoyne and Boydell's self-help book for managers (2001, 2004) and Stewart's end-of-chapter exercises (1999).

6.2.5 Learning and the self

Before passing on to consider the collective forms of learning theory, there is one issue which cuts across all the learning theories we have considered. It is a profound issue and one which has taxed many social philosophers and we can only raise it here as something to meditate upon without giving it the real attention it needs.

The harder, more positivistic end of MD is concerned with the absorption of knowledge from the outside. We accommodate to new knowledge, absorb new models and techniques. However, once we start talking about 'self development', the question is immediately raised of whether there is a coherent and unified 'self' that can learn (Cunningham and Dawes 1997). Postmodern, Buddhist and constructionist views (e.g. Silverman's 1970 'action frame of reference') all deny that a single, unitary, consistent self which is continuous between one situation and another, one period of life and another, actually exists.

Does the 'I' exist independently of others' definitions of 'me' or is identity constantly being negotiated and renegotiated in varying social contexts? Is my construction of self precariously dependent on how others see me? This is of more than philosophical interest. How can I take charge of my 'self development' if that self is partly inferred from others' perceptions of me?

Many commentators say (e.g. Mangham 1996) that 'doing management' with any sort of competence seems to require a good self-image, self acceptance and a high self-concept. However, if we accept the 'mirrored view of the self', then a robust self acceptance may require far more of a dialogue between self/others' perceptions of who I am, in a variety of situations, than the standard literature allows. However, this may just be another way of saying real self-awareness is a journey which lasts as long as your career, a sentiment which many commentators (e.g. Pedler et al. 2001) would share.

There is a further point raised by Stewart (1999): if the self is nebulous, then surely the end point of development must also be unknown. Although development is concerned with change towards some goal, if we take a decentred view of the self how would we know if that goal had been reached? Would the end point always be a subjective and inter-subjective construction among key actors who have an interest in the issue? Can we only talk about a self journey and self emergence, not achievement of an end state?

The kind of thinking which ultimately holds that the self is fluid and co-constructed by the community in which we are part also raises the other perplexing issue of whether 'self development' can ever be an appropriate form of management learning. Perhaps meaningful development can only be a collective experience in which an individual builds a reputation within a social context which has no other life beyond it (i.e. moving to another community means self making and self developing anew).

These themes are not introduced to discredit the 'self managed' or 'experiential' learning projects, merely to help developers appreciate the problematic nature of what they are about and to avoid obvious 'solutions' which turn out not to address real issues.

6.3 Organisational learning and the learning organisation

The shift of interest towards organisational learning and the learning organisation arises from an increasingly competitive environment, constant change and the consequent need for continual learning.

The days when 'super brains' at the top of the organisation – a Ford, a Watson or a Carlson – were enough to ensure that the organisation made the adjustments that were needed may have gone. To survive, let alone prosper, organisations now believe that they have to harness the skills, tap the commitment and enable the learning of people at all levels.

Organisational learning is a response to what is defined as poor organisational performance: bureaucracy, control, lack of commitment to development and the inability of organisations in the past to use the creative powers of their staff to the full. Top managers now look to 'learning organisation' ideas as a strategy for improving quality and encouraging learning and commitment so that the organisation remains constantly flexible and adaptive (Beardwell and Claydon 2007).

However, despite managerial interest in organisational learning as an OD strategy of transformational change, it is interesting that few practical examples of successful learning organisations exist and managers often naively link organisational learning with a commitment to training rather than an enriched climate of stimulation which encourages each individual to make a full commitment. There are many issues to be explored here: the links between individual and organisational learning; the meaning of organisational learning; how it connects with more traditional intervention strategies in OD; how the learning organisation is to be operationalised as a concept and turned into practical programmes of action.

6.3.1 Organisational learning

Organisational learning is the study of the individual and collective learning patterns and processes aimed at helping organisations develop and use internal knowledge to improve themselves and become more competitive. Organisational learning inevitably involves the study of how individuals in management are developed, but it goes beyond that to consider how the learning of individuals interrelates with others and has an effect on the organisation. Organisational learning is more than the accumulation of individual learning efforts. It is possible for individual managers to learn effectively while the organisation does not (e.g. a manager may learn how to serve the customer better without sharing that knowledge with other members of the company). Conversely, organisations may learn in the sense that improvements are made in work design and processes which leaves the social processes of organisation untouched.

Individual learning and collective learning become mutually reinforcing when the generation, analysis and dissemination of knowledge through learning has an impact on organisational behaviour, that is, when it results in doing things in an improved way, when the process of interaction is changed (e.g. learning becomes part of work; learning is embedded in strategy etc.) and those changes become a permanent part of organisational memory (i.e. the benefit they confer is not lost when people leave the organisation) (Easterby-Smith et al. 1999).

In the end, the influence of individual and collective learning is reciprocal. The quality of learning within an organisation depends on the approaches, energy, mental models and values of managers interested in improving their skills and knowledge. At the same time, the individual learner can be helped or hindered by the ethos of the organisation in which s/he works (e.g. is there a real commitment to planning the learning of managers? Are there mechanisms for sharing ideas and insights for development?). Yet, there is another turn: strategies of individual learning can cumulatively shape the culture and institutional system of the organisation and build its learning capability, so taking the interactive learning process around another loop in the cycle.

Ultimately, organisational learning focuses on learning at all levels – individual, group and corporate – and it involves close study of how people create or fail to create, flexible and self-renewing organisations which value learning for the competitive edge which it gives. Implicit in this thinking is the importance of transformative change which goes beyond OD interventions to construct organisations which have the capacity to be self-sustaining, i.e. generating a climate which values learning as a way of life; which acts to remove blockages to learning; which establishes mechanisms for capturing and disseminating good practice.

Expressed in this way, organisational learning can seem vague and difficult to grasp. When we look at the literature in the field, it seems fragmented, reified (i.e. there often seems to be an assumption that 'organisations learn' which many readers would see as a 'mystification', when it is surely individuals, not abstract categories, that can do such things) and the concepts lack clarity. All the same, several approaches are available to understand organisational learning to which we now turn.

6.3.2 Learning and organisational process

One strand of thinking defines organisations as 'residues of thinking' (Grey and Antonacopolou (2004). It focuses on deep processes of culture. What are the routines by which organisational knowledge is acquired? Argyris and Schon (1978) talk of the 'master programmes' by which people become mentally conditioned to define and deal with situations. Through socialisation, people develop 'habits of thought' or 'routines' which predispose them to interpret information in particular ways. These habits of thought can prevent recognition of changing conditions and displace effective learning when the routines are 'defensive' and 'closed'. As in 'group think', these blinkers inhibit the reception of new ideas and process is allowed to swamp innovation. Argyris and Schon (1978) emphasise that organisational learning is greatly improved when organisational actors develop the sensitivity and reflective insight to recognise self-defeating routines which hinder change and the search for new solutions to old problems.

Argyris elaborates this thinking by talking of Model 1 and Model 2 forms of learning. In Model 1, the dominant values and norms stress task performance, control and the protection of the self from negative information. This defensive routine blocks learning (e.g. strict linear reasoning, withholding information, playing safe, cutting off available feedback). In its place, Argyris advocates Model 2 learning, that is, dialogue, holistic thinking, free flow of information, informed choice and a spirit of inquiry. Argyris argues that an organisation with these reflective 'routines' is best placed to adapt to the turbulence and unpredictability of modern business.

Another important 'process' model, also developed by Argyris and Schon (1978), defines organisational learning as a series of learning loops at different levels (box below).

Argyris and Schon: learning process model

Level 1: *Single loop learning*. Also sometimes known as 'inner loop learning', this involves problem-solving when an error is detected so that operational processes can proceed more smoothly. It is learning about how to improve on what we are currently doing so that we become more efficient at it.

Level 2: *Double loop learning*. Known too as 'outer loop learning', involves *why* questions in terms of the value of what we are doing rather than doing what we presently do more efficiently. Double loop learning means rising above immediate organisational problems, reframing issues and embedding them in deeper structures of meaning.

Level 3: *Triple loop learning or deutero-loop learning*. This learning is difficult to achieve but can be extremely important for paradigm changing. It implies shifts in ideological models of organisation, challenging purposes, principles and strategies and creating a climate of 'learning how to learn'.

Of course, all these levels of learning are connected and an organisation which is really aligned to continuous learning will develop multiple streams of learning appropriate to problems of varying kinds.

Source: Adapted from Argyris, C. and Schon, D. (1978) *Organisational Learning: A Theory of Action Perspective*, Addison-Wesley

6.3.3 Organisational learning and cognitive processes

Much of the literature on organisational learning is concerned with cognition. How we think about the organisation will shape processes of learning and behaving. So Karl Weick (1995) talks about 'interpretive processes' as the key to organisational learning. How people in the organisation 'enact' their environment, that is, make sense of the opportunities, constraints, threats and so on facing them will determine how the organisation behaves. This has implications for learning.

The 'social action' approach of Silverman (1970) takes the idea of sense-making further by suggesting that organisational members are engaged in a process of socially constructing their organisation as they continually act and interact with each other. Consensus on what is taken as true provides the underpinning for organisational action. However, when the pictures of the world held by organisational members become disconnected from objective conditions, then organisational effectiveness is undermined. Argyris (1999) suggests that this may be an important source of learning. When dominant mental maps of the organisation ('theories in use') become out of touch with the realities they seek to describe, pressure builds to find alternative theories. Argyris believes that organisations that are truly geared up for organisational learning will be aware of the subtle filtering effects of dominant theories in use and will be constantly testing them for their effectiveness as guides to action.

Both Senge (1990) and Argyris (1999) claim that developing self-awareness of our cognitive models of the organisation can be a vital intervention strategy, helping people to bring to the surface inherent conflicts (e.g. between espoused beliefs and actual 'theories in use') and experiment with new mental models which may be more relevant to the context. For example, many managers espouse a theory of participation as a management philosophy and yet approach situations with an implicit theory in use which is authoritarian and controlling. Real learning happens when people reflect and change their '*theories in use*' (understandings and definitions which guide our actions) not just change our '*espoused theory*' (what we claim to believe). Confronting contradictions of this kind and modifying mental constructs throughout the organisation so that they are more coherent and relevant can become a critical source of leverage, the cognitivists argue, for adaptive organisational learning.

6.3.4 Organisations as communities that learn

As we have seen, organisational learning goes beyond individual learning, to create conditions which encourage reflection, challenge existing paradigms and stimulate new thinking.

Dixon (1994) has done a lot to define the collective learning process based on shared meaning. This is her representation of an iterative cycle of collective thinking and reflection – of acting, assessing, acting again and building a collective memory of effective action – which is meant to represent organisational learning when it is flowing smoothly and freely.

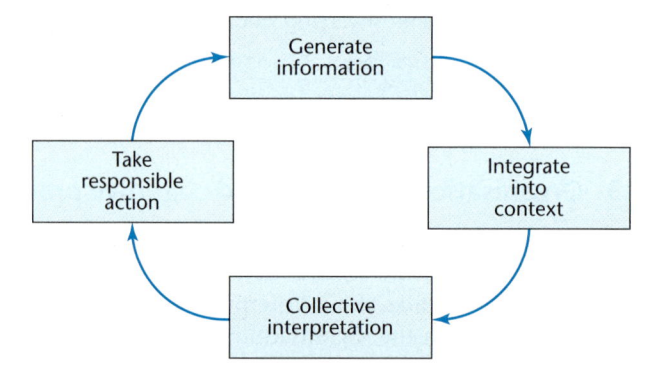

Figure 6.3 Dixon's organisational learning cycle

Source: Adapted from *The Organisational Learning Cycle*, McGraw Hill (Dixon, N. 1994).

Trying to capture the nature of organisational learning is like freeze-framing something in motion. Although it gives a snapshot it denies the process. To partially overcome this, Pedler et al. (1991) suggest that organisational learning can best be understood by seeing the organisation as an organism animated by vital energy flows. He tries to represent this in an interactive model, shown in Figure 6.4.

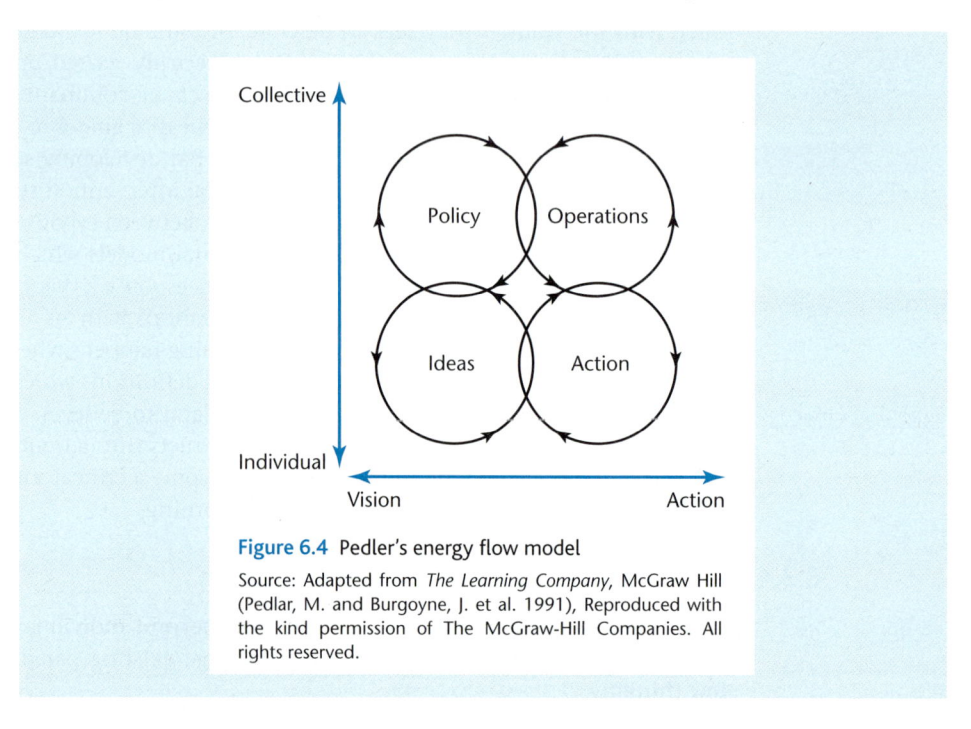

Figure 6.4 Pedler's energy flow model

Source: Adapted from *The Learning Company*, McGraw Hill (Pedlar, M. and Burgoyne, J. et al. 1991), Reproduced with the kind permission of The McGraw-Hill Companies. All rights reserved.

Figure 6.4 shows how individual and organisational learning are reciprocal and the energy of one flows into the other.

However, perhaps the most important recent contribution to theorising about organisational learning has been the notion of 'communities of practice' proposed by Brown and Duguid (1991). We touched on this idea when we considered 'situated learning' (above). COPs are conceptualised as groups of people who are involved in making sense of their work experiences. Through the sharing of stories about work, the community comes to a consensus on 'good practice'. This becomes part of workplace folklore and is embedded in the collective memory.

COPs are based on processes of sense-making, collaborative decision-making and shared understanding. They are important because they show that organisational learning, at the micro-level, is really about learning through action and then building that learning into the fabric of the culture, so that it becomes a taken-for-granted common sense.

The practical implication of these insights is that a management concerned to build learning within the organisation will want to facilitate a climate of learning to support experimentation, sense-making and the codification of knowledge which arises spontaneously in the group as it addresses its task. It is by creating a culture in which workers are free to interpret and improvise the rules and make them fit the demands of the structure that the organisation can become genuinely adaptive (Orr 1990),

Far from being a deviation from prescribed work processes, elaborations around the rules by work groups can be a source of creativity and innovation in dealing with unanticipated contingencies. Managers are exhorted to recognise such creativity and harness it to design systems which consolidate the learning as a permanent feature of the organisational knowledge base.

Pause for thought

Peter Senge's thoughts on the future role of the leader

The leader is a teacher . . . this is not about teaching people how to achieve the vision. It is about fostering learning, for everyone. Such leaders help people throughout the organisation develop systemic understandings. Accepting this responsibility is the antidote to one of the most common downfalls of otherwise gifted teachers – losing their commitment to the truth.

Question
If Senge is right, what qualities will this new generation of leaders, as architects of learning process need to have and how can they be developed?

Source: Senge, P. (1990) *The Fifth Discipline*, p. 356, Century Business.

6.4 Knowledge management

Much of the thinking about organisational learning shades into knowledge management. This is defined (Scarborough and Swan 1999) as

> Any process, practice of creating, acquiring, capturing and using knowledge, wherever it resides in the organisation, to enhance learning and organisational performance.

Successful companies seem to be those that consistently create new knowledge and disseminate it widely. They also quickly embody new thinking in procedures and practices and the latest technologies and products. Organisations which are committed to knowledge management find ways of generating knowledge, of capturing new ideas and experience, sharing it with interested parties and using it for innovation and organisational improvement.

Knowledge-creating companies are said to be effective in recognising that most learning within organisations actually arises from the natural demands of the work, where people solve problems on the job. However, in the typical organisation much of this learning by individuals and within COP is lost because no attempt is made to codify and institutionalise it within an established knowledge base.

Knowledge-creating companies such as Honda, Canon, Matsushita, NEC and so on recognise that most learning actually arises from the natural demands of work (Walton 1999). However, unless institutional procedures are put in place, much of that learning evaporates. These organisations recognise the importance of tacit knowledge (Lam 2000). This is the taken-for-granted knowledge embedded within a COP. It is the know-how of older, experienced employees which is passed on to the next generation through socialisation. This is context-bound practical knowledge of how things work, the informal solutions to problems which a work group has improvised from formal rules, accidental work-based discoveries and the unarticulated wisdom of the group encoded in collective memory. Unless this knowledge is transferred from the minds of people into a permanent record it will disappear as groups dissolve and reform around other projects and people leave the organisation.

Practical techniques for organisational learning

It is unlikely that reflection will develop naturally in most organisations because of operational pressures, but the consequence of not reflecting as a corporate habit is that important collective lessons are not drawn and the organisational amnesia that results means that the organisation will have to go around the learning loop again. Techniques for creating collective learning include the following.

- Set up periodic review and debrief sessions at the end of a major project, crisis and so on to critique the processes and record the corporate learning (what went well and badly) for next time.

- Commission an officer to write an experiential learning record of the event, for example, interviewing key players and bringing together the community view of the meaning of the experience for the organisation.

- Commission an officer to write a historical overview of a recent period of organisational history, bringing out the key themes which are likely to recur; creating a coherent account of what the organisation has been through and what this implies for the future.

These reviews and experiential learning accounts might be integrated in the existing KM systems of the organisation and would be useful for performance review, appraisal, development and induction purposes.

Nonaka and Takeuchi (1995), who have researched widely in knowledge management, argue that the rate of organisational learning and creativity is much enhanced if 'tacit knowledge' can be made explicit. They talk of the 'spiral of knowledge', in which the experiential knowing of the individual (Polanyi 1996) is made collective, codified and turned into 'explicit knowledge'. In this way, everyday, individualised transitory knowledge can be translated into permanent, collectivised knowledge which can be stored, retrieved, shared and accumulated for the organisation as a whole. By degrees, the accretion of practical learning can transform the organisation so that it becomes ever more responsive and effective.

In the same way, organisations driven by an ethos of knowledge management seek to create interdependencies among knowledge workers. Linking the diverse talents of employees around projects, creating networks of roles around information flows and deliberately building the conditions for synergy, can engender new streams of creativity and innovation. As Dixon (1994) says:

> The challenge is to build information saturated organisations . . . where organisation no longer filters from the top down, but branches out into every imaginable direction and flows away from information creators towards information users.

On the 'hard' side that means IT systems which free up the circulation of information and make it accessible to all, in the form they need for the tasks that confront them, for example, internets, intranets and e-learning systems customised for the user. On the 'soft' side, it involves interweaving knowledge into cultures and systems of working so that data can become real learning with tangible outcomes of commercial value.

It is this area of conversion of data which requires most attention. Merely improving the dissemination of information will not generate greater organisational learning. Indeed, the links between data flows, knowledge generation, individual and group learning are still obscure to us and studies in knowledge management which are largely based on cybernetic theories lack socio-psychological sophistication. Transmuting knowledge into learning requires attention to social concerns – how to make the massive changes required in attitudes, behaviours, trust relations and politics; how to create cultures of real openness for free dialogue, collective reflection and creative thinking become a way of life? These are themes which are taken up in a closely related area of inquiry, that of the 'learning organisation' (LO).

6.5 The learning organisation

The idea of the LO has been developing over the past twenty-five years. It remains a vague concept and more of a promise than an enacted reality. Much of the writing on the LO is, in Easterby-Smith's words (1997), about building 'normative models for creating change in the direction of improved learning processes'. This can amount to advocacy by consultants, rhetorically harmonising positive findings from their own assignments with selectively chosen insights from the organisational learning literature.

Another major issue in the field is the plethora of definitions. Here are just two, which may give you a flavour of debate.

Peter Senge (1990) defines the LO as:

> An organisation where people are continually expanding their capacity to create the results they desire, where patterns of thinking are nurtured and collective aspirations are set free . . . so that people can learn how to learn together.

In a definition which has wide currency, Pedler et al. (1991) define the LO as:

> An organisation that facilitates the learning of all its members and continually transforms itself.

The roots of the LO seem to spread broadly. The concept owes a lot to the 'excellence' movement of the 1980s and its values of organic, flexible organisation, quality, communication and culture-building. It also has elements in common with 1970s organisational development and the philosophy of openness, trust, personal growth, participation and so on. It seems to have affinities with quality of working life approaches and TQM. It also accommodates the cognitive, interpretive and gestalt approaches in learning theory and aspects of strategic HRD. However, the idea of the LO goes beyond all of these influences to suggest a process of constant organisational transformation.

6.5.1 Characteristics of the learning organisation

In defining the philosophy and principles of the LO we are faced with both the nebulous form which this concept takes and the fact that commentators in the field have defined it in very different ways. All the same, it may be possible to define some consistent features and common assumptions underpinning the body of work on LO.

- *Learning and competitive advantage*: The LO concept seems to have found its time because organisations have come to realise that competitive pressures require new forms of organising which use the mental powers of everyone in the organisation to their full capacity and encourage continual thinking, reflection and learning. Constant updating of organisational knowledge through learning is no longer just desirable but simply essential for survival.
- *Systematised learning*: The quality and quantity of learning can be increased if it is organised deliberately. Accidental learning is happening all the time, but the value of this is compounded if it is systematised and processes exist to review the learning and share lessons with those parts of the organisation best placed to use them. This prevents the waste of effort involved in constantly reinventing the wheel because learning is not captured.

- *Shared learning*: Learning is best achieved if it is shared with others – through dialogue, team learning and evaluation. Data becomes knowledge when people act together to discuss its implications, link it to judgements, hunch, intuition, metaphors and symbols which form something new – an idea, a product, new systems or policy – which has the legitimacy conferred by participative process.

- *Climate of learning*: LO theorists insist that it is a management responsibility to build a climate in which learning is valued and people feel motivated to learn. This means replacing an atmosphere of defensiveness and fear with one of forgiveness and trust. It means developing structures that identify learning processes and explicitly support opportunities for development and learning from past mistakes (i.e. learning 'why' is seen as important as learning 'how'). It also involves recognising and rewarding those who have taken the risk to experiment and create new knowledge which improves the capability of the organisation.

- *Learning across boundaries*: The learning culture of the LO encourages collaboration across boundaries. It involves drawing on the insights of key stakeholders – customers, suppliers, outsourced workers and so on – as well as people inside the organisation. The aim is to build a self-reinforcing community of learning in which creativity is valued. Open boundaries between departments, units and companies allow ideas for good practice, product information, customer satisfaction and benchmark data to flow freely throughout the organisation so that the probability of new creative synergies is greatly increased.

- *Learning as empowerment*: Finally, the LO is empowering of learners. It replaces hierarchy with systems of minimum control and facilitates networks of groups and agents who have autonomy to act independently for change. Learning is a central value of the organisation (i.e. HRD-led) and resources are put behind these values to help people to become genuinely self-developing innovators. People are encouraged to run their own projects and experience the personal satisfaction of making a real difference within the organisational space they control.

Much of this may seem to you to be vague, even vapid. This is because concepts of the LO are still developing. However, greater clarity may be brought to bear by considering the contributions of the most influential theory of the learning organisation.

6.5.2 Senge's model of the learning organisation

Peter Senge's writings such as the *The Fifth Discipline* (1990) and *The Dance of Change* (1999) have had a major influence on thinking in this area and any review must critically consider his contribution.

Throughout his work, Senge presents a very positive vision of what organisations can achieve. He believes that organisations, as we currently experience them, are not conducive to reflection, engagement or empowerment. They concentrate on 'adaptive learning' when the real need is for 'generative learning', or learning which builds the capacity of the organisation to position itself favourably for the future. To move towards this happy position, Senge advocates action in relation to five disciplines (see box on the next page).

Senge's learning disciplines

- *Systems thinking*: This is seen by Senge (1990) as the most important of the disciplines on which all the others are dependent. Thinking in 'systems terms' means an understanding of the interrelatedness between the parts which make the whole and focusing on process. In terms of practical action. It means being able to see how action in one part of an organisational system will have consequences elsewhere. Although Senge regards this as an injunction to all members of a progressive organisation, it applies particularly to those who have directive power and is intended as an antidote to management by sectional politics.
- *Personal mastery*: The foregoing notwithstanding, this category reminds us that we can get bound up in concepts of the organisation which are abstract and removed from actual behaviour. As Senge (1990) says: 'Ultimately organisations learn through individuals … without individual learning we cannot speak of organisational learning'. Personal mastery underlines the importance of continuous development of personal knowledge and skill.
- *Mental models*: This involves the importance of challenging the assumption, implicit definitions and pictures of the world which key stakeholders hold (i.e. their world-view in one tradition, or 'theories in use' in another). They can block change and the acceptance of new ideas. Senge advocates 'learningful conversations' to articulate these assumptions (i.e. put into words what may be tacit) and discuss the value for thought and action.
- *Building shared visions*: This emphasises the importance of agreeing a common purpose, vision or picture which inspires people and creates bonds of trust and unity. A genuinely shared vision only emerges when the dialogue between team members is tolerant, open and mutually supportive.
- *Team learning*: Senge puts a lot of emphasis on developing the capabilities of the team, that is, thinking together as a team so that ideas clash and are reconciled into new modes of thinking through dialogue and debate.

Source: Adapted from Senge, P. (1990) *The Fifth Discipline*, pp. 5–11, Century Business, London.

Senge (1990) advocates that managers thoroughly understand these disciplines of learning and implement their spirit to create a culture of sustained learning. However, he acknowledges that this is not easy. There are many barriers to change, not least, inadequate resources, fear and anxiety, diffuse organisational strategies, politics and lack of clarity to what management intends. Overcoming these and other blockages requires determined, clear-sighted leadership.

There are three critical roles for the leader of learning. As a *designer*, the leader is involved in developing systems for participative involvement and learning; as *teacher* the leader acts as a facilitator of learning so that everyone understands the threats and opportunities facing the organisation; as a *steward*, the leader demonstrates belief in the organisation's strategy and tells a narrative of past, present and future so that all can feel involved.

6.5.3 The learning organisation in real life

The problem with the LO principles is how to apply them in the real world. The truth is that many managers find difficulty in owning the LO concept and the reasons are not hard to find. For one thing, LO philosophies are an assault on the legitimacy of management. If the goal is to strive for an organisation which *renews* itself, the role of the manager begins to look redundant. There is also the problem of how to operationalise the concept in terms of the actual behaviours which will be needed. It is not surprising that many managers dismiss the LO as 'just another HRD fad' (Easterby-Smith et al. 1999).

However, a number of writers including Mumford (1999), Garvin (1993), Lundy and Cowling (1996) and Garratt (1990) have suggested practical forms for realising the spirit of the LO and spelling out the implications for management behaviour. *Inter alia* these writers have suggested the following elements.

- *Leadership*: Top managers have to be seen to drive the learning environment. By their actions they model the behaviour which others will emulate. So, the top management needs to demonstrate openness, questioning, creativity, strategic thinking and its own willingness to learn. Higher levels need to show that learning is part of the vision and that thinking and innovation are truly valued.

- *Management*: Managers need to be encouraging learning as a way of life, as much by their own behaviour as by exhortation. They should be trying to build learning and development into the design of work and acting to create a climate in which all experience is reviewed and lessons derived for learning.

- *Teams*: Team leaders need to help members see their activities as part of a learning forum. Norms of collaboration, sharing knowledge and experience, adaptability and thinking in terms of 'systems' rather than disembodied 'problems' are the key to a sustained learning process. Multidisciplinary teams help people to understand different perspectives. Action learning sets help members to reflect on experience and learn about interaction, group dynamics and decision-making as well as outcome. Self-managing groups responsible for an entire project learn about the complete management process and have a wider picture of how the organisation works. Quality-management systems provide data for joint decision-making and team review of its own performance.

- *Boundaries*: Everything possible should be done to learn from others. 360-degree appraisals and customer involvement at all stages of the development process provide vital feedback. Joint learning across teams provides a common vocabulary as well as the generalisation of good practices. Sensitisation attachments to other organisations allow benchmarks to be established and lessons captured which can be brought back home.

- *Self learning*: People at all levels, not just managers, need to commit themselves to the concept of lifelong learning. This has many implications for the structure of work, not least that it should be linked to planned learning. Within this system, tasks would be designed and delegated so that people can develop. Learning would be seen as part of the work. Learning contracts would be based on maximising learning opportunities. Time would be allocated in daily schedules for reflection, analysis and the generation of new knowledge. Support networks, mentoring frameworks, learning resource centres, local learning cells and customised IT would provide an environment for self-managed learning.

There are very few organisations which, at the time of writing, have attempted to introduce a full-blown LO. However, this is not to say that a good number of organisations have not attempted learning arrangements which owe an obvious debt to LO ideas. For example, Monsanto has produced a 'knowledge management architecture' based on sophisticated electronic knowledge flows and learning forums which are multidisciplinary and project-based. Motorola's TQM system is based on a deliberate attempt to integrate performance standards, customer feedback and quality measures in a continuous learning process. GEC has an institutionalised system of 'town meetings' in which work groups pool their experience around ideas for change (Walton 1999).

There are also some formalised models and tools for learning and change which have been widely applied in corporate settings and can trace their origins, in part, to the LO concept, such as the European Foundation for Quality Management Model, the Balanced Scorecard and the Investor's In People Standard. While serving the useful function of focusing the attention of management on learning, quality and change as interconnected elements, these models can seem mechanistic and deny the 'process orientation' which is at the heart of the LO project.

More useful, perhaps, are stories of organisational attempts to introduce change which is infused with the values of the LO (see case study below).

Case study — Anglian Water Services plc

Anglian Water is one of the largest water authorities in the UK. In the 1990s it was decided by top management to try and replace its highly structured, even bureaucratic culture with one which was more flexible and innovating to help the company respond to a newly deregulated and demanding market.

After much painful restructuring in which a lot of disparate initiatives were taken up and dropped, the top team decided to move to a LO. In pursuing this ambition the following initiatives were taken.

- Top management attended an 'executive stretch' workshop to sensitise it to the importance of learning and empowerment.
- The HRD strategy was revised to proclaim 'learning' as a core value of work at Anglian.
- Work groups were encouraged to come forward with ideas for learning projects which were intended to help workers grow in confidence, experiment with innovative ideas and become accustomed to working in multidisciplinary teams. A number of projects were undertaken; the most ambitious involved work outside Anglian, including renovating a children's hospice and digging a well in Africa.
- The company provided facilitation for the team development processes, coaching and mentoring for change roles, intranet learning resources and support for debriefing and disseminating lessons from each learning experience.
- A collaborative venture was also established with a local university to augment skills, help with knowledge generation and provide wider learning support networks.

An evaluation after three years showed that there was a lot of support for these initiatives among the workforce, but continuing concern about further plans for reorganisation which promise not only further job cuts but also a tightening of central control around business values.

Questions:

Do you think that these experiments at Anglian suggest a sincere attempt to move towards an LO? What more would you like to see for development towards this goal? What factors threaten to derail progress?

Source: Adapted from Morton, C. (1998) 'Waterproof' *People Management*, 11 June 1998 and lecture by C. Morton at Roffey Park School of Management.

6.5.4 Critique of the learning organisation

In view of the amount of emphasis that has been given in this chapter to the LO, it seems a little cavalier to move on without some critical review of the concept. This is particularly appropriate here because the LO shows no signs of receding as a force for leadership and organisational development. However, there have been a number of criticisms of the LO concept:

The LO concept is often advanced with evangelical vigour as a panacea to all organisational problems. The commercialisation of its ideas also means that some very superficial approaches have been advanced under the banner of the LO. Some of the gurus in this field have taken these comments to heart (e.g. Easterby-Smith et al. 1999; Burgoyne and Reynolds 1997; Senge 1999). They have recently emphasised that LO should not become an article of faith and stress that LO is not just another consultant's 'fad': it is a strategic orientation based on humanistic ideology which is unlikely to disappear.

The LO concept is said by some to deny the real conflicts of interest between stakeholders in favour of a unitary concept of organisation (i.e. common vision, purpose and practice). LO theorists counter by acknowledging that this is a legitimate interpretation. However, even if there are objective conflicts of interest, they can find rough consensus in an order which reconciles conflict within an overarching goal of *shared* interest in learning and the survival of the organisation as a whole.

The LO concept is also criticised for its lack of clarity, its abstraction and almost mystical belief in the power of learning. Critics talk of the lack of measurable outcomes, the utopianism and the failure to distinguish between relevant and irrelevant learning, as it conduces to the good of the organisation. The response of the LO supporters is to underline the importance of learning as a liberating and empowering force, and to also reaffirm the incremental nature of the movement. Building an LO is not one grand project, but a working out of general principles in relation to the experience of a particular organisation. In the end, the LO is not a set of 'actionable parts', but the development of a process which requires experimentation with different forms of learning and development. Senge (1990) suggests that this requires a sophistication of 'corporate mind' which is not often found in the organisational world.

Finally, the concept of the LO is often criticised for its naivety about organisational politics and power. This is a criticism which may have hit a nerve. So much of LO theorising appears unworldly because it seems to deny the politics, power struggles and manoeuvrings which are part of all organisational process. It seems to imply the willingness of key groups to embrace a democratic open ethos which flies in the face of the commonly experienced reality that information is power in most organisations and will be closely guarded, and that management is a political process. The response of the LO theorists is to concede this point but to remind their detractors that the LO movement is about changing the metaphors by which we think of organisational process so that we can change behaviour towards a greater unity of purpose (Easterby-Smith et al. 1999)

In the end, the LO emerges as an attractive concept. It promises a virtuous cycle of participation, empowerment, creativity and learning. It is less about fulfilling a set of institutional criteria but generating a sense of learning as a way of being and becoming. It is not an end state but an attitude of mind which appreciates that the journey of learning and becoming never ends.

Mumford (1997) emphasises that mastering the LO philosophy and applying it seriously will have major consequences for the function of management. After all, managers will be champions for learning within the organisation as a whole. Helping others to learn and setting a good example in this becomes a central part of the managerial role. Mumford also thinks that managers are turning into developers, consultants and researchers, diagnosing the nexus of forces within the organisation and designing systems which advance work-centred learning of all kinds and at all levels. If management continues as a separate category of work, its main justification is likely to be that of facilitating the learning process.

Case study: So near to a learning organisation and so far from market success

Mona (name changed) is a well-known, UK-based global engineering consultancy with a strong culture and explicit mission, well known for its highly professional advice throughout the world.

Mona already has a number of characteristics which might be interpreted as expressive of the spirit of an LO.

- Mona has a profit share scheme with all staff; the organisation is owned by a charitable trust and profit is distributed among employees. This provides a strong sense of shared vision, trust and unity.

- A sense of common purpose results in a shared culture and identity. The founder's mission of creativity and excellence in design and social purpose continues to galvanise the organisation and ensures a strong culture.

- Mona is learning at the same rate as external change outside the organisation and learning continuously in terms of its technical capability, required by most definitions of an LO (Pedler 1991; Senge 1990)

- Mona is a culture of continuous learning geared up to review performance and professional development and constantly adapt in order to retain world-class competitive edge. Some of the departments of this organisation have a sharpness in technical excellence and experimentation which make the organisation unique.

In so many ways, Mona does exemplify the LO ideal. It is 'the organisation that learns continuously and transforms itself' (Watkin and Marsick 1993). It is the organisation that is 'constantly seeking to collect, manage and use knowledge for success; which empowers people within the company as they learn to work' (Marquardt 1996).

Mona does allow experimentation, permits failure, encourages internal discussion and dissent, builds close relationships with colleagues and customers, the hallmarks of the LO as the theorists define it, but some essential elements are missing.

- Mona may be learning at the same rate as the environment in technical terms, but in organisational, management and market terms it is falling behind.

- Learning and development values have not been applied to organisational capabilities. The management and leadership stock is not being replenished or developed. Mona is lopsided; its technical capability outbalances its strategic, organisational and managerial learning.

- As a result, Mona, so technically dynamic, so close to being an LO in its professional culture, may still fail as an organisation in the marketplace.

- The strategy needs to rebalance the economic and managerial elements so that they are aligned with the technical to create the harmony of parts which the LO requires and the market rewards.

Source: Personal communication and research

6.6 Conclusion

This chapter has attempted a broad overview of learning. There are a range of theories which offer useful insight into individual learning. Some are general theories from developmental psychology, others are specific to adult learning. All are controversial; all have strengths and weaknesses, although some seem to be worked through rather more than others. Each is linked with development techniques.

What seems to emerge is that adults (including managers) learn in different ways and no theory or technique will be successful in explaining the learning of all people all of the time. Certainly no simple model seems to represent adequately the complexity and endless differentiation in professional (including managerial) learning at work. Certainly, managers themselves are usually unable to say how they have learnt their skills. Further themes for inquiry in individual learning may include a closer analysis of the conditions in which managers derive lessons from experience of different kinds and the principles that impel the genuinely curious, self-directing and effective learner. Then there is the mystery of why one person can learn in a given set of conditions and the other does not, and the mechanisms involved.

Similar ambiguities plague organisational learning. The interface between individual and collective learning requires further conceptual clarification. Organisational learning is obviously more than the sum of all individual energies directed to learning within a community. However, much theory in this area seems reified and excessively abstract, not to say rhetorical. The interplay between micro-individual experience and macro-collective process, between the learning agendas of the individual and the organisation may become fruitful areas for future research inquiry.

Review questions

1. Which theory of learning do you find most persuasive in describing how you learn and why? Would you want to critique any of the models in terms of your own experience?

2. How would you react to the proposition that andragogy and experiential learning have established such 'ideological hegemony' (look this up if you don't understand it) in learning theory and practice that other approaches to learning have become marginalised?

3. Do you agree that the link between emotion and learning needs more consideration in the literature? From your own experience, how does emotion influence learning?

4. Make a case for your organisation becoming a learning organisation. What are the steps it will need to take?

5. 'The theory on organisational learning is all very well but it offers little practical assistance to the busy manager?' Do you agree with this contention?

Web links

A website of debate on learning:
http://www.newhorizons.org/lrnbus_marchese.html

An interesting and recent article on the characteristics of effective adult learning:
http://www.newhorizons.org/article-bllington1.html

An important project of the Learning and Skills Research Centre looking at the value of informal learning and the contribution it makes:
http://www.lsda.org.uk/pubs/dbaseout/download.asp?code=LSRC447NR1

A website on informal learning in government:
http://www.lsc.gov.uk

On Bandura's social learning theory:
http://chiron.valdosta.edu/whuitt/co/soccog/soclrn.html

For information on learning styles see:
http://www.support4learning.org.uk/education/lstyles.htm/General

For Argyris and his famous categories of learning:
http://tip.psychology.org/argyris.html

Recommendations for further reading

Those texts marked with an asterisk in the bibliography are recommended for further reading, especially the following;

Argyris, C. (1999) *On Organisational Learning.* Argyris has had a fundamental impact on how we think about learning in organisations at the individual and collective levels. Although he is not easy to understand, the effort is worthwhile.

Pedler, M., Burgoyne, J. and Boydell, T. (1991) *The Learning Company: A strategy for Sustainable Development.* A stimulating and accessible introduction to organisational learning.

Honey, P. and Mumford, A. (1986) *The Manual of Learning Styles.* You cannot go far in the area of management learning before encountering this model, so rather than rely on other people's representations, go to the source yourself.

Bibliography

*Argyris, C. (1999) *On Organisational Learning*, Oxford, Blackwell.

Argyris, C. and Schon, D. (1974) *Theory in Practice: Increasing Professional Effectiveness*, Jossey-Bass.

*Argyris, C. and Schon, D. (1978) *Organisational Learning: A Theory of Action Perspective*, Addison-Wesley.

Bannister, D. and Fransella, F. (1971) *Inquiring Man*, Penguin.

Bandura, A. (1977) *Social Learning Theory*, Prentice Hall.

Bandura, A. (1986) *Social Learning Theory*, Prentice Hall.

Bandura, A. (1996) 'Social learning', in Manstead, A. and Hewstone, M. (1996) *The Blackwell Encyclopaedia of Social Psychology*, Blackwell.

Bartlett, F. (1932) *Remembering*, Cambridge University Press.

Beardwell, J. and Claydon, T. (2007) *Human Resource Management*, 5th edn, Prentice Hall.

Beckhard, R. and Pritchard, W. (1992) *Changing the Essence: The Art of Creating and Leading Fundamental Change in Organisations*, Jossey-Bass.

Blackler, F. (1993) 'Knowledge and the theory of organisations: organisations as activity systems and the reframing of management', *Journal of Management Studies*, 30/6, 863–84.

Blagg, N., Ballinger, M. et al. (1993) 'Development of transferable skills in learners', Employment Department, Sheffield.

Brotherton, C. (1991) 'New Developments in research into adult cognition', Nottingham University.

*Brown, J. and Duguid, P. (1991) 'Organisational learning and communities of practice', *Organisational Science*, Vol. 2, No. 1.

Brundage, D. and Mackeracher, D. (1980) *Adult Learning Principles and Their Application to Programme Planning*, Ministry of Education, Ontario.

Burgoyne, J. and Reynolds, P. (1997) *Management Learning*, Sage.

Buzan, T. (1974) *Use Your Head*, Macmillan.

Buzan, T. (1988) *Harnessing the Para Brain*, Colt Books.

Champy, J. and Nohria, N. (eds) (1996) *Fast Forward: The Best Ideas on Managing Business Change*, Harvard Business School.

Cheetham, G. and Chivers, G. (1996) 'Towards a holistic model of professional competence', *Journal of European Industrial Training*, Vol. 20, No. 7.

Cunningham, I. and Dawes, G. (1997) 'Problematic premises, presuppositions and practices in management education and training', in Burgoyne, J. and Reynolds, M. (1997), Sage.

Dalton, K. (1993) 'The Performance of Narrative and Self in Organisational Culture', PhD thesis, Bath School of Management.

Dewey, J. (1938) *Experience and Education*, Indianapolis: Kappa Delta Pi.

Dixon, N. (1994) *The Organisational Learning Cycle: How We Can Learn Collectively*, McGraw Hill.

Easterby-Smith, M. (1997) 'Disciplines of organisational learning: contributions and critiques', *Human Relations*, Vol. 50, No. 9.

*Easterby-Smith, M., Burgoyne, J. and Araujo, L. (1999) *Organisational Learning and the Learning Organisation*, Sage.

*Edmonson A., and Moingeon B., 'From organisational learning to the learning organisation', in Grey, C. and Antonacopoulou, E. (2004) *Essential Readings in Management Learning*, Sage.

Elkjaer, B. (1999) 'In search of a social learning theory', in Easterby-Smith, M. et al. (1999) *Organisational Learning and the Learning Organisation*, Sage.

*Fox, S. (1997) 'From management education to the study of management learning', in Burgoyne, J. and Reynolds, M. (1997) *Management Learning*, Sage.

Freire, P. (1978) *Pedagogy in Process: The Letters to Guinea Bissau*, Writers and Readers Publishers.

French, R. and Grey, C. (1996) *Rethinking Management Education*, Sage.

French, W. and Bell, C. (1990) *Organisation Development*, Prentice Hall.

Gagne, R. (1970) *The Conditions of Learning*, Rhinehart and Winston.

Gagne, R. (1985) *The Conditions of Learning and Theory of Instruction*, Rinehart and Winston.

Garratt, B. (1990) *The Learning Organisation*, Fontana/Collins.

Garvin, A. (1993) 'Building a learning organisation', in *Harvard Business Review*, Vol. 71, No. 4.

Goodstein, L. and Burke, W. (1991) 'Creating successful organisation change, *Organisational Dynamics*, Vol. 19, No. 5.

Gregory, R. (1970) *The Intelligent Eye*, London.

*Grey, C. and Antonacopolou, E. (2004) *Essential Readings in Management Learning*, Sage.

Harrison, R. (1995) *The Consultant's Journey*, McGraw Hill.

Hayes, N. (1997) *Successful Team Management*, Thomson.

Honey, P. and Mumford, A. (1986) *The Manual of Learning Styles*, Maidenhead.

Jarvis, P. (1987) *Adult Learning in Social Context*, Croom Helm.

Kelly, G. (1955) *A Theory of Personality*, Norton and Co.

Kelly, G. (1959) *Personal Construct Theory*, Norton and Co.

Klein, G. (2003) *Intuition at Work: Why Developing your Gut Instincts Will Make You Better at What You Do*, Doubleday.

Knowles, M. (1980) *The Modern Practice of Adult Education*, Cambridge Books.

*Knowles, M. (1984) *The Adult Learner: A Neglected Species*, Gulf Publishing.

*Knowles, M. (1990) *The Adult Learner: A Neglected Species*, Gulf Publishing.

Kohn, M. and Slomeczynski, K. (1990) *Social Structure and Self Direction*, Blackwell.

*Kolb, D. (1984) *Experiential Learning*, Prentice Hall.

Lam, A. (2000) 'Tacit knowledge: organisational learning and societal institutions', *Organisational Studies*, Vol. 21, No. 3.

Latham, G. and Frayne, C. (1989) 'Increasing job attendance through training in self management: a review of two studies', *Journal of Applied Psychology*, Vol. 24.

*Lave, J. and Wenger, E. (1991) *Situated Learning: Legitimate Peripheral Participation*, Cambridge University Press.

Lawrence, D. (1985) 'Improving self esteem and reading', *Educational Research*, Vol. 27, No. 3.

Lewin, K. (1935) *A Dynamic Theory of Personality*, McGraw Hill.

Locke, E. and Latham, G. (1990) *A Theory of Goal Setting and Task Performance*, Prentice Hall.

Lundy, O. and Cowling, A. (1996) *Strategic Human Resource Management*, Routledge.

Mangham, I. (1996) *Power and Performance in Organisations*, Blackwell.

Margerison, C. (1991) *Making Management Development Work*, McGraw Hill.

Marquardt, M. (1996) *Building the Learning Organisation*, McGraw Hill.

*Marswick, V. and Watkins, K. (1990) *Informal and Incidental Learning in the Workplace*, Croom Helm.

Maslow, A. (1954) *Motivation and Personality*, Harper Row.

Morton, C. (1998) 'Waterproof', in *People Management* 11 June.

Mumford, A. (1995) 'Four approaches to learning from experience', *Industrial and Commercial Training*, Vol. 27, No. 8.

Mumford, A. (1997) *Management Development*, CIPD.

Mumford, A. and Gold, J. (2004) *Management Development, Strategies for Action*, CIPD.

Nadler, L. (1979) *Developing Human Resources*, Austin: Kogan Page.

Nadler, J. Thompson, L. et al. (2003) 'Learning negotiation skills: four models of knowledge creation and transfer', *Management Science*, Vol. 49, No. 4.

Nonaka, L. and Takeuchi, H. (1995) *The Knowledge Creating Company*, Oxford University Press.

*Orr, J. (1990) 'Sharing knowledge, celebrating identity: war stories and community memory in a service culture', in Middleton, D. and Edwards, D. (eds) *Collective Remembering in Society*, Sage.

Pedler, M., Burgoyne, J. and Boydell, T. (1991) *The Learning Company: A Strategy for Sustainable Development*, McGraw Hill.

Pedler, M., Burgoyne, J. and Boydell, T. (2001) *The Manager's Guide to Self Development*, McGraw Hill.

Pedler, M., Burgoyne, J. and Boydell, T. (2004) *A Manager's Guide to Leadership*, McGraw Hill.

Perls, F. (1973) *The Gestalt Approach and Eye Witness in Therapy*, California: Sundown Books.

Piaget, J. (1926) *The Language and Thought of the Child*, New York: Harcourt Brace Jovannovich.

Polanyi, M. (1964) *Personal Knowledge*, Harper and Row.

*Polanyi, M. (1996) *The Tacit Dimension*, Macmillan

Pun, A. (1990) 'Managing the cultural differences in learning', *Journal of Management Development*, Vol. 9, No. 5.

Rogers, C. (1980) *A Way of Being*, Houghton Mifflin.

*Sadler-Smith, E. (2006) *Learning and Development for Managers*, Blackwell.

*Salaman, G. and Butler, J. (1990) 'Why managers won't learn', *Management Education and Development*, Vol. 21, No. 3.

Scarborough, H. and Swan, J. (1999) *Knowledge Management: A Literature Review*, CIPD.

Schaffer R. and Thomson, H. (1992) 'Successful change management programmes begin with results', *Harvard Business Review*, Vol. 70, No. 1.

*Schon, D. (1987) *Educating the Reflective Practitioner*, Jossey-Bass.

Senge, P. (1990) *The Fifth Discipline: The Art and Practice of the Learning Organisation*, Random House.

Senge, P. (1994) 'The leader's new work: building learning organisations', in Mabey, C. and Iles, P. (1994) *Managing Learning*, Open University.

Senge, P. (1999) *The Dance of Change*, Doubleday Books.

Silverman, D. (1970) *The Theory of Organisations*, Heinemann.

Stewart, J. (1999) *Employee Development Practice*, Prentice Hall.

Sweller, J. and Chandler, P. (1994) 'Why some material is difficult to learn', *Cognition and Instruction*, Vol. 12, No. 3.

Tolman, E. (1959) 'Principles of purposive behaviour', in Koch, S. (ed.) *Psychology: A Study of a Science*, McGraw Hill.

Torrington, D., Hall, L. and Taylor, S. (2005) *Human Resource Management*, Prentice Hall.

Walton, J. (1999) *Strategic Human Resource Development*, Prentice Hall.

*Watkin, K. and Marsick, V. (1993) *Sculpting the Learning Organisation: Lessons in the Art and Science of Systematic Change*, Jossey-Bass.

Watson, J. (1930) *Behaviourism*, University of Chicago Press.

Watson, T. (2001) 'The emergent and processes of management pre-learning', *Management Learning*, Vol. 32, No. 2.

*Weick, K. (1995) *Sense Making in Organisations*, Sage.

Weick, K. (1996) 'Organisational learning: affirming an oxymoron in Clegg, S., Hardy, C. et al. (eds) *Handbook of Organisational Studies*, Sage.

Wood, D. (1988) *How Children Think and Learn*, Blackwell.

Woodall, J. and Winstanley, D. (1999) *Management Development*, Blackwell.

7 Informal management learning

Learning outcomes

After studying this chapter you should be able to understand, analyse and explain:

- the shift from 'instruction' to 'on-the-job learning' or experiential learning;
- the strengths and weaknesses of experiential learning;
- the meaning of 'incidental' and 'informal' learning; 'retrospective' and 'prospective' learning;
- blocks and opportunities in experiential learning;
- self-development and managed learning: philosophy, skills and conditions of practice;
- the skills of the self developer;
- the organisation and self-development; continuous professional development;
- methods and approaches to experiential learning, that is, learning from changes in job design; one-to-one and group process.

7.1 Introduction

Can managers only learn to be managers by 'doing managing'? Learning through the 'doing' of management and reflecting on it ('learning by experience') is the orthodoxy of the age; how did this happen; what rationale underpins it and what does it imply?

In recent times the model of instructor-led learning has been turned upside down. The priority is no longer how to make the trainer/educator/instructor more effective, but how to facilitate learning from experience in a way which helps people learn their own lessons. The move is towards action-based, experientially focused, individually led management development. Another way of saying the same thing is that in the past few decades there has been a seismic shift from *formalised training and education* to *workplace-based learning; informal learning; natural learning or 'learning on the job'*, all terms which are treated as more or less synonymous in this text.

However, the term which is preferred is *experiential learning* because it captures the *in vivo* spirit of refection on lived experience, but this is not to suggest that the only experiences that managers learn from are experiences at work. Experience in the classroom can be very real and very valuable, as we discuss in the next chapter.

7.2 The irresistible rise of experiential learning

Part of the attraction of experiential learning is the widespread disenchantment with formal management development. There are many critics of the taught course and in recent times there has been a growing realisation that the complexity of the management process cannot be reproduced in class. Managers learn far more from day-to-day work, from colleagues, from observing others and drawing out lessons for the future than they ever can in formal programmes (Mumford 1997). Indeed, as an introduction to management, it is said that formal training can be actually disabling because it gives people the impression that they know how to manage when they really only know about some concepts, techniques and tools (Mintzberg 2004).

The case against formal education is further strengthened when we consider the claims of writers such as French and Grey (1996), that the formal model of Anglo-American management education inhibits critical questioning and reduces participants to the status of dependent recipients of knowledge untested and unsubstantiated by the direct personal experience of those imbibing it. This, they describe, as the 'banking' model of learning. 'Deposits' are made to this cerebral 'account' which grow cumulatively and are drawn upon as enhanced human capital. Another way of saying this is that empty vessels are filled up with knowledge so that they become competent practitioners.

For many senior development practitioners and theorists alike, this is anathema. Mumford (1999) and Woodall and Winstanley (1999), for example, believe that MD should *not* be something *'done'* to people but something they *'do'* for themselves. Besides, merely giving people knowledge, skills and a good appreciation of orthodox thinking about management is not enough. It falls far short of the true potential of MD which should be about helping individuals achieve no less than a 'different state of being' (i.e. a generic change in character and orientation) which equips them for the demanding world of modern management (Mumford 1999). This commitment to 'whole person' development provides an ideological rationale for experiential learning (and MD) as a 'totalising process'.

However, other factors also explain the new hegemony of informal (experiential) learning. One of these factors is the changing role of the manager. As we saw in Chapter 2, modern research on the manager emphasises the human skills and behaviours of managing. The manager is coach, mediator, lynchpin of groups, enabler of the social process of organisation. S/he uses predominantly lateral relationships to stimulate divergent thinking, build the confidence of others and encourage the conditions for creativity and empowerment. These roles require self insight, sensitivity to the social process and to self/other interaction. Experienced managers say that they are more likely to develop these skills through reflection on naturally occurring experience than through off-the-job methods such as simulations, role-plays and exercises. However well designed, these formal techniques lack the immediacy and the real-time authenticity of live action (Hill 2004).

Other contextual factors have also come together to give impetus to informal learning processes. For example, with downsizing and re-engineering managers are now expected to do larger jobs and time pressures at work are increasing. Managers find it more difficult than ever before to take time to attend formal programmes off-site. This combines with the contemporary view that as part of their coaching role, line managers have a responsibility to develop the people they are responsible for and to use work-based incidents and experiences as learning opportunities. The declining commitment of organisations to longer-term career development and the shift to self-managed careers further strengthens the focus on experiential learning as the form of learning most appropriate to prevailing conditions. From the perspective of the organisation this also has the advantage of being (for them) a relatively inexpensive form of personal development.

The box below captures the dimensions of this new turn to experiential learning.

From instruction to learning: trends in MD

In a classic article Margerison (1994) suggested that MD is shifting from a focus on 'there and then' (and the technologies of case studies and reconstructions of 'dead' experience) to 'here and now' and the immediacy of 'live' experience within the work situation. These are the dimensions he suggested. Many of these themes will reverberate throughout this chapter.

- *From teaching to resourcing*: The trend is away from lectures and explicit teaching towards more interactive self learning. Increasingly teachers are becoming consultants and facilitators helping managers to define their own problems and work through them.
- *From programmes to contracts*: More locally designed learning; less standardised packages based on predefined programmes of education. Less teaching as an end in itself; more learning as a process of more individualised discovery.
- *From individual to group orientation*: While the traditional training emphasis has been on developing individuals, increasingly management learning is through the group, with teachers acting as facilitators of a 'learning community'.
- *From standard cases to real cases*: Moving from the study of case histories written up by professional developers to learners considering cases which are current and real to them so that work experience is brought into the arena of learning.
- *From delegating to developing*: Line managers are increasingly involved in MD. They are required to allocate tasks not just on the basis of functional efficiency but also as a vehicle for development. They are increasingly held to account for their development of others.
- *From inputs to outputs*: Moving from an ethos of filling people with knowledge and giving them skills to shaping a climate in which people develop their knowledge and skills through projects and tasks which are supervised and guided.
- *From fixed term to continuing education*: Continuous professional development (CPD) is replacing education and training as a one-off or episodic input for the

> emerging professional. Learning is becoming more flexibly organised so that it becomes embroidered throughout a professional life.
>
> - *From management education to experiential and 'existential' learning for managers*: Formal development still has its place but the educational process is moving nearer to managers' lives, to connect with their existential reality. This means that learning is increasingly becoming embedded in the fabric of managers' work and directed by them.
>
> Source: Adapted from Margerison, C. 'Action learning and excellence in management development', in Mabey, C. and Iles, P. (1994) *Managing Learning*.

Of course, the new enthusiasm for experiential learning can set up a false sense of contrast between informal and formal development which elevates the one and denigrates the other. However, as we examine in forthcoming chapters, in truth formal and informal both have their advantages and disadvantages and are of value for supporting very different kinds of learning. Indeed, defining them as polarities is misleading. Increasingly, in the most progressive organisations, formal and informal are becoming blended and mutually reinforcing. Sophisticated management courses incorporate the informal in the formal. They try to capture the experience of managing by becoming highly participative and led by the experiences of participants. Participants can bring in issues they are working on, share them with others in an atmosphere of support and challenge and test them against concepts and theories.

In the same way, the formal can support the informal by helping the individual with self assessment and self monitoring through appraisals, development planning and continuous professional development. Formal input at strategic points (e.g. when a manager moves to a new job, when s/he makes the transition from a functional to a general management position, etc.) can be extremely important for giving focus to informal, self-development processes and providing a broader framework for structuring and conceptualising the disjointed micro-experiences of organisational life (Murray 2003).

7.3 Experiential learning: only two cheers?

All the hoopla around experiential learning can blind us to its limitations. At its most populist, experiential learning means 'learning from the school of hard knocks': that is, you learn by trial and error, from making mistakes, getting punished then getting rewarded, finding things out by improvisation and then emphasising the positive. It is true that the lessons you learn in this way will go deep; however, this may be a rather laborious and time-consuming process of developing competence, not to say a little masochistic. As Mumford (1999) says, relying just on experience for your learning means that 'you get the test first and the lesson afterwards'.

Learning from experience alone can also lead to 'learned incapacity' in which people just learn how to avoid punishments, how to keep their heads down and get by. It can mean that people develop 'defensive routines' (Argyris 1995), tried and tested practices in which they feel competent in their comfort zones, but will not attempt anything unfamiliar. There is also the issue that the fast-paced, superficial processing of work and the constant shifts in wavelength involved in modern management all cut against learning reflectively from experience.

The primacy of the 'now' does not encourage retrospective reflection. 'Things that happen to you' do not promote personal growth, unless they are actively identified, deliberately analysed and positively reflected upon, then they become 'personal experience'. However, all the evidence (Mintzberg 1973; Watson 2001) suggests that most managers are not naturally reflective people, but action-oriented and most organisations are more likely to give lip service to experiential learning than actively promote it. Exclusively relying on 'learning by doing' that is blind to theory and is not set within a context of planned, conscious and supportive reflection may lead to far less real learning than the more demonised model at the other extremity – a menu-led, formal programme of development.

Mumford (1999) and Woodall and Winstanley (1999) perceptively sum up the main drawbacks with the experiential learning approach when it is used alone, unsupported by more formal approaches, unconnected to the planned processes of development. By itself, experiential learning is narrow and localised: the manager would find it difficult to appreciate the relevance of more general themes to the practice of managing. Learning for yourself in one organisation can also lead to romanticising parochial experience ('our ways are the best ways'). The pragmatism of direct experience needs to be supplemented by wider professional and academic knowledge.

There is also the point that we cannot experience everything directly in life: we have to learn from the experience of those who have gone before us which is passed down to us and which we draw on as truths learned vicariously (e.g. it is better to learn that stoves are hot by instruction rather than direct contact with them; Cunningham 2007). Then there is the issue that to rely on workplace learning as your main source of learning is to be a ticket-holder in a lottery. It may be that your boss is sympathetic to continuous development; you may have supportive colleagues and good role models. However, the very opposite of these conditions could equally apply as the organisational reality into which you have been thrown, with negative consequences for learning from work.

This last point is particularly important because it should puncture any sense of complacency that experiential learning is always superior to other forms of learning. Some of the literature on informal learning seems to take a rose-tinted view of the workplace as a crucible for learning, as if all organisations are seeking to become learning organisations. Many organisations are run by authoritarian bosses, with prescriptive systems and tight performance regimes. Doing the task always comes first and can endlessly displace the reflection and thinking needed to derive lessons for the future. In these circumstances, reliance on experiential learning will result in a very lopsided learning and could even mean learning the wrong lessons and developing the wrong behaviours.

'*Non schola sed intra indiscimus*', or 'we learn not for school but for life' was the slogan of young men in ancient Rome preparing for a life in politics. That also seems to be a fitting epithet for young people in the twenty-first century preparing for the use of legitimised power, or authority in management. It seems inconceivable that practical professions like Roman politicians or modern-day managers would prepare the next generation through any other means than experiential learning. The principle is sound, but the question remains. What are the conditions by which people are most likely to learn significantly from experience and what are the practical means by which these conditions can be met? MD as a discipline is still exploring these questions.

7.4 The nature of experiential learning

Whatever developers might wish or advocate, many studies (e.g. Daudelin 1996; Hill 1992) suggest that managers tend to value techniques over concepts, prefer the tangible to the abstract, are impatient with theory and are most likely to learn when the subject promises immediate practical application which will help them solve pressing problems. Despite the many individuals who defy this generalisation (who any teacher of management will have met), managers, by and large tend not to be reflective thinkers but pragmatic activists (See Chapter 2). As hyperactive 'doers' a learning experience which is embedded in the present and in the real-life work context with its pressures, politics and ambiguities is entirely appropriate.

The central tenet of experiential learning is that most of what we learn and understand comes from doing, that is, we take action, reflect and learn. Managers who have to handle constant interruption and juggle a relentless barrage of demands, think and learn in the context of action (Weick 1983). Typically, they get into things, do something, then reflect on the experience by making a series of adjustments to their actions so that a better fit between the 'needs of the situation' and the 'logic of the intervention' emerges. In Kierkegaard's phrase, managers 'live forward but make sense of life by thinking backwards'. It is through reflection that managers learn, but this can take various forms.

An important distinction suggested in the literature is that between unstructured and structured informal learning. Mumford (1989), in his famously influential model of learning types, made a differentiation between Type 1 or 'accidental/incidental' learning processes within an informal management process and Type 2 or 'opportunistic' learning processes within an integrated or planned management process (see box).

Mumford's famous 'learning types'

It is difficult to go very far in considering the literature on management development without coming up against Mumford's model which has been very influential in shaping thinking in the field and also this chapter.

Type 1: Informal management development – incidental/accidental learning

- occurs within management activities
- occurs incidentally to doing a task
- not planned in advance
- unstructured development
- owned by managers.

Learning is real, direct, unconscious and insufficient.

Type 2: Integrated management development – opportunistic learning

- occurs within management acivities
- task performance and development

- clear development objectives
- planned beforehand and reviewed
- structured for development by boss and subordinate
- owned by managers.

Learning is real, direct, conscious, substantial.

Type 3: Formalised management development – planned learning

- often away from normal managerial activities
- explicitly developmental
- clear development objectives
- structured by developers
- planned beforehand, reviewed as learning
- owned more by developers than managers.

Learning is conscious, relatively infrequent.

Source: Beardwell, J. and Claydon, T. (2007) *Human Resource Management*, p. 364; the material first appeared as Mumford, A. (1989) *Management Development: Strategies for Action*, CIPD.

7.4.1 Incidental learning

'Incidental/accidental learning' (Mumford's Type 1) happens all the time in management jobs. It is learning which is 'incidental' to doing something else, perhaps the handling of some instrumental management task or a social interaction. Despite not being planned or intentional, the learning can be very real and very valuable. So for example, during a selection interview, the manager gains some new insights into her patterns of talk and listening. Perhaps she notices that she listens selectively and is unduly influenced by emotional trigger words. Perhaps she realises for the first time that her phrasing of questions signals the responses she wants to hear or that she jumps in too fast with follow-up questions which foreclose on the candidate expressing his true position. It is like noticing things from the corner of your eye. All of these perceptions provide the self-developing manager with valuable data with which to experiment with different ways of behaving (Marsick and Watkins 1990).

Various commentators (Mumford 1989, 1999; Raelin 1998) believe that this type of learning offers excellent chances for insight and knowledge. It provides the best opportunities for flash-bulb moments or epiphanies, that is, sudden revelations of meaning, heightened self-awareness and the appreciation of new connections and patterns. Because the learning often centres around some highly charged incident, perhaps a personal setback or mistake which has unsettled us, the raw emotions which are evoked provide a spur to reflect. The lessons of experience go deep and are very memorable. Often the experience and the learning involved surprises us so much that it creates a sense of unease with the ordinary and familiar, causing us to look at it again freshly from a different angle. This provides the conditions for new thinking and the reframing of old problems in new terms.

Incidental learning is unpredictable, spontaneous and very real. Although Mumford (1989) describes this as 'accidental' learning, in fact it only happens when the manager is mentally prepared to recognise its value and reflect. This is learning which spins off of everyday process because the manager is intellectually curious and is receptive to learning when it emerges.

Marsick and Watkins (1997) and Mumford (1989) suggest that many situations, at work, in the family and in the community, have the potential for significant management learning. The fact that management is such a generic role and ultimately involves 'doing social life with skill and sensitivity' (Mangham 1986), means that the whole of life can become a field for personal discovery. For example, a business trip abroad may sensitise the manager to the influence of culture as a variable in his business calculations; being involved in a major restructuring and watching how it is handled may provide an *in vivo* case study of the listening, persuading, influencing skills which are needed. Equally it might provide a case study in how not to do it (Mumford 1997).

The value of incidental learning and the importance of being open to the lessons of experience seems incontestable. However, as most of the commentators in this area suggest (e.g. Smith and Morphey 1994; Salaman and Butler 1990), incidental learning is often only partly conscious. As we saw in Chapter 6, much is subliminal and involves tacit knowing (e.g. Nonaka and Takeuchi 1995; Polyani 1966), which is not always clearly articulated, even by the self to the self. It is also a random and haphazard form of development, certainly a rather hit-and-miss basis on which to establish a corporate MD programme.

It is for these reasons that those who champion experiential learning usually advocate the harmonisation of tacit and explicit learning. For example, Mumford's Type 2 approach, which he calls 'learning opportunistically', could perhaps without loss of meaning also be termed deliberate, structured and guided informal learning. Informal learning is whole-person learning based on the workplace, but, unlike incidental learning, is structured by the individual and/or the organisation, to maximise opportunities for reflection and development. It usually involves accomplishing a task, but it also challenges the manager to explicitly review the process of handling it.

7.4.2 Guided informal learning

Guided (or structured) informal learning, a synonym for 'opportunistic' learning (or Type 2) in Mumford's typology, involves both 'learning retrospectively' and 'learning prospectively' (Mumford 1989). By 'retrospective learning' theorists mean that managers are encouraged to step back from what has happened to them to review, analyse, consider and think. This requires the manager to deliberately take time out to reflect on what happened in a particular situation of success or failure (say the loss of a contract) or on a strand of behaviour over a period of time (e.g. the quality of decision-making in a committee) to define the variables which seemed important (e.g. interactions, identities, styles of behaving and cultural differences etc.). Is there any general learning here which can be transferred to situations which are likely to recur in future?

The truly experiential learner will be setting aside a regular period of time for reflection to consider 'What did I learn today?' or 'What are the lessons from my time working on the review committee?' S/he may be deliberately collecting stories of experience using perhaps a learning log or diary and reviewing it for continuing themes and insights. So, in the spirit of reflection, on returning from a difficult client meeting or presentation, the experientially-aware manager may be engaging in self dialogue around a series of searching questions.

- How effective was I and did I get the result I wanted?
- Did I really do adequate and appropriate preparation?
- Was I able to interpret the agendas of the actors and did I allow for these in my handling of the process?
- Who made the most influential contribution?
- What strategies and skills did they use, that is, what was their style and why did it impress me?
- What could I imitate in the future?
- If I had my time again would I do anything differently?

This self dialogue might also form the basis of a discussion with others. This is structured informal learning from real life. Managers often like this sort of learning because it is close to their realities, although initially they may be sceptical of the value of reflection on the mundane and ordinary and may regard the process as 'commonsense' (McCall and Lombardo 1988).

With practice, often using a facilitator, mentor and learning group (as we will see later on), managers learn to pull the fragmentary threads of experience into a coherent whole, to sense the deeper social processes involved and the context which provides the ground spring for action. Essentially, they learn to give a plausible account of experience, tell a story that makes sense – to themselves as well as the world. This can lead to the sort of breakthrough Argyris (1995) seems to mean in his term 'double loop learning'.

Practised regularly, enthusiasts say that retrospective reflection leads over time to an attitude of mind which recognises the value of learning as you are doing it, which understands the importance of transforming blind experience into usable knowledge and creates meanings which allow experimentation with new forms of behaviour more likely to be effective.

The benefits of retrospective learning

Here are some of the self-assessed learning gains which managers have reported from reflecting on past experience. Ultimately, it is about making 'learning how to learn' a living reality in the conduct of everyday life:

- learning more about self; strengths and weaknesses; habits of dealing with situations;
- understanding your preferred thinking and learning styles;
- knowing when to ask for help and how to ask;
- learning how to manage the relationship with your boss; developing the confidence of knowing when you are competent to operate on your own and when you need thier continuing involvement;
- learning how to scan the environment, discern patterns before they crystallise and anticipate problems that may come up;

▶

- learning how to ask critical questions; to play devil's advocate and ask what-if questions;
- learning how to appraise a situation and consider questions from a variety of viewpoints;
- learning about the social processes in groups and how to shape these in terms of group differences;
- learning how to operate with a variety of styles; knowing when to push, when to back off, and so on; how to work with people to gain their commitment;
- learning how to operate in ways consistent with a culture in order to change it;
- learning how to use power structures and networks of relationships to achieve organisational goals.

Source: Adapted from Smith, B. and Morphey, G. (1994), 'Tough challenges: how big a learning gap?' *Journal of Management Development*, Vol. 13, No. 9.

A commonly cited spur to retrospective reflection is the desire to learn from tough challenges, adversity and setbacks. Managers typically focus most seriously on mistakes as foci for meditation and seek to find generalised learning to avoid falling into similar traps in the future. However, Smith and Morphey (1994) and McCall and Lombardo (1988) have found that managers are less likely to subject their success to the same degree of rigorous, post-mortem dissection. Success is likely to be seen mainly as vindication of our great good sense and the conditions which brought forth good fortune often remain unexamined. Smith and Morphey (1994) suggest that this is a complacent attitude which inhibits learning.

By far the main stimulus to reflection seems to be the challenge of unfamiliar circumstances (e.g. a promotion with more demanding responsibilities; a stretch assignment, etc.) where managers become painfully aware that their old behaviours and skills no longer seem to work. Mumford (1989) talks of the 'jolt' or 'shock of the new'. Novelty forces the managers to reframe issues and sensitises them to new thinking, especially if they have an enquiring attitude of mind which is responsive to fresh learning.

Retrospective learning is the prelude to 'prospective' learning (Mumford 1989). So, we have learnt 'x' from analysing the past, what can we do with it in the future? Will it be possible to develop a plan so that we will behave differently in the future? This is what experiential learning really means. It is about diagnosing opportunities for learning; recognising key incidents as 'growth points'; thinking aloud as you find a way through the treacle of ambiguity and complexity; finding words to make some kind of sense of confusing phenomena; hearing yourself talk in fumbling to discover rules of practice and the conditions in which they probably apply. Some managers can do this alone; most need a structure for reflection, usually a form of structured dialogue, one-to-one or group.

Prospective learning is usually planned learning. As we will see, experiential learning is often at its most successful when criteria of development and personal growth are incorporated in managerial decisions about the allocation of tasks, the setting of work priorities, the organisation of assignments, performance appraisal and development plans. Experiential learning is also planned when experience is explicitly shared through a team, mechanisms are set up to capture learning and people are helped to critically distance themselves from experience through mentoring so that they avoid the mistake of replaying the scripts of the past.

7.5 Conditions of experiential learning

7.5.1 Blocks to learning

If experiential learning was natural to managers and easy to do, most managers would practise it as a matter of course. However, commentators agree that most managers will not do explicit reflection unless the process is formally organised and, even so, many managers find this difficult to do (Marsick and Watkins 1997; Mumford 1997; McCall 1988).

There are many reasons why day-to-day opportunities of informal learning are not seized by managers. Perhaps the most common reason is that they fail to understand that tasks also contain within them the potential for learning. Managers may focus so much on the instrumental aspects of doing that they miss the lessons of development which these embody. Others will understand the growth potential of mundane forms of management experience but lack the discriminating constructs to freeze-frame the flow of managerial life to extract important lessons. This sense-making is particularly difficult where anticipation of future learning involves imaginative projection into the future and preparation for the requirements of more challenging jobs as their careers unfold. Because the lessons do not seem immediately relevant to the immediate situation, they can be ignored. Too often, managers fail to value their own experience highly enough or give it serious attention as a catalyst for professional and personal growth (Raelin 1998).

In this the culture of the organisation is important. It will seem unnatural for managers to think about learning at work if the task is given overwhelming importance and the pace, volume of work and reward system stresses constant activity and meeting tight deadlines. A blame culture will inhibit people from experimentation with new behaviours or looking back dispassionately at experience to derive lessons. Authoritarian, rule-dominated cultures may block people from thinking and acting creatively or breaking with cycles of repetitive activity and finding new ways. Complacency about current practices or fatalistic disengagement – that change is not possible or will lead to desired improvements – will also dilute the motivation to learn on the job.

Politics can hold back the spirit of self learning. For example, managers are hardly likely to develop change management skills by finding opportunities to innovate in their job if they believe that top management is insincere in its rhetoric and that taking initiative may even damage their careers. Managers have well-worked constructs for getting by, constructs of survival behaviour in their employing organisation, and will only embrace experiential self learning when they believe there is ample evidence that top management will reward what it says it wants.

7.5.2 Opportunities for learning

As Thomson et al. (2001) suggest, experiential learning only really prospers where senior managers are proactive in building a climate of support and facilitation. For this to happen they need to be sympathetic to the values of informal learning, recognise its importance and be trained in identifying development opportunities. They will also need to mitigate the increasing intensification of work by redesigning jobs and deliberately building-in protected space for thinking and learning.

An environment supportive of informal learning values a planned, explicit and integrated approach. Informal learning is blended with formal learning; programmes are led by performance review and learning goals; assessment of learning needs is jointly agreed between the individual and the organisation; support mechanisms are set up to allow guided self analysis and to embed self-development in group process; there is periodic review to ensure that learning is truly integrated in daily work.

Organisations that are best geared up to maximising the conditions for learning of their managers try to replace the randomness of chance learning with ordered processes which enhance learning of all kinds. The box (below) provides an example of a blue-chip company which has attempted to create a systematic and supportive learning climate.

How Shell does it: 'blended learning' in a multinational

Royal Dutch/Shell has long been regarded as a model for progressive MD among blue-chip companies. In recent years Shell has diversified its corporate structure and developed a new global strategy; it has made similarly transformational changes to its MD system.

Until recent times, the philosophy of MD at Shell could be described as 'growing your own timber'. Shell used common criteria for job descriptions and performace management system ratings to plan MD for cohorts of managers and for individuals. But in recent years the shift has been away from standardised promotion criteria to individualised appraisals and assessment using balanced score card and 360-degree feedback. Central planning of job assignments has been replaced by individuals and line managers taking ownership of flexible development opportunities.

The old approach of 'planned development' is being replaced with departments 'growing their own' and individuals 'growing themselves'. While planned job rotation, action learning and formal training still have their place, a more flexible pattern has emerged.

Opportunities for Type 1, informal, unstructured and unconscious learning, are deliberately built into patterns of job rotation and the design of assignments which bring the manager into contact with colleagues from other cultural backgrounds and allow them to work across boundaries. Working at Shell seems to offer many opportunities for developing cultural sensitivity and observational learning from role models.

However, it is in Type 2 learning where the Shell programme seems to come alive. Different kinds of assignment, that is, line *v* staff; turnaround business situations *v* starting-up business situations; at home *v* at 'arms length', provide a variety of management experience. An open-resourcing approach to career development and experiential learning tailored to the ambitions of the individual allow people to apply freely for internal vacancies which come up, supported by a system of internal referrals.

Experiential learning also finds support in action learning and action reviews. Shell sees these as opportunities for people from different disciplines and different levels of seniority to work together on commonly perceived problems and for real-time learning to take place. They are also seen as a means by which young staff can meet with senior executives and gain something through the social interaction with those revered in the company for their competency and *gravitas*.

At Shell, up-and-coming managers have mentors. Line managers are also expected to take on a proactive role in developing others. The system puts a lot of emphasis on people admitting what they don't know and using social networks to get (ultimately political) advice on what works and what won't work in the culture. There are a lot of opportunities in this system to reflect on how you have learnt; what you have learnt; the conditions for your learning and what you will do with it.

Finally, Shell offers Type 3, more formalised learning experiences. Leadership programmes are available not just for the most senior executives but for staff who put themselves forward as leaders. In these programmes leaders develop leaders by becoming coaches to their reports. Part of the process involves aspiring leaders to build a portfolio of evidence of their leadership effectiveness and coaches/mentors help to find business situations where leadership skills can be developed and tested.

Questions

- Which aspects, if any, of Shell's development programme impress you as progressive?
- Do you think the experiential learning parts of this programme will be as influential as those which are more formalised?
- If you were an MD adviser, are there other issues you would want to consider for a blended programme?

Source: Adapted from Mahieu, C. (2001) 'Management development in Royal Dutch/Shell', *Journal of Management Development*, Vol. 20, No. 2; also Shell website available at www.shell.com.

Experiential learning prospers where managers define themselves as responsible for developing others. This encourages them to go further than just letting informal learning happen. They actively set up mentoring, coaching and group learning so that learning becomes an unexceptional, institutionalised part of everyday activity.

Managers concerned to build a learning climate will recognise their personal symbolic value as leaders and act as exemplars of learning, keeping abreast of new developments and showing that real managers are learning all the time in a rapidly changing world – if they are worthy of the description 'manager'. Senior role modelling is vital for lower management to understand why continual learning is important for personal growth and for it to become embedded within culture.

Building the culture is all important in creating a climate of informal learning. Daudelin (1996) suggests that you learn by observing what you have done time and time again and finding patterns in the familiar. However, the right conditions need to be present for the learning potential in everyday experience to be brought to the surface. Organisations committed to learning are adept at spotting informal opportunities for learning. They understand the importance of giving time and support to encourage reflection on what is taken for granted. They invest in building a climate in which people are prepared to recognise their strengths and weaknesses and address the emotions involved in making changes. They encourage the sharing of experiences, the surfacing of tacit knowledge and a spirit in which alternative viewpoints can be debated openly and in an atmosphere of trust.

All this amounts to using reflective practice as a deliberate tool of management learning. The manager acts as coach and brings in professional facilitation to help people admit mistakes, own up to what they don't know and learn with and from each other. Often that requires as much humility from the senior managers as it does from their reports; it means being committed to developing the self by acting as a catalyst for developing others (Raelin 1998).

Building a reflective process so that learning happens naturally and continually in the midst of practice can be one of the most important things any manager can do. Through reflection, people are encouraged to articulate their problems, to generate hypotheses about them, to test out theories of practice and evaluate the appropriateness of action. People reflect in different ways – one-to-one; with a peer group; with a boss; keeping a learning diary; often a professional facilitator can help, but not necessarily. Developing the habit of mind is more important than the precise technique. Reflection which questions experience, which provokes questions which would otherwise have gone unasked, which helps you look at a problem in another light, which creates a virtuous self-reinforcing process – retrospective learning; prospective learning, action and reflection – is surely central to any creative management process (Marsick et al. 1992).

7.6 Self-development

Conventional development programmes have often been accused of encouraging the passive acquiescence of learners in their learning. Self development (SD) on the other hand, actively engages managers in designing and taking forward their own development process. When learners are truly self-managing they are taking responsibility for their own careers. They do not wait for the HRM department to tell them where they will be placed next. They take their own development in their hands; they organise their own projects, secondments and career moves and build their own network of contacts (Marsick and Watkins 1997).

This sits well with the 'New Deal' at work. Declining job security and competitive markets encourage managers to acquire a wider range of skills than ever before. In a future where there will be fewer but more sophisticated managers, it is those who have flexibility, who are self-starting, self-motivating and self learning and can adapt to constant change who will be the winners. Self-development seems an approach well suited to changing times and is also a sign that individuals no longer trust organisations to manage their development or their careers. Indeed, Handy (1985) goes as far as to say that self-developing managers may be the only managers who will survive in the age of portfolio careers and dynamic, virtual organisation of the future.

However, in the more progressive organisations, the responsibility for learning is not just left with the learners. As self-development, often tied to continuous learning, becomes established as a new orthodoxy, so the employment contract shifts to the employer, abdicating responsibility for employment in the longer term but instead providing continued opportunities for 'employability' while the individual is on the payroll. Organisational support for learning while doing, for helping people take advantage of development opportunities at work, for self-development in its various forms, is part of that new 'psychological contract'. Sometimes this is formalised in explicit 'learning agreements' or 'learning contracts' which spell out how the organisation will help the manager to become the infinitely flexible person who the organisation says it wants (we look at the 'downside' of SD in Chapter 10).

However, when the conditions are right, the advantages of SD for the individual can be considerable. Self learners typically engage in distance learning leading to new qualifications; they achieve higher levels of performance, develop new portfolios of skills and powerful CVs which give them enhanced promotion prospects (Megginson and Whittaker 1999) However, testimony by participants suggest that it is at the level of self-concept, self-awareness, self-motivation and self-confidence that SD shows the biggest pay-offs. People talk about finding new meaning in their work and greater job satisfaction when they embrace an ethic of continuous learning and improvement. They feel they are achieving more of their potential, growing in management mastery and wisdom. SD develops their sophistication as a player and raises their self expectations of what they can achieve in a management career.

At its best, SD helps managers to become 'reflective practitioners' (Schon 1983), which we discussed in Chapter 6. SD helps people to recognise and articulate the tacit theories of the world by which they operate, problematise routine situations and taken-for-granted assumptions by challenging people to look at the familiar with new eyes. Those who enter fully into its spirit become Schon's 'practical theorists', able to reframe situations using a repertoire of constructs they have worked out from their grounded experience. They develop the capacity to improvise tailored solutions and act imaginatively beyond the deadening effect of standard models and a narrow rationalistic logic. In sum, they interpret and make sense of experience for themselves. The evidence suggests that real self developers not only greatly improve their life chances but those of the organisations in which they are based.

7.6.1 The philosophy and practices of self-development

Where self-development is embedded, managers take control of their learning. They take primary responsibility for choosing what, when and how to learn. They decide on their own development objectives, and how to achieve them; they initiate learning activity and evaluate the outcome (Antonacopoulou 2000). Ultimately SD is based on the belief that managing self is the first step for empowering others. As Yukl (1998) provocatively asks, 'unless I can take charge of myself, how can I take charge of situations and of people?' Taking responsibility for yourself and directing your learning, becoming self-aware, self-confident and culturally sensitive, is perhaps an essential test of your maturity and fitness for management. Pedler et al. (1990) memorably calls this 'managing from the inside out'.

Self-development is an active form of learning and is consistent with the values of *andragogy* (Knowles 1990) which we discussed in the last chapter. It is active, self-engaged learning in which the individual manager drives the process of learning.

Self-development can take many forms, but real SD involves the development of the whole person, not merely technical capabilities, however important these may be. It is therefore learning which goes deep and is consistent with the ambitious definition of MD as a totalising process mentioned earlier. When it is done skilfully, it fundamentally alters how you understand the world and brings into play latent talents. It relies ultimately on the motivation of individual learners wishing to push forward to achieve their potential and informal groups of learners networking together to create new synergies by sharing their thoughts and feelings. However, SD works best where there are some structures which substitute for trainers yet allow flexibility (facilitators, learning contracts, mentors, peer support, ALS, etc.), and the organisation is supportive and creates opportunities for self learning to happen (Pedler et al. 1990).

There is no formula for doing self-development. SD is about exposing yourself to new situations and understanding more about yourself through self-reflection. In terms of SD techniques, the only guideline seems to be discovering what works for you in the organisational conditions in which you find yourself. There are no techniques specific to SD; they are continuous with those used in experiential learning as a whole (Pedler and Burgoyne 2004).

Megginson and Whitaker (1999) suggest that SD should start with personal stocktaking. They suggest the use of *diagnostic tools* such as a 'learning life line' or a 'dissatisfaction mind map' or 360-degree feedback, workbook exercises or even attendance at an assessment centre. Learning style inventories can generate insight, although for some managers the abstract categories can shut down imaginative thinking. Informal CPD plans can be used by the individual to define priorities for development and mobilise the inputs of significant others, helpers in self learning.

Keeping a written record of your experiences, a *learning log*, perhaps categorised by key themes or issues which seem important, may help you find patterns which suggest vicious cycles of thought, emotion and action you will want to break in the future. As with the keeping of a diary, this requires self-discipline, but enthusiasts say that the learning is well worth the effort because it provides a basis for periodic self review. The learning log (which could be an e-log) will become even more valuable if you can make it into a portfolio in which trusted helpers in your learning can share personal interpretations of experience and give you feedback. For those of you interested in learning logs go to Barclay's (1996) review of best practice in the area.

A development of this is the new interest in *storytelling*. Telling stories of yourself to others is a way of making sense of complex and often contradictory life experience. They are a valuable way of understanding situations as a whole and representing them as human dramas with characters, storylines and archetypal themes of the human condition. The value of sharing stories is that people soon come to realise that their experiences are just variations on recurring human scripts (see Dalton 1993; Gabriel 2000). Storytelling is increasingly being used as a way of understanding the emotions, beliefs and values which drive us and are a powerful tool for provoking discussion and self insight.

As we will see, *mentoring* is also a valuable medium for hearing yourself put into words issues which have been bottled up within. Group reflection also helps SD and *action learning sets* (ALS), we look at later, have been described as self learning through the group process. Developing others can also be a self-development approach. As this author can personally testify, acting as a facilitator for an ALS, as a mentor/coach or being a teacher forces you to reflect very clearly on what *you* have learnt as a manager and what is involved in the mysterious process of managing.

Some, all or none of these techniques may help the self developer. The most important factor is having a ceaseless spirit of enquiry, a real desire to have a clear understanding of yourself and others within the organisation.

7.6.2 The skills of the self developer

While the case for self-managed learning seems strong, for it to become a living reality managers must want to take responsibility for their own learning and have the sensitivity and skill to do so. The most committed self developers are likely to be those who are dissatisfied with their performance and want to do better. Very often it is early failure or the shock of the new which brings managers to question their existing understandings and acts as the spur to self-development. Typically too, it is at the early stage in the typical management progression within a job (i.e. the 'taking-hold' phase) when the manager is still adjusting to its demands, and it is a challenge, that s/he is likely to engage in self learning. Katz (1982) suggests there are three stages of an individual's tenure in a job – early, responsive, unresponsive – and most learning happens in the first two when the manager still feels challenged.

Although committed, purposive self-development may always be a minority activity, there is much that organisations can do to create the right climate for it to become a widespread practice. The trick is to encourage managers to be curious, to convince them that they will feel more in control if they regard their whole field of lived experience as a valued source of learning, that experimentation with informal feedback can lead to real self-discovery which will improve their game and much of this can be planned.

So what mind-set and micro-personal skills do managers need to be self developers?

Diagnosing your own learning needs

As well as a good understanding of self, managers need to have a fairly clear picture of what they want to achieve in their career. The skills which are needed here are the qualities of self-knowing, of being honest with yourself about strengths and weaknesses and being realistic about future prospects. In short, it means being able to stand back and evaluate your performance from the viewpoint of an imagined, critical judge. For many people this is an extremely difficult task. However, if done in a spirit of candour and resisting self-delusion it is also self-empowering. Unlike a management development programme where the design is based on what a development specialist perceives to be the learning needs of an entire management population, self-testing allows a far more sensitive appreciation of your learning needs. It also gives managers confidence in selecting appropriate learning opportunities and motivates them to constantly seek to deepen and extend their skills, not relying on the organisation to do this for them (Mumford 1980).

Organising your own learning

From this personal stocktaking, the self developers will probably go on to design their own learning objectives and action plan. This plan will go deeper than the official PDP and be more personal. Truly self-managing learners have broad plans for their careers in the longer term. They have a picture in their mind's eye of how their careers may progress, that is, the experience they will need in different functions at different points in the career cycle; the qualifications they will need; how they can gain a personal profile in the eyes of those higher up by being associated with the right prestigious project at the right time. The personal plan will be endlessly flexed around the vicissitudes of organisational life but it will remain a steady fixed point which guides work agendas.

> **Pause for thought**
>
> ### Socrates and the examined life of self-reflection
>
> Socrates famously advocated the search for wisdom by examining prevailing norms of behaviour and commonsense views, subjecting them to sceptical inquiry. What is obvious and natural often turns out not to be so on critical examination. The knowledge into which we are socialised can dissolve into contradiction and myth when considered critically and in the light of our own life experience, if we reflect seriously upon it. Equally, things that look easy, like dancing or making a pot from clay, only seem easy from a distance, but are very difficult to do, and often we can only understand these activities by trying them ourselves. Managing and leading can be like this.
>
> #### Question
> *How far do you think the Socratic model of seeking wisdom from reflective experience has relevance to the modern manager?*

Recognising and using opportunities for personal growth

As the self developer practises, s/he is likely to become aware that learning opportunities are all around him or her at work and in social life and begins to develop a critical understanding of the different benefits they can confer. This means accurately recognising the learning potential of serendipitous experience, for example, accidental involvement in a project which gives access to potential sponsors, a network of contacts, the chance to learn new skills and to learn from others. As a self-starter and self-organised learner, s/he will not be waiting for the experience to happen but seek out the experience needed (Pedler et al. 1990; Mumford 1980; Megginson and Whittaker 2003).

When self learners develop the mind-set which sees the broad field of everyday experience as material for personal development, they come to pay more attention to behaviour in a wide variety of human settings. They find themselves asking: What is really happening here? What can be learned from observing people trying to get what they want from situations? What learning can be gained from accidents of personal history and fortuitous contacts, both inside and outside of work? Although I may be currently doing something that bores me, are there some skills and knowledge I can learn here and from others that will help me in the future?

Reflecting on yourself

'Only know thyself' was the plea of the Delphic oracle (Mumford 1980). All thoughtful action stems from our concept of the self. Self-reflective managers who want to grow in maturity and self-awareness will turn the searchlight on themselves. They will be self-critical, self-reviewing and self-testing. They will be looking at their self-presentation in terms of the perceptions which they impute to others. So, if there is a mistake at work involving their leadership, self-reflecting managers will risk the possible loss of self-esteem involved by recalling events in their head and empathically placing themselves in the minds of others. It becomes a sort of stream of consciousness which might go like this:

> Was there something in what I said, how I constructed the argument, how I gave instructions and delegated the tasks that could have caused the misunderstanding that led to the 'cock-up'? In hindsight, why did Jim look puzzled and Joan have a quizzical expression? Perhaps I didn't communicate clearly.

It seems that people differ in the degree to which they can undertake this imaginative empathy and reconstruct an accurate picture of others' perceptions of their behaviours. However, it is this sense-making that can lead to real breakthroughs in self-insight so that the flat words on the appraisal report, 'Joan's interpersonal skills of leadership and communication need attention', take on a living meaning for you, and you know what to change.

Of course, looking at ourselves from the perspective of others is emotionally difficult because it forces us to own up to aspects of ourselves which we might prefer not to examine. Critical self-examination may show a performance gap, make us sensitive and dent our self-confidence. It is a fine balancing point. Managers need self-understanding to become life-long learners. However, too much self-analysis can be disabling in a profession which is all about self-confidence, having the courage to make judgements, taking a line in ambiguous circumstances, being resilient and determined (Pedler et al. 1990, 1999). Neurotic paralysis is the last thing the manager needs.

Seeking out and attending to feedback

It follows from the above that self-awareness implies an ability to listen and reflect on the comments of others. This information may be critical and upsetting and threaten our self constructs, but it is also an important stimulus for learning.

What distinguishes the genuine self learner from others is that they are prepared to take some social risks such as admitting insecurity or incapacity by asking for feedback and then of opening themselves to criticism which may prove wounding. Are there consistencies in the commentary which the manager has to address? Reviewing negative comment and considering it impartially is part of the 'self watching self' capacity all managers need to have (Mangham 1986).

Mumford (1980) believes that active listening is one of the key skills of effective developers. He says that they should listen for cues about their behaviour. What is being said which can be used as practical data to work with for behavioural change? Good listeners concentrate on what is being said, not screening out comments which do not conform to their 'ideal self' construct, not making assumptions in advance about what commentators are going to say and not filtering reception of the message through their feelings about the speaker. Good listeners learn more about themselves because their listening encourages candour and disclosure. They show 'attentiveness' and responsiveness', so people tell them more. By degrees, active listeners can become privy to much of the gossip which swirls around them in organisations; they come to understand their reputation and the labels which are applied to them. This is valuable information for any adjustments to 'self in the world' they may want to make.

Being honest with yourself

What managers then do with this data will tell us a lot about whether they are genuinely committed to self-development or just going through the motions. Do they try to deny the credibility of the data with excuses rather than examine it impartially? Do they try to undermine the credibility of the reporter? Do they impute malevolent intentions? Do they insist that the criticisms only apply historically or to specific circumstances not to the generality of their behaviour? (Mumford 1980). All these are the reactions of a manager who does not want to face up to personal issues and regards self-development more as a rhetorical exercise or 'impression management' than a genuine tool for personal growth. We all know when we are being intellectually self-deceiving and SD requires authenticity, especially with ourselves (Pedler et al. 1990; Dent 1999).

However, this is not to say that the self-learning manager has to take on board others' definitions without examination. Their data is useful because it often expresses a community's definition of an individual filtered back to them; it needs to be taken seriously but considered in a discriminating way. For example, if someone at work says that people think you too accommodating and seek to please, the reflective response would not be to immediately incorporate this isolated perception in your general construct of the self but to look for evidence more broadly (Mumford 1980). What exactly have you done to merit such a definition? Are you guiltily aware that there may be some substance in the claim? Can you recall times when your behaviour may have been interpreted in this way or are we dealing here just with the selective perception of one partial observer (Mumford 1989; Raelin 1998)? You may want to check this perception with those you trust, and are in a position to comment with authority.

Choosing and observing good role models

Truly self-developing learners seem to have the capacity to observe others' behaviour with perceptive understanding. This is no mean feat. Firstly, it requires the ability to choose good role models, an understanding of who is doing a good job and why. It also means being able to 'role take', to empathically enter into the 'life world' of those you model. What strategies are these exemplary managers following when they are acting effectively? This means having well-developed and sophisticated constructs for making sense of managerial behaviour and developed social skills to encourage role models to articulate their behaviour. It also means having the skill and courage to selectively experiment with those behaviours which you admire and mesh them into your personal style so that they seem organic. Again, this is something which is not easy to do (Mumford 1980; Dent 1999).

Reviewing your learning

As self-reflection becomes part of everyday life, for the true self developer the desire to learn can become insistent and self-generating. The pragmatic career reasons which may have first impelled self-directed learning becomes replaced by a sense of curiosity and a genuine desire to become a truly well-informed, insightful and wise manager, to practise as a master of the craft.

Taking experiential learning seriously, the self developer may set aside regular periods of time for self-reviewing, not in a mode of masochistic fault-finding but more in a spirit of thoughtful enquiry. S/he may take to keeping stories of experience. Review may be undertaken as a solitary stream of memory and consciousness exercise, but its real potential may be best realised when self insights are shared with others in peer groups (Pedler et al. 1999).

As we have said, managers tend not to be reflective analysts; they prefer to immerse themselves in experience and learn by trial and error, developing rules of practice as they go, which they use in future situations. However, reviews which are embedded in some models of learning help managers to think beyond mere *events* (e.g. 'In interviews I have learned not to talk too much') to reflect conceptually on *process* (e.g. 'I find that I have to resist a tendency to seek for certainty and force myself to accept ambiguity which is often the only way of solving the problem. I can do this best when I allow things to take their course, resist making early judgements and allow the reality of the situation to emerge').

This is the basis for 'watching yourself doing', the process by which you begin to conceptualise your learning, judging, thinking and so on and the conditions under which you work well and when you work less well and make the necessary adjustments, building on strengths and compensating for weakness (Mangham 1986).

Pause for thought

Where are you as a self-developing manager?

If you are already a manager you might like to consider these questions in terms of your professional practice. If you are not yet a manager you might still like to consider how you are learning from everyday life.

- What do you know about yourself as a learner? Under what conditions do you learn best?
- Which experiences in your career so far have been most important to you as influences on your personal growth?
- How far has your learning been accidental or planned by others rather than planned by you? Are you happy with this pattern?
- Can you think of instances when you have tried to seize opportunities for learning? How did you feel when you did?
- Could you define the conditions when you are most creative; think most clearly; make the best decisions; memorise data, act most confidently?
- Have you tried to find ways of maximising these conditions in your work environment?
- Does your organisation help you to become a self-managing learner?
- Do you think you are good at identifying other people as helpers in your learning and cultivating them?

7.6.3 The organisation and self-development

For the employer, self-development has a number of benefits. The conflict between organisations striving for economic efficiency through downsizing and delayering and managers seeking career progression can be softened through self-development. Self-development, if it is supported by resources, offers employees a rationale and an opportunity for flexibility, greater independence and an opportunity to continue to learn and develop their skills. For many managers personal growth is one of the most important reasons for staying with a company. Self-development programmes which provide organisational support in the form of horizontal moves, a choice of secondments, projects, time off for study and so on helps recruitment and retention of self-motivated learners and enhances their commitment to the organisation (Megginson and Whitaker 2003).

Where the organisation recognises a commitment to help the individual with self-directed learning and explicitly integrates learning with work, we can talk of 'continuous professional development'. Marsick and Watkins (1997) define CPD as a process in which learning is an ordinary part of work; learning is continuous and life-long (although conducted in different organisations during a career); learning involves not only the improvement of individual performance but also that of the work unit. CPD becomes a reality, not just a slogan, when the organisations acts to remove barriers to learning, gives rewards for self-development, builds a climate in which teaching others to learn is part of the culture. Usually this is expressed through 'learning partnerships' in which the organisation commits itself to support the managers' own goals for development, not those forced on them. While this has long been established practice in Japan, it is very new in the West.

Where CPD is flourishing it is an indication that the organisation has turned away from a culture of training and is moving to a culture of learning. It is a sign that the organisation understands the importance of harnessing the brainpower and commitment of all its members and is well on the way to creating a climate in which everyone takes responsibility for learning and self-improvement.

The continuous professional development cycle

Figure 7.1 The continuous professional development cycle

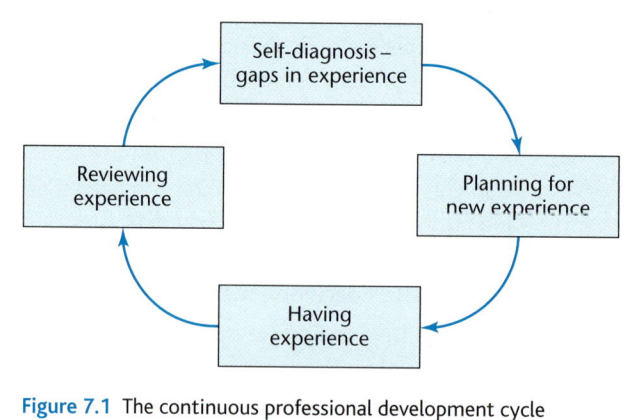

Where CPD is a living reality within the organisation, the self developer will be supported at different stages in the cycle above.

Self diagnosis: can be encouraged with workshops, psychometrics and self-test exercises linked to the PDP.

Planning for experience: involves career advice, guidance and preparation for work opportunities.

Experience: involves rotational schemes, secondments, shadowing and so on.

Reviewing experience: includes feedback, discussion and support to reflect on personal styles of thinking, learning and behaving and gives the developer the protected space that may be needed to experiment with different approaches.

All this is very good for the organisation's prospects for the future. A continuous learning culture in which managers are genuinely concerned with professional development helps the organisation to learn faster and to keep its competitive edge (Cunningham 2007). If individual learning can be facilitated and integrated with collective learning processes the organisation may be well on the way to creating the conditions in which learning and reviewing experience becomes a reflex of ordinary behaviour. It might even be on the road to making learning integrated and synonymous with work and putting in place the foundations of a real-life learning organisation. In these happy conditions, rarely achieved, CPD becomes one of the main drivers for integrating MD and OD in building a culture in 'which learning how to learn' is the guiding value.

Pause for thought

The Apprentice: a study in self-development

At the time of writing, *The Apprentice* – a popular BBC reality show with cult status, now sold to the rest of the world – was showing on British TV. It follows a simple format. A group of aspirant job seekers are giving various tasks to determine their suitability for higher management which they conduct competitively. The contestants find that the twelve weeks of exercises and projects is very demanding. Interviewed on camera afterwards, almost all the contestants reflect on how they have developed as learners.

Here is what one of the contestants says:

> The whole structure of the show with its winners and losers theme, boardroom visits, critical feedback from the boss and from your colleagues, focuses your mind on how you are perceived . . .

Part assessment and development centre, part learning community, part performance appraisal, part self-development exercise, *The Apprentice* formula seems to encourage real reflection on the practical art of management, at least at the operational level.

Questions
If you know the show, do you think that it is a realistic simulation of management life? In terms of the foregoing discussion, what opportunities for self learning are available and what skills do contestants use to develop themselves?

Source: *The Apprentice*, with Sir Alan Sugar; BBC TV

7.7 Methods of experiential learning

As we have argued above, informal learning is most effective when it is planned; there is an attempt to explicitly identify experiential opportunities for learning in the structure of work and incorporate analysis on what has been learned. The rest of this chapter examines the way work can be organised to release the potential for development and the main methods of on-the-job learning.

Planned informal learning starts with a PDP-led assessment of learning needs. As we have seen, assessment can take various forms. At a minimum it should involve an identification of the conditions under which the manager learns best, a review of their core skills (observation, decision-making, judgement, analysis, etc.) and a review of current and potential learning opportunities at work. This assessment provides the rationale for then combining the methods of informal learning into a plan which exposes the managers to new situations in a graduated way so they can grow.

A common feature of this class of workplace learning is that it increasingly involves evidence-based evaluation. It is often linked to the keeping of a record of personal experience as demonstration of personal and professional achievement and development. Building a portfolio of accumulated personal data (learning logs, independent testimony of behaviour and attainments) is claimed to help individual, reflective insight (in the process of assembling the fragments, new ways of seeing emerge) and helps to drive review around the learning cycle (Fee 2001).

7.7.1 Learning from new responsibilities

This cluster of methods involves changes in job content and job context, usually involving the enrichment of work so that opportunities for learning are increased.

Secondments and attachments

We examine this form of work-based development in some detail in Chapter 12 to which the interested reader is referred. Here we will just consider some general themes.

Secondments involve moving individuals from their normal work situation and placing them in a different work context where the experience will be unfamiliar. Secondments can be part of a structured rotation programme for a group of managers to give them a standardised experience or they can be bespoke and designed around the individual.

It is common for someone groomed for a general management position to be found temporary placements in a range of functional departments as a way of broadening horizons, giving an overview of the complexity, diversity and challenge of management and understanding how specific disciplines gear into the general policy process. It is also a tool for immersing learners in the subcultures of key departments or the varying parts of an international business so that they gain a good appreciation of multiple interdependencies, multiple perspectives and work practices (Yukl 1998). In some exceptional cases secondments are used to help senior management keep in touch with the pressures of working at the sharp end, as used by Japan and strongly advocated by Revans (as in the *Back to the Floor* series on UK TV).

Big organisations are also keen on sending chosen managers at senior or middle level for a tour of duty to outside organisations. In some cases this may be a cynical exercise in getting rid of a sidelined or 'misfit' manager or sending a 'plateaued' manager on 'gardening leave'. However, it is also a serious development tool. So, secondments might be arranged with customers and suppliers to capture their perspectives on the organisation. A civil servant may be given the deliberate culture shock of a period of service in a commercial enterprise; a senior manager of a blue-chip company may be seconded to a charity, appointed as project manager on an aid project in the developing world or sent as a professional adviser where s/he will have to learn to use his or her organisational skills in an entirely different context. Sometimes it is a 'job swap' with an officer from a parallel, but different organisation.

Where the secondment is based on a sensitive definition of learning needs, is done by consent, happens at an appropriate juncture in an individual's career and is well planned and implemented, the learning gain can be considerable. Attachments can be a dramatic means of forcing managers to think afresh about their role and competencies, their fundamental values and modes of working. Attachments can give them new skills, cultural sensitivity and knowledge which can be transferred back home. Those who have had the experience often speak of it as broadening their understanding of management, often creating 'dissonance' which has forced them to re-examine their fundamental assumptions and management philosophy (Fee 2001). They talk of being more self-aware and tolerant of different approaches. This and the 'halo' effect of having done something different is usually held to outweigh the possible disadvantage of being politically marginalised or being given insufficient recognition for personal growth at the point of re-entry, which often happens. A well-planned and successful secondment, especially if it is augmented by a deliberate attempt to reflect on the experience (e.g. learning log, mentoring, knowledge transfer) can be a vehicle for promotion to a larger job.

Most evaluation studies (e.g. Yukl 1998) show that secondment encourages skill development and transfer. The main drawback (and this can be considerable in the average organisation) is that job rotation/secondments tend to lower productivity at the beginning as the attached person comes up to speed. This means that managers are unlikely to want to lose experienced workers in return for temporary substitutes, especially if these are on a fast track and will soon be moving on. Flourishing job rotation schemes seem to presume enlightened line managers committed to workplace learning and politically savvy MD specialists who can present programmes in terms of local interest.

Acting up

Another form of on-the-job learning from job enrichment is the time-honoured practice of 'acting up'. This involves junior managers temporarily taking on the role of their boss for a limited period of time. If this involves cover for longer than holiday relief (e.g. maternity leave, secondment, etc.) the knowledge and self-awareness gained can be significant. Where it is well planned, 'acting up' is an opportunity for the individual to appreciate the broader scope of decision-making, greater responsibility and different skills needed in the higher position and to experiment with different styles. It is also an opportunity for the organisation to consider their eligibility for promotion (Woodall and Winstanley 1999). The value of this learning experience can be augmented by the judicious use of 'helpers' for self-reflection (e.g. mentors, colleagues, etc.).

Tasks, projects and task forces

Projects can be of various kinds. Nothing tells the observer more about the sincerity of the organisation's commitment to learning than how it allocates responsibility for projects. Projects and tasks can be parcelled up and allocated to the manager with the most expertise, or tasks can be allocated on the basis of potential and development need (Yukl 1998). So, for example, HSBC has a system for matching the learning opportunities in different kinds of assignment with the development needs of managers as assessed by the learning plan. Assignments are graded in terms of complexity and matched against the growth needs of varying individuals. 'Talent spotting' lists are used as the basis for choosing people. Work is deliberately allocated with an eye to developing a cadre of internationally-minded managers. Other multinational companies (e.g. Ericsson, Unilever, etc.) operate a central clearing-house system in which subsidiaries propose local candidates for international assignments advertised on the corporate intranet and a panel of top managers selects on the basis of a matrix which includes task, career and personal development factors (Barnham and Oates 1991). Whatever the details, organisations genuinely committed to MD build development criteria into their placement decisions.

Projects might involve internal consulting, investigating the cause of a problem in depth – why the recruitment and retention rate for one group of staff is falling; why sales for a particular product are up in one market but down in another, and so on. The work will involve information collection, analysis and the presentation of results. The project might be a one-off investigation running alongside existing work or it could be part of a bigger programme involving participation in a cross-cultural working party cutting across the organisation.

Well-designed project work, with appropriate coaching support, can develop many management skills – problem-defining and problem-solving; analysis; teamworking; coordination; innovation. It is therefore the learning vehicle of choice of many organisations. Typically projects straddle the divide between formal processes of learning and informal learning. So, a typical project might start off as a formal inquiry into a company issue with a task component and planned development element but then become elaborated into an action-learning set with groups of managers helping each other derive personal insight and experiential growth (Mumford 1999; Yukl 1998).

Assignments, often used by multinationals for their high-flyers, involve troubleshooting commissions to some remote or ailing unit. This may be a turn-around situation where roving managers are required to make decisions in a stand-alone situation, taking on far more responsibility than they would at home and using their own judgement in difficult circumstances. Another type of stretch assignment would involve setting up a new operation in an unfamiliar setting with limited local or HO support. Perhaps there is a difficult local boss, no procedures to follow, no one immediately available to turn to for help – factors which are outside your control.

Most stretch assignments call for very visible leadership with little local support and your success or failure is apparent for all to see. That is why they are often used as part of management succession. McCall and Lombrado (1988) provide some excellent accounts of the coping strategies of managers in stretch assignments and the accelerated learning that seems to arise.

In these situations the risks of failure are high and they are extremely stressful. However, those who rise to the challenge often say that the learning involved in making independent decisions and living with the consequences is the best possible preparation for higher management. It tests your ability to operate on a larger stage, to use real business judgement, pull together a multidisciplinary team, handle the politics and get results despite adverse conditions. Participants believe they grow in resilience, flexibility, self-confidence and sophistication in managing people and power. Managing a major business or division of a company before the age of 35 seems to be the 'royal road' to the top in global companies and, despite the relative lack of research on the effectiveness of stretch assignments, they are very useful for gaining early visibility at the top and providing demonstrative evidence of having the 'right metal'.

Other planned experiential methods often used to expose young managers to the demands of higher levels and to broaden their skills include international task forces, leading investigative studies, acting as a representative on an important committee or working as an assessor in a management assessment centre. These experiences expose the 'up-and-coming' manager to the complexity of interwoven management problems which cross functional competencies and call for a corporate response. These are opportunities for relatively junior managers to be involved in genuine problems where risks have to be balanced and their decisions could have real effect on the company's fortunes. Involvement in these development experiences helps people learn quickly, to pitch above their level of seniority, gives them profile with the higher reaches and access to valuable networks across the organisation. They also, sadly, give you a high parapet from which to fall (very publicly) from grace (Margerison 1991).

Other work experiences

One of the strengths of Mumford's famous *Strategies for Action* (1989, 1999), and one which resonated with this author in his own erstwhile career as a manager, is its inclusion of life experience beyond the immediate context of the job as a source of relevant development in management. This is surely right. In a time when people are coming into management via unorthodox routes, it is empowering to suggest that life experience can be a preparation for managing. For example, there is much 'broadening and maturing' (whatever these terms really mean) to be gained from taking a position of responsibility in a charity, voluntary organisation or public body (e.g. board member, health authority member, school governor, etc.). Equally, serving as a representative of a professional organisation or industry association, becoming a counsellor in local government or holding an office in a union can be very valuable experiences for deepening awareness of the delights, responsibilities and frustrations of using authority. Indeed, these experiences may offer more insight into how power works than most jobs within a line hierarchy. So much of life experience is relevant to management, if reflected upon in the right spirit, that SD, imaginatively defined, can ultimately mean the analysis of everyday life for its lessons.

7.7.2 Learning from one-to-one

Managers often say that some of their most powerful learning has been through the influence of individuals. These may be inspirational senior figures in the organisation who have given emotional support to the aspirant manager, helping her to deal with the tensions of introducing change or confronting difficult challenges. They may be difficult or bad bosses who have unwittingly provided lessons in what not to do in a senior position. They may be colleagues who have infected you with their enthusiasm for a particular style or approach (McCall and Lombardo 1988). It is in social interaction that synergies arise; we become aware of new self insights and we are influenced to try new things. It is one of the reasons why the successful manager invariably has a rich and diverse network. In terms of planned experiential learning, there are several classic ways that managers can learn one-on-one.

Shadowing and observing

As we saw when considering self-development, managers often say they learn from observing skilled practitioners. Experiential learning programmes can go beyond casual observation. Shadowing 'star' managers and watching how they address problems allows observation to be systematic and focused. How do they chair a meeting, handle a disciplinary, make a presentation, win round a recalcitrant colleague, or make a case for a budget increase? These are opportunities for inexperienced managers to reflect on their own style and selectively imitate those they would seek to emulate. Evaluation of shadowing arrangements shows that learning is most effective when there is a careful matching between practitioner and observer (learning style; traits; values), and the observer is given some help in how to observe (Woodall and Winstanley 1999). For example, observers seem to often need a framework of behavioural categories to make sense of the stream of disjointed activity within management and practice in asking searching questions of the practitioner to understand the logic of their behaviour (Mumford 1989).

Learning from observation is an inexpensive form of experiential development which can be combined with other methods. The development potential of role modelling and shadowing often informs decisions to assign inexperienced managers of high potential as executive assistants to senior managers and to help induct women into management. For example, 'Network Ireland' helps management women to be matched in shadowing relationships so that the experiential wisdom of older women of surviving in the (still) male world of managing is passed on to the next generation (Fee 2001).

Coaching, mentoring, counselling and sponsoring

In recent years coaching and mentoring have moved to the centre stage of experiential approaches to development. Because so much has been written in this area, we only consider the main themes here and the interested reader is referred to one of the many specialist books on this subject (e.g. Parsloe 1999; Megginson and Clutterbuck 1995; Watson and Harris 1999, and so on). We will consider executive coaching when we look at leadership development. Although coaching, mentoring and counselling seem to blur together (at least to this author's mind) and distinctions are fine, they are treated here as separate entities.

Coaching is an essential part of the management job. Indeed, in recent times, the shift of the manager from directive controller to coach and facilitator of those doing the operational work has become part of the Zeitgeist. The essence of coaching is that a senior person, usually with authority, helps a more junior person become more effective. The harder end of coaching (directive coaching) which conjures up images of the manager as sports coach, is supervisory and task-led. It involves the manager giving clear instruction on what needs to be done, standards of performance and monitoring (Downey 1999; Mumford 1999). Coaching in this mode is very results-focused. It is about helping a colleague (often a subordinate) solve problems, make good use of their skills and become more proficient. It involves the manager-coach in defining standards and good methods and modelling desirable behaviour. The manager becomes the lesson s/he hopes to impart.

Non-directive coaching is the softer end of coaching. It implies an open facilitative style in which the coach doesn't so much instruct as guide the subordinate to a solution. Typically the coach helps the learner identify the reality of their situation, bring them to an appreciation of the balance of constraints, demands and choices (Parsloe 1999) inherent in the context and ask pointed questions to help the learner come to his or her own conclusions about appropriate action. This kind of coaching merges naturally with mentoring which we consider below. However, coaching is not just a management style of on-the-job learning, it is also a technique for planned development. In a recent Hays Group survey (Anon. 2003) over 70 per cent of respondents saw coaching as being a more effective method for changing behaviour than traditional training courses, and second only to learning from experience and feedback, as delivering real results management.

A CIPD survey in 2006 (CIPD 2006) found that 80 per cent of large organisations use external coaches for 'catalytic coaching' with their middle and senior managers. Coaching of this kind seeks to challenge existing habits of thought, provoke new thinking through a kind of Socratic questioning that is supposed to reveal deep values and encourages new behaviour within a context of feedback and guidance. Done well, this type of coaching can be a valuable tool for change management resulting in individual and organisational learning (Clutterbuck and Megginson 2005).

Bluckert (2005) suggests that the relationship between the coach and the coachee is the critical factor in coaching effectiveness. The coach's capacity will obviously be an issue in effectiveness but so will be the linkage to business strategy, values and objectives and top-management support. Coaching seems to work best where there are particular problems to address, where the coachee takes ownership of the situation, uses the coach as a resource for thinking and accepts responsibility for the outcome (Burdett 1998). Bluckert's (2005) conclusion has plausibility: 'one of the greatest values of having a coach can be the experience of someone really being there for you and encouraging you to believe in yourself and achieve your goals'. Finding convincing ways of evaluating coaching will be one of the priorities of MD in the future.

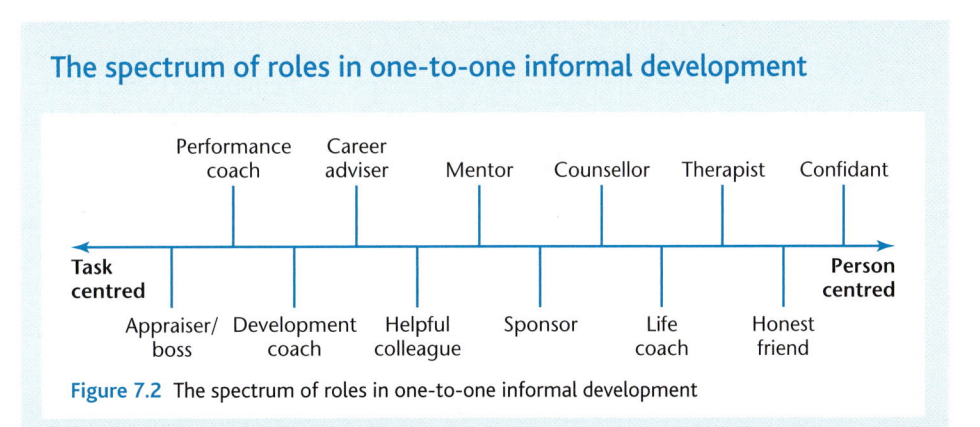

The spectrum of roles in one-to-one informal development

Figure 7.2 The spectrum of roles in one-to-one informal development

Learning one-to-one ranges from the very task-oriented to the very person-centred, through many gradations of which these are just a few.

Mentoring is about an experienced person providing guidance, encouragement, feedback and support to a learner so that they can better manage their learning and achieve their potential. Some forms of mentoring are formal and seen as an integral part of the development process; other forms occur quite spontaneously and may be every bit as influential but are not formally structured.

Being a mentor is about acting as an adviser, counsellor, enabler, sounding board, role model, broker, even advocate and 'organisational friend'. The word 'mentor' comes from Greek mythology. Mentor was the Greek nobleman sent by the goddess Athena to act as a friend and guide to Telemachus, son of Odysseus, when Odysseus was on his twenty-year travels. The mentor/protégé relationship is more intense than most other relationships in the organisation; it is a relationship of support and encouragement. The mentor is a mixture of concerned parent and experienced colleague and licensed friend offering friendship and support. The essential defining characteristics of mentors seem to be that they are older and more senior than the protégé and respected performers. Usually they have trodden the same path that the protégé now hopes to follow and can draw on their experience to help the younger person. It is also important that the mentor does not have a line relationship with the protégé (which would blur relationships of authority with relationships of support).

Mentors perform a number of functions. The following is a synthesis of the observations of some of the main authors in the field (Clutterbuck and Megginson 2005; Hunt and Michael 1983; Parsloe 1999; Burdett 1994, 1998).

- The mentor helps the learner solve problems by acting as a facilitator, gently probing, questioning, summarising and suggesting different lines of action. The mentor proceeds by drawing out lessons from the experience which the mentee shares with him or her, suggesting ways of reframing problems and tentatively offering ideas on how to solve them. Experienced mentors avoid direct advice which can be disempowering but instead help the learner work through his or her own cognitive and emotional processes.

- The mentor typically models the management role by demonstrating how issues might be handled and the competencies involved.

- The mentor provides a safe space in which innermost experiences, doubts and fears can be raised in an atmosphere of trust. This may mean gently challenging assumptions which are blocking performance, helping the learner gain greater self-awareness and confidence through guided reflection. It is also about helping him or her to own up to mistakes and confusion, giving non-judgemental feedback and creating a climate for experimentation with new behaviours.

- The mentor is also an important source of career advice and facilitation. The mentor may help the protégé move into a position best suited to his or her talents. S/he may also act to bring the protégé into networks of influence to increase his or her profile within the organisation.

Generally, the mentor is there to share expertise and experience and build the confidence and professional maturity of the protégé. The mentor is not supposed to be the fount of all knowledge and the guardian of the 'one right way'. However, s/he is likely to have acknowledged wisdom and the social skill to help the protégé learn how to learn.

More research is needed on how mentors facilitate the development of protégé skills. Inevitably much relies on the compatibility of the mentor and the protege (e.g. in terms of race, gender, personality, learning style, etc.) and on how the mentoring relationship is established and maintained. Armstrong and Allison (2002) suggest that synchrony of cognitive style may be the most important factor in predicting compatibility, although gender composition, especially female mentors and male protégés, was found to be a predictor of poor results. A problematical issue is the lack of suitable female mentors in most organisations (a reflection of the relatively low numbers of women in positions of seniority) and the issues of poor rapport which can often result from mixed-gender mentoring. A free choice of mentors and protégés seems most calculated to build trust and mutual understanding, although the most important indicator of success is personal chemistry which often allows for unpredictable combinations of people.

What qualities and skills do you need to be a mentor?

There is a consensus in the literature that effective mentors have the following qualities and skills.

- By definition, *mentors are success stories*. They are generally high performers with credibility and status. This prestige is important for role modelling. They also need to have power in the organisation to give protection to the protégé and to help career progression.
- *Mentors need the skills of a good therapist*. While it would be expecting too much that mentors have therapist training, they should at least have an understanding of psychotherapy as an approach. The values of mentoring are those of humanistic and counselling psychology (e.g. Carl Rogers, see Korel 1983), so mentors need the ability to empathise with another's 'internal frame of reference'; to have active listening skills; the ability to mirror back what has been said so that the protégés hear themselves talk and the ability to give *unconditional positive regard* and show sensitivity in giving feedback.
- *By definition, mentors are self-aware*. They know how they appear in the world. They know how their words, their silences and their body language send signals which create psychological meaning for others.
- *Mentors are good teachers*, able to stimulate discussion, guide without directing. Typically they question skilfully, helping the protégés make their own analysis and infer the lessons. However, they also provide a safety net if things don't work out as intended. Mentors understand the learning process and know how to build trust and rapport.
- *Mentors are sincerely interested in taking on the role of the mentor*. They are also genuinely interested in the person with whom they are twinned and hope to see him or her grow in skill and confidence. Mentors generally have qualities of sincerity and commitment to others; non-possessive warmth and genuineness in how they relate to others.

> **Questions**
> - *Do you think you have the capabilities to be a good mentor?*
> - *Who do you know in your circle at work or college who is or might become a good mentor? Why?*

For mentoring to be effective, the mentor and learner have to meet regularly, become familiar with each others' styles and develop a relationship of mutual understanding. Synchronisation only happens by degrees. As familiarity develops, the protégés typically disclose more of themselves and are prepared to take more social risks. The mentors may then find themselves speaking for less and less of their time together and becoming less directive. Most of the literature emphasises the importance of moving as soon as possible to a relationship of rough equality. When mentoring is working well, the commentators say (e.g. Parsloe 1999), the learners feel challenged but secure, supported but not dependent. The learners feel in control of the agenda and can raise anything for discussion; they also feel that the interactive process is genuinely angled to their personal development. Where the matching is good and real trust emerges the relationship can greatly help the learner's growth and be immensely satisfying for the mentor as well as mentee (Walton 1999). Mentors can learn about themselves from the mentoring experience and it is enjoyable to help shape the mind-sets of the next generation.

Evaluation of mentoring suggests that it can be one of the most important relationships for aspiring managers (Clutterbuck and Megginson 1999). Managers with mentors seem to have more successful careers and more satisfaction in them (Hunt and Michael 1983). Mentoring has been shown to be a significant factor in breaking the glass ceiling for women progressing into higher management (Davidson and Cooper 1992). It also seems important for retaining high-flyers and for helping others to cope with the stress and emotional exhaustion which can come with management work. For executives, it is the organisational method of choice for leadership development (Hall et al. 1999).

Mentoring is a 'broad church' of roles. However, sometimes it can develop so far in one direction that it becomes something else – counselling. Where the mentor is *counsellor*, s/he becomes heavily involved in the identity, self-esteem and personal growth issues of the protégé. Here the mentor will be engaged in building confidence, helping the protégé to deal with emotional issues which may be damaging performance and manage difficult relationships at work. At the extremes this may mean acting as a 'de facto' psychotherapist without the training and qualifications. This is a dangerous situation and the wise mentor will know when s/he is out of his or her depth and seek outside, specialist support.

Sponsoring is another elaboration from mainstream mentoring. Where powerful mentors take an interest in young managers on the way up, they may be active in pushing the protégés forward, ensuring that they are considered for high-profile assignments, that their names are well known in influential places and they are in line for promotion. Here the fortunate protégés have an opportunity to demonstrate their skills to be noticed and gain from the reflected glory of the mentor. Many high-flyer business leaders admit to the power of an active mentor-sponsor at early stages in their career (e.g. Welch 2001) Of course, sponsoring can be rewarding for the sponsor as well as the sponsored. Networks of protégés give the sponsor greater corporate influence and an impact on the policy agenda.

Most people who experience mentoring regard it as a positive experience (Parsloe 1999). In some cases they are surprised just how powerful it can be. A survey carried out in 2004 by Borderless Executive Search among senior executives in the chemical and pharmaceutical industries found 98 per cent of managers who had been mentored in businesses across Europe believed it to be a valuable experience. They said they had gained in confidence, sophistication and professional skill (Lester 2004).

Mentoring might be regarded as the management equivalent of a craft apprenticeship in which the master of a craft helps the apprentice progress. It is guided supervision in the responsible use of corporate power and, as such, is a progressive form of MD. However, despite the effectiveness of this tool, there is a crisis of mentoring in the large organisations of the West. Restructuring and downsizing have taken their toll. The loss of so many experienced, capable managers has left a shortage of credible leader-mentors who can give one-to-one guidance to younger people on the way up. Mentoring is said to be far less institutionalised as an element for empowering management than it was ten years ago (Lester 2004). This remains true despite the massive growth of an industry in freelance coaching and mentoring. Finding good quality mentors remains a constraint on the use of this tool for developing future managers.

Pause for thought

Everybody needs a mentor

When Tony Blair, recently the PM of the UK, became Leader of the Opposition in the 1990s, he invited Lord Jenkins and others to a dinner at his home in Islington. Alexander Irvine QC, Blair's former boss in chambers where he trained as a barrister, was also there. Lord Jenkins later noted in his diary how Blair seemed to hang on Irvine's every word and deferred to his wisdom, as if he was a mentor. Later, Tony Blair acknowledged his debt to Irvine for helping his development by appointing him Lord Irvine, Lord Chancellor and Speaker of the House of Commons.

Social scientists might talk here of social exchange theory at work. Mentoring is part of the reciprocal exchange of support and favours which we engage in through management *networking*. Here the protégé may have gained in knowledge, political understanding, gravitas and contacts from association with his mentor; the mentor gained vicarious influence and the patronage of a former pupil now in a high office of state. Such are the foundations on which many professional (including 'management') careers are built.

Questions
- *How far do you agree with this view of mentoring as part of a political process?*
- *Within your own networks do you have any potential mentors who may help you in your career?*

7.7.3 Learning through group processes

Team building is discussed under organisational development (Chapter 13). Self-development is helped by group participation, and group learning helps to develop the organisation. Managers working together in multidisciplinary teams learn together. They learn about the most effective way of tackling tasks and in the process often gain personal insight and grow in emotional intelligence. They also learn about the dynamics of group process and how meanings emerge from the collision of very different perspectives on management. The learning is likely to be most explicit and planned in self-directive groups where the team leader is also a facilitator and coach. There are many group learning techniques and opportunities. Here we just consider two of the best known.

Personal group sessions

Also sometimes called *peer support groups*, these are informal groups of colleagues who come together to develop their interpersonal skills and help each other grow in self-awareness and personal maturity. This is an experiential form of learning which can be integrated into work (e.g. a long-standing team periodically reviews how it behaves as a team) or take the form of off-the-job personal growth workshops or 'away days'. Either way, the focus is on the psychodynamics of the self in the group. It may involve scenario analysis, critical incidents, stories and hypothetical situations, or analysis of different approaches to professional practice. Sometimes repertory grids and metaphor analysis (diagnostic techniques used in OD and personal therapy) are used to tease out tacit theories in use and articulate the constructs we regularly use to define people and situations. How do they help us in our sense-making and how do they blind us to the complexities of experience?

A growing trend is the emergence of *EQ workshops* in which participants examine emotions at work, emotions and working relationships and emotion rules in the office. They aim to raise awareness of personal style and help people act more naturally, with greater expressive range and personal skill.

These sessions often use various feedback methods (as in T-groups, see Chapter 12) to help people become more aware of how they are perceived and get in touch with their inner feelings, essential values and latent fears. Although the role of a facilitator is obviously very valuable in this setting, and will probably do much to improve the sophistication of the process, where there is sufficient trust between members of a long-established management team, the group can regulate itself. Personal growth sessions of this kind can be very strong emotional experiences in which people become aware for the first time of the psychosocial barriers which inhibit them from self-critical examination, and blocked emotions which stop them from confronting situations head-on. The result can often be cathartic.

We can also learn through others in *networking situations*. Professional and social interaction provides us with opportunities to build on our interpersonal, communication, data-gathering, influencing, observational and listening skills. The opportunities for reflection and learning are greatly increased if you have a wide variety of others with whom to share stories of experience.

Action learning sets

One of the most powerful methods of development to emerge from the 1970s and 1980s is action learning, a philosophy developed by the famous pioneer of MD,

Reg Revans (1982). His work originated from experiments in learning communities developing their own solutions in the coal industry and an internal communications project opening up managers to the definitions of nurses in a hospital (Levy 2000). Action learning also owes a debt to 'Coverdale Training' in which groups of managers engage in 'trial and error', discovery learning with others, experimenting with different behaviours in a safe setting as a rehearsal for real organisational life.

Action learning is a way of developing people through valuing their experience and, by extension, developing the organisation. This is not a new concept:

> One must learn by doing the thing; for though you think you know it you have no certainty until you try.
>
> (*Sophocles*)

However, AL is more than just learning by doing. It is based on the belief that a process that brings people together to find solutions in an atmosphere of trust provides the best conditions for finding good business decision-making and developing self-awareness. However, the real distinction between ALS and other group learning techniques is that ALS are based on problems taken from real life, and members of the group have an emotional investment in addressing them. This is more than just learning by doing. Set members share experience by working on their problems and supporting others working on theirs'. In the process they learn about themselves, about others and about processes of decision-making in groups (Beardwell and Holden 2003).

At meetings of the set each member presents his or her work-based problem and the others in the set give their observations, reflections, insight and advice drawn from their experience and expertise. The group follows the progress of each member at regular meetings. Time is taken to check perception of the problem, to consider differences in perspective and strategies for proceeding. In between meetings members collect information about their problem and experiment with different solutions. At each step members return to the set to learn from the experiences of others and consider their counsel for the next stage. In the process they often reframe how they see things and come to terms with their blind spots, the limitations of their constructs of situations and of received wisdom in management.

Case study: What's it like to be involved in an ALS?

One way to examine the nature of action learning is to look at it from the perspective of the participants. It is through the words of those with first-hand experience that the newcomer to ALS can come to appreciate what is involved.

'Helping Hands', a London-based charity with a mission to help the single homeless, has been running ALS as a vehicle for managerial and professional development over the past five years. The sets are advertised internally and attendance is voluntary. Each set is made up of officers at roughly the same level of organisational seniority. Each set runs for ten sessions. It starts with an introductory meeting in which the ground rules of behaviour, the philosophy of AL and its purpose are discussed. Subsequent monthly sessions are given over to members of the set who take it in turn to present a problem or project they are working on followed by feedback from peers, asking questions, providing gentle challenge and reflection. The facilitator helps the group keep focused and the discussion relevant. Sometimes this may require attention to how the set is working. The emphasis is on set members critiquing each other's approach, sharing their perceptions, supporting people in working through dilemmas and reflecting on lessons for their own practice. There is an end session in which progress on each of the participant's projects is reviewed, common themes from the collective set experience are analysed and learning is shared.

This is a familiar pattern found in many ALS programmes. Typically they result in learning about personal strengths and weaknesses, the dynamics of groups and real-life business problem-solving. But can we capture something of the 'lived experience' of those involved? This is a digest of some of the responses from five sets.

At the beginning of the programme

People who are about to start a programme of AL are likely to be more nervous than those beginning ordinary training programmes because they sense that this may require a high degree of personal openness and exposure. This was the case at Helping Hands. Some were worried that there may be a secret agenda; top management might want to use it to probe for their weaknesses.

> I wasn't looking forward to it. Why did we have to bring a task with us? Was this going to be used to reveal our inadequacies in management?

The organisation can do a lot to reassure participants and address their concerns at an early stage so that the programme can go ahead on the basis of trust.

The first action-learning set session

Nervousness and apprehension remained high. There was a lot of milling around and much argument over ground rules. There was also frustration and anger that the facilitator seemed unwilling to define what the rules should be.

Typically set members take a while to understand that they are responsible for creating their own sense of order, as at Helping Hands.

> It all seemed chaotic at the beginning; although the facilitator explained the philosophy of AL, we didn't quite know what was expected of us . . . we kept looking for guidance but the facilitator stood back.

Later in the programme

It often takes a number of meetings before set members really get what AL is all about. This was definitely the case at Helping Hands. Suspicion and frustration usually gives way to enthusiasm. People begin to understand the value of a sounding board for their ideas. They begin to realise that AL is very unlike a didactic learning experience (and often the participants' last experience of formal learning was school); it is practical and involves learning through a community of peers.

> I like this sort of learning because it is about real things and you are not being talked at by a teacher.

End of the AL programme

At HH, the completion of the programme did not mean the end of the action-learning set. It continued as a non-facilitated learning set, although perhaps more precisely it became a peer-support network. People had acquired the taste for learning through others and wanted the 'support and challenge' to continue.

> I now recognise the importance of group learning and thinking beyond the everyday with others, but networks lack the focus of the ALS and we need to try and recapture this.

Lessons from the ALS experience

Respondents at HH mentioned a wide range of positive outcomes from the programme which are typical benefits of an ALS programme. In their words:

> The set provided a safe space to explore business problems but also to examine our own anxieties and consider our own behaviours.

> Sharing problems helped us to understand each other better and that built trust which outlasted the learning set.

> The learning set was a forum to understand more clearly what managing means and how our organisation really works.

> The set was a place for managers to think away from the ordinary pressures and to test their thinking against other minds. Drawing on the skills and insights of others can be very useful.

> However, although enthusiastic, HH-set members were not uncritical of their experience.
>
> > The set was very scary at the beginning because of the amount of exposure it involved. More could be done to make it 'safe' for people to take personal risks.
>
> Action learning will only really work if top management is committed to it. That means giving time off to attend, agreeing the projects to be worked on and doing something with the project reports . . . I think there were some issues of top management support here.
>
> Source: Based on action research and evaluation done by the author

At its root, AL is based on Revan's view that for managers 'programmed knowledge' (gained from books, manuals of good practice, tried-and-tested solutions) is less important than 'experiential knowing'. By bringing together 'comrades in adversity', committed to solving difficult problems, and opening up decision-making to diverse perceptions and critical questioning, elegant, original solutions can emerge. The solutions seem fresh and appropriate because they express a process of thinking anew, not marginally adapting a familiar solution to a different set of circumstances. In Revan's terms programmed knowledge (P) and questioning insight (Q) has been brought together to form new contextualised knowledge which fits the needs of the situation (Revans 1982).

This 'reflection in action' is often supplemented by 'reflection on action'. As members learn from each other and independent thinking is stimulated, there is also the opportunity for learning at other levels. Typically they become more aware of group process, interpersonal dynamics, creativity and thinking. They develop a more sophisticated understanding of 'how things go', perhaps the beginnings of managerial wisdom. These 'things' are often subtle, difficult to articulate *inter alia* : an appreciation of the value of the well-placed question; insight into the power of language to persuade; the potential of all group members to both facilitate and stifle the creative flow; the interwoven nature of emotions and cognition in the group process; the connectedness of the small and the large in management; how your assumptions may turn out to be part of the problem; how the charismatic speaker in the group may not be the most insightful or the most creative; how acting impulsively to satisfy a 'cult of decisiveness' may be less effective than acting more slowly and with careful consideration. Of course, this just scratches the surface of the 'process understanding' which is possible from AL, but it does give some glimpse of the deeper learning about social process which can emerge when Revan's spirit of reflective enquiry is released (Pedler 1996).

Pause for thought

Picturing ALS outcomes

A graphic representation of the learning gains from an ALS (captured from a workshop session evaluating a development programme) was included in Chapter 6 when we considered mind-mapping techniques. You might like to turn back to this.

Question
If you have recently been on an ALS, how does your learning and the learning of your group compare with the recorded experience of this set?

ALS are important for personal and professional development. As we mention in Chapter 12 they can also be effective as an OD tool for stimulating collective learning by developing a culture of listening, questioning and open relationships. Networks of ALS in which people share ideas, knowledge, insights and experiences can create the conditions for a learning organisation based on virtuous cycles of action, learning and reflection. ALS can become the grounding for a culture that values questioning, experimenting and innovating. They can form the framework for a genuine 'community of learning and practice' which challenges 'defensive routines' and makes support and challenge part of ordinary organisational process (Pedler et al. 1999). However, the potential of ALS for organisational transformation is rarely realised in practice. Too often hierarchies block the co-creation of new behaviours and authoritarian values displace fresh thinking and unorthodox ideas. Sadly, the empowering effects of ALS – giving people self-confidence in their ability to manage change, to question organisational assumptions and suggest alternative visions of the future – are often perceived by higher managers not as a breath of fresh air, but as a threat to the existing culture of management.

This leads to a consideration of the limitations of ALS. The first point which should be made is that AL has grown in popularity in recent times and there is a tendency for it to be seen as a panacea for all manner of development problems. This uncritical use of AL is a mistake. It will only be effective where conditions (especially political conditions) are favourable, the top management is involved in the process (e.g. being engaged in defining the problems to be worked on and committed to implementing outcomes) and ready for the radicalising effect which AL often brings. Secondly , there is the issue that diverse development programmes tend to be labelled as ALS when they actually lack the spirit of Revan's philosophy (Clarke et al. 2006). For example, ALS can often be reduced to a technique. Programmes with an AL tag may turn out to be task-led internal consulting projects with little opportunity for process reflection and questioning. This interpretation of AL adopts too closely a conservative, risk-averse management agenda and denies the critical challenge implicit in a full-throated acclamation of ALS. Other organisational programmes, defined as AL, are really support groups more concerned with issues of self-development, group bonding and mutual help than with organisational problem-solving. Again, this only partially fulfils the requirements of an ALS.

However, even at its most well worked through, ALS is not without its critics. Some say that ALS show a tendency to become 'talking shops' (Bourner and Weinstein 1998) in which the development process seems to take precedence over results and it is therefore out of joint with the realities of modern business. Others take the view that ALS may be a valuable means of experiential learning but only allows partial learning and in itself is insufficient preparation for management. Too often, they say, AL is divorced from the historical context of policy, is unconceptual and focused on problems which leave the bigger values and wider strategies untouched. As such, ALS tend to be rather insular and heuristic in emphasis and need blending with formal, more conceptual inputs to ensure the intellectual as well as the pragmatic development of the manager.

Wilmott (1997) advocates a more critical approach to ALS which avoids what he sees as the 'psychologising' of problems and the denial of power relations. Instead, an alternative AL could become a vehicle for critical reflection on the social and economic forces at play in the workplace, scrutiny of received wisdom in management against personal experience and the construction of new ways of seeing and behaving.

The view of this author is that AL promises much both in personal and group learning. It is a versatile approach which can be combined with other experiential and formal learning processes and OD practices to develop the organisation as a whole. Some large companies are using AL in new more advanced forms. Exxon Oil, for example, has moved beyond single-case ALS to progress team members through a variety of roles in overlapping projects (e.g. participant, project leaders, facilitator for an ALS in another unit, etc.), so that the emancipatory experience of thinking afresh is sustained. Other organisations are trying to deliberately create a shock of the new to force teams to think beyond conventional responses and stock categories, unlearn old lessons which have hardened into dogmas and experiment with a questioning style which, it is hoped, will become a permanent part of management behaviour.

These developments are encouraging but there are conditions for the effective use of AL. It will only work when the climate is enlightened, where empowerment is a core value and top management recognise its importance as a catalyst for change. A supportive culture is still more the exception than the rule.

7.8 Conclusion

Experiential learning has become the new orthodoxy in MD. There are many opportunities for learning in the everyday world of the manager – incidental learning but also learning which can be guided and structured around management tasks. At its best, experiential learning can be rich and deep, emerging directly from reflection on professional management practice. However, it requires the manager to have sensitivity, imagination and commitment and for the organisation to provide the right supportive culture for learning – conditions which are not always present. Self-development is an important trend in learning how to learn and an essential requirement for management success in demanding times. The techniques of experiential learning are numerous and involve learning through planned changes in the nature of the work, one-to-one relationships and learning through group reflection and discussion.

Review questions

1 Sir Winston Churchill, a British prime minister, once said that he liked to learn but often resented being taught. Do you feel like that sometimes? What is it about the formal learning experience which may have inhibited you from learning?

2 As a manager or as a student, reflect on learning which you believe has helped you be effective in social life as it applies to management (e.g. listening; influencing; leading a group, etc.). Define the skills involved here and consider *how* you are learning them (and will continue to do so throughout your life).

3 Do you learn most from the 'devil of failure' or the 'goddess of success'? Reflect on your thinking processes. In this context does the devil or the goddess offer the best tunes for personal growth?

4 How real do you feel the advocacy of the self-development lobby to be in the average organisation where the 'doing' of work is increasingly unrelenting and the spaces for reflection increasingly unavailable? What are the responsibilities of the organisation in developing an aware, self-developing workforce?

5 The chapter talked of defensive routines and tacit theories in use which guide us in ordinary organisational life. If you were put on the spot, would you be able to identify some assumptions, habits of thinking or blind spots which stop *you* from thinking and seeing clearly?

Web links

The web link for the International Foundation for Action Learning:
http://www.scu.edu.au/schools/gcm/arp/actlearn.html

The web link for the Revans Collection at Salford University:
http://www.isd.salford.ac.uk/specollect/revans.php

A useful web link on action learning theory and practice:
www.12manage.com/methodsrevansactionlearning.html

The website of the Centre for Self Managed Learning:
http://www.selfmanagedlearning.org

DVDs/Videos

Working Girl (1988) directed by Nichols, M; featuring Sigounery Weaver and Melanie Griffith
Contains an amusing but telling scene between Melanie Griffith and Sigourney Weaver which points up the dangers of choosing the wrong mentor.

Back to the Floor (2007) Channel 4
An interesting series depicting top managers returning to the operational end to refresh their experiential learning.

Recommendations for further reading

Those texts marked with an asterisk in the bibliography are recommended for further reading, especially the following:

Davies, J. and Easterby-Smith, M. (1984) 'Learning and developing from managerial work experiences', *Journal of Management Studies*, 21 (2). A very useful review of the techniques and processes of informal learning.

Pedler, M., Burgoyne, J. and Boydell, T. (1990) *Self Development in Organisations*. Helpful 'self help' guide to becoming focused and creative in self managed learning.

Schon, D. (1983) *The Reflective Practitioner: How Professionals Think in Action*. A classic account of the orientations and skills of the thinking practitioner with lessons for all of us.

Bibliography

Anon. (2003) 'When executive coaching fails to deliver: is it time to kick sporting metaphors into touch?' *Development and Learning in Organisations*, Vol. 17, No. 2.

*Antonacopoulou, E. (2000) 'Employee development through self development in three retail banks', *Personnel Review*, Vol. 29, No. 4.

*Argyris, C. (1995) 'Action science and organisational learning', *Journal of Managerial Psychology*, Vol. 10, No. 6.

Armstrong, S. and Allison, C. (2002) 'Formal mentoring systems: an examination of the effects of mentor/protégé cognitive styles in the mentoring process', *Journal of Management Studies*, Vol. 39, No. 8.

*Barclay, J. (1996) 'Learning from experience with learning logs', *Journal of Management Development*, Vol. 15, No. 6.

Barham, K. and Oates, D. (1991) *The International Manager*, Random Century House.

Beardwell, J. and Claydon, T. (2007) *Human Resource Management*, Financial Times Press.

Beardwell, I., Holden, J. and Claydon, T. (2003) *Human Resource Management*, Prentice Hall.

*Bluckert, P. (2005) 'Critical factors in executive coaching – the coaching relationship', *Industrial and Commercial Training*, Vol. 37, No. 7.

Bourner, T. and Weinstein, K. (1998) 'Just another talking shop?' *Journal of Workplace Learning*, Vol. 8, No. 6.

Burdett, J. (1998) 'Forty things every manager should know about coaching', *Journal of Management Development*, Vol. 17, No. 2.

Burdett, J. (1994) 'To coach or not to coach – that is the question!', in Mabey, C. and Iles, P. (1994) *Managing Learning*, Open University Press.

Burgoyne, J. and Reynolds, M. (1997) *Management Learning*, Sage.

CIPD (2006) *Latest Trends in Learning, Training and Development*, CIPD.

*Clarke, J., Thorpe, R. et al. (2006) 'It's all action; its all learning: action learning in SMEs', *Journal of European Industrial Training*, Vol. 30, No. 6.

Clutterbuck, D. and Megginson, D. (2005) 'How to create a coaching culture', *People Management*, 21 April.

Cunningham, I. (2003) 'Sheep dip to strategic intent', *People Management*, May.

*Cunningham, I. (2007) Do we really want all learning to be experiential? The hot stove effect', *Development and Learning in Organisations*, Vol. 21, No. 3.

Cusins, P. (1996) 'Action learning revisited', *Employee Counselling Today*, Vol. 8, No. 6.

Dalton, K. (1993) 'Presentation of the Self through Organisational Narrative', PhD thesis, Bath School of Management.

Daudelin, M. (1996) 'Learning from experience through reflection', *Organisational Dynamics*, Vol. 24, Issue 3.

Davidson, M. and Cooper, C. (1992) *Shattering the Glass Ceiling*, Paul Chapman Publishing.

Davies, J. and Easterby-Smith, M. (1984) 'Learning and developing from managerial work experiences', *Journal of Management Studies*, Vol. 21, No. 2.

Dent, F. (1999) *The Self Managed Pocket Book*, Management Pocketbooks.

Downey, M. (1999) *Effective Coaching*, Orion Business Books.

Eglin, R. (2000) 'Directors jump on the coaching bandwagon', *Financial Times*, 7th June.

Fee, K. (2001) *A Guide to Management Development Techniques*, Kogan Page.

French, R. and Grey, C. (1996) Re-thinking Management Education, Sage.

*Gabriel, Y. (2000) *Storytelling in Organisations*, Oxford University Press.

Hall, D., Otazo, K. et al. (1999) 'What really happens in executive coaching', *Organisational Dynamics*, Winter.

Handy, C. (1985) *Understanding Organisations*, Penguin.

Hill, L. (1992) *Becoming a Manager: Mastery of a New Identity*, Harvard Business School Press.

Hill, L. (2004) 'New management development in the 21st century', *Academy of Management Review*, Vol. 18, No. 3.

Hunt, D. and Michael, C. (1983) 'Mentorship: a career training and development tool', *Academy of Management Review*, Vol. 80, No. 3.

Katz, R. (1982) *Career Issues in Human Resource Management*, Prentice Hall.

Knowles, M. (1990) *The Adult Learner: A Neglected Species*, Gulf Publishing.

Korel, J. (1983) *A Complete Guide to Therapy*, Penguin.

Lester, T. (2004) 'An urgent need for top quality mentoring', *Financial Times*, 12th July.

Levy, M. (2000) 'The sage of reason', *People Management*, 28 Dec.

Mabey, C. and Iles, P. (1994) *Managing Learning*, Open University.

Mangham, I. (1986) *Power and Performance in Organisations*, Blackwell.

Margerison, C. (1991) *Making Management Development Work*, McGraw Hill.

Margerison, C. (1994) 'Action learning and excellence in management development', in Mabey, C. and Iles, P. (1994) *Managing Learning*, OUP.

*Marshall, J. and Reason, P. 'Collaborative and self reflective forms of inquiry in management research', in Burgoyne, J. and Reynolds, M. (1997) *Management Learning*, Sage.

Marsick, V., Cederholm, L. et al. (1992) 'Action-reflection learning', *Training and Development*, August.

*Marsick, V. and Watkins, K. (1990) *Informal and Incidental Learning in the Workplace*, Routledge.

*Marsick, V. and Watkins, K. (1997) 'Lessons from informal and incidental learning', in Burgoyne, J. and Reynolds, M. (1997) *Management Learning*, Sage.

Mathieu, C. (2001) 'Management development in Royal Dutch Shell', *Journal of Management Development*, Vol. 20, No. 2.

McCall, M. (1988) 'Developing executives through work experiences', *Human Resources Planning*, Vol. 11, No. 1.

*McCall, M. and Lombardo, M. (1988) *The Lessons of Experience*, Lexington Books.

Megginson, D. and Clutterbuck, D. (1995) *Mentoring in Action*, Kogan Page.

Megginson, D. and Pedler, M. (1992) *Self Development*, McGraw Hill.

Megginson, D. and Whitaker, V. (1999) *Cultivating Self Development*, CIPD.

Megginson, D. and Whittaker, V. (2003) *Continuing Professional Development*, CIPD.

Mintzberg, H. (1973) *The Nature of Managerial Work*, Harper and Row.

Mintzberg, H. (2004) *Managers not MBAs*, Prentice Hall.

Mumford, A. (1989) *Management Development: Strategies for Action*, CIPD.

*Mumford, A. (1997) *Strategies for Action*, CIPD.

*Mumford, A. (1980, 1999) *Making Experience Pay*, McGraw Hill.

Murray, S. (2003) 'Homework is out, real work in', *Financial Times*, 23 Nov.

Nonaka, I. and Takeuchi, H. (1995) *The Knowledge Creating Company*, Oxford University Press.

*Parsloe, E. (1999) *The Manager as Coach and Mentor*, CIPD.

*Pedler, M. (1994) 'Applying self development in organisations', in Mabey, C. and Iles, P. (1994) *Managing Learning*, Sage.

Pedler, M. (1996) *Action Learning for Managers*, Sage.

Pedler, M. and Burgoyne, J. (2004) *A Manager's Guide to Leadership*, McGraw Hill.

*Pedler, M., Burgoyne, J. and Boydell, T. (1990) *Self Development in Organisations*, McGraw Hill.

*Pedler, M., Burgoyne, J. and Boydell, T. (1999) *A Manager's Guide to Self Development*, McGraw Hill.

People Management (2005) Coaching at Work, Vol. 1, No. 1, Special edition, various short pieces.

*Polanyi, M. (1966) *The Tacit Dimension*, Routledge.

*Raelin, J. (1998) 'Work based learning in practice', *Journal of Workplace Learning* (1998) Vol. 10, No. 6/7.

Revans, R. (1982) *The Origin and Growth of Action Learning*, Chartwell-Bratt.

Revans, R. (2000) 'Sage of reason', *People Management*, Dec.

Salaman, G. and Butler, J. (1990) 'Why managers won't learn', *Management Education and Development*, Vol. 21, Part 3.

*Schon, D. (1983) *The Reflective Practitioner: How Professionals Think in Action*, London: Maurice Temple Smith.

Sills, C. and Critchley, B. (2003) Pause for Reflection, *Training Magazine*, April.

Smith, B. and Morphey, G. (1994) 'Tough challenges: how big a learning gap?', *Journal of Management Development*, Vol. 13, No. 9.

Thomson, A., Mabey, C. et al. (2001) *Changing Patterns of Management Development*, Blackwell.

Walton, J. 1999) *Strategic Human Resource Development*, Prentice Hall.

Watson, T. (2001) *In Search of Management*, Thomson Learning.

Watson, T. and Harris, P. (1999) *The Emergent Manager*, Sage.

*Weick, K. (1983) 'Managerial thought in the context of action', in Srivasta, S. (1983) *The Executive Mind*, Jossey-Bass.

Welch, J. (2001) *Jack Straight from the Gut*, Warner Books.

Wilmott, H. (1997) 'Critical management learning', in Burgoyne, J. and Reynolds, M. (1997) *Management Learning*, Sage.

Woodall, J. and Winstanley, D. (1999) *Management Development: Strategy and Practice*, Blackwell.

Yukl, G. (1998) *Leadership in Organisations: Developing Leadership Skills*, Ch. 13, Prentice Hall.

8 Formal management development: management training

Learning outcomes

After studying the chapter you should be able to understand, analyse and explain:

- the relationship between informal off-the-job and formal on-the-job management learning;
- debates and trends in formal management development;
- the distinctions and relationship between management education and management training;
- design processes in formal MD;
- issues in delivering management training;
- the strengths and weaknesses of short courses;
- the range of methods in management training, their strengths and limitations.

8.1 Introduction

As we have seen, *informal on-the-job experiential* development, which we explored in the last chapter, scores highly in terms of relevance and immediacy; it appeals to the practical thinking of many managers and empowers by encouraging them to take their own experience seriously. However, there are limits to what can be learnt from experience alone, however guided and reflective.

Formal off-the-job development also has a part to play in helping managers find their own voice, their own unique style of managing. The main case for separating managers from the daily pressures of their work is that they can concentrate on the *learning* rather than the *doing* of tasks and can be exposed to new ideas which will hopefully have a positive impact on their knowledge, skills, attitudes and behaviour.

This chapter is the first of two linked chapters which explores the rich diversity of techniques for the formally developing managers by focusing on management training. It also explores professional practitioner knowledge concerning the design and delivery of training and examines trends within this field.

8.2 The 'informal' v 'formal' debate

Until the 1980s the formal, structured approach to developing managers was the orthodoxy but it is now on the defensive. There are many reasons for this. The problems of transferring knowledge from off-the-job education and training events and claims that they encourage single loop or one-dimensional learning (Burgoyne and Reynolds 1997) have raised doubts about their effectiveness. There is also growing scepticism about whether there is a body of professional knowledge to be taught in management. However, it is the irresistible rise of informal, experiential learning and the emergence of a broad consensus that managers only learn within their work context that has been decisive in threatening to marginalise formal MD (which includes management training, management education and planned formal development away from the job) to a secondary role in support of on-the-job learning.

As we saw in the previous chapter, recent trends in MD have tended in the direction of experiential, work-based methods of management development. Because effective management is now seen as first and foremost a practical craft based on the development of social skills, behaviour and attitudes, best learnt by doing it with support and guidance, fashion has shifted decisively in favour of off-the-job or experiential approaches. Formal management development (on-the-job) is increasingly relegated to a secondary role, to inculcate the instrumental skills and knowledge which the manager will also need as part of an all-round competency.

It is a consistent finding of researchers that when managers are asked to recall formative memories in their growth as managers, they tend to recount experiences at work. They recall emotionally charged incidents, often mistakes, on which they reflected and drew lessons to become better managers. For practical thinkers, like managers, learning through reflecting and sharing of experience has an undoubted edge, in terms of both relevance and resonance, over other less immediate, more institutionalised development methods.

However, it is not hard to see some problems with this new hegemony of experiential learning. As Woodall and Winstanley (1999) shrewdly observe, there is a danger of on-the-job learning becoming an *ideology* which is highly critical of the management training and education establishment, yet does not apply the same standards of critical evaluation to itself. Informal methods are notoriously difficult to evaluate and often practitioners don't bother, yet experientialism is championed as a matter of faith by the contemporary development establishment and many senior academics. At its most extreme this ideology can proclaim a creed in which doing and activity in learning is always to be preferred to thinking and reasoning. Here, words and phrases like 'academic', 'developing a philosophy of managing', 'thinking abstractly', 'ruminating meditatively' (perhaps the last is a little provocative) have negative meanings. This extreme and exclusive emphasis on experience is captured by Alan Mumford (1980), himself, ironically, a strong advocate of informal, experiential learning:

> I remember the horror with which a course tutor received the news that I proposed to start a morning on leadership styles with a twenty minute talk on different ways of defining leadership: 'But Alan, our style is to get people to learn by doing; can't you give them some exercises?'

There are a lot of issues involved here. It would certainly be bizarre to claim that the practitioner skills of the manager are best taught in the classroom, and many of the great management practitioners would have derided such a suggestion (e.g. imagine how a Sloan, Watson, Roddick, Ford or Barnard would have reacted). Yet although experiential learning may be engaging for many managers who are accustomed to think in the midst of action, it is surely romantic to believe that most organisations are geared up to creating a climate of learning at work. In many, the primacy of the task means that any learning from experience is incidental and haphazard. Tasks themselves may not be developmental; the press of events may squeeze out opportunities for discussing and reflecting on process. In these conditions, learning on the job happens by accident, if at all; there is no organisation of learning and what is learned can be very narrow, parochial and organisation-specific.

This brings in a larger point. The assumption that managers only learn when they are confronted by immediate demands, when their responsibilities exceed their current competencies, as cynics might have it, are inherently pragmatic in their orientations and do not want ideas, theories or concepts, is a little condescending (Woodall and Winstanley 1999). It certainly flies in the face of most management educators' experience of their students. Many managers do have instrumental attitudes to learning, but a lot *are* inquisitive and thoughtful, looking for a philosophy of management practice to make sense of their confusing realities. Many are keen to experiment with new ideas and find coherent conceptual frameworks to guide their everyday actions. The best are developing their own frameworks of meaning by testing out ideas to develop their own 'theory in use' (Argyris 1982) The 'anti-intellectualism' of much that passes for experiential learning (e.g. the action learning sets that are all action and little learning; the mentoring which is really organisational therapy not debate; the coaching which is perfunctory; the projects which pay lip service to individual growth, etc.) raises questions about the critical element in informal MD and the reality that experience is often not reflected upon because the process does not involve systematic learning.

On the other hand, the strengths of off-the-job approaches can be considerable. Well-designed formal programmes provide managers with a cocoon of protected learning free from the pressures and politics of organisational life. They can offer a time for personal stocktaking and reflection. They can also expand consciousness by linking personal experience to larger orbits of thinking and broadening vision. Finally, they give managers 'credentials', which afford the manager, forced to be self-developing in turbulent times, a more appealing CV. This is a more transportable asset than the most enriching workplace learning which requires the manager to have good narrative powers to persuade a future employer of its worth.

However, in the end, as Woodall and Winstanley (1999) say, the issue does not resolve itself into an either/or choice. This is a false polarisation. Can developers find ways of blending the best of the formal and informal and create new synergies? What is teachable within management and what can only be acquired by experience? How can the element that is teachable be harmonised with self learning to acquire the social, political and practical skills of managing?

For formal MD the challenge is how to convincingly capture the real-life choices, dilemmas, judgements and skills of managing in the artificial world of the classroom. The big challenge for experiential management learning is how to help people articulate the lessons of experience and turn tacit knowledge and unarticulated feelings about relationships and events into generalisable lessons for managing. The big challenge for all those who hope to see an enlightened MD in the future is how to make it a total process in which planned and incidental, formal and informal, analytical and reflective, doing and thinking are mutually reinforcing. For concepts like self-development and continuous personal development to mean anything, they surely involve managers taking responsibility for learning through guided practice, through a framework of planned but flexible development which draws on the best of formal and informal learning processes. These are important themes which we will return to throughout this chapter and the next.

However, fashions come and go in MD; the pendulum may have swung too far towards 'experientialism' so that it becomes a bland and unrealistic panacea. It could still swing back to a new equilibrium between formal and informal approaches.

8.3 Patterns of formal management development

8.3.1 Mapping the field

So what constitutes off-the-job learning? For the purposes of this book the range of activities we are concerned with can be categorised as:

- In-house or internal courses, seminars, workshops and conferences. As we will see, these are designed to address company-specific management learning needs, as defined by training needs analyses (TNAs), surveys or other assessment techniques. These activities may be delivered by corporate staff or external agencies contracted in for the task.

- Externally run courses. These may be open enrolment courses which will contain participants nominated from a range of organisations *or* custom-designed courses run by external development consultants for a cadre of managers from different departments but at the same career level or managers at all levels within a division of the nominating company.

- Externally run accredited courses. These tend to be longer-term management courses leading to a recognised qualification, for example, an MA, MBA, executive MBA, and so on. Historically this has involved sponsorship of selected managers to attend business school courses. However, as we will see, new corporate/university partnerships and corporate universities are now emerging which complicate the patterns of provision.

In this chapter we will consider the first two of these main categories of off-the-job *training* (the next chapter will consider the last category – *education*), which provokes further attempts at definition.

- *Management training*: is concerned with developing particular skills or knowledge, often company-specific; building usable competencies; learning how to do your current job more effectively; building the profile that the company wants of its managers. Training is often delivered by in-house or commissioned external providers. It is often very technicist and vocational. The company remains in charge of the event/s and has considerable control over course design and implementation (e.g. Latham and Seijts 1998; Fee 2001).

- *Management education*: is concerned with facilitating a broad range of abilities needed by managers: social, political, conceptual, cognitive. It is often concerned with conceptualisation, critical thinking, self-awareness and having a larger perspective on organisation and managing. Often it involves preparing managers for 'total life' in the organisation. Courses are often off-site, away from the company and service providers; external accrediting agencies have an important input into the content and implementation. The participants have more control than in training over the nature of the experience and their commitment to it (e.g. Latham and Seitjs 1998; Fee 2001; Mullins 2004).

The training/education fault-line is traditional in MD. Med is broader and less specific than MT. However, some say that the distinction is becoming blurred. Qualifications offered by Med are often taken for vocational reasons and the best training is critical, intellectually challenging and encourages the development of the whole person. Besides, with business schools trying to become more responsive to their corporate customers and management educators trying to balance academic work with training consultancy, it can look as if both parties are trying to steal each others' clothes. However, we believe there is still sufficient distinction between these two modes of learning to divide our focus between two chapters.

In designing an MD programme it is perhaps useful to see the distinction in terms of tendencies. So, it is easy to overemphasise the Med dimension and create learning processes which are too philosophical and remote to be applied or to overdo training and make the experience narrow and unreflective. Keeping a balance is one of the key skills of the developer.

As we shall see, off-the-job development can be diverse in purpose, design, methods and implementation. At its best, it is strategic, aligned to the business plan and its monitoring and review processes. It is the culmination of the structured process of objective setting, assessment/appraisal, career planning, delivery and review (development cycle planning) which we discussed previously (chapters 4 and 5). Seminars, workshops, short courses, executive seminars and so on are the expression of a deliberate process of targeting priorities for individual and collective learning and the marshalling of resources to the design of appropriate programmes (Stewart 1999).

There certainly seems to be a link between a planned, systematic process and the use of formal courses (Thomson et al. 2001). A formalisation of process seems to favour formal tools of development. Formal MD, unlike experiential, work-based learning which is often below the radar, is the highly visible, public, tangible and (importantly) the more measurable part of the MD strategy. It is also often seen as the organisation's MD not the manager's, i.e. 'what they do to us'; not 'what we can do for ourselves'.

The trends we have discussed have forced formal MD on the defensive. The once extensive apparatus of MD has been partially dismantled. The removal of structured career pathways and the shift to self-development has meant that the suites of courses to mark each stage of a manager's progression have been drastically cut back. The shedding of the HRD staff which maintained this apparatus, the focus on outsourcing management training that is needed and the delegation of responsibility to strategic business units have also reduced its influence on development policy.

Then there is the issue of the cultural meanings assigned to formal management development. Historically, MT has acted as the calibration by which managers marked progress in their careers. Invitations to management courses were critical points in management progression, often signalling transition from one status level or tier in the hierarchy to the next. For example, going on the 'advanced management development course', or something similar in your organisation, was a mark of arrival into senior management. If the invitation arrived in your 30s or early 40s, it was taken as a sign of potential elevation to the highest levels. However, with the shrivelling of planned career development, the cult of the in-house course as a symbolic benchmark has faded.

Yet, here is a paradox. Despite these forces, Thomson at al. (2001) found that the volume of formal MD, as well as the range, has increased considerably from the mid-1990s. Much of this is corporate activity. In the following chapter, we look at the evidence that there is a far greater variety of formal MD activities of all kinds than ten years earlier. By 2009, most large companies could now claim to offer a good range of in-company courses; sponsorship for attending accredited courses; executive seminars, workshops and conferences, and so on linked to formal assessment and development systems. All this seems to suggest that on/off' the job MD are not in head-to-head competition for scarce corporate resources. Both pedagogies are seen by organisations as valuable, mutually supportive and of sufficient strategic importance for budgets to be devoted to them.

> **Pause for thought**
>
> ### An offer you can't refuse
>
> As part of an interview question for a management job, candidates were asked how they would spend £5,000 and a month off of work for their development. It was intended to test their capacity for defining learning need and choosing appropriate methods.
>
> *What would you have said?*

All the same, even if the level and variety of formal MD is increasing, there are subtle changes in the balance between types of formal provision. For example, managers increasingly perceive in-company courses as of low status and low impact; the use of external providers has increased for corporate development (partnerships and contracted-in training) but less open enrolment MD is being commissioned and company residential courses are slipping in favour along with the time-honoured conference 'jollies' for company executives (Thomson et al. 2001). However, on the upswing is a massive surge in support for postgraduate management qualifications, the type of formal MD most appreciated by younger managers. So too is an increased demand from top managers for master classes to meet and discuss the ideas of leading-edge thinkers and, of course, the mushrooming demand for distance learning.

The reasons behind these trends will be complex. However, underpinning some of it will be a disillusionment with the standardised 'menu of courses' approach, once central to the concept of development, and a switch in demand to more complex, customised learning processes, towards partnerships in thinking about experience which can be adapted to the busy lives of modern managers. Strong too is the demand for institutions of higher education to act as a stimulus to creative thinking for busy practitioners and validation of experience through credentials.

Even as the pendulum of fashion swings away from the formal approach to a new orthodoxy of *in situ* learning, an irreducible core of formal MD, both its logic of planned process and its pedagogy of teaching *ex situ*, will remain. Off-the-job seems to have an enduring future as the expositor of functional knowledge in management expertise, as a vehicle for managerial professionalism and as a catalyst for deep thinking on the doing of managing.

Who benefits most from formal development programmes?

Harrison (2002) suggests that formal development programmes are particularly effective for four types of management staff:

(a) young potential managers who have yet to specialise and need a grounding in organisational culture and practice;

(b) managers recently given substantially increased responsibility, for example, change management and need immediate help in developing abilities and skills against a tight agenda;

(c) managers who are set in their ways and may be blocking the development of others;

(d) managers being prepared for more strategic roles within the organisation and need the broadening of vision and values which only formal development can bring.

To categorise these learning needs a little more abstractly, they may be characterised as: (a) socialisation (b) role transition (c) remedial (d) leadership – in the sequence above.

It is interesting to note in passing here that senior managers who are experienced in their roles are notoriously difficult to coax on to courses unless they believe that there may be some business opportunity (e.g. networking) or they will be exposed to new ideas which may give them some business edge. Another group which is very difficult to activate with a company short course is the MBA graduate, for reasons which would be interesting to speculate upon (Thomson et al. 2001).

Question
From your own experience and observation, would you want to extend the range of categories and the groups of managers who would benefit well from development?

Source: Adapted from Harrison, R. (2002) *Learning and Development*, CIPD.

8.4 Designing management training

Let us now turn to the detailed issues of programme planning and design. Here we are moving into the area of professional skills and knowledge associated with HRD as a whole. The methodologies and techniques used in vocational training or staff development are not qualitatively distinct from those used in MD, although there may be differences of emphasis and detail. What follows is a discussion drawn from textbook best practice and the attentive reader will notice that the tone becomes a little more procedural, more managerialist, than is usual in this book. Some readers will be looking for this. Others who believe that there are no certainties or universals in management and that it is ultimately a thinking subject may want to retain a critical perspective and consider cases where these generalisations may not apply.

8.4.1 Stages of programme design

Individual programme development can be regarded as a subsystem of the cycle of development planning which we considered in Chapter 5. What follows is a distillation of professional advice taken from a number of textbooks in the field (e.g. Harrison 2002; Stewart 1999; Reid and Barrington 2000; Huczynski 1986).

Stage One of designing a formal in-house programme for managers requires a consideration of the *development needs* of a group of managers. This will involve interaction with the framework of strategy, the overall business plan, the HRD/MD plan and the priorities which they identify (see Chapter 4). It will also involve a consideration of flows of data from assessment and appraisal systems, TNA, surveys, specifications of new standards and many other sources which inform the MD strategy (Chapter 5). The role of the management developer here is to translate the general priorities of MD strategy pitched at the organisational level into the more detailed statement of learning needs for a specific group of managers (Reid and Barrington 2000; Stewart 1999).

Stage Two of programme design is to *establish objectives for developing managers*. Again the process involves interaction with the MD strategy and aggregating data (e.g. individual appraisal results) to identify patterns of learning needs. Through iterative and interpretive dialogue, broad intentions in the strategic plan (e.g. 'We hope to change the management from one dominated by values of technical expertise to one which is more entrepreneurial.') are turned into more specific, measurable and achievable goals (e.g. 'We intend to change the behaviour of middle managers in divisions a/b/c so that individual initiative is encouraged and rewarded.') (Stewart 1999).

Establishing learning objectives is not easy. To be effective they have to be coherent in terms of the larger framework of corporate objectives. There also needs to be a clear and direct line of sight between identified learning needs and the strategies of learning development within a proposed programme. Enclosed within these larger considerations other questions of philosophy and methodology have to be resolved, for example, what really needs to be learnt on the programme and how the organisation can satisfy itself that managers can now do what they claim after the experience.

Because management is a synthesis of thinking, knowing, valuing and sensing, it is tempting to set learning objectives which define management as a total process. However, this is the ideal. Most organisations find that this approach raises too many problems of definition and measurement. The usual practice, and one advocated by the writers in the field like Stewart (1999) and Reid and Barrington (2000), is to set 'behavioural objectives' which spell out clearly the behaviours needed to reach the standard required. Often a hierarchy of behavioural objectives is established with high-level statements incorporating lower-level 'enabling objectives' specifying in progressive detail the behaviour required, the performance needed and the standards by which people will be judged. Well-designed objectives allow a degree of clarity and focus and give orientation to the direction of learning. An indicative element is often seen as valuable in describing representative behaviour which successful learning should exhibit. Behavioural definitions also provide reasonably objective benchmarks for measuring performance (Simmonds 2004).

Stage Three requires the designers of the MD programme to be clear about the *types of learning* they hope to promote. However clearly formulated the objectives, the learning strategy which flows from them is never deterministic. Learning objectives may suggest some guiding considerations of learning processes but they do not lead naturally to a selection of appropriate methodologies. Further judgement is needed to couple intention and action. This involves reflection on assumptions. Is the learning intervention intended to develop attitudes, knowledge, thinking or social skills? Is the main learning need defined as conceptual or procedural understanding? Is the programme really about building comprehension or practical skills? Is surface learning sufficient or should it go deeper, touching assumptions, values and world-views? Is emotion involved as well as reason? Is the learning concerned with longer-term holistic development or short-term acquisition of instrumental skills (Reid and Barrington 2000)?

Several *taxonomies* of types of learning exist and can be useful for clarifying the learning which intervention hopes to stimulate. For example, Bloom et al. (1956) emphasise several *'domains' of learning.* These are the cognitive (knowledge, facts); the affective (emotions and values); psychomotor (movement); interpersonal (influencing) and self-knowledge (awareness) domains. Developing complex management behaviour may involve building capabilities across a number of these domains, but clear thinking will also be needed to ensure learning outputs are not over-complex or incompatible. Pedler (1974) has also developed a classification system of learning to help in making intervention choices. He talks of levels of learning, that is, from the very specific and tangible to the open and philosophical; from 'learning of parts to learning of the whole'; from simple recall to complex discursive thinking. Intervention patterns become less structured and the content less clear-cut as the programme moves up the hierarchy of learning. Without suggesting an easy 'read across', Pedlar suggests some logical linkages between learning levels and appropriate methods (see Table 8.1 below).

Linkage between learning methods and level of learning

Level	Type of learning	Description	Off-the-job method	On-the-job method
1	Memory checklists	Learner can recall facts; define and describe	Lectures; talks/ programmed learning	Algorithms
2	Understanding	Learner grasps concepts, ideas; can explain, argue; justify	Talk; discussion; case study; business game; incident study	Projects Assignments
3	Application	Learner can apply concepts to relevant situations	Role play; simulations; projects; in-tray	Supervised practice; coaching
4	Transfer	Selecting from 'toolkit' of ideas and techniques to solve non-standard problems. Finding creative solutions	Experimental learning; dialogue; brainstorming; creativity, etc.	Counselling; process consulting; mentoring

Table 8.1 Linkage between learning methods and level of learning

Source: Adapted from: 'Learning in management education', *Journal of European Training*, Vol. 3 No. 3 (Pedler, M. 1974).

As well as defining the learning types and level which will be needed, this is also the stage of design when other values are considered. Do the designers have an explicit *philosophy of learning or learning model* (e.g. Revans 1982; Honey and Mumford 1992; Kolb 1984) in mind which is persuasive in terms of the outcomes they hope to achieve? (see Chapter 6 for a detailed examination of popular models of learning). If so, are they aware of the weaknesses as well as the strengths of this approach and have they thought through the practical consequences of following the model (Huczynski 1986)?

In the same way, are the designers led by a *philosophy of management,* that is, a clear view of what management is about and how managers learn? What balancing point do they want to achieve between giving managers what they, as developers, think is good for them (i.e. perhaps more conceptual, strategic, political development) and what managers typically demand (i.e. often techno-specific, easily applied skills like time management or financial techniques)? As a general rule, the more that implicit assumptions can be made explicit and made part of a conscious agenda of programme decisions, the more likely it will be that choices in learning approach will be aligned to objectives and a principled basis for action (Yukl 2002).

Stage Four is the point at which learning needs, learning objectives and learning models are transmuted into a *detailed learning plan or strategy.* Again, judgements are needed, but at an even greater level of discrimination than at earlier stages. Often there is no obvious rationale for choosing a method to match the learning need. Although, as we have seen, taxonomies of learning do suggest different learning methods, tutors will also differ in how to interpret and use the same method. Issues of professional judgement, educational philosophy and experience of how people learn are all involved in choosing appropriate content for the learning strategy (Harrison 2002; Matthews et al. 2004; Reid and Barrington 2000; Stewart 1999).

In fact, the criteria for developing a coherent intervention strategy requires a series of structured choices. For example, should the selected activities within the programme show a preference for on or off the job? Should there be a blending of formal and informal; internal and external? How do you relate what managers do every day to what they will do on the day of the course and how do you ensure that the learning on the course flows into learning back in the workplace (Harrison 2002; Reid and Barrington 2000; Huczynski 1986)?

Again, careful judgements are needed between a range of variables in constructing the programme.

- Is the programme content and balance compatible and integrated with the career development strategy of the organisation?

- Is the learning anticipated realistic within the resources available for development?

- Is the mix of proposed elements the best possible compromise between the desirable and the possible; between satisfying the organisation's needs and the individual's expectations; between meeting the learning preferences of all and retaining the motivation of the most able?

- Is the programme really appropriate to the level of managers it aims to engage – in terms of age, attitudes, maturity, skill and aspiration?

- Will the approaches and techniques employed maximise the opportunity for transfer of skills and insight to the workplace?

Stage Five is the level of the individual learning event (e.g. a short course, workshop, seminar, etc.) within the larger development programme. When you have set the coordinates of the overall learning strategy, a final set of fine-tuned decisions are needed about the form of delivery for each event. For example, a development programme for, say, graduate management trainees might consist of residential blocks of formal tuition; individual away-days; conferences; seminars on the *formal* side; ALS or peer support groups; reading groups; self-development and so on the *informal*. Decisions will be needed at the level of the programme on the combination of approaches into a coherent whole and each learning event will also require design decisions. It is this interface, between the learning strategy of the programme and the programme delivery of each event within it, that makes or breaks the learning experience as a whole (Yukl 2002).

Reid and Barrington (2000) and Harrison (2002), among others, suggest the types of issues which may be considered here.

- How do the objectives of this part of the programme link in with the programme strategy as a whole?
- Is the selection/nominating process working as it should (e.g. do nominating managers understand the objectives of the programme and criteria for nomination? Are the nominees volunteers rather than conscripts?). If the participant doesn't want to be there very little learning will take place.
- Are the chosen methods compatible with the programme objectives and both varied and relevant?
- Does the structuring of the event reflect the learning expectations and preferences of the group (e.g. has any attempt been made to define the learning expectations of the target group)?
- What is the nature of the group (e.g. size, the age profile; organisational seniority, attitudes to learning, likely motivation, etc. will all have implications for methods that can be used, the tempo of the event the balance of instructional/participative involvement etc. – e.g. beyond a certain number of members participative exercises are impossible)?
- At the micro-level, how is the programme structured? Are the objectives of each session tied to the outcomes of the programme as a whole? Does the material flow on coherently with logical connections between each topic? Is each learning event tailored to the whole? Does the programme allow good pace without rushing and blurring? Is there a sense of purpose and direction so that participants are not left wondering where the process is heading?
- How will the formal elements of the learning be delivered (e.g. through in-house staff or external contractors)?
- Is the proposed programme of learning really compatible with the culture of the organisation?
- What arrangements will be made to ramp up involvement (e.g. getting commitment from line managers, reassuring participants and getting senior management involvement)?
- Are the resources available (equipment, accommodation, etc.) adequate for the purpose?

- Are the key elements, venue, timing, scheduling of work and so on all planned with an eye to inclusion and do not indirectly discriminate by imposing barriers to involvement (e.g. a residential course at a weekend may indirectly discriminate against women with young children)?
- Is there any provision for follow-up at the end of the programme to help implement learning (e.g. peer support networking; post-course tutoring etc.)?

Because this detailed programmatic planning is not a science operating to universal rules, tensions between what may appear pedagogically to be the best solution and what is pragmatically possible will force many compromises. For example, faced with a development brief, the programme designer may believe that attitudinal/behavioural change is most likely to happen through a planned learning experience which blends a range of activities over a period of time. However, organisational contingencies such as cost, immediate demands and the task commitments of the target group of management trainees may dictate a two-day course. If s/he cannot change the constraints, the role of the developer in these circumstances is to suboptimise and choose a feasible solution which will provide the best possible learning outcome in the circumstances. 'Rough and dirty' as this may be, it is ultimately the juggling art which the developer is paid to perform (Reid and Barrington 2000).

Case study: 'A damp squib': the MD programme that failed

SMEs (small and medium sized businesses) are often criticised for not giving attention to MD programmes or done in an *ad hoc* and tactical way without proper planning and professional management. This is an example of what can go wrong.

'Voicebox', a provider of call-centre services with a staff of 150 on three sites in South-east England, had not yet attempted any formal MD. However, it became apparent that there were significant skill gaps within the management team and evidence of friction and mistrust between the call-centre managers with a client interface and the account managers concerned with operational support.

It was decided to run a twelve-week management course (one day a week) to improve specific management skills which were identified as important (e.g. appraisal, handling grievances, financial control) and also to build the management team. The sessions were run in-house by two junior HR staff (the HR department itself only consisted of four people) and consisted mainly of group activities. Class sessions were supported by a distance-learning package which had been bought off the shelf from a commercial training consultancy. There was a test at the end of the 12 weeks and a certificate was given to those that passed.

Attendance was sporadic but the pass rate was good and the 'happy sheets' were positive; however, a focus group held one month after the programme suggested that the programme had not really achieved its ambitions. The problems which emerged held salutary lessons for the organisation going into MD for the first time.

- The managers asked to attend the course were given no relief from their usual duties and the culture of 'immediate pressures' and 'finger pointing' meant that managers could not 'let things slip' a little to invest in their development.
- Having authorised the programme, top managers seemed to take no interest in it.

- The facilitators were seen as too young and inexperienced to have credibility.
- Participants were unsure of the objectives of the course and why they were being asked to attend.
- No attempt had been made to design the course in collaboration with the participants and it was seen as 'something dreamt up by HR'.
- The managers did not see how it fitted with the business strategy or, indeed, any of the big issues which confronted them.
- For most, it became an exercise in cramming for the test so that they could demonstrate to their bosses that they had 'gone through the motions'.
- There was certainly no evidence that bringing the two sets of managers had improved working relationships and built a more cohesive culture.

A negative experience of MD such as this can do much to discredit its value, resulting in apathy or even hostility towards future learning events. However, for the organisation that wants to become more professional at MD, there are many lessons here – the importance of good diagnosis, strategic alignment of learning, the value of a learning model in choosing appropriate methods, and the crucial involvement of top management are just some of these. What also emerges is that a knee-jerk reaction ('We haven't tried a management training course') to an entrenched problem like poor teamworking is likely to prove disappointing. The top management needs to start by analysing the fundamental issues, deciding on the nature of the problem that confronts them and choosing from a range of interventions which are wider than just a formal programme.

Question

Faced with these results, if you were in top management at 'Voicebox' what would you now be doing?

Source: Personal experience and observation

8.5 Management training courses

8.5.1 Patterns of management training

Every year thousands of in-house courses are run in and for companies, large and small. Some are held at comfortable management retreats, some are held at the training suite of a commercial supplier, most happen on site at the client's premises. Management training is big business worth millions of pounds each year and the volume of this activity is increasing all the time. Attending a two-day course on 'communications' or a week-long workshop on 'team building' or a one-day event on 'emotional intelligence' is part of management culture (at least in the West) and a mark of belonging to 'the management'. Indeed, attending some courses is almost a rite of passage which publicly demonstrates that you have reached a certain level of organisational status. Attending the course is symbolic of your achievement.

The high end of the short-course syndrome is the 'management of change' executive seminar or fast-track development programme for 'young managers of potential' at the company's residential training facility (e.g. BA's prestigious Young Professionals Programme in a leafy park country house, the three-week NHS Leadership Development Programme for high-flyers at the prestigious King's Fund). Executive development, which is not usually qualification-based, is usually provided by universities, independent management colleges (e.g. Ashridge, Roffey Park, Sundridge Park, etc.) or independent consultants. The range here is vast. For example, it includes: very sophisticated seminars by leading academics and practitioners to business leaders at elite institutions like Warwick or London Business School; skills development courses for middle mangers or leadership for professionals as well as a three-day programme on 'time management' for the supervisors in a company's 'Accounts' department. We examine the evolving partnerships between business and educational providers in the next chapter.

That sinking feeling: *They* say I have to go on another course!

I hate going on short management courses. They are just not my thing. I hate the 'creeping death' of introductions and then the 'ice breaker', where you throw the cushion to someone and say their name. I hate getting into small groups and then having to 'report back' if you happen to catch the tutor's eye or the group pressurises you. I don't really want to 'brainstorm' with people I don't know or trust or pretend to build a team with them. Then all that nonsense about learning styles and bullet points on flip charts . . . When you leave the two days later, you get on that train to come home in a mood of complete euphoria and then something miraculous happens . . . it's as if your memory of the event and everything associated with it has been removed by a hypnotist. Next day, can't remember a thing.

These are the comments of a management friend who is clearly not a fan of management training. However, other managers are always asking for time off and funding to 'develop themselves' on the latest training programme. Mumford (1980) wisely advises the thoughtful manager to break free from any institutionalised system that defines the development needs of 'people in his position' by putting them on courses (e.g. 'We always send our best people to Harvard'). Instead be critical in deciding if you need to go on a course and, if so, choose which is best for you, that is, make enquiries, first of yourself (i.e. your learning needs in terms of personal objectives; the conditions under which you learn best) and then of providers about what is on offer and what you might expect to learn. A genuinely self-directive learner does not settle for marketing speak but probes and gets third-party testimony to find the best possible fit. Quite often the result of this will be that attending a course is just not a good use of time.

Questions
What's your experience of going on courses? Were they mainly fulfilling or frustrating for you? Under what conditions did you learn something useful?

Company training often takes the form of catch-up to help managers fill in gaps within their portfolio of experience (e.g. giving them a full range of practical management skills; a taste of some specialist areas of management; an introduction to strategy). It is also 'competency maintenance', that is, helping managers keep up to date in fast-changing areas like legislation and technology and new ideas in management (e.g. 'process re-engineering', 'learning organisation' *ad infinitum*). Courses like this are useful in helping managers acquire knowledge and at least the rudiments of skill not reliably acquired from work experience alone. Indeed, where the workplace is not conducive to learning, courses are an alternative learning environment, free from the immediate tasks and pressures of organisational life: *time-out for real thinking*.

Short courses can be offered in-house or as part of open programmes. In-house courses have the advantage of being tailored specifically to the company's needs and are consistent with wider company culture. This helps the facilitator connect learning on the course with continuous learning in the workplace and integrate knowledge transfer with everyday experience. The course can make explicit use of company material and refer to company history for compelling examples. However, there are also well-known drawbacks with in-house courses. The range of experience among participants may be narrow; there will be none of the synergies which new blood and fresh outside perspectives can bring. Participants may have trouble relaxing, admitting doubt or experimenting with new behaviours if the course is part of the appraisal process, or their performance on it may affect their career prospects. Mixing levels of seniority on the same course can inhibit spontaneity because of the issues of continuing relationships and reputation which are involved. Finally the in-service course can seem rather insular and parochial, culturally bound by the horizons of the organisation and in-house trainers, however good, are always compromised by the taint of over-familiarity (Mumford 1997).

Open programmes at commercial management training colleges can overcome some of these problems. In a 'stranger' environment managers may be more prepared to take risks with learning and be more relaxed about accepting vital feedback on their practice of skills (i.e. their performance on the course will not affect their position back in the office) (Mumford 1997). A wider range of material can be used; there is likely to be more scope for conceptualisation; a wider mix of participants may generate creative ferment and facilitators may have more sophistication and credibility. However, all these advantages must be weighed against greater problems in contextualising and applying learning to an action programme at the end of the course (Eastburn 1980).

8.5.2 The problem with courses

In recent years the culture of the short course as a means of developing managers has come under sustained attack as contributing to a piecemeal approach to development which is merely tokenistic in building usable learning and can be actually disempowering for managers by encouraging a false sense of knowing. Mumford and Gold (2004), Handy (1988), Storey (1989) and most other leading members of the development establishment, have all expressed their reservations about the value of the short course. Here is a distillation of their observations.

Managers need to be motivated to come on a course. In practice, the wrong people may be sent on the wrong course at the wrong time. If 'sheep dip' procedures operate in the company (i.e. You've been with us for two years but not yet been on the social skills development course . . . So, we're sending you!') then it is likely that attendance will be seen as a ritual rather than a vehicle for personal development. In the same way, if there is limited discussion on why they have been proposed for a course, or even worse, a system operates by which people are expected to fill in gaps created by first-choice nominees who are unable to attend, commitment is likely to be low.

There are other reasons why people may not want to attend a course. Perhaps their pride is hurt that the system has identified weaknesses in their skills or knowledge and they are resentful. Perhaps they dislike the philosophy or methodology of a course (e.g. many managers resist outdoor development because they disapprove of the physicality and competitive nature of the experience). Perhaps there is fear of embarrassment in front of a group of peers or of assessment which might undermine their standing at work. Some people have had bad experiences of learning at school and even in adult life have phobias about formal learning. Pressures at work and disdain for the quality of learning or the credibility of the trainers may deter others. In the case of senior managers, they may harbour the belief that their seniority suggests that they have little more to learn about management and their time is valuable, so management courses are not for them (Handy 1989).

Managers may be committed to the purpose of the course yet feel that it is distant from what they do at work. This is a perennial criticism of management education as a whole and we will return to it later when we consider accredited programmes. Handy (1989) talks of short courses as 'cultural islands of learning' which are experienced as isolated from their everyday reality of management. Mumford emphasises that 'successful courses start where the managers are, not where the developers are'. For courses to resonate intellectually and emotionally with participants they must engage with the disjointed, experiential social processes of management (as we describe them in Chapter 7).

However, because developers' definitions often prevail in practice, short courses can often seem like artificially sealed packages of knowledge (marketing; finance; quantitative methods; communication skills, etc.) and abstract best-practice models which are distant from the *felt experience* of managing (Mangham 1988). Short courses are also accused of trivialising management by turning complexity into oversimplified principles and checklists. This can have the effect of giving some managers a false sense of security, a sense that they know about, say, 'motivation' because they can reproduce the mnemonic of an explanatory diagram, while others will intellectually switch off from a body of material which seems to reduce the complex judgements they have to make into a shopping list of obvious sounding steps. Too often a collusive relationship can develop between the tutor providing the 'standard management education kit' (Watson 2004) and students uncritically accept the nice pictures, diagrams and undemanding mantras to please their bosses without hope of learning anything relevant.

However, management courses can be practical, relevant, sensitive to the perceptions of participants and still fail to have a significant impact. It is a common experience of developers to have great days away with the executive team of an organisation during which ideas are exchanged, problems confronted and conceptual models developed. But these 'seven-day wonders', although fun and stimulating, often fail the test of knowledge transfer (Margerison 1991). Nothing changes back in the office. The problem seems to lie in the confusion participants can feel about what they were supposed to learn from the course or what they were supposed to do with the learning once they had gained it. Here the failure is a lack of coupling between formal learning with continuous learning on the job.

Courses are also criticised for being vehicles for corporate propaganda and managerial culture building. Heller (1986), in a tongue-in-cheek critique, suggests that in-house courses in some of the bigger companies have the feel of a secret society or a conference of the Soviet Communist Party. The educational element on a course is hijacked by top management seeking to use the event as a vehicle for outlining their business vision and legitimating their authority to a captive audience. Events are orchestrated to whip up loyalty to the leadership; indoctrinate people into core values, anoint heroes and demonise fools and villains.

At some residential retreats, Heller (1995) claims there is a sense of being part of a doctrinaire cult or a cell for 'ideological brainwashing'. Isolated from the world in comfortable residential cocoons, managers are ego-stripped and reborn through rituals like T-groups and team games so that they can emerge purified with a new culturally approved identity (e.g. become a more self-aware activist of the new organisational vision).

Of course, Heller is exaggerating for effect, but there is certainly something very evangelical about many management courses, and it is apparent that ideological agendas are being played out which have little to do with management learning. However, in the end, the symbolic role of the course may be more important. For example, mere invitation to attend the course may be its main point because it is a sign of favour, that the organisation is prepared to invest in you as one of a small circle of the faithful destined for higher rank. Certainly these are the political meanings which are often read into attendance on key courses by the many 'organisation watchers' which modern organisational conditions now breed.

Excessive use of management training for ideological and political ends is a dangerous game, to be played with care or it will induce a widespread, corrosive cynicism about the value and purpose of formal management learning.

Are providers of commercial management training patronising their clients?

Imagine the scene: a group of about 20 middle-aged managers in HRM/HRD/Organisational Development, gathered together in a well-lit and elegant training room in a very reputable commercial training centre. There was quite a lot of well-paid talent in the room. It had started with:

> If you had to represent your management style as an animal, what animal would you be? Break into pairs to discuss.

Then:

> Right, all the group stand up and shake yourselves. Are you feeling relaxed? Now I'm going to say some things to you about change in organisations. Now if you agree with the statement jump forward, if you don't agree jump backwards. If you're not sure jump to the side . . .

Never liking 'Simple Simon Says' games at primary school, this author decided to sit on the margins despite comments that he was not showing the right spirit.

Salaman and Butler (1990) and Ready and Conger (2003) have suggested that the modern consensus that managers are practical thinkers and doers may have gone too far. It leads to assumptions that managers are not capable of conceptual thought, sustained attention or critical thinking. In the name of relevance, course designers often attempt to boil down complex ideas into lists of 'factors' and are heavy on 'prescriptions' and 'action plans' without real discussion of context or conditions of application. An 'edutainment' ethos requires variety in themes and teaching media; the use of highly simplified, even childlike language and at least three simultaneous forms of communication (e.g. Powerpoint, handouts and oral exposition). Formal input is kept short; everything has to be illustrated with simple diagrams or 'fun' pictures; abstraction is minimised in favour of stories; philosophical discussion is discouraged and 'instant comprehensibility' dominates.

Ready and Conger (2003) argue that the 'commercialisation' of management training is a form of 'dumbing down'. Techniques, activities, games and general 'busyness' become a substitute for real thinking and critical inquiry. Tutors are turned into crowd pleasing 'performers' with their main eye on the aptly named 'happy sheets' at the end. If you can send them home excited, engaged and with a smile on their faces, you have done your job. The consumer has purchased the marketed product and is satisfied. It is a 'commodification' of learning which offers a 'rush to action' package, instant solutions to complex problems.

Salaman and Butler believe that this approach only really appeals to extreme 'activists'; it risks disabling real learning by infantilising the (adult) students and putting them in a 'passive' role, debasing thinking and demotivating independent thinking. It can also be seen as ultimately patronising and contemptuous of the punter.

This is not a pedagogy which seems to have any place at a university but is it appropriate even within a corporate setting which has serious learning intentions? It is *ironic* that the participants on these courses increasingly have one or two university degrees gained by more traditional pedagogies which involved the demonstration of considerable sustained intellectual ability. In their managerial work they are often confronted with human and technical problems of great complexity and sophistication. It is *ironic* too that management training often ignores the proven intellectual ability of participants and uses the pedagogy of the primary school.

Questions

Do you agree with this perception about the 'infantilisation' of managers in training? Perhaps you think these views are those of a killjoy, when learning should be light hearted and fun? Justify your arguments.

Note: To consider these issues in further depth see: Salaman, G. and Butler, J. (1990) 'Why managers won't learn', *Management Education and Development*, Vol. 21, No. 3; Ready, D. and Conger, J. (2003) 'Why leadership development efforts fail', *Sloan Management Review*, Spring.

8.5.3 Conditions for success in course design

From the foregoing we can understand why Mumford and Gold (2004), as writers of the leading textbook in this field, are so sceptical of management training as formal, planned developer-led learning which is 'done to' people rather than learning for themselves (Type 3 Learning in Mumford's model, see Chapter 7). It has its place, but not as a substitute for other forms of learning, only as a supplement to reinforce coherent webs of integrated learning. All the same, can we go on from what we know to define the conditions most likely to encourage success in course design and implementation? What is offered here is not last-word prescription but a summary of thinking from the literature which may stimulate thoughtful managers to their own response.

Osbaldeston and Barham (1992) remind us that any MD programme should be linked to organisational objectives, address defined challenges and follow systemic assessment of need. These general considerations, apart from short courses, are likely to be considered in only part fulfilment of defined learning need. Professional consensus suggests that courses should not be simple stand-alone units of development. Like a set of Lego bricks put together to build a wall, their value lies in collective connection with other units of learning to form coherent chains of learning. *Courses work best when they are part of a deliberate, planned learning programme* in which formal and experiential learning are sequenced and dovetailed so that learning happens in the form and the time when it is needed (Sadler-Smith 2006; Yukl 2002)

Setting the learning objectives of the course and designing its content should involve the managers who will participate in it (Fee 2001). What are their understandings, the issues which need addressing, their own weaknesses? To avoid the course becoming developer-led it needs to be designed around the perceived needs of participants. However, this is not to say that participant definitions are the only legitimate ones and the course designer may be open to accusations of pandering or indulging the client if s/he abdicates a professional responsibility to balance expectations of immediate relevance and populist values with a consideration of wider issues and bigger objectives.

The option of the short course may be most viable when there is a need to learn a discrete skill (e.g. financial planning) or when removal from the everyday emotional context is needed to reframe attitudes and behaviours (e.g. by creating an artificial social laboratory in the class room, T-groups can help people experiment with new social strategies in a safe learning situation before applying them on the job). Taking managers out of their daily environment can help them to focus on analysis and self-awareness beyond the restrictive horizons of the job.

A major concern for course designers should be how to create *favourable conditions for managers to engage with the course content and be energised to use their learning at work*. This has many implications for micro-design. Professional orthodoxy suggests that successful courses are likely to build on familiar learning experiences and processes at work. So, as Mumford and Gold (2004) suggest, learning methods on the course should reinforce these patterns of learning. For example, if managers are not used to listening critically to lectures (or presentations) in their work they may not know how to derive benefit from them in class; many adults have an emotional resistance to being taught in a formal setting and are suspicious of implicit agendas in courses. Setting tasks to illuminate concepts may make more emotional connecion because they echo familiar experiences of problem-solving in the workplace. The challenge for the facilitator is to find tasks which may be enjoyable in themselves, which are not trivial and allow a practical link to be made to the life situation of the manager. The argument is that if participants can see the link they are more likely to use the knowledge behind it as a tool for action.

However, there are other issues which inhibit knowledge transfer, not least the lack of reinforcement, resistant cultural factors and politics in the workplace. If courses are to have a real behavioural impact, it is suggested that time be set aside for mapping these anticipated obstacles to change and developing an action plan in the classroom for implementing new approaches on return to the office. Sessions might also be usefully given over to the politics of implementation (Harrison 2002).

Successful courses seem to be underpinned by coherent learning philosophies. Effective trainers will be sensitive to differences in the typical learning patterns of academics (e.g. learning through abstraction, reflection, conceptualisation) and the management students they teach (e.g. typically learning through trial and error; guided experimentation with a few key concepts) and make appropriate adjustments to pedagogy, *whilst avoiding crude stereotyping* (Mumford 1980; Handy 1989).

Good course designers will also recognise that different MD techniques reflect varying learning concepts and advance different learning objectives. They will appreciate that a guiding logic is needed to select and combine methods to address multiple learning styles and preferences in learning strategy. This will be led by detailed profiling of participant learning definitions, an understanding of the strengths and weaknesses of the MD methods available and the types of learning they promote (see next section).

Good course designers often use a variety of methods. They will strive for a good balance between thinking and doing; between stimulating the mind and engaging the emotions; between stretching people so that they feel the shock of the new, but not leaving them feeling upset and unsettled. However specific and functional the course, good design surely finds space for process. Courses provide conditions well suited to helping people to understand how they learn and how they can help learning in the organisation as a whole. This linking of content and process, of single and double loop learning greatly improves the chances of extending learning into practical action beyond the course. It also serves to blur the false distinction between formal and experiential learning. Properly designed, they are symbiotic (Yukl 2002).

What an effective course should do

As we will discuss in Chapter 14 when we look at 'evaluation', the more ambiguous the purpose of a course the more difficult it will be to measure its effect. If the subject is something like change, culture and/or leadership the effects may not show up for months or years. Besides, 'effectiveness' can be interpreted in different ways. For example, if you go on a course and learn nothing new but meet some people with ideas that stimulate you to make changes back at work, was the course nevertheless successful because it enabled you to think and try something new?

Here is the author's rough guide for deciding that a course was successful.

- It captured your attention and interest.
- It seemed relevant to your current issues or future plans.
- It connected with your existing experience.
- It offered you concepts and ideas which provided a new way of seeing (the shock of the new).
- It engaged with your emotion (it was exciting and seemed intuitively right).
- It enlightened you not just about a technique (which may easily become obsolete) but also about ideas and perspectives which helped you conceptualise process.
- It energised you to take action to make concepts real.
- It emboldened you to overcome the obstacles in implementing change.
- It gave you some new knowledge and skills you can use or bolstered your confidence in the skills you already have.

Question
Perhaps you have your own criteria for looking back and deciding if a course was a good use of your time. What are they?

8.6 Off-the-job MD methods

8.6.1 The 'field' of methods as a whole

As we have seen, MD methods are not effective in themselves, but in combination. Choosing MD methods and putting them together in ways which embody a guiding theory, give expression to varying learning styles and satisfy defined learning outcomes, represents the 'art' element of MD. As we have seen there is some evidence-based guidance on the relationship between method and factors like domains and type of learning, learning preferences, the maturity, size, cultural diversity and so on of the learning group (Huczynski 1986); much remains within the area of professional judgement (i.e. pedagogical values and heuristic rules of thumb which are part of the folk wisdom of developers).

As we will see, this is probably reflective of the relatively unevaluated nature of MD as a professional body of knowledge. According to Mumford and Gold (2004) very little has been written about the link between method and learning theory and between method and outcome. This leaves MD unprotected against fads, fashion and charlatanism.

What follows is a cursory, but critical survey of the best-known MD methods used in formal management training which have stood the test of time or seem to go beyond mere 'here today and gone tomorrow' faddism. Here we can only scratch the surface. The serious student will consult Andrew Hucyzinski's encyclopaedia of MD methods (both the 1986 and 2000 editions) which is comprehensive and sweeping in its scope.

In considering the armoury of weapons which the developer has at his disposal in developing formal programmes, several themes stand out.

- The two editions of Hucyzinski's work (1986, 2001) illustrate the dynamism and turbulence of this area. Many methods which were fashionable in 1986 seem to have vanished from sight by 2000. Others are recognisable but re-branded for a new management generation.
- Some methods are significant development tools and are likely to have a continuing place in the arsenal of approaches. They have a broad focus and are linked to pedagogies of learning. Others are narrow techniques (e.g. the Managerial Grid) which may have longevity but no theoretical grounding and, fun events (e.g. fire-walking to build management confidence) which will probably be transient (but only time will tell).
- Some methods seem to be tutor-centred and others are student-centred. Despite the swing to participative, active learning, directive learning still has a part to play.
- Some methods seem to be on the way in and others on the way out.
- A few methods are OD-led and span the divide between collective and individual learning. Where the technique seems to have a broad management of change focus it is held over for consideration in the chapter on OD.

8.6.2 A Critique of MD methods

Lectures

Lectures and related methods such as talks, demonstrations, keynote speeches at conferences score strongly as vehicles for conveying information, especially if the material is theoretical. The effectiveness of the lecture depends on the perceived relevance of the material, the care with which the lectures are prepared and the stage presence and oral skills of the lecturer. It is generally held that the impact of the lecture can be enhanced if it is accompanied by visual aids (e.g. Powerpoint; OHP; flipchart, etc.) and includes participation by the audience (e.g. Q/A sessions). The use of films and DVDs can also dramatise the lecture. Moving images can reinforce themes in the lecture and make the subject come alive. If stopped at key points DVDs can act as a stimulus for discussion.

The lecture/presentation is much criticised in the literature and evangelical proponents of experiential learning will dismiss it as didactic because it implies a directive form of learning. Typically the lecturer takes on the role of expert and controls learning, focusing mainly on the content rather than the process of learning. The lack of participation can be demotivating for some students who can become bored and switch off. There is also the problem that the method gives little feedback to the lecturer that people are understanding what is taught or can apply the lessons. All the same, this technique has the advantage that it gives the student an orientation to an unfamiliar body of knowledge; it is not intimidating to participants and if the lecturer is lively it can stimulate thinking and inquiry. If the lecture is complemented with other techniques – classroom aids, games, case-study reading, and so on – it still has a powerful role to play in management development and education (Fee 2001; Huczynski 1986).

Pedagogies of teaching and facilitation

Formal training programmes are likely to oscillate between these two polarised pedagogies, between sessions or even within the space of a single session.

Tutor-centred learning	*Student-centred learning*
Directive learning	Facilitative learning
Focus on a learning agenda offered to the group	Focus on the group; defining its agenda
Expert role of tutor	Tutor facilitates group; surfacing their experience
Concentration on content	Concentration on process; social and technical
Tutor remains detached	Tutor works to build rapport with group
Participation is limited to functional tasks	Encouraging participation for general development
Presenting ideas and solutions	Helping the group find solutions
Detailed learning plans	Learning plans are flexible to meet learner needs

Table 8.2 Pedagogies of teaching and facilitation
Source: Adapted from *Facilitation Skills*, CIPD (Bee, F. and Bee, R. 1999).

Watson (2004) believes there is a tendency for management knowledge to be offered as packages of formalised information which do not have an obvious connection to the everyday practice of managing as experienced by the students. The danger is that students absorb the models and theories uncritically without their relevance to the doing of managing being discussed, interpreted and applied. Lecturers present models and leave the students to make the connections. Watson calls this 'surface level processing'. Students recognise that there is a gap between what they learn in class and what they do in management but they cynically go with the flow in order to satisfy their bosses and 'win badges'. Watson argues for a more critical and interpretive approach in MT which 'discomforts and challenges students to think for themselves'.

Raab (2004) echoes these views by suggesting that trainers should become 'experts in not knowing'. They should de-structure their sessions, embrace the facilitated end of the spectrum (above). He stresses that trainers should not be 'people pleasers'. Helping the client really learn may require a move beyond consumerism. The trainer should act as a facilitator who resists prescription, resists student pressure to act as the expert and creates a safe space in which learners can escape from dependency to explore their own experience and the relevance of theory in helping them reflect. The role of the tutor is to challenge and support the group in its learning, to give it confidence in the value of its own experience and take some risks in learning. This is easier said than done. The group will project its anxieties on to the facilitator, push for structure to meet its need for security and blame the tutor for not giving them authoritative knowledge. Raab believes that the wise tutor will resist these pressures, push the expectations back and continue to help the group create meanings from its own experiences.

> **Pause for thought**
>
> ### The modern way: 'do it yourself'
>
> How do you respond to pedagogies such as these which reframe the trainer as facilitator and consultant helping people to 'learn for themselves'? Do you think they are always valid or only under certain conditions?

Discussions

Located towards the tutor-led end of the continuum, seminars and discussions are useful for reinforcing points raised in lectures. Discussions can be quite controlled, with the tutor guiding discussion according to an agenda of issues which are considered important, or they can be relatively open and unstructured.

The value of discussions lies in the opportunity they provide for a free exchange of information and views. This creates a forum for course members to participate in the dialogue and reach their own conclusions on where they stand on the issues. It promotes shared attitudes and understandings and team coherence. Discussions also offer direct feedback to the facilitator on group progress in learning and sends signals for assessing further interventions which may be necessary.

On the downside, discussions can be time-consuming if the discourse moves away from the topic at hand and process issues become complex and overwhelming. This faces the facilitator with the choice of allowing the discussion to ramble onto new and interesting themes with the benefits of greater personal involvement and group cohesion or foreshortening the talk in order to keep to a schedule for the session. The strategy which the facilitator adopts will tell us a lot about whether s/he is fundamentally tutor or student-centred (Latham and Seijts 1998).

Dialogic methods

These vary considerably in the degree of structure and direction which is involved. Didactic (instructive), Socratic (questioning) and facilitative (drawing out) methods are all involved, although the balance will shift from one technique to another and in relation to the tutor's style of teaching.

- *Panel discussions* involve assembling a panel of experts which discusses complicated themes in front of a largely passive audience whose involvement is largely restricted to asking questions.
- *Buberian debate* is a formally structured debate in which the pros and cons of an idea are presented with examination of the cases, questions, discussion and concluding statements and sometimes votes.
- *Syndicates* are small groups separated off from the main discussion group which discuss parts of a larger issue in depth and report back to a plenary session. This is a method which often draws people out and helps with team building.
- *Buzz groups* are smaller and more informal versions. They may be set up during a learning session to discuss key issues as they emerge. They are useful for breaking the ice at the beginning of a formal programme, for varying the rhythm and giving people confidence in explaining their view.

See A. Huczynski (2001) for a more detailed discussion and critique of these methods.

Case studies

These can take a number of forms. Vignettes or critical incidents allow a close examination of a single incident, as it casts some light on deeper management themes and processes. These can be useful teaching tools in support of didactic presentations and also facilitative devices for soliciting attitudes, values and beliefs.

Case studies provide richer and more complex illustrations of management behaviour. Case studies of all lengths have always been popular in management education. For example, the case study method is the cornerstone of Harvard Business School's teaching and the mainstay of training for a million in-company management training programmes.

The advantages of the case study approach are considerable. It focuses on real-world management problems. It encourages active learning through practical problem-solving. It helps students hone their vital decision-making and communication skills. It stimulates interest in the abstract as a means of making sense of the whole and is useful for illustrating conceptual material. Students say that it gives a feel for management and provides insight into the messy, cross-functional nature of business life for those new to management. Case studies can also help students to develop generic thinking (central to general management) and builds the self-confidence which comes from thinking for yourself.

In the hands of imaginative teachers, case studies can serve as an embodiment of facilitative learning and a vehicle for the Socratic method of inquiry in which people are encouraged to examine the deep assumptions on which their beliefs are based through meditation on a series of penetrating questions.

How the Socratic method works

- Someone proposes something which might be described as common sense (perhaps a student makes a pronouncement about management from a reading of the case study which s/he believes is unproblematic and universal e.g. 'Management is always about searching for what is efficient and effective').
- The tutor believes that, despite the self-confidence of the proposer, the statement may not be universally true and suggests situations where this may not apply.
- If an exception to a general rule is found, then the general rule is either false or only partially true.
- If so, then the initial statement needs to be modified.
- This may go on a number of times before a general principle or a proposition with contingent conditions emerges which everyone can agree.

The question and answer method of inquiry (Socratic dialectic) often couples with pretend ignorance (Socratic irony). These techniques are useful for helping people to examine the roots of their long-held assumptions and for clearing the mind to think afresh.

Question
How could you use the Socratic method in your study or at work?

Source: Adapted from de Botton, A. (2000) *The Consolations of Philosophy*, p. 24, Hamish Hamilton.

However, despite its strengths, there are many criticisms of the case study method. It focuses mainly on past experience which may be no guide to future management. Because most of the available case studies have reported Western management problems, cases can seem ethnocentric. Doing cases where answers are derived from complex problems can mislead newcomers to management into believing that they know more about managing than they really do. It is difficult to reproduce the political context in case studies and this encourages an unrealistically technicist approach to management problem-solving. It has also been claimed (Latham and Seijts 1998) that case study analysis involves a relatively static form of learning based on single loop learning and groupthink norms which rarely result in imaginative solutions. By suggesting that there is a right answer which the neophyte has to discover, case studies can be part of the process by which young managers are socialised into being a 'safe pair of hands' rather than 'finding their own way' reformers (Woodall and Winstanley 1999; Yukl 2002).

Games and simulations

Games have always been popular with management developers; they can be computerised or non-computerised, simple or complex, interactive with others or interactive with a machine.

Games attempt to reproduce elements of business situations. They involve understanding a situation and coming to terms with it by carefully balancing factors in making skilful choices. Games develop a variety of management skills, for example, decision-making, judgement, improvisation and teamworking under conditions of stress. Teams are often asked to compete, performance results are fed back at intervals during the game and participants are required to manage the consequences of their decisions. A classic example of this is the 'action maze' in which participants select action paths from a variety of alternatives within a complex net. Working within the net they come to understand how actions have consequences and how fine the dividing line is between success and failure. Sophisticated board games, based on corporate ethics and computerised in-tray exercises which feed back the results of decisions taken on a batch of miscellaneous documents, also operate on similar principles.

Other games give attention to the interaction within and between groups. Competitive team decision-making games like 'building a tower of cards', 'constructing a paper aeroplane' or the now infamous 'landing on the moon' game are well known to thousands of middle managers. With proper facilitation and discussion they are valuable for giving people an appreciation of the strengths and weaknesses of the team process.

Simulation is a safe space in which managers can practise new skills with little risk to the company that employs them. It is learning by doing within a formalised programme and that is attractive to many managers. The best games are fun. They break up the ennui of a lengthy development programme and make a dry subject interesting. People often have a good time and come away energised.

However, games and simulations have many disadvantages. They can foster a misleading sense that ambiguous business conditions can be structured so the right answer emerges. They appeal more to activists and pragmatists than theorists and reflectors who often criticise them for being artificial and contrived. There is also the problem that this is a tutor-led technique and some managers may rankle at the degree of structure which is imposed on the learning, especially if they have problems in entering the spirit of the game, and define it as trivial or irrelevant to their working lives.

To work, the games have to be related to clear learning objectives and participants need to be good at abstracting from reality, accepting the artificiality of the situation and imagining its relationship with real life. However, critics, like Mumford, ask whether there is any need to simulate reality when there are many experiential processes to examine the real thing (Huczynski 1986).

Pause for thought

Taking things seriously

Many of the MT exercises in the classroom, for example, psychodrama, games, role-plays, simulation and so on require you to suspend disbelief and get into the right spirit for them to work.

Do you find you can do this?

E-learning

The growing use of on-line learning, IT-based learning and learning using electronic means (e.g. CD-ROM; virtual reality technology, etc.) will be examined in the next chapter in relation to distance and open learning and master's courses at university. It is probably sufficient to note here that IT is growing rapidly and will probably have a major impact on how managers learn in the years ahead.

Computer-assisted learning, especially when it is integrated with telecommunications, allows managers to learn in their own time and at their own pace. Interactive digital screens allow individuals to explore complex decision-making issues through business simulations. Virtual reality platforms provide authentic-seeming 3D worlds in which managers can gain vicarious techno-experience before they are immersed in the real thing. Chat rooms and intranets provide a means for group interaction and the creation of networks of electronic learning communities which stimulate new ideas and provide support and encouragement.

At present e-learning systems are impacting faster on technical skills training than on MD which involves more social learning, but it is probably true to say that electronic systems are developing faster than MD practitioners know how to apply them. Pedagogy is lagging behind technology. However, it does seem that the IT revolution will greatly increase the volume, availability and access to MD. It may also encourage more self learning by managers and potentially replace much classroom teaching with periodic small tutorials backed up with continuous electronic facilitation. However, nothing is certain. At the point of writing it is probably just about acceptable to devote a paragraph or two to these radicalising forces; in ten years' time e-learning may be the new orthodoxy but it is unlikely to replace face-to-face and most packages will be a skilful blend of electronic and humanistic modes of learning (Fee 2001; Latham and Seijts 1998).

Case study: Does e-learning have a human face?

Many companies used to have big training establishments delivering training in-house. Now they have shifted to e-learning which gives them greater flexibility and cuts costs.

At one company, which we will call Big Technology Co of India, management training has been largely placed on-line. It has opted for a blended package which mixes e-learning with short one-week modules of traditional class training. Basic management training introduces managers to key skills through on-line articles, questions, answers and scenarios to be addressed. Higher level e-learning involves navigating simulated situations with interactive scenarios, a menu of advice on handling them and links to a myriad of related databases.

For middle and senior managers there are virtual modules which allow videoconferencing with teams in the spread of multinational businesses. There is also a facility for chat rooms and virtual discussion with other managers, peers on their course and tutors. Training for this level often involves virtual classrooms and problem-solving with virtual groups, simulating the hot-wired flexible form organisation of the future and helping managers with vital networking across boundaries and collaboration through virtual links.

All management e-learning is blended with classroom participation and coaching both on-line and face to face. All teaching is project-based and team-led with virtual peer learning emphasised quite as much as learning through the tutor.

The organisation believes that e-learning has helped it implement its management learning programmes across the levels of management faster and in a more collaborative way. It has cut the time required for training, reduced overheads and provided the infrastructure for internal knowledge-building. Although e-learning is not seen as a substitute for face-to-face interaction, e-technology is regarded as a vital tool for a high-quality learning and cost-effective learning experience.

Source: From private conversation with students.

Interactive skills exercises

We have considered T-groups, encounter groups, sensitivity and team process development in the chapter on organisational development. Work in organisations usually involves teamwork and management training can do a lot to simulate these conditions by giving students experience of group participation in various roles (chairing group discussions; acting as spokesman for the group, etc.) and 'process observation' (e.g. developing sensitivity to group emotions, competing demands, problem-solving, etc.). Typically management training helps students develop group skills as an incidental part of the content aspects of the course and explicitly in sessions dedicated to close observation of group process.

Interpersonal and social skills training also form a major part of formal MD. This often takes the form of role-play, giving managers behavioural modelling in effectively interacting with others. Through role-play, participants come to understand the importance of emotional literacy and empathy with others. It is a technique which can be used for a range of social situations typically encountered by managers, for example, disciplinary meetings, motivating others, overcoming resistance to change. In all role-plays participants are asked to suspend disbelief and take on imaginary roles around a situation which is defined for them by the facilitator. Every effort is made to duplicate the real-life context. Sometimes CCTV is used so that people can see themselves acting within a public arena.

The potential of role-play for reframing our experience and building understanding of how others see our behaviour is considerable. With proper debriefing and analysis after the interactive sessions, participants can gain real insight into recurring behaviours which may be self-defeating and have an opportunity to try out different social strategies in a protected environment. Self-awareness can be further enhanced by role-reversal techniques where protagonists are asked to adopt a role contrary to their usual work (e.g. the boss is asked to play the subordinate; the manager becomes the HR adviser, the manager, the shop steward etc.). This can often bring fresh perceptions, typically a new depth of empathy with others' needs and the logic underpinning their behaviour.

Role-play works best where participants are confident and prepared to engage with the social process of support and challenge. However, many people feel self-conscious and ill at ease in role-play (e.g. they are so engaged in the social interaction they have no emotional energy for the 'self watching self' which is needed for real personal development) and this places a heavy onus on the facilitator to make the experience both insightful but also safe for everyone involved (Huczynski 1986).

Drama

Drama is a logical extension of role-play. Short plays, sometimes scripted, sometimes improvised, help people act out situations which they deal with in real life. *Socio-drama* of this kind is sometimes combined with 'fishbowl' exercises in which an out-group watches and feeds back observations or questions while an in-group dramatises an organisational experience where appropriate behaviour is problematical. The groups then switch places.

Psycho-drama is a little different. It is the process by which individual managers play out work or even life scripts within an open space. This can take various forms but classically the student uses the 'empty chair' technique to talk to different parts of the self (i.e. sitting in the empty chair) to surface conflicting personal roles, contesting emotions and professional identity. The facilitator guides the self-talk and the group gives gentle support and challenge to help the individual resolve internal tensions and develop greater self-awareness.

A new development is the use of professional troupes of actors who perform little scenes of corporate life around key themes. The course participants can stop and start the action, feed in new contingencies, question the actors-in-role and ask for alternative patterns of events or alternative endings to be played out. When this is well done it can be an exciting and imaginative use of theatre to capture the complexity of the organisational world and involve participants intellectually and emotionally.

Case study Using drama for development

Until recently the Royal Shakespeare Company (RSC) had a consulting arm, Directing Creativity (DC) which has used theatrical techniques for management and organisational development with a range of blue-chip companies.

The Principal of DC believes that managers can learn a lot about managing creativity from dramaturgical principles. Any theatrical production starts with a 'misty vision' in the director's mind which is then clarified by the designers and explored and developed by the 'ensemble' of actors in rehearsal. The ensemble with its vigorously democratic self management and commitment 'to finding the play' suggests the kind of social framework that stimulates creativity in the management of change. The Principal suggests that innovative companies should aim to build a process resembling the rehearsal of a play if the abstractions of the vision are to become cemented in business culture.

DC has used consulting based on principles of 'image theatre' to help managers in a post-merger situation express their emotions through tableaux: 'In one organisation someone picked up a pole lying on the ground, lifted it vertically and stood at attention. Everyone then stood up and rallied around'.

This was seen as an 'aha' moment; people were expressing their allegiance to the company's principles and signalled a need for clear leadership.

Because theatrical consulting is dealing with emotions, the issues are ambiguous and so are the solutions, but they give managers a chance to go deeper and explore the 'real world' of contradiction and paradox in management.

Other training companies use theatre to enact scenes from everyday organisational life which can be used to demonstrate management skills. Actors play out a piece of theatre and then discuss the issues. They can ask the characters why they behaved in certain ways and ask them to play out different strategies. The value of drama is that it is emotionally involving but people can still retain an analytical distance. It is far more powerful than discussing a case study because it is more interactive and people become involved in the problem being played out and in considering other approaches.

The facilitator controls the theatrical space, managing group discussion, allowing the group to stop and start the action and questioning them about choices of behaviour; people learn from each other and 'learn through doing' in a safe space.

When the method works the learning can be considerable and proponents suggest that the method motivates managers to try new behaviours at work.

Source: Adapted from Lloyd, T. 'Management training hits bard times', *Financial Times* 10 July 2003.

The use of all interactive events is a risk. They are less predictable in terms of learning outcome than most of the other methods considered. They are most likely to be successful when learning objectives are clear, when people have some social sophistication and emotional maturity (most of these techniques are used with more senior staff), they are willing to commit themselves to learning through social process and the event chimes with organisational culture. A lot depends too on the facilitators and their ability to help participants disengage and review the psychological lessons involved. When they go well these techniques are catalytic – they provoke deep learning and may fundamentally change behaviour. When they go badly, the learning situation can become unsafe and people can even be psychologically damaged. These methods are definitely not for the developer who lacks specialist training or the faint-hearted (Fee 2001).

Creativity Exercises

As management is increasingly held responsible for learning and innovation in the workplace, creativity becomes an important theme in management training. Managers look for tools to help them live with uncertainty and flux and move beyond linear rational thinking. They want help in defining problems, seeing the interconnectedness between things, transcending the blinkers of the past to bring something new into the world. They want techniques for remaining comfortable with creativity despite its muddled and unpredictable nature. Like the character in the famous Zen parable they want to know how to enjoy the raspberry growing from the under cliff as they dangle precariously from a vine with tigers growling above them and tigers prowling beneath them.

Of course, this is a vast area and those interested are referred to some of the key texts in this field such as Weisberg (1986), Adams (1987) or de Bono (1970). In keeping with the subject it purports to develop, creativity training is on the wilder fringe of MD. Of course many of its techniques have not been systematically evaluated and some would not fit all organisational cultures. However, this is not to deny the sheer frame-bending originality and clever ingenuity which lies behind their construction.

Brainstorming is a technique well known to managers. Here a decision-making group agrees to temporarily suspend critical judgement to stimulate the flow of ideas and the chance of unusual 'bi-sociations' of ideas (Koestler 1960). Later, a more analytical approach will be used to sift the ideas for their practical utility.

Creative dialogue is a technique to help managers deal with unexpected and unstructured situations. The facilitator deliberately presents a dilemma which is open-ended and ambiguous. The group is left to find ways of coping with the uncertainty which this creates. In review sessions afterwards there is discussion on the efficiency of the methods which it collectively employs. This technique is often used in leadership training to help future leaders balance rationality and intuition in their thinking and take decisions without complete data, in conditions which are fluid.

Lateral thinking is the brainchild of Edward de Bono (1970). It involves games and discussions using constructs which are said to help people approach problems from new angles. Using different lenses, people begin to see possibilities which had not been noticed before and to take risks with their decision-making.

Edward de Bono's six 'thinking hats'

In this tool, Edward de Bono tries to define six different ways (or hats) of looking at the world. The idea is that once you become aware of these differences, you can adapt your thinking style so that it is appropriate to the circumstances.

- **White hat:** Information available and needed.
- **Red hat:** Intuition and feelings.
- **Black hat:** Caution, difficulties and weaknesses.
- **Yellow hat:** Benefits and value.
- **Green hat:** Alternatives and creative ideas.
- **Blue hat:** Managing the thinking process.

Each problem or each stage of a problem has an appropriate hat. It is not a good idea to wear a green hat for reviewing, but green is needed for envisioning.

If you get stuck on a problem or similar problems keep recurring, you need to consider whether your preferred thinking style is appropriate. You may need to think with a different hat. The creative team may need a variety of hats and know which hat is needed for each problem or each phase of solving it.

Source: de Bono, E. (1986) *Six Thinking Hats*.

Divergent thinking involves the use of the 'right brain' to think synoptically and connectively; using 'upside down' thinking (see Handy 1990) to see the familiar in a totally new light. There are many famous exercises which are used by facilitators within this tradition, for example, the candle game in which a group is asked to find an elegant solution to the problem of attaching a candle to a door; the egg game in which competing teams are set the task of devising a way of safely projecting an uncooked egg from one side of the room to another; the list game in which participants are asked to list all the uses they can think of for a *brick* or all the edible things which are *white*; the nine-dot problem in which participants are asked to link all dots with just three lines which are not allowed to bend (Weisberg 1986).

Protocol analysis is a technique which is intended to help people understand how and why they get blocked in problem-solving. A group which is set a problem is asked to talk aloud (perhaps tape-recorded) on the decision choices they used to solve it in the process of working it out. With feedback and discussion, it is claimed that this technique provides lessons on the conditions under which thoughts get blocked and creativity is encouraged.

Mind mapping involves writing down ideas associated with a concept in the form of a broad spreading diagram in which the relationship between elements can be defined. It is claimed that by reiteratively working between the parts and the whole, new connections can be made which offer genuinely creative insights (Buzan 1974).

All these methods are offered to managers as heuristic techniques to increase personal awareness of thinking styles and to develop social processes which increase the chances of good ideas emerging. Although the manager does not have to be the most creative member of a team s/he has to be able to recognise creative potential where it exists, spot good ideas when they emerge and create conditions in which energy will be released. However, the jury is still out on whether creativity on management development programmes achieves any of these things.

Does crazy mean creative?

'Horse whispering', international folk dancing, chicken herding and motorised toilet-bowl racing have all been used as creative activities to develop management skills. But does any of it work? Here is one journalist's experience.

> Last Friday evening in the freezing rain, in a car park in Nottingham, I found myself engaged in that most clichéd of corporate training activities, walking across burning embers.

> To find out why companies continue to encourage employees to firewalk given the evident stupidity of it, I arranged for a motivation coach to give me some training. The preparation he gave me didn't explain why an activity popularised by 'empowerment guru', Tony Robbins, decades before was still going strong. Sitting on a beanbag in a purple room, my motivation coach churned out the usual pop psychology/neuro-linguistic programming guff that typifies most management training, before talking about the importance of 'personal sovereignty' . . . and creating your reality through language.

> However, then something unexpected happened. Or rather, something expected didn't happen. The coach didn't launch into shamanistic talk about 'protective auras' or 'elevating the frequency of your energy to that of the fire'. Instead he explained rationally why firewalking is possible because the soles of your feet are 25 times thicker than the rest of the body and a short distance of hot charcoal doesn't hurt.

> Firewalking is often the finale to team building and corporate away-days. It is often presented as an analogy with the business world. For example, the mental state you have to put yourself into before taking the first step on to burning ash is claimed to be not dissimilar to the mental state needed when making an awkward sales call, firing someone or preparing for a difficult interview.

> As a quick confidence building exercise, firewalking has something to recommend it but in the past I have got a similar buzz just going into Wolverhampton city centre on a Friday night. However, the real issue is why 'corporate clowning' persists despite all the evidence that more conventional development methods achieve more.

Question
What do you think of events like this as opportunities for learning?

Source: Adapted from I will never again pour cold water on corporate firewalking, *Financial Times*, 17/03/2006 (Sathnam, S.).

Outdoor development

The final form of off-the-job learning we should consider is that of outdoor management development (OMD), also known as Outward Bound or Adventure Training. The idea here is to use outdoor settings to develop qualities of 'rugged individualism', initiative, entrepreneurism and skills of leadership and teamworking. The harshness and physicality of nature exposes managers to challenges of leading and cooperating with others which make the lessons more real and memorable to them. It is certainly at the creative end of structured MD techniques.

OMD seems to have developed from military tests and activities designed to select and develop officers. Even now it has something of this military flavour although commercial organisers are careful to avoid any parallels with commando courses or weekend paintball warriors. Over the twenty-five years of its existence groups at all organisational levels have been involved in OMD, but the method is most often used with team leaders/first- line managers.

OMD is based on the idea that the unpredictability and challenge of performing physical tasks which require judgement and thought in the unforgiving environment of the countryside can simulate the stresses of modern business. The mantra is: 'providing real tasks to real people in real time with real constraints and real consequences' (Banks 1994). The tasks involved all require physical energy: orienteering, abseiling, climbing a mountain peak, white-water rafting, collecting symbols on a desolate moor and navigating back to base. In all cases the tasks themselves, although demanding, are far less important in themselves than in what they reveal about your own character and skills in tackling them (Badger and Sadler-Smith 1997).

So, do the orienteering well and you and your team escape from the moor and are snug that evening in the bar at the residential management centre. Do it badly and you will be camping on a moor in the driving rain that night. Advocates say these tasks lay bare the real conditions of business – winners and losers – and the nature of management itself.

Unfortunately OMD lacks systematic evaluation and its effectiveness is largely a matter of faith. Perhaps unsurprisingly, a survey of participant reactions by Badger and Sadler- Smith (1997) found that outdoor development appealed to younger managers. They liked the practical tasks. The stress, physical discomfort and slight frisson of danger had an emotional charge which activated the learning significance and made it seen highly relevant. The shared experience also had a positive effect on team bonding. As a method for personal development, for example, stimulating awareness of your strengths and weaknesses and how people see you, it was seen as very valuable. It also seemed to encourage entrepreneurial values of robustness, self-reliance, risk-taking and self-confident leadership.

However, there is no shortage of detractors. A Channel 4 *Cutting Edge* programme in the 1990s showed the potentially harmful psychological effects of this sort of development (Beardwell et al. 2004). The programme claimed that it encouraged hyper-competition, excess of zeal, aggressive and bullying behaviour and over-identification with the roles allocated for the purpose of the exercise (with consequences very similar to the famous 1960s' prison experiments with 'prisoners' and 'guards' conducted by Zimbardo (1973)).

As things stand the evidence base for OMD remains largely anecdotal and the claims of enthusiasts remain unproven. However, a consensus of opinion seems to be forming around the following points.

- Although OMD may draw on all learning styles, it seems to appeal mainly to 'activists' and is concentrated largely at the doing stage of the learning cycle. This is likely to demotivate a good number of the participants.
- Personal learning seems to be greatly increased if OMD is linked to more established methods of MD (e.g. classroom learning) which allow an opportunity for debriefing

and conceptualisation of the experience in terms of an explanatory framework (Badger and Sadler-Smith 1997).

- The quality of the learning experience is likely to be proportionate to the quality of the facilitation. Using staff experienced in outdoor activities who are also psychologically skilled is essential where participants have stressful experiences and may feel vulnerable. Building a safe learning environment seems paramount. Equally, facilitation is needed to help people examine the meaning of experience for identity and translate its relevance for managerial behaviour.

- Outdoor programmes need to be guided by clearly defined objectives so that participants can put their experience in context and they have criteria for assessing outcomes (Latham and Seijts 1998). Fee (2001) tells us about the Oki Electronic Industry Company which teaches Westerners at its subsidiaries the values of Japanese teamworking through OMD. Before the residential periods of OMD a lot of emphasis is given to personal assessment and objective setting. Effort is devoted to identifying individual development needs in relation to a corporate competency framework; PDP goals and career development objectives are also agreed. The OMD experience is framed by the logic of these plans which are tested by the challenges of outdoor development.

It seems that OMD works best where all members of the outdoor programme are of roughly the same status. This is less threatening to those with supervisory authority over others. However, the incidental effect of sending established work groups on outdoor programmes is that group solidarity can be reinforced. According to Woodall and Winstanley (1999), this can create a 'them and us' feeling back home. A mix of people from several organisations might create the 'safest' conditions for participants to take risks with new modes of behaviour.

The big problem with OMD is demonstrating that the emotionally stimulating learning derived from climbing rock faces really translates into improved working in the office on Monday morning. Old Mr Plum from accounts may prove himself unexpectedly resourceful at using a compass and getting his team across the 'ravine' with only an oil drum, a pulley, a plank and some ropes, but do these skills transfer readily to leading the accounts team to achieve its performance targets (Woodall and Winstanley 1999; Fee 2001)? Unless the physical nature of activity is very closely related to organisational experience, and lessons are drawn out, OMD can amount to 'fun and games' in the country with no change in the office because knowledge transfer and cultural/contextual issues have not been properly addressed.

Other critics claim that OMD is using a sledgehammer to crack nuts. A large wedge of opinion suggests that the self-awareness and leadership development involved can be achieved more directly and less expensively in conventional ways, with less physical risks and less celebration of aggressive, heroic values.

At its best (e.g. a programme run at a well-established facility like Ullswater Outward Bound Centre in the Lake District), OMD may combine significant social learning and personal growth with fun and camaraderie. At its worst, it is an expression of anachronistic 1980s' 'macho' values. It is interesting that the 'glory days' of OMD were in the late 1980s and early 1990s, and interest has subsequently fallen off. There are still at lot of residential centres in the Lake District, Wales and Scottish Highlands dedicated to the method but the industry is now overstocked and some of these centres are likely to close. However, OMD remains an interesting hybrid between the experiential and conceptual strands of learning in management and still has potential for stimulating imaginative challenges to the manager which cannot be reproduced in the classroom. Despite the apparent decline in OMD, there is definitely a growing interest in 'reality simulation' using real-world settings that try to capture something of the pressures of the management role which the highly popular *Apprentice* series on British and American TV (2008) demonstrates. As we consider elsewhere, there is also growing interest in community-based, real-world projects to help managers learn skills and develop a sense of social responsibility. In the view of this commentator, this may be a sign of things to come.

8.7 Conclusion

Despite the tendency in management to celebrate experiential *in situ* learning above all other formal off-the-job development continues to flourish. Here we have concentrated on the in-company management programme, so much part of Western management culture. Designing formal MD programmes requires a sophisticated appreciation of learning needs, learning preferences, learning strategies and the link between methods and learning objectives. Management courses often fail to deliver what they promise for varied and complex reasons but course designers can do a lot to increase their success. Many formal techniques exist; however, they are as good as the facilitation which directs their use. Formal methods may be most effective when they are used as challenge and support to encourage participants to think for themselves and value their experience. Although experiential and formal learning are often contrasted, in reality they are mutually supporting, and blended learning which makes planned use of the strengths of both approaches is probably the way of the future. Certainly, 'off the job' does not have to deny experiential learning and the best formal programmes try to bring the real world into the classroom through storytelling, *in vivo* case studies, co-counselling, drama, project work and reflective exercises. This is a theme which is continued in the next chapter where we consider that other sphere of formal development, management education.

Review questions

1. 'Informal, experiential development is very critical of formal MD but it does not apply the same standards of critical reflection to itself.' How would you react to this statement?

2. 'MD is driven by fashion: at present it is all coaching, mentoring and self-development. In five years' time formal courses will be re-discovered.' Critically consider this opinion.

3. It has been claimed in this chapter that formal MD doesn't encourage double-loop learning. What does this mean and do you agree?

4. 'Formal and informal need each other. Neither is complete without the other. The trick is to draw out the strengths of both for any group of learners.' Do you agree?

5 Outdoor Management Development is largely a matter of faith. It is said you will gain a lot from it if you enter into the spirit and believe in it. If you were a prospective course member, what questions would you want to ask the course organisers before you enrolled?

6 'Going on courses is just something that managers do; it's part of the culture.' How would you react to a comment like this? Consider the social functions of courses and the reasons why some people go on many courses while some people seem to avoid them.

Web links

Website on OMD with information of suppliers and users:
http://www.users.zetnet.co.uk/research/index.htm

Council for Excellence in Management and Leadership (CEML) website which contains a useful appraisal of various MD methods:
http://www.managementandleadershipcouncil.org

The Chartered Management Institute (CMI) is a useful source of information on 'good practice' in management training design and delivery:
http://www.managers.org.uk

A website for Ashridge Management Institute courses:
http://www.ashridge.org.uk/

Recommendations for further reading

Those texts marked with an asterisk in the bibliography are recommended for further reading, especially the following:

Fee, K. (2001) *A Guide to Management Development Techniques.* Very useful handbook of techniques for the MD practitioner.

Harrison, R. (2002) *Learning and Development,* Ch. 18. Harrison is very good on the professional frameworks for designing formal development programmes.

Huczynski, A. (1986; 2001 editions) *An Encyclopedia of Management Development Methods.* An absolute 'bible' of exercises, games and methods for use in management training.

Bibliography

Adams, J. (1986) *The Care and Feeding of Ideas*, Penguin.
Adams, J. (1987) *Conceptual Blockbusting*, Penguin Books.
Argyris, C. (1982) *Reasoning, Learning and Action*, Jossey-Bass.
Armstrong, A. (2003) *A Handbook of Human Resource Management Practice*, Kogan Page.

*Badger, B. and Sadler-Smith, E. (1997) 'Outdoor management development: use and evaluation', *Journal of European Industrial Training*, Vol. 21.
*Banks, J. (1994) *Outdoor Development for Managers*, Gower.

Bibliography

Beardwell, I. and Holden, L. et al. (2004) *Human Resource Management: A Contemporary Approach*, Ch. 9, Prentice Hall.

Bee, R. and Bee, F. (1999) *Facilitation Skills*, CIPD.

Bloom, B., Engelhart, M. et al. (1956) *The Taxonomy of Educational Objectives*, Longmans Green.

Burgoyne, J. and Reynolds, M. (1997) 'Introduction', in *Management Learning: Integrating Perspectives in Theory and Practice*, Sage.

Buzan, T. (1974) *Use Your Head*, BBC Books.

De Bono, E. (1970) *Lateral Thinking: Creativity Step by Step*, Penguin.

De Bono, E. (1986) *Six Thinking Hats*, Penguin.

de Botton, A. (2000) *The Consolations of Philosophy*, Hamish Hamilton.

Eastburn, R. (1980) 'Management Development' (offprint)

Fee, K. (2001) *A Guide to Management Development Techniques*, Kogan Page.

Graham, H. and Bennett, T. (1999) *Human Resource Management*, M and E Books.

Handy, C. (1989) *Understanding Organisations*, Penguin.

Handy, C. (1990) *The Age of Unreason*, Arrow Books.

Hargreaves, P. and Jarvis, P. (2000) *The Human Resource Development Handbook*, Kogan Page.

*Harrison, R. (2002) *Learning and Development*, Ch. 18, CIPD.

Heller, R. (1986) *The New Naked Manager*, Ch. 24, Coronet Books.

Heller, R. (1995) *The New Naked Manager for the Nineties*, Ch. 24, Coronet Books.

Honey, P. and Mumford, A. (1992) *Manual of Learning Styles*, Maidenhead: Honey.

*Huczynski, A. (1986 and 2001 editions) *Encyclopedia of Management Development Methods*, Gower.

Koestler, A. (1960) *The Lotus and the Robot*, Harper and Row.

Kolb, D. (1984) *Experiential Learning*, Prentice Hall.

Latham, G. and Seijts, G. (1998) 'Management development' in Drenth, P. and Thierry, H. (eds) *Handbook of Work and Organisational Psychology*, Vol. 3, Psychology Press.

Lloyd, T. (2003) 'Management training hits bard times', *Financial Times,* 10 July.

Mabey, C., Storey, J., Thomson, A. et al. (2001) *Changing Patterns of Management Development*, Blackwell.

Mangham, I. (1988) *Power and Performance in Organisations*, Blackwell.

Margerison, C. (1991) *Making Management Development Work*, McGraw Hill.

Matthews, J., Megginson, D. et al. (2004) *Human Resource Development*, Chs 5, 10, Kogan Page.

Mullins, L. (2004) *Management and Organisational Behaviour*, Ch. 23, Prentice Hall.

Mumford, A. (1980) *Making Experience Pay: Management Success Through Effective Learning*, McGraw Hill.

Mumford, A. (1997) *Strategies for Action*, CIPD.

Mumford, A. and Gold, J. (2004) *Strategies for Action*, Ch. 6, CIPD.

Osbaldeston, M. and Barham, K. (1992) 'Using management development for competitive advantage', *Long Range Planning*, Vol. 25, No. 6.

Pedler, M. (1974) 'Learning in management education', *Journal of European Training*, Vol. 3 No. 3.

*Poulet, R. (1997) 'Designing effective development programmes', *Journal of Management Development*, Vol. 16, No. 6.

Raab, N. (2004) 'Becoming an expert in not knowing', in Grey, C. and Antonacopoulou, E. (2004) *Essential Readings in Management Development*, Sage.

Ready, D. and Conger, J. (2003) 'Why leadership development efforts fail', *Sloan Management Review*, Spring.

Reid and Barrington (2000) *Training Interventions*, Ch. 10, CIPD.

Revans, R. (1982) *The Origins and Growth of Action Learning*, Chartwell Bratt.

*Sadler-Smith, E. (2006) *Learning and Development for Managers*, Blackwell.

Salaman, G. and Butler, J. (1990) 'Why managers won't learn', *Management Education and Development*, Vol. 21, No. 3.

Sathnam, S. (2006) 'Does crazy mean creative?' *Financial Times*, 17 March.

Simmonds, D. (2004) *Designing and Developing Training*, CIPD.

Stewart, J. (1999) *Employee Development Practice*, Ch. 9, Prentice Hall.

Storey, J. (1989) 'Management development: a literature review and implications for future research', *Personnel Review*, Vol. 18, No. 6.

Syrett, M. and Lammiman, J. (1999) *Management Development: Making the Investment Count*, Economist Books.

Watson, T. (2004) 'Motivation: that's Maslow isn't it,' in Grey, C. and Antonacopoulou, E. (2004) *Essential Readings in Management Learning*, Sage.

Thomson, A. Mabey, C. et al. (2001) *Changing Patterns of Management Development*, Blackwell.

Weisberg, R. (1986) *Creativity: Genius and Other Myths*, Freeman and Co.

Woodall, J. and Winstanley, D. (1999) *Management Development: Strategies and Practice*, Chs 7 and 8, Blackwell.

Yukl, G. (2002) *Leadership in Organisations*, Ch. 13, Prentice Hall.

Zimbardo, P. (1973) *Proceedings of the American Psychological Association Conference*, APA, Montreal.

9 Formal management development: management education

Learning outcomes

After reading the chapter you should be able to understand, analyse and explain:

- trends in the development of management education;
- historical themes in the development of management education in the UK;
- management education and the professionalisation of management;
- the main elements of management education;
- debates in postgraduate management education;
- the nature of the MBA;
- the controversies surrounding the MBA as the dominant formal qualification in management;
- the value and effectiveness of business schools;
- issues in strategic partnerships and the rise of corporate universities;
- prospects for management education in the future.

9.1 Introduction

As we defined it in Chapter 1, management education is a constituent part of management development, which is the larger category and assimilates a wider range of learning approaches. As a rough rule of thumb, management education is concerned with developing functional and theoretical knowledge and management development is concerned with applied skills and self-development as a practitioner. However, this crude distinction breaks down when we begin to examine it. Increasingly management education is about developing the whole person drawing on experiential reflection, and development involves the critical application of ideas in a real-world context as a thinking and reflective practitioner.

An inescapable dilemma for management education is that studying management is not the same as studying engineering, medicine or law. Like management, these are practical and professional subjects which are studied in institutions of higher education. However, here the similarity ends. Most professional subjects claim to train people so they are equipped with the competencies they need to serve as a practitioner. However, management education is different. Despite the marketing hype around many higher education courses in management, there is little evidence that a qualified manager is necessarily a better manager.

This does seem rather odd, but it probably has something to do with the practical nature of managing, the importance of experience, maturity and judgement in being an effective manager, the diversity of management activity and the relatively undeveloped state of the managerial learning base. While the principles of a subject like engineering apply everywhere, management ideas seem to be culturally and contextually bound. There is only so much that the successful manager can learn in the classroom.

These factors explain, at least partially, the recent shift to experiential methods of development in the West, the new urgency of debate over the purpose and effectiveness of the MBA and the extent to which management is a science which offers techniques that allow managers to act rationally, exercise control and plan the future. Sceptics, often pragmatically inclined businessmen, wonder if there really is a core of generalised practitioner knowledge in management; even if there is, can it be taught? There is a lingering suspicion that management education is essentially an act of faith and management itself is more a craft than profession with a lot of art as well as science.

However, despite the scepticism of business elites, management education has never been more popular or its provision more extensive. So how do we explain the apparent contradiction between establishment doubt about the effect of management education on business performance and the surge in management education driven by popular demand? Management education is also changing: are we seeing the beginnings of a new form of management education in which usable theory is becoming increasingly integrated in wider learning repertoires within the workplace?

These are issues which will be considered further in this chapter. We take a critical view of the nature of management education: its growth; its diverse forms; the definitions of its main stakeholders and prospects for the future. The intention here is to build a clear picture of where management education is in the first decade of the new millennium. Throughout, the focus will be on management education within Anglo-American culture with special attention to the situation in the UK. While some readers may bridle at this and regard it as yet further evidence of the ethnocentrism which besets this subject, the focus is justified on the grounds that alternative management education and development systems are considered when we turn to cross-cultural development in Chapter 11. It is also the case, for better or worse, that the Anglo-American model is still the dominant, universalistic model for the growing of managers. Despite the mediating influences of national models, there are distinct signs of convergence around the totem of the MBA. It is therefore reasonable and justifiable to consider the hegemonic system of management education, which is offered as a exemplar to the rest of the world, in some detail. However, this is done in anticipation that as geopolitical power shifts, that hegemony may be breaking up and a pluralistic post-MBA pattern with separate paths to management education, more adapted to local cultures, may now be in the process of emerging.

9.2 Management education: the British case

In Chapter 13 we consider the history of management education in the UK up to the late 1980s (to which the interested reader is referred) Here we merely need to know that in 1989, management education in the UK was in crisis. A debate had erupted about the alleged relationship between the quality of management and the state of the national economy. Was national economic decline attributable to the poor capabilities of British managers? Was the pragmatic and anti-intellectual culture of British management failing the country and jeopardising its future?

This debate was provoked by a number of highly critical reports on management education. In 1985, Coopers and Lybrand (1985) produced a survey, 'A Challenge to Complacency', which showed the widespread ignorance among top management of how their company's management training programme performed compared with competitors. Hard on its heels, a report by Mangham and Silver (1986) showed that most managers in the UK received no formal training in the skills vital for economic success. Then the Constable and McCormick report (1987) demonstrated that British industry had neglected the development of its management stock and that was a major reason for relatively poor national economic performance. It confirmed that in 1988 only half of managers received any education or training at all and those that did, rarely more than two days per year.

However, the killer report was Handy's (see Chapter 13 for more detail), which concluded that Britain lacked a coherent, modern system of management education and development and was badly in need of reform.

The cumulative effect of these reports was to provoke a three-cornered battle for the future of management education. In an important article on the strategies of managerial professionalism through educational reform, Reed and Anthony (1992), set out the key agendas of the groups who have manoeuvred for the soul of British management education on the eve of the millennium.

In one camp were older and more established managers, members of the BIM, leading lights in the Institute of Directors. These vociferous movers and shakers, all successful top managers, argued that management was a practical subject and was best taught on the job. If professional membership was to be introduced as a *sine qua non* for managerial practice, only a proven track record in management should count.

In the second camp were those who had a technocratic view of management and management education. This was the view taken by the government-backed National Training Agency and the National Forum for Management Education, a powerful lobby group. They wanted to see management education and training under the control of employers and the government, with qualifications based on NVQ-style competency frameworks.

The third camp might be called the academic position and was headed by the Council for University Management Schools. It argued that the low standards of education among British managers could only be overcome by empowering institutions of higher education to introduce validated qualifications which would become a requirement for entry to a management job. It was through an agenda of harmonising abstract knowledge and specialist skills through the agency of the academy that managers might build the self-regulation of older professions.

Thomson et al. (2001) bring the story up to date. The main tangible legacy of the debate was the formation of the Management Charter Group, a group of leading companies which agreed to a code of conduct or charter based on Charles Handy's model for MD in the future. Soon the Charter Group had transmuted into the MCI (Management Charter Initiative). Conceived as an independent body to improve standards of management education benchmarks of good practice, the MCI soon became a vanguard for a technical, credentialist, 'bottom line' oriented, highly vocational concept of management education.

Later, MCI became the lead body for developing national standards in management performance and an advocate for NVQs (the government's competency frameworks). More recently, it has again morphed into the Management Standards Centre, strongly wedded to a competency-based development approach but less concerned with developing national generic standards and more responsive to enterprise-level definitions of management performance.

Soon state sponsored bodies like the national Forum for Management Education and, later, the Council for Excellence in Management and Leadership (CEML) took up the call for a vocational approach to management education. In this they have been heavily influenced by the practical needs of employers and the technocrats (above) in defining standards and a corpus of knowledge in management and how this should be taught.

The influence of these bodies is behind the competencies revolution and the rise of the NVQ system for establishing a generic set of practical qualifications based on measurable standards of performance. This approach tends to be skills-focused, highly pragmatic and concerned with proficiency in specific tasks. Despite many criticisms of its narrow behaviourism, its anti-theoretical and technocratic bias, the NVQ approach has gone on to dominate management education at the sub-degree level, the level at which most people first encounter management subjects (usually as part of a professional or technical course). City and Guilds, BTec, National and Higher National certificates and diplomas all reflect the influence of this philosophy of vocationalism. It is in this area of government-sponsored training that there has been the most dramatic take-up of management and business training. There was a 90 per cent increase in NVQs between 1994 and 1997. By the end of the 1990s 120,000 students were graduating each year with vocational qualifications in management (Thomson et al. 2001).

Although technocratic vocationalism is dominant at the lower end of management education, the situation is more mixed at undergraduate and postgraduates levels. Here the main axis of debate is between those who believe that management education is about developing critical thinking, analysis, reflection and judgement, and those who believe that the first duty of higher education is to ensure the mastery of skills essential to management. While some management educators at university believe that it is quite possible to reconcile the agenda of thinking with the agenda for skills, others believe that the pressures to vocationalism threaten to displace management as a discipline of critical and thoughtful inquiry. They believe that vocationalism is increasing all the time through government controls over higher education and by the back door through the requirements imposed by accrediting and professional monitoring organisations like the Chartered Institute of Personnel Development (CIPD), the Chartered Institute of Public Finance accountants (CIPFA) and the Association of MBAs (AMBA). Some believe that learning to be a thoughtful practitioner is being displaced by a rush to gain technique-led qualifications which may not mesh with the processual realities of managing.

Management education in Britain has been helped by more general government support for training and development in the British economy. National Training and Enterprise Councils, 'Investors in People', Learning and Skills Councils, the Dearing Report on Higher Education, while unspecific to management, all had implications for management education. They consolidated the trend to vocationalism, confirmed the skills agenda in higher education and legitimated the functionalist approach. In a broad-brush way they may have also helped to raise standards of general education in adult life, an issue which has always been at the root of poor management performance in the UK, going back to the nineteenth century. In this context, as Thomson et al. (2001) suggest, the expansion of higher education from the early 1990s onwards (a tenfold increase in graduates in 30 years) will have had an effect on the educational level of national management population as a whole.

So what is the balance sheet on Med in the UK almost 20 years after the watershed of 1989? In the 1980s there was too little education for too few managers. Now it seems that the vast majority of managers receive significant and increasing amounts of education and training every year. By 1997, Mumford could suggest that only 4 per cent of managers across all industrial sectors received *no* training at all, a massive reversal of what Mangham and Silver (1986) had discovered just a decade before. Employer attitudes towards education seem to have become more positive and the managerial stock more qualified, with more postgraduates.

However, it is not all good news. Taking the national system of management education in Britain as whole, it seems that many of Handy's criticisms from the late 1980s are still valid. It is still poorly organised, with no qualification which is recognised as a licence to practise management in Britain. Nothing came of Handy's (1988) dream of a professionalised model of educational development for managers, in which managers serve apprenticeships of study and supervised practice before they are allowed to operate autonomously (not dissimilar to the training of doctors).

As Thomson et al. (2001) suggest, in the opening years of the new millennium there was no shortage of players concerned with Med. In fact, there was now an overstocked market with wide variations in standards between providers, leaving both students and employers confused about the relative status and value of their products.

There was also a good number of agencies with an interest in developing managers: the Institute of Management (IMI); the Association of Business Schools (ABS); the Association of MBAs (AMBA); the Foundation for Management Education (FME); the Association for Management Education and Development (AMED); the Confederation of British Industry (CBI). All had their policy agendas and issued guidelines for good practice in management education and development. However, these agencies were not linking up or coordinating their efforts. In 2001 a new body was set up by the government, the Council for Excellence in Management and Leadership (CEML). This is a non-executive body composed of businessmen, trade unionists and academics with an ambitious remit to raise consciousness about management education and work for its integration with national policy in education (see box below)

The centre for excellence in management and leadership

There is much hope invested in the CEML that it will put MD firmly on the centre stage of national learning and development policy. The CEML is charged with the following responsibilities.

- Identifying issues relating to managerial leadership
- Articulating a vision for MD/Med in the future through an MD strategy for the UK which links with the government's strategy for national education and skills
- Reviewing the quality and range of support for MD/Med across the range of management issues
- Monitoring progress on issues identified by the Council
- Improving the quality of business school graduates
- Enhancing the standard of British business schools and helping them to become international in their focus
- Helping to make life-long learning in management a common practice
- Reporting annually to government and other stakeholders on progress

Question
If you were appointed to the Council, where would you be urging it to concentrate its energies?

Source: CEML publicity literature.

Taking the Med scene as a whole, although it remains fragmented, there may be some first signs that the bipolar division between the 'skills development' of the competency movement and the 'whole-person development' represented by the academy is breaking down. Perhaps we are witnessing a new convergence around a model of learning that values direct experience and reflection in action and is led by competencies which are geared to the realities of the management process. Perhaps too, the growing consensus that the new millennium requires managers who are not just technically proficient, but also can address concerns of social and moral responsibility, will form a rallying point for rival camps.

9.3 Is management a profession?

The British experience helps us to examine an issue which concerns managers in all countries. Interwoven in the debates about management education, in Britain and abroad, is the 'professionalisation project'. Behind the agendas of alternative futures for management education is the persistent question of whether management is a profession, or should be a profession and, if so, how the next generation should be prepared for professional practice.

This is not just a question for after-dinner speculation, because on it hangs the future of management education. If a clear body of knowledge exclusive to management can be found and there is the right political will, the discourse of professionalism can be used to regulate entry to management, define the educational agenda and control standards of managerial conduct. A lot of the debate on educating managers, all around the world, is actually about status building and gaining social recognition for professional closure. Claims to professionalism are ultimately an ideological discourse, used as a resource, to elicit recognition for material and social privileges.

As we have seen in the British case, the educational agenda underpinning the professionalisation project is an issue to be hotly contested. Creating pools of well-educated and qualified young people from which to select future management leaders is an important step on the way to professional status, yet it is unlikely that management will achieve legal and social recognition as a profession in the foreseeable future. Why should that be?

Unlike other occupations which have achieved closure, it is difficult to see a body of management knowledge and expertise which is universalistic and can be transferred from one setting to another. Critics of those who lay claim to professionalism in management say that many managerial competencies are organisationally dependent and skills are highly 'particularist' (Reed and Anthony 1992): that is, the knowledge and skills you need for managerial effectiveness are contextualised. Because you are successful as the manager of a supermarket does not necessarily mean you will be equally successful as the manager of a hospital. The well-established professions control transferable knowledge (think of medicine or law) but managerial knowledge is more local.

Secondly, it is difficult to identify a body of abstract knowledge in management which is essential to practitioner effectiveness. What abstract knowledge is associated with management – for example, psychology, sociology, administrative – seems only tenuously connected to the actual work of managers. Perhaps the nearest that management gets to defining a body of knowledge germane to its work is through behavioural science, but managers do not have a monopoly of control over this diverse intellectual field and it is too nebulous to inform day-to-day managerial practice.

Then there is no clearly teachable component. Many of the skills managers use are craft skills based on experiential or tacit knowing. It is difficult to discern professional knowledge which informs and directs everyday management practice in all settings and situations or 'sacred practices' of the profession which define its identity (Reed and Anthony 1992) in contrast to, say, engineers.

Unlike doctors or lawyers, managers lack autonomy and control over their work. There are always external constraints (shareholders, owners, political, institutional expectations) which limit independent judgement. Managers are ultimately dependent on a hierarchy of authority which controls and directs them according to priorities which are not exclusively those of professional competence.

Managers as a class in society are highly stratified and divided. There is functional differentiation and cleavages between senior managers who are increasingly strategists/decision makers and lower managers who are increasingly restricted in the autonomy. This heterogeneity dilutes the sense of professional community. Managers do vastly different things and have very different spheres of autonomy and competency. Differentiation also inhibits the potential of managers to unite in collective action for professional control (Reed and Anthony 1992).

The established liberal professions can claim to be regulated by a code of ethics that ensures their accountability to the public interest. They are also perceived to perform a civic role and provide a public service (e.g. the doctor, the accountant, etc.). This is often cited as the justification for professional prerogatives. However, it is difficult for managers to make such assertions. After all, managers are ultimately agents of capital who have to act to maximise shareholder value whatever the consequences for communities, the environment or the public interest as a whole. Despite movement towards socially responsible management, is management just too interwoven with the logic of profit-making and capitalism for a professional code of ethics to become established or be policed? Certainly the many corporate scandals in recent years (Enron, WorldCom, etc.) give us little reason to believe that management is or could be regulated as a moral order aligned to purposes beyond those of the self-seeking interests of elites (Thomson 2001).

Pause for thought

Is 'management professionalism' a contradiction in terms?

How far do you agree with the analysis above? What do you think would have to happen before management become a profession like, say, the law?

The professionalisation debate in management continues unresolved. In the UK it is gridlocked in the contested claims of different groups seeking to control the educational agenda. As Handy (1988) says, this leaves us with the uncomfortable situation that 'of all the responsible jobs in society, only the role of the manager requires no licence of proficiency to practise'. However, some ideas do not go away and it is likely that we will renew efforts to professionalise managers in the years ahead.

9.4 An overview of management education

Management education in the UK has been criticised for encouraging a much lower proportion of managers into further and higher education than in the USA. In 1988 Handy found that only 12 per cent of UK managers had degrees while 85 per cent of Japanese and US managers were graduates (although the position for corporate managers was better at some 40 per cent in 1988).

However, since the late 1980s there has been a quiet revolution in management education. Higher education as a whole has expanded to the point where perhaps 30 per cent of eighteen-year-olds are participating, and Business Studies is the most popular subject taken on undergraduate courses. At the postgraduate level Thomson et al. (2001) suggest that about 40,000 managers were studying for Master's in Management in 1998, up from 18,000 four years previously.

It is easy to exaggerate the changes. The UK had to pull itself up from a low base level and management is far from being the graduate profession found in other advanced economies. However, the trends are clear – university education for managers is of a higher quality than in the past and a larger proportion is at Master's level. While universities tended to regard business and management as too vocational and insufficiently academic up to the 1980s, by the late 1990s even the most prestigious were running business programmes which attracted a lot of student interest. When Oxford University opened its Said Business School in the late 1990s, its business programme received more applications than any other, a seismic shift from just 20 years before when the study of management had not been possible at Oxford.

All this probably reflects a shift in public attitudes to business, the eulogising of free enterprise, the glamorising of managing big organisations and money-making. Especially among the young, the image of the manager in the grey flannel suit, the symbol of conformity, his career owned by the company, has given way to the manager as dynamic business leader.

As in America, this surge in the provision of management courses in British higher education has been accompanied by a good deal of hand-wringing about its effectiveness and appropriateness. These criticisms will be examined in depth later. However, first let us consider the main strands of management education. While the international student may feel that much of this discussion reflects Anglo-American trends, the same developments are happening in all corners of the globe and it is likely that you will find resonances with debates in your own country.

9.4.1 Undergraduate business degrees

One-fifth of all undergraduates in the UK are now taking business courses in over a hundred business schools. A quarter of all part-time students in British universities are taking a business degree, often sponsored by employers. Students who might have once chosen Economics or Humanities are now opting for a BSc in Business and Management. At the prestigious end are Oxford (Said and Templeton) and Cambridge (Judge) aimed at high-flyers who want a career in business (as opposed to doing Business Studies). These courses aim to provide a broad liberal education which has long been favoured as preparation for the world of business (as arts were in the inter-war years and classics in the days of Empire). Studies in sociology, anthropology, international politics and psychology are balanced with more business and financially-oriented subjects in a crowded curriculum (Currie 1999).

Most undergraduate business courses focus more traditionally on business, but there is a wide range of choice on offer. Three-year degrees in business administration exist alongside four-year sandwich placement BA business studies and a range of European business degrees sometimes requiring a year at a foreign university.

While courses vary in style and focus, they all cover the key material in law, accounting, IT, quantitative methods, organisational behaviour, economics and so on and often a European language. There are also specialist electives in HRM, financial management, operations, production management, marketing and so on. Sometimes there is also a consulting exercise or a placement in a company, often abroad.

All courses require mastery of a range of subjects, both human and technical. This multidisciplinary mode of study places demands on students which may be greater than for those studying a single subject. Teaching styles are likely to be more interactive than in many university disciplines, with project and group activities forming a major part of the activity. Often there is a focus on problem-solving through case studies, games and exercises and much emphasis is given to developing practical management skills as well as management knowledge. The best courses draw on personal experience for the illustration and application of ideas and help students to be critically analytical in argument (Lock 1998).

Placement work is often crucial to the overall learning experience Students learn to cope with the pressures of the workplace in a junior management job and have an opportunity to apply some of the analytical techniques they have learnt in formal education. Properly organised, the placement can be a very maturing experience and gives students a clearer focus on what they want for their future career. It is also often a bridge to a job after graduating.

Undergraduate business courses have been much criticised in recent times for giving an unrealistic picture of business. Some are condemned for an overly analytic, narrowly quantitative approach to business. They are also criticised for glorifying business values and the capitalist world-view. Most schools have attempted to confront these criticisms by broadening their curricula, guarding against an excessively rationalistic view of business, including case material from the public and voluntary sectors and incorporating subjects such as business ethics, the social responsibilities of business, and green issues in management. Whether the business degree does indeed prepare students for business, let alone management, remains controversial. Mintzberg (2004a) is a great sceptic. As we shall see, he argues that educating managers is different from educating undergraduates, and a business degree can only give a general appreciation of business. Becoming a businessman or a manager comes later and involves a lifetime of development.

Despite this counsel of modesty to newly minted business graduates and business school deans, the success of business students in finding jobs in tightening graduate markets suggests perhaps that the degree programmes are meeting many of the expectations of employers. All the same, as we will see, they remain open to criticism about their purpose and the kind of learning they provide.

9.4.2 Certificates and diplomas in management

This is a mixed bag of qualifications provided in a range of institutions – colleges of education, universities and professional institutes. They range from sub-degree Higher National Diplomas to specialist management qualifications recognised by professional bodies, for example: Association of Accountancy Technicians, Chartered Institute of Financial Accountants; Chartered Institute of Personnel Development, and so on. This group would also include the post-experience Diploma in Management Studies taught at universities.

Often students have not had experience of higher education or are returning to formal study after a long absence. Students may also lack experience of management because they come from a technical background. Often students are taking the qualification as a catch-up to fill in gaps in knowledge and skill or as a vehicle for career change. This means that a lot of attention has to be given to remedial teaching and study skills development. These courses are often tightly tied to competency structures and benchmarks set by the Management Standards Centre (successor to the MCI) and/or criteria for professional recognition. This tends to condition the content of the courses, that is, very skills-focused; functionalist and vocational.

The pedagogy emphasises the integration of work experience and didactic learning. There is a strong focus on practical tasks, participation, group work and learning best practice. Assignments are often based on portfolios with multiple sources of assessment, learning logs and projects (Woodall and Winstanley 1999).

While the 'competency standards' logic underpinning this education does ensure consistency in the curriculum and ensures basic management skills are acquired, there is a danger of imposing a straitjacket of conformity which encourages the belief that all management problems can be solved by the application of the right technique. This is in danger of precluding a truly reflective and critically thoughtful approach to the practice of management which is needed at higher levels.

9.4.3 Specialist postgraduate qualifications in management

These take many forms and are an area of great expansion in management education, for example, Master's in Human Resource Management; Business Technology; Organisational Change; Production Management, and so on. MAs can usually be taken in a variety of different modes (full-time; distance learning, part-time, etc.), which can flex around the work demands of the student.

Unlike the MBA which is concerned to turn specialists into generalists, MAs are aimed at the manager who is still at a relatively early stage in his or her career (e.g. mid-20s to mid-30s) who wishes to build on previous experience and qualifications in management and become more specialised in a selected field. Quite often, the course is used as a bridge for shifting from one career in management to another and, as such, these qualifications are a form of credentialism. However, again unlike the MBA, the management MA usually does not require the student to have previous management experience, so is also an entry-level qualification for postgraduates wishing to make a career in management.

At their most exciting, MAs are used for continuous professional development (CPD) and personal development. Take, for example, the MSc in Organisational Development and Consulting, run jointly by Brunel University and Roffey Park: this is an exciting blend of conceptual thinking and action research in which participants act as change agents within their organisations. The course aims at developing critical thinking skills, conceptual sophistication and consulting experience through a process of mentoring and learning sets (*Roffey Park Newsletter* 2003). Commentators claim that MAs often seem to offer creativity in course design and a gestalt approach which is said to be lacking in many MBA programmes.

> **Pause for thought**
>
> ### Just why are you doing a management degree?
>
> *Many of you reading this book will be engaged in studying for a management qualification. Be absolutely honest with yourselves: what is your primary motivation?*
>
> Management education can be about developing some of the skills and knowledge needed for management. It can also be a form of credentialism, to obtain magic letters after your name. It may be a form of socialisation, a rite of passage in which the aspiring manager shows s/he has the true grit needed and acquires the values and language to fit into the world of management.
>
> *What does your management course do for you?*

9.5 The Master's in business administration

It is the MBA which receives disproportionate emphasis when management education is considered because it is the most deliberate and most ambitious attempt yet devised to prepare people for powerful general management positions within the organisation. For this reason we consider it as a separate category.

In the past 20 years, the MBA has grown from a post-experience degree offered in only a few places and intended for a tiny managerial elite, to a mass programme taught at most universities, intended for postgraduates with a bit of management experience hoping for a business career. There has been much debate about the purpose and value of the MBA programme which has aroused considerable passion among its critics and its defenders. For example, Harold Leavitt (1989), the famous social psychologist, believes that 'the weird, almost unimaginable design for MBA-level education takes well proportioned young men and women and distorts them into critters with lopsided brains, icy hearts and shrunken souls'. Henry Mintzberg (2004a), the equally famous Professor of management at McGill University, says that MBAs 'train the wrong people in the wrong ways with the wrong consequences'. He has refused to teach on the MBA at McGill and has instead developed an alternative International Master's Programme in Practising Management (IMPM) offered by a consortium of five international business schools. However, advocates of the MBA point to the continuing popularity of the qualification with students and employers alike. The MBA remains buoyant because it provides good starting salaries and benefits and dramatically improves career prospects. Many employers strongly defend the MBA degree as laying the groundwork for a career in management, even if the graduates they produce are not 'finished articles', but 'goods in progress' who require more guided experience to become mature managers (Linder and Smith 1992).

9.5.1 The nature of the degree

The MBA is a curious hybrid. It provides vocational training in management, but the content of the course is largely academic. The aim of the MBA is to develop future general managers by introducing students to a range of management subjects. This is valuable to people with technical degrees or degrees in liberal arts who want to shift career and move into general management but lack knowledge of the building blocks of management. The

MBA claims to synthesise specialist knowledge in management with an appreciation of international business and the development of professional/personal skills in leadership.

Providers of the MBA do not claim that they are able to transform the person, to turn ugly ducklings into management swans, nor do they say that they provide a finishing school to make candidates with an already established professional background desirable to well-paying blue-chip companies. However, the MBA is about developing analytical, decision-making capabilities, a broader outlook on business and the social skills and cultural knowledge of management which will allow him or her to be accepted by the management community.

The MBA degree is an import from America dating from the 1950s. It only established itself in the UK in the mid-1960s and for a long time was run at just two elite institutions – London Business School and Manchester Business School – which had been set up by the government to improve standards of management education in Britain. Now there are around 130 programmes in the UK graduating about 12,000 MBAs a year (about 200,000 in USA) (Woodall and Winstanley 1999).

American and European MBAs differ considerably. The US model is traditionally that of the two-year MBA, with considerable emphasis on quantititative, analytical subjects. The European MBA is likely to be shorter, to give more weight to the softer subjects in management (e.g. communication, leadership, organisational change) and provide students with a more multicultural experience by virtue of the diverse background of faculty and students. Typically, there is also more focus on testing business theory in practice and on project teamworking. American and European schools also differ in the importance they ascribe to the GMAT test (an internationally recognised test of symbolic and numerical reasoning ability). In American universities getting a high score here is of overwhelming importance; in European schools other variables such as social skills and character are also given credence (*The Times* MBA supplements 1997, 2001, 2004, etc.).

9.5.2 The benefits of the degree

At one time the MBA degree was rare and exclusive. It had a 'catchet' which conferred on its holders an 'edge' which showed itself in a high starting salary and accelerated promotion to high levels of management. However, the MBA qualification was oversold in the 1970s and 1980s and its graduates did not prove to have the qualities of 'super managers' which were claimed for them. It was soon recognised that an MBA did not guarantee leadership potential, managerial acumen or even managerial competence. The analytical ability assessed on the MBA did not transfer automatically into managerial capability. Recruiters came to realise that they had to look beyond the qualification. The MBA has now come to be seen increasingly as a necessary, but not a sufficient, requisite for success in management.

Although the glamour of the letters MBA may have faded, the qualification is still held in high respect within business and even if it doesn't open all doors it does significantly improve career prospects by giving its holders an extra lever for success. What exactly does the MBA degree do for the person who holds it?

Periodic surveys of students carried out by the Economist Intelligence Unit (annual surveys; see bibliography) suggest the following advantages.

- The MBA seems to be a good longer-term investment in career development. Although it does not guarantee a big jump in salary from your previous job (although that can also happen), it is still an internationally recognised vehicle for social mobility into the higher reaches of management. It seems that most MBA students embark on the arduous training more for the material benefit it may bring (e.g. higher salaries, career security) than any intrinsic interest in developing character or understanding the workings of international business.

- The MBA can open up new career opportunities. Many graduates use the qualification to switch careers, typically into consulting or financial services, which pay more and are arguably the occupations which make most use of the formal skills developed on an MBA course.

- The MBA broadens knowledge of business processes and encourages holistic thinking about the organisation. It sensitises MBA graduates to the relationship between functions and how they are geared into the purpose of the organisation as a whole.

- The MBA develops problem-solving skills using formal, analytical techniques. MBA graduates are often flawless at dissecting issues using statistical techniques. The intellectual rigour of the course is said to give those who experience it a sense of confidence that they have a bag of intellectual tools from which they can draw in any management situation they may confront.

- While the MBA cannot implant managerial qualities of sensing, feeling and understanding if they are not there, it can sharpen those skills by promoting self-awareness. Leadership may not be something which can be taught in the classroom, but the experience of learning together in teams in conditions of stress can bring early maturity in judgement and the use of social skills as well as helping to cultivate a coherent philosophy of management which may last a lifetime.

- Finally, the MBA gives access to an international network of peers and faculty. It is argued that this gives opportunities to develop the cross-cultural sensitivity and communication skills which will prepare graduates for international roles in multinational companies. The international contacts made on the course can also be of great value in future business dealings.

Although the MBA is not a magic wand to transmute base metal into gold, it is a powerful catalyst. It can supplement relevant professional experience; it can enhance personal talents; give new skills and give the credibility to make the transition into general management. It is also a guarantee of employability and provides a currency widely recognised which allows mobility between organisations.

From the point of view of employers, the value of the MBA seems to lie not in the skills you develop but the fact that you were selected, especially if your MBA is pursued in a high-status business school. The tough admissions process acts as a pre-selection screen guaranteeing (for many potential employers) that the applicant 'has what it takes'.

9.5.3 The contents of an MBA

The typical MBA usually involves the following elements.

- Modules in the main functional elements of management (e.g. finance, quantitative methods, marketing, HRM), usually about eight core subjects.
- A programme of quantitative methods.

- A good choice of electives which allow the student to take specialist interests in management to a deeper level.
- A company project. This is usually a consultancy task in which students do research within a company, prepare a report and make recommendations to both the company executive and the school faculty.
- A balance between exercises to develop technical skills and the softer skills of managing (e.g. communicating, influencing, persuading, motivating, teamworking, etc.).
- A programme of external speakers drawing from experts in management and the school's network of alumni.

There are usually three main methods of teaching on an MBA.

The case study method

Following the Harvard example, case studies have always been important to the MBA curriculum anywhere in the world. The use of business narratives usually involves a management dilemma which tries to capture the messy, interwoven nature of business life where there are no clear-cut issues and no obvious right answers. The great advantage of case studies is that they offer an overview of management problems and encourage critical, even creative, thinking to address them. The downside is that case studies can be ethnocentric and culturally limiting.

Typically in an MBA class, a student is chosen at random to present the analysis to the rest of the class and make some recommendations. Then the case is opened for discussion by the group and the tutor facilitates a consensus and a summing-up. The case study method is seen as a useful stimulus for class discussion, forcing students to think for themselves and to apply management techniques in terms of the unique conditions which it presents (EIU surveys; *The Times* MBA supplements).

Group work

This is an essential element of the MBA because it simulates the social/political context of real management. Programmes try to put students in situations where competing demands have to be resolved and individuals have to defend their vision against the pressures of group conformity. In many programmes students are assessed in terms of their group involvement and there is peer assessment of individual performance.

Group working can be enriching for MBA students but it is also a source of stress and emotional discord. In teams, some people can feel 'frozen out'; difficult members have to be conciliated; there are battles of power and status. Emotions can run high. A common reflection of students looking back on the MBA experience is that they would have liked more preparation in how to work effectively in groups.

Projects

Any well-established MBA will have a consultancy or company project element. The quality of the placements will reflect the richness and diversity of the school's corporate links. The challenge is to find companies willing to commit time to accommodate student teams of consultants. Projects allow students to practise their new-found mastery of management techniques and knowledge in real-world management situations. Here is an opportunity to show insight into organisational politics and to demonstrate the vital social skills needed for presentation and implementation. From these consulting projects host organisations often get free consultancy and a chance to spot talent. Many projects act as a bridge to a new employer even before the student has finished his or her MBA.

What's it like to do an MBA?

The professor moved his eyes across the amphitheatre, emphatically inviting us to approach the course with a 'willing suspension of disbelief'. Was I to disbelieve the teachings of my professor? No, he seemed to be implying something deeper like, 'Don't take my word for it, try it for yourself' and 'This may not make sense or seem important but it will do later'.

I quickly forgot this wise advice and became consumed by the MBA. It is very demanding and all absorbing, a way of life in itself. The intense workload materialised immediately. Period 1 at INSEAD, affectionately known as P1 and the first of five academic periods encompasses core courses in Prices Markets (translation: macroeconomics); Data, Uncertainty, Judgement (translation: statistics) and Financial Markets Valuation (translation: finance). P1 and P2 are meant to establish the core competencies of an MBA, while P3 and P5 provide the opportunity to choose electives in an area of interest.

The rapid pace continued throughout the year. There were numerous campus presentations by external speakers; there were numerous exercises, case studies assignments and exams. INSEAD purposely overwhelms its students with too much to do in too little time. Eighty-hour weeks are not at all uncommon. The whole course is structured so that students learn the art of balance and prioritisation.

One of the highlights has been an international business game in which INSEAD students compete with business school players around the world in running a virtual cosmetics company in uncertain business conditions. It was exciting and fun and showed me that business itself is a game; success lies in knowing how to apply the rules.

It was my 'willing suspension of disbelief' that got me through the course and helped me to bring the pieces together. I have indeed learned concrete business concepts, but I have also picked up something more. Yes, I have learned to use the capital asset pricing model to evaluate the pricing of risky securities, and yes, I have learned how the F-test, a statistical test, can tell me if my regression model has any hope at all. But I have also discovered that I can use these concepts in a range of situations. I never imagined for example that I would watch a basketball game and explain to my fiancé that if the coach had only understood the economic theory of absolute and comparative advantage, he would have played Robinson at centre, instead of forward, and they would have won the game.

Equally, I never thought that my INSEAD experiences would lead me to the shores of Thailand to study the effects of the tsunami devastation where I would be part of a team doing a marketing feasibility study to evaluate long term projects to benefit a small fishing village hit by the enormous wave. I was using techniques which only a few weeks ago were just technical exercises. I feel I've been transformed into a true MBA.

Question
This is the reality of an MBA. How would you cope with the intellectual and emotional demands?

Source: Adapted from From chaos comes order and composure, *Financial Times*, 30/05/2005 (Huang, L.).

9.6 Trends in the MBA

The MBA has been subject to much criticism for being overly analytical; too concerned with techniques at the expense of developing mature judgement and understanding; too distant from the actual process of doing management. We consider these issues later on in the context of the continuing debate around the future of business schools, but here we consider the various ways in which the MBA is changing.

9.6.1 Changes in curriculum

In the last decade, many schools, even the most prestigious, have revamped their MBA programmes. For example, Harvard, stinging from criticism that its programme produced 'number crunchers' not leaders, has moved from teaching functional subjects (marketing, finance, etc.) to teaching management as a cross-disciplinary process in which problems are examined from a variety of perspectives. LBS has adopted a model of cross-modular integration focusing on problem-solving. Many schools are sensitive to charges of ethnocentrism and are now using study material which is less Anglo-American. Most are making their courses more skills-based and incorporating more qualitative subjects (e.g. organisational behaviour; team building; creativity; management culture) alongside the technical subjects. They are also aligning their programmes with practical workplace skills and embracing the challenge of knowledge management and the learning organisation.

Many elite programmes are experimenting with more imaginative use of projects and simulations to bring home to students the real conditions of managing. For example, the HEC School of Management in France includes a complete elective in which students shadow top managers of a large French company and observe board level decision-making in action. They are then asked to provide consultancy support by drafting marketing and promotional strategies to put real management decisions in the company into practice. This may include writing the MD's speeches and doing the background analysis for press and TV presentations. Alongside the real consultancy there is shadow simulation in which students role-play parts and undertake the same activities as their real-life counterparts. The final twist is that students are asked to videotape their experience which becomes part of the assessment. Students say that the opportunity to observe and then apply learning in this way makes the theory come alive (Syrett and Lammiman 1999).

Other schools take a different approach to integrating theory and practice and broadening the consciousness of students. So at IMD, all students are required to do the 'team initiated exercise'. As part of the course requirements, students are asked to implement a project which has nothing to do with their studies. It may be anything, from organising an expedition to climb Mount Blanc to coordinating a children's theatre company, running a soup kitchen for the homeless or visiting refugee camps in a developing country (*The Times* MBA supplements).

> **Pause for thought**
>
> ### Can the MBA help make managers become more ethical?
>
> In the post-Enron period, there is a new interest in making managers more socially and ethically conscious and encouraging them to develop a personal philosophy of management which is principled. Business schools have responded to this need in different ways. Many run ethics and corporate responsibility seminars interwoven with the core courses, but some schools go further.
>
> At the University of Michigan, all MBA students undertake a 'global citizenship' and ethics course. The course deliberately raises prickly issues. Is the use of child labour always wrong? What if the alternative is no job, poverty, even starvation? What if getting that international contract involves complicity with practices which may be questionable? Part of the programme involves students spending periods of attachment at shelters for the homeless and centres for battered women to build empathy with social issues.
>
> At the French business school, ISA, the compulsory ethics module is taught at a St Benedictine monastery. The teachers are monks, many of whom have been successful businessmen before taking a spiritual path. Hard-headed MBA students are asked to consider issues of business and moral purpose and what it takes to develop a 'community of belonging' at work. Although the monastery is not explicitly offered as a model, it is certainly there as an exemplar of a work community with a common purpose to which all are committed.
>
> #### Question
> *If you were responsible for designing the ethics part of an MBA programme, how would you approach the task?*

Another important development on the MBA is the changing criteria for selection. While it was once possible to enter an MBA with just a first degree, the trend now is to make the course post-experience. Increasingly, candidates are required to have had several years of management-related experience before they are considered. This means that the average age of MBA recruits is now 28, with a large proportion in their 30s. Accreditation regimes are increasingly policing this requirement. This marks off the British (and indeed, European) MBA from the American, where entrants are typically in their early 20s. Whether aspirants to management need some experience to make sense of the theory or theory first to make sense of the experience is an unresolved question in management development to which there are no easy answers.

9.6.2 Differentiating the MBA

MBAs are becoming more varied. One trend is for MBAs to become more specialist. Some might regard this as a contradiction in terms. After all, the MBA was always regarded as a general management programme that encompasses all the functions of managing and seeks to develop generic skills. All the same, one of the most dominant trends in business schools is towards specialisation. This is by function (e.g. an MBA with a slant towards marketing) or geographical (e.g. an MBA with a bias to business in China) or by company (i.e. the corporate or consortium MBA; see below).

Bowing to pressure from employers who say that MBA graduates are too broadly educated, schools are offering MBAs in HRM, Information, International Business and so on. Other schools are following the American option of combining an MBA with an MA in a more specialist subject (e.g. MBA and healthcare; MBA and law). These have a lot to recommend them in a business climate where people are supposed to be immediately effective when they are appointed.

MBAs are often aligned to the corporate links of the business school. For example, at Imperial College students who want to be strategic consultants can elect to study mergers and acquisitions which will involve live projects and attachments with McKinsey and Co. and Arthur Little. There is a Whitehall MBA at Cranfield which fuses business and public service principles of management. At the Royal Agricultural College, Cirencester, it is possible to do an MBA in agribusiness which integrates the principles of an MBA with agriculture and allows periods of study in three European countries (*The Times* MBA Supplements).

MBAs are also becoming differentiated in terms of the length and mode of programme they offer. In the USA, the two-year full-time programme is still sacrosanct. However, in the UK most schools have succumbed to business pressure for a short, sharp qualification by pruning back to one year. This means that the one-year MBA is very intensive and far too much is attempted in the time available. Increasingly, students are opting to do part-time MBAs in which they combine study and work. This has the virtue of allowing students to keep their jobs while they become qualified. It also means that students are often sponsored by their employers and can readily apply what is learnt in the classroom to practical organisational issues.

As with all postgraduate courses in management, the problems of balancing an MBA with a job are considerable. There is always a delicate juggling act between study, work and family, especially difficult if the student doesn't have an understanding employer. There is also the problem that the part-timer misses out on the total immersion and group camaraderie of the full-time course which is often cited as the most stimulating part of doing an MBA.

9.6.3 The distance-learning MBA

Distance learning (DL) accounts for the main growth in MBAs. Business schools like Henley and the Open University have thousands of students scattered around the world. The attraction of the distance-learning MBA to students is not hard to see. Using electronic media, students can study in their own time and at their convenience. This appeals particularly to the new cadres of geographically mobile, international managers who cannot commit to regular attendance on a conventional course. For employers and sponsors of the MBA, the distance-learning option is cheaper than other study alternatives and has the benefit of synthesising learning with day-to-day work.

Distance learning has its origins in the old correspondence course. However, the days of ring-pull binders full of glossy notes and paper-based materials has been largely replaced by electronic links. For example, Henley Management Centre uses IT-based learning called Lotus Notes – the electronic classroom – to introduce students to the more formalised number-crunching aspects of the course while reserving precious class hours for 'presence' teaching to behavioural skills and team-building activities. Computer networks also allow students to keep in touch with each other and with business school faculty wherever they are in the world. Multimedia link the student through study notes to virtual learning groups and provide them with an on-line guide to internet data sources. Computer conferencing/seminars and blackboard-style intranets allow interactive discussion and learning (Bickerstaffe 1995).

Evaluative studies of DL MBA courses have shown that this format is an effective way of transferring the functional knowledge in an MBA but virtual elements need to be supplemented by social learning (e.g. summer schools; weekend seminars; local study groups; tutor hotlines and periodic facilitated learning) to overcome the isolation of self study using this format. The 'atomised' form of learning which DL implies is the main drawback to this mode of delivery. Students have to be very motivated self-starters to work consistently on the course. It appeals more to 'theoretical' and 'reflective' learning styles than 'activists' and 'experiential' learners. Even with good support networks it takes a lot longer than other forms of study to complete (i.e. 3–4 years). As a result, a large proportion fail to ever do so. There is also the issue that much of learning to be a manager involves social interaction and group involvement which is inevitably far less evident with the DL model than in other approaches (EIU 2003; Bradshaw 2001).

Despite all the drawbacks, innovative DL MBAs which skilfully blend on-line and experiential learning are likely to be the force of the future. It is a cheap, convenient form of learning which empowers the student and is appropriate to the fluid nature of modern working. Even now, there are signs that students feel unwilling to take the risk of giving up a job to take a full-time MBA; even day release and evening classes do not fit in with the new frenetic and unpredictable styles of working. (Tysome 2000). Future electronic forms of learning which are visually appealing; which bring excellent lectures into home study; which make teaching material available in major world languages; which allow easy interactive links with responsive tutors and with an international peer group, will probably prove irresistible to the thousands, or is that millions, of eligible people who want a management qualification (Mathews and Megginson 2005; Anon. 1999).

Pause for thought

A miscellany of views

Below are a number of quotations from commentators on the MBA.

> 'Business Schools are the massage parlours of the 20th century. MBA stands for 'moral bankruptcy assured'.
>
> *Reg Revans, famous management guru*

> An MBA at Henley is a 'Mould Breaking Ambition'.
>
> *Henley advertisement*

> 'I've recently started running an '80-Minute MBA course', a kind of Reduced Shakespeare Company approach to business education. A couple of MBA graduates have complained that we were devaluating the MBA brand. Quite a few have said, 'Eighty minutes is a bit long; any chance you could do it in an hour?'
>
> *Richard Reeves, MBA graduate and course founder* www.the80minutemba.com

> 'The MBA is a lot of hard work and the pace is fast . . . don't expect depth and don't expect miracles when you graduate . . . an MBA is not as good as having natural 'smarts' or entrepreneurial talent, but it does get you to 'first base' in the management rat race and then the rest is up to you'.
>
> *An MBA graduate*

Questions

Do any of these observations appeal to you? Do you have any thoughts of your own?

See too: Reeves (2008) 'A degree of confidence', *Management Today*, July 2008.

9.6.4 The company MBA

A growing trend is the rise of corporate MBAs. These are either in-company MBAs tailored to the strategic needs of one company, or consortium programmes for a cluster of non-competing companies. Examples of the former include the Lancaster MBA for British Airways and the Bradford MBA designed for managers in the BBC. Of the latter, consortium programmes include executive MBA programmes run by Cranfield and LBS for small groups of contracting blue chip companies. Both involve the adaptation of the standard MBA programme to the company's business and aim to add value to corporate investment. Sometimes the MBA is offered as part of a strategic partnership between a corporate learning and development department and a business school, so that teaching on the programme is a combination of inputs from the university and in-company staff. Accreditation is through the host business school (Latham and Seitjs 1998).

Company MBAs are controversial. On the one hand they do provide a mechanism for immediate knowledge transfer for management problem-solving. Project work can be focused on the key issues facing the company. In consortium companies there is an opportunity for joint projects between companies. This gives participants a chance to understand the cross-cutting nature of many management problems, the universality of experience in management which may have seemed personal and the opportunity to observe how other companies tackle issues so that good practice can be benchmarked. Sometimes this can be catalytic in helping managers to re-evaluate their standards and behaviours.

On the other hand, critics argue that students on company programmes miss out on important aspects of the MBA experience. Limiting participation to candidates from a single organisation or a small number of organisations restricts the pool of collective experience, reduces the range of contacts and the cross-fertilisation of ideas. Students also miss out on the normal campus experiences during which most learning comes through informal relations between the students themselves. Then there is the issue of academic rigour. An important concern is that employers have an undue influence on the programme, diluting the theoretical material and making the content consistent with their company culture. All this could compromise the balance and objectivity of the degree.

Advocates of the company MBA argue that the degree of tailoring is likely to be quite small in practice. According to Henley Management College, which has been running company MBAs since the 1980s, most companies are careful to respect the core programme. Corporate programmes, they believe, do not displace theory but place it within the context of the sponsoring company's business. The real pressures to compromise come not from corporate disdain of theory and pressure to be technique-oriented, but the conflicting timescales of business and academic priorities. Business often presses for a fast completion of the company MBA which is only possible if corners are cut and the curriculum watered down. These are the real dangers of company linkages.

Consortium programmes face special problems – in becoming established, agreeing a curriculum which satisfies all the partners, respecting confidentiality, harmonising philosophies of learning and maintaining momentum when some participating organisations pull out, as they invariably do. Although consortia can create a rich ferment of synergies for learning, they are difficult to pull off.

9.6.5 The executive MBA

Another trend is the rise of the executive MBA. This is a post-MBA and/or an MBA for experienced managers for which there is growing demand. These are part-time courses aimed at high-flying younger managers (mid-30s) and executives at a later stage in their careers. Quite often EMBA students are postgraduates in management who are seeking to recreate the stimulating environment of thinking and debate which they enjoyed at university and which they do not find in the workplace.

The EMBA is described as employer-friendly because it is usually quite short, about a year, and is concentrated in short intensive blocks of residential study supplemented by distance learning and international projects. It is a way of retaining or motivating valued managers and helping those who missed out on formal education in the past to fill in gaps within their armoury of management skills. The EMBA can be both 'finishing school' and a 'brains trust'.

From the viewpoint of students, a company-sponsored place on an EMBA at a good school is attractive because it allows them to obtain an MBA while retaining their jobs at a point in their career when time for study is at a premium and time out of the organisation could be fatal to their ambitions. The programme exposes them to business leaders and spokesmen of leading-edge concepts. It also brings them into networks of international peers to create the ferment that they are really looking for at the business school – the shock of new usable ideas and intellectual challenge of colleagues at the same level. The managerial experience of participants often makes them high-quality, challenging students and their seniority means they can trial ideas from the classroom immediately in the workplace.

In the UK there is a boom in EMBAs and London business schools lead the world in this area. In return for high fees the schools deploy their best teachers and most innovative teaching, and run events in luxury hotels and conference centres. International companies are enthusiastic and although the cost may put EMBAs beyond the purses of most small business, there is likely to be demand from entrepreneurs and public sector high-flyers. However, it is in China where the market demand for executive development is likely to be greatest and partnerships between Western and Chinese business schools already exist (Syrett and Lammiman 1999).

The DBA: in search of a unique selling point

With MBA graduates fast becoming almost commonplace and even the executive MBA losing some of its lustre, it is little wonder that some business schools are developing another tier of qualifications for their best and brightest. The DBA, the elder brother to the MBA is on offer at a small number of schools, including Henley, Bath and the Strathclyde School of Business.

The motivators for taking a DBA seem to be the desire to upgrade CVs and get a distinctive edge, but also to develop yourself intellectually. The DBA candidate is likely to be in his or her mid-40s with middle/senior management experience.

Although billed as a doctoral programme and leading to the title 'Doctor', it is seen by BS and employers as performing a different function to the traditional PhD degree. It is less about theory and the development of new knowledge and more about researching concrete management problems. So, recent DBA research at Henley has included patient management in the NHS, career leadership and management development in the Royal Navy, emotional management and modelling risk. Most of the DBA candidates study a project linked to their jobs and this is seen as contributing to better decisions at work.

Question
As management becomes more involved in organisational research and internal consulting, is the DBA likely to become more mainstream or is it always destined to remain of exclusive minority interest?

Source: Adapted from FT report: Business education: an ever more exclusive degree, *Financial Times*, 9/09/2002 (Matthews, V.).

9.7 Are business schools doing a good job?

9.7.1 Critique of the business school

In recent years criticism of the value of the MBA has merged with wider criticism of the purpose and effectiveness of management education. For example, Bennis and O'Toole (2005) claim that business schools lost their way when they tried to escape the stigma of narrowly vocational 'trade schools' in the 1950s by embracing a model of 'science' which was out of step with the realities of practising managers. The business school curriculum became dominated by quantitative, abstract, financial and economic analysis. Management became defined as an academic discipline which aped the 'positivism' of the natural sciences and arguably misapplied its methods to the *social* experience of managing. The model of management as a *liberal* profession based on experiential insight and enlightened practice was ignored.

Scientism remains entrenched, although it is unclear that the obsession with techniques, statistics and sophisticated modelling produces a better manager. The empirical studies on the doing of management (see Chapter 2) concur in their observation that the best managers often operate very successfully with back of the envelope calculations and with heuristic methods of decision-making without knowing any higher mathematics (Heller 1986).

With this epistemology underpinning the MBA curriculum, it is hardly surprising that MBA graduates are often accused by the employers who recruit them of being too preoccupied with techniques and of having unrealistic assumptions about the value and application of techniques to real management situations. The mindset of the typical MBA graduate is said to be technocratic. MBA graduates have a reputation for being strong on abstract reasoning, analysis and problem-solving but weak on path-finding, communication, culture building, leadership and implementation. Since the 1980s there have been calls for business schools to adapt their curriculum to overcome functional myopia, to develop practical wisdom and build an holistic understanding of the multi-strands of management problems which defy easy technical classification or analysis. Business schools have been encouraged to help students become more conceptual, to work with an appreciation of power and politics, to be more ethically aware, more synoptic and more imaginative in their approach (Pfeffer and Fong 2002).

These criticisms have hit home. As we have seen, most business schools have been revising their curricula to address the concerns of their main corporate customers. There have been many initiatives (e.g. projects, consultancy assignments, etc.) to take learning out of the classroom and give students a taste of decision-making in the resistant medium of the typical organisation. Leadership skills now feature strongly in many, as is personal effectiveness using a dynamic balance of coaching, interactive learning and experiential projects (Purcell 2003). In many places, teaching methods have been revised to stimulate students to think thematically, to think holistically, to think creatively and with real understanding of the softer issues of managing (Linder and Smith 1992).

While the degree of radicalism involved in curriculum reform has varied greatly between programmes (one of the reasons why employers are as concerned with where you get your MBA as much as how well you perform on it), it seems that the average MBA in the new century is very different in character to an MBA taken in, say, 1985. In this respect, commentators say that European schools have often gone further than their American counterparts in recruiting faculty with management experience; changing selection criteria in favour of older students who have held positions of responsibility; recasting curricula so they involve the social, political and moral issues of managing; emphasising experiential not just 'surface' knowing or learning just to satisfy course requirements, and so on. However, controversy still dogs the business schools.

Some highly respected critics from within the fort, like Henry Mintzberg who was once an evangelical advocate of the MBA but now refuses to teach it at McGill University, believe that the fundamental model of the MBA as a generic preparation for management is flawed. Ironically, in view of some of our earlier discussion, his view is that management education goes wrong when it defines management as a profession, like law, which requires the absorption of knowledge before managers can practise (a view also echoed by Raelin 1990). Because management is a practical subject, he argues, the time for some formal input is later, when the fledgling manager has learnt some experience-based craft skills and, even then, long periods of involvement at a university may not be the best solution.

Henry Mintzberg on MBAs and business schools

Question: What is your argument against the MBA?

Mintzberg: The conventional MBA is aimed at fairly young people with limited management experience. It gives the false impression that they are being trained as managers. You can't train managers in the classroom. What you can do is take people who are experienced managers and, if you design the programme properly, enhance their understanding of management, so you make them better managers.

Conventional MBAs and many Masters in Management, train the wrong people in the wrong ways with the wrong consequences.

Question: And the executive MBA?

Mintzberg: Here you train the right people in the wrong ways with the wrong consequences. Its ironic, well more than that actually, that you take a programme designed for people without management experience then not only do you give the same programme to people without experience but you boast about it.

Question: The counter argument is that 100,000 people graduate with MBAs and find good jobs, so the schools must be doing something right?

Mintzberg: No, they teach them to talk a good game, how to move fast and do a lot of analysis. All these things can be good in the short term; they do projects and studies; they are very busy and energetic. However, in the long term these things may be very dysfunctional. For example, the way people are trained to think about strategy is that it's a generic sort of thing using analyses. But that is disconnected from context, what you are making strategy about.

That's true of the case study method that business schools love. I'm questioning cases as an artificial way to force people to make decisions based on things they know almost nothing about, but they think they know. This leads on to all sorts of bad practices including George Bush, a Harvard MBA graduate, making decisions on Iraq. It's the 'you give me a 20 page case study and I'll give you a war in Iraq' approach that concerns me.

Question: What is the right way to develop better managers in the classroom?

Mintzberg: First don't let anyone into the classroom who is not a manager. The students should be connected to their jobs; that means they should be sponsored by their companies who value their learning and want to use it. Then you build as much of the classroom as you can around them using and sharing their experience and connecting it to useful concepts . . . As a teacher you try to find ways of bringing key company issues into the classroom.

Source: Adapted from interview: Mintzberg, H. and Dearlove, D. (2004) *The Times*, 4 October; and Mintzberg (2004a) *Managers not MBAs.*'

Another thrust of criticism of business schools emanates from the radical fringe of management educators, often sociologists of management and 'critical management theorists' (e.g. French and Grey 1996; Wilmott 1997). Their arguments are complex but they seem to resolve around the following claims.

- Postgraduate management education is saturated with the 'American management mystique' and the assumption that US management principles are both universal and superior to management practised elsewhere. Unfortunately, as many MBA graduates find, these techniques do not provide magic spells which work everywhere regardless of context (Grey 2006).
- Management is taught on MBA courses as if it is non-problematical and provide optimum, technical rational solutions. This, despite the fact that there is little evidence that the techniques offered really do predict and control as their designers

claim (Grey 2006). The implication is that much of management education is rhetorical; it makes claims which are not backed up with hard evidence that it can really have a significant impact on performance in a world of inconsistency and contradiction.

- Because of the dominant ideology of rationality and technicism in business school education, subjects are taught as 'positivistic certainties' (Roberts 1996). There is a dominant 'engineering ideology'. As a result, subjects are taught as non-problematical slabs of knowledge (e.g. 'motivation', 'change management', 'strategy', etc.) which are packaged and prescribed as a body of facts and scientific knowledge which the student absorbs (Watson 2004). While some students may have critical reservations about the value of the knowledge presented to them, they collude in a cynical contract of ingesting the information to pass exams, not because they see the concepts as tools to help in their managerial sense-making (Roberts 1996).

- The pedagogy of management education is marketing-led. Management teachers largely act as entertainers and salesmen of management ideas. They define their role as agents for making the received wisdom of management palatable to easily bored students. The social construction of the technical knowledge or its cultural contextualisation is rarely examined on MBA courses. It is little wonder then that management education typically homogenises the learning experience and contributes to the creation of identikit MBA graduates when business *says* that it wants independent, critical thinkers (French and Grey 1996).

- But this result should surprise no one, the radical critics would say. Although management education is nominally part of the liberal university tradition, its real function is not to develop critical thought or critical thinkers (whatever the rhetoric); MBAs are really about selecting and socialising those who are screened as suitable for management work (and this pre-selection for management may be the main value of an MBA for most employers). Some of this involves a sort of indoctrination into the ideology of management as a rational–technical system and into appropriate cultural behaviour. In this task, management education has arguably served its business sponsors well but the downside may be that socialisation also brings with it conformity and a conditioned outlook when business says that 'high potential' managers are 'mavericks' with flair (Thomas and Anthony 1996).

Pause for thought

Do the radical critics protest too much?

- How persuasive do you find the views presented above? If you are a student on a management course, do you recognise the force of some of these comments?
- Is your course content 'over analytical' and 'technicist' and do you feel you are being indoctrinated into the 'world views' of management?
- Do you think you can retain critical distance?

9.7.2 Moving beyond the business school

Ironically, the radical attack on business schools from the critical theorists finds its nemesis in a critique of these same institutions from within mainstream big business. Although objections to university-led management education may vary greatly between the factions, they are united in the degree of emotion which animates them.

By the 1990s many large companies were expressing their dissatisfaction with business schools. Business school courses were too academic, too conceptual and unrelated to their business needs. Their monopoly as providers of management education now seems increasingly threatened by a range of other providers – independent training centres, management consultancies and solo suppliers (Arkin 2000). Although universities may have an edge over their competitors in being research-oriented, presenting leading-edge thinking to senior managers and have the draw of famous names, it was claimed that their pedagogies were old-fashioned and the quality of their facilities insufficient. Over the past decade or so, many universities, especially those heavily dependent on MBA revenue from sponsoring companies, have made real efforts to renew their products so that they are more acceptable to corporate clients.

Syrett and Lammiman (1999) give the example of LBS which until the mid-1990s was perceived by big business to be old-fashioned and insular, international in rhetoric rather than in substance. In recent years, LBS has become less scholastic, internationalised its curriculum, introduced multidisciplinary, thematic courses and moved closer to the corporate market. This has meant involving companies more closely in decisions about course content and delivery; introducing more experiential elements such as live consultancy attachments; forming partnerships with clients around action research programmes and commissioning courses linked to continuous learning within their organisations. Part of this new commercialism has involved setting up new 'think-tanks' and platforms for new ideas (e.g. The Foundation for Entrepreneurial Management) which bring together businessmen and academics to create new synergies and provide electronic databases for clients to network with each other. It has also meant using its distinct brand identity to become a leader in executive education (Dealtry 2000).

However, large organisations are not just becoming more demanding in what they want from business schools, they are also becoming more proactive in defining their learning and development needs and designing programmes in partnership with business schools which will be integrated into their internal career development systems. A few companies have taken the next step by developing their own *corporate universities*. Motorola, Anglia Water, McDonalds, Natwest and so on have all set up corporate universities and commentators claim that a large number of blue-chip companies are likely to follow (Arkin 2000).

These are more than just residential retreats for in-house programmes. Corporate universities are often sophisticated organisations which provide a focus for programmes co-designed between the host organisation and external providers contracted in. At their best, these institutions can become the hub of learning and development networks across the organisation; a mechanism for linking together diverse groups within the company; a force for developing a company-wide culture; a platform for leading change and a means of providing management development which is academically sound but relevant to business needs. Forty per cent of corporate universities are planning to run programmes in partnership with a range of providers, coordinated by the corporate university, quality-managed and accredited by a business school (e.g. Henley is working with the Cable and Wireless Company college to run an accredited MA programme; the course was co-designed, that is, Henley teaches the management aspects, Cable and Wireless the telecommunications elements) (Syrett and Lammiman 1999).

The rise of corporate universities (CUs) is an ambivalent trend for the business schools. The corporate universities also offer a business opportunity to the universities because most company schools want external validation. But here lies a dilemma. At present, most business schools see themselves as institutions of higher education which do some executive development. However, strategic partnerships with corporate universities will raise important questions. Can universities continue to maintain traditional academic standards while also offering the practical forms of management development based on different teaching models which the corporate world will want? Can business schools be academic institutions and training consultancies at the same time (Anon. 1999; Arkin 2000)?

The main fear is that the performance-driven imperatives of business and the culture-building purpose of the corporate universities will dilute the independence of thought of participating academics, replace conceptualisation with narrow utilitarianism and limit the breadth of the curriculum. Corporate-aligned qualifications may also place limits on the diversity of experience and breadth of perspective available to students in the learning process. Then there are ethical and political issues. CUs will want the aura of respectability and credibility of association with a well-known university, but the university has a lot to lose if the company's behaviour is questionable. For example, how embarrassed would the partner university be if it had participated in the Enron University MBA (Moore 2002)?

Managing the partnerships will not be easy, but CUs are unlikely to disappear. When business schools and corporations join forces it can be a win–win situation for both. Business schools have access to the highest reaches of the company and the opportunity to integrate education programmes into the fabric of the organisation, from performance reviews to succession planning, so guaranteeing influence and continuing work. Client pressures can serve to raise standards requiring business schools to sharpen skills, embrace DL technology and develop innovative blended learning opportunities. CUs benefit from their access to broader ideas and skills which feed into internal development programmes. When everything is working well a high-quality accredited, customised MBA run through a strategic partnership can have real impact on the organisation as a whole by linking new ways of thinking to new ways of working. It is MD at its best, but is sadly a phenomenon rarely seen in the real world.

Case study: Building the global corporate university

Deutsch Bank University (DBU) is based in Germany but works with company employees worldwide to offer the latest technology and service-driven processes for learning and development.

Soon after its foundation in 2001, DBU helped Deutsch Bank to build a global culture and fulfil its new corporate strategy. It developed a top-level corporate training philosophy and provided education programmes for executives in the hope that senior members of the organisation would act as mentors for the next generation of bankers and embed the strong values of the organisation at progressively lower levels of the bank.

DBU also helped the company by aligning learning and development with business strategies. The university formed specialised units called 'business schools' (e.g. the 'Sales and Training School of Business'; the 'Trade Finance School of Business', etc.) charged with assessing needs and developing MD strategies with linked corporate divisions.

The university was set up as a field service agency. The staff were not 'corporate centre' but 'shared service people' who were required to compete with external training organisations on price and quality. It is thought that this internal competition generates the most robust development solutions. The future goal is for its programmes to receive international accreditation. The university is developing partnerships with business schools around the globe that are willing to offer credits for completing DBU training.

To extend the reach of the DBU's work to far-flung subsidiaries, the DBU places emphasis on e-learning. This is offered in support of local programmes which use one-to-one mentoring and hands-on teaching. The DBU example shows that while a corporate university undoubtedly requires significant outlays of time and resources, especially if the level of delivery is to match that of the established business schools, the benefits can be very compelling. A successful corporate university can serve as a vehicle for promoting cultural change, transmitting corporate vision, enhancing organisational learning and improving management capability on a global basis.

Question

This case has been written to 'emphasise the positive' in defence of corporate universities. If you were given the brief for the prosecution, what line would you take?

Source: Adapted from Dzinkowski, R. 'Building the global corporate university', *Financial Times*, 5 September 2002.

9.8 Prospects for management education in the future

9.8.1 Experimental programmes

The dominance of the MBA may be waning but what will replace it? This section has deliberately omitted discussion of alternative futures in leadership development so as not to steal the thunder of the concluding chapter. However, it would be wrong to miss the opportunity to say a few words about interesting lines of experimentation away from the MBA and signal some of the author's own thoughts about possible new directions for Med.

Mintzberg's International Master's Programme for Participating Managers at McGill, the 'New MBA' at the Judge Institute, Cambridge, the AL-based MBA at Buckingham Independent Management Centre and the self-managed learning MA at Roffey Park have all attempted in recent years to provide a robust and intellectually rigorous alternative to the MBA as generic programmes of management education. Although they differ in particulars, a common theme linking them is an experimental attempt to integrate experiential understanding and learning through conceptual insight. They all try to dissolve the false dichotomy between reflection on learning at work and theoretical learning in the academy. Through the sharing of stories from the manager's world in the classroom; analysing how others defined and handled situations; listening to the accounts of master managers brought in to share their philosophies of leading; engaging in personal projects and reflecting back to others in small groups with the assistance of skilled facilitation, a climate of genuine experiential learning can be created in the classroom. In the same spirit, individually tailored action plans, outreach supervision by the tutor in the workplace and *in situ* ALS can help people apply the ideas of the academy to the real world and test theories in action.

All the programmes we have mentioned honoured these values. For example, at the Judge Institute, a one-year full-time course to build business appreciation is followed by two years' full-time work experience interspersed with six one-week blocks back at the Institute. Study sessions at the Institute give considerable emphasis to reflection on the meaning of experience in the sheltered conditions of the Institute. It is an opportunity to disengage, reflect and reengage with new meanings that can be tested in the field. Back at work, students are encouraged to test ideas in management against their own experience, look out for new relationships between elements which become 'working hypotheses' to be shared with classmates in facilitated student sessions during the one-week blocks (Talbot 1997). At Roffey Park and Buckingham, ALS drive the programme. Organisational consultancy and action research are mediated by peer feedback, discursive analysis (in the field and at the academy) and expert facilitation to help participants develop their own philosophies of practice informed by reflection (Talbot 1997).

At its best this learning is individualised and seamless. Talking about managing and doing managing are no longer distinct; knowledge of managing and experience of managing are no longer separated. Thinking and doing come together in an endless dialectic which connects the academy and the workplace. Perhaps Fox (1997) captures what is intended here – to develop managers who can 'do' and 'talk about doing'; to build communities of practice (COP) which overlap the workplace into the academy and are enlivened and directed by the interplay of fields of thought and fields of action. In this way, formal management education is offered the promise of more than an incidental part in management learning (managers rightly claim they learn most about managing at work) to become the catalyst for the reflective manager who values thinking in action.

It is in Mintzberg's IMPPM, deliberately designed as an alternative to the standard MBA and intended for the successful, mid-career manager that ideas of this kind find their most concrete expression so far. On this programme formal study is divided into five two-week class blocks around key learning themes: reflection, analysis, worldliness, collaboration and action. Between the academy modules, there are regular visits in the organisations of the class participants, learning group discussions, guided experiential reflection and self-managed learning. Facilitators try to contextualise management theory in the experience of participating managers, draw out their deep assumptions about issues and show the relevance of theory. The learning agenda is an agreement between the facilitator's definition of what the manager needs to know and what the manager sees as important.(Mintzberg 2004a). This helps ownership of the corpus of knowledge in management and the development of an informed inquisitive approach. Tutors also work individually with participants to clarify their learning priorities, work together with others in 'support and challenge' groups, define development agenda and track the implementation of ideas on return to the organisation.

9.8.2 A new agenda?

Innovative and different as the IMPPM is, there is a sense that it is work in progress. Drawing on the contributions of a number of writers (Gosling and Mintzberg 2006;

French and Grey 1996; Pfeffer and Fong 2002; Sadler-Smith 2006) can we discern some pedagogical principles for management education in the future?

In line with the new shift to developing *managerial leaders*, we are likely to see the gradual disappearance of management programmes which fragment the teaching of management into a set of disciplines. Increasingly the learning will be thematic around the qualities which are needed to be an effective leader of talented groups of workers; how to help him or her address the interwoven problems in any complex management situation that cannot be easily separated out into neat functional pigeon holes (Mangham 1986).

In the same spirit, we can expect curricula to become more geared up to helping managers with path-making and future-making skills, seeing things holistically and making connections, using imagination and judgement and acting with flair. The emphasis will be on finding ways to develop inquiring, even philosophical managers, who can think across disciplines, think counterfactually, think critically and are comfortable engaging in a constant dialectic of deductive and inductive reasoning, of ideas and action. It is also likely that there will be a new valuing of 'character' in management – the ability to be self-analysing and self-critical, sensitive yet robust enough to make decisions in the conditions of uncertainty and stress which management involves. Of course, social skills will also be highly regarded – persuasion, influencing, facilitating; having the facility to use symbols, ideas and narrative to motivate a team. More than ever before, the task of Med is becoming focused on the development of the total person – with social, cognitive, organisational, political and cultural understanding needed for leadership.

Under pressure from this agenda, business school curricula are likely to become transformed. Certainly, less knowledge filling and more character building; more development of the whole person and not just the mind; more on implementation not just analysis; more on mindsets and less on knowledge sets (Gosling 1996). By degrees, the Med syllabus, traditionally so weighted to the technical and formal, could give way to the political, cultural and experiential. There are signs this is already happening.

However, the turn to a leadership agenda may have deeper implications for pedagogy. The ideological bias to market liberalism and rugged individualism which many have detected in mainstream Med (Aspen 1994; Delves-Broughton 2008) may become softened (it would be idealistic to say replaced) by a new ethos of social and environmental responsibility. Can we expect to see a new recognition of corporate citizenship, social and environmental responsibilities, business ethics and corporate governance in the syllabi of business schools? Will issues of social justice (e.g. equity, human rights, work–life balance and the social accountability of multinationals) and diversity have more than walk-on parts in the curriculum, tokenistic classes which students skip because they don't get credits for them? Will core courses become led by issues of sustainability, respect and protection of the environment and an eco-management which balances 'turning a profit' with saving the planet?

A pioneering example of this 'alternative' approach is the New Academy of Business, set up by Anita Roddick of Body Shop with Bath University, which runs an MA in Responsibility and Business Practice. It tries to integrate social, environmental, ethical, even spiritual issues, with successful business practice (Roddick 2003).

How will the business schools respond to new leadership agendas? So far, the response has often been tokenistic. Can we expect to see more guided practice and assignments to learn to use power with ethical consciousness? Will there be creative opportunities for learning about cross-cultural issues to truly appreciate the meaning of diversity and multiple perspectives in organisational behaviour? What about collaborative learning from peers and facilitated simulations to build critical, political awareness?

Business schools are still experimenting with ways of meeting this social and political agenda which will be important for the moral and cultural development of future leaders. But what about the creative agenda: how to build the cultivated, self-aware, independent-minded philosopher–activist who may be needed for leadership in the future? This has long been the concern of many cultures – how to select and develop thoughtful, principled rulers, administrators or 'men of action'. It is a question as old as Plato who tried (unsuccessfully) to help Emperor Dionysius of Syracruse become a 'philosopher king'. It was the same concern to develop a enlightened executive class which required eighteenth-century Chinese mandarins and British civil servants (until very recently) to become steeped in classics and humanities before being given the opportunity to govern. The common theme here is a good, broad, liberal and philosophical education. Unfortunately, this has also become code for a class-based, expensive and exclusive education for 'gentlemen'. However, if we strip away the classism and the elitism, is there something to be said for exposure to a broad range of ideas and cultural movements and the refinement of critical sensibility as an apprenticeship for the privilege of wielding power? This chimes with Drucker's (1989) view that management is ultimately a liberal or humanistic art which draws for its insights from social sciences and humanities and requires 'wisdom' to practise effectively. The implication is that leadership development should be based on a broad cultural education and an educated ability to see things whole and with a critical appreciation.

If this is a trend, perhaps we can anticipate a shift to the greater integration of the arts in the Med syllabus. We can envisage the innovative and imaginative use of drama, music, art and philosophy to develop critical sensibility, interpersonal understanding and group learning. Many organisations want to move beyond homogenised MBA graduates to developing stylish, counter-cultural leaders who can think afresh and have the imagination and flair to create anew, despite paradox and uncertainty.

Aspen (1994) advocates a new type of Med with a postmodernist curriculum (relativistic philosophy, chaos theory, 'end of history' models, aesthetics theory). Grint (2001) talks of the need for twenty-first century managers to draw on an ensemble of arts (fine art, philosophical and performing arts) to understand 'the deeper structures of leading'. Jackson and Parry (2008) cite Chester Barnard (1938) who wrote a classic work on the *executive process* which he defined as needing feeling, judgement, a sense of balance, appropriateness and elegance of outcomes. These are aesthetic qualities and perhaps there is an artistic dimension to managerial leadership. Morgan (1986) calls for organisational sense-making through metaphor and image-making. Boje (2001) emphasises the value of narrative analysis to see things as a whole and 'enact leadership' through transformative visions and persuasive arguments for change. Literary criticism may help managers develop a mindset of 'appreciative inquiry' and the skills of the wordsmith to engage others with symbolic and rhetorical meanings. Mangham and Overington (1987) have explored drama as a lens for understanding organisational process and for helping managers develop the text within. By recognising that much of leadership is a form of acting, managers can be encouraged to move beyond predetermined and limiting scripts through a process of dissociation (mentoring, 360-degree feedback, etc.) to examine the meanings behind their actions. It is likely that we will hear a lot more about the parallels between thinking like a leader and thinking like an artist, leadership as an aesthetic process, and Med experimenting with the arts as tools for leadership development.

In terms of curriculum content, another emergent theme in Med is the search for new ways of embedding ethics in the pedagogy of management learning. This will mean going beyond tokenistic gestures to business ethics, to help managers face moral dilemmas and develop a coherently thought out ethical code of conduct which is more than hot air and gives the individual a fixed compass point in their leadership style. Spirituality and leadership development are likely to be strong items in future practice.

So far we have concentrated mainly on possible changes in the *content* of university-based programmes of management learning. However, the processes are also likely to change. Burgoyne and Reynolds (1997) suggest that if universities are to become more experientially led then the environment of learning has to change. The whole ethos of detached analysis and individualised professional knowledge building has to give way to a climate in which analysis takes place in action, students share ideas in peer support and there is more integration of work and study through practice supervision. Burgoyne and Reynolds also anticipate that assessments systems will reflect the new experiential culture with more use of portfolios of achievement using evidence of organisational impact, not just technical proficiency.

Fox (1997) takes up this theme. Management education has to reflect and assess the realities of management work, for example, the thinking, interacting, sense-making skills which Kotter (1992) and Watson (2001) identified. It must also move away from being an arena where students 'talk about' management to creating 'communities of discourse and practice' which tie together academy and workplace. Managers need to learn how to think while they innovate work practice within the organisation.

These ideas are echoed and amplified by recent work by Gosling and Mintzberg (2006) who effectively outline a radical manifesto for the future of Med. They emphasise that management education should be for managers, not a preparation for management. Med is best where it facilitates a learning group of people who are already managers to explore the dilemmas and choices involved in doing management. If the student is also a practitioner, there is less chance that academic work will seem abstract and disembodied from practice. Ideas from the university can be woven into daily organisational experience and reflected on in a work context. This encourages the manager in learning to appreciate that Med is not about denying past experience by replacing it with the abstract knowledge of the academy but building on that experience by looking back on it and deriving usable lessons. Formal models become meaningful when they connect with issues that really concern managers. As Mintzberg (2004a) says, when your learning community is also your work community, a discussion of, say, managerial ethics becomes more than a course requirement and more a consideration of the grounds for principled behaviour in daily management within a familiar setting. It becomes more real and engaging.

Gosling and Mintzberg (2006) advocate 'thoughtful reflection' as the key to tomorrow's Med. That requires faculty to facilitate discussion of work issues, help managers reframe their meaning and experiment with new approaches to work. This is appropriate for the development of the 'craft' skills (not 'science') of managing; participants are constantly testing ideas against their experience, trying out new approaches at work and sharing the results with trusted others in a 'discursive community' (Beddowes 1994).

However, to achieve an atmosphere of reflection and interactive learning, current pedagogies have to be thrown over. The pressure cooker of the MBA – Mintzberg talks of the 'military drill' of packed timetables, vast reading lists, constant assignments – is not conducive to the surfacing of thoughts and feelings, bringing to mind experiences and relaxed discussion with supportive colleagues, all of which is needed for self-insight. The curriculum has to change, but so does the pedagogy and role of the tutor. This is a point also made by Raab (2004), who anticipates that the future requires faculty to be less focused on oratory in large lecture theatres, but more on facilitation and coaching in small groups. This means helping people to value their experience and tell good stories about it; stimulate discussion; ask probing questions and offer interpretations based on a conceptual knowledge of the field. This implies a different relationship of the tutor and his or her class; s/he is no longer the salesperson of ideas under pressure to entertain and please the students by filling them up with memorable knowledge, but more a group catalyst, ironically mirroring the new role of the manager in post-industrial organisations.

Tutor-led classroom facilitation and coaching at work may be supplemented by learning circles or sets formed of participants themselves and on-line support (chat rooms, and electronic aides) to make learning a continuous process of critical thinking and experiential inquiry.

These are paradigm-breaking reforms and if they could be implemented and made to work would transform Med from a model of specialised, professionalised and prescriptive development to one which is flexible, interactive, experiential and closely tied to the realities of managing as a social craft.

9.9 Conclusion

This chapter has looked at management education, focusing particularly on qualification-based courses concerned to build generic management skills. It has considered recent attempts to build management as a profession and looked at the dual strands of vocational and academic routes in Med. Emphasis was given to an appraisal of the MBA as the most ambitious, international course in management and how it is becoming refined and differentiated and customised to meet the changing needs of career managers. The continuing debate about the role and value of the MBA in all its forms was examined. So too were the prospects of higher education of developing a less techno-functionalist syllabus, more in line with the experiences of managers themselves. Future prospects for Med were considered, including corporate partnerships, corporate universities and radical pedagogies which have attempted to integrate formal and informal management learning around a new leadership agenda.

Review questions

1 'Using the classroom to develop people already practising management is a fine idea, but pretending to create managers who have never managed is a sham' (Mumford 1997). How would you react to this proposition?

2 Business schools have had their day. The future lies with new forms of MD – experiential learning and with corporate universities who can provide down-to-earth, practical programmes aligned to the strategies of the organisation. Do you agree?

3 Management is not, and cannot be, a liberal 'profession', as common parlance defines this term. It is a practical craft based on experiential knowing. This is not teachable. How far do you agree?

4 People enrol on courses in higher education not because they want the knowledge but because they want the 'credential' which will bring status, money and power. Management education is all about social climbing. How would you react to this?

5 Students like to complain about the lack of relevance of the business school curriculum, but they conspire in this by taking a largely passive role, are not generally critical of the theories they imbibe and fail to do the thinking needed to make theories into living tools of management analysis. Students get the business schools they deserve. Respond to this statement.

6 It is all very well to criticise the business schools, but at least they do not dumb down complex things into checklists, acronyms and simple rules of thumb, infantilise students with playgroup activities or make their teaching a tool for corporate propaganda – all of which you are likely to get in the commercial sector. Consider this statement thoughtfully as a defence of Med.

Web links

The Centre for Excellence in Management and Leadership (CEML) has a website for their publications at:
http://www.managementandleadershipcouncil.org/

The Association for Management Education and Development (AMED) is at:
http://www.amed.org.uk

The British Academy of Management (BAM) which encourages scholarship and good practice in management education is at:
http://www.bam.ac.uk

The Association of Business Schools (AMBA) can be found on:
http://www.leeds.ac.uk/bes/abs/abshome.htm

A website of the Management Standards Centre (formerly MCI):
http://www.management-standards.org/

Recommendations for further reading

Those texts marked with an asterisk in the bibliography are recommended for further reading, especially the following;

Bennis, W. and O'Toole, J. (2005) 'How business schools lost their way', *HBR*, May. *Interesting article on the loss of purpose and direction of American business schools.*

French, R. and Grey, C. (1996) *Re-thinking Management Education.* An excellent collection of contributions on the ideological debates within management education and possible ways forward.

Mant, A. (1979) *The Rise and Fall of the British Manager.* Classic, iconoclastic attack on the irrelevance of management education to the British manager.

Bibliography

Anon. (1990) 'The best business schools', *Business Week*, 29 Oct.

Anon. (1999) 'Business class', *Voyager Promotion*, Sept.

Anon. (2003) Roffey Park Newsletter.

Arkin, A. (2000) 'Combined honours', *People Management*, 12 Oct.

Aspen, P. (1994) 'Carp pool reflections on the art of doubt', *THES*, 22 April.

Augar, P. (2001) 'Cash in on MBA Talent', *THES*, 5 Jan.

Barnard, C. (1938) *The Functions of the Executive*, Harvard University Press.

Beardwell, I. and Holden, L. (2000) *Human Resource Management: A Contemporary Approach*, Ch. 9, Prentice Hall.

Beddowes, P. (1994) 'Re-inventing management development', *Journal of Management Development*, Vol. 13, Issue 7.

*Bennis, W. and O'Toole, J. (2005) 'How business schools lost their way', *Harvard Business Review*, May.

Bickerstaff, G. (1995) 'Switching on the electronic classroom', *The Times*, 16 Oct.

Boje, D. (2001) *Narrative Methods for Organisational and Communicative Research*, Sage.

Bradshaw, D. (2001) 'Tougher to attract the top level', *Financial Times*, 4 June.

*Bradshaw, D. (2004) 'London leads the world in MBAs for executives', *Financial Times*, 12 July.

Burgoyne, J. and Reynolds, M. (1997) 'Introduction', in *Management Learning*, Sage.

*Chia, R. (1996) 'Teaching paradigms shifts in management education', *Journal of Management Studies*, 33, 4 July.

Collin, A. (1996) 'The MBA: the potential for students to find their voice in Babel', in French, R. and Grey, C. (1996) *Re-thinking Management Education*, Sage.

Constable, J. and McCormick, R. (1987) *The Making of British Managers*, BIM.

Coopers Lybrand Associates (1985) *A Challenge to Complacency: Changing Attitudes to Training*, London, NEDO.

Currie, J. (1999) 'All sewn up', *THES*, 15 Jan.

Dealtry, R. (2000) 'Case study in the evolution of a corporate university', *Journal of Workplace Learning*, Vol. 12, No. 8.

Delves-Broughton, P. (2008), 'Harvard loses its lustre', *Prospect'*, Sept.

Dogar, B. (1998) 'Capitalist schools', *Newsweek*, 28 Sept.

Drucker, P. (1989) *The New Realities*, Ch. 15, Harper and Row.

Dzinkowski, R. (2002) 'Building the global corporate university', *Financial Times*, 5 Sept.

EFMD (1993) *Conference Proceedings*.

EIU: *Which MBA?* (1996), (2002), (2003).

Fee, K. (2001) *A Guide to Management Development*, Kogan Page.

*Fox, S. (1997) 'From management education to the study of management learning', in Burgoyne, J. and Reynolds, M. (1997) *Management Learning*, Sage.

*French, R. and Grey, C. (1996) *Re-thinking Management Education*, Chs 2, 8, Sage.

Gosling, J. (1996) 'Plato on the education of managers', in French, R. and Grey, C. (1996) *Re-thinking Management Education*, Sage.

*Gosling, J. and Mintzberg, H. (2006) 'Management learning as if both matter', *Management Learning*, Vol. 37, No. 4.

Greenhaigh, T. (1994) 'Business education', *THES*, May.

Grey, C. (1998) 'The business of being allies', *THES*, 25 Sept.

Grey, C. (2006) *A Very Short, Fairly Interesting Guide to Organisational Analysis*, Ch. 5, Sage.

Grey, C. and Antonacopoulou, (2004) *Essential Readings in Management Learning*, Sage.

Grint, K. (2001) *The Arts of Leadership*, OUP.

Handy, C. (1988) *Making Managers*, Pitman.

Haynes, P. 'Passport to prosperity', *Economist*, Vol. 318, Issue 7696.

Heller, R. (1986) *The New Naked Manager*, Coronet Books.

Hodges, L. (1993) 'Big bang for business schools', *THES*, 10 Dec.

Huang, L. (2005) 'From chaos comes order and composure', *Financial Times*, 30 May.

Hubband, G. (2006) 'Do not undervalue the impact of business education', *Financial Times*, 29 June.

Jackson, B. and Parry, K. (2008) *A Very Short, Fairly Cheap Book about Studying Leadership*, Ch. 6, Sage.

Kotter, J. (1992) *The General Managers*, Free Press.

Latham, G. and Seijts, H. (1998) *Handbook of HRD*, Psychology Press Ltd.

Leavitt, H. (1989) 'Educating our MBAs: on teaching what we haven't learnt', *Californian Management Review*, Spring.

*Linder, J. and Smith, J. (1992) 'The complex case of management education', *Harvard Business Review*, Oct.

Lupton, T. (1984) 'University business schools: looking to the future', *Creativity and Innovation Network*, April.

Lock, A. (1998) 'Makes you think doesn't it?', *Guardian*, 8 Dec.

*Mabey, C. and Thomson, A. (2000) 'The determinants of management development: the views of MBA graduates', *British Academy of Management*, Vol. 11.

Mangham, I. (1986) *Power and Performance in Organisations*, Sage.

Mangham, I. and Overington, M. (1987) *Organisations as Theatre: A Social Psychology of Appearances*, J. Wiley.

Mangham, I. and Silver, M. (1986) *Management Training: Context and Practice*, ESRC.

*Mant, A. (1979) *The Rise and Fall of the British Manager*, Pan Books.

Mathews, J. and Megginson, D. (2005) *Human Resource Development*, Ch. 5, Kogan Page.

Matthews, V. (2002) 'Business education: an ever more exclusive business degree', *Financial Times*, 9 Sept.

Merritt, J. (2001) 'The MBA programmes are going back to school', *Business Week*, 7 May.

Miles, R. (1985) 'The future of business education', *California Management Review*, Vol. 27, 3, Spring.

*Mintzberg, H. (2004a) *Managers not MBAs*, Prentice Hall.

*Mintzberg, H. (2004b) 'Leadership and management development', *Academy of Management Executive*, Vol. 18, No. 3.

Moore, T. (2002) 'Survey of business education', *Financial Times*, 25 March.

Morgan, G. (1986) *Images of Organisation*, Sage.

Mumford, A. (1997) *Management Development: Strategies for Action*, CIPD.

*Pfeffer, J. and Fong, C. (2002) 'The end of business schools? Less success than meets the eye', *Management Learning and Education*, Vol. 1, No. 1.

Pilewski, M. (1997) 'Still the ticket to the top', *Spotlight*, May.

Purcell, J. (2003) 'Criticism fails to recognise changes in the business schools', Letter to the editor in *Financial Times*, 23 Sept.

Raab, N. (2004) 'Becoming an expert in not knowing', in Grey, C. and Antonacopoulou, E. (2004) *Essential Readings in Management Learning*, Sage.

Raelin, J. (1990) 'Let's not teach management as if it were a profession', *Business Horizons*, Vol. 13, No. 3.

*Reed, M. and Anthony, P. (1992) 'Professionalising management and managing professionalisation: British managers in the 1980s', *Journal of Management Studies*, 5, Sept.

Reeves, R. (2008) 'A degree of confidence', *Management Today*, July.

Roberts, J. (1996) 'Management education and the limits of technical rationality', in French, R. and Grey, C. *Re-thinking Management Education*, Sage.

Roddick, A. (2003) 'New academy of business prospectus', *Roffey Park Newsletter* (2003).

Sadler-Smith, E. (2006) *Learning and Development for Managers*, Blackwell.

Shipman, A. (2002) 'Is the master plan coming unstuck?', *THES*, 8 Nov.

Syrett, M. and Lammiman, J. (1999) *Management Development: Making the Investment Count*, Economist Books.

Talbot, C. (1997) 'Paradoxes of MD: trends and tensions', *Career Development International*, Vol. 2, No. 3.

The Times, MBA Special Supplements: Oct. 1994; Oct. 1995; Jan. 1997; Oct. 2004.

THES (1993) Special Supplement on Business and Management; various short articles, reviews, etc.

Thomas, A. and Anthony, P. (1996) 'Can management education be educational?', in French, R. and Grey, C. (1996) *Re-thinking Management Education*, Sage.

Thomson, A., Mabey, C. and Storey, J. (2001) *Changing Patterns of Management Development,* Ch. 8, Blackwell.

*Trehern, S. (2002) 'A corporate university brings learning to life', *Financial Times*, 30 Oct.

Tysome. T. (2000) 'A human face still beats the net', *THES* 8 Dec.

Watson, T. (2001) *In Search of Management*, Thomson Learning.

*Watson, T. (2004) 'Motivation: that's Maslow isn't it?', in Grey, C. and Antonacopoulou, E. (2004) *Essential Readings in Management Learning*, Sage.

*Wilmott, H. (1997) 'Critical management learning', in Burgoyne, J. and Reynolds, M., *Management Learning*, Sage.

Woodall, J. and Winstanley, D. (1999) *Management Development*, Ch. 8, Blackwell.

10 Management careers, succession and talent management

Learning outcomes

After studying this chapter you should be able to understand, analyse and explain:

- the main trends in the nature of managerial work over the past twenty-five years;
- decisive shifts in the nature of the 'psychological contract' in managerial careers;
- changing concepts of the 'managerial career';
- debates in career management;
- methods and processes of career management;
- the rise of self-development and its implication for the individual manager's career;
- the philosophy and practice of succession management;
- management audit and succession management;
- the rise of talent management.

10.1 Introduction

An important aspect of MD is ensuring the right numbers of managers of the right quality, in the right place and at the right time so that the strategic purposes of the organisation can be served. These issues are part of the strategic development planning process which we discussed in Chapters 4 and 5 Succession planning, talent management and career management are all links in the development cycle.

The organisation has its concerns about ensuring the right supply of managers, but the individual manager also has a right to concern about how s/he is developed. These perspectives and interests may harmonise but can also conflict: the organisation has its succession plan, but the manager has his or her 'career'.

This chapter examines changing concepts of a career in management and considers issues such as the balance of responsibility between the organisation and the individual for career development and the consequences of recent shifts in perception of the 'psychological contract' underpinning managerial careers. It also looks at the tools and techniques for identifying and grooming talent, their strengths, limitations and contexts of application and raises questions about the future direction of career management. This is a complex area to cover in a single chapter, which has had to omit some interesting themes, such as how managers choose their careers, individual career self concepts and identity and career transition, but the interested reader is referred to Baruch (2004) or Arnold (1997) in the bibliography, which are excellent introductions to this area. It is also an area in which a standardised language is elusive. One commentator's 'succession planning' is another's 'succession management' or, to be modish, 'talent management' strategy. However, this author tries to move beyond the labels to consider real-world themes and tendencies.

10.2 Trends in management careers

In the past 20 years the corporate landscape has been re-modelled by top management to improve competitiveness in a globalised economy. Here we merely touch on some of the effects of restructuring on management, management development and the careers of managers. For more detailed descriptions of the changing context and realities of management careers, the reader to referred to Arnold (1997), Arthur and Rousseau (1996) and Osterman (1996).

10.2.1 The transformation of management work

In the past, up to the late 1980s, managers were largely immune from economic changes. It was blue-collar workers who were laid off during a business downturn. For most of the post-war period, the manager, the 'organisation man', the 'man in the grey flannel suit' (Whyte 1956) was a social hero, the torch-bearer of corporate efficiency and progress (see the *Power Game* on DVD for a sense of the spirit of those times). Managerial numbers increased steadily and managers and paternalistic cultures thrived, with annual pay rises, good job security and the expectation of a steady rise up the hierarchy to larger and more lucrative jobs. If the company valued you at all highly then you would be promoted, almost always in a vertical functional hierarchy; lateral shifts, reserved for those perceived to be cut out for general management material were rare. During periods of retrenchment, cuts were usually deflected to support functions and the front line. The implicit psychological contract was security and a planned career of steady progress for most managers in return for loyalty and diligence in quite narrowly defined roles. A good popular film which captures the dominant management culture at that time is *The Apartment* from 1960, or *Mad Men* (2008) which is a very insightful retrospective commentary on office life.

However, by the 1980s the tide was turning. There was growing concern that the big corporate bureaucracies had become complacent, self-serving and had lost touch with the ground. There was also a shift to entrepreneurism, with a focus on pleasing shareholders by cutting management costs. It is in this period that we see the rise of institutional investors who realised their hitherto latent power to compel companies to improve financial performance and corporate raiders who took over companies to break them up. These forces concentrated the minds of executive boards on restructuring their companies, drastically reducing overheads and streamlining operations, including the reduction of management numbers and a redefinition of their roles. Intensified international competition added to the pain by creating pressure for efficiency and workforce productivity. Plant closures, company mergers, downsizings, selling-off of business units decimated the ranks of managers (Sampson 1995).

By the 1980s too, the computer had become a threat to corporate jobs for the first time, helping to flatten organisations, replacing the managers who had once acted as essential intermediaries between levels of authority with electronic networks which allowed greater control at lower levels.

Then, there was the impact of new organisational processes, models and techniques. More unstable business conditions encouraged the search for more flexible forms of organization – Japanese team processes, JIT, matrix management, process re-engineering, TQM, lean production systems, competency-based systems, outsourcing and so on – had a decisive influence on the nature of managing. Self-managed teams and cross-functional systems replaced hierarchies; management numbers were reduced and roles became broader with more responsibility attached to them (Sampson 1995; Osterman 1996).

In responding to these pressures senior managers transformed their organisations and in the process transformed the world of the manager. By the mid 1990s the old loyal company man – working steadily up the organisation, expecting annual increments and a guaranteed pension – was a figure of the past. The main impact of change has been to change the rules of the game for those managers who survived.

Declining job security

While some press reporting may be alarmist (e.g. the end of the career for managers), and the displacement rates for managers seem well below that of many other groups, managerial employment seems more insecure than ever before (Bridges 1994). With the flattening of organisations and the introduction of process engineering, many organisations are employing fewer managers than previously. Whole levels of management have been stripped out and some technical and coordinating roles have vanished. The slimming down of HO functions and the consolidation of plants into bigger units has often resulted in a loss of managers. Middle managers, now often seen as unnecessary links in the chain, have suffered disproportionately in restructuring. Outsourcing has often meant that people have been put on short-term contracts or forced to do the same work for the old company on poorer conditions of service. Many managers feel a sense of marginalisation and less part of a managerial community (Useem 1996; Arnold 1997).

Changes in the nature of managerial work

We consider this issue in more depth in the concluding chapter. Here we should note that the cumulative effect of the changes has been to dramatically remould managerial roles. Those who remain within the corporation claim they are doing twice as much work, with tighter performance targets and fewer safety nets. With fewer managers but escalating demands on them, the survivors of culls experience an intensification of work. Managerial roles are larger with broader spans of control and more general management responsibilities.

The context of managing is also seen as more difficult. It is certainly experienced as more ambiguous and contradictory. Teamworking, matrices and flexibility often mean constantly shifting relationships and confused accountabilities to multiple bosses. Ideologies of organisation and expectations of behaviour are now more complex and ambivalent than ever with clashing values which the individual manager is left to reconcile. Empowerment and decentralisation ideologies emphasise more managerial discretion and responsibility for decision-making, but IT-led performance management and control systems point in the opposite direction, towards standardisation and conformity. Rhetorics of involvement and participation can sound hollow to unit managers who see their real independence eroded by computerised financial systems which offer the mirage of more control while in reality centralising authority at higher levels. The same may apply to an emphasis on 'empowerment' or 'intrapreneruship' while 'headcount' is being reduced by edict from on high (Thomson et al. 2001; Herriot and Pemberton 1995).

New management skills

As one of the acute observers of the modern corporate world (Useem 1996) has put it, 'Senior managers pulled up the ladders that had taken them to the top and dropped down new ladders with different climbing skills'. Useem suggests that the rise of investor capitalism has prioritised investment and financial competency as the key competencies in senior management jobs. Board and top-level managers are now seen to need skills with investors – securing external funding; bolstering share price; translating strategy in terms of ROI; strong leadership presence. This sets the ethos for the rest of the organisation. Professional specialists who were once at the top of functional divisions have often been sidelined by management generalists with strong financial and leadership skills who run the new business units. The skills now in strong demand are general rather than technical: change management, performance against targets, strategic management, producing shareholder value and giving clear direction. Increasingly higher-level managers live by results: security and promotion contingent on proven business performance.

The end of an era: even IBM 'eats its own children'

A symbolically important turning point in the relationship between the manager and his employer occurred when IBM massively reduced its management ranks in the early to mid 1990s. IBM had long been known for offering job security in exchange for commitment. The company was able to provide many benefits because it enjoyed a quasi-monopolistic position in a growing market. However, IBM was slow to recognise the new demand for mini computers and was out of touch with its customers. To re-establish its market position IBM retreated from its progressive HR practices and made massive redundancies among its managerial staff (called the 'Great Grey Cloud' in the industry), so breaking its social contract with its employees.

When they were made redundant many of these managers didn't know what to do. They had performed very narrowly defined technical jobs linked to IBM technology and processes. Their skills didn't translate into what the market wanted. They had always assumed that IBM would care for them forever; they had never done a job search or drawn up a CV. As Sampson (1995) tells it, many found it difficult to find another job, adjust to self-employment or to working for a small company. Many felt rejected, without identity. Some blamed themselves. Many gave up and never worked again in a career job. Others came to realise that the company's strong career development and paternalism had made them dependent. These were the people who realised that building a marketable skill base, keeping up to date with the market and having a strong external network was the best insurance policy against layoffs and a far better personal strategy than relying on the promises of a single employer, however benevolent they might seem.

By the late 1990s, no one wanted middle managers: a safe pair of hands, who knew a business process thoroughly and could play the part of technocratic adviser (Sampson 1995). The new 'hot prospects' were the young 'high-flyer' (e.g. with an MBA and leadership skills); the intellectual manager-consultant who traded in ideas and could offer new solutions and the interim manager who could adjust quickly and manage the paradoxes of change. These managers embraced insecurity, accepted the concept of variable performance-based reward and were content to move from project to project, nomads living by their wits (Osterman 1996; Useem 1996; Arthur and Rousseau 1996).

However, the bulk of any organisation is made up of ordinary managers who did not have and could not acquire these skills. One of the most profound effects of the changes has been a fracturing of the management community of an organisation. At one time, someone who entered 'management' had 'arrived'. S/he was part of a select group. Doing a management job meant internalising the official organisation's values and culture and representing it. Part of the tacit understanding was that higher management would protect and support them. However, in recent years the top has pulled away, rewarding itself disproportionately, deflecting blame for poor performance on others and withdrawing from any sense of social responsibility for the managers within their team. Declining opportunities for upward mobility and the larger social and reward gaps between the managerial layers have reduced the sense of social solidarity within management and sowed the seeds of mistrust (Sampson 1995; Arnold 1997).

As Osterman (1996) suggests, the middle managers who remain in the big organisations, especially those in middle age, have had to reconcile themselves to careers which resemble those of technicians – horizontal and project-based. The main source of satisfaction left to them is professional delivery on essential organisational tasks, not aspiring to rise to higher levels of power and status. While some may be content with this diminished role and reduced compass of expectation, others have revised their personal loyalty and commitment to the organisation, using it instrumentally as a stepping stone for their own career plans.

10.2.2 The changing 'psychological contract' at work

The last point in the paragraph above suggests that the traditional psychological contract at work is changing. Arthur and Rousseau (1996); Rousseau (1995) define the 'psychological contract' as the individual's belief regarding the nature and level of the reciprocal exchange between him/herself and the employer. The traditional management career was a 'social exchange' in which the employer gave a guarantee of continued employment in return for loyalty and competence. It implied a long-term relationship based on trust and mutual support. However, in the 1990s top management in many companies unilaterally changed the employment relationship by shattering the old contract. A 'new deal' was imposed, which is more about a 'transaction' of economic exchange than a 'relationship' of mutuality (Arnold 1997; Arthur 1994). Employees are now expected to work longer hours, take on more responsibilities, improve productivity, develop a broader portfolio of skills, be flexible around change and remain as committed as ever. In return, the organisation offers no commitment to the individual, except to pay a higher rate for those with skills the organisation values highly while it needs them and perhaps some help in building a skill base. It is a shift from a 'job for life' to a 'job for now'.

Many managers responded to the breaking of the old psychological contract with disappointment, frustration, anger and despair. Many felt that promises on pay, promotion, development and job security had been violated, their sense of self-worth and identity undermined. As employment security and a clear career path with steady progression was removed, the response of many younger managers, especially Generation X and Y, has been to become career agile. They neither expect nor desire a job for life. Instead, they move frequently, taking their talents to whichever employer will offer the best conditions. By the early years of the twenty-first century it was not uncommon for a young knowledge worker or manager to have changed jobs nine times by the age of 32. This brings in its wake new challenges for the organisation in terms of recruitment, retention, motivation and commitment (Manville 2008; Lawrence 2008).

10.2.3 Conceptualising management careers

The undermining of the old psychological contract did not end the traditional career in management, but it did usher in new trends in the world of work, for example, more lateral rather than vertical job moves; more movement in and out of organisations; more short-term contracts and interim employment around projects; more self-employment. Gunz (1989) talks of the trend away from the 'career ladder' towards the concept of the 'climbing frame'. A 'ladder' assumes a series of vertical steps involving accumulating increments in prestige, skill and authority. In a 'climbing frame' people enter at various levels and move from rung to rung as vacancies arise, sometimes higher sometimes at the same level but in different parts of the frame. Sometimes they may cross over to a lower rung to be better placed to make a subsequent vertical move.

As organisations fragment and deconstruct, turning into attenuated networks, so the climbing frame extends to take in various organisations and disciplines. In this environment, careers are becoming 'boundaryless' (Arthur 1994). Managers cross boundaries – organisations, functions, product areas, technologies, skill sets – in a succession of assignments, projects, tasks and jobs during their working lives. Commentators talk about the rise of the 'protean career' in which people engage in experiments, explorations and frequent career moves in search of a personal identity and a distinctive competence (Beardwell and Holden 2001; Beardwell and Claydon 2007). This involves periodic reskilling and a succession of work identities over the period of a working life. In this spirit, Driver (1982) provides a taxonomy of career patterns which add to our vocabulary for describing matters of this kind.

- *Steady state careers*: Where the manager stays in the same or related roles throughout a working life, perhaps with small career movements. Professional and technical careers are often like this: e.g. the radiography manager will have a short professional ladder and his/her roles in management would vary only in terms of the size of the unit s/he manages.
- *Linear careers*: These are the classic corporate career ladders. The manager typically moves up a functional ladder and either reaches the top of this professional tree or makes a transition to a parallel but higher ladder in general management in mid/late career. Of course, many of these ladders are being massively reduced in scale.
- *Transitory careers*: Where the manager has no permanent job set or field. This captures something of the restless 'job hopping' of younger managers and professionals, often experimenting with different disciplines. It also captures the multidisciplinary background of many modern managers and the effect of multiple project work in matrix-style organisations.
- *Spiral careers*: Where managers make frequent lateral job moves to gain experience and breadth of perspective. It also captures something of the spirit of the 'boundaryless' career where, at different stages, in a working life the manager might be working in different functional areas in different organisations, in a corporate strategic role, doing outsourced work and running his/her own business or offering consultancy.

As this chapter suggests, in recent years there has been a move away from steady state and linear patterns towards more spiral/transitory career paths. In this new environment, people concentrate on being employable, being flexible, multi-skilled and up to date in the skills which the market wants, because it gives them flexibility and choice in their work. This is especially true of Generation Y (or is that 'Z' now?) managers who have very high career expectations. They are impatient for recognition and reward for their hi-tech skills but they also want to 'live life to the max', to have fun while they work and combine work flexibly with their leisure pursuits. They are likely to be the most cosmopolitan workers without much identification with the organisation that employs them (Manville 2008).

Some of these managers see themselves as 'portfolio workers' (Handy 1988), working outside the conventional job matrix, following freelance consultancy careers, relishing the freedom this brings and adjusting to the insecurity and irregular flows of income of this pattern of working. They market themselves and retrain in the periods searching for new work. Managers following the portfolio route find there is a lot of work to be done as ad hoc tasks' rather than parcelled up as 'jobs'.

This is the extreme end of 'boundaryless' working and many managers would not have the portable skills, learning agility, temperament or self-marketing ability to survive in this environment. All the same, many organisations are replacing jobs with projects, and individuals are employed on a rolling succession of short-term contracts around assignments. Success means moving between projects of increasing complexity, higher value and greater length. The manager's status in the company flows from his/her mix of skill, expertise, experience and the value s/he can add to the company's strategic purpose at a particular point in time (Waterman et al. 1994).

However, in discussing shifts in the nature of work it is important to avoid hyperbole. Predictions about the 'end of the job' (Bridges 1994) and the rise of the 'free agent' supplanting the 'career manager' made in the 1990s seem to have been exaggerated. Perhaps there has been too much (but understandable) crystal-ball-gazing based on the successive restructurings and social dislocation of that period and the sense of crisis which this caused.

Overell, reporting in 2005 for the *Financial Times*, found that there were a record number of managerial and professional jobs available in Western countries and many were good, high-status, high-paying jobs. The numbers of people acting as consultants and doing portfolio work remained constant at around 7 per cent of the population. Permanent jobs were growing faster then temporary jobs and people were staying longer with employers.

All the same, some other micro-trends reported in the same survey may also be significant for the future. Mid-level jobs in organisations did seem to be shrinking. Organisational hierarchies remained flattened and promotion opportunities were limited. Young people changed jobs more frequently than ever before and had more of an 'economic exchange' mentality, expecting high pay for the work they did now rather than 'deferring gratification' as part of a career contract. A growing number of people were in part-time work while also running their own businesses (e.g. managers who were also consultants) and people relied more on their own judgement in managing careers whatever investment the organisation made in their development.

All of this merely reinforces the earlier point that the old certainties of the traditional career in management have been replaced by ambiguous and even contradictory trends which do not yet form into a clear pattern of behaviour.

10.3 Career management and development

10.3.1 The concept of career management

Burgoyne (1988) defined management development as 'the management of managerial careers in an organisational context', which presents a different picture of MD to the one we have explored so far. Certainly, the continuous war for talent means that the supply of high-quality future managers is a major priority for many organisations. However, the key question today is whether the changes in the nature of work, which we have considered above, mean that organisations still have a role to play in managing careers or that this is now the responsibility of the individual.

First, a quick note on definitions. Some writers like to make a distinction between 'career planning' and 'career management'. While these are often used as synonyms in the literature, here the author will define planning as the older more bureaucratic and top–down process of organising an individual's career. 'Career management' has the connotation of something more open, more flexible and jointly determined (Arnold 1997).

Career management (CM) is the 'design and implementation of organisational processes which enable the careers of individuals to be planned and managed in ways which optimise the needs of the organisation and the preferences and capabilities of individuals' (Mayo 1991). Organisations need the capability to identify and foster the skills, knowledge and experience required by the individual to perform effectively in the current job and in jobs of different kinds in the future.

Taking this further, Armstrong (1993) claims that career management has three overall aims:

1. ensuring that the organisation has a constant supply of managers in the right numbers, the right quality and type to satisfy organisational needs;
2. providing individuals with a sequence of development and experience which will prepare them for the level of responsibility which is equal to their level of ability;
3. giving individuals with potential the guidance and support they need to pursue a successful career.

Although this is a perfectly adequate description of the aims of CM, as traditionally conceived, it begs the question of whether recent shifts in the nature of management work and of employment relationships are challenging the values which underpin it.

10.3.2 Debates in career management

In CM terms, all organisations have choices to make – whether to develop their managers and, if so, to develop all of them or only some of them and for what.

How important is the labour market to CM?

A major factor distinguishing between organisations in their commitment to CM is the labour market in which they operate. Essentially, does the organisation seek to make its own managers or does it choose to buy them in? Another way of saying the same thing might be: does the organisation rely on its own internal labour market for its flow of managerial talent or does it rely more on the external labour market?

An internal market focus is likely to correlate with a planned career structure and a strong disposition towards developing the manager over the longer term. An external labour market is quite the reverse. Here, top management may take a short-term view, recruiting for the job, not encouraging expectations of a long-term career in the company or investing in their development. A famous categorisation of labour markets in terms of their HR and career orientations is included in the box below (Thomson et al. 2001).

Classifying labour markets and career patterns

In a classic study, Sonnenfeld, Peiperl and Kotter (1988), suggested that firms (and indeed whole industries) can be placed in the following categories.

- *Academies*: Firms with internal labour markets; characterised by stability and low turnover. They tend to hire mainly at entry level (e.g. graduate management trainee) and expect their managers to stay for long periods. Careers here tend to be very planned and orderly, with development heavily geared to the needs of the organisation. Typical sectors here would be: pharamaticals, electronics.

- *Clubs*: Also rely heavily on internal labour markets. Promotion tends to be graduated and based on careful assessment at each career stage. There is a clear career trajectory and those at the top have usually been through the system. Typical sectors are government, utilities and the military.

- *Baseball teams*: Are open to the external market. Employees are taken on fully skilled and there is little internal development except in terms of the specific needs of the organisation at any point in time. The career pathway may be sketchy with a balance of internal promotion and external hire. Typical sectors are consulting, medicine, banking, and so on.

- *Fortresses*: Are firms focused on survival so do not focus much on the development of the individual or give them much career grooming. Typical sectors are airlines, retailing, publishing and hotels. External recruitment dominates with some selective internal promotion. Career development focuses on developing core talent.

Each of these categories has a different implication for MD and career management, with internal labour economies giving higher values to these factors.

Source: Adapted from Baruch, Y. (2004) *Managing Careers: Theories and Practice*, Prentice Hall, p. 109; original article: Sonnefeld, J., Peiperl, M. and Kotter, J. (1988) 'Staffing policies as a strategic response: a typology of career systems', *Academy of Management Review*, Vol. 13, No. 4

Other factors also shape the extent to which organisations are committed to career planning and development. One of the most apparent is *strategy*. Thomson (2001) suggests a useful framework for linking HR systems, including career management and MD, to corporate strategies. Miles and Snow (1978) identify four basic organisational types: prospectors, defenders, analysers and reactors. Very briefly, *prospectors* are organisations which seek to find and exploit new business opportunities. They are likely to seek managers who are creative and innovative. The emphasis tends to be on recruitment from the external market, but those with scarce technical skills will be managed with care to ensure retention. *Defenders* are likely to operate in a stable market. HR systems will be geared to recruiting, developing and promoting long-serving staff. The reliance on the internal labour market is likely to favour planned CM, at least for those staff who are seen as 'core' to the business purpose. *Analyser* organisations are not as 'leading edge' as prospectors, but are innovative in developing new goods and services. The HR systems here are geared to hiring people who take moderate, calculated risks but remain loyal to the company. CM is likely to be a balance of internal development of talent and the external hiring in of particular specialist skills. Finally, *reactors* are organisations which display little ability to anticipate, adapt and survive. CM is likely to be primitive, except perhaps for a handful of 'high-flyers' who may be seen as organisational 'saviours'. The external market will be used for temporary staff and the focus will be on retrenchment.

Although the Miles and Snow model can seem simplistic (as well as a little dated), it does serve the useful function of reminding us that MD practice, including CM, happens within a structural context which defines the form it takes.

What are the key policy debates in CM?

While contextual factors may well define the overall nature of career management/planning in an organisation, it is the policy decisions which shape the actual processes of CM in any particular setting. Armstrong (2001) debates some of the choices facing organisations. Some organisations will commit themselves to developing managers for the future, which implies a career in the organisation, others will buy in from the outside. If the latter, then again there will be policy differences. Some organisations will deliberately source staff from the external market to bring 'fresh blood' into the organisation and because they have a policy of 'buying in' managers for particular tasks or for a particular stage of the company's history (e.g. a 'turnaround stage'). An organisation like this has a minimal commitment to career management and development. However, another organisation may rely heavily on the market to fill shortfalls of managers with specialist skills or transient skills but show a career commitment to promoting managers with 'core skills' that the organisation will need for the long haul (Baruch 2004).

Organisations vary too in their timescales for encouraging and investing in careers. Where the focus is on *short-term performance*, they will recruit managers who will perform well in the present job. If they achieve their performance targets they will be promoted. In this culture, the top management tends to question the value of developing managers for a future that is uncertain. The dominant view here is that the best managers sourced from outside will prove themselves, develop themselves on the job and be ready for promotion. If there are shortfalls of particular skills, the organisation can always poach from the market when the time comes. Armstrong thinks that this approach appeals particularly to small and medium sized businesses. However, since Armstrong's writing there is evidence that this approach may be gaining ground as the psychological contract at work shifts.

At the other extreme, are the organisations which *actively plan* the careers of their professional and managerial staff. Planned career management means that careers progress along routes defined by the organisation. Career guidance is regular and focused at key points in the career journey; potential is periodically assessed and development offered for growth. Assessment centres (ACs) are generally involved to provide reviews of performance and potential and there is usually a 'high-flyer' scheme running alongside a career path for ordinary-level performers. Until recently, this was the model adopted by the larger, more bureaucratised organisations which were led by forecasting and planning: that is, blue-chip companies such as Shell and ICI and the Civil Service in the UK and many other countries.

Armstrong (1993) also suggests a third model of career management, that of *long-term flexibility*. Organisations adopting this policy are concentrating on good performance now but they also recognise that good performers should be developed for strategic roles in the future. That means broadening the experience of the 'high potentials' with challenging assignments, job rotation, mentoring and coaching and so on, without guaranteeing them a secure route to the top. This strategy attempts to steer a middle line between a short-termist focus (with all the implications that has for commitment and retention of talent) and the rigidity and potentially unrealistic approach of the structured, planned approach. It recognises that in modern conditions it may not be possible to plan careers in detail for the longer term and, organisations need to be strategic and flexible in developing their people.

Do organisations still need CM?

As we can see, there is a current disenchantment with planned career strategies. This actually pre-dates the 'end of career' discourse. Writing in the 1980s, Charles Handy (1988) was forceful in claiming that CM schemes did not work. There are many examples of expensive, high-profile management development schemes which failed to provide the recruits to the top management positions for which they were designed. Handy (1988) also went on to suggest other problems: planned systems encouraged dependency on superiors who had the power over the ticks which went into the assessment boxes; planned careers could be directive and homogeneous, people were put on a well-trodden path with no deviation; mavericks were penalised because there were no opportunities to show their creative difference. Yet, despite the bureaucracy, powerful line managers had no problem in circumventing the rules and hoarding talent at the expense of overall organisational performance and the best deployment of talent.

Handy (1988) also went on to suggest that CM, as practised by the big corporate bureaucracies, created the conditions of an artificial obstacle race. Candidates had to clear each hurdle (i.e. each assignment or posting) before progressing to the next. Fumbling and falling at any point would be recorded and count against you in the race for the places at the top. Indeed, falling at an early stage might debar you from further participation in the race altogether. The obstacle race of spiralist, short 'tours of duty' also had the effect of encouraging the 'wrong' sort of management behaviour – an obsession with quick, flashy results to secure the next rung on the corporate ladder, before your mistakes in the last position became apparent. The whole system, Handy (1988) believed, was antagonistic to anyone who hoped to build anything lasting and anyone who was in the least bit entrepreneurial and creative. With this form of career development, real leaders were screened out early on.

This brings us to the current position regarding CM strategies. For the reasons discussed in the opening sections of this book, this seems to be a time of flux and transition. While the claim that we are witnessing the end of the career concept may be exaggerated, a lot of organisations have dismantled the old career structure but still keep an internal market, support individual development plans and remain engaged in more limited forms of planning such as succession management. Elsewhere, there are real attempts to move towards 'partnership' and practical assistance to managers to remain 'employable' and 'career resilient', although this can take a number of forms as we will see. The box below is an impressionistic glimpse of the spectrum of career management strategies, and associated methods that may be found across the organisational divide.

A mixed picture of career management activities

Pole position 1: Organisationally led career management
This is traditional CM using succession management; talent management techniques; career-oriented appraisals; planned job moves; design of work for development and so on.

Median position: Partnership or joint responsibility
Can involve a range of interventions, individually and corporately initiated: for example, use of development centres to assess potential; high-flyers more likely to

have their careers actively managed than ordinary managers; career discussions through appraisal process; PDPs; career counselling and workshops; mentoring; some secondments and so on for development.

Pole position 2: Individual career management
Individuals are largely left to manage their own careers by self-directed development with residual support from the organisation for example, self-assessment; career workbooks; career seminars, networking support; mentoring; information on company plans and so on.

As a general trend, the shift seems to be away from 'top down' planned and programmed development (e.g. scheduled 'tours of duty' or executive development programmes at set points in a management career) towards more bottom–up and flexible development of the individual. Organisations are also taking a more short-term view of the future of people in the organisation and there is a consensus that individuals now have to take primary responsibility for steering their careers. However, the new post- 'New Deal' orthodoxy is that it is in the enlightened self-interest of organisations to assist them. By and large, it appears that organisations have not abandoned commitment for career development but they do now draw limits to that commitment and it is far more provisional than before (Herriot and Pemberton 1995; Walton 1999).

Case study: Breaking the mould in CM is never easy

'Brewco' is a medium-sized company specialising in brewing and distilling in Taiwan. Until recently management careers have been planned by the organisation. Although this process was directive and took little account of individual preferences, managers felt part of a principled system that assessed and progressed people fairly. However, just recently market pressures have caused the board to restructure, with some management roles and levels being removed. For the first time in the company's history managers have been made redundant. This flies in the face of the paternalism of the company culture and, indeed, the paternalism of wider societal culture.

The board has explained that there are fewer opportunities for promotion and managers should lower their career expectations. Career trajectories will now be more horizontal, with greater use of job rotation and job exchanges. Individuals will also be required to take more responsibility for their own careers, although the company will give some support on learning and development.

At the same time, the board has woken up to the fact that many of its top managers are ageing and need to be replaced, but the process of succession is haphazard, so a coherent SM needs to be established.

Unfortunately, the reaction of the management workforce has not been enthusiastic:

- Many managers now feel demoralised and betrayed. Promotion which they had worked for and sacrificed for is no longer there. They feel that long-standing promises have been repudiated. There are issues of loyalty and trust.
- As part of the new shift to self-development, these same managers have been given more responsibility to facilitate the development of their line reports. However, they resent the imposition of what they regard as 'counselling' responsibilities. They do not identify with this development role; they feel they are already too busy to do it and will not be rewarded for it. What is more, the introduction of horizontal career processes

(e.g. project assignments and rotational schemes) only makes the position of these managers worse because they will potentially lose their best people and receive others they have no say in selecting but have to take time out to develop.
- Line managers are stalling on introducing practical support for the new self-development-led career system. As a result, the spirit of partnership is not growing. Lower-level managers are feeling uneasy; career paths have been removed and the promised support for SD has not yet materialised. The situation is not eased by the secretive criteria by which a few managers have been selected for the fast-track succession plan, still tightly managed by the top. These 'chosen ones' seem to be offered a 'royal road to the top' as one disgruntled manager put it. Women managers are particularly angry. The barriers to female career progression have always been considerable in this patriarchial company. Now it seemed that the old boys' network would determine everything.

Question

Changes in the career structure are in danger of destabilising the management culture of the company and affecting performance. As HR director or MD adviser, who would you talk to and what would you say?

Source: Confidential conversation and discussion.

10.3.3 Career management interventions

A key question which emerges from the foregoing is how organisations can build a consensus that joint responsibility for careers is more than just a platitude. There appears to be no obvious answer or best practice in the fluid conditions of modern business. However, Jackson (2000) suggests that any framework of CM must satisfy the expectations of employers who want to deliver strategies which harness the potential and develop the skills of their valued people and the expectations of individuals who want support in managing their careers, especially career transitions (i.e. promotion, job moves, redundancy, etc.).

From the point of view of the organisation, Jackson (2000) goes on to suggest that the detailed purposes of CM are fourfold.

1. *Assessment*: activities to provide the organisation and the individual with the chance to understand individuals strengths and weaknesses and patterns of competency (which may be assessed by formal competency criteria) as well as values across the organisation.
2. *Vacancy filling*: activities to manage the internal labour market so that there is a regular supply of managers with the right profiles for the jobs which become available.
3. *Capability development*: activities to build the skills and wisdom of the management community as a whole and the individuals within it.
4. *Career positioning*: activities to help individuals and their managers find square pegs for square holes and reduce the misfit of square pegs and round holes which causes so much upset and is found in all organisations.

To fulfil these worthwhile ambitions, and to satisfy the needs of organisation and individual, there are a range of CM interventions available. Any CM programme will need to choose between these alternatives and combine them in ways which satisfy the expectations of the organisation and the individual.

Under the new partnership arrangements for managing careers, an implicit division of labour seems to be emerging. The organisation accepts responsibility for helping people to update their skills and provides a spirit of challenge so that they can remain marketable and adapt rapidly to finding work elsewhere, if necessary. Essentially this means that line managers and HR people accept a responsibility for developing staff (i.e. appraising performance, identifying career potential, looking for development opportunities). In return, employees take responsibility for their own career development, showing flexibility in adapting to new challenges and engaging in lifelong learning. This is reflected in the distribution of responsibilities between the parties (see box below).

Shared responsibility for career management

As a rough rule of thumb, this is how the concept of partnership in career management is likely to translate into career interventions.

Tasks in which the organisation takes a lead:

- succession planning
- development centres
- career development workshops
- career counselling/mentoring
- learning resource centres/career action centres
- performance appraisal
- design of work/work assignments/project work, etc.
- outplacement

Tasks in which the individual may take a lead:

- networking
- PDPs/creating career plans
- self assessment, self-development and continuous learning

Some organisations such as the large US company, Johnson Wax, have introduced learning partnerships along these lines which formalise the involvement of both parties. Linked to PDPs individuals accept responsibility for striving towards some learning goals and the organisation agrees a level of support to help their careers as part of the employment contract (Walton 1999).

There are many possible categorisations of activities which could be defined as part of a CM programme. Indeed, most of HRM – that is, HR planning, recruitment, reward, performance management and so on – have a CM element. In the best-organised systems CM is explicitly integrated into all HRM practices. So, for example, a new 360-degree appraisal system will be angled so that it helps the individual with self-development and self-assessment to build transferable skills (see our development planning system in Chapter 5). We can now look at some of the main

> interventions which an organisation may choose to combine together in a CM programme. A number of these techniques have already been considered in other places in the book (to which the student is referred); here these methods are reviewed briefly in terms of their career development aspects.

Organisationally driven CM methods

The spectrum of available methods and approaches include the following:

Succession management/planning/talent management: This is considered in depth, as a special case, later in the chapter.

Development centres: We discussed the philosophy and practice of DCs in Chapter 5 DCs use techniques such as simulations, role-plays, group discussions and presentations to establish performance levels and potential. Often led by competency criteria they can be used to select for promotion and to decide on an appropriate form of development tailored to the individual. For example, they are often used as the main screening process for identifying candidates for fast-track schemes. In addition the data collected helps line managers and HRM in planning a candidate's future career development (e.g. identifying weaknesses which might be addressed in the next assignment; determining suitability for another more senior appointment) and in reviewing the stock of managerial talent overall for strategic decisions on how to use MD resources (Arnold 1997; Jackson 2000; Mabey and Iles 1994).

Career development workshops: Give groups of managers the chance to undertake exercises, computerised tests and discussions to take stock of themselves and clarify their career plans and preferences. When these are well designed there will be opportunities for people to examine their life goals, core values, lifestyle preferences and so on in some depth through multimedia techniques, intensive discussions and counselling. Many large organisations (e.g. Esso, Cable and Wireless, Wellcome Pharmaceutcals) have CD workshops which are seen by higher management as useful not only for signalling a shift to self-development in career management but also for providing another stream of data into decisions on job posting, work allocation and formalised training (Walton 1999; Arnold 1997).

Career counselling: Organisations are increasingly providing career counselling support. As career pathways become less certain, work itself becomes more insecure and self-development of primary importance, it is inevitable that people will seek supportive relationships with those who can listen, help them formulate their problems, consider different alternatives (perhaps even re-define experience in new terms) and assist in developing a career plan. Career counselling may involve professional input funded by the company but may equally involve line managers as part of their responsibility for developing their line reports: that is, helping individuals to gain a sense of their own value and how they are valued by the organisation; showing them how their career aspirations are compatible with business plans; indicating how they can seize opportunities to build personal profiles which the company is seeking. Although these are important CM activities, it is also a potentially time-consuming addition to the already overcrowded roles which managers are required to perform (Baruch 2004; Arnold 1997).

Learning resource centres/Career action centres (CACs): These form another element of the systems which large-scale organisations are establishing to allow people to become more 'career resilient' (i.e. benchmark their skills against the demands of the job market). For example, the BBC has a system of 'career points' scattered across its locations where staff can access career information and services from wherever they are (Arnold 1997). CACs are drop-in centres (both physically and electronically) where a variety of career services are available. Waterman et al. (1994) describe them as 'havens' in the hurly burly of organisational life where people can work on their self-assessment, attend career seminars, talk to a career counsellor, attend job-finding seminars, seek out job vacancies within the company and learn about the future HR plans of the organisation. Usually there are also resources for electronic networking, labour markets, professional associations and opportunities for on-line learning (e.g. CD-Rom, DVDs etc.). CACs are an increasingly important aspect of career management, helping managers (and indeed all grades of staff) to be self-directed in their learning, flexible and saavy about their career opportunities. The downside is that they help talented individuals, who the organisation may want to keep, to all the more easily find jobs with rival companies.

Performance appraisal: As we have seen, appraisals are moving beyond 'top down' judgemental reviews to involve a wider range of assessment: that is, peer ratings, 360-degree data, client satisfaction reports, end of project reviews and so on. Increasingly too they consider development need. This makes them potentially more valuable as sources of data for career-planning decisions by the individual and the organisation.

Work redesign, work projects, assignments: As we have seen elsewhere, the design of work can be used to develop skills and experience. Project work, lateral moves, cross posting, rotational schemes can be deliberately planned as career enhancing. Job rotation can be part of a deliberate preparation of the manager for a broader role. Lateral moves can be engineered as career bridges for promising managers to negotiate career blockages. Project work can be organised for 'plateaued' managers who are still of value to the organisation, for specialists who need to learn team leader roles and for generalists who need to develop more specialist skills within a multidisciplinary team. The task and roles structures of the organisation have always been used to support career movement. But under current conditions of reduced promotion opportunities, the initiative for a secondment or lateral shift is as likely to come from individuals keen to get some vital experience based on their assessment of promotion criteria as the organisation concerned to plan a balanced repertoire of experience for each of its managers (Woodall and Winstanley 1999; Jackson 2000).

Outplacement (OP): This is a career management tool for people who are leaving the organisation, often involuntarily. As organisations restructure themselves more frequently and redundancy becomes an established part of organisational life, the demand for help in preparing for departure and finding alternative employment is increasing. This involves a wide range of services which need to be tailored to the needs of the individual: for example, personal counselling, psychometric testing and self-assessment; advice on job-search skill; training on CVs, self-presentation and networking. Although CAC facilities lend themselves to this form of support, Jackson (2000) suggests that outplacement should not be seen as the function of the CAC or people will be suspicious of the service. There are many tensions and contradictions surrounding outplacement, not least the exact motives of the providers, the effectiveness of the support and whether OP can be considered an elitist intervention – usually provided for higher-level managers and professionals but typically not for other groups of staff who may arguably need the assistance rather more. See Arnold (1997) for a discussion of these issues.

So the range of CM techniques at the disposal of the organisation is considerable. The logic by which they are chosen and combined will be driven by the values of the MD plan and other HRM policies. However, a common theme is that they are usually animated by an organisational philosophy of returning career decision-making to the individual while acquiring data about competencies and development needs which can be build into PDPS. Increasingly too, from the organisation's perspective, CM is less and less for preparing people for promotion and more and more about keeping people motivated and continuing to contribute to organisational performance in their present jobs or sideways moves.

Individually driven CM methods

Networking: As careers become less structured with less obvious career paths, more frequent job moves, 'boundaryless' career shifts and unpredictable developments such as redundancy, informal social networks are increasingly important as career resources. Networking is based on the view that the deeper and more interwoven our network of influential people and the more who know of our talents the more chance there is of progressing our careers. Through networking we can 'win powerful friends and influence others'. From contacts we learn of upcoming jobs, even impress someone sufficiently to be given the job informally or have a new vacancy created around what we have to offer. Networking is important for getting the right mentor, the right international posting, the opportunity to shine in front of an important talent scout. Effective networking requires good social skills, an ability to cultivate the right people, self-presentation, getting people in power to regard you favourably and being useful to them. Although this 'impression management' (see Goffman 1959) may seem deceitful and ingratiating, it can also be reframed as the exercise of persuasion and power, the use of which managers have to be adept, and the exchange of favours for personal career advancement (Arnold 1997; Sims et al. 2003).

PDPs and personal career planning: As we have seen, managers who are proactively managing their careers will be taking their PDP very seriously and ensuring that it is based on accurate assessment data; the plan milestones are appropriate and realisable and they have a committed mentor and resources to achieve their goals. They will also be using the PDP to get the experiences, sponsorship of qualifications, responsive involvement of HR and sponsors and so on to achieve their personal career goals.

Self-assessment and self-development (SD): Self-management of a career requires the manager to have a number of skills. As we have seen (Chapter 7), successful SD means exposing yourself to experiences and feedback to learn about your strengths and weaknesses. It means forging your work identity and your future by identifying learning opportunities within work roles to enhance your marketability. It means having a clear idea of the work environment which allows you to shine and finding others who can help you. Self-awareness is the key; it is having a clear self-concept or 'career anchor', that element of the self which is essential to you in work (see Schein's typology of career anchors, Woodall and Winstanley 1999) and then matching your knowledge and skills to the work which is available and will give you satisfaction. Sometimes this may require reinventing the self as well as your skill set. The self developer then has to build the profile which s/he needs to do the work which s/he wants to do by continuous learning and benchmarking. Here the progressive organisation can help with CACs, mentoring, appraisals and advice from top managers even if the initiative remains with the individual.

> **Pause for thought**
>
> ### Remaining employable and career resilient
>
> Whatever the stage of your career, have you engaged in any personal stocktaking to identify your 'career anchors', core life values and your profile against the demands of different management jobs?
>
> If not, have a look at Nelson Bolles (2008) *What Colour is Your Parachute?*, an international self-help guide to career selection and development, well endorsed by those who have used it.

However, despite the heroic rhetoric, there are problems with the ideology of self-development. With declining opportunities for upward mobility, only a very small proportion of even the most motivated self developers will be given promotion. The question for the top management is how to maintain a commitment to continuous self-learning among the vast proportion of the management population in any organisation in the face of growing everyday work pressures for performance, heightened insecurity and with little prospect of reward except the prospect of eventually finding a good fit between who you are and the work you do. In these circumstances it is not surprising to find that SD is squeezed by the 'long hours' culture and well-meaning initiatives such as CACs remain conspicuously underused. Here is an example of a multinational that has taken real steps to redesign its management career system to make 'learning partnership' more than just a form of words.

Case study Career management at Unilever

Unilever is a Dutch company and one of the largest multinationals in the world. It has operating units in 90 countries and many successful brands. It employs 255,000 people.

In the early years of the new century, Unilever experienced a process of rapid change in terms of technology, employment relations, structure, process and skills profiling and MD. Building on existing HRM, an integrated system of performance management linking competency development, appraisal and CM within a new job classification for managers has been introduced.

Focusing just on the CM and MD aspects, these seem to be the main issues driving the change:

- *A team approach to change*. People are expected to move from project to project, team to team; from being a team leader to being a team player and back again; to being in a team on site and being in a virtual team. Flexibility and multitasking are seen as essential in management and the career/development system attempts to promote it.

- *A continuing commitment to the development of managers*. This is to ensure the company has the range of skill sets to deal with new situations. It means that the organisation does not have to recruit a new tranche of managers as the business situation changes.

- *A high value is put on personal and professional growth* and development by the company, both through formal training and challenging assignments. Development is seen as a genuine partnership in which both the individual and the organisation have responsibility for development.

- *Internationalism and diversity are values much celebrated.* Managers are expected to think and act across borders and between cultures, and careers are expected to be international, although Unilever recognises the need for work–life balance. Family and dual career pressures will be accommodated where possible.

- *A new psychological contract.* In the past, putting in time and effort for the company was seen as an investment by managers in their future careers. Now, younger managers are less likely to believe in promises of graduated promotion in organisations that can be delayered and re-engineered. Instead, people are looking for a decent package, personal satisfaction and reward for work performed now. The company accepts this and its appraisal, reward and CM systems reflect these new expectations.

These are some of the characteristics of the MD and CM systems:

- Unilever has radically overhauled its job classes at management level so that there are now only four managerial work levels below business group president. Moving from one level is therefore a big step change. Decisions to move people from one work level to the next are absolutely critical and involve a range of performance measures (i.e. reports, DCs, assessment against a skills profile which is used to make the proficiency levels of each job transparent and the relative performance of different candidates). Posts are advertised internally and individuals can ask for their names to go forward for consideration by an internal review panel.

- The responsibility for development is shared between the business and the manager. Unilever encourages managers to take an active role in their own development, especially if this involves promotion. Managers are expected to be continuously improving their skills. However, they can also expect help from the organisation in the form of assignments, design of work to facilitate learning, mentoring and so on.

- Building a career at Unilever requires a range of skills developed in various operating environments. Managers need detailed understanding of one key business process but also acquiring breadth of experience in overseas postings and an ability to show versatility. In the new system, reaching your potential may not necessarily mean moving up the hierarchy: it may actually mean becoming an expert and taking on increasingly sophisticated work in this sphere. Good jobs are available at all levels and Unilever does not view 'plateauing' as a career consolation prize.

- Finally, at the heart of Unilever's career and development system is performance development planning. Unilever uses a 'competencies directory' to assess performance at each level. However, performance discussions are expected to cover issues well beyond the agenda of a standard performance appraisal. HR and line managers are involved in appraisal and assessment of potential, and tasks are agreed with the manager with this in mind and in terms of preferences, recognising work–life balance needs. Managers are also advised on whether they are ready to apply for promotion. It is the PDP system which is also used to spot future leaders early and give them help in developing their talent but no explicit fast-track exists because it is seen as elitist and divisive.

Commentators on the Unilever approach to CM often hail it as a model of career management at a time when many organisations have reduced it to a residual form (e.g. Boxall and Purcell 2007). It balances tight control of CM at the centre with a networked system of lateral movement of managers between functions, businesses and countries. As well as exposing managers to a wide range of experience, this allows Unilever to foster a common culture in management, building trust, social and intellectual capital across boundaries and creating a sense of shared purpose. As such, CM becomes a tool of organisational development and is seen as a reflection of the consensual model of Dutch society as a whole.

Question

On paper Unilever's attempt to develop a partnership system seems designed to satisfy many of the expectations of the key stakeholders, but where would you expect some tensions to arise?

Source: Adapted from Reitsma, S. (2001) 'Management development in Unilever, *Journal of Management Development*, Vol. 20, No. 2, pp. 131–44.

10.4 Succession planning and management

Succession planning (SP) is defined as the process of identifying future candidates to fill key roles in the organisation and developing successors to be ready to take over when these roles are vacated. The literature suggests (e.g. Arnold 1997) that SP is one of the techniques by which career management strategies are operationalised. If career planning is the overall design of organisational processes which allow the careers of individuals to be planned and managed (Mayo 1991), SP attempts to identify the potential gaps in organisational capability which set the priorities for development and the mechanisms for career planning. SP is also the linchpin which brings together the needs, interests and expectations of both the individual and the organisation. Performance management, appraisal and assessment systems harmonise succession and career management activities and coordinate their overall effectiveness. The diagram below shows the central, potentially pivotal role of SP in focusing career and development activity.

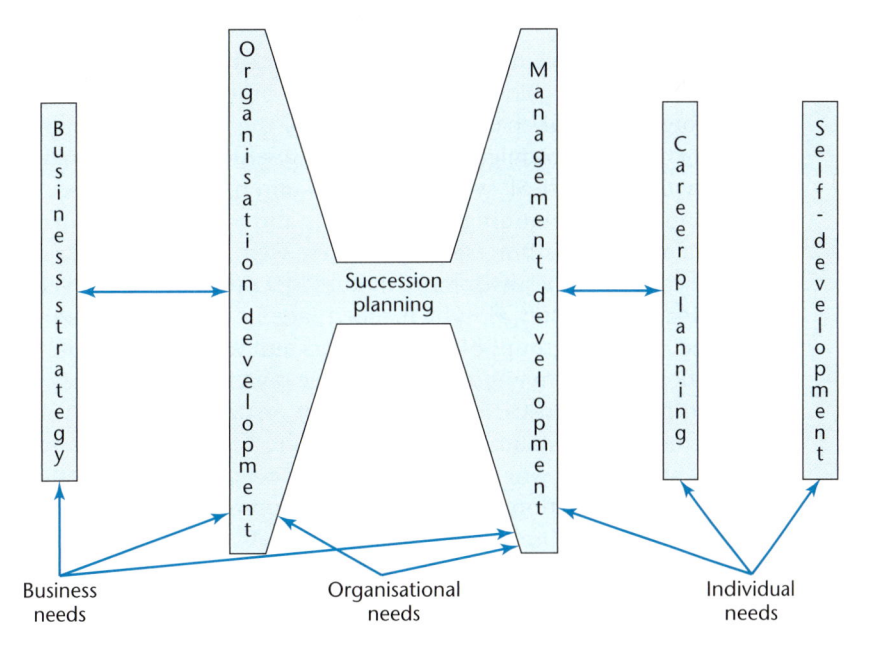

Figure 10.1 Succession planning: the lynchpin of development

Source: *Management Development: Strategy and Practice*, Routledge (Woodall, J. and Winstanley, D. 1999).

In practice, there is no one 'best way' approach to SP that has been adopted across the board. However, all approaches are based on the view that intelligent organisations do not wait for the right people to come along to fill the organisation's vacancies for managers and higher-level professionals. It is far better to be proactive in finding successors for those undertaking important roles so that key tasks in management can continue even if the role incumbent leaves the organisation or has to switch jobs (retirement, reassignment, dismissal, resignation, etc.). It is considered particularly important to be grooming a successor or a number of successors to be ready to fill the top slots when the time comes. As Mumford (1997) puts it, the organisation needs to have a contingency plan if the CEO, or a key senior manager disappears under a bus. The alternative is management by crisis.

10.4.1 Traditional forms of succession planning

Traditional processes of SP focused on very narrow tiers of the organisation: the CEO, higher and senior managers a few levels down. It was therefore a very elitist form of HR planning. Typically, it involved an assessment of the current performance of senior managers in terms of strategic business goals and priorities. Using data from appraisals, 360-degree assessments, line manager reports and so on, managers were assessed against competency profiles, definitions of future leadership and the strategic plans of the organisation. Tentative judgements were made about the positioning of managers in relation to one another on a career trajectory and against organisational objectives and their longer-term potential. Where were they expected to be in three years' and five years' time and what action may be needed to deliver the plan (Berke 2005)?

In its most sophisticated forms of expression, in the giant multinationals, the process of identifying successors for key posts could be very elaborate: for example, sophisticated arrangements for plotting anticipated career pathways (e.g. vast walls with a myriad of multicoloured pins and names provisionally placed in boxes advancing up the organisational chart covering most of the wall) and computerised simulations of how chains of jobs might be filled when a senior post was vacated.

Typically, these SP systems, detailed and highly structured, brought together HR resourcing and planning, skill analysis and audit of the management stock, development and job filling/selection. These were the frameworks beloved of large hierarchical companies with more mature MD processes (e.g. level 3/4 of the Burgoyne ladder, see Chapter 4), which relied largely on internal labour markets. They focused on select groups of top managers and were highly centralised, led by HO and its HR function. In annual performance reviews of candidates, high potentials were identified early in their careers and put on an executive development or fast-track scheme. More established managers were 'pencilled in' as successors for specific jobs at the top when they emerged. The overall assumption was that of long tenure, organisational loyalty and career progression along routes defined by the organisation in preparation for specific jobs earmarked for the individual by the planners (Hirsh 2000).

As we will see, shifts in patterns of work and the employment relationship have largely invalidated traditional forms of SP, which are now widely viewed as mechanistic, bureaucratic and out of touch with the modern world. However, even in the halcyon days of the corpocracy and planned, predictable careers, SP was often honoured more in the breach than the observance. The usual pattern was for SP to only be used in emergencies, where there was a shortage of some vital management skill, key people had been lost or there was some immediate recruitment and retention issue at the higher reaches of the organisation. Succession planning then became de facto 'crisis planning'. Very few organisations ever consistently and carefully prepared the next generation of managers to fill the shoes of their elders.

Even where top management fully embraced SP, its processes were usually hobbled by the cost of setting up and maintaining the system (e.g. the IT involved could be considerable); poor performance management and auditing systems; the resistance of corporate culture; the secrecy surrounding the process and the reluctance of top management to discuss succession. The result could be plans which were often short-term, sketchy and very provisional. Even in the most propitious circumstances SP tended to be reserved for the higher levels of management and rarely stretched to the middle, let alone further down (McArthur 1994).

Mumford (1997) captures many of the problems of SP. He talks about how disconnected they can be from real life. Then there is the politics. The mere knowledge that the board has a plan based on an assessment of individual potential, around which there is an air of secrecy (which is usually the case), can be enough to engender an atmosphere of paranoia and mistrust. It can create the conditions for organisational politics and intense jockeying for position. It is perhaps understandable if many top managers have always been reluctant to enter this territory. It is understandable too that top managers may dislike discussing hypothetical situations which may require the replacement of work colleagues or make definite judgements about an individual's potential. Fast-track decisions can be like this. There are so many imponderables involved that picking winners can seem very much like gambling. Also, if the SP is made public, 'hostages to fortune' are created; people may feel that implicit promises of promotion had been made which need to be honoured. However, doing the SP in secret creates other equally intractable problems of mistrust. It is not surprising if the CEO might prefer to dispense with planning altogether and rely on the stretch assignments or Allan Sugar style knock-out challenges to identify those with the 'right stuff'.

Mumford (1997) wisely suggests that the real test of an SP is not its sophistication, thoroughness or cleverness, but its ability to engage the interest of all the key stakeholders (which implies transparent processes) and do a thorough audit of your management stock.

He also counsels that in the real world, management succession decisions will, in the end, be made 'subject to the exigencies of the conditions', which may mean putting aside the most coherent and wisely crafted succession plans because of variables which could not be anticipated.

10.4.2 Succession management and management audit

Succession plans are a coming together of data from DCs, appraisals, personnel files, commentaries by line managers, talent-spotting reports, psychological tests and panel interviews on individual managers within the system. We examined these techniques in detail in Chapter 5. This assessment data on the existing management stock allows an overall appraisal of the individual performance of managers and forecast of an individual's likely performance in future positions. However, setting the data against the values and priorities of the MD strategic plan, competency criteria and development planning benchmarks also allows some generalisations to be made about the diversity of management skills, attitudes and experience within the organisation as a whole. It enables questions to be posed and tentative conclusions inferred, for example:

- *In terms of our corporate strategy, how far away are we from having the right number of managers, with the right skills, in the right jobs and available to us at the right time?*
- *What do we know about the spread of talent in our organisation?*
- *Where are the strengths and weaknesses of the talent pool? Do some stock need to be replaced (redundancy and outplacement)? Some replenished (recruitment and development)? Given fast-track opportunities?*

A thorough audit provides *collective* data on the talent which will feed back into the strategic plan and inform decision-making about profiles against the criteria of the plan (see Chapter 6). It will doubtless provoke debate about the balance of emphasis to be given to internal development and external resourcing from the marketplace; the groups of managers who are priorities (e.g. the plateaued older managers who need new challenge or replacement; the thrusting 20-something youngsters; the 'technos' who need to become team leaders; the generalists who need technical skills, etc.) (Hirsh 2000).

Demographic data may also be considered against people in the pipeline. Should succession decisions be influenced by gender, ethnic, even the class mix of the future team of senior managers? Should succession be used as a form of social engineering, promoting cultural change by changing the criteria by which people are promoted?

Then the audit gives *individual* data for deciding on who should be developed and for what purpose. The data allows assumptions to be made about potential, promotion and progression. Who fits the profile and will be promoted? Who is board-level material and requires 'stretch opportunities'? Who needs to be given sheltered work until they can be allowed to retire early, with dignity? Who is no longer needed and has to be pushed out?

Organisations handle these sensitive discussions in different ways. Typically, they involve annual reviews of managers in which data on particular jobs and groups of jobs are combined with profile data on the individuals – their assessed capabilities and preferences – to reach some conclusions about potential, career direction and development needs. Although every attempt will be made to ensure the discourses of assessment are disciplined, systematic and balanced, judgements are being made about other people's careers in 'smoked filled backrooms' or, if that imagery is now rather dated, at least in corporate retreats away from the everyday organisational arena.

Malcolm Odiorne (see Beardwell and Claydon 2007) captures the kind of thinking (if not the exact categories) and the spirit of judgement which underpins the assessments made on managers from auditing data. In his 'portfolio' approach to classifying managers in terms of diversity he talks of:

- *Stars*: High-performing and high-potential managers who will need challenge and incentives to encourage them to perform at even higher levels. Should be promoted before they leave.

- *Workhorses*: Good solid performers with good potential who need both motivation and reassurance. Opportunities are needed to make use of their experience. Should be deployed so that they are content and their skills can be used properly and developed for intermediate-term promotion.
- *Problem employees*: Managers who have potential for further growth, even promotion, but are currently underperforming. Appraisal is needed to understand the source of their weaknesses and help them develop but also monitor them closely in terms of standards.
- *Deadwood*: Managers who are low-level performers with poor potential. Can their weaknesses be overcome or should they be 'let go'?

Most succession discussions focus just on candidates who fall into the first two categories (the obviously promotable ones at a higher level), but even within these categories there is room for fine-grained assessment of people. In the end succession management is part of HR planning as a whole which is concerned with managing the flows of people into, within and out of the company by matching skills to a strategic understanding of organisational need. Collins (2001) in his recently acclaimed book *Good to Great* has distilled the essence of HR planning and succession planning for managers as:

- getting the right people on the bus;
- throwing some of the people off the bus;
- getting the people who remain into the right seats;
- deciding who will drive the bus;
- deciding where to drive it.

It's a nice analogy.

Pause for thought

What's ethics got to do with it?

How did you react to this talk of 'auditing management stock'? 'Stock' is usually cattle or 'stocks and shares'. We are really talking about individuals and their hopes, dreams, their livelihoods. What about the Odiorne classification; what was your emotional reaction to the labels which were used? Do you think this is a dehumanising way to consider groups of managers? Do you think it is reflective of deeper attitudes and assumptions in (Western) management culture? What is your own psychological response to this?

Large organisations usually take great pains to ensure that succession discussions are based on good evidence, balanced assessment and clear judgement against a strategic plan. At the same time, there is always a large element of art mediating the science of this process. The following dramatised discussion at a review meeting tries to capture this flavour (IOD 2000; Berke 2005).

Case study: Is he really one of us?

Here is an extract from the meeting of the board succession committee considering the prospects of Keith, a promising member of a talent pool, for advancement to general manager of a division. Facilitated by HRM to ensure fair play, this is one of a mesh of conversations which will take place to reach a balanced view of the relative strengths and weaknesses of available candidates. Although this is a dramatised account, it is based on the experiences of the author.

Jane (Head of HRM): Thanks for reminding us of Keith's profile and his recent record. Keith's a great bloke but do you think he lacks confidence?

Jim (Keith's immediate boss): Yes, I think he does. He does seem to doubt his judgement when the stakes are high and that makes him hesitant.

Jack (Head of Marketing and Keith's former boss): Yes, I've noticed that. I think he can also procrastinate because he is frightened of doing the wrong thing . . . Sometimes I've noticed he will put things off if he is uncertain of his ground, as if events will take care of themselves.

Jane: Is he a good decision maker?

Jill (Head of Corporate Sales, a senior collaegue): Oh, he's a clever chap alright and can reason things through.

Fred (Head of Corporate Communications who has worked with Keith): He's very solid when the issues are tangible . . . quantifiable . . . and at the task end but it's the fuzzy stuff and the bigger picture stuff . . .

Jane: What you mean that he's not really a visionary?

Fred: No, I think that's right. He seems to need structure. He likes someone to frame the issues for him, then he can usually find an answer which is good enough in the circumstances.

Jack: I suppose I'd go along with that. Keith is a bit reactive. He's a real 'terrier' a 'go for it kind of guy' when the issue is concrete and he can see the boundaries. However, when it's all interwoven with other policy and politics and the soft intangibles, he seems to lose his footing.

Jill: There's one other thing I've noticed. Although he's good at fixing problems, one after another as they come at him . . . fire-fighting, he's not so good at anticipating problems coming up or planning for them, especially if they're not easily parcelled.

Jim: While all that is true, Keith is a very good team player, a great facilitator, smoothing things over, building consensus in our multi-cultural team which has some headstrong people in it, as you know.

(Everyone laughs)

Jane: I'm getting the sense that here we have a good troubleshooter and management diplomat but not someone who is a great strategist or a visionary leader. Is he going to go much further?

The group concludes that Keith needed to prove his ability at longer-term strategy, synoptic thinking and organisation-building before being considered in the frame for a board-level position. The group agrees too that Keith needed to build on his strengths – his ability to motivate teams and achieve results in difficult conditions – but in a context which challenged him to develop more conceptual understanding and strategic vision. The next assignment he was offered should be designed to help this development.

Source: Author's fieldwork notes.

10.4.3 Trends in succession planning/management

In the traditional model of SP, the long-term business plan and assessment data were used as a basis for identifying SP needs, especially for identifying the high-flyers at an early stage and developing longer-term MD plans for grooming them for senior positions in the future. However, this model assumed a stable, hierarchical organisation in which roles remained largely unchanging and people stayed with the organisation in the long term. As we have seen, since the 1980s organisational structures have become flatter and more fluid; there are fewer opportunities for vertical progression and individuals are encouraged to take responsibility for their own careers. How can SP work in the age of the 'restless organisation' and the 'boundaryless career'? Focusing on preparing people for specific jobs is futile if organisations are constantly restructuring to adapt to changing market conditions. Planning is undermined if managers are career resilient and mobile.

However, although the static, bureaucratic forms of SP which acted as a form of 'replacement planning' for those in higher positions may have died, SP as a concept is still very much alive. The search for talent has become one of the top priorities of organisations; most companies believe that they have too little leadership talent and 40 per cent of externally hired managers fail within 18 months on the job (Zhang and Rajagopalan 2004). In these circumstances it is hardly surprising that many businesses feel that they need to be proactive in identifying and developing their own managerial talent. SP is changing from and adapting to the new realities. It is becoming succession management, a more sophisticated process which integrates HR and strategic planning with new flexible processes of talent management.

The majority of large organisations in the West have an SM process and use their internal market more frequently than the external to fill leadership vacancies. However, most have updated their existing practices in terms of some general principles.

- Modern thinking emphasises the importance of simple SM systems tailored to the unique needs of each organisation.
- Modern SM is flexible and flows naturally from the strategic business plan. This should indicate priorities for leaders in the future and the skill profiles which may be needed (Berke 2005).
- New model SM goes beyond merely developing people for specific jobs or to replace those in particular roles. Instead talent is identified and developed for a range of higher-level tasks.
- By the same token, the new emphasis is on building capability at all management levels. This involves selecting pools of promising candidates at various stages in their managerial careers and formulating development plans for each to ensure that they acquire the competencies needed for promotion. Although there may be an 'acceleration pool' of high-potential candidates (IOD 2000), modern SM is based on 'slates' of candidates with potential to be developed for a range of management at different levels of seniority. Planning involves enriching, refreshing and renewing these pools of talent (Hirsh 2000; Huang 2001).
- The SM model is usually far more devolved than traditional SP. It is likely that only the planning for top management roles and high potentials will remain with the corporate centre; most SM tasks – assessment, selection, review and so on – will be conducted at SBU level. In recent times planning for succession planning has moved away from top management to include lower levels of management (Conger and Fulmer 2004; Kakabadse and Kakabadse 2001).
- Modern SM is usually open and inclusive. The emphasis is on everyone owning their own development; the criteria for selection to the talent pool are openly

agreed; reviews of performance and potential are more candid discussions with the candidates than top–down assessments.

- Finally, successful SM usually requires the visible commitment of the top management to developing the next generation of senior managers. The CEO has to symbolically act to legitimate the talent agenda and overcome the political dynamics which may subvert it (e.g. top managers trying to influence their choice of successors so that their legacy is continued; SBU managers advancing talent to increase their organisational influence or hiding talent because they focus exclusively on their own unit's performance). SM is ultimately a part of corporate governance (IOD 2000) because the business strategy will only be as effective as the quality of the managers who have to implement it. This requires the close attention and active support of top management.

At its most successful, SM is a forward-looking and flexible tool for planning the future workforce in uncertain conditions. It is based on continuous review and development and focuses not on fulfilling static needs, which may be displaced by the unpredictable experience, but on building the competencies that support strategic intent. When it is working well, SM recognises the new competition for top talent, the new ethos of self-development, the new 'job hopping' which the removal of job security has created. It concentrates less on 'crown prince' succession to structural positions and more on developing pools of talent for future job roles which may not yet exist and alternative future scenarios which the organisation may face. Competency frameworks are often useful here for developing rich and varied pools of talent which can feed into the organisational process as gaps in management capabilities are exposed by new business challenge (Berke 2005; Arnold 1997).

SM systems which work are well integrated with performance management, development and other HR systems. They are also designed to create a sense of shared involvement. Crucially the line must feel ownership of the process (even if HR facilitates it) and staff see it as a fair and impartial regulator of career progression (Hirsh 2000).

The balance sheet for succession planning/management

Here the philosophy of SP/SM (rather than its specific forms) is considered. It has always been controversial in management. This is a digest of arguments often found in the literature arguments, *for and against*.

Planning for succession is a good thing:

- It helps short-listing quickly for important job vacancies. There is always a pool of high-quality internal candidates who can be considered to ensure continuity.
- There is tailored career development, personal and professional development for selected 'high potential' individuals. They have graduated from programmes which selectors know, which is a guarantee of standards and gives higher-level confidence in selection.
- SM, with customised career planning, individualised development and fast-track, helps recruitment and retention of the best talent.

- With SM there is no concern that the candidate may not 'fit' with the culture (a risk with external appointments) because they have been socialised by the organisation and are aware of its issues.
- Having a talent pool helps in OD decision-making. 'Knowing the stock' gives top management an informed understanding of the capabilities of its managers in adjusting to change and is valuable data for designing enabling roles and processes.
- Systematic review and development of high potentials helps to build a strong corporate culture by embedding shared values and shared experience within the management community.
- It would be unwise, even irresponsible, for an organisation to leave the supply of future top managers to the chance and the availability of talent in the external market at the point when they are needed.

But not everyone agrees. These are the arguments of those opposed to SM:
- Hiring from the outside may bring in new ideas and experience and act as an antidote to 'inbreeding'.
- Succession plans can so easily become old boys' networks, or charmed circles which may restrict the pool of real talent and demoralise those outside the loop.
- SM can become a means by which the top clones itself by selecting its successors in its own image.
- Modern conditions make it difficult to predict the work roles which will be needed in the future or the skills required. Time and effort may be wasted in developing people for roles (even whole categories of roles) which may not even exist when they are ready to take them on.
- The new career mobility means that specially groomed talent may leave before they reach the levels of responsibility for which they are being prepared.
- SM is by its nature elitist and divisive within the organisation, especially if it seems that an managerial elite have their careers carefully nurtured by the organisation while everyone else has to cope for themselves.
- SM is also centralised and directive (whatever concessions are made to decentralisation and empowerment). This is at odds with a rhetoric of self-development and undercuts the devolved responsibility of line managers to do their own staff resourcing.

Questions
Where do you stand in this debate? As an MD adviser which way would you be pressing?

10.4.4 Talent management

As a reflection of the new priority given by companies to building knowledge capital and sourcing talent for competitiveness, a new style approach to development has emerged which calls itself 'talent management'. In fact much of it is not new and is often indistinguishable in practice from the most flexible and progressive SM. However, TM is probably a broader concept involving not just the creation of a pool of well-prepared talent (also called a 'leadership pipeline') but also recruitment, development, performance management, feedback and workplace planning elements as well. This raises the question of how TM differs from good practice in HRM in general (Williams 2000).

This is a developing field and its focus remains fuzzy. According to Cornwall (2008), drawing eclectically on Athey (2004) and other recent practitioner literature:

> Talent management is an enabler of career development and provides a succession planning structure to identify the right people for the right roles. Talent management can be used as a framework by organisations to connect strategic intent to the demand for talent required and acts as a mechanism for aligning the organisation's view and the individual's view of career self concept through feedback.

Essentially it seems that TM involves the integration of a variety of HR tools and processes in a broad and strategic approach in identifying and managing talent. It concentrates on doing leadership audits of the next generation of managers against the strategic priorities of the organisation, finding the 'best and the brightest' and then ensuring that they are deployed in the right roles with the right support to maximise their opportunities for personal growth to reach their full potential.

In seems that TM owes its origins to the McKinsey report (1997) 'The War for Talent' (See too Chambers et al. 1998) and some new grading and performance review systems introduced by GEC and Enron in the late 1990s. These initiatives were based on the idea that having the best talent at all levels of management was the more assured way of outperforming the competition. However, it was often difficult to know who had talent. Too often in the past the best performers in their current jobs were selected as top talent but these may not have been 'learning agile', able to learn quickly and progress quickly in management. At GEC and other large corporations, in a system nicknamed 'rank and yank', employees have been ranked into A/B/C categories in terms of their ability to learn rather than their experience or current performance. The As form the fast-track – well-rewarded, well-supported and systematically developed. They are seen as crucial to competitive success and are formed into talent pools from which future leaders can be selected. Bs and Cs are not priorities for development. These principles which are increasingly being adopted (e.g. by the Treasury, the Bank of England, the Royal Mail etc.) are coming to be seen as central to talent management (Cohen 2005). They are also associated with career systems based on 'up or out' (law firms, consultancies) and performance management which annually slices off the bottom 10% performers.

In practice, TM means very different things in different companies. However, common themes seem to be:

- systematic monitoring sweeps to identify current and potential management talent gaps;
- a commitment to auditing the entire management stock for potential as well as current performance;
- building talent pools of highly valued talent chosen as much for their 'intrinsic quality' against agreed competencies as their experience;
- a commitment to recruiting systematically and only the best in terms of agreed criteria;
- taking a comprehensive and integrated approach to career management of the high-flyers, for example, leadership development; performance management; reward and so on;

- deep and active involvement of top management in all aspects of TM as a demonstration of its vital strategic value (e.g. CEOs are said to spend about 20–30 per cent of their time developing promising talent (McGee 2006; Faragher 2006);
- constant evaluation of the results of the talent management process and fine-grained readjustments, depending on the performance records of participants.

One of the key issues facing the architects of TM programmes is selecting the right people for the talent pools. The assumption underpinning McKinsey's initial model of TM was that identifying the best people would be easy and that ability would be apparent even in the face of organisational influences which might inhibit performance. However, it seems that in practice defining the qualities of the top talent and then finding them is more difficult than might be expected. For example, Maitland (2003) describes how one major US company invested $100 million in a 'high potential' programme and put 300 people through it. Yet after 15 years, only three had reached senior management and none of the board-level designated successors were graduates of the programme. It seems that candidates were selected for their outstanding sales or technical skills rather than for their leadership potential. DDI, the consultants brought in to evaluate the programme, recommended more attention to defining selection criteria and 'casting the net more widely to catch people who may not fit the classic mould, or internal preconceptions, of a high-flyer'.

Case study: Can you spot the winners?

In the 1990s while many large organisations 'were cutting off heads', career ladders were being removed and the 'one-company career' was being discouraged, some companies rode out the backlash of leadership shortages and declining employee loyalty by investing in their succession programme.

One of these companies, a well-known British multinational in the aerospace industry which we will call Aero Plc always saw its 'high potential' programme as an important part of its business strategy. As one of the forerunners of modern flexible succession development and talent management, Aero Plc eschewed elite graduate programmes in favour of talent-spotting in which lists of people with leadership potential were composed from unit level upwards. The lists usually emerged from discussions about qualities and behaviours of outstanding individuals between senior/line mangers facilitated by HRM.

The talent spotters were looking for several key qualities which Aero Plc saw as applying to leaders at all levels:

- outstanding current performance;
- ability to 'live' the company values;
- flexibility and adaptability;
- intellectual curiosity;
- always innovating and improving.

Although senior managers may also need some further qualities to operate at the corporate level (e.g. managing complexity; leading change programmes, etc.), the architects of this programme believe that all managers exemplified the five qualities listed above.

Using these criteria Aero Plc always had a strong line of succession and a pool of good people to draw on for positions of responsibility at all levels. Constantly refreshing and renewing the talent means that the skills profiles were always geared to changing business conditions. Its advocates claim that its far-sighted talent management policies demonstrated themselves in the 'bottom line'.

Question

What other information would you want here to form a balanced assessment of this programme?

Source: Oral account from confidential source.

Most organisations that have adopted TM turn to assessment and development centres to help in the selection of candidates: 360-degree data, psycho-metric and ability tests are standard. Sometimes there are role-plays and simulations which try to capture the types of decisions which senior managers face in their daily work and test the core competences of the individual. Often the assessors are looking for the multiple abilities needed at higher levels – being able to think from first principles, being able to reflect and that elusive quality 'learning agility'. Lombardo and Eichinger (2000) have defined this as the ability to learn from experience; being able to learn new skills in novel situations rather than merely applying pre-existing knowledge and expertise to an unfamiliar problem. This is a skill which is quite rare but vital in the fast-moving turbulence of modern business. The most sophisticated processes also probe the psychology of the candidates. Being good and bright may not be enough. Business psychologists may be called on to test the candidates' ambition and resilience: do they have aspects of character which may cause them to fail in exposed and stressful leadership positions or do they have the profiles of longer-term success (Gladwell 2002)?

Another issue for embarking on TM is deciding on the exclusivity of the talent pool as the feeder system for promotion. Should it be a requirement for promotion to the senior ranks that candidates have been selected and developed within it? There are issues here of elitism and the demoralising effect on those steady capable performers who have not been selected but without whom the organisation could not function. For this reason, some organisations downplay their 'fast streams' in promotion decisions. Some recognise that people may flower at different rates and allow late developers to be included later (IOD 2000). Other organisations hold by their philosophy of 'creaming off' the best as early as possible but showing commitment to the stable, consistent performers by providing them with challenge and job enrichment even if their careers have plateaued. Other organisations, such as Vodafone and Virgin Holidays, offer a suite of talent schemes so that staff at every level have an opportunity to excel within localised orbits of advancement. At Lloyds TSB and Prudential there is a small exclusive scheme for executive development and a larger talent pool for staff progressing into middle/upper middle management (Roffey Park 2006).

A final challenge for organisations committed to design the fast-track programme is that TM must be integrated horizontally with other HRM strategies (eg: performance management, recruitment, career management, development, etc.) and vertically with the business strategy. All the moving parts of TM must be synchronised together and mutually supportive of other systems.

Most organisations who are following this route have stepped away from the 'one size fits all' graduate high-flyer schemes of the past to more customised development which recognises individual learning styles and capabilities. Of course, the emphasis in leadership development on these schemes is likely to be experiential with opportunities for senior-level support and reflection: for example, coaching, mentoring, projects, ALS, cross-functional posting, stretch assignments and so on – all those techniques which have been discussed in other parts of this book. The assumption is that talented people will want to take responsibility for their own development, have the capability to seek out their own and can draw their own lessons from experience. However, most schemes also recognise that top talent needs to feel encouraged and supported by the organisation. Here the importance of involving senior managers in helping high potentials learn and develop is apparent. This means senior people agreeing to act as mentors, facilitators of ALS and to tell 'war stories' about organisational experience at the top from which acolytes may learn (see Chapter 7).

For example Roger Enrico, the CEO at Pepsi for much of the 1990s spent much of his time coaching aspiring executives (IOD 2000). Often he would talk to groups or individuals about his career, successes, failures and the strategies he had used to address 'knotty' problems. He would give 'support and challenge' to ALS groups, making recommendations on a 'live' organisational issue, and act as a consultant to management groups which needed a larger corporate view. At Pizza Express high-performing managers have the opportunity to pitch business ideas to 'Dragon's Den' groups of board directors. The involvement of the top management gives the programme credibility, signals its importance to line management and provides a means by which management wisdom can be passed from one generation of leaders to the next (Davies and Easterby-Smith 1984; Barrett and Beeson 2002).

Whatever the programme design that is chosen, there will be a need to align people with roles and roles with people (Cunningham 2007). That is, choices have to be made about who in the relevant talent pool is ready for promotion. Should someone be given the chance to take on a new role, even though they may not be ready, as a 'stretch experience'? Should an aspiring manager be given the choice of a sideways move to address some perceived weakness before moving further vertically? A good feedback system also needs to be put in place to let people know how they are doing and sensitive arrangements to give accelerated opportunities to the truly outstanding and the relocation of poor performers out of the programme. 'Weeding out' may be a necessary function if the scheme is to have credibility in the eyes of those not chosen. All this has to be done without regressing to the old model of moving people around on a chessboard, and being sensitive to the market freedom of young, talented people. This highlights the importance of linking TM plans with active career support.

Of course, the concept and implementation of TM is open to criticism as an obviously elitist practice which favours only the people with top potential at a time of flattened structures when there are perches on the higher branches for only a select few. However, having said that, many organisations are trying to ease the sense of disappointment among their ranks of sold corporate citizens by building job enrichment and variety into their work (Arnold 1997).

However, the main thrust of criticism seems to be over how the high-flyers are selected. 'Learning agility' criteria is a very nebulous basis on which to select the master managers of the future (even when that concept is deconstructed by Lombardo and Eichinger (2000) as: people agility; results agility; mental agility, change agility). As Sennett (1998) suggests, some among the middle-aged may feel that a selection system which is so biased to 'youth', 'brightness' and 'potential' at the expense of painfully acquired 'experience' is a little one-sided and denies the value of character as it grows with maturity. Indeed, it has been cited as one of the reasons for Enron's downfall that it fostered a culture of 'bright young things'. The talent mindset of top management meant that glibness and intelligence was hired and disproportionately rewarded to the exclusion of social skills, team skills, integrity and, in the end, even the ability to get results (Cohen 2005).

People in management feel passionately about their careers. Talent management schemes will only command popular legitimacy if the criteria for selection to high-potential accelerated promotion is seen to reflect relevant multiple abilities and real performance and there is continual review. Certainly stories like the one below do nothing to create a sense of normative justice or confidence in the career/succession systems of the organisation.

> Mr X, part of the senior executive team of an international pharmaceutical company, played an important role in integrating the staffs of the two companies that merged in 1999. At the time, he said, the company identified 'the absolute key people who could make or break the merger' depending on whether they stayed or left. The 650 people, he said, were 'touched' by a top manager whose job it was to take them to one side and say: 'Whatever you're feeling during this period of instability don't worry, you are part of our core leadership talent and have a significant job in the new organisation'. Those who were not needed were told by e-mail.

(Donkin 2004)

Case study: Talent management in a Turkish multinational

The XYZ Group is a large conglomerate in Turkey with 70 companies scattered around the world. There is a business partner view of HR at board level and the long tradition of an internal labour market for career development.

In the past few years, the Group has introduced the Organisational Transformation Project, aiming to integrate all aspects of HRM with business strategy to help facilitate change towards desired values and leadership competencies. This important change management programme is supported by MD, which is seen as a 'critical success factor' for organisational renewal and the succession planning process.

As part of the change process, the traditional SP system, based on periodic reviews with individual candidates about their 'future job', has been replaced by a broader talent management programme where the aim is to identify talent as a generic quality, wherever it may exist within the organisation. Identified candidates who may be 'high potential' and 'good potential', are then developed in a range of competencies and experience to form a pool of potential successors adaptable for a variety of future roles which may appear as the organisation flexes to remain competitive.

To help with the identification and assessment of talent, the Group uses assessment and development testing against a well articulated and validated competency framework. DCs, along with 360-degree reviews, appraisals and referee's reports provide audit data for gap analyses of management stock from which PDPs and learning contracts are agreed to prepare promising candidates for upcoming roles. With top managers and high potentials a very sophisticated battery of diagnostics are used for talent review.

Career management is varied and targeted on individual needs and organisational SM/talent management plans. Higher-level managers and high potentials are developed in longer-term career plans; the rest of the managers will be developed in intermediate and short-term programmes dependent on the outcomes of appraisals, assessments and reports and their own career aspirations.

Since the introduction of the Organisational Transformational Programme, the career and succession management systems have become more varied and open. The old centralised and secretive system of plotting the expected career trajectories of individuals and marshalling them into development programmes has been replaced by systems which are more devolved and transparent. Advertising internal job openings, appraisal-based career conversations, jointly agreed PDPs, internal job moves and so on are all part of the new partnership ethos. Opportunities are available for 'portfolio' and 'boundaryless' careers within the Group which often appeal to the young; older managers who are more likely to expect a traditional career ladder also have their preferences met to the extent that organisational conditions allow. The use of more broad-based talent management approaches means that both external and internal market solutions for sourcing leadership ability are used and people from a much wider swathe of social experience are being brought into senior management, which brings creativity and new perspectives.

Questions

- What are the main assumptions about succession and career management which are apparent in this case?
- Would you see this as an example of good practice in talent management?

Source: Adapted from Hicsonmez Kilic, A. (2008) from whom permission has been kindly granted to use this material.

10.5 Conclusion

Despite all the liberating effects of more flexible forms of working and the empowerment that comes when the individual embraces self-development, there has not been a seismic shift in cultural attitudes among managers to accommodate the new realities. Typically the 'new deal' has been seen as something imposed rather than a real contract freely entered into. Many outsourced managers in mid-career do not so much relish the flexibility which project work brings them as resent the new uncertainties forced upon them and their families. Psychologically many managers still have a 'tournament' concept of the career in which they joust with other managers at all levels until they reach the powerful positions at the top to which they have always aspired. For many managers in mid and late career, the reality is that the end of the planned career has come at an inconvenient time – they can no longer build on their past in a linear way and probably lack the skills and potential to progress further.

For younger managers with the right skill profiles and personality, the 'new deal' has brought opportunities for those who are flexible and competitive and have the self-discipline involved for continuous learning. This new generation of managers resents paternalism and detailed control of their careers by a paternalist organisation. They want to be paid for their skills now rather than accept promises of promotions which may never come. As a trend, organisations seem to be passing beyond the phase of showing minimum support for the manager's career (except where immediate services are needed) to reaffirming the importance of career management and offering development opportunities to keep people marketable without accepting an obligation for their long-term employment. Increasingly too, career management is paradoxically becoming both more generalised for all groups of staff and also more segmented, with different levels of support given to high potentials and the rest.

Review questions

1. Is the model of the 'boundaryless' career where people are constantly moving from one short-term contract to another, working in a 'portfolio' way, reskilling and retraining at different stages of their lives, a vision of work heaven or work hell?

2. 'A lot of career management, career partnerships and so on is just good intentions but not very effective.' What are your feelings about this statement?

3. Do you think that succession management and career management are dying as the structure of work and employment relations shift, or are they just refocusing?

4. Do you think it is realistic to expect 'plateaued managers' to remain committed and self-developing if they have no hope of advancement? What would you do to keep them motivated?

5. Do you think the values of Generation Y/Z, especially the emphasis on work/life balance and the demand for work that is stimulating, enjoyable and well paid, will transform all the tools of career and talent management and development planning that we use today? Explain and justify your answer.

Web links

An on-line career planning and development site:
http://www.cdm.uwaterloo.ca/steps.asp

There is a wealth of careers advice in management on the CIPD website:
http://www.cipd.co.uk

If you are interested in work–life balance and professional/managerial working, try:
http://www.dti.gov.uk/work-lifebalance/

Ed Schein's concept of the 'career anchor' and its practical application for getting a good fit between the person and the management job on:
http://web.mit.edu/scheine/www/home.html

DVDs/Videos

The Power Game (1965–69) ATV series; starring Patrick Wymark
Captures the sense of hope invested in managers as a dynamic force for social progress during the 1960s.

The Apartment (1960) Directed by B. Wilder; starring Jack Lemmon; Shirley MacLaine
Iconic film about managerial life and careers in the giant organisations of the 1950s.

Working Girl (1988) Directed by M. Nichols; starring Harrison Ford; Melanie Griffith
Classic film about career success for a working-class woman in a corporate finance house.

Enron: The Smartest Guys in the Room (2005) Directed by A. Gibney

Excellent documentary on Enron which includes footage on its 'rank and yank' performance appraisal/talent management system.

Mad Men (2008–09) Made-for-TV series. Lionsgate Productions
Simply brilliant representation of office life, management and careerism in the 1960s which holds insights for our own time.

Recommendations for further reading

Those texts marked with an asterisk in the bibliography are recommended for further reading, especially the following:

Arnold, J. (1997) *Managing Careers into the 21st Century*. Very useful book for understanding the context of the 'new deal' at work and techniques of career development.

Berke, D. (2005) *Succession Planning and Management: A Guide to Organisational Systems and Practices*. A digest of research findings and summaries of articles in the field. Excellent for putting together a bibliography.

Osterman, P. (1996) *Broken Ladders: Managerial Careers in the New Economy*. Excellent compendium of essays on changes in the roles, employment conditions and careers of managers.

Bibliography

Anon. (2003) 'Succession planning top of Barclay's agenda', *Financial Times*, 6 Feb.

Appelbaum, S. (1994) 'Revisiting career plateauing: same old problem avant-grade solutions', *Journal of Managerial Psychology*, Vol. 9, No. 5.

Armstrong, M. (1993) *Human Resource Management*, Kogan Page.

Armstrong, M. (2001) *A Handbook of HRM Practice*, Kogan Page.

*Arnold, J. (1997) *Managing Careers into the 21st Century*, Chapman Publishing.

*Arthur, M. (1994) 'The boundaryless career: a new perspective for organisational inquiry', *Journal of Organisational Behaviour*, Vol. 15. pp. 295–306.

*Arthur, M. and Rousseau, D. (1996) *The Boundaryless Career*, Oxford University Press.

Athey, R. (2004) *It's 2008: Do You Know Where Your Talent Is? Why Acquisition and Retention Strategies Don't Work*, Deloitte Development LLC.

Barlow, L. (2006) 'Talent management: a new imperative?' *Development and Learning in Organisations*, Vol. 20, No. 3.

Barrett, A. and Beeson, J. (2002) *Developing Business Leaders for 2010*, Conference Board.

Baruch, Y. (2004) *Managing Careers: Theory and Practice*, Prentice Hall.

Bate, R. (1996) 'From bureaucracy to enterprise: the changing jobs and careers of managers in telecommunications', in Osterman, P. (1996) *Broken Ladders*, Oxford University Press.

Beardwell, I. and Claydon, L. (2007) *Human Resource Management*, Prentice Hall.

Beardwell, I. and Holden, L. (2001) *Human Resource Management: A Contemporary Approach*, Prentice Hall.

*Berke, D. (2005) *Succession Planning and Management: A Guide to Organisational Systems and Practices*, Centre for Creative Leadership Management.

Boxall, P. and Purcell, J. (2007) *Strategy and Human Resource*, Palgrave.

Bridges, W. (1994) 'The end of the job', *Fortune*, 19 Sept.

Burchell, B. and Ladipo, D. (2002) *Job Insecurity and Work Intensification*, Routledge.

Burgoyne, J. (1988) 'Management development for the individual and the organization', *Personnel Management*, June.

Chambers, E., Foulon, M. et al. (1998) 'The war for talent', *The McKinsey Quarterly*, Vol. 3.

*Clutterbuck, D. (2005) 'Succession planning: a developmental approach', *Development and Learning in Organisations* Vol. 19, No. 5.

Cohen, N. (2005) 'The Bank borrows an idea – from Enron', *New Statesman*, 24 Oct.

Collins, J. (2001) *Good to Great: Why Some Companies Make the Leap and Others Don't*, HarperCollins.

*Conger, J. and Fulmer, R. (2004) 'Who's next in line?' *Strategic Decision*, Vol. 20, No. 6.

Cornwall, S. (2008) *Talent Management: A Framework for Succession Planning and Career Planning*, Westminster Business School.

Cunningham, I. (2007) 'Talent management: making it real', *Development and Learning in Organisations*, Vol. 21, No. 2.

Davies, J. and Easterby-Smith, M. (1984) 'Learning and developing from work experiences', *Journal of Management Studies*, Vol. 21, No. 2.

Donkin, R. (2004) 'Talent management: make sure the cream rises to the top', *Financial Times*, 18 Oct.

Donkin, R. (2005) Appointments: time to pay attention to management succession', *Financial Times*, 15 Sept.

Donkin, R. (2007) 'Appointments: the best way to put talent to work', *Financial Times*, 18 Jan.

Driver, M. (1982) 'Career concepts: a new approach to career research', in Katz, R. (ed.) (1982) *Career Issues in Human Resource Management*, Prentice Hall.

Faragher, J. (2006) 'Spotlight on talent', *Personnel Today*, 10 Oct.

Gladwell, M. (2002) 'The talent myth: are smart people overrated?' *The New Yorker*, 78, p. 28.

Goffman, E. (1959) *Presentation of Self in Everyday Life*, Penguin.

*Gunz, H. (1989) 'The dual meaning of managerial careers', *Journal of Management Studies*, Vol. 26, No. 3.

*Guest D. and Mackenzie, H. (1996) 'Don't write off the traditional career', *People Management*, 22 Feb.

Handy, C. (1988) *Understanding Organisations*, Penguin.

*Herriot, P. and Pemberton, C. (1995) *New Deals: The Revolution in Management Careers*, J. Wiley.

Hicsonmez Kilic, A. (2008) *Is Succession Planning and Career Planning for Managers Dead?* Westminster Business School.

*Hirsh, W. (2000) *Succession Planning De-mystified*, IES.

Hirsh, W. and Rolph, J. (2003) 'Snakes and ladders', *People Management*, Vol. 9, No. 9, May.

Huang, Tung-Chun (2001) 'Succession management systems and HR outcomes', *International Journal of Manpower*, Vol. 22, No. 8.

IOD Pocketbook (2000) *Developing Tomorrow's Leaders: Improving Business Results through Succession Management*.

Jackson, T. (2000) *Career Development*, CIPD publications.

Kakabadse, A. and Kakabadse, N. (2001) 'Dynamics of executive succession', *Corporate Governance*, Vol. 1, No. 3.

Khurana, R. and Carr, N. (2002) 'Secrets of succession', *Financial Times*, 6 Dec.

Kyriacou, S. (2008) *The Talent Pipeline for NHS Managers*, University of Westminster.

Lawrence, V. (2008) 'Unlocking the talent of Generation Y', *Management Today*, July.

Lombardo, M. and Eichinger, R. (2000) 'High potentials as high learners', *Human Resource Management*, Vol. 39, p. 321.

Lundy, O. and Cowling, A. (1996) *Strategic Human Resource Management*, Ch. 2, Routledge.

*Mabey, C. and Iles, P. (1994) 'Career development in the UK: a participant perspective', in Mabey, C. and Iles, P. *Managing Learning*, Open University Press.

MacArthur, C. (1994) 'Keeping donkeys out of the boardroom', *Executive Development*, Vol. 7, No. 4.

McGee, L. (2006) 'CEO's influence on talent management', *Strategic HR Review*, Dec 2006, Vol. 6, Issue 1.

Maitland, A. (2003) 'Leadership management: a difficult task', *Financial Times* 27 Oct.

Manville, G. (2008) 'Generation Y is all wired up and ready for action', *Times Higher Education*, 14 Aug.

Mayo, A. (1991) *Managing Careers*, CIPD.

Miles, R. and Snow, C. (1978) *Organisational Strategy, Structure and Process*, McGraw Hill.

Mumford, A. (1997) *Management Development: Strategies in Action*, Ch. 5, CIPD.

Mumford, A. and Gold, J. (2004) *Management Development*, Ch. 10, CIPD.

Nelson Bowles, R. (2008) *What Colour is Your Parachute?*, Ten Speed Press.

Newing, R. (2007) 'Talent management: secret weapon in global war for talent', *Financial Times*, 19 Nov.

*Osterman, P. (1996) *Broken Ladders: Managerial Careers in the New Economy*, OUP.

*Overell, C. (2005) 'The sinking of the 'free agent' myth', *Financial Times*, 19 Sept.

Reitsma, S. 'Management development in Unilever', *Journal of Management Development*, Vol. 20, No. 2, pp. 131–44.

Roffey Park (2006) *The Talent Management Journey*.

*Rousseau, D. (1995) *Psychological Contracts in Organisations*, Sage.

*Sampson, A. (1995) *Company Man: The Rise and Fall of Corporate Life*, Harper Collins.

Schein, E. (1988) *Organisational Psychology*, OUP.

*Sennett, R. (1998) *The Corrosion of Character*, Norton.

Sims, D., Fineman, S. and Gabriel, Y. (2003) *Organising and Organisations*, Sage.

Starbuck, W. (2005) 'Four great conflicts of the 21st century', in Cooper, C. (2005) *Leadership and Management in the 21st Century*, Oxford University Press.

Thomson, A., Mabey, C. et al. (2001) *Changing Patterns of Management Development*, Chs 2, 3, 10, Blackwell.

Useem, M. (1996) 'Corporate restructuring and the restructured world of senior management', in Osterman, P. (1996) *Broken Ladders*, OUP.

Walton, J. (1999) *Strategic Human Resource Development*, Ch. 8, Prentice Hall.

*Waterman, R., Waterman, J. et al. (1994) 'Towards a career-resilient workforce, *Harvard Business Review*, July–Aug.

Watson, T. (2001) *In Search of Management*, Thomson Learning.

Whyte, W. (1956) *The Organisation Man*, Simon and Schuster.

Williams, H. (2000) *The War for Talent*, CIPD.

Woodall, J. and Winstanley, D. (1999) *Management Development: Strategy and Practice*, Ch. 3, Routledge.

Zhang, Y. and Rajagopalan, N. (2004) 'When the known devil is better than an unknown god', *Academy of Management Journal*, Vol. 47, p. 483.

11 Cross-cultural management development

Learning outcomes

After studying the chapter you should be able to understand, analyse and explain:

- the relationship between 'convergence' and 'divergence' in the practice of management and MD;
- various models for categorising cultural differences in management;
- similarities and contrasts in the national systems of MD in key industrial companies in France, Germany, Japan, USA, UK, Central Europe, China and developing countries;
- trends and prospects for the future which cross-cut national traditions;
- how insight into cross-cultural traditions demonstrates the relativity of techniques in MD.

11.1 Introduction

As international business grows in volume, models of organisation and styles of management are starting to converge; at the same time it is more important than ever to understand and manage across the many cultural differences which persist. Globalisation, increasing world trade and freedom of capital flows around the world are all serving to harmonise management practices. Transnationals are rising above differences in societal culture. Managers within these organisations use techniques and approaches which are tried and tested and effective everywhere in the service of the new globalising capitalism. The forces of industrialisation, technologies, markets and the logic of a new super-charged capitalism are combining to create common patterns of organisation, common forms of management practice and development. Within this spirit, MD is becoming internationalised around the business school, the MBA and the planned, competency-led and blended learning practised by large Anglo-American companies. We will examine this perception and its implications for management development in Chapter 12.

However, there is another viewpoint which holds that the 'convergence' thesis based on global management culture is superficial. There may be limits to convergence in management practice. National differences in how managers define their work and how they are developed seem very persistent and have the force of history on their side. This position is based on the view that management is not a universalistic set of principles, certainly not a science with iron laws of certainty. Countries continue to define management and practice management development in very different ways according to their educational and historical traditions (Hickson and Pugh 1995; Sparrow and Hiltrop 1994).

Certainly it seems beyond dispute that countries do educate their managers differently. Handy et al. (1989) provide some useful examples. Most Japanese and American managers have degrees, while far fewer British managers are graduates. MBAs are well respected in the USA and many managers have them but the MBA is still hardly known in Germany and in Japan. In the UK many top managers have an accountancy background but not so in Europe. Why is general education and technical education valued more highly as preparation for management in France and Germany than in UK? Why is on-the-job learning so much more prized and organised in Japan than in other countries?

This chapter concentrates on these differences, the cultures which lie behind them and the separate national traditions for developing managers, while also noting that internationalisation is a variable which may be causing some blurring of these distinctions.

11.2 Variations in national management culture

This is not the place to examine the vast literature on cross-cultural differences. What seems to emerge as a general theme from this literature is the sheer diversity of national traditions on how management should be practised. Assumptions about what management is, what it takes to be a manager and how managers should be developed are strongly shaped by national cultures which have a long history. This finding casts serious doubt on claims about the universality of (generally Western) management principles and emphasises the importance of understanding management in terms of cultural difference. It follows from this that MD has to be appropriate to the culture in which it is embedded if it is to command any degree of popular ownership. Alien transplants will be rejected.

The most famous work on cross-cultural variations in organisation and management is that conducted by Geert Hofstede (Hofstede 2001, 1994). We examine it here in quite a cursory way because it is so well-known. Hofstede provides us with an organising logic and vocabulary to discuss national differences in management even if it is rather one-dimensional and a little simplistic. The interested reader is referred to Hofstede's work itself or the many critiques of it.

Hofstede famously identified four key elements in understanding national culture and its impact on management.

11.2.1 Individualism v collectivism

In individualistic societies the ties between people are loose-knit. Society expects people to be responsible just for themselves and their immediate families. There is acceptance that interests will diverge and a good measure of acceptance of social conflict. A collectivist culture expects people to subordinate their own desires to the good of the social unit. The powerful are expected to look after the less powerful in return for loyalty. Conflict tends to be seen as deviant.

The implications for management are significant and point up issues of universality. For example, motivation theory, largely based on the experience of individualistic (Western) societies, makes little sense in places where managers expect conformity to elite control. Equally, performance related pay (PRP), job enrichment and many other practices of Western HRM would be unworkable because 'belongingness' has a higher cultural value than techno-rational 'performance' and obedience is the rule, not initiative.

As we will see, there are also consequences here for the forms of MD which will be acceptable. The implicit values of Anglo-American management development programmes – that the manager should be a critical, independent thinker, entrepreneurial and mould-breaking – is unlikely to play well in cultures where the manager is expected to do what s/he is told by clan elders and national elites.

We don't have conflict here . . .

Acceptance of organisational conflict differentiates management cultures. Hickson and Pugh tell the story of giving an impromptu talk to their Chinese hosts at the beginning of an overseas management programme. They talked about the manager acting as a broker of conflict between organisational groups. Suddenly, the translator broke off his translation in mid-flow and turned to the English speakers: 'We do not see things like that here. We don't have conflicts at work'. China is a 'collectivist' society in Hofstede's terms. The orthodox ideology is that a harmony of interests prevails in society; conflict is exceptional and shameful.

Source: Hickson, D. and Pugh, D. (2005) *Management Worldwide*, 1995, p. 25.

11.2.2 Masculine and feminine cultures

This is the second of Hofstede's categories. According to Hofstede, in 'high masculinist' societies the dominant values express achievement, material reward and individual performance. In 'high feminine' societies value is placed on cooperation, solidarity, community, environment and being of service to others.

By implication these differences prescribe very different styles of management. In some places managers are expected to be competitive and performance-led. Material success and winning will be highly regarded. Elsewhere managers will strive for consensus, balancing short-term success with longer-term growth and development. Social criteria as well as economic criteria will be significant in measuring outcomes. Again this is likely to play into MD programmes. Some may see a masculinist bias in dominant forms of management education in much of Western society (e.g. the allegedly free market, accumulative values of the MBA; the technocratic materialism of the French model, etc.) which is only now being addressed with new concerns about social responsibility and environmentalism and commonweal ideas drawn from other management traditions (e.g. Scandinavia) (Sparrow and Hiltrop 1994).

11.2.3 High and low power distance

Hofstede believes that in 'high power distance' societies, subordinates expect to look up for direction and are deferential to authority. They do what they are told and are frightened of expressing disagreement with the boss. Inequality and status differences are accepted as part of everyday life. 'Low power distance' societies reduce differences to a minimum; subordinates expect to be consulted and share decisions with the manager. There is a participative ethos and power has to be democratically legitimated to be effective.

The implications for management style are considerable. For example, 360-degree feedback, 'upward communication' and 'participative decision-making', all fundamental to liberal, Western models of management would not work in many parts of the world. In many Asian or African or former East European countries managers are not used to consulting or sharing responsibility and would ignore participative approaches. They would see participation as undermining their authority. Indeed, in some parts of the world a collaborative approach would be seen as a sign of the manager's weakness. People expect the boss to know the answer and give authoritative guidance. In France and Italy, for example, the authority of top management is sacrosanct and a directive style is the social norm. In many Asian societies the workforce would be acutely embarrassed to be asked to give feedback to the boss on his management (e.g. 360-degree) because it would be seen as insulting and cause him to lose face. These values will shape the form of MD which is acceptable. Much of the experiential learning which we have discussed in this book based on a self-awareness through feedback and learning through support groups using open communication would be unacceptable to managers in many cultures (Kreitner 2002; Sparrow and Hiltrop 1994).

'High power distance' also translates into the elitist education of managerial cadres (e.g. the French system) where the emphasis is on 'knowing', 'analytical powers' and 'having command of technical knowledge' (often law, engineering, finance, etc.) or 'apprenticeship systems' (e.g. the Japanese) where the neophyte learns at the hands of the 'master', with the hierarchical assumptions that are implied built into the process of management learning.

Culture goes deep in the bone

Consider this story which circulates around business schools and may be apocryphal but may also be true. A group of international management students at a leading business school were asked to write a diagnosis of a management problem which involved conflict between two departmental heads in a Western organisation. In their answers students took up positions which may have been predicted from their national culture. So, the French, expressing a hierarchical orientation, thought that the conflict required *force majeure* applied from a higher level. The Germans, taking a structuralist perspective, saw this as an example of poor organisation, so roles and lines of accountability should be redesigned. The British, true to form, taking a pragmatic, interactive approach saw the conflict as mainly about interpersonal communication and proposed that managers be helped to develop better social skills.

Question
Do you think there is something in national stereotypes of managing after all?

11.2.4 High and low uncertainty avoidance

Hostede suggests that some societies are more security conscious than others. Some show a lot of anxiety about the future and try to plan and control it. There is relatively little tolerance of conflicting views and ideas and they are uncomfortable with ambiguity. This seems to find expression in the emphasis on unity, the preference for formal planning, control and structure. It also implies an avoidance of conflict as a negative and disruptive force. Other cultures seem far more prepared to accept the risks and uncertainties of life.

Uncertainty avoidance is likely to show up in management cultures. For example, Dutch and British managers work in a culture where the risk involved in delegating responsibility is seen as far more acceptable than in France, Italy and other countries with a more centralised, hierarchical and risk-avoiding tradition. The successful manager in some societies will be pictured as decisive, outward-going and risk-taking, even buccaneering; elsewhere s/he will be seen as cautious, careful, procedural, the guardian of a planned system. While one management tradition may embrace 'empowerment' through the building of 'semi-autonomous' teams of knowledge workers, another tradition might use the same vocabulary but it would mean something else – more a qualified rebalancing of authority between organisational levels within the context of managed debate led from the top (Senior 1997).

There will also be implications for MD. Planned formalised cultures of management are likely to give rise to MD which is reflective of these values, that is, systematic assessment of need, careful career management with an emphasis on management techniques (especially planning and evaluation tools) and formal methods of development to gradually develop the manager for positions of increasing authority (e.g. as in the Japanese system). Less cautious and formalised systems are more likely to emphasise self-development, project-led forms of MD tied together by performance management systems which focus on key indicators.

Hofstede's work has been subject to much criticism as being too general and sweeping and even of repeating national stereotypes dressed up as research. However, along with similar typologies by Trompenaars (1993); Kluckholm and Strodbeck (in Robbins (1996)); Laurent (1983), these frameworks do provide us with some simple ways of discussing something which is very complex. However, they only offer the beginning of thinking, not an end point (Kreitner 2002; Beardwell and Holden 2001).

There is much to suggest that the influence of national culture goes deep and the forms of MD practised by a culture will have to reflect dominant assumptions about management and managing if it is to command any degree of popular ownership.

> ### Inter-cultural differences in managing
>
> Differences in national style appear most pronounced when managers of different nationalities are brought together in an international training programme. Mabey and Iles (1994) report some of these cross-cultural differences from a week-long international management training course. The international participants, acting as observers of each other's styles, reported the following facts.
>
> - On negotiation skills, the English consistently tried to draw out the views of others and looked for consensus; the French were seen as more concerned to 'win', whatever the consequences for others.
> - In all exercises the French seemed to adopt a similar style of analysing situations, looking for the root causes and summarising areas of agreement and disagreement.
> - Germans typically worked for a 'structural' solution, for example, bringing in mediators; changing the rules of the bargaining situation; changing the team composition, and so on.
> - Even putting aside differences between individuals and allowing for stereotyping, some nationalities seemed to be more assertive than others; some more reserved; some more flamboyant and impersonal.
>
> Although this little study is hardly conclusive, it is tantalising in suggesting that differences in national styles of management may be expressed even at the interpersonal level and can cause misunderstanding when groups of different nationalities come together. There are consistencies of style which transcend differences in individual personality and reflect issues of national culture, basic values, education and socialisation. Interwoven in all this are variations in how management is defined.
>
> Source: Berger, M. and Watts, P. 'Management development in Europe, in Mabey, C. and Iles, P. (1994) *Managing Learning*, Open University, p. 248.

11.3 National systems of management development

Here we briefly consider five distinct national approaches to developing managers. The countries have been chosen because they are important industrial powers and offer distinct alternative models of management development which have often inspired emulation elsewhere.

11.3.1 Developing managers in France

The French system for educating and developing managers derives from French concepts of management-as much as a badge of social status as a set of tasks or a bundle of capabilities. Arguably it is as much as about legitimating the exercise of authority by an elite (or 'cadre', those who control) as inculcating the skills of management (Sparrow and Hiltrop 1994).

Reflecting perhaps the strong role of the State in French society, 'management' is not easily distinguished from the civil service. The model is that of the well-qualified technocrat who is concerned with efficient running of the machine. Management itself is seen as an intellectually demanding task in which abstract reasoning and mathematical calculation are regarded as far more important than social skills.

Managers in France are often figures of considerable authority, who expect and are given social respect. They are expected to exercise personal authority very visibly, take the lead and show confidence in addressing all issues which arise. French managers have a reputation for being autocratic, demanding and highly directive. Encouraging debate, discussion and participation is often dismissed as a sign of managerial weakness. Formality and 'going through channels' are also very pronounced aspects of managerial culture (Sparrow and Hiltrop 1994).

The qualities most valued in managers are primarily intellectual, that is, rhetorical ability in French (important in a culture which emphasises written communication), numeracy, rigorous analysis and rational decision-making. However, political skills – judgement, coalition-building and negotiating skill in achieving favourable outcomes through bureaucratic infighting – are also highly regarded. The cerebral aspects of managing are emphasised far more than the social (e.g. communicating, motivating, leading), although managers are also expected to have the social confidence, poise and style which are associated with a position of social authority.

Various commentators have seen the French system of management development as reflecting these dimensions of management behaviour. It has been described as elitist and intellectual (Handy et al. 1989), highly formalised, theoretical and didactic (Sparrow and Hitrop 1994) and as much about selecting members of a technocratic elite as creating effective managers in a globalising world (Beardwell and Holden 2001). It may be that the system both reflects dominant management culture and models the norms of behaviour which French managers absorb, so perpetuating that culture from one generation to another.

The elitist nature of French management development is symbolically represented by the *grandes écoles*. Entrance to the *écoles* is highly selective. They are the royal road to success in management whether in the public or private sectors. Their stranglehold on the educational and development processes experienced by participants destined for senior and top management is revealed in a few statistics. In 1996, 80 per cent of higher managers in France's top 200 companies had graduated from *grandes écoles* and of that number 50 per cent had attended just three institutions: the École Nationale d'Administration (ENA), the École Polytechnique and the École des Mines. These elite institutions provide a highly intellectual grounding in engineering and administration as a prelude and grooming for membership of the managerial elite or cadre (Sparrow and Hiltrop 1994).

Getting into ENA

'The most difficult part of the selection process for ENA is 'le Grand O' (Grand Oral). It is a test of knowledge, quick wittedness and the ability to argue and debate. In formal surroundings a five-person jury can question the candidates on anything, and in public.' This is adapted from Jean Benoit Nadeau's account.

> The Big O began with an usher announcing the candidate's name. Antoine was 33, black haired and impeccably dressed. The second he sat down the clock started. Like all candidates, Antoine had 45 minutes to impress the jury. During these 45 minutes the jury bombarded him with 65 questions on a wide range of management and public administration issues. Typically, some of the questions will be notoriously unfair and examiners interrupt candidates in mid-sentence with other questions to destabilise the candidate and to see how they recover. Should the minimum wage be indexed to national growth? What elements of your personality would help in a foreign posting and what ones would be detrimental . . . Good recoveries are the stuff of legend like the story of the candidate who was asked the depth of the Danube river and replied: 'under which bridge, sir?' It's the kind of brilliance that the French expect from their civil servants and managers.

Source: Adapted from Jean Benoit Nadeau and Julie Barlow (2005) *Sixty Million Frenchmen Can't be Wrong* p. 63/193, Robson Books.

The *grandes écoles* stand much higher in status in the pecking order than the *écoles de commerce* (the nearest equivalent in France to business schools) or the French universities in preparing students for a 'fast-track' career. Indeed, so strong is the aura of social exclusivity associated with membership of a *grande école* that commentators cynically speak of a 'mafia' or 'old boys network' which reserves access to management jobs for privileged members of the '*école* alumini' (Handy et al. 1989).

Inevitably, competition for places at these prestigious schools is intense. Selective entry means those who enter the *grandes écoles* are intellectually bright in the formal sense. The selection tests are heavily skewed to identifying good problem solvers skilled in analytical rationality. It is said by critics that this selection system reinforces a conception of management which is rationalistic and technicist and downplays values which are arguably more important in the global economy (e.g. social sensitivity; empathy; managing across cultural boundaries). However, the truth is that companies remain much attached to the type of intelligence screened and nurtured by the *grandes écoles*. For those at the top, who are of course the beneficiaries of this system, selection by a *grande école* is a sort of gold standard guarantee of management quality which should ensure rapid promotion to the highest levels (Kumar 2004).

Getting into a *grande école* is the most difficult part and young students prepare intensively for it. Once selected the student is almost assured of their diploma. Although the training is becoming more demanding, the tendency of business to look to the *grandes écoles* for their selection of the best and the brightest (at least in its own terms) and not its training is perhaps a reflection of a widespread view in France that management capability is largely innate and cannot be developed in a systematic way (Kumar 2004; Nadeau and Barlow 2005).

The training which is delivered at the *grande école* is likely to be highly formalised and didactic, with little classroom participation or attempt to build the social and interpersonal skills of managing. The curriculum concentrates on the quantitative and strategic aspects of management and ignores the softer aspects of managing like HRM and experiential, reflective development. Again, it has been claimed that this pedagogy helps to mould the authoritarian-technicist mindset often associated with the French manager (Kumar 2004; Handy et al. 1989).

Pause for thought

How do you hold a meeting?

These are some of the differences in cross-cultural style which international students have reported (inevitably filtered through their own cultural frameworks of meaning.

'Italians and Romanians never stay with agendas; they don't pay attention in meetings, chatter with each other in small groups and are always interrupting the flow to take phone calls.'

German manager talking about other managers in an international team

'The Dutch do prepare well for meetings and so do the Germans, living up to their reputation for thoroughness. But I can't say the same about the Brits; they arrive opening the envelopes with the agenda papers inside. However, that doesn't stop them from offering opinions and trying to dominate the meeting.'

Swedish manager commenting on managerial colleagues

Other observations were made by the students.

'In France, you can expect a management meeting to have a detailed agenda, formal briefings, which are like little speeches to the floor, and all interaction is through the chair. You will have to catch the chairman's eye to speak or you may be declared "out of order".'

'In Italy meetings are very informal. People come and go throughout. Side conversations are tolerated. Even if there is an agenda this may be discarded by everyone, including the chairman, if interesting items are raised by delegates. The process is very freewheeling, very flexible and accommodating.'

'For Greeks and Spaniards informal networking and discussions outside the formal setting will be as important as what is discussed in the meeting. Often the meeting is there just to 'rubber stamp' decisions made informally before.'

Question
Of course, there is a danger of stereotyping here. However, there do seem to be real societal differences in management style which become highlighted in varied definitions of appropriate behaviour within a meeting. In your own experience, have you noticed any cross-cultural differences in behaviour which may suggest something essential about cultural variations in managerial style?

Despite the dominance of the *grandes écoles*, there are other elements of the national system of management development which may be emerging in ways which provide a counterweight to the weaknesses of traditional practice.

Although the *French universities* have always been peripheral to management training because they are regarded as too left-wing, too unselective and too academic by business elites, in recent years they have been raising their credibility as business educators. At local level, French chambers of commerce sponsor schools of commerce and business which provide a more vocational approach to management and balance theoretical training with practical on-the-job experience (Handy et al. 1989).

In terms of *corporate training*, the requirement that all organisations should spend a proportion of their wages bill on training has increased the provision of in-house and external training for lower levels of management and helped the development of systematic training policies. There is also a growing appreciation of the need for experiential learning of softer skills through coaching and mentoring and in this respect French organisations are turning to Anglo-Saxon models.

As a system of identifying and developing management talent to its fullest potential, the traditional French system has come under increasing attack in recent years.

- There are concerns that the *grandes écoles* system provides a one-shot chance of development and ignores a lot of potential talent. There is a need for more varied types of development at different stages of the occupational life cycle and more flexible career tracks (Nadeau and Barlow 2005).

- The dominance of the *grande école* agenda is in danger of producing managers who are comfortable with the abstract areas of management but lack emotional literacy or the social skills for an increasingly democratic workplace.

- The French *grande écoles* and the schools of commerce and business are arguably inward-looking and closed to outside influences. Despite the lip service paid to internationalism, this is within a framework which is ethnocentric and fails to recognise the energising effects of diversity (e.g. in the *écoles* all instruction is in French and neither the students nor the faculty are usually international) (Kumar 2004).

- There is a lack of postgraduate provision. Young-manager development programmes are rare and although there is a growing recognition of the need for continuous professional development (CPD) to satisfy the demand for a growing number of managers and to build specialist skills on top of the generalism of a first degree or diploma. This explains the growing interest in master's level qualifications, including MBAs.

- There is increasing recognition that globalisation requires strategic leadership, holistic thinking, creative judgement, cross-cultural sensitivity and commitment to a learning organisation, yet the French system may not be geared up to develop these skills. There is a fear that French management education is not producing managers who can operate on an international stage and, while it would be unwise to slavishly imitate the Anglo-American model, some commentators (Kumar 2004) have suggested that its values of informal learning, reflective experience and learning through social interaction might usefully counterbalance the formalism of the French approach.

Some believe (Kumar 2004; Sparrow and Hiltrop 1994) that the French system is too parochial for the new world economy and is more likely to be adapted by forces playing upon it than offer a model for others to follow.

11.3.2 Developing managers in Germany

The traditional German conception of management is as distinctive as that of the French. As in France, the German manager has always been a technocrat, but here the similarities end. Germany has traditionally had a weak concept of management as a discipline separate from production or the provision of a service. German companies see management as about specialised knowledge and technical expertise. The term 'management' is used to describe technicians and skilled craftsmen quite as much as senior executives and board level directors.

The German ideology of *Technik* is also interwoven with popular notions of management. Germany has always prided itself on being a society which produces well-engineered, high-quality artefacts. This means that the professional expert, the technologist or the technician are folk heroes and management is defined as an adjunct of the task. Managers at lower and middle levels are professionals first and managers second. Their primary 'career anchor' is the technical skill. Only at top management levels do you see the cult of the generalist manager often associated with Anglo-Saxon concepts of managing (Handy et al. 1989).

The idea of the *techniker* permeates and guides the system of management education and development in Germany. At each level the educational system is vocationally oriented and attempts to build high levels of skill in a society which prides itself on the excellence of its production values.

Management is entered at a number of levels. The lowest level of entry is through the *apprenticeship*. By serving articles and moving between apprentice, skilled worker and master craftsman, people can progress into management. Despite the increasing credentialism and academising of management, many senior managers still start off this way.

Another portal into management is through the completion of technical or grammar school (gymnasium) training (the *Abitur*) which allows entrance to specialised training schemes, some of which act as a bridge to management.

The final level of entry is by graduating from a *university or polytechnic*. This is the fast track into management, although management entrants are in their late 20s by the time they graduate. University graduates have a more rigorous academic training but polytechnic graduates have the edge in terms of practical skills and experience. Of the subjects studied business economics offers the best route into management, although graduates of all subjects enter management training schemes.

A much larger proportion of German students entering management study for a doctorate than in other countries in the West. This is because the doctorate is highly regarded as a preparation for the intellectual work of higher management in the larger companies, and in some industries like chemicals, banking, insurance it is *de rigueur*.

German graduates are regarded as mature, responsible and well grounded in their specialist areas but lacking in business understanding and practical experience. In keeping with the *techniker* tradition, graduates enter a functional discipline in management; the concept of the fast-track generalist management training programme is almost unknown. Graduates in management may be seen as people with high potential but promotion depends on proven performance and nothing is guaranteed.

Corporate management development varies widely. Lower managers generally receive more development than middle managers and the top is rarely exposed to formal development. Larger organisations are far more likely to provide systematic, planned development than small and medium enterprises. For lower managers the themes are generally technical–vocational, building on university skills. For higher management the topics are more generic (e.g. quality assurance, problem-solving, HRM, budgets, etc.), but there are far fewer events on corporate issues (e.g. leadership, strategy, financial management, etc.) than you would find in other countries like the UK. Even at the highest levels there is suspicion of the mystique of managing as a body of knowledge separate from production.

A plethora of external MD programmes are offered by external agencies. Universities also offer programmes, often in partnership with corporate clients. The chambers of commerce provide practical training for smaller companies with an entrepreneurial tradition which tends to deny the value of business training. Despite all this activity, it is the exception rather than the rule that MD is led by explicit philosophies or strategic objectives and is rarely evaluated.

The key themes which German management development will be addressing in the coming years may include the following points.

- The German education system is very effective at providing a good specialist education for functional management, but the provision of general management development is limited.

- It is surely a reflection of the German concept of management as technical professionalism that there are few German business schools. To get an MBA Germans usually go abroad. Increasingly, senior managers are adding an MBA from a prestige institution like INSEAD to their specialist doctorate. All the same, the MBA is not always well received in German companies. MBA graduates are criticised for their (perceived) arrogance, their high expectations of starting salaries and poor team skills. Most German companies do not know how to make the best use of them.

- Another issue for German management development is the haphazard organisation of corporate MD. It is not always led by explicit objectives or plans and tends to consist of short courses in specific topics. There is also the problem that German management tends to be insular and this does not encourage the cross-fertilisation of ideas which comes from personal development through mobility.

- There is much concern that Germany may not be developing the right kind of manager, the manager capable of meeting the serious business challenges and shifts of technology in the modern world economy. The professionalism of the expert *techniker* tradition seems to encourage a parochialism and conservatism which inhibits the development of generalist management with an international focus. The bias to production and the neglect of HR issues are particular blocks to progress.

Paradoxically, the professionalism always associated with German management may be more of a liability than an asset in changing times and the future may lie in more varied approaches to MD.

11.3.3 Developing managers in Japan

Worldwide interest in Japanese management began in the 1980s because of the penetration of Western markets by Japanese products, with high growth rates, quality products, high productivity and exemplary HR practices which promoted employee commitment. The 'Japanese miracle' inspired a search to unravel the 'secret' of Japanese management techniques.

However, even a superficial examination shows that there is no distinct entity recognisable as 'Japanese style' management. Within Japan, the nature of managing in the large companies is entirely different from managing in the SMEs and it is difficult to generalise about a consistent cultural experience. While large companies might exemplify the model of management in Japan which the West knows very well, that is, internal labour markets, seniority promotion systems, long-term planning, consensus decision-making, long-term development and so on, the smaller companies which make up most of the Japanese market show none of these features. This bipolarity applies as much to management development as to anything else. While the larger companies give great emphasis to developing managers, in the highly competitive world of the internal Japanese market the smaller companies lack the time and resources to train any group of employees, especially managers (Handy et al. 1989; Berkley-Thomas 2003).

There is also the issue that the traditional management systems of Japan are in a period of rapid transition as they absorb more of globalised, predominantly Western, management culture. This adds to the problem of making sensible generalisations because so much is in flux. With these caveats in mind and in the full knowledge that this commentary is mainly oriented to the larger companies, how can we make some broad generalisation about Japanese management?

Overall, it seems that management culture in Japan is *collectivist*. In Hofstedte's terms, managers are expected to subordinate their individual desires and ambitions to the good of the group. Decision-making involves extensive consultation (the *Ringi*), leading to an elaborately engineered consensus. It is a slow process but encourages group involvement and a sense of shared responsibility for the performance of the organisation as a whole. Power distance is deliberately kept small with single-status operations and flat hierarchies.

Loyalty to the organisations and to higher authority are valued and rewarded. In return, many organisations accept a responsibility to give as much security to their staff as possible. While changing times may make lifetime employment impossible, in an economic downturn Japanese management is likely to make far more effort than their Western counterparts to keep people employed, even transferring workers to a subsidiary during hard times to retain workforce loyalty. A commitment to quality, reliability and productivity are values widely shared through the holistic relationships which bind people together in a nexus of trust, mutual understanding and commitment.

These are aspects of Japanese management culture at its best. However, the negative is captured by the popular saying in Japanese: 'The nail that sticks up gets hammered down'. As a generalisation, Japanese management culture seems conservative and dominated by corporate politics. Fresh thinking and dissent which might disrupt the harmony of the whole are likely to meet with official disapproval. Risk-taking and individual initiative are less likely to be rewarded than conformity. Promotion is as least based in seniority as merit. In this context, it is an interesting sign of changing times that a *manga* or cartoon character, Kosaku Shima, has become a celebrated countercultural hero as the 'salary man' who stands up to the conservative gerontocracy which is seen to dominate national management.

These are the coordinates for understanding management development in Japan. Given what we have said, it would be unlikely that systems for developing managers in such a context would have much in common with the individualistic, entrepreneurial and leadership-obsessed MD of the West. And that proves to be the case.

In the Japanese system management development starts with recruitment. Selection from high school or university is into the company, not into management. There is careful screening of applicants and selection is quite as much on the ability to work in groups as the display of outstanding individual talent. Although things are changing with the impact of Western market values, selection is still with an eye to long-term employment and the continuous development of the individual (Handy et al. 1989).

In the larger companies managers still expect a long period of employment and gradual promotion within a single firm. The manager is the 'company' or 'salary' man (less often the 'company woman') and the backbone of the organisation. He can expect a career of long-term assessment and seniority-based promotion to larger and larger jobs up the hierarchy. Assessment of potential is a slow burn. There is very little of the fast-track, early talent spotting common in the West. Typically, Japanese graduates have to prove themselves in a succession of technical jobs before they are considered suitable for management and there is no guarantee that anyone recruited to the company will make the transition into management ranks. In this context, it perhaps comes as no surprise that graduate management training programmes common in the West do not exist in Japan (Handy et al. 1989; Sparrow and Hiltrop 1994).

As we might expect of a system which is committed to internal labour markets and internal promotion, career planning is highly sophisticated and based on long-term goals. It is used to build not just skills but also attitudes such as team commitment, shared understanding and loyalty to the company. Development has the purpose quite as much of socialisation into the culture of the organisation as of building competence. It is about creating a sense of involvement in the collective and personal growth through understanding company culture, not preparation for greater individual challenge and risk-taking as it often is in the West.

Development is systematic, structured and led by a personal development plan which is agreed with the individual and periodically reviewed at key points in his or her career. Careful regular monitoring of performance, usually involving a Japanese version of 360-degree assessment, drives all development decisions.

Early training of recruits who may later enter management involves a series of functional assignments, usually at the same horizontal level. This reflects the Japanese belief that management is best learnt from a technical base, by watching and emulating masters at work. When mastery has been achieved the individual may then be recommended for further development in another functional area so that s/he obtains a broad view of the different elements of management (Beardwell and Holden 2001).

Consistent with this spirit, most development in Japanese companies is company-specific on-the-job, company-specific training *(OJT)*. No doubt reflecting the Confucian tradition which accords such high status to the teacher, managers are very interested to act as mentors and trainers of subordinates. Training departments supplement OJT with additional coaching and instruction in techniques. Job rotation is also used extensively to broaden experience and obtain feedback on strengths and preferences for work (Handy et al. 1989).

Although OJT is central to the Japanese model, it is reinforced by other forms of learning. At each stage self-development is strongly encouraged. Correspondence courses are popular in Japan and there is an ethos of continuous professional and personal development (CPD), including self-investment in training and keeping professionally up to date through seminars, conferences and reading, which makes Western managers' personal growth programmes seem amateurish by comparison (Berkley-Thomas 2003).

Case study: John Hughes tries to think cross-culturally

The XYZ Construction Company had always had a good reputation as a training company. However, the long-established training system was breaking down because it was perceived as failing to develop the management profile needed in changing times.

A new MD director, John Hughes, was appointed with the remit to establish a reformed system for developing the management stock of the company. John took the first few months to familiarise himself with local conditions and discovered the following facts.

- Many managers, even those at the top, had received no systematic training in management.
- There were real shortfalls in skills related to HRM, marketing and leadership although the company was trying to expand into new markets.
- Most managers had narrow functional skills.
- The bias of development was towards formal rather than experiential approaches and little use was made of planned rotation to develop a broad portfolio of management skills.

The MD director wrote a confidential report to the board suggesting a radical shift in approach in MD. It emphasised the importance of integrating MD plans with the business plans of the units. MD should be led by clearly defined performance goals. Succession and career planning systems should be intertwined with development. Local learning partnerships criss-crossing the organisation and linking in with external providers, including a business school to offer external validation of courses were also suggested.

John leaned back from the report on his desk and smiled to himself with pride. He thought his ideas were bold and imaginative. But then some doubts crept in. Would they really be enough to overcome the entrenched anti-intellectualism within the corporate culture? Senior managers had largely reached their positions through experience, not development, and were yet to fully recognise its value. To make real changes would mean a cultural shift in attitudes. Would his recommendations go deep enough to dislodge the macho 'sink or swim' attitudes of his colleagues?

It was then that John remembered the report he had read on MD in Japan. He liked the ideas of general 'capability development', of slow-burn development, of progressive appraisal and development. He liked the idea of group learning, of the manager feeling proud to act as mentor and coach. But how to introduce these ideas in the conservative culture of a middle England, medium-sized, construction company?

Questions
- If you were in John's position, how would you set about evaluating the relevance of the Japanese experience for this company?
- What auditing and pilot arrangements would you want to put in place?
- What cross-cultural lessons in MD might go into the action plan?

Formal off-the-job training is also well developed and increases as the individual progresses in seniority. Classroom-based training begins with specialist knowledge and continues with more generalised organisational concepts when the individual progresses into management. Although there is still a dearth of Western-style business schools (e.g. few undergraduate departments of business and not many MBA programmes), there are many external providers of management training, including well-regarded professional management organisations. The larger companies supplement this activity with their own residential courses. Although teaching seems to be tutor-focused and didactic from the viewpoint of the Western observer, there is an increasing shift to interactive learning as Japanese companies try to build innovation and creativity, still seen as the Achilles heel of a system which, despite its many qualities, is often criticised for encouraging conformity (Handy et al. 1989).

Like their German equivalents, Japanese companies avoid the cult of general management (e.g. strategic management, leadership, etc.) and courses do not concern themselves much with philosophies of managing. Management is regarded as a practical matter which has its roots in functional knowledge and the technical process.

Although the Japanese model of management and management development is likely to retain its distinct identity for many years to come, there are signs of blurring with Western models of development (especially the American model) as the world becomes more homogeneised through globalisation. These are the trends which may become even more pronounced in the future.

- Competitive pressures have caused many Japanese companies, even the largest, to revise their commitment to lifetime employment and planned development. As in the West, individuals are increasingly required to develop themselves, although company paternalism and corporate commitment to helping individual development remains strong.

- The Japanese system seems to score well in terms of systematic integration of diagnosis, performance review and development and provides a rich palette of development techniques, but does not make optimal use of the talent. It is said to be weak on recognising and promoting diversity. There are claims that the system is so thorough that it stifles individuality and fails to give opportunities for creative, maverick talent. There is national concern that Japanese managers lack entrepreneurial talents or attitudes.

- Social trends may well challenge the supremacy of the model. The younger generation of Japanese seem increasingly dissatisfied with slow-burn assessment and promotion and there is pressure for giving high-flyers earlier experience of management. The rise of hi-tech companies with entrepreneurial values can make life as an 'organisation man' in the big Japanese corporations appear less attractive. There is also the issue of how to create a more inclusive environment for women, more marginalised in management than in any other major industrialised country.

- Although there is still little sign that Japan is interested to embrace the business school model and the only MBA course are in private universities (e.g. Keio Daigalu Business School), leading Japanese companies still like to send their best and brightest executives to study at elite institutions like Yale or Harvard and Western business schools are keen to open up operations in Japan.

The effect of these pressures may be to ultimately redefine the main principles of Japanese management development.

Learning wisdom from the shop floor

Gerba-Shingiis is a Japanese term meaning 'respectable shop floor'. It is a traditional part of Japanese management training and refers to the idea that a period spent on the shop floor labouring in a machine shop or serving behind the counter in a large departmental store is not demeaning to the junior manager or even the middle manager who returns to the frontline to keep in touch with what the organisation is ultimately all about. It is a reminder of the dignity of manual labour in which most employees are involved and a reminder of what the real business is all about.

Teaching the business from the ground up and giving managers 'stay in touch' experience is, in the view of this author, an attractive form of MD which could be applied far more widely. It helps to give the manager a direct understanding of the business and all its functions, helps build a common company culture, mutual trust and empathy which cuts across hierarchical levels.

However, when G-S has been transported as an MD technique to other cultures, it has not always been successful. Western managers sent to work on the shop floor often saw it as demeaning or even as a punishment and their discontent often alienated the workers around them. In the age of the portfolio career and the footloose manager constantly changing jobs and companies, G-S may not make sense. However, as this author discovered in learning to be a healthcare manager in the 1970s where a similar system operated, there are few substitutes for direct experience in learning how an organisation functions. Also, respect for operational work and those who do it, exemplified by this Japanese model, are important cultural qualities which should not be lost.

Questions

Do you agree that there are some values here which need to be built on for developing the managers of the future in any culture? Do you have any ideas about incorporating the spirit of G-S *into your own organisation?*

Source: Adapted from Teacher Shop Floor Principles to the Executive Suite, *Financial Times*, 13/08/2002 (Witzel, M.)

11.3.4 Developing managers in Anglo-Saxon countries

When we consider the Anglo-American approach to management and development we are actually defining the features of the dominant model of MD in the modern world. However, although Anglo-American ideas of managing are distinct from other approaches, they are not homogeneous. While Americans and British systems share many values they also exhibit significant differences and it may be best to consider them as separate subsystems.

Developing managers in the USA

'The business of America is business', a cliché perhaps but one which nevertheless explains something of the centrality of business and management education to core American values.

In the USA, businessmen have always been folk heroes and people grow up exposed to the all-pervading culture of business. This ethos is reinforced by the open society ideology which insists that America is a meritocracy and success is possible for all those who are willing to seize the opportunities. An important avenue for self-development is through business and it is by investing in yourself, through business/management education, that life chances are seen as improved (Handy et al. 1989). The strength of this folklore explains the long history of management education in the USA (Harvard Business School was founded in the 1880s) and the large number of degree-giving business schools which exist.

In America management has high professional and social status, but in a different way to the status it enjoys in a country like France. In France, being in management means that you have entered a highly selective meritocratic elite. In America, entrance into management is far more democratic and the title of 'manager' is applied far more liberally to a wide range of people from the supervisor to the company president. Managers are seen as the embodiment of the entrepreneurial values which forged the pioneering spirit of America, that is, gumption (or showing initiative), versatility, opportunism, risk-taking and drive. At the higher levels, where the term 'manager' shades into 'executive', management has very high status indeed. Corporate executives have achieved the American dream, they are socially successful, respected, greatly rewarded and move easily in the shadowland between business and politics.

Americans also believe that management is a subject which is teachable on MD programmes, which accounts in part for the large profusion of them. This is in stark contrast to the French view that management capability is innate or the traditional British view that it is ultimately bound up with character. The American view of management is that it is a profession in its own right, similar to law or accountancy with its own values, ethics, skills and knowledge. There is a strong cult of general management as something separate from the doing of functional work. This again contrasts with the dominant perspectives of most Europeans that management is merely an extension of demonstrated skill in a professional–technical area (e.g. engineering, law, accountancy, etc.) (Handy et al. 1989; Woodall and Winstanley 1999).

The way that management is constructed as a concept in America accounts for the form which MD takes. In the States MD is seen as an activity of personal development separate from professional training. Management development is about building effectiveness in general management rather than professional training. It is about personal growth but is also a strategic tool of HRM contributing to business performance. This strategic linkage is more explicitly defined in the USA than just about any other country.

Americans respect universities and see no paradox in teaching an ultimately practical subject like management in that setting as practitioner preparation. Education has always supported business in America and this accounts for the large number of undergraduate business studies and postgraduate management courses which are available, of widely varying quality. Universities, local colleges and training consultancies of all kinds proliferate, flourishing on funding for corporate education provided by big business. An important stimulus for development has been the long-standing custom of corporate reimbursement of a proportion of study cost for external qualifications. This is widely practised and powerfully supports the American norm of self-improvement through self-initiated education, but with corporate assistance. Formal education has high status and it is fashionable to 'go back to school' in adult life to acquire management qualifications (Handy et al. 1989; Sparrow and Hiltrop 1994).

America is also the land of the *Business School* modelled on the longer-established Law School, and the MBA is seen as the equivalent of a professional legal qualification which provides a professional licence to practise. The MBA is the most popular business qualification, with many thousands of new graduates being produced every year. However, not all MBAs are equal. Where the MBA is received is also important. There is a status pecking order among institutions offering the qualification, with the Ivy League colleges dominating (Handy et al. 1989; Beardwell and Holden 2001).

> **Pause for thought**
>
> ### Is a qualified manager a better manager?
>
> The Anglo-American tradition favours generic management qualifications (e.g. the MBA and other Master's in management) as the route for developing an educated managerial workforce. However, it is not at all obvious that qualifications in management translate into greater achievement, and the cult of the management training course is far less entrenched in other cultures. German, Japanese, Swedish and Norwegian managers are often extremely well educated and have high technical qualifications. Indeed, some might say that they often seem more sophisticated and better able to cope with new technology and changing conditions than their Western counterparts with their university degrees in managing.
>
> #### Questions
> *This is a theme that runs through the entire book. What really is the best preparation for a management career and what should continuous development involve? What are your thoughts, having considered how some other countries do it?*

In recent years business schools have been differentiating their products, so that schools become known for their specialisms. There have also been a number of trends which are being copied elsewhere.

- Local universities are often contracting with big business to provide *tailor-made courses* which balance academic rigour with sensitivity to the development needs of management groups within the organisation.
- An extension of this is the provision by business schools of executive education, including *executive MBAs,* often designed in part to satisfy the needs of particular organisations. These provide a crash course in management for senior executives who may be travelling light in terms of academic credentials and an updating for those who already have an MBA. A new turn is the growing number of doctorates in business administration programmes aimed at high-flying specialists.
- An increasing number of big companies are setting up corporate universities or *'learning centres'* (e.g. Dana University, McDonalds University, Xerox Learning Centre, etc.) to provide their own post-experience and postgraduate courses in association with traditional business schools (which may provide faculty and validate standards).

As extensive as the formalised system of management education may be, most MD in America takes place within companies. In broad simplistic terms these are the themes (Handy et al. 1989; Beardwell and Holden 2001; Hiltrop and Sparrow 1994):

- A growing appreciation of the need to develop people in a planned and progressive way based on periodic diagnosis of development needs. This had led to an explosion of in-house activity, including seminars, work shops, mid-career development and so on, increasingly integrated with career management strategies and appraisal systems.

- Much corporate development takes place in residential learning retreats where executives broaden their thinking and skills in an atmosphere of corporate comfort intended to send signals to those who attend that the organisation is investing in them and recognises their contribution quite as much as developing them for more senior positions. MD in corporate America is often bound up with recognition, reward, management perks and culture building.

- Formal development is becoming increasingly blended with experiential learning (mentoring, planned assignments, group working) and anchored in workplace development which ensures that the lessons of the academy and the lessons of pragmatism are mutually reinforcing.

- Managers are under increasing pressure from their companies to develop themselves and stay abreast of contemporary developments (like their Japanese counterparts). Increasingly the ethos in the big companies is *'building learning partnerships'* (Handy et al. 1989). The individual is seen as responsible for his or her own career and the organisation is backing away from paternalism, but sponsorship is available for helping people to become the flexible, innovative polymaths which sophisticated post-industrial companies say they want.

American managers in the larger companies (unlike managers in the smaller companies) certainly have many opportunities to become educated in management. However, the American system of MD has come under attack in recent years from a number of different sources.

There is concern that much in-company MD is ritualistic and concerned as much with reward and retention of 'rising stars' in the organisation as developing skills and understanding. At its best, corporate MD is a force for cultural change as well as experiential development. At its worst, it is claimed that MD in America is disconnected from the realities of managing, an expensive form of corporate junketing and a vehicle for corporate propaganda (Handy et al. 1989).

The business schools have been savagely criticised by businessmen as too narrow and specialist, too concerned with analytical techniques at the expense of generic development. There may be some truth in this. Business schools continued with the same basic curriculum from the period of the 1960s to the early 1990s. It was only with the formation of an accrediting body for MBAs (the AACSB) that more flexibility has been built into the curriculum; attempts have been made to include neglected management subjects such as culture, HR, leadership and international management, and courses have been more aligned to practitioner concepts of relevance. Even now there are claims that business schools are out of touch and courses like the MBA encourage false expectations and an arrogance among their alumni when the need is increasingly for empathy and understanding in management (see Chapter 8).

The future suggests that MD in America will become increasingly strategic, increasingly led by explicit business needs and used for culture change as much as individual development. It also seems to be readjusting the balance between external and on-the-job learning, so that experiential learning receives greater prominence (on the Japanese model).

Is Harvard in decline and with it a model of management education?

The USA used to see globalisation as the vehicle for spreading the American way of business.

For an institution like Harvard Business School which makes a tidy living from selling US business 'knowhow' to the wider world America's economic decline is worrying. American business prowess is part of the draw for foreign students. HBS doesn't teach a specifically American variant of capitalism but a big part of its appeal stems from instinctive respect felt by students from Europe, Asia and Latin America for a certain American business education method – heavily statistics based – versus the more intuitive, culturally varied ways one finds elsewhere. It is precisely this sense of respect that is being challenged by macro-economic events . . .

Could HBS follow the path of the great Victorian educational institutions designed to educate an imperial ruling class? Consider the once swaggering Indian Institute at Oxford, founded during a period of imperial might. These days it is little more than a dusty library tucked away at a corner of the Bodleian.

Source: Broughton, P. (2008) 'Harvard loses its lustre', *Prospect*, September 2008.

Developing managers in UK

The UK shares many of the concepts and values of the USA in its definitions of 'management' and pathways of development. For example, norms of individualism, proactive leadership, efficiency and the bottom line predominate. However, there are differences. In UK, managers are less of a vanguard for entrepreneurism than in the States; they enjoy less social status; have less publicly recognised professionalism and less reward. There are differences too in terms of development approaches. By and large, the British have not shared American optimism about higher education as the vehicle for developing professional skills (Thomson et al. 2001).

Equally, there are contrasts between British perspectives on development and those of the other traditions. Historically the British have eschewed the *elitist model* of the French, the *technicist model* of the Germans and the *planned model* of the Japanese. By contrast, the British approach might be characterised as a *pragmatic model* emphasising liberal education over technical education and putting ad hoc learning and self-development above organised programmes of MD.

It is a strange paradox that Britain, the first country to industrialise, was the slowest of the major Western industrialised nations to recognise the importance of professional management or to appreciate that managing was a distinctive role requiring knowledge and skills which had to be systematically developed. The standing of managers has always been low in UK society. Management has always had an underdeveloped sense of its professional identity. Reed and Anthony (1992) suggest that managing in Britain always drew for its legitimation on a discourse of social status rather than professional expertise and technical competence. Mant (1979) takes up the theme by suggesting that MD in the UK was always preparation 'to be' (i.e. take on a status position) than 'to do' (i.e. be a skilled practitioner). Also, managing as a process was identified more with structures of administration (e.g. of a fading empire) rather than with innovation and entrepreneurism (dynamic business).

Until the end of the Second World War, management was not seen as a prestigious profession in UK and the role of manager had a much lower status than in America or Europe. This was partly a reflection of the British class system and an expression of the contempt in which trade was held. For people with talent, management was seen as a less fitting occupation to join than the professions (e.g. law, accountancy, the media, etc.) (Wiener 1981). Management potential was held to be attributable more to character, energy and interpersonal skills (e.g. 'the capacity to lead' was often taken as code for membership of the educated middle classes) than intellect or technical ability. Having the 'right stuff' in management was a mixture of competitiveness, courage, determination, charm and forcefulness, characteristics which might be held to have a 'class basis'(Mant 1979). Social criteria for membership of the management community was as important as intellectual criteria.

The system which grew up for developing managers largely reflected these values. Until the late 1940s training for management was not taken seriously in the UK. Most companies were managed by their owners, so management succession was a matter for the family. Because of the prevailing essentialist view that management capability was an expression of character and common sense, it was widely regarded that the skills and knowledge required could be picked up on the job. The best preparation for management was widely seen to be a good 'public' school education and professional qualifications in accountancy (Mant 1979; Thomson et al. 2001).

Education away from the place of work was often viewed as unnecessary, even irrelevant. MD of any kind was an afterthought, often seen as remedial and regarded by many as unnecessary interference in the Darwinian struggle by which those most fitted to manage rose to the top in a battle for survival.

If higher education was valued it was for the social polish and connections it gave, rather than the acquisition of critical thinking skills which were desirable rather than essential. For a few elite high-flyers, a background in humanities (classics or PPE) was useful for its social kudos and exclusive networks. Many managers were recruited from public school, from family linkages or from the socially mobile, up from the shop floor. Not surprisingly, most graduates avoided industry which was regarded as philistine and dull. Industry, for its part, preferred practical experience and good character to brains, which they could find within their own restricted gentrified circles (see Thomson et al. 2001; Reed and Anthony 1992 and Mant 1979, for a full account of British social attitudes to management).

It was not until the late 1950s that large companies began to recruit significant numbers of graduates on to specially designed management development programmes (Handy et al. 1989). It was also at this time that concerns about national economic performance concentrated the minds of politicians and those in top management positions. Increasingly there was an awareness of the amateurishness of

British managers and the need for investment in management development to improve national competitiveness (Mangham and Silver 1986).

However, even by the 1960s, despite flagship MD programmes in blue-chip companies such as Unilever, ICI and Shell, there was little organised MD in business or the public sector with the exception of the Civil Service, and management education was in its infancy (Handy et al. 1989). The British higher education system was remarkably reluctant to embrace 'management' as a subject which was intellectually respectable and could be taught. This seems to have been the result of an unholy alliance between the inward-looking complacency of the British academic establishment and the continuing resistance of employers to recruiting 'too clever by half' business-educated managers, especially if their education made managerial labour more expensive (Reed and Anthony 1992; Thomson et al. 2001).

The main impetus to the spread of management education in the 1960s/1970s was the establishment of the first two business schools in the UK – at Manchester and London – following the American model (a recommendation of the Franks Report of 1965 which had been commissioned by government to find ways of improving the quality of the national stock of managers as a stimulus to national competitiveness).

However, the business schools were not easily established. They wanted to produce a vanguard of bright, young, thinking managers who could act as shock troops for business innovation. But business conservatism and anti-intellectualism remained strong. The cult of the self-trained amateur was entrenched. Many business leaders were untouched by management education and, as pragmatists, were disparaging of its value (Thomson et al. 2001). The contrast with elaborately trained managers in France, Germany or Japan could not be greater. Thomson et al. (2001) note that UK in the 1960s was only then catching up with the point reached by these competitor nations in MD at the end of the nineteenth century.

Although more business schools appeared, business education in the UK became more geared to the needs of students in demanding management jobs (e.g. distance learning, modular programmes, etc.); more commercial providers appeared offering professionalised post-experience short courses and company training in management began to take off, MD as whole remained a neglected Cinderella function.

By the late 1980s there was serious concern that the national system of management education and development was failing the country. Writing in 1989, Handy et al. spoke of the haphazard and uncoordinated nature of MD in Britain. They claimed that there was no coherent route into management in the UK. Where managers did follow a path of development it might be one of three kinds.

1. *Formal study in one of the established professions* like law, accountancy or surveying which resulted in membership of a professional body which conferred status and involved some generalised management.
2. *Training by one of the large companies* (Unilever, BP, British Telecom, ICI, etc.) on a corporate management training scheme. This usually involved company-specific functional management experience supplemented by on-the-job supervision and periods of formal training at company training centres.
3. *Academic training*, for example, sub-degree courses (like the HND); postgraduate diplomas (like the Diploma in Management Studies) or MBAs. In the late 1980s the status of these qualifications was generally unclear and employers were uncertain how much value to give to them.

Handy et al. (1989) were scathing. Other competitor countries educated their managers to a much higher level than in UK. Where managers were educated in Britain it tended to be in technical/functional skills, not in general management. Only 12 per cent of managers had degrees and the vast majority of managers received less than one day a week of training a year (Handy et al. 1989; Mangham and Silver 1986). Planned progressive development was rare; often business education only happened later in career and then in a haphazard fashion; preparation for executive responsibility and executive development were particularly neglected.

Of Handy's three tracks, the *professional* was the most popular. This is was a characteristically 'British' way of preparing managers – through a long period of formal training (articles in law or accounting), leading to membership of a professional institute. Handy concluded that this might be sufficient training for a functional profession like accountancy, but it was insufficient preparation for the political, social and conceptual understanding needed at the higher corporate levels of managerial policy-making. There was also the problem that the three pathways in management were separate from each other and mutually incompatible.

Handy concluded that the British system of MD in 1989 was uncoordinated and unplanned, anti-intellectual and short-term in its focus. As he said, a yong person stepping out on a career in management had no obvious path to take. The UK was still searching for a pattern of MD which suited its culture and would address its functional needs.

Pause for thought

The British amateur tradition

Consider this observation made by one of the most controversial critics of British management culture.

> There is an enduring amateurism about the British manager. Even today managers refer to 'theory' with a sneer as if it had nothing to do with practice and 'academic' is the ultimate sneer. At just the point when Continental educational institutions were beginning to theorise about new industrial processes, the British engineer was moving into a second phase dominated by improvisation of a typically British kind: 'If the boiler blew up you strapped another band round it; if the bridge collapsed you bolted on more cast iron next time' . . . From the very start there was a tradition of the resourceful management amateur, self taught on the job, not the man specially and elaborately trained.

Question
Compare and contrast this view with what you have read about management in other countries. If you are a foreign student, do managers do it differently back home?

Source: Mant, A. (1979) *The Rise and Fall of the British Manager*, Pan Business Books.

The Handy report and other critical commentary created a crisis of confidence in existing systems of MD which stimulated debate and adjustment, resulting in the patterns we see today. Since the late 1980s British MD has seen various changes (Thomson et al. 2001; Reed and Anthony 1992).

- UK organisations have gradually come to understand the significance of management training and development as a key process in delivering organisational change, adding value and contributing to the strategic business, and are prepared to invest in it.

- There has been a proliferation of undergraduate courses in business and postgraduate courses in management education. There is evidence that the American interest in management credentialism is now quite established in UK. The MBA has become an aspirational benchmark for young people following a managerial career. Although it has not yet established itself as the 'sine qua non' for management practice, selection and promotion in management relies more heavily on professional qualifications and younger managers are far more formally qualified than their predecessors.

- Employers have become more committed to building the effectiveness of their managers and are more supportive of individuals acquiring external qualifications as well as internal experiential development programmes. Most large organisations now run their own MD programmes and the average annual number of training days received by British managers is about eight (in 2004).

- MD and education is more of a balance between developing practical skills and developing the whole person for leadership.

- Patterns of MD are also changing. Fast-track graduate programmes of development are being replaced by broad-funnel training for a large swathe of employees in their early years with a deliberate holding back on the selection of leaders until talent has had a chance to emerge (although this needs to be set against 'talent managed' development of potential leaders).

- As in America, there are many experiments in blending formal, planned MD with informal, self-reflective, peer and experiential learning. In some cases these initiatives work; in others they are the old British reliance on pragmatism and 'incidental learning' repackaged as 'self-development' and 'action learning'. Increasingly competency-based diagnostic systems lead the programmes of MD which takes place.

We examine all of these recent trends in different parts of the book. However, as a national approach to developing management capabilities, it seems that the British 'system' (which still deserves inverted commas) is still finding its way. Handy's criticisms still apply, if with less force today. British managers still lack the educational levels of their foreign counterparts; their professional status continues to be lower; law and accountancy remain the main routes into management; the Japanese ethos of continual professional development (CPD) is still not embedded and the American reverence for 'management' as a teachable subject still meets with scepticism among practitioners and academics alike. More than most, the British approach to MD is a hybrid, synthesising influences from abroad, particularly those of America and Japan, with a traditional no-nonsense spirit of pragmatism. This eclecticism may be a strength and reflective of a truly internationalist spirit but one suspects it is more an expression of an unreflective empiricism which lacks a coherent philosophy of management and how to develop it.

11.3.5 Developing managers in the wider world

Most of the MD systems in the rest of the world derive their design from one of these previous models, although some countries are struggling to develop approaches which are eclectic in form and provide a better fit with their cultural, economic and social context.

In the *developing countries*, the tendency has been for countries to look to the model of the former colonial power as the exemplar of management development. Alternatively, they have adopted a international model which on closer inspection usually means absorbing the implicit values of the American approach.

In Asia and Africa, MD means either 'ad hoc' informal patterns of workplace learning or formal programmes offered at universities and management institutes focused on remedying skill deficiencies and providing catch-up opportunities for those new to management. For the elite, MD usually means periods of study abroad in prestigious institutions in Europe or America leading to MA or MBA qualifications. Management qualifications often confer social standing and status and are valued for this reason quite as much as any functional advantage they may offer.

It is not unusual to find that managers are exposed to quite inappropriate management development – individualised, technocratic and Western, when the need is for collective approaches which allow the use of intermediate technology and the opportunity to build a precarious national identity from cultural diversity. An encouraging trend, however, is the number of distance-learning MD programmes which are emerging based on close collaboration between Western providers and/or international institutions like the UN, and Third World clients. At their best, these balance formal input from Western MD institutions with local learning networks and are sensitively adapted to local conditions.

In *Central Europe* the need to create a new generation of managers capable of navigating the difficult transition from a planned to a market economy (if that is what is happening) has often led to the wholesale adoption of Western models of MD. Inevitably, programmes provided by Western-oriented business schools seem to be 'out of sync' with local realities. There is also considerable local resentment towards free-market philosophies which often underpin Western programmes bought off the peg and resistance to the evangelical tone of missionary developers going to Eastern Europe and Russia. A common criticism of managers in these countries is that their experience under Communism, which often involved subtle negotiating and 'pseudo-entrepreneurial' behaviour to make planning structures work, is overlooked by outside management educators who assume rather too readily that the West is a repository of all good practice in management.

The best hope here may lie in the formation of new management models for post-socialist economies which build on the best of the old and are responsive to the best of the new. This will only come about through *collaborative partnerships* between providers and clients which are based on mutual respect and a willingness to experiment.

Is much of what passes for management development in East Europe ideology in disguise?

Here are two quotations from Poles who have been on the receiving end of MD directed at managers in former Communist countries.

> There are two categories of Western developers as 'management missionaries': the free marketers and the 'culturally sensitive'. While the former concentrate on free market values and typically address the intellectual elite, the latter show concern for the 'Polish common man' . . .

> With the management theory are myths – the myth of hard work, the myth of the free market, the myth of economising. An example of the myth of hard work is the story of the 'shoe shiner' who becomes a millionaire. This 'American Dream' story is told to the Poles and the lecturers emphasise the moral message: all you have to do is work hard and believe in your product. Success will inevitably follow . . . the market is a just judge and a fair distributor of rewards . . . But Poles want education in management not the teachings of a Messiah.
>
> Source: M. Kosteva 'The modern crusade: the missionaries of management come to Eastern Europe', in Grey and Antonacopoulou (2004) *Readings in Management Learning*, Sage.

Finally, in view of its growing importance in the world economy, perhaps we should consider MD in *China*. Here there is a great need for sophisticated managers who can operate in an emergent international market and a chronic shortage of MD. At the same time, for political reasons, there is considerable local resistance to pedagogies which are central to Western management practice (e.g. participation, self-awareness, critical evaluation, open discussion, etc.). At present much of the typical management syllabus (especially people subjects like HRM, organisational analysis, etc.) is regarded with much suspicion as agents of Western liberalism and/or capitalist values (e.g. marketing and finance). Experiential learning is regarded as potentially subversive because of the critical consciousness which it encourages. The Chinese preference is for formal, technicist, classroom-based instruction on the technology and tools of management without the accompanying values. China is the great exception to the homogenisation which some see as central to Western-led MD. Because of China's separate historical path, it is difficult to believe that even if Chinese managers receive the full programme of a Western business school they will end up thinking like their Western counterparts. Other counterbalancing influences will be too strong.

It will be interesting to see what form of MD emerges in China from the clash of state ideology and managerial internationalism which seems to lie in the future. Given the collectivist and high power distance nature of China, it is unlikely that any arrangements will work unless they 'bend with the bamboo' in recognising core values: the principle of the organisation as a family unit, the entrenched sense of hierarchy in social relationships, complex obligations of loyalty and protection and a fatalistic mindset.

11.4 Comparative MD approaches

What emerges from a comparative study of national MD systems is that there is no general consensus on the best way of developing managers. MD is not a science with universal principles. What works in one place signally fails to work in another. The role of the manager is variously defined and each country has its own way embedded in its historical and cultural environment.

Of course, it is easy to overgeneralise about *cosmopolitanism* at a time of massive international change, but national assumptions about the nature of management and different patterns of historical development are still powerful in shaping cross-cultural variations in MD. However, continuing diversity does not, in itself, deny the concept of international convergence in making managers. It is quite possible to acknowledge the importance of national models yet argue that convergence could still happen in the long run. However, the form which an international style of development might take (e.g. it could be the ultimate hegemony of the Anglo-Saxon model of a new global eclecticism) are questions for the future. In current circumstances is it possible to see similarities of experience lacing through the differences? This is a personal reading, intended to provoke others to take issue and find their own interpretations.

- The MD systems of all countries recognise the importance of giving managers an *international perspective* even if different countries have various ways of making this a reality (e.g. Japanese interest in sending managers abroad and incentives for people to be world-class in their professional knowledge; American faith in internationalising the curriculum of the business school, etc.). Some countries, like France, seem to have further to go than others in becoming internationalist in their patterns of MD.

- There is a tendency for a *management career in all countries to require further or higher education.* Although this is less true in UK with its historical anti-intellectualism and amateur tradition of accidental learning, even here management is now on the way to becoming a graduate preserve. Everywhere *credentialism* in management as part of the criteria for selection and development in management is increasing. The jury is out on whether this will always be the case.

- In most countries the idea of the 'crown prince' development programme, in which an elite management group is selected at an early stage for long-term management progression, is giving way (except in France) to more *diversified talent spotting.* As organisations become flattened, more people will start as specialists and move into management later in their careers and development will increasingly involve the building of broad horizontal experience in a range of functions. Indeed, the concept of young graduates choosing a career in management may become a thing of the past. This seems to be a trend cross-cutting many national cultures.

- Increasingly, large organisations everywhere are forming *learning contracts or partnerships* with their management talent which combine personal responsibility for learning with corporate support for education and training. Larger corporations increasingly recognise that they must invest in the next generation of managers, but it is now a cross-cutting theme between cultures that individuals are increasingly investing in themselves.

- *All countries are searching for new ways to learn.* Japan champions the 'mentor role' and the shadowing of 'masters' of competency. The UK values 'action learning' and Germany the model of the 'apprentice'. Although these approaches operate on different principles, they all involve the development of professional and personal skills in supportive conditions within the organisation. In this respect there is a rough consensus between many countries, that although classroom teaching can help refine and deepen the understanding of management, the holistic, experiential skills are best learnt at first hand in the work environment.

- Finally, there seems to be a trend in all countries towards *harnessing MD as a vehicle for broader corporate strategy* and for evaluating it in business terms. Although decisions about committing MD resources still involve considerations of special pleading, sectional interests, fashions and the enculturation of the next generation of managers in the values of the top and so on, as they always did, increasingly the rigour of evaluation and the bottom line has become an imperative in organisations of all kinds and in all societies.

Case study: Management development institute in a small island state

This case study is a short report of the author's experience as Director of the Seychelles Institute of Management (SIM) in the late 1990s. It is offered as an example of the problems of building management capability in a developing country and the cultural issues involved.

The management culture of the Seychelles

The Seychelles are a group of tropical islands situated in the middle of the Indian Ocean. Historically, the Seychelles has suffered from problems of scale, resource deficiency, remoteness of location, an undiversified economy and the long shadow of colonial experience. Until the 1990s it was a one-party state. It also had a continuing pattern of centralised authority, state control of the economy, a slow growth rate and dependency on volatile industries such as fishing and tourism.

This was an authoritarian society which placed emphasis on top–down communication, limited transparency and debate. People expected leadership to come from the top. These societal values permeated into the management ethos within the organisation. Using Hofstede's dimensions, the prevailing spirit was that of *high power distance*. Obedience was given a higher value than creativity; management style tended to be directive. It was predominantly an administrative culture with the accent on procedures and operations rather than strategy; it was also task-oriented with little appreciation of HRM and behavioural sciences ideas in management. Used to 'doing' not 'thinking' and conscious of the prevailing ethos of compliance not debate, people tended to be measured in what they said in public, upward communication was poor and low-trust relations were common.

On the *collectivism/individualism* index, the Seychelles was a strong collectivist culture. Social networks were tight-knit, family roots went deep. A micro-state with a small population made it difficult for Seychellois managers to be strictly impartial in their management behaviour. The high density of kinship networks in this collectivist society created social obligations and patronage demands (some family clans had considerable political leverage) which the manager ignored at considerable personal cost.

On the *masculinity/femininity* scale, matriarchcal 'caring' values were well to the fore. Communal caring through the village and state paternalism including protectionist legislation at work and a blind eye to informal practice in the workplace, were entrenched. At the same time, management style could be tough and masculinist, very punishment and blame centred with very little recognition of psychological or development needs at work.

Finally, in terms of *uncertainty avoidance/ acceptance*, Seychellois managers appeared generally reluctant to take risks, were reactive and defensive. Conservatism dominated over innovation. Many managers were reluctant to take initiatives, to stand out or of being visible at higher levels. They were frightened of being perceived to have made mistakes because these were more likely to be punished than innovation rewarded. This mindset inevitably conditioned an approach to management which valued policy maintenance over policy development; the status quo, not change; conformity not initiative and avoidance of personal accountability.

Other tendencies in management culture included a low awareness or respect for entrepreneurial values (the privately owned small and medium business sector was still quite embryonic but growing) or strategic envisioning or development (organisational, team, individual). Many key management and technical positions were held by expatriates who brought their expertise (which they were supposed to pass on but often did not) and were probably more easily controlled by government elites than Seychellois equivalents. Seychellois managers tended to be young for the responsibility they commanded (a Permanent Secretary of a government ministry might be in her early 40s), who were usually technocrats with limited preparation for corporate roles.

The Seychelles Institute of Management Development

SIM is the only management development agency in the Seychelles, indeed in the Indian Ocean. When the author was unexpectedly appointed as director, it seemed obvious that the organisation had great potential to act as a vital resource for national development. In particular, it could provide a catalyst for building management capability and aligning management skills to the government's plans for a more internationally facing, market-oriented economy.

However, it soon became clear from the focus groups with stakeholders which were set up that SIM was not the vehicle, in its existing form, to build new management skills and attitudes. SIM lacked a coherent corporate philosophy and strategic plan. The college had long been operating as a civil service college running specific skills courses for middle managers and in relative ignorance of national development objectives.

SIM was diagnosed by informants as insular and reactive, giving little priority to assessing learning needs of management constituencies, marketing its courses or evaluating effectives. It was essentially a civil service and accountancy training college which provided very narrowly defined training for middle and lower level managers. Its courses were seen as very standardised, inflexible and concerned with technical skills rather than general management. There were few internationally accredited courses and course content was essentially public administration, with little attention to business disciplines, strategy or HRM. Although SIM had 'management development' in its title, this was not what it was delivering. Senior managers either looked overseas for their development or assumed they did not need further development. The private sector regarded the college as a creature of government and irrelevant to its needs.

Change management at SIM

The situation at SIM required change at all levels. The first step was to start a debate about the role of SIM in the future economy of the Seychelles. This involved discussions with a wide range of current and future stakeholders. This participative process led to the development of a strategic plan which defined SIM for the first time as an emergent business school offering competency-led development, externally validated professional courses and learning partnerships with sponsoring organisations. It also stressed our commitment to the development of small business managers which seemed to represent the future of the country.

A lot of internal changes were made to build the skills of the teaching staff, the professionalism of our processes and the quality of our product. Local courses were run to challenge existing management mindsets (e.g. enabling, not controlling; strategy as well as operational process, etc.) and give the next generation of managers the skills and knowledge to become more proactive. Counter-cultural values of 'participation', 'empowerment', 'business leadership', 'creativity and innovation' were heavily stressed in our course programmes and our development consultancy. Overtures to Western universities and international funding agencies led to a distance-learning MBA, ACCA-licensed training and an MAHRM, run in partnership with a leading British business school and targeted at the future leaders of the economy.

On paper much was achieved. SIM increasingly came to be seen as a vehicle for building vital management skills for all levels of management and across the sectors of business. Good linkages were formed with the private sector, leading to executive development programmes linked to the learning and development plans of various organisations. Conferences and seminars at the college with visiting international speakers created opportunities for debating alternative approaches to management to be considered.

However, there were limits to what SIM could achieve. Although many courses were resource-based, most were culturally bound. SIM's influence depended on change within wider spheres of management, government and the economy. Top management and political leaders stayed aloof from our debates over the future of the college and its place in the Seychelles economy. Although they did not oppose our changes, neither did they take ownership of them. This meant that our modernisation programme always lacked legitimation by the top. As a result, many of our initiatives, intended to be counter-cultural, had less of an impact on conservative management attitudes than we would have liked. Reframing 'management' from a mechanistic to an enabling process and redefining the manager as an 'innovator' and 'internal change consultant' and 'cultural leader' was a hard message to sell in such a resistant culture. Even if managers were sympathetic, they often lacked autonomy and faced real constraints of higher-level control, staffing and dysfunctional performance systems to experiment with new forms of behaviour.

There was also the issue of cross-cultural translation of ideas. Were we in danger of assuming that a model of management that worked in the West, especially Anglo-American society could be imported to the Seychelles? Although the faculty of largely expatriates at SIM was always careful about making the assumption that the West had all the answers and tried to adjust these models to local conditions, in retrospect more could have been done. For example, the internationally accredited Master's courses were largely purchased 'off the shelf' and although professionally run, more attention could have been given to adjusting the package to Seychelles. For example, 'participative management' and 'responsibility autonomy' values saturated the course programmes, which may have been inappropriate to a hierarchical society based on 'managed' forms of debate. Perhaps the 'rationalism' of the MBA programme and corporate techniques were really more disabling than helpful in the context of the Seychelles. Perhaps it was always unrealistic for SIM to believe that it could shift wider cultural values about managing, even if shifts in macro-economic strategy seemed to require this, and perhaps the debates should have been led by Seychellois themselves, not by foreigners seeking to act as catalysts.

The future of SIM, as with other management colleges in the developing world, lies in creating an open dialogue between international management trends and specific conditions so that models of management and development evolve naturally from a local consensus.

11.5 Conclusion

Despite many signs of cosmopolitanism and convergence within MD which transcend national and corporate boundaries, cross-cultural differences in how managers practise and how they are developed persist. This chapter considered some distinct national traditions of management, attempting to link development processes to tendencies in national culture. Although many of these distinctions are likely to remain, there are some consistent themes, such as increased management exposure to higher education; talent management replacing fast-track; self-development replacing planned, structured development and increasing emphasis on experiential learning, which seem to cut across cultures and may be helping to standardise MD worldwide. The chapter includes some examples of what can happen when models of management and development fail to mesh with the culture in which they are based.

Review questions

1. Are there signs that the similarities between national processes in developing managers will soon outweigh the differences? Critically discuss.

2. If you were an international MD adviser called in to a former Communist country to design an MD programme for senior managers, what issues would you want to consider?

3. An American training agency hoping to do business in Japan has decided to make a pitch at a trade fair in Japan. They have made a video which celebrates a visionary, charismatic style of leading. You take a look as an experienced 'Japan watcher'. What are you likely to say?

4. How could you help a provincial French *école de commerce* to become more international in its orientation? What resistances would you anticipate?

5. How would you react to the view that the MBA is a 'dinosaur'? As the world changes, can we expect the next wave of ideas about developing managers to come from places in India, China and Brazil, not from Harvard Business School?

Web links

For information on Hofstede's theories see:
http://geerthofstede.com

For research using Hofstede's categories in relation to the countries covered in this chapter see:
http://www.pittstate.edu/mgmict/culture.html

Recommendations for further reading

Those texts marked with an asterisk in the bibliography are recommended for further reading, especially the following:

Doyle, M. (2007) 'Management development', in Beardwell and Holden (2007) *HRM: A Contemporary Approach.* The Doyle chapter on MD is good in many ways, but particularly for clearly setting out the key elements of different national systems of management education and development.

Hickson, D. and Pugh, D. (1995) *Management Worldwide.* A good introduction to cross-cultural management with some references to differences in development, Amusing stories throughout.

Sparrow, P. and Hiltrop, J. (1994) *European HRM in Transition.* The chapter on comparative managing and MD for European countries is well written and helpful.

Bibliography

Beardwell, I. and Holden, L. (2001, 2004, 2007 editions) *HRM: A Contemporary Approach*, Ch. 9, Prentice Hall.

Berger, M. and Watts, P. (1994) 'Management development in Europe', in Mabey, C. and Iles, P. (1994) *Managing Learning*, Open University Press.

Berkley-Thomas, A. (2003) *Controversies in Management*, Ch. 9, Routledge.

Broughton, P. (2008) 'Harvard loses its lustre', *Prospect*, Sept.

*Doyle, M. (2007) 'Management development', in Beardwell, I. and Holden, L. (2007) *HRM: A Contemporary Approach*, Prentice Hall.

Fincham, R. and Rhodes, P. (2004) *Principles of Organisational Behaviour*, Oxford University Press.

Grey, C. and Antonacopoulou, E. (2004) *Essential Readings in Management Learning*, Sage.

*Handy, C., Gordon, C. et al. (1989) *Making Managers*, Pitman.

*Hickson, D. and Pugh, D. (1995, 2005 editions) *Management Worldwide*, Penguin.

Hofstede, G. (1994) *Cultures and Organisations: Software of the Mind*, Harper Collins.

*Hofstede, G. (2001) *Culture's Consequences*, Sage.

IEBM *International Encyclopaedia of Business and Management*; section on international management development and education.

Iles, P. (2000) 'International HRD', in Stewart, J. and McGoldrick, J. (2000) *HRD: Perspectives, Strategies and Practice*, Prentice Hall.

Kosteva, M. (2004) 'The modern crusade: the missionaries of management come to eastern Europe', in Grey and Antonacopoulou (2004).

Kreitner, R. (2002) *Organisational Behaviour*, Ch. 10, McGraw Hill.

*Kumar, R. (2004) 'Management education in a globalising world: the French experience', in Grey, C. and Antonacopoulou, E. (2004) *Management Learning*, Sage.

Laurent, A. (1983) 'The cultural diversity of Western concepts of management', *International Studies of Management and Organisation*, Vol. 13, No. 2.

*Mabey, C. and Iles, P. (1994) *Management Development in Europe*, Open University Press.

Mangham, I. and Silver, M. (1986) *Management Training: Content and Practice*, ESPC.

Mant, A. (1979) *The Rise and Fall of the British Manager*, Pan Business Books.

Nadeau, J. and Barlow, J. (2005) *Sixty Million Frenchmen Can't Be Wrong*, Robson Books.

*Reed, M. and Anthony, P. (1992) 'Professionalising management and managing professionalism: British management in the 1980s', *JMS*, 29(5), 1992.

Robbins, S. (1996) *Organisational Behaviour: Concepts, Controversies and Applications*, Prentice Hall.

Rollinson, D. (2002) *Organisational Behaviour and Analysis: An Integrated Approach*, Prentice Hall.

*Scarborough, J. (1998) *The Origins of Cultural Differences and Their Impact on Management*, Quorum Books.

Senior, B. (1997) *Organisational Change*, Prentice Hall.

Shackleton, V. (1995) *Business Leadership*, Ch. 12, Routledge.

*Sparrow, P. and Hiltrop, J. (1994) *European HRM in Transition*, Ch. 10, Prentice Hall.

Tayeb, M. (2003) *International Management: Theory and Practice*, Prentice Hall.

Thomson, A., Mabey, C. et al. (2001) *Changing Patterns of Management Development*, Blackwell.

*Trompenaars, F. (1993) *Riding the Waves of Change*, Economist Books.

Wiener, M. (1981) *English Culture and the Decline of the Industrial Spirit 1850–1980*, Penguin.

Witzel, M. (2002) 'Teaching shop floor principles to the executive suite', *Financial Times*, 13 Aug.

Woodall, J. (1994) 'The transfer of managerial knowledge to Eastern Europe', in Kirkbride, P. (1994) *HRM in Europe: Perspectives for the 1990s*, Routledge.

Woodall, J. and Winstanley, D. (1999) *Management Development: Strategy and Practice*, Ch. 12, Blackwell.

12 International management development

Learning outcomes

After reading the chapter you should be able to understand, analyse and explain:

- trends in the globalisation of business;
- modelling the stages of growth to transnationalism;
- the implications of transnationalism for management processes and management roles;
- categories of managers in the international organisation;
- the knowledge, skills and attitudes of the international manager;
- issues in developing international managers;
- techniques for developing international managers.

12.1 Introduction

The pace of globalisation and the depth of its penetration means that international business has expanded massively in recent times. As a consequence, many organisations, not just the transnational giants but also medium-sized companies, are concerned to develop their managers (or at least a select cadre of them) to operate in a new, more dynamic environment.

The internationalisation of production means far tighter interdependence between skills, knowledge and capital than ever before. So, take the manufacture of something like an office machine, say a printer or photocopier. This presumes an international organisation of some complexity and management of some sophistication. The elements which compose it – having an idea, designing the structure and process to translate that idea into a product which is then targeted to segmentalised markets – are the essential principles of *international management*. Bringing it all together – the design in Britain, the digitalised parts made in USA; the shell made in Japan; the inner parts machine-tooled in Asia, the assembly in Singapore – requires a management with an international outlook which is culturally sensitive, expert in collaboration and has the capacity for the larger thinking that can bring world-beating creativity out of chaos.

Managers are increasingly called on to manage geographically and culturally diverse businesses – joint ventures, mergers and acquisitions – and to balance the demands of global integration with local responsiveness. This chapter looks at the nature of the management skills involved in this and the tools which organisations use to develop managers who can work across frontiers to enable the planning, manufacturing and marketing which sophisticated products require.

12.2 The globalisation of business: modelling the process

International business has expanded massively since the Second World War. There are far more organisations doing business on a global basis than ever before. Typically, organisations with ambitions to trade internationally pass through a number of stages in their growth. At each stage the management needs of the organisation will be different and so will the processes for developing the vital cadre of managers who will run it. There are a number of typologies which try to represent the transition of a domestic company into a global player. Here the elements of four well-known typologies are fused into a composite model synthesising insights from Barney and Griffin (1992), Bartlett and Ghoshal (1991), Adler and Ghadar (1990) and Perlmutter (1969).

In the model below we consider the life stages of an international organisation and the management processes associated with each stage of the organisation's development.

The national or domestic stage. Although the organisation may be large, its dominant focus is the home market. Exports are largely through local distributors or local operations set up from the parent company.

At this stage, control is centralised and exercised from the parent company in its home base. Perlmutter calls this the *ethnocentric* mindset.

The international stage. Here, although the organisation continues to derive most of its revenue from a single country, it is taking major steps to become an international organisation. At this point some modest overseas operations may be established – these may be foreign agents, small operating subsidiaries or licensing arrangements.

At this stage the emphasis will be on transferring technology from the centre to overseas production sites. Products will be standardised for all markets and the foreign operations will be seen mainly as delivery platforms for the home base to reach into global markets. The organisational form most associated with this stage of growth is that of the *centralised hub*, that is, control through an international cadre of expatriates and top managers responsible for integrating subsidiaries into a total organisation with global reach.

Adler and Bartholomew (1992) call this the *ethnographic* stage. When the international company is trying to establish new business processes in another country, most key management positions will be filled by parent country nationals (PCNs), that is, expatriates sent out from HO to the host country. The parent company assumes that its systems represent best practice and are imposed from above.

Although control is centralised in the home base and downwardly directive, it is a system which allows the smooth transfer of technology, techniques and systems. The expatriate managers act as a source of expertise. They pass on skills and knowledge to locally recruited employees and act as reliable change agents during the early phases of internationalisation.

The multinational stage. Here the firm is becoming increasingly dispersed with diverse markets and subsidiaries. Typically this is the stage at which subsidiaries are given a higher degree of operating autonomy (e.g. the authority to vary the design of company goods and develop their own marketing strategy) to meet the needs of local markets. This is the model of the conglomerate (e.g. ITT, Unilever, etc.).

At this stage, international organisations can be regarded as collections of divisionalised operating units serving different national and regional markets. The centre is still powerful, setting standards and processes, but overseas subsidiaries are given margins of freedom to create slightly modified products and services and each host country subsidiary has its own sales approach. This is the *decentralised federation* model.

At this stage of development (often called the *polycentric stage* by Adler and Batholomew (1992) and Perlmutter (1969), some diversity in management will be allowed. Host country nationals (HCNs) are recruited to manage the subsidiary in their own country. Expatriates may still be in evidence as advisers, troubleshooters and consultants, but authority is increasingly devolved to qualified and experienced local staff who have a measure of independence in how they interpret their role.

HO will want to keep a balance between local sensitivity and global vision. Developing the skills of HCNs will be seen as a progressive development in terms of releasing local commitment, but controls will be needed to ensure that corporate goals are not displaced by local projects.

The global stage. At this point the firm is becoming truly worldwide in its focus. It is not tied to any single nation. Goods are branded but marketed in different ways in different markets. The company operates effectively as a set of independent firms coordinated through sophisticated management systems and key performance indicators laid down by the centre.

This is the situation of many of the giant companies (IBM, GE, Phillips, etc.). They are *coordinated federations* of businesses 'globally integrated by strategy and structure'. There is a loose–tight system in which the centre retains tight control of core performance issues but discretion is granted on other issues to allow local flexibility and empowerment.

This is the point (also called the *geo-centric stage* by Adler and Bartholomew (1992) and Perlmutter (1969) at which a cadre of top managers for each of the businesses is developed from country of origin, host country and third country staff (TCNs). No longer are positions reserved for managers from particular origins, good people from all parts of the worldwide organisation are recruited into a cadre of international executives responsible for integrating a sprawling and complex global organisation.

The transnational stage. Few organisations have made the transition to this stage. Here the corporation develops strategic capabilities to compete globally while remaining closely in touch with local markets. It implies an *integrated network* of units. Radical decentralisation allows subsidiaries to make adaptations to their local markets, yet the flexible model of organisation also encourages networking with all parts of the far-flung organisation so that it can benefit from the knowledge of each.

Work is organised in a spider's web of contracts, alliances, corporate ventures and cross-boundary project teams. Rapid knowledge transfer through intranets and interlinked networks mean that local innovation can be picked up and disseminated internationally. All the business units are dependent on each other for products, resources and technology, and functions such as R/D and marketing are shared internationally.

The role of the centre here is largely that of coordinator of strategic objectives, policies and the flow of information to and between the separate units. It also acts as a sort of switchboard linking together units with complementary skills where opportunities for synergy may be considerable.

This is the stage (often called the *pan-centric stage*) where a truly global view is taken of products and markets. The company operates worldwide in a variety of regions. All distinctions between local and expatriate managers have become obsolete because managers from all parts of the company and all parts of the world need to be able to collaborate effectively. Cultural diversity through boundary-spanning teams have become the normal way of conducting business and most managers perform an international role, acting as a broker linking parts to the whole.

Pause for thought

Time to go truly global?

Sometimes organisations need to restructure and reorient themselves to become truly global in their scope. Take Centro, a worldwide telecommunications company based in Belgium. It has expanded incrementally over 25 years by mergers and acquisitions as well as export-led growth.

It has now reached a critical point in its development. It has a worldwide constellation of operations, but there are problems.

- The HO makes most policy decisions and there is little discussion with the foreign operating units on strategy.
- Most products are still developed at HO in Brussels.
- The flow of technical assistance and support is only one way, from the centre outwards.
- Although local nationals largely run the subsidiaries, board decisions at local and international levels are largely made by Belgian managers.
- Although the local units have some operational freedom, a lot is standardised. There is also the problem that the system seems sluggish in sharing good ideas and good practice.

Although the company continues to grow and remain competitive, there have been problems of declining sales; new products seem to be slower to market than in competitor companies; there are claims of long bureaucratic chains and evidence of low morale among local managers.

Questions

Do you think this company needs to change its structure and redefine the roles of its managers? If you were a consultant, what would you suggest?

12.3 Managers and transnationals

Much of the literature suggests that pancentric transnationals are the aspirational model of many global companies. If this is so, what does it mean for the role and behaviour of the managers within them?

Organisations such as Shell, ABB and Ericsson are moving beyond hierarchy and the notion that national subsidiaries are spokes arranged around the hub of the wheel to networked systems in which cross-flows between subsidiaries are encouraged. This is based on the growing belief that national subsidiaries have legitimate relations with subsidiaries in other countries based on understanding customer needs and providing flexible solutions, for example, trading partnerships, joint ventures, strategic alliances and multiple project groups (Barney and Griffin 1992).

As the corporation becomes more polycentric, the HO role becomes less that of instructing and more that of facilitating and evaluating, ensuring that the parts are geared together in a common direction and all are aware of the innovation which emerges. Indeed, some organisations, like Shell, are dispensing with central offices completely. In the place of a controlling centre, teams of senior managers from local subsidiaries and functional departments coordinate projects which add value to the organisation as a whole. Top management teams emerge which are no longer formed and chosen by the top but reflect and represent the diversity of businesses, cultures and expertise within the entire corporation (Kanter 1989).

In the 'newspeak' of these global modernisers, 'hierarchies' are giving way to 'heterarchies' (Barham and Oates 1991). Flatter corporate structures are emerging coordinated, not by rules and systems but multiple points of expertise. Heterarchies involve the radical disaggregation of traditional HQ functions to dispersed subsidiaries which elect to undertake strategic global roles for the whole company where they have claims of expertise and talent. So, subsidiaries begin to specialise in areas where they have an advantage and share learning, knowledge and ideas. Integration is provided by multidisciplinary task forces – genuinely cross-cultural, pluralistic and independent of the 'power embrace' of the centre – and by shared strategies and cultural values. However, the main cement is learning and communication (Ohmae 1990).

At its fullest development, heterarchy is presented as an infinitely flexible form of organisation which encourages local subsidiaries to rise above their parochialism, generate knowledge and share it across boundaries. Each subsidiary has a position in a value chain. Through the quality of its ideas pooled with others, subsidiaries rise or fall in credibility. Complex divisions of labour emerge as countries specialise in what they do best and new creative synergies arise through the collision of cultural differences (e.g. American individualism and Japanese teamworking; the design skills of the Italian team are combined with the marketing knowledge of the Germans, etc.). Some centres of excellence arise as fertile sources of innovation, serving as nodal points in the dissemination of good practice; other subsidiaries take the role of leaders in product development for a global brand (Gooderham and Nordhaug 2003).

Binding the creativity together is a sophisticated overlay of knowledge management circuitry. Electronic networks coordinate diverse 'communities of practice' (Brown and Duguid 1991) and link scattered bases of knowledge and expertise. New interdependencies, arising from technological systems, new patterns of working and institutional processes lacing across the system create new opportunities for collaboration. Education and training, management project groups, transfers of staff and reciprocal visits provide the basis for building common understandings, shared knowledge and mutual trust. From such focused social interaction informal learning networks build up which provide pathways along which ideas for innovation flow.

Case study: 'Anglo-Dutch': in the vanguard of the transnational company

Anglo-Dutch (name changed) is a household name for consumer white goods. It used to be a typically globalised organisation managing dispersed interests and constituent businesses through a traditional hierarchical structure. The company was a 'collection of independent villages'. However, in recent times A-D has moved towards a more transnational model based on interactive global networks.

So, businesses are now clustered into small nationally based production units which have global responsibility for designated products. For example, the British A-D plant is responsible for its own national production but also for freezer design, development and production internationally. Multidisciplinary task forces, responsible for product design and development, draw on the contributions of national teams from various countries so as to maximise the skills of each. The aim is to change attitudes – from being a good British, Dutch or French manager of refrigerators to being a brand manager of A-D products marketed globally.

In the new age of networked functions, every part collaborates, shares information and decisions.

The thinking of the whole, of corporate strategy, is embodied in the values and behaviour of every part (the 'hologram' organisation). This is the A-D ideal. Each national subsidiary can retain its individuality because it knows its place in the larger commercial order and links its actions to those of others through shared norms and values.

In a multi-centred system such as this, controls from the centre are no longer needed. Central authority can be pushed down and the HO becomes a resource for consultancy and coordination. This is largely what has happened at A-D. The company does not hold together through a structure but through an organising logic – of international teams promoting mutual understanding; of intensive virtual communication disseminating ideas and innovations; of senior managers travelling the globe, reinforcing trust through face-to-face interactions, building synergy and involving people in common purpose (see also Ohmae 1990).

This is the very antithesis of bureaucracy and implies a new role and skills for the manager.

Of course, it is easy to get carried away by a grand narrative of futurology around the transnational. The model of a turbocharged, polycentic, multicultural, networked super-organisation is not much in evidence in the real world. Equally, the implicit idea of a global corporate village in which a new elite of super-managers act as the unifying force for shared good practice in business is more dream than reality. It is also easy to exaggerate the novelty and rate of change (Victorian Britain probably saw an even faster rate of innovation) implied by ICT, electronic networks and the virtual organisation.

The truth is that most multinationals have not shed their skin to become transnationals. More typically, multinationals use the rhetoric of synergy and flexibility while remaining centralised and directive. While some international managers are building networks of knowledge management, many are concerned to use the new technology for ever more precise systems of control.

From the perspective of our concerns in this book, this raises the issue of whether developments in international business have fundamentally changed management process, the skills managers need to be global players and how to develop them.

12.4 What makes an international manager?

It is clear that some qualities are universally required for any manager with international responsibilities. Other qualities will be role-specific and a final class of competencies will reflect the international culture of the employing organisation.

A number of studies over the past twenty years have attempted to define the main attributes of the successful international manager (e.g. Adler and Bartholomew 1992; Barham 1989; Barham and Oates 1991; Wills and Barham 1994). What emerges most clearly from these various surveys is the consistency of their findings. There are some attributes of international management (over and above being an effective manager in a domestic setting) which seem universally desirable. There is also a high degree of consensus that the qualities most needed and most scarce in the labour market are soft skills rather than the professional skills of functional management. So what might these qualities be?

Global mindset. An essential quality, universally valued, is the ability to 'think global and act local'. Although a cliché nowadays, this epithet still captures something of the essence of being an international manager. Having a 'global mindset' means being able to rise above ethnocentrism and the interests, plans and purposes of the country in which the manager is based. It means being able to see the interconnections between the parts of a business within a competitive world market. It means understanding the world standards against which the organisation has to successfully compete. It also involves being able to balance the specific and the general and make choices for the good of the whole. For example, a commitment to a global culture may require the manager of a subsidiary to forego the advantage of new investment or accept retrenchment locally because it is the best decision for the corporation as a whole. The corporate statesmanship, vision and gestalt understanding involved here is considerable and the possession of these qualities is an important distinguishing factor among those aspiring to become an international manager (Barham and Oates 1991).

Strategic awareness. This involves the ability to comprehend the whole situation, to take a long-term view of how things develop and be able to understand the linkage between specific action and larger behaviour, between operational detail and the big picture. It means focusing on what is essential by using bifocal vision: alternating your perspective from one context to another, shifting attention from foreground to background and back again as the key dimensions of a problem emerge in their entirety.

Intellectual and analytical ability. The above implies a good level of analytical ability, that is, keeping ends in sight while being engaged in means; being able to accept ambiguity and paradox as part of the environment of decision-making and not to strive for false rationality; being able to see connections and patterns in the swirl of events; being able to keep conflicting perspectives in mind while still acting coherently and with purpose; searching for tailor-made approaches to problems, not relying on standardised solutions; having maturity of understanding and judgement.

Personal qualities. These involve the skills of personal effectiveness, both cognitive and affective, that is, self-awareness and self-knowledge; personal maturity; having emotional intelligence, psychological toughness and resilience to stress; having self-esteem and self-confidence.

People orientation and skills. These are the people and political skills of management, for example, team building and leading skills; being adaptive to people and experiences; social empathy; active listening; being able to enter into others' minds and understand their perspectives; building networks of talent and informal communication networks (Bartlett and Ghoshal 1992).

The skills of a lifelong learner. This means having curiosity to learn – to grasp opportunities for personal development and experiential learning. It also involves creative thinking, the search for creative solutions and helping to build learning networks by putting people together who may spark new synergies.

Technical knowledge and skills. While many of the 'soft factors' are crucial, managers cannot operate with credibility at the international level without solid grasp of the fundamentals of business and technical skills. These would include knowledge of technology, knowledge of strategic and financial instruments, knowledge of competitive markets, knowledge of global business trends (Barham and Oates 1991).

Inter-cultural competency. Above all else, international managers need qualities of cultural sensitivity, respect for cultural difference, linguistic skills (including fluency in foreign languages) and cultural adaptability. Effective international managers rise above ethnocentricity, avoid judging by the absolute standards and operate on the basis of informed understanding rather than stereotypes. This often requires them to have a deep understanding of their own cultural roots as well as the culture in which they operate.

These characteristics of insight, tolerance and breadth of outlook are essential for many of the roles which international managers have to perform (see Adler and Bartholomew 1992). As *champions of corporate strategy*, international managers are responsible for building a strong shared culture which embraces national subsidiaries without suffocating them; they are also responsible for educating people at the centre about local conditions and brokering appropriate adjustments.

As *cross-border coaches and coordinators*, international managers act as enablers of local teams, building skills and developing plans which mesh with the corporate vision. As *inter-cultural mediators* international managers act as OD consultants and change agents, helping local people manage change, moderate in conflict situations and build diverse multicultural teams in which creative difference is a potential strength. Finally as *knowledge facilitators*, international managers act to integrate diffuse knowledge and build common understandings. This often means acting as 'intellectual brokers' translating tacit and socially embedded knowledge in terms which make sense in terms of the meanings of other communities (Barnham and Oates 1991; Bartlett and Ghoshal 1992).

While many of the qualities required by the international manager are also required of the domestic manager (see Chapter 2), it is apparent that global management (especially in organisations which are transmuting into transnationals) is of a far higher order of complexity, subtlety and skill. The role requires combinations of qualities (e.g. great sensitivity and respect for others mediated by high self-confidence and self-esteem) which are rare. It requires great reserves of energy, intellectual and personal maturity, flexibility, sophistication, imagination and vision as well as robustness and determination, which are not easily found. (Barham and Wills 1992). What role can MD play in developing these attributes?

> **Pause for thought**
>
> ### Do you have the 'right stuff'?
>
> Opportunities for graduates to work abroad were once limited. With more global companies having satellite offices around the world, opportunities have increased. Graduates sent to work overseas fall into three categories:
>
> 1. those sent to develop skills which working abroad will help to acquire;
> 2. those sent because their expertise will allow them to make a real contribution;
> 3. those who are sent because they have been selected for leadership, and overseas experience is part of the grooming and developing process.
>
> It is this last category which has grown most in importance. At any one time KPMG will have 500 of its employees working abroad, many in their 20s. Here is the view of a senior manager of the company:
>
>> You won't make partner in the firm without doing a number of overseas postings. You have to understand the nature of the international market and be where the clients are. That requires a lot of 'stand alone' responsibility.
>
> A career in international management and working abroad are among the most popular aspirations of graduates.
>
> *Are you one of this group? If so, do you have a realistic view of the demands of the job?*
>
> *Do you think you have the background and potential to be a good candidate?*
>
> *What do you think you could do to improve your chances of selection?* (e.g. international travel; working abroad; demonstrated capacity with languages; having general management experience; showing evidence of independent working and leadership experience).
>
> However, even if you are successful in finding one of these international jobs, do look at the fine print of the employment contract and retain a healthy scepticism about the company propaganda. You may find yourself in the back office in Slough for a number of years using your French on the phone talking to your counterpart in Lyons before you are considered for any international project work.

12.5 Who are the international managers?

This question is important because even large organisations which are committed to internationalism may require only a proportion of their managers to be truly internationalist in outlook and behaviour. A crucial issue for large companies is to decide which groups of managers should be exposed to international experience and expected to be part of the 'global mind' of the organisation. Should only an elite of high potential corporate managers be so exposed or should the ordinary managers, the bedrock of the organisation, also be given global responsibilities? Certainly if the company is really concerned to develop a cosmopolitan spirit and global perspective which permeates through its work, then it makes sense to build capability throughout the company and make this part of a clearly formulated HRD strategy. At the same time, broad involvement may dilute the resources available for development and fail to build the degree of sophistication necessary for those who are the key players in global management.

Within the typical large-scale international organisation there will be various categories of managers differently oriented to internationalism with different development needs. Bartlett and Ghoshal (1992) in a classic article on strategies of globalisation mentions five types of managers.

1. Managers managing across boundaries within the whole geographical area covered by the business. These are the real 'global brains' of the organisation, the global generalists or *corporate managers* involved in complex negotiating across frontiers, monitoring and leading.
2. Managers based abroad and operating corporately within the context of several countries. These are the *business managers* heading up product divisions. They act as strategists for an international product line; coordinate the company's activities for competitiveness and efficiency on a global scale.
3. Managers mainly operating within their own country but with significant interaction with foreign units and other markets. Typically, this is the *country manager* leading a subsidiary, ensuring its efficiency within the global matrix and the effective implementation of global strategy in the local setting.
4. Managers based in one location, often HO, with an advisory relationship with other units. This is typically the position of the *functional manager* or specialist, transferring knowledge, scanning for expertise, identifying good ideas and generalising good practice and systems around the world. Although more technician than manager, these functionaries need as much sensitivity to strategy and culture as any of the previous categories.
5. Finally, the managers who need to be competent in a domestic market. However, even these *locals* need an appreciation of the company's global strategy.

From this typology it follows that overseas tours of duty and managing multicultural projects are only one form of international management. Although the truly 'transnational' corporate managers concerned with cross-cultural synergy and integration may only be a small elite in any corporation, many other managers with more incidental overseas contact still need to have cultural sensitivity and a mindset which sees the organisation's activities within a global context.

12.6 Developing the international manager

MD has become increasingly central to the corporate strategy of large organisations. It is no longer defined as just the development of individual skills and attitudes but also includes building group competence, learning across boundaries and shaping an international culture of continuous inquiry and improvement.

What follows is a critical consideration of the main issues facing those responsible for international management development.

12.6.1 Strategic issues

Barnham and Oates (1991) show how organisations vary greatly in how they organise their MD activities. For example, some organisations try to raise the general level of international awareness among all levels of management. Others focus resources on developing those who are seen as the next generation of high-flyers, to be prepared for their demanding international roles.

Organisations vary in the degree to which MD is defined as a strategic function. Where the organisation is genuinely committed to organisational learning, there is a tendency to take a large view of MD as linked to corporate strategy and key drivers such as succession planning and the career-planning system. For example, at some of the transnationals there is a gradual process of internationalising managers by systematically exposing them to foreign experience at key points in their careers and developing explicit criteria for selection to higher management based on successful foreign appointments. So, in organisations of this kind selection for an international appointment would be made on the basis of 'suitability for development' quite as much as the demands of the task to be done. Promotion to a larger job would mean demonstrating the ability to cope in stand-alone foreign postings of increasing demand and complexity. In very planned and structured career systems of this kind, appointments are likely to be made by a corporate development committee which compares jobs on a system of weighted responsibility and attempts to match people to positions with a built-in stretch element for development in an international environment.

As this suggests, a strategic approach to MD often involves quite centralised development structures. Unilever, for example, has long believed in taking a worldwide view of its management resources, assessing talent and planning their careers to gain broad experience from an early stage. Top management is closely involved with the MD process, which is explicitly used to build a culture of cosmopolitanism. International experience is incorporated into planned careers based on regular assessment and dialogue about succession. The usual pattern is a series of lateral moves to foreign locations, all monitored by HRD, before elevation to corporate responsibility (Barham and Oates 1991).

However, this is not the only multinational model of MD (and it is interesting that Unilever is changing its MD system to introduce more flexibility and self-management of careers by individuals (see Reitsma 2001)). Some large companies have adopted a decentralised approach. The responsibility for the early development of managers is left to the subsidiaries on the basis that local people are better placed to assess development needs. The centre only becomes involved in career development and MD placements when managers rise in the hierarchy and take on more senior jobs. The form which any organisation's international MD system takes will be a reflection of many variables, not least top management's interest in MD, the extent to which developing an international ethos is seen as valuable for the organisation as a whole rather than just a corporate elite and how the debate about whether subsidiaries should be run by local or expatriate managers is resolved locally. A professionalised cadre of managers with an international remit is likely to shape a different pattern of MD to an organisation which believes in building cosmopolitanism from the bottom up.

12.6.2 Recruitment and development

Because of the difficulty in recruiting managers with international experience and skills in global markets, many multinationals are now trying to develop their own managers.

Increasingly the tendency is to recruit for an 'international career' which attracts high-quality graduate applicants and select those with international credentials, for example, with language skills, experience of living abroad; who come from cross-cultural families and where there is evidence of cultural sensitivity. Companies are looking for breadth of outlook, intellectual ability, emotional maturity, early signs of being able to think and act on a global stage. Often they are then recruited to the worldwide company, no matter what their national background, and can be deployed anywhere within its sphere of operations (Gooderham and Nordhaug 2003).

Selection of an international cadre of managers usually involves bringing trainees on to a management training programme which will be the prelude to systematic planning throughout their careers. The first phase usually consists of formal training at a corporate development centre or retreat. This is about orientation, but also helping future senior managers build a peer group through which they are socialised into organisational values and linked into a network of cultural support, information and contacts which will help them in future management positions. Later, this cadre of high-potential managers will be sent on international assignments where their potential can be assessed and they can build self-knowledge to make reasoned choices about areas of specialisation.

The entrance programme at McKinsey's

McKinsey's selects future international consultants who are smart and have good analytical skills, but it also looks for human qualities of character, for people who have well-rounded interests and are good team players who have gone out and achieved something. They look for social skills and the ability to communicate to people who may be twice their age and far less qualified.

The two-week introductory course introduces recruits to the McKinsey analytical approach, but it is also about helping them to have empathy and cultural sensitivity so that they can operate internationally. The course is concerned to socialise them into the norms of the company culture, imbuing them with a sense of *esprit de corps* and giving them a network of professional support for the future. While some might see this as brainwashing, others who have been through it look back on the experience as giving them a sense of belonging to the corporate culture and building their confidence for international work at an early age.

Source: *Masters of the Universe*, documentary series (1999), Channel 4

These elite programmes can be effective in giving candidates early experience of working abroad, interpersonal and cross-cultural learning and MBA-style formal management development. Bringing together management trainees periodically helps to build a common culture of shared values which reinforce confidence in stand-alone assignments in far-flung places. These programmes help top management develop a pool of internationally experienced managers capable of assuming the highest level jobs when they become available.

This is the chosen model of the blue-chip companies, especially the banks and international businesses. Good selection, systematic career development, varied experience, appraisal and recommendation should ensure a good flow of skilled and experienced people with a background of achievement in two or three foreign cultures before taking on board positions. The downside of this 'crown prince' approach to international MD is that it smacks of elitism which may provoke resentment as well as restricting the available talent pool (Rothwell 1992).

12.6.3 Corporate education and the international manager

Most organisations concerned to develop the international perspective in their managers blend on-the-job development with periods of training and development at corporate management training centres. Barham and Oates (1991) give useful examples of different patterns of formal MD. For example, Unilever runs formal courses focused on the needs of managers at various stages in their careers. At each stage the international content of the course is increased with case studies in global business and multicultural skills-learning involving a range of nationalities. By the time a manager reaches the top s/he will have attended half a dozen international development courses and mixed with colleagues from all round the world. This progressive introduction to global issues is seen as preferable to intensive special courses in international management at the threshold of entry to higher management.

Often organisations have complex sequences of courses linked to stages of managerial careers. For example, GE has courses for newly recruited graduates; for functional managers making the transition to team leader; for experienced managers to help them develop leadership skills; for higher managers developing advanced strategic skills and, finally, courses for executives in global leadership of complex, networked, multinational organisations (Barham and Wills 1992).

Approaches to formal development vary widely. However, most organisations are sensible to the importance of building cross-cultural awareness and creative synergy from an early stage, and training-centre faculty and course participants are chosen for their diversity. Most companies also realise the importance of creating a climate of critical inquiry which goes beyond standardised teaching. They try to build a climate in which people can learn from each other and test out business skills in real-world situations. This is far more involving than simulations, case studies and scenarios. So, many companies bring in leading-edge management thinkers or 'movers and shakers' of the business world to encourage discussion and debate. Others enlist the help of top management of the company to act as facilitators of thinking and interaction.

Usually there is an *experiential* element. This might be an ALS, perhaps involving some consulting through immersion in a foreign culture. It could mean data collecting and reporting on a real issue in the business. Sometimes, as at GE, an element of competition is introduced so that teams are set up for the same project to report and defend their recommendations in debate before a panel of top management.

Sometimes internal corporate management development is interlinked with external business school involvement. Some companies believe that learning partnerships with business schools offer a broader, external perspective. Involving a business school allows high-flyers exposure to the latest ideas in international management, helps cross-fertilisation of ideas between participants and encourages managers to think more strategically.

In recent years business schools have been under attack for their lack of imagination and lack of experiential process. However, some, like the MBA at Ashbridge and the London Business School Consortium Programme have developed programmes as joint ventures with organisations which are highly regarded as preparing leaders for global management. These often involve cross-country teams of managers learning about handling complexity through project work, usually at arms length from the usual base of operations. The focus is on developing skills of diagnosis, analysis and reporting while engaging creatively with colleagues whose world-views are diverse and the opportunities for cross-cultural misunderstanding are considerable. The usual pattern is for team and project work to be interlinked with learning group and residential input to conceptually contextualise learning. However, in the most imaginative programmes there might be Outward Bound elements for team building, cultural diversity exercises, insights into comparative management thinking and the development of sophisticated process skills which help the trainee to connect global thinking, strategy and action. The involvement of a recognised academic centre also ensures that trainees acquire internationally recognised credentials as well as a thorough grounding in the dynamics of international business (Syrett and Lammiman 1999).

Case study: A corporate management development centre for an international elite

Every year hundreds of GE managers are sent to the John F. Welch Leadership Centre in Crotonville, New York, a bucolic town nestled in the Hudson River Valley.

The participants come from all the foreign subsidiaries within the GE empire; they read case studies, do experiential exercises, take classes and pull 'all nighters' on real-life business problems, putting together recommendations for senior management.

The Leadership Centre, which opened in 1956 as part of an initiative to train its managers better, offers various courses ranging from a few days to several weeks.

This is where managers tackle the specific, nitty-gritty issues that GE faces in its international businesses – how to improve a supply chain in its jet engine division and how to market a product for the plastics unit as well as more general leadership skills, *in the company of peers around the globe.*

Anne Alzapiedi has taken a number of courses at the centre during her eight-year career with GE. She says that the courses help her 'feel connected to the company'.

> When I come here, it's a big deal because I feel the company is investing in me. I get to meet people from all over the world and exposure to business leaders I wouldn't ordinarily get to see.

The sessions are intensive and hard work, but the emphasis is also on networking with others, creating synergies and having fun.

The centre's in-house staff facilitate most of the learning, but there are often lectures by Harvard and Wharton College professors and top executives of GE are strongly encouraged to stop by. This is not just education, managers are looking for talent. Does someone have a skill or a brilliant idea which the organisation should be using?

The GE Leadership Centre also offers tailored courses to its customers – free of charge. Typically, a company's senior management team arrives at Crotonville with a particular project or issue they'd like to consider. Through discussions, workshops and other exercises, Crotonville facilitators help teams work through their problems. This is good marketing and PR but it is also an excellent demonstration of Learning Organisation principles in action:

> We help customers to come up with their own solutions, but we also learn from them. There are instances when we are scribbling as fast as the customers are talking.

This hints at Crotonville's other aspiration: to become a 'strategy' or 'synergy' centre. By acting as a synthesiser of ideas, linking people across boundaries; building shared interests in the transnational net; putting people in search of solutions with people who may have the skills for solutions, Crotonville can act as a catalyst for new systems of collaborative learning. Of course, there is a long way to go, but by degrees Crotonville might become a hub of global learning for the organisation as a whole.

Questions

What are your thoughts and feelings about Crotonville as a centre for international MD? What do you think of Crotonville's ambitious mission to stimulate organisational learning?

Source: Adapted from GE's corporate boot camp cum talent spotting venue, *Financial Times*, 20/03/2006 (Knight, R.).

12.6.4 International assignments and expatriates

International assignments are an important way of broadening cross-cultural awareness and developing the skills needed by higher management in the worldwide marketplace. However, overseas assignments can take various forms.

At one end is the single-shot, short investigative visit or consultancy placement. The manager may be involved in some data collecting in a foreign setting, giving advice to an overseas operation, doing a tour of duty with an international task force or investigating problems which cross international boundaries, mentoring or training up local talent. It could involve local managers visiting HO to become sensitised to global strategic issues or making the centre more aware of issues at the periphery. It might include visiting world-class organisations to identify benchmarks of excellence which can be fed back to help organisational development at home. In all these cases, the international posting contains an inherent development opportunity which may offer benefits which go beyond the demands of the task. Travel, exposure to foreign cultures and the shock of the new in collision with alternative values and perspectives can help people grow as managers and assist the development of a 'global mindset' within the transnational (Barham and Oates 1991).

However, most enculturation and learning is likely to happen through longer-term attachments when the manager transferred has a real opportunity to become deeply involved in the host community. This may be an ad hoc posting when the organisation decides to post an expert to tackle an intractable local problem and transfer expertise to host country managers or it may be part of a rotational programme to build international awareness in its cadres of international managers. For example, many large organisations have exchange programmes and foreign placements in stretch assignments as part of programmed development. These may involve expatriating HCNs to worldwide foreign offices or HO to develop their breadth of experience and international grasp and/or sending HO managers for a tour of duty in one or more subsidiaries to build appreciation of local expectations and needs. Japanese companies, which rely heavily on expatriates to run their extended operations, often have sophisticated rotational programmes involving assessment-based 'job swaps' and foreign postings graded in terms of complexity and challenge to develop the capabilities of managers at different stages in their career.

The trend is for international companies to make increasing use of international assignments for all levels of management. There is also a tendency towards specialist assignments to share skills rather than general management responsibilities with a geographical remit. Foreign postings also tend to come earlier in the manager's career than ever before, to give young managers a taste of international management and develop cultural sensitivity and management resilience. Assignments are also used for testing the capabilities of a high-flyer before appointment to a key position at home. They can be used for older executives who may be 'plateaued' but still have much experience to contribute. In many cases international assignments are melded with other forms of career and management development (Handy and Barham 1990; Mabey and Iles 1994).

However, while the use of international assignments is increasing, the employment of professional expatriates who make their careers in a succession of foreign postings is on the wane. Traditionally, expatriates were the peripatetic 'officer corps' of an international business. They were the backbone of the organisation. Expert and experienced, they could be relied on to maintain HO control at the periphery, implement corporate strategies, diffuse a common corporate culture, transfer know-how, put out 'forest fires' and build local skills. However, in recent years professional expatriates have been used less frequently, mainly in turnaround situations where there are severe issues of underperformance or in 'hard to fill' positions where an extensive input of technical consultancy is needed (Woodall and Winstanley 1999).

The reasons for the declining popularity of the career expatriate are not hard to find. Expatriate contracts are expensive when all the supplements of travel, accommodation, schooling for children and allowances are added in. Developing nations often resent what they see as a continuing neocolonial relationship in which outposted managers are perceived locally more as overseers than experts – even 'de facto' agents of HO direction, Western culture and Western management techniques. It is also claimed that the ethnocentricity inherent in the expatriate model reinforces hierarchical relations between the centre and periphery, inhibits the assimilation of the expert to the local setting and checks local empowerment. It also masks the reality that knowledge transfer is not usually just a one-way process and the expatriate learns from the locals. Certainly an expatriate class usually acts as a glass ceiling to the promotion of HCN managers (especially in Japanese companies) which stimulates resentment and creates a barrier to building the skills and independence of thinking which managers will need in the decentred transnationals of tomorrow (Woodall and Winstanley 1999; Gooderham and Nordhaug 2003).

In recent times the advantages of building internationalism by developing local talent has been reckoned to outweigh the risks of creating parochial blocks (powerful local barons) to a globalised, 'boundaryless' organisation. The loss of the old expatriate class may also be counted as progressive if it encourages the centre to focus on shared values and learning as the social cement of the organisation and gives organisational space for local people to exercise real management responsibilities. The evolution of the organisation on these lines would also mean that MD resources become focused on HCNs who will be linchpins in the networks of reciprocal learning exchanges crucial to successful large organisations in the future, rather than on the expatriates who may represent a fast-vanishing organisational model.

However, whether the foreign assignment is a professional expatriate contract, a rotational attachment for an 'ad hoc' test for a rising new star, foreign postings are fraught with problems and need to be organised with care. Large companies keep the failure rate of their foreign placements secret, but the recall rate of US expatriates was probably about 30–40 per cent in the 1980s (Barham and Oates 1991) with all the costs to the organisation and the individual which this entails.

12.6.5 Selection for foreign assignment

Good *selection* greatly reduces the odds against failure. A key factor is the motivation of staff. Does the manager really believe that this is an opportunity for personal development which will enhance his/her career? Can the company address the fears and resistances which are likely to arise (e.g. the disruption of the children's education; the quality of working life abroad; issues of personal security; effects on a spouse's career and issues of corporate re-entry). There is a good case to be made for organisations asking for volunteers for international development opportunities. This would make ambitious, self-developing managers largely self-selecting.

Pause for thought

Opening up to Chinese wisdom

A Western manager based in the Far East with a Western multinational speaks of a dilemma concerning the next posting of a young manager. He was aggressive and difficult, but had been highly successful in his last assignment. Only two openings were available – a quiet, safe job at HO or a difficult assignment away from base with little support. Although the latter would be challenging and stimulating, the young man had just come out of a stressful posting.

The Western manager mentioned this development issue to a Chinese colleague. Drawing on his organisational experience (and knowledge of Chinese folklore) he pronounced: 'Tigers don't eat grass'.

The young manager was offered another tough assignment; he thrived on it and did very well.

Question
Do you think organisations should be more like this man – open up to the intuitive and take more risks in agreeing assignments for their 'rising stars'?

However, there is also the issue that foreign assignments are expensive and a valuable tool of corporate MD for cultivating a seedbed of future top international managers. The offer of an international posting should therefore be at least partly contingent on an audit of management capabilities and succession planning within the organisation. However, in organisations truly committed to using their entire talent pool, assessment of suitability for an international assignment should involve a thoroughgoing review of potential in the subsidiaries as well as HO, support and line functions and those at all levels of their career. This ensures that all available talent is assessed.

The mechanism which some international companies use is to hold internal competitions for placements using the company intranet. Individuals demonstrate their motivation by applying for consideration; the selection panel then considers appraisal reports, management audit assessments, MD strategy and succession plans in deciding who to choose. In making their choices selection committees are likely to be considerably influenced by a candidate's track record, but wisdom may lie in looking for generic qualities; the effective practitioner in one setting may be a good risk for adapting readily to a cultural context which is very different (the traditional view of American multinationals) but then again, perhaps not. Weighting might also be given to other relevant intangibles such as the cultural sensitivity, adaptiveness to new experience, tolerance, openness and family situation of the candidate (Reitsma 2001).

12.6.6 Preparation for foreign assignments

However wise and thoughtful the selection, a successful assignment requires *preparation*. A key factor here is the host culture. Has the ground been properly laid so that the host organisation will be welcoming of an outsider? Do they recognise the potential benefits to local organisational development? Unless the culture is accepting, there will be no learning for organisation or individual (Barham and Oates 1991).

Evaluation of assignments that go wrong suggest that family unhappiness is a major cause of failure. It therefore behoves the organisation to do what it can to prepare the whole family for the culture shock and help them make a smooth transition. As we will see, this can include inter-cultural sensitisation but also language training, country briefings by former assignees, role-play of typically stressful situations and even pre-assignment visits. The company can also help in practical ways – paying for tuition fees and annual home leave; help with accommodation; applying for a work permit for the spouse in dual-career families, and so on – can make all the difference between an assignment which achieves its functional and development goals and one which is a costly embarrassment for everyone (Iles 1996; Barham and Oates 1991).

12.6.7 Support during a foreign assignment

The assignment needs to be supported if real development is to happen. The referring unit can do much to reassure local people that the visiting assignee is not a 'spy' from HO and is there as a potential local resource. The referring organisation (probably the HRM department) can also establish appropriate mentoring and support arrangements. For example, less experienced managers can be paired with more experienced 'godfathers' at home base. Technically skilled with good social skills, professional reputation and gravitas, these managers can act as sounding boards for working through problems, a resource to mobilise for overcoming organisational roadblocks and a direct link to higher authority if necessary. There may also be a need for 'buddy managers' who know the local culture and the informal ways of working. At Unilever these are called 'contact managers', who are well versed in the practical issues of living in the new setting (tax, schooling, transport, accommodation problems), have a fund of 'instructional stories' for socialisation and can act as a focal point of contact, inducting newcomers into local support networks (Barham and Oates 1991; Beardwell and Holden 2001).

Good practice also emphasises the need for good 'keeping in touch' arrangements. For the assignee to believe that his sojourn overseas is part of a progressive development plan, s/he needs to feel part of the communication net. It helps therefore if the referring organisation organises periodic events to bring far-flung assignees together for networking opportunities and peer support. International seminars and conferences keep them abreast of new thinking in their professional fields and with changes of policy back home. Sponsorship and time-off agreements with host organisations can allow assignees to build their credentials by taking advanced qualifications (perhaps by e-learning/open learning) during their period of attachment so that they remain up to date in knowledge and skills (Gooderham and Nordhaug 2003; Isles 1996).

12.6.8 Re-entry from a foreign assignment

The final issue which has to be addressed in designing developmental assignments is that of *re-entry* or *repatriation*. The common experience of managers sent abroad on stand-alone assignments is that their global understanding of the business increases substantially; they develop new skills and grow in maturity, independence and judgement. Because they lack the immediate specialist inputs available at home and they are at the end of long communication lines they have to improvise, take on new responsibilities and deal with complex situations and stresses at a much higher level than they have previously faced. In short, foreign assignments often have an accelerator effect in developing management skills and confidence (Walton 1999).

However, the problem comes on return. Managers are often required to readjust to smaller jobs, more bureaucracy and controls and the organisation seems oblivious to their achievements in difficult circumstances abroad. MD which is systematic and progressive will be involved in early planning for the re-entry. This will involve agreeing an appropriate re-entry point and sourcing available opportunities well in advance of the end of the attachment. It will also mean reassuring managers that their achievements are recognised, helping them to culturally readjust and capturing their experiences, perhaps through peer support groups, as part of institutionalised organisational learning. However, the sad fact that this rarely happens is testimony to the failure of so many organisations to take international MD as seriously as they should (Gooderham and Nordhaug 2003; Barham and Oates 1991).

Case study A cautionary tale

International MD can go badly wrong. We usually only hear the success stories but more can be learnt from mistakes and failures. Take the case of an Austrian organisation we will call 'Ersaz' which took over a Romanian engineering company. The company had been under state ownership during the Communist period. The idea was to introduce a coaching system in which Ersaz engineers would pair with a Romanian equivalent to develop their management skills.

Unfortunately, the HO Ersaz managers were selected purely on their technical competence, not their process understanding or their track record for people development; they were given no preparation as coaches and they received no cultural sensitisation. Equally, the Romanians received no instruction on how to act in the role of coachee.

It was a disaster. What went wrong?

- The Ersaz coaches defined their role as 'experts in best practice'; the Romanians were cast in the role of inadequately trained professionals, learners with a lot to learn. This offended their sense of professional pride and was seen as arrogantly dismissive of their considerable technical achievements in the former system.
- Lacking cultural sensitivity, the Ersaz coaches refused to listen to the Romanians about what had worked in the past.
- Instead of developing the Romanians in a supportive and encouraging way, the Ersaz engineers showed their professional disdain by taking on all the responsible work and delegating operational duties to the Romanians who they came to see as their subordinates.
- Feeling deskilled, resentful and angry, the Romanians reacted by working closely to instructions, effectively freezing the Ersaz people out of the informal communication system.

Very soon the Ersaz coaches found that their technical solutions didn't work in a society with a different cultural history. Offended by the patronising manner of their Western 'partners', the Romanians offered no support. Indeed, far from developing as managers they regressed to the 'getting by' and 'passive disengagement' behaviour which they had practised under Communism, where the prevailing management style had been similarly hierarchical, critical and controlling. They took no initiative or responsibility, offered no comment and acted with begrudging compliance. It is difficult not to feel some sympathy with them.

This MD scheme was a major embarrassment for Ersaz and did much damage to working relationships with its subsidiary before a more culturally sensitive form of development was put in place.

Question

If you had been a Western manager in charge of this project, what would you have done differently?

Source: Author's fieldwork on management culture in Romania

12.6.9 Cross-cultural sensitivity training

Cross-cultural development is a specialist aspect of management development. Cross-cultural awareness can help managers to become more acute observers of situations which involve cultural diversity. It can improve social and communication skills across cultural boundaries. It can encourage managers to develop an attitude of respect, non-judgemental attitudes, tolerance of difference, even celebration of the creative vitality which the interplay of perspectives from different backgrounds can bring.

HRD interventions to bring out the benefits of cultural pluralism can take various forms. Cultural awareness workshops can create a climate in which participants feel able to examine their stereotypes, their implications and their origins. Simulation exercises and role-playing around concrete examples of cultural dilemmas can stimulate people to reconsider their notions of common sense and draw out diverse, but equally acceptable, approaches to an issue. Sensitivity and 'encounter training' can improve skills of active listening and imaginative empathy with the perspectives of others. Problem-solving cases around real situations or dramatised critical incidents, in which participants can direct the flow of the action and reflect on experiential lessons, can help the development of social confidence, openness and flexibility in experimenting with different styles of behaviour. Cultural briefings and assignments on the history, religion, customs, values and business practices of other communities can help build respect, understanding and the ability to see things from the viewpoint of the other (Harris and Moran 1987; Tayeb 2003).

Well-organised and properly integrated into a larger MD programme, cross-cultural training can be highly effective in overcoming stereotypes and helping to create the sophisticated cosmopolitan globe-trotting manager, much sought after by the big companies yet in such scarce supply throughout the world.

Cross-cultural training as a growing force in management development

The need for cross-cultural training is ever more urgent, as companies' operations, particularly those in Europe, span across an increasing number of nations. Without awareness of cultural distinctions, misunderstandings can arise. For employees this can bring frustrations because of wasted time resulting from miscommunication. For the business, this means low morale as well as the missed opportunity to benefit from the contributions of a diverse group of employees.

Cultural differences can materialise in very different ways. For example, if you have a team of managers from different countries they may have different concepts of what 'being on time' for a meeting means. So how do you, as the 'flown in' expert, start a meeting and still respect local cultural differences?

When it comes to overseas postings many companies use long-term cultural training programmes to help employees become integrated. Lehman Brothers, for example, hosts interactive theatre programmes with the help of actors. Business teams come together to discuss their reactions to what they observe in the plays enacted for them and in their own interactions with the actors. It helps if managers can see their impact on others and listen to their feedback.

Accenture has developed a computer-based cross-cultural awareness tool covering communication and cultural attitudes towards gender, which is used with managers in multicultural teams. Again, the learning comes from the sounding board others offer to you.

More difficult to deal with are the subtler differences in attitudes and working practices that create obstacles to efficient collaboration for a culturally diverse team. With on-the-job learning it is possible to interrupt the behaviour which is causing difficulties and then encouraging people to see how it happens and how they can make a different choice next time.

Question
Addressing the difficulties that arise when people from different cultures work together is one thing; how would you develop some ways of using this same diversity to improve organisational creativity?

Source: Adapted from Murray, S. 'Cross cultural training: learning to make the most of increasing internationalism', *Financial Times*, 11 May (2005).

12.7 International MD and organisational learning

Finally, perhaps a short note about international MD as a vehicle for cross-national learning. The future of big business seems to lie in networks of information and ideas coordinated around nodes of synthesis, integration and transmission. As we have seen, MD is important in helping managers from diverse backgrounds to become real, cohesive teams which use difference as a creative force to produce something new. But it goes beyond this. Corporate MD centres, like Crotonville and many others less illustrious institutions, are beginning to act as catalysts for collective learning and knowledge management. At GE the creative solutions of cross-cultural teams of managers are 'blown through' the organisation. They become the ideas which circulate through the system, stimulating new developments and offering good practice which others can emulate.

This is a theme picked up by Gooderham and Nordhaug (2003) who suggest that in future innovation (e.g. product development) will increasingly become the expression of the organisation, not the hierarchical preserve of the 'big brain' at corporate HO. Increasingly transnationals are becoming circuits of ideas in which some of the subsidiaries will be the prime movers for ideas, informal sharing and distribution of knowledge. Centres of excellence are emerging in the subsidiaries, focal points for managerial learning and creativity (small-scale versions of Crotonville, either physical or virtual) which act as powerhouses of thinking and transmission and brokerage of ideas about organisational development and innovation across the world, building the company from within.

12.8 Conclusion

Organisations typically follow a sequence of development on the path to becoming truly international; and the management processes, management roles and competencies which managers need to display vary from one stage to another. The move to flexible form, transnational organisations seems to require far more of effective managers, especially in terms of social skills and cross-cultural sensitivity. However, there is no identikit global manager and no formula for developing him or her. Sensible organisations will recognise that international MD has to take account of the scope on global activity, the type and level of manager involved and the cultural context of the operations. They will also recognise that the development of cross-cultural managers has implications for broad policy areas such as career development, succession management, competency frameworks and assessment. They will appreciate that the flow of international managers through the organisation will affect the corporate culture (for good or ill) and provide knowledge management opportunities which need to be managed every bit as carefully as the more technical aspects of cross-cultural assignments.

Review questions

1 'In a globalising world, management development has become *international* management development and sensible organisations are concerned to develop cadres of cross-cultural managers'. *How do you react to this opinion?*

2 'There is nothing distinctive about international MD; it's the same models, processes and tools of MD but applied within a global organisation'. *Do you agree with this?*

3 'The importance of cross-cultural training can be exaggerated; a manager sent on an overseas posting will be more concerned about getting the quality assurance system they use in Rotterdam to work in Thailand than causing offence to his hosts, because he doesn't thank them in the right way for their hospitality or he commits the gaff of showing the soles of his feet in public'. *How would you respond to this view?*

4 If you were responsible for selecting a manager for a high-profile Asian posting where traditionalist gender values prevailed, would you think twice about sending a woman, however technically competent she might be? Explain the grounds of your decision.

5 Do you think the days of the career expatriate are numbered or will the need for coordination in diverse organisations (as well as issues of politics and power) continue to make their presence inevitable?

6 What would you do to ensure that the learning of assignees on foreign assignments is captured to improve the knowledge base of the organisation?

Web links

An organisation that takes the development of managers *sans frontieres* very seriously is the European Foundation for Management Development:
http://www.efmd.be

The International Institute for Management Development is also at the leading edge in developing global managers:
http://www.imd.ch

So is the London Business School and INSEAD:
http://www.lbs.ac.uk
http://www.insead.fr/

Among the corporate development providers, Ashridge Management College has an international reputation:
http://www.ashridge.org.uk

DVDs/Videos

Gung Ho (1986) Directed by T. Howard; featuring Michael Keaton
An amusing satire on the problem of cross-cultural management which engages with differences between Japanese and American management styles. Despite much stereotyping, some serious messages.

Outsourced (2008) Directed by J. Jeffcoat.
A love story set against the backdrop of changes in work contracts, external postings and the disruptive effect on personal lives. Becoming an international manager has its personal costs as well as satisfactions. What is your personal bank balance?

Recommendations for further reading

Those texts marked with an asterisk in the bibliography are recommended for further reading, especially the following:

Barham, K. and Oates, D. (1991) *The International Manager.* Very useful introduction to the issues of developing the international manager from the perspective of the individual and the organisation.

Bartlett, C. and Ghoshal, S. (1989) *Managing Across Borders: The Transnational Solution*, Harvard Business School Press, Sept. An influential article in the literature which introduced a categorisation of managers/international managers still used today.

Gooderham, P. and Nordhaug, O. (2003) *International Management: Cross Boundary Challenges.* An up-to-date account of changes in the structures and processes of transnational organisations, including the development of managers.

Bibliography

*Adler, N. and Bartholomew, S. (1992) 'Managing globally competent people', *Academy of Management Executive*, Vol. 6, No. 3.

Adler, N. and Ghandar, G. (1990) 'Strategic HRM: a global perspective', in Pieper, R. (ed.) *HRM: An International Comparison*, De Gruyer.

Armstrong, M. (2001) *A Handbook of HRM Practice*, Kogan Page.

*Barham, K. (1989) *Developing the International Manager*, The Ashridge Management Research Group.

*Barham, K. and Oates, D. (1991) *The International *Manager*, Economist Books.

*Barham, K. and Wills, S. (1992) *Management Across Frontiers: Identifying the Competences of Successful International Managers*, Ashridge Management Research Group.

Barney, J. and Griffin, R. (1992) *The Management of Organisations: Strategy, Structure and Behaviour*, Houghton Mifflin.

*Bartlett, C. and Ghoshal, S. (1991) *Managing Across Borders: The Transnational Solution*, Harvard Business School Press.

*Bartlett, C. and Ghoshal, S. (1992) 'What is a global manager?', *Harvard Business Review*, Sept.

Beardwell, I. and Holden, L. (2001) *HRM: A Contemporary Approach*, Prentice Hall.

Berkeley-Thomas, A. (2003) *The Future of Management*, Ch. 10, Routledge.

Brewster, C. (1991) *The Management of Expatriates*, Kogan Page.

Brewster, C. and Mayrhofer, W. (2004) *Human Resource Management in Europe: Evidence of Convergence?* Butterworth-Heinemann.

Brown, J. and Duguid, P. (1991) 'Organisation learning and communities of practice: towards a unified view of working, learning and innovation', *Organisation Science*, Vol. 2, No. 1.

Burgoyne, J. and Reynolds, M. (1999) *Managing Learning*, Ch. 15, Sage.

*Foster, N. (2000) 'The myth of the "international manager" ', *International Journal of Human Resource Management*, Vol. 10, No. 5.

*Gooderham, P. and Nordhaug, O. (2003) *International Management: Cross-Boundary Challenges*, Blackwell.

Handy, C. and Barham, K. (1990) 'International MD in the 1990s', *The Journal of European Industrial Training*, Vol. 14, No. 6.

*Harris, P. and Moran, R. (1987) *Managing Cultural Differences*, Gulf Publishing.

Hegewisch, A. and Brewster, C. (1993) *European Developments in HRM*, Routledge.

Hislop, D. (2005) *Knowledge Management in Organisations: A Critical Introduction*, Oxford University Press.

Iles, P. (1996) 'International HRD', in Stewart, J. and McGoldrick, J. (1996) *HRD: Perspectives, Strategies and Practice*, Prentice Hall.

Kanter, R. (1989) *When Giants Learn to Dance*, Simon and Schuster.

Kirkpatrick, P. (1993) *Human Resource Management in Europe*, Chs 12, 14, Routledge.

Knight, R. (2006) 'GE's corporate boot camp cum talent spotting venue', *Financial Times*, 20 March.

*Lessem, R. (1998) *Management Development through Cultural Diversity*, Ch. 1, Routledge.

Mabey, C. and Iles, P. (1994) *Managing Learning*, Open University.

Micklethwait, J. and Wooldridge, A. (2000) *The Witch Doctors*, Ch. 10, Mandarin Books.

Murray, S. (2005) 'Cross-cultural training: learning to make the most of increasing internationalism', *Financial Times*, 11 May.

Ohmae, K. (1990) *The Borderless World: Power and Strategy in the Inter-linked Economy*, Collins.

Perlmutter, H. (1969) 'The tortuous evolution of the multinational corporation', *Columbia Journal of World Business*, Vol. 8, No. 18.

*Reitsma, S. (2001) 'Management development at Unilever', *Journal of Management Development*, Vol. 20, No. 2.

Rollinson, D. (2002) *Organisational Behaviour and Analysis*, Chs 19, 22 Prentice Hall.

Rothwell, S. (1992) 'The development of the international manager', *Personnel Management*, Jan.

Smy, L. (2003) 'Working overseas: global companies open more gateways', *Financial Times*, 17 Oct.

Sparrow, P. and Hiltrop, J. (1996) *Human Resource Management in Transition*, Ch. 10, Prentice Hall.

Stewart, J. and McGoldrick, J. (1999) *Human Resource Development: Perspectives, Strategies and Practice*, Ch. 4, Prentice Hall.

Syrett, M. and Lammiman, J. (1999) *Management Development: Making the Investment Count*, Economist Books.

Tayeb, M. (2003) *International Management: Theories and Practices*, Prentice Hall.

Trompenaars, F. and Hampden-Turner, C. (1997) *Riding the Waves of Change*, Ch. 12, Nicholas Brealey.

Walton, J. (1999) *Strategic Human Resource Development*, Chs. 1, 18, Prentice Hall.

*Wills, S. and Barham, K. (1994) 'Being an international manager', *European Management Journal*, Vol. 12, No. 1.

Woodall, J. and Winstanley, D. (1999) *Management Development: Strategy and Practice*, Ch. 12, Blackwell.

13 Management development and organisational development

Learning outcomes

After studying the chapter you should be able to understand, analyse and explain:

- the relationship between MD and OD;
- definitions of OD;
- the nature of OD and its cardinal principles;
- a brief history of OD;
- techniques and intervention strategies of OD;
- the skills of the OD practitioner;
- politics, power and OD;
- the future of OD.

13.1 Introduction

Management Development is about developing the learning individual, but it is also about developing the system of organisational learning. Managers can only achieve their full potential when the conditions for learning are positive. Rigidities in the context of managerial learning inhibit managers from being truly experimental, creative and innovative. An open learning system will have the opposite effect. At the same time, management learning styles shape attitudes, values and behaviours which can decisively influence the culture of learning, either for good or ill. The development of the organisation and the development of the manager are symbiotic. Neither can be done in isolation from the other. Ultimately this makes progressive management development conditional on building a form of organisation that is self-developing and puts learning at the centre of its processes.

13.2 The relationship between MD and OD

As we have seen in earlier chapters, in recent years MD has become more strategic and more contextualised. As Doyle (2000) suggests in his 'relational perspective' (considered in Chapter 3), modern MD is broadening its knowledge base to include learning of all kinds and at a number of levels. It is busy combining its traditional concerns with regard to planned, individualistic development with larger interventions which contribute to learning and effectiveness within the overall organisation. MD is also focusing beyond individual managers and groups of managers to influence the organisational context in which managers operate. Patching (1998) looks at the link between management development and organisational development:

> MD is organisational development . . . management and organisational interventions make no direct physical impact on organisations as such . . . yet they change things. What they change is managers' minds and as managers' minds change, so do their organisations.

Storey (1989) talks of MD as a force for organisational change, as a catalyst for addressing issues of climate, culture and promoting innovation within the organisation as a whole. Doyle (2000) also takes up this theme, claiming that MD is becoming holistic and transformative, addressing social , political and emotional issues of organisation. At the minimum level this can mean having MD programmes which transmit a message, like reorienting middle managers in British Telecom (now faced with a competitive environment) to the core principles of the organisation's mission. But it can go much further than this. In the NHS, for example, leadership development programmes are being used to redefine the total organisation as client-centred.

In many organisations, MD in all its forms – coaching, mentoring, learning sets, project work and so on – quite as much as formal programmes, can become tools to build a shared culture and a common sense of identity within management. MD can stimulate organisation-wide debates to raise awareness of corporate governance, ethical behaviour, social responsibility, diversity and cross-cultural issues and other challenges facing the organisation and provide the arena for the constituent parties to agree a coordinated response.

Increasingly the priority is to link MD interventions with organisational strategy to ensure improvements in effectiveness (Mumford and Gold 2004). There is growing recognition that the successful development of managers depends on the organisation and its culture. Learning is contingent on establishing a culture that promotes inquiry, openness and trust. This requires action of an OD nature to build an enabling climate to help managers to develop. By the same token, gearing micro-level management learning to change initiatives contributes to the overall effectiveness and culture of the organisation (e.g. developing a management community with greater cultural awareness).

As MD becomes more strategic and takes on a broader agenda, so it comes within the larger umbrella of OD. Much of what is termed MD is now about aligning personal goals and organisational goals, balancing individual and collective needs and helping managers to achieve their own potential while contributing to the potential of the organisation they work in (Garavan 1999). OD and MD become so closely intertwined that they become indistinguishable, and drawing distinctions between them is hardly worthwhile. If this is a future line of development of MD, then we need to know more about OD as field of activity in which it is becoming contextualised.

OD as 'total system' change

OD usually involves change in multiple spheres of activity or subsystems to bring about desired, planned change in the organisation as a whole.

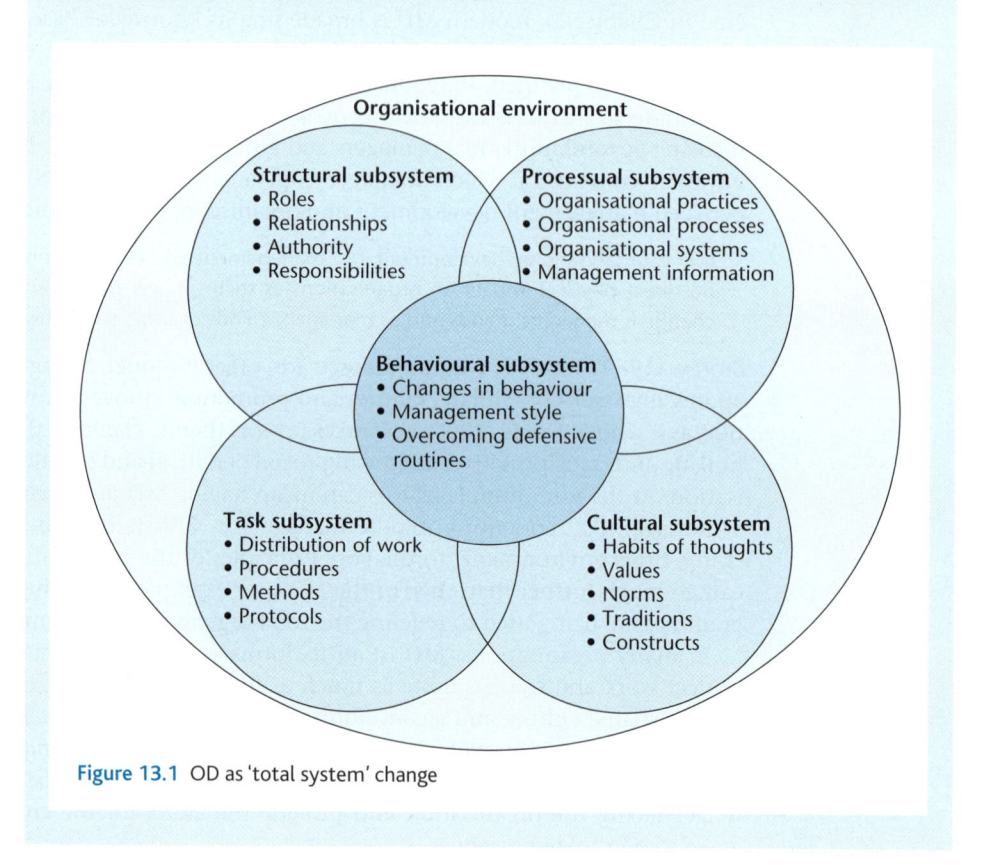

Organisational environment

Structural subsystem
- Roles
- Relationships
- Authority
- Responsibilities

Processual subsystem
- Organisational practices
- Organisational processes
- Organisational systems
- Management information

Behavioural subsystem
- Changes in behaviour
- Management style
- Overcoming defensive routines

Task subsystem
- Distribution of work
- Procedures
- Methods
- Protocols

Cultural subsystem
- Habits of thoughts
- Values
- Norms
- Traditions
- Constructs

Figure 13.1 OD as 'total system' change

13.3 The nature of organisational development

Over the past two decades the scope of the business environment has been transformed and organisations have had to position themselves to accommodate radical changes. The fast-paced, complex nature of change requires organisations to learn how to find innovative ways of meeting new demands. OD is an influential field of theory and practice which enables organisations to work towards strategies for managing change. OD involves 'whole systems change' and the selective use of interventions that shape the invisible, intangible but essential aspects of organisational process – values, norms, beliefs, symbols, ideologies, relationships and behaviours. OD holds many weapons in its arsenal to help organisational members address key issues confronting them in transitional times, e.g., managing change, developing leadership skills, building organisational culture and climate, defining vision and strategy, developing business process and work organisation.

13.3.1 Defining organisational development

OD is a vast field and theorists and practitioners come at it from a number of different angles. This means that there is a plethora of definitions. However, one which stands out is from French and Bell's (1999) classic study:

> A top management supported, long range effort to improve an organisation's problem solving through an effective diagnosis and management of culture involving improved quality of life, team process, group and inter-group dynamics. The focus is on improving the total system with the assistance of a consultant facilitator and the use of techniques of behavioural science and action research.

OD is fraught with paradox. It is science but also art. It is a toolkit of techniques which contains some fashionable gimmicks, but also well-tested and proven methods derived from social science and systematically evaluated management practice. OD is concerned with small-scale developments (e.g. 'quality of working life' initiatives, person-centred empowerment, team development, etc.), yet it also engages in large-scale strategic management, restructuring and redesign work. The term OD has been diluted in recent times as OD approaches have become absorbed into the mainstream of management process. At the same time, there is still consensus that for an intervention to be regarded as OD certain basic criteria need to be satisfied.

OD is holistic. Most definitions recognise the 'total organisational system' as the target for change. OD is concerned with holistic development. So, while an OD intervention may be targeted at a particular subsystem of the whole (e.g. tasks, structures, strategies, leadership, etc.), it is also concerned with the impact of change in one part of the organisation on the totality. This often means progressive interventions to trace inter-linkages (e.g. how changing the reward system has implications for leadership and culture change) as they ripple out from the epicentre of change.

OD is strategic. It is never a quick fix to a particular management problem. The 'total systems' approach requires a fusion between analysis, vision and techniques. All need to be aligned to achieve effective change which takes time and patience. It means helping the top managers, who are the ultimate architects of the change, to articulate their values and expectations and then move consistently and with purpose to shift the culture in ways which support desired behaviours that will ultimately have a transformational impact.

OD is planned change. It is about adaptation and process development, anticipating the need for change and consciously embarking on an agreed course of action. OD tends to be incrementalist in its approach to change (i.e. a series of small steps, increasing in strides as the momentum builds, adding up over time to dramatic change) rather than a sharp 'rupture', especially if that means following an overarching blueprint for change superimposed from above in a directive and disjunctive way. However, the important feature of change which can be characterised as 'OD' is that it is deliberate, systematic and guided by a clear vision for the future.

OD is participative change. From its beginnings, OD has always celebrated the involvement of those who will have to live with the consequences of a change programme. OD typically emphasises the collaboration of a range of stakeholders in diagnosing the organisational problems to be worked on and empowering people to find solutions which build ownership and commitment to change. This is the essence of the 'process consultation' model of consultancy and of 'action research' led approaches which aim to encourage shared meanings through guided facilitation and reflection.

OD is based on behavioural science. OD is a form of change management guided by the concepts and models of social science. There is not one theory underlying OD activities, only a variety of contributions from behavioural science such as social psychology; group dynamics, organisational analysis, social learning theory, role theory, personality theory and so on. Behavioural science provides the conceptual tools for analysing and influencing the ideological processes of organisational process, that is, the interpretive meanings, cognitive maps and values of different stakeholders within the organisation.

OD is an educational strategy. OD is concerned with development through learning. Ultimately it is about cognitive restructuring, that is, shaping how different groups of people construct their realities and relate to each other so that larger organisational goals can be achieved. In the hands of a wise practitioner of the art, OD is about helping people to understand how they think and act and how they might think and act differently in future for the greater good of the whole organisation.

> **Pause for thought**
>
> ### An OD consultant's admission
>
> Consider this quotation from Roger Harrison, one of the all-time great OD practitioners:
>
> > I tell my management clients now, 'Don't ask any questions you don't really want the answers to.' Every time we consultants ask how people would like things to change, we create an implicit understanding that we intend to take action. But, too often management is just fishing to see what is down there beneath the glassy surface of employee attitudes, a surface that in normal day-to-day interaction reflects only the comforting image of the manager's own face. Faced with the deeper reality of employee attitudes, many managers turn and run.'
>
> **Question**
> What ethical obligations do OD consultants have to the people who will be most involved in change and will have to live out its consequences every day of their working lives?
>
> Source: Harrison, R. (1995) *The Consultant's Journey.*

13.3.2 A brief history of organisational development

The origins of OD can be traced to the 1950s and 1960s. French and Bell (1999) and Grieve (2000) provide a comprehensive account of the history of OD. A cursory overview would emphasise the work of Kurt Lewin (1951) on group dynamics and force field analysis and the introduction of T-groups in the 1960s (Argyris 1970; Schein et al. 1964). The 1970s were characterised by team development, action research, socio-technical systems and ideas for personal development derived from psychotherapy. OD was increasingly seen as the answer to improving organisational effectiveness, with major programmes introduced in large-scale companies such as General Motors and ICI, many of which were evaluated as successful.

The 1980s saw the rise of concepts such as organisational culture, systems thinking and quality management, while the 1990s witnessed the emergence of learning organisation concepts which were philosophically in accord with traditional, humanistic OD values and also business process re-engineering principles which were based on strict business logic (Grieves 2000).

In recent years the accelerating pace of technological change, an increasingly competitive market, the growing rate of buyouts, bankruptcies and mergers, globalisation and new organisational designs (Hussey 1996; Champy and Nohria 1996) have challenged OD to redefine itself. Considerable attention is now being given to what is being called 'second generation' OD or 'organisational transformation'. While practitioners still use first-generation OD approaches, the demands of modern business seem to require more complex, multifaceted interventions. Second-generation OD places more demands on organisational vision and leadership, paradigm shift and the management of an increasing number of variables. Writers contrast the fine-tuning and the incremental change of the past (see above) with the fundamental 'frame bending' which top management now requires of change (Goodstein and Burke 1991; Barczak et al. 1987; Beckhard and Pritchard 1992).

A major focus of OD interventions is now cultural change – interventions to help managers identify their cultural assumptions and build agreements with subcultures on developing new norms of behaviour. Another new turn is the integration of OD with organisational learning (a theme which is considered in a separate chapter on learning). Then there is the renewed interest in teams. Recent years has seen an intensified focus on high-performance teams, cross-functional teams and self-managed teams. Team building and team learning initiatives are often linked to efforts to build a climate of participative involvement in quality improvement and systems development. Further areas which are encompassed in the new scope of OD include envisaging and 'scenario planning' (future search conferences), the valuing of diversity, developing political skills and exploring radical fringe issues such as spirituality, the 'psychological contract' and organisational change. The latest turn is to an approach called 'appreciative inquiry' which emphasises the special strengths and unique qualities of the organisation. Rather than identifying problems beneath the surface, which will be perceived as pointing the finger of blame leading to resistance, the consultant concentrates on what is already good with the organisation and builds on these foundations (Fitzgerald et al. 2002).

The development of effective management is at the heart of 'new' organisational development and performance management. This showcases the specifically MD aspects of OD. Competent managers are now required to have much wider skill sets to manage complex systems and conduct the sophisticated, collaborative change which OD implies. The strategic decisions taken by managers are now central to business success. Managing change and innovation have become fundamental skills for managers alongside the art of delegation, facilitation, empowerment. Second-generation OD puts high value on building these leadership skills and integrating them in organisational process for transformational change.

Case study: OD at South-East Asian Airlines

An airline company who we shall call SE Asian Airlines discovered a couple of years ago that intensifying international pressures in the marketplace and internal changes such as turnover in leadership, new flights and new schedules meant that existing processes were no longer adequate. This caused top management to bring in their internal OD team to investigate the airline's strengths and weaknesses and facilitate transition to a new order.

The change model guiding the interventions here was continuous, evolutionary change concerned to improve the organisation's effectiveness within a framework of strategy. It was planned change involving a series of incremental steps which would eventually build up to transformational change. On the face of it, Lewin's (1951) famous model of change in which the organisation must first be *unfrozen* (i.e. realise a need for change) so the debate and transition can lead to new behaviours which are *refrozen* (i.e. institutionalised) seemed to guide the OD consultants. However, as Weick and Quinn (1999) suggest, 'in the face of continuous change a more plausible sequence may be freeze, rebalance and unfreeze'. The rebalancing stage is 'time out' in which people reflect on how they have been moving. This is a time for iterative readjustment to the strategy; tightening and refining, not lurching from one initiative to another. Certainly this seemed to capture the spirit in which OD was practised at SE Asian Airlines.

The aims of the OD intervention were defined in quite an abstract way before the project and involved talk of 'building a stronger healthier organisational culture that would support SEAA's crew members and customers'. This was deliberate. The OD approach is usually an exploratory journey rather than a predetermined trajectory, concerned with the process of changing as much as the change itself. Certainly top management hoped that the OD team would offer an insightful outside perspective, a 'look under the hood' to identify what was working well and what could be changed. All parties seemed to understand that 'soft was hard' here, that designing roles and processes to help personal growth and give work meaning, developing leadership that was supportive and facilitating and building cohesive teams would have an effect on the quality of service and ultimately the bottom line.

The OD consultants started with a feedback survey of the front line (airline and control staff), inquiring about the factors which helped and hindered their work. Then they asked the same questions of the senior managers. A significant perception gap emerged. The patterns which seemed to emerge suggested five areas for improvement which were largely behavioural in nature: poor communication of company goals; weak personal development; insufficient customer focus; lack of management understanding of the local culture and some unwillingness to change.

The survey feedback was the beginning of the rebalancing stage aimed at capturing the current situation so that it could be analysed and then rebalanced – reframed, reinterpreted and patterns of activity reorganised. During this stage, the five areas were discussed at all levels of the organisation. True to the spirit of OD as a collaborative change process, a programme of weekly meetings were held between senior management and front-line staff to discuss the issues in depth, examine the reasons for variations in perception and agree an action plan to address them. This participation was seen as crucial to getting buy-in to change from all parties. During these sessions the OD consultant acted as facilitator helping people to articulate their interpretations of events and brokering a consensus.

From these dialogues broad agreement was reached on action within each of the five problem areas. One of the fundamental principles of OD is to ensure that decision-making and implementation remains in the hands of the client. This principle was honoured here. The task of the consultant was to help clients generate useable data, create opportunities to clients to search for solutions and create conditions where people felt committed to their choices and make them happen. So, in the programme OD consultants performed a variety of support roles, for example, helping managers 'walk the talk' and align their behaviours with the 'participative' rhetoric; team building to give front-line staff a sense of belonging; designing an organisational decision-making process in which front-liners had a sense of ownership; searching with the client for opportunities to show short-term wins so that the momentum and excitement was sustained. In this process the OD consulting team moved between a number of interlocking roles – researcher, facilitator, coach, systems designer, therapist.

By all accounts, the OD consultants did their job well at SEAA. An atmosphere was generated in which the main parties could question and reflect on their basic assumptions and how certain behaviours in the past had become 'self defeating scripts' (Argyris and Schon 1978). This is essential for generating a culture of emergent change which is directed by the people themselves. Reflection and conceptualisation are fundamental to an organisation learning how to learn (i.e. Argyris's double loop of learning; see Chapter 6) and can only be achieved by engaging people in thinking through action, and the most valuable and most lasting outcome of this successful OD programme.

Questions

This case study was deliberately presented to emphasise the positive. However, as a critical reader, does it all sound 'too good to be true'? What reservations might you have accepting this as an account of change?

Source: Internal company literature and informal communication.

13.4 The techniques of OD

OD intervention strategies focus on development at all levels, that is, the individual, the group, the organisation as a whole, and they cover a broad and varied spectrum of activities. OD interventions are situational actions and vary from case to case. OD can be used to address problems as diverse as poor morale, low productivity, poor quality, interpersonal and inter-group conflicts, strategic failures, poor leadership, poor team performance, structural issues and any number of these in complex combinations. There is no standard way in which OD strategies are designed and implemented. Each OD intervention is essentially a unique response to a set of problems and opportunities. There are really only two consistencies. One is that OD consultancy considers the organisation as a total system and will therefore focus on the interrelationships, interactions and interdependencies between variables. The other is that action is not pre-determined but stems from diagnosis which will usually involve the people who will be most affected by the change and/or who will have to make the change work.

OD involves a broad spectrum of techniques (French and Bell 1999; Cummings and Worley 2001). In the space available, here is an appraisal of some of the key approaches. Of course, the list is not exhaustive and may incorporate other methods such as those we associate with core MD and/or HRM practices. Each intervention should be a careful combination of selected techniques to create packages which will address the interwoven technical, structural, cultural, political and social issues involved and allow change to progress in a relatively planned way.

13.4.1 Action research/survey feedback approaches

Traditionally the guiding philosophy of OD has been to make change collaborative. It is about listening to the organisation, listening to the accounts of people at all levels as they define situations, make sense of experience and construct their realities from assumptions, images and stereotypes. This involves a diagnostic or action research approach.

Action research is about the change agent being actively involved in planning and understanding the change process by being part of it themselves. AR is increasingly the key methodology driving OD. It is participative and based on the belief that real change stems from data collected with those who are at the receiving end of change.

The process of AR-led change is cyclical. It is also change which is planned in a step-by-step manner. (See Beckhard and Pritchard 1992 and Reason and Bradbury 2001 for a good discussion of the strengths and weaknesses of AR).

The action research process

Typically an AR project follows a number of steps.

- *Diagnosis of organisational themes to establish the map of issues.* This involves carrying out research with the people concerned. Here a wide range of issues may be relevant, for example: How are people motivated? What are the leadership styles? Can anything be said about the relationship between structural and cultural factors?
- *Feeding back the results* to those who have supplied the data. Does the diagnosis make sense to them? Can they recognise their experience in the results?
- *Discussing the results with wider circles of interested parties.* Here the OD consultant/action researcher acts as facilitator. What does the data mean for change in the system as a whole?
- *Action planning* is the next stage. What are the practical consequences of the research findings? What steps have now to be taken to help organisational transition?
- *Action* involves implementing the OD programme. This is likely to be a blending of techniques such as envisioning, institutional change, team development, formal and informal personal development.
- *Evaluating the action.* This means having the objectivity and openness to consider tough questions. Has the change been successful? Are there issues here which have not been addressed? Were there problems of initial diagnosis or implementation? Is there a need for another turn of the AR cycle, more data gathering, review and action?

At its most sophisticated (Marshall and Reason 1997) AR can become a radical force for change, a strategy for cooperative inquiry within a work community. Using a participative approach in which the facilitator engages work groups in collecting their own data, ideas can be explored in action. Through support and challenge, the facilitator can provoke the group to explore organisational meanings which might be taken for granted. How are problems being defined, and knowledge socially constructed in this culture? What if we represented experience in a different way? Will managers then come to recognise the 'defensive routines' by which they habitually screen out certain factors and insulate themselves from self-reflection? (Argyris and Schon 1978). AR can act as a catalyst for critical independent thinking at work which has a permanent impact on the collective consciousness of the culture and its everyday processes of behaviour.

Of course, most AR interventions do not go this deep. But, as a general rule, where action research is working well, a research-led, diagnostic approach to OD greatly increases its chances of success. However, because it is so front ended, so reliant on the diagnostic skills of the consultant and the quality of the relationships which can be formed, this is an approach which often goes wrong. It also requires a reasonably long timescale which management is often loath to grant in the conditions of modern business where change happens against tight deadlines.

OD consultants can also be involved in less intensive diagnostic activities. These usually involve *vertical or horizontal slicing*, gathering data about how issues are perceived and then building a collage of perspectives to map the culture or the 'field of forces' within the organisation. In this survey work the emphasis tends to be on uncovering the meanings of different sub-groups within the organisation as these are socially contextualised.

13.4.2 Team building and team learning

As we have seen, recent pressures on organisations to respond adaptively to customer needs, to be faster to market, empower workers and release creativity have led to the break-up of bureaucracy and a proliferation of teams. These can take many forms: customer and supplier interface teams; multidisciplinary teams, self-managed product and project teams, quality circles, strategic management teams. As we discuss later, teams are at the heart of the modern organisation and building teams is a major OD activity. When you consider that researchers tell us that senior management groups often fail to function as teams; they often show signs of 'pathology' and behind most corporate failures there are issues of team leadership (Hackman 1990; Garratt 1996), the scale of the challenge facing OD becomes very concrete, very real.

Team building based on behavioural science knowledge through OD interventions, offers the prospect of many positive returns. Through team building a collection of people brought together in an ad hoc group can be forged into a cohesive team. John Hunt (1986) suggests that members of cohesive teams have many advantages. They experience fewer work-related anxieties, are better adjusted to their organisations, respect each other's contributions, work together in a coordinated and productive way. Distilling the work of Katzenbach and Smith (1993), Glenn Parker (1990) and Larson and LaFasto (1990), strong, cohesive, high-performing teams seem to have the following characteristics.

- members can influence each other naturally and directly in face-to-face interaction; there is much discussion and participation;
- there are shared goals and common values animating team members;
- there is a sense of mutual trust and openness;

- members are mutually supportive; people listen to each other, ask questions, summarise and so on;
- conflict is not avoided but is handled with goodwill;
- decision-making is largely by consensus;
- communications are open; feelings as well as reasons can be expressed; individual agendas to not displace team agendas;
- team members identify with the team;
- they have a feeling of responsibility for the team to achieve its purpose;
- leadership shifts between members;
- members understand their roles and responsibilities;
- the team accommodates a variety of thinking, learning styles; task and process roles.

It will probably come as no surprise to hear that teams like this are rare and most work teams would benefit from team building. Team building usually involves a third party, a trusted external consultant, working with the team to help its members become more aware of how they work together and what they might do to become more effective.

Team building can be used for established long-term groups and also for temporary project groups. With new teams the emphasis is on the whole team developing a common framework of understanding and agreeing common goals within which people can work. A facilitator works to help the team move through the various stages of development, that is, *forming, storming, norming and performing* (Tuckman 1965) or *dependency, counter-dependency, cohesion, interdependence* (Schein 1988), so that it can become mature and productive as quickly and as painlessly as possible.

With existing teams, the team as a whole looks back over the recent past to determine what problems there have been and how they have been dealt with. The reflection is likely to involve 'task' issues but also 'process', such as the nature and quality of relationships between team members and between members and the leader. Is the team of a manageable number? What are the agendas of participants and are they compatible? Is there a rich mix of team roles (e.g. Belbin 1993; Margerison and McCann 1991; Bales 1950). Is there a good balance between 'task' and 'maintenance' roles (Hunt 1986), between learning and thinking styles (e.g. Kolb 1984). Is there an ethos of participation and openness to new ideas or are there aspects of 'group think'? How is the team led and what role does the leader adopt in relation to the others?

Typically, the facilitator will help the team confront these issues; come to a joint understanding of the core purpose of the team; visualise its future role, how roles can complement each other and the new expertise that should be brought in. This is never a straightforward process. Often people are not prepared to change behaviours or admit limitations; they do not want to accept responsibility for the performance of the team as a whole; they have unrealistic expectations of the leader or the leader is unwilling to share power. Very often, the team facilitator is faced with the irony that everyone in a management team understands the importance of organisational change but they do not appreciate the new learning and new behaviours which will be required of *them*. That means that teams need to be helped to question old behaviours and attitudes and draw experience from them. Often this implies an outside perspective to question experience and replace old habits of thinking and action with new processes (Marsick and Watkins 1997).

Team building occurs over months or even years and will involve a range of activities, group discussion, cognitive mapping to surface and share mental models, diagnostic feedback by the facilitator, self/group reflection, scenario analysis, critical incident analysis, repertory grids and role-plays. Getting the team into a more balanced state will generally require mutual readjustment between team members and experimentation with new, more productive behaviours which will help the team develop. None of this happens quickly. There will be emotional knots to unravel as well as habits of thinking and behaviour which have to be worked through and good will accumulated before the dynamics of the team will really change.

While much team building involves building the micro-culture of the team using the special skills of the social scientist as facilitator, some aspects of team development are more obviously traditional MD. For example, new team leaders may need help in coordinating teams based on empowerment and involvement. This may involve executive coaching and counselling to help managers reflect on their habitual scripts, provide feedback on feedback on how others see their behaviour and 'support and challenge' while they experiment with more adaptive behaviour. Dyer (1984) believes that high-performing leaders need to be able to move seamlessly between 'leader as educator', 'leader as coach' and 'leader as facilitator' with the team as conditions demand. Team members may also need learning and development input, acquiring skills of communicating, problem-solving, creativity and so on, to play an active role. As hierarchical roles break down and leadership becomes rotated or shared, this will be increasingly important. All these interventions represent different aspects of OD and should be tailored as a crafted programme of mutually supportive activities.

13.4.3 Sensitivity training

Straddling personal and team development, the *T-group* or *learning laboratory* is a vehicle for increasing the sensitivity to emotional transactions within a group and using that feedback for developing social skills (French and Bell 1999). T-groups involve about 10 people brought together to examine intra-group processes, interpersonal styles and how people impact on each other. Usually T-groups are made up of people drawn from the same department or perhaps at the same organisational level but spanning different departments. They are concerned to give participants a better understanding of what makes them tick and what makes groups function as they do.

T-group sessions are left largely unstructured. The group is given only hazy instructions about its tasks. Interpersonal interactions are then observed as group members try to clarify their objectives and the process of working together. Developers adopt a non-interventionist style. Their purpose is to encourage group members to reflect on how they are reacting to events and building a sense of order in which the group defines roles and rules of behaviour (Cummings and Worley 2001).

At a later stage, the developer will help the group reflect on its experience by raising themes for discussion. How does the group make decisions? What are the problem-solving processes and how rational do they seem? How are people negotiating identities within the team? How are agendas set? Is the team stuck in self-defeating routines of thought so that certain issues cannot be considered and creativity is stifled? What are the micro-processes of communication? Why does the group not listen to Jill?

Why is Jack always interrupted? Why is John allowed to dominate the agenda? Typically, the developer will be acting as a group therapist, helping the group to articulate its fears, work though the intractable issues and reach a consensus on the problems facing it and how it should evolve.

Overlapping with T-groups are *encounter groups*. These are facilitated interactive sessions to help groups of managers be aware of their impact on others. Sensitivity training often involves a variety of exercises, simulations and role-plays, with the OD consultant acting to manage the process by which we come to see themselves as others see them. Psychotherapeutic techniques such as Transactional Analysis (Berne 1973) are often used to identify behaviour which is dysfunctional (destructive game playing, avoidance of authenticity, etc.) so that people can act with more self-awareness and with greater social effect. French and Bell (1999) provide a far more detailed account to which the interested reader is referred.

13.4.4 Inter-group meetings

Organisational mirroring is a process by which an organisational group gets feedback from other groups about how it is perceived and regarded. Often it involves bringing together two groups which have a history of conflict. The objective is to help members of the two groups increase their awareness of the other's activities and reduce a sense of 'them and us'.

The technique benefits from the support of an outside facilitator who manages the 'open space' of interaction. The process involves both groups producing two lists. The first is 'the complaints we have about them'; the second is 'the complaints we think they have about us'. The lists are then shared between the two groups. Typically, it emerges that many of the complaints can be resolved quite rapidly because they result from simple misunderstanding and poor communication. Also the lists of both sides show a lot of congruency, that is, 'we know what they think about us and they know what we think about them'. In subsequent discussion, the lists form the basis for an exploration of the causes of submerged feelings, frictions and finger-pointing. By surfacing these issues within a climate of candour and openness and mixing the groups in subsets to work on problems identified as contentious, relationships can often be dramatically improved (see Warner Burke 1994).

A variation on mirroring is a technique called *role negotiation*. This can take place between teams and within teams. It involves individuals and teams 'contracting' with each other to change their behaviour. Using 'support and challenge' techniques, participants are asked to say what they want others to do more of, less of, or stay as they are. A follow-up meeting a few weeks later can review progress and set up new contracts if needed.

13.4.5 Process consultation

Process consultation is the quintessential OD technique (see Schein 1988). It is a participative approach in which the consultant acts as observer, counsellor, researcher and facilitator for a group. In this function the OD consultant acts to help people share in the process of interpreting issues within the organisation which need to be addressed. S/he encourages them to define what the issues are, what problems are being avoided, how presenting problems may have their roots in culture and structure.

The consultant also acts as a probe, offering observations about how processes (e.g. decision-making, communication, etc.) seem to work, hypotheses about behaviour, and challenges to consider alternative approaches. The consultant will also help groups and individuals to become more self-aware of process issues so that they can maximise the opportunities for creativity, learning and self-management in the future.

Typically this form of intervention starts with a structured observational instrument used to measure team interaction, for example, sociograms, interaction charts or a team climate inventory (see West 1994) to provide the team with something concrete on how meetings are conducted and possible areas of improvement, but then the facilitation is likely to become far more open, hopefully leading to a facilitated agreement on further, focused OD intervention.

13.4.6 Third-party facilitation

Facilitation is a general skill which cuts through most OD work. It involves a sensitive, knowledgeable and skilled third person who can act to mirror behaviour, encourage 'reflection in action' and draw out lessons for future behaviour. It involves diagnosis, questioning, managing debate and drawing conclusions. Quite apart from the other categories of intervention we have discussed, there are particular areas where skilful facilitation is at a premium.

Third-party peacekeeping interventions involve the facilitator in helping antagonists confront the causes of conflict by agreeing a diagnosis of its causes, work though negative feelings and agree changes to behaviour which may avoid flashpoints in the future. The facilitator will play a key role in interviewing principals separately to understand their construction of the situation, setting the agenda of the confrontation meeting, policing the interaction and regulating the dialogue, providing a conceptual understanding of the issues involved and brokering an agreement (French and Bell 1999).

A slightly different form of facilitation, *third-party debriefing,* is used when a manager needs objective, disinterested feedback on his or her style and impact on others. Here the consultant's job is to shadow the manager for about a day and observe the content and process of how s/he behaves. Then the manager and the consultant review the day, discuss his or her style in terms of management models and possible ways it could be improved.

13.4.7 Strategic management and organisational design

Although the foregoing concentrates on the softer end of OD, increasingly the discipline has to justify itself in terms of tangible, bottom-line results. This second-generation OD can involve the following processes.

- *Strategic management*: helping managers 'enact' their environment (Weick 1995) and 'envision' the future (e.g. scenario planning; 'future search'; vision workshops; performance gap and strategic choice analyses).
- *Organisational design work*: advising managers on how to develop the building blocks of the new organisation, for example, greater differentiation; flattened structures; improved lateral relations; autonomous teams; greater flexibility, and so on. It also means micro-work, for example, designing interlocking roles; more involving work; building learning and development into work, and so on.

- *Performance management systems*: designing systems which will support the management agenda and give expression to values of equity and fairness. Linking PM with appraisal, quality management, reward, strategy and development.

See Hussey (1996) for a good introduction to the hard-edge tools of OD.

13.4.8 Education and learning interventions

As we have seen, OD is ultimately educational and we discuss its linkage with organisational learning in another chapter. There are informal workplace learning elements in all the methods considered above. OD interventions are usually clusters of mutually supporting techniques and will draw on the core MD methods which we consider throughout the book (e.g. coaching, counselling, life and career planning, leadership development, etc.).

Pause for thought

Just who is the client?

Although the OD consultant may be invited in by a specific manager, the systematic and iterative nature of OD means that no one manager can define the OD agenda. In the course of any contract the OD consultant immerses himself/herself in the social context of the host organisation and talks to many organisational actors. So, is the 'client' the commissioning manager and his/her subordinates within a subculture? Does the contract actually stretch to other managers and their wider networks through the organisation? Is the OD consultant actually accountable to the total organisation and the greater good of the whole? These are perplexing questions which have an impact on the real world of consulting.

Questions
If you were an OD consultant what would your position be? What would you want written into the consulting contract?

13.5 Power, politics and OD

OD philosophy is based on humanistic values of trust, openness, collaboration and participative decision-making (French and Bell 1999; Burke 1994). Changing beliefs through education, culture building and open confrontation of problems are the stock in trade of the OD consultant. S/he is there to provide useful information, promote open discussion and help clients make free but informed choices. The philosophy of OD defines him/her as a facilitator, not a power-broker or political fixer. In this spirit, it is not at all unusual for OD interventions to proceed without any explicit discussion of conflict, differences of interests or the sources and expression of power.

This apparent blindness to organisational power and politics is perceived by some (e.g. Greiner and Schein 1988) as potentially discrediting to the OD project. Change always releases political forces because the equilibrium of power within the organisation is upset, yet OD seems, by its silence on 'realpolitik', to take the romantic position that organisational reality can be changed without engaging with these processes. Indeed, power and OD are seen as contradictory approaches to managing change.

However, some writers have tried to reconcile OD and power. Pettigrew (1985) in a superb study of a failed OD programme at ICI emphasises that OD needs to recognise the pluralistic power games of organisations and play them skilfully and strategically to achieve greater ends. He argues that OD has no choice. As an innovating group pioneering a shift in organisational culture, the OD team will inevitably be seen as illegitimate by some and subversive by others. As change agents, OD consultants always have a fragile political position and can be easily neutralised and discredited by coalitions of conservative forces, so they need to be aware of organisational manoeuvring.

Pettigrew in his very detailed account, suggests that OD interventions at ICI failed where OD practitioners took a techno-rational view of their input and were insufficiently aware of the shifting ideological and political contests. He concluded that OD needs networks of supporters at nerve centres of power within the organisation. It needs political sponsorship in high places and a top management that is not just permissive with regard to collaborative change but enthusiastically engaged in legitimating it (and defending the OD team against criticism). To have any chance of impact, the OD department also needs to have senior practitioners (i.e. OD specialists as senior managers), good skills, resources and access to demonstrate its value to the operating units. Most of all, the OD team needs the skill of infiltrating into the cultural and political system, showing adaptability to the shifting ideological and political contexts of the top and visibility in its achievements.

These requirements tick most of the boxes on French and Raven's (1959) classic taxonomy of power sources and power use (structural, expert, referential, etc.) and demand behaviours which are quintessentially political. OD specialists need to see the organisation as a system of shared and contrasting perspectives and beliefs; change comes about by modifying meanings through language and symbols (Pfeffer 1981). Bargaining, influencing and persuading are crucial to OD.

Greiner and Schein (1988) and French and Bell (1999) have taken this debate further by suggesting a distinction between the negative and positive faces of power and how OD practitioners can reconcile the use of organisational politics with ethical principles. However, the modern consensus is that OD has no option but to play the power game; otherwise it will become a pawn in the power games of others and ultimately be offered up as a sacrifice when a scapegoat is needed.

13.6 The skills of the OD practitioner

Ultimately success in using an OD approach to facilitate change will be an expression of the qualities of those who act as change agents. Below is an attempt to capture the qualities required of a good OD consultant. You will notice that these include knowledge, skills, attitudes, emotional maturity and an ethical orientation which are not easily found in the combination required.

The qualities OD consultants need

- *The ability to think afresh.* Each OD situation is unique and what worked before may not work here. It is best to embrace the ambiguity and address situations freshly and without fixed assumptions.
- *The ability to act professionally.* Knowledge of a variety of OD techniques, their strengths and weaknesses and how they may be used. Deep knowledge of research methods, organisational behaviour, social psychology and management disciplines.
- *The ability to network.* Being able to make useful contacts and develop cooperative relationships with people who can help with the OD project.
- *The ability to elicit information.* Knowing how to gather reliable information from individuals and groups involved in change. This means the ability to listen, to empathise and to win the trust of clients so they speak openly. It means being able to understand others' 'life worlds' so that you can act appropriately.
- *The ability to critically assess and synthesise.* The capability to collect data from different sources, discriminate between what is important and what is less so and weave it into a coherent picture of the issues requiring intervention.
- *The ability to diagnose.* The capacity to turn the client's diagnosis (which may only be an appreciation of symptoms) into a construction of organisational issues which all parties can agree. It also requires the ability to conceptualise using the language and ideas of social science.
- *The ability to persuade.* Part of the process above also implies a capacity for persuasion and an instinct for power, that is, being able to sell ideas and influence political coalitions to embrace a line of change.
- *The ability to inspire.* Persuasion also involves the ability to tap into others' energy and to radiate personal enthusiasm so that others have the confidence to try new ways of behaving.
- *The moral courage to address issues.* Much of OD involves surfacing issues which others would like to ignore and keeping them focused despite resistance.
- *The ability to develop others.* This is the counselling side of the role (e.g. helping teams experiment and learn new skills) and also the facilitative. It is about finding 'teachable moments', opportunities to challenge existing mindsets and demonstrate the value of alternative approaches.

Source: Personal observation and discussion with practitioners; competency profiles of large organisations.

Weick (1996) brings these threads together neatly when he talks of the OD consultant as a 'conceptual therapist'. Much like a psycho-therapist, s/he is helping people to represent their experience, directing attention, asking questions, provoking new thinking, encouraging them to link together experiences and hinting at new ways of seeing. Like the therapist, s/he hears lay descriptions and recycles them back in new language or uses different symbols so that clients may reframe their meanings. By changing the language and the constructs, old scripts of behaviour which had just been run off in the past are now seen to be problematic; then the way we construct situations which we had taken for granted suddenly seems absurd. This creates the climate of introspection and interpretation from which a commitment to genuine change can emerge.

The consultant role is a difficult one to play because s/he has to remain on the boundary of a group, neither inside nor outside. S/he has to join but also remain detached. S/he has to be involved enough to fully understand group members' perceptions and feelings but distant enough that s/he does not lose perspective. S/he has to be part of the stream of action by, say, facilitating a team-building meeting but resist leading in or imposing his/her definitions. The role is also difficult to play because it requires mastery of so many sub-roles – educator, process specialist, diagnostican, researcher, reflector, therapist, facilitator – and an appreciation of what is required at each point in a complex, fast-moving social process.

Historically, OD practitioners have been external consultants brought in when management sensed that fundamental change was needed. However, with the recognition that change is now constant and that managers should be facilitating change, there is a trend towards managers becoming OD practitioners in their own right. Increasing numbers of senior managers are being seconded into an OD role. For example, a recent Roffey Park survey (Anon. 2005) defined the essential management skills of the future as organisational awareness, strategic understanding, self-awareness, knowledge of change management techniques, facilitation skills, micro-political skills and the ability to manage conflict. These seem very similar to the skills of the OD consultant we have distilled above. The day may not be that far off when OD effectiveness will be a general management skill.

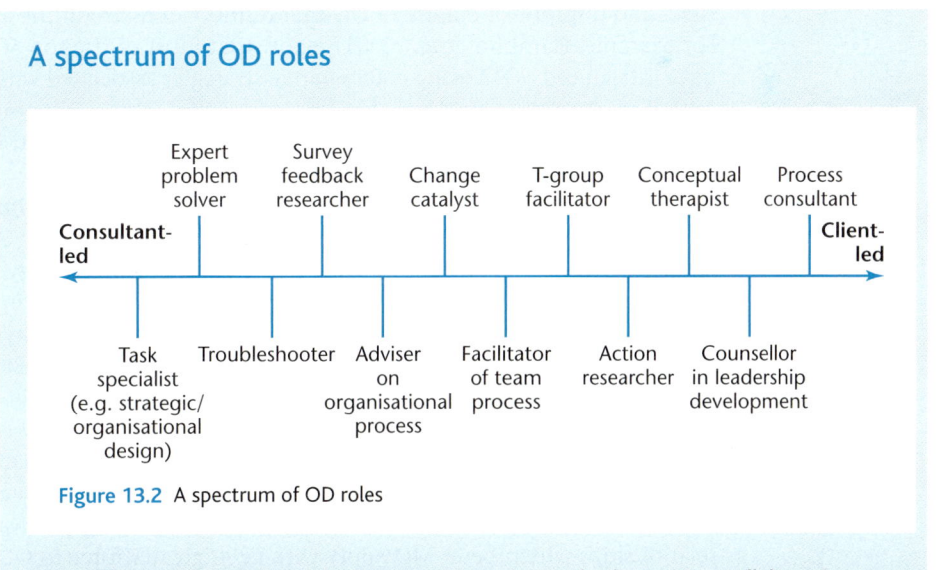

A spectrum of OD roles

Consultant-led ← → Client-led

Above the line (consultant-led to client-led):
- Expert problem solver
- Survey feedback researcher
- Change catalyst
- T-group facilitator
- Conceptual therapist
- Process consultant

Below the line:
- Task specialist (e.g. strategic/organisational design)
- Troubleshooter
- Adviser on organisational process
- Facilitator of team process
- Action researcher
- Counsellor in leadership development

Figure 13.2 A spectrum of OD roles

Although the classic role of the OD consultant is as a facilitator in a collaborative relationship with the client, in practice the role will shift backwards and forwards along a spectrum as tasks and relationships change.

13.7 A critique of OD and its future

OD is now a significant and influential field of change management. However, it is not without its critics. Research (e.g. Hamblin 2001; IRS 1997) suggests that 55 per cent of all change programmes fail and a massive 80 per cent of OD/cultural change programmes fail. French and Bell's (1999) review of the literature across a broad swathe of organisations found 'little conclusive evidence that OD programmes produce positive changes at the organisational or individual levels'. Schaffer and Thomson (1992) go so far as to say that performance improvement efforts, including OD, have as much impact on real results as a 'ceremonial rain dance has on the weather'.

Many of the failings of OD programmes can be attributed to the managerial expectation of quick results when OD processes are necessarily longer-term; to organisational politics and the failure of top management to throw its weight behind OD initiatives; to the loss of key management patrons during the life cycle of a behavioural intervention; to the lack of skills in corporate management to maintain momentum after the OD consultant has left (Pettigrew 1985). When we use a magnifying glass to observe the reasons for project failure, so many of the real causes of disappointment lie in top management's treatment of people and dominant management philosophies which are ultimately antagonist to the participative, culture-building values of OD.

All the same, OD must share some of the blame for managerial disenchantment with the perceived gap between its claims and its delivery. Too often, techniques get slotted under the label of OD without being part of a whole systems framework or the core of theory and practice which is OD (e.g. there has been a diffusion of the OD approach into total quality management, performance management and continuous process improvement initiatives, even business process re-engineering). The impoverished and unprofessional use of OD that results can discredit the approach as a whole. For example, Hamblin et al. (2001) report that most of the top 500 companies in UK have introduced TQM using collaborative strategies associated with OD, yet only 8 per cent of managers believed they had been successful. This result points to a need for OD to police its professional boundaries. If OD is so widely diffused that everything is OD, it becomes nothing and easily ignored.

There are other issues which OD needs to address. One is the image that OD retains of being preoccupied by the interpersonal and social aspects of organising when top management perceives the priorities of the future to be strategy, tasks, technologies and structure. There is also the problem that foreshortened timescales in business mean that managers want fast response. However, the philosophy of OD is essentially continuous planned change which doesn't allow quick results. Then there is the problem that OD relies on certain cultural assumptions which may not hold in all societies. Openness, expression of feelings and critical discourse may play well in Scandinavian societies with their democratic tradition but in more authoritarian countries this may be seen as subversive and disabling. Finally, there is the issue of evaluation. The issues of conducting rigorous evaluation and establishing straightforward cause and effect relationships which beset MD apply with even greater force to OD. Evden (1986) suggests that 'success' in OD, more than in other aspects of MD, must be regarded as intersubjective, with consultants convincing managers of the value of intangible benefits (a 'strong' culture; 'cohesive' teams, etc.), and managers reaching a consensus on the value of an OD initiative which is then communicated down the line.

Despite the problems of demonstrating value, OD methods will continue to be used. Indeed, we might be seeing something of a resurgence of interest in OD after the phase of 'heroic', often 'directive' leadership of the 1980s and 1990s. Contemporary themes – continuous professional development, TQM, high-performing teams, self-managing teams, employee involvement and culture building all lend themselves to the OD philosophy and technique. Organisational learning will be a particularly strong theme in the future (see Chapter 6) and OD may eventually become absorbed into organisational learning as an experiential process for perpetual organisational transformation.

In addition, we can expect to see OD become more diverse with 'twin track' OD programmes offering 'fast response, result-driven programmes' (Schaffer and Thomson 1992) which promise relatively quick systems change and measurable performance (e.g. TQM, BPR, etc.) running alongside programmes which allow longer-term benefits (e.g. organisational renewal, vision sharing, culture building and the learning organisation, etc.). This may set up tensions causing OD to review its essential philosophy in tune with competitive, bottom-line obsessed times.

We are also likely to see a tendency for OD consultants to give more attention to knowledge transfer, involving clients even more fully in the change process so they have the awareness and skills to maintain programmes beyond the start-up stage. As Cummings and Worley (2001) suggest, the field of OD is in creative flux and constantly growing. With more evaluative research on the conditions under which OD interventions are successful (e.g. Burke 1994), the full potential of OD as an approach to planned change has still to be fulfilled.

Case study: The professional 'craft' of organisational development

It is all very well to describe the 'tools' of OD, but real insight into OD as a professional 'craft' comes from a description of OD interventions which shows how the wise OD practitioner diagnoses the issues and then selectively combines interventions to build the capacity of the organisation.

Here is an account of OD consultancy in a joint venture, part State owned, part owned by a major American-based multinational, concerned with the processing and canning of fish products. This was the largest manufacturing company in the Seychelles islands and a major earner of foreign exchange for the national economy.

At the time that the OD consultant was involved, the organisation was in trouble. There were quality, production and control problems. Recently a top manager from Head Office in Seattle had visited this remote subsidiary of the big American corporation and had declared himself shocked by what he had seen. He wanted this division 'transformed' within nine months or HQ would withdraw from the Seychelles operation. This would mean a loss of many thousands of jobs in a small country with few employment opportunities and the loss too of valuable foreign exchange to a fragile developing economy.

The Director of the Seychelles division recognised that the writing was on the wall and immediately took a number of steps to address the problems, as he saw them. He held crisis meetings with senior managers; he made selective replacements of existing managers; he spent time 'walking about' the shop floor reassuring and motivating front-line workers and supervisors and introduced some training programmes. Nothing seemed to work.

It was at this point that he decided that an OD consultant was needed.

The phone rang; the consultant picked it up. 'We need some help, can you advise us?' the client asked. The consultant immediately said that he was not in the business of authoritative advice but he would help management with their thinking processes. The client agreed.

The first stage of the consultancy involved an exploratory visit, talking to the general manager, observing the work processes, meeting informally with the top teams . . . to get a flavour of things.

The consultant then went away to consider a methodology to probe deeper. He came back a couple of weeks later. He interviewed a 'vertical slice' of managers and staff, starting with the top managers. What came out of the interviews was that the division's goals lacked clarity and were not specific enough for people to know what they had to do. There were also some inter-departmental/ interpersonal problems, for example, conflict between certain senior managers and feuds between departments. As a result, sectional infighting seemed to displace the ends of strategy.

However, the consultant still felt that he didn't understand the culture sufficiently. This led him to take soundings about the division's culture through interviews and focus groups. What he found was that the division was very bureaucratic – most of its energies seemed to be absorbed in internal communications, handling internal tensions and balancing sectional pressures. The bureaucratic culture seemed to create a narrowness of focus: committee skills were more valued than risk-taking or change-making. It was hierarchical and slow-moving.

The consultant believed that his first priority was to deal with the team issues. He organised a special meeting with the senior management at a hotel in the hills around Victoria, the capital of Seychelles. What emerged from a day-and-a-half of discussions, self-test exercises, group encounter and mirroring was that the conflicts in the organisation went further than mere tensions between individuals at the top of functional departments. There were issues of group interdependencies and conflict based on differences in values and perception about the purpose of the organisation and where it was going.

The next step was another off-site meeting with those departmental heads and their teams who were most at loggerheads. The consultant used mirroring to help the groups clarify their differences and seek a way of overcoming them. This session helped with communication and team integration. It helped to unite management around some core shared values of change and development.

However, the outcome of the inter-group meeting suggested another step. A major problem needing attention was that the production division was not working as a team. This resulted in a process consultation and team-building session with the top team. The sessions involved exercises in defining roles, giving feedback on team relationships, agreeing the distribution of tasks, ways of working to improve collaboration and team goals.

But the consultant remained troubled. At this point, he came to the conclusion that the interventions so far had addressed symptoms not causes. He felt that the culture of this 'machine bureaucracy' also needed to be tackled. Booking a meeting with the divisional director, he suggested some 'root and branch' reforms, for example, redesigning structures so that they were more project-team based; systematically reviewing all procedures and systems to determine if they could be simplified or discontinued; redesigning work so that it was more enriched and involving; building more autonomous teams based on TQM; encouraging a climate of empowerment and learning; investing in learning and development and changing the reward system so that it gave recognition for commitment and performance.

The divisional director was shocked. But surely this would require a massive shift in management style and culture? He didn't think the organisation was yet ready for this order of change and corporate HQ was bound to oppose it. However, he was prepared to recommend that the Seychelles division review the distribution of job responsibilities and invest in some skills-based training. Beyond this, he could not commit himself.

Not surprisingly, soon after this meeting, the consultancy involvement came to an end; or rather, it just petered out. The division never was 'turned around' and within a year the American company had withdrawn from its partnership with the Seychelles governments, and its managers and staff were made redundant.

What this little case study shows is a fairly typical OD intervention. The patterns are familiar.

- It proceeds *iteratively*, that is, in waves, with diagnosis, feeding back, discussion, getting agreement on action and review.
- It involves a range of techniques brought together to support diagnosis and action.
- At each stage, the client is involved in defining and agreeing the change and implementing it. When the client cannot be involved then the consultancy becomes marginalised and may be brought to a premature end.
- As the consultant becomes more familiar with the organisation it is possible to attempt more fundamental change. The problem that the client defines may not be the most significant problem but only a symptom of something larger. Also, fixing one problem may suggest others which require further interventions.
- It is not always possible to complete the whole OD cycle. The agendas of sectional groups, the mindsets of managers, power and politics can become blocks which prevent the consultancy from going deeper, that is, to explore cultural issues such as beliefs, values, ideologies, norms and implicit definitions which ultimately shape the nature of organisational behaviour.

Questions
Were you surprised at the result? If you had been the OD consultant here, would you have handled things differently?

Source: Personal observation, discussion and reflection on experience.

13.8 Conclusion

In this chapter we have considered OD as a body of knowledge and technique that helps managers bring about change. The values of OD are humanistic and educational. They are based on the view that people at work can develop throughout their lives and the organisation that harnesses their energy to enable them to achieve their full potential will also achieve its own. OD interventions emphasise collaborative learning, systems understanding, empowerment, participative involvement, shared culture and responsible autonomy. Always there is a tension between short-term business pressures and the longer-term social processes which OD tries to handle for the greater good of the organisation in the future. OD consultants are facilitative and work with the grain of the client's definitions while helping to conceptualise them in behavioural terms as part of the workings of the social system of organisation as a whole. In the process, the consultant typically plays a number of roles – diagnostician, reflector, enabler, therapist, educator and strategist – and switches between them as the change process passes through its vital stages.

Review questions

1 How can OD build managerial effectiveness?

2 With the shift to second-generation OD, do the guiding values and philosophy of OD need to be revised?

3 What skills do you regard as key to effective organisational development? Are these the preserve of the specialist consultants or can general mangers also act as OD practitioners?

4 Why do you think most OD interventions fail to achieve their objectives? Does this mean that the OD approach is flawed or does the onus of responsibility lie with managers in knowing how to make effective use of OD interventions?

5 What arguments would you use to support the proposition that despite the unitarist principles of OD, consultants need to be organisational politicians to survive?

6 How far do you agree that OD has been hijacked by change models that do not share its fundamental values? If so, what should be done?

Web links

For a selection of excellent papers and further links on contemporary OD go to:
www.roffeypark.co.uk

For information on Action Research try:
www.scu.au/schools/gcm/ar/arp/actlearn.html

For very useful information on all aspects of OD and networks of OD practitioners try:
www.amed.org.uk

DVDs/Videos

Can Gerry Robinson Fix the NHS? (2007); *Can Gerry Robinson Fix the NHS? One Year On* (2008) Open University DVD Interesting case study in 'de facto' OD and planned management change and an opportunity to see a change agent in action.

12 Angry Men (1957) Directed by R. Rose, featuring Henry Fonda
Classic ethnographic study of a dysfunctional team crying out for team development interventions.

Recommendations for further reading

Those texts marked with an asterisk in the bibliography are recommended for further reading, especially the following:

French, W. and Bell, C. and Zawacki, R. (2005) *Organisational Development and Transformation.* One of the classics in the field; a comprehensive coverage.

Hamblin, B., Keep, J. et al. (2001) *Organisational Change and Development: A Reflective Guide for Managers.* OD models and approaches described in ways which are friendly to managers.

Warner Burke, W. (1982) *Organisation Development: Principles and Practices.* Very well written introduction to OD to someone who has been there and done it.

Bibliography

Anon. (2005) *The Management Agenda*, Roffey Park Management School, www.roffeypark.co.uk

Argyris, C. (1970) *Intervention Theory and Method: A Behavioural Science View*, Addison-Wesley.

Argyris, C. and Schon, D. (1978) *Organisational Learning*, Addison-Wesley.

Bales, R. (1950) *Interaction Process Analysis*, Addison-Wesley.

Barczak, G. et al. (1987) 'Managing large scale organisational Change', *Organisational Dynamic*, Autumn.

*Beckhard, R. (1969) *Organisation Development: Strategies and Models*, Addison-Wesley.

Beckhard, R. and Pritchard, W. (1992) *Changing the Essence: The Art of Creating and Leading Fundamental Change in Organisations*, Jossey-Bass.

Belbin, M. (1981) *Management Teams*, Heinemann.

Belbin, M. (1993) *Team Roles at Work*, Butterworth-Heinemann.

*Bennis, W. (1969) *Organisational Development: its Nature, Origins and Prospects*, Addison-Wesley.

Berne, E. (1973) *Games People Play*, Penguin.

Champy, J. and Nohria, N. (eds) (1996) *Fast Forward: The Best Ideas on Managing Business Change*, Harvard Business School.

Cummings, T. and Worley, C. (2001) *Organisational Development and Change*, South Western College Publishing.

Doyle, M. (2000) 'Management development in an era of radical change', *Journal of Management Development*, Vol. 19, No. 7.

Dyer, J. (1984) 'Team research and training: a state of the art review', *Human Factors Review*, Jan.

Evden, D. (1986) 'OD and the self fulfilling prophecy', *Journal of Applied Behavioural Science*, Vol. 22.

Fitzgerald, S. et al. (2002) in Waclawski, J. et al. (2002) *Organisation Development: A Data-driven Approach to Change*, Jossey-Bass.

*French, W. and Bell, C. (1999) *Organisation Development*, Prentice Hall.

French, J. and Raven, B. (1959) 'The bases of social power', in Cartwright, D. (1959) *Studies in Social Power*, Institute for Social Research.

French, W., Bell, C. and Zawacki, R. (2005) *Organisational Development and Transformation*, McGraw Hill.

Garavan, T. (1999) 'Management development: contemporary trends, issues and strategies', *Journal of European Industrial Training*, Vol. 23, No. 4.

Garratt, B. (1996) *The Fish Rots from the Head*, Harper Collins.

Garvin, A. (1993) 'Building a learning organisation', in *Harvard Business Review*, 71(4): 78–91.

Goodstein, L. and Burke, W. (1991) 'Creating successful organisational change', *Organisational Dynamics*, Vol. 19.

Greiner, L. and Schein, V. (1988) *Power and Organisation Development*, Addison-Wesley.

Grey, C. and Antonacopoulou, E. (2004) *Essential Readings in Management Learning*, Sage.

Grieve, J. (2000) 'Introduction: the origins of OD', *Journal of Management Development* 19(5): 345.

Goodstein, L. and Burke, W. (1991) 'Creating successful organisation change', *Organisational Dynamics*, 19: 5–17.

Hackman, J. (1990) *Groups that Work and Those that Don't: Conditions for Effective Teamwork*, Vol. 23, Jossey-Bass.

Hamblin, B. (2001) Lecture on OD in the NHS; NHSP organised conference, Birmingham.

Hamblin, B., Keep, J. et al. (2001) *Organisational Change and Development: A Reflective Guide for Managers*, Prentice Hall.

*Harrison, R. (1995) *The Consultant's Journey*, McGraw Hill.

Huczynski, A. (2000) *Encyclopaedia of MD and OD Change Methods*, Gower.

Hunt, J. (1986) *Managing People at Work*, McGraw Hill.

Hussey, D. (1996) *Business Driven Human Resource Management*, J. Wiley.

Industrial Relations Service (1997) 'Cultural change', *IRS Management Review*, Vol. 11, No. 4.

Kakabadse, A. (1991) *The Wealth Creators*, Kogan Page.

Katzenbach, J. and Smith, D. (1993) *The Wisdom of Teams*, Harvard Business School Press.

Kolb, D. (1984) *Experiential Learning*, Prentice Hall.

Larson, C. and LaFasto, F. (1990) *Teamwork*, Sage.

Lewin, K. (1951) *Field Theory in Social Science*, Harper and Row.

Lippitt, G. (1982) *Organisational Renewal: A Holistic Approach to Organisational Development*, Prentice Hall.

Lundy, O. and Cowling, A. (1996) *Strategic Human Resource Management*, Routledge.

Margerison, C. and McCann, D. (1991) *Team Management*, Mercury Books.

Marshall, J. and Reason, P. (1997) 'Collaborative and self-reflective forms of inquiry in management research', in Burgoyne, J. and Reynolds, M. (1997) *Management Learning*, Sage.

Marsick, V. and Watkins, K. (1997) 'Lessons from informal and incidental learning', in Burgoyne, J. and Reynolds, M. (1997) *Management Learning*, Sage.

Mumford, A. (1997) *Management Development*, CIPD.

Mumford, A. and Gold, J. (2004) *Management Development, Strategies for Action*, CIPD.

Parker, G. (1990) *Team Players and Teamwork*, Jossey-Bass.

Patching, K. (1998) *Management and Organisation Development*, Prentice Hall.

*Pettigrew, A. (1985) *The Awakening Giant: Continuity and Change at ICI*, Blackwells.

Pfeffer, J. (1981) *Power in Organisations*, Pitman.

Reason, P. and Bradbury, H. (2001) *Handbook of Action Research: Participative Inquiry and Practice*, Sage.

Schaffer, R. and Thomson, H. (1992) 'Successful change management programmes begin with results', *Harvard Business Review*, Vol. 70 No. 1.

Schein, E. (1988) *Process Consultation,* Vols. 1 and 2, Addison-Wesley.

Schein, E., Bennis, W. et al. (1964) *Interpersonal Dynamics*, Dorsey.

Silverman, D. (1970) *The Theory of Organisations*, Heinemann.

Storey, J. (1989) 'Management development: a literature review and implications for future research', *Personnel Review*, Vol. 18, No. 6.

Tuckman, B. (1965) 'Developmental sequence in small groups', *Psychological Bulletin*, Vol. 63, No. 6.

Warner Burke, W. (1982) *Organisation Development: Principles and Practices*, Boston: Little Brown.

*Warner Burke, W. (1994) *Organisation Development: A Process of Learning and Changing*, Addison-Wesley.

Weick, K. (1995) *Sensemaking in Organisations*, Sage.

*Weick, K. (1996) 'Organisational Learning: affirming an oxymoron', in Clegg, S., Hardy, C. et al. (eds) *Handbook of Organisational Studies*, Sage.

Weick, K. and Quinn, R. (1999) 'Organisational change and development', *Annual Review of Psychology*, Vol. 50.

West, M. (1994) *Effective Teamwork*, BPS Books.

14 Evaluating management development

Learning outcomes

After studying the chapter you should be able to understand, analyse and explain:

- why evaluation of MD often does not happen;
- what purposes evaluation serves and the benefits it confers;
- a number of frameworks and models for conceptualising the evaluation of MD;
- the types of evaluation and the conditions under which they might be used;
- the special nature of MD and why it presents particular difficulties of evaluation;
- different philosophies and approaches to MD evaluation;
- various methodological choices in MD evaluation;
- political and cultural issues in conducting MD evaluation.

14.1 Introduction

Employers spend vast amounts on training and development. In 2007 the figure was something like £13 billion in UK alone, and a lot of this was devoted to management development. In the USA the figures are much larger. Large American corporations spend $50 billion a year on executive education; 20 billion work hours are devoted to it (Ready and Conger 2003). Since the millennium the annual budgetary growth in MD and leadership development has been of the order of 10 per cent. Although the credit crunch will take its toll, the bouyancy in spending on development is likely to continue as organisations seek to stay ahead of technology and develop the creativity and responsiveness of their key workers, not least their managers. However, in the midst of this boom, only a minority of organisations seem to regularly evaluate their training in terms of business impact and a much smaller percentage do a 'return on investment analysis' (See Eadie 1999).

The more nebulous the training (e.g. attitudes and behaviour rather than specific skills), the less effort that tends to be expended in evaluation because the methodological problems to be overcome are just too great. However, as we have seen, MD is renowned for its questionable (or is that 'creative'?) programmes. Calypso dancing, outdoor adventure, walking on hot coals and so on are all offered to promote better teamwork, leadership, creativity or motivation. Developing management capabilities is universally seen as of strategic value but disquieting questions remain about its effectiveness. If truth be told, the body of tested development method is still in the process of emerging. Lewis and Thornhill (1994) quote the memorable words of one top manager 'One half of our MD budget may be well spent but we don't know which half'.

Just because these courses are unusual does not necessarily mean that the events are ineffective or a form of charlatanism, but if no evaluation is done it obviously means their value is unknown and that is an Achilles heel for developers at a time when development is under pressure to show its effectiveness.

This is a relatively new experience for MD. Historically, as Mant (1977) claims, MD has been largely regarded as an act of faith. The traditional assumption has been that developing our managers must be good for the organisation as a whole. Even if the learning objectives of the course are not met, the assumption is that something will still spin off and that will be for the good for organisational players with the strategic importance that managers have for the future of the organisation. Walton (1999) claims that this is suggestive of a 'gentlemen and players' mentality. Until recently, MD was historically for 'officers' who didn't need the same tight control or evaluation as training for 'other ranks'. There was an assumption that as figures of authority deriving intrinsic satisfaction from their work, managers could be relied upon to develop themselves with periodic formal inputs, and done without detailed monitoring.

However, all this is changing. The new emphasis on bottom-line results and the alignment of all activity to the strategic purpose of the organisation means that activities which cannot show a measurable 'value added' are vulnerable to retrenchment. The outsourcing of development to contractors and the integration of development with performance frameworks also set up new pressures for accountability through evaluation. The growing professionalism in delivery and the search for ever higher standards in development design adds another turn of the screw. Management development, like training as a whole, is big business and needs to show its effectiveness.

As John Burgoyne (2001) has said:

The extraordinary thing is that there is no proof that MD works. At the macro level, there s some evidence indicating that organisations with sensible MD practices derive performance gains, just as they do from good HR practices generally. But the growth of MD methodology, which is vast and quite eccentric in some ways, is a massive act of faith. It's weird and – even stranger – we have lost sight of the fact it's weird.

This poses great challenges for MD practitioners taxed with the responsibility of demonstrating their effectiveness.

14.2 Why evaluation is often not done

Organisations know that they should evaluate their MD activities. Evaluation is part of the training/learning cycle (Stewart 1999) (as below), but it is the phase of development which is most neglected and least well done. This is true for HRD as a whole, but particularly MD with its special issues of clarity and measurement. In the 1990s, Lewis and Thornhill (1994) suggested that only 15 per cent of British organisations made any real effort to assess the benefits of MD and this was at the most basic, customer-reaction level. It would be interesting to know if the figure has changed much 15 years on.

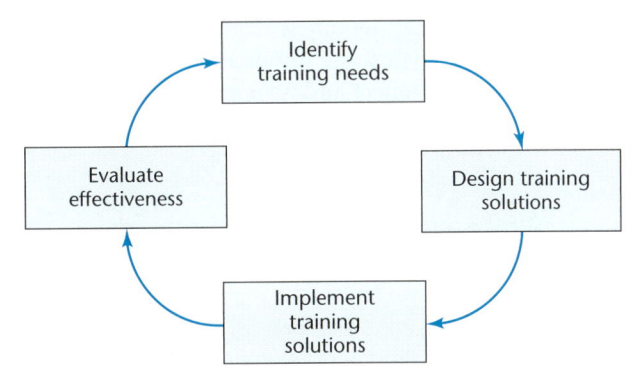

Figure 14.1 The systematic training cycle
Source: Adapted from *Employee Development Practice,* Pearson Education (Stewart, J. 1999).

It is easy to dismiss the reasons cited by practitioners for not effectively evaluating as 'excuses'. However, they are very real for the people concerned. The main reason cited by developers for not evaluating is lack of time and resources. It is time-efficient to use straightforward end of intervention evaluations, such as 'happy sheets'. However, these only gauge the satisfaction of participants with a learning experience; they do not measure changes in performance.

Evaluation methodologies which assess the contribution of an intervention to individual and organisational effectiveness and come to some conclusions about cost-effectiveness and strategic value will involve time and skill which developers often lack. Sensible organisations will source the resources which are needed. However, the reluctance to evaluate beyond the superficial may go deeper. Developers themselves are often imbued with an ideology of individual development rather than collective learning or organisation development and this conditions their focus on immediate responses (i.e. 'if the sponsors are happy then so are we').

With a tendency to be 'activists' rather than 'reflectors', developers are also more likely to be interested in delivery than results. Their 'doing' mentality will be compounded by the values of line managers who may feel little investment in evaluation and may merely want training programmes which satisfy the requirements of a strategic plan or some performance gap which needs to be addressed (Mumford and Gold 2004). In organisations with a 'tick box' style of managing this will be particularly likely. Then there is the problem of learning objectives. It is not at all unusual for MD programmes to be designed with vague objectives. This makes evaluation methodologically difficult. Lack of measurable objectives means lack of measurable achievements. Equally problematic are the politics involved. As we will see, evaluation can be perceived as a political process and this may prejudice the commitment of key players to a deep evaluative study (Harrison 2002).

Finally, in the case of MD, even more than in other HRD activities, successful programmes involve blended experiential and informal processes which go beyond discrete training events and call for an evaluation of the system of development as a whole. This may require a degree of conceptual and methodological sophistication which goes beyond the resources and skills of most MD departments even where the motivation to reflect and review is strong.

Why is evaluation done badly?

The rest of the chapter will implicitly return to this box. Indeed, much of what follows is really an elaboration on the issues raised here. What are the reasons for ineffective evaluation in development?

- *The cost of evaluation often seems to outweigh the tangible benefits.* This is particularly true of under-resourced development departments who are assessed on volume not outcome.
- *There are difficulties of measurement.* The more ambitious the learning programme, the more difficult it is to measure it. Did that executive course for directors really improve the quarterly results or was it due to movements in the wider economy?
- *There are difficulties in disentangling the effect of development from other variables.* The action learning sets (ALS) for middle managers was probably a good thing but could the experiential wisdom they gained have been acquired in other ways?
- *There are ideological blocks.* Often organisations have a religious view of MD. MD is seen as good, almost as an act of faith. It is an absolute value because other organisations we admire are doing it. It is also a good thing because managers are such important players in an organisation and they will surely derive something of benefit from it which will translate into organisational effectiveness.
- *There are cultural issues.* Where there is a hire/fire ethos rather than a culture of growing people, development is either not done at all because employees are not valued as future assets, or it is not given any real value for strategic purposes. Equally, a defensive corporate culture may be reluctant to evaluate because it may raise awkward questions about effectiveness and strategic direction about which both developers and top managers may feel sensitive.

- *Finally, as we will see, organisational politics always plays a part in evaluation.* There are always issues of who evaluates and for what purpose. The results of evaluation exercises can be used as political ammunition in inter-factional manoeuvring.

For these and other reasons, we can expect that organisations will typically either ignore the evaluation stage of the learning process, undertake it with reluctance or in ways which are compromised or partisan.

14.3 Why evaluate?

14.3.1 What is evaluation?

Despite the foregoing, the pressure is on for MD to collect data and analyse it to demonstrate that it is adding value to the business. Increasingly, there is agreement that a learning process has not run its course unless there has been a deliberate attempt to evaluate its effectiveness (Beardwell and Claydon 2007).

But what is evaluation? Definitions of evaluation can be more or less inclusive. A focused 'exclusive' definition (Rae 2001) has it that:

> Evaluation is the assessment of the worth of development in terms of both value and cost effectiveness.

However, a more 'inclusive', more ambitious definition is suggested by Staines and Patrick (2003):

> At its best the evaluation of learning is concerned with producing evidence of learning outcomes as they contribute to strategic intent and insight into how such outcomes are produced.

Evaluation may be concerned with the outcome of a specific learning event or the changes brought about by a more unstructured, informal learning process (e.g. an ALS linked to self-development) which is far less discrete in nature and output. Of course, the more intangible the process and the more strategic the link which needs to be demonstrated, the more difficult the evaluation will be.

A classic approach to evaluation makes a clear distinction (Reid and Barrington 2000):

(a) *Validation* (or internal validation): have people learnt what was intended from the programme or experience? So, were the learning objectives achieved and were the expectations of the management participants satisfied?

(b) *Evaluation* (or external validation): have people put what they learnt to good use? This implies the question of whether performance has improved because of the learning intervention. Following this track may mean examining the issue of whether the objectives achieved were necessarily the most useful objectives. Did the learning really lead to improvements in behaviour; was the achievement of objectives worth the investment?

A moment's thought will probably tell the reader that demonstrating *validation* (often required by outside bodies, e.g. ISO 9000; 'Investors in People', etc.) is usually easier and requires less depth of investigation than demonstrating effectiveness which is implied by *evaluation*. Studies which look at the total value of a learning experience (which may go beyond defined objectives) and puts learning within the wider frame of organisational change require the most sophisticated methodologies.

Types of evaluation

Evaluation comes in many forms, with different approaches and methodologies. The evaluation type should be chosen to fit the development questions that need to be asked. Sometimes various evaluation types will be combined, perhaps at different stages in a programme.

- *Evaluation assessment*: considers the feasibility and suitability of an evaluation strategy.
- *Programme monitoring*: is a form of validation to ensure conformity to standards, requirements and policies.
- *Quality assurance*: is very similar and involves monitoring to ensure compliance with previously agreed standards.
- *Self-evaluation*: where the learner engages in self-critique.
- *Cost-effectiveness/benefit evaluation*: where the main interest is in return on investment in terms of service delivery.
- *Meta-evaluation*: a summary and critical appraisal of a number of evaluations to determine common themes.
- *Process evaluation*: a study of the behavioural processes and quality of the climate and social relationships within a learning event.
- *Formative evaluation*: this is the information collected while the programme is running to determine if learning goals are being achieved. Usually involves taking soundings from participants and making adjustments to the programme as it progresses.
- *Summative evaluation*: measurement of the final result; assessing changes in relation to objectives. Also known as 'outcome evaluation'.

Source: Adapted from Robson, P. (1997) *Real World Research*, Chapter 7, Blackwell; Gibb, S. (2002) *Learning and Development*, Palgrave.

14.3.2 The benefits of evaluation

The value of evaluation is ultimately about joining up various strands: development, business strategy, development needs, development methods and development outcomes. It is the quality control part of training and development and, as such, is of importance to any of the many stakeholders to a development project or process who hope to see an improvement as a result of an investment of development resource.

Simmonds (2003), Reid and Barrington (2000) and Megginson and Banfield (2000) provide us with a detailed assessment of the potential advantages of carrying out evaluation. In most cases their concern is with training but many of their points apply equally to MD. All these writers quite correctly suggest that different evaluation strategies will yield very different kinds of data and satisfy the needs of different groups of stakeholders. All the same, there are common advantages which are summarised below.

Evaluation confirms the extent to which learning objectives have been achieved. It is perhaps the litmus test of any learning programme: does the scheme achieve what it set out to achieve? Have the processes set up produced demonstrable results which were anticipated from the needs analysis and development plan? As we suggested above, this is the validation aspect of the evaluative process. It is concerned with whether the learning gap assessment was accurate, learning objectives were properly identified and deficiencies in skill, knowledge and behaviour are being remedied. Essentially, has the development completed what was required and delivered what was expected? (Simmonds 2003).

Evaluation demonstrates the costs and benefits of investing in MD. The concern here is whether the programme has delivered in terms of economy, efficiency and cost-effectiveness. The cost is likely to be more than the formal elements of learning (e.g. what about the cost of organising the event; of covering for absent staff; 'opportunity costs' of them not being at their desks). Has it been a good investment?

The evaluation may seek to provide data on how effectively resources such as money, people, space and equipment have been used. Just how much is the learning programme costing the company? This may involve a comparison of the costs and benefits of different development methods. We consider some of the methodologies for establishing return on investment later on. Well-conducted exercises usually use monetary values as a proxy measure to represent tangible and intangible costs/benefits and seek to present a balance sheet of the value of investing in MD against the costs.

Evaluation shows the link between learning intervention and performance. This equation is at the heart of learning process. Is there evidence that those involved in the development are benefiting from it? Does it seem that their work performance is improving because of it? This is essential data for assessing whether there has been any real added value as a result of development. Evaluation in this mode can show the sponsors of MD if there has been knowledge and skill transfer resulting in better performance on the ground (Reid and Barrington 2000).

Follow-up evaluation studies can show measurable performance gains using objective indicators. They may also call on 360-degree assessment to map stakeholder perceptions. Have there been measurable effects on learners? Has decision-making behaviour changed? Do managers display different attitudes and values? The self-perceptions of participants might be also captured (do *they* think they are now more effective)?

As well as measuring the effect of learning on individuals and showing an improvement in competencies, evaluation can also provide evidence of the value of the development process for collective learning and the strategic performance of the organisation as a totality. As we will see, the more attenuated the relationship between the particular and the global, the more difficult it is to make a plausible case of cause and effect. However, this is not to deny that evaluation has the potential to provide valuable feedback data for organisational development as well as particular learning programmes and it is to be hoped that more organisations will recognise this in future (Simmonds 2003).

Evaluation provides data for future learning development. A major benefit of intelligent evaluation is that it gives feedback to the designers of learning programmes. It adds to the body of development experience which becomes a part of the intellectual property of the professional group. The data shows developers where their efforts have been most fruitful and where the return has been low. It demonstrates how far learning needs have been met and defines further learning needs which the development has uncovered incidentally. It provides evidence for resetting learning objectives and revising learning designs so that they remain current and relevant (Megginson and Banfield 2000).

Politically the evaluation data gives feedback on the effectiveness of the MD function, justifies its use of resources and provides a platform to build its profile for a more ambitious organisational role.

Evaluation gives important feedback to individuals to help them focus their energies. Feedback rewards learners with knowledge of their success or feedback on improvement needs. The results of evaluation help the learners reflect on their performance, consider gaps and change behaviours where that is necessary. Evaluation allows them, with the developer, to assess further individual learning needs and the blend of formal and informal development which may be needed in the future.

Evaluation feedback gives developers usable performance data to assess their effectiveness. Were the tests and exercises on the course effective? Should the theoretical models and techniques used now be refined? Can the learning process be streamlined? Do developers need to acquire new skills (Simmonds 2003; Lundy and Cowling 1996)?

Evaluation gives managers of MD information for their business case – on the success of their programmes, the cost-effectiveness of their choice between alternative lines of provision, the competence and satisfaction of learners and their managers. It strengthens their arm in asking for more support from the top.

Of course, evaluation feedback can just as easily provide key stakeholders with unwelcome surprises as welcome validation of their competency and effectiveness. However, the claim of the advocates is that evaluated learning is always of benefit, because it provides the stimulus for continuous improvements to be made to programmes as learning accumulates.

Easterby-Smith's model: purposes of evaluation

Easterby-Smith (1996, with Thorpe 1997) has published some of the most incisive work on evaluation of MD practices and processes. He categories the reasons why anyone would want to evaluate and the benefits which they may derive.

Proving. The motive here is to demonstrate some improvement has occurred because of development activity. This is often led by management expectations – to see value, impact or outcomes – which can be defended in terms of strategy and organisational objectives (e.g. the development programme has led to a rise in productivity, higher competence, reduced labour turnover, etc.). The concern here is for systematic analysis with tangible measures of success and failure.

Improving. The benefit of evaluation within this category is the demonstration that development programmes are being revised and streamlined. They are becoming more satisfying and more effective for participants.

Learning. Here evaluation seeks to show how MD helps the learning process. Evaluation seeks to monitor and facilitate the informal learning by reflection on results on which progressive MD relies.

Controlling. This is often the motive for evaluation. The benefits it confers here will be uneven. Higher management, the sponsors of development programmes and managers of development are likely to benefit more than developers and individual learners from evaluation of this kind, but the feedback may raise standards overall. Here evaluation data is used to ensue that developers are performing to agreed standards, learning objectives are being met and formal programmes are being run according to accreditation criteria (e.g. the type of evaluation a university accrediting a corporate programme might adopt).

Ritualism. This is the last function which evaluation can perform. If, as we have seen elsewhere, MD is seen as a social and symbolic as well as a learning process, this is important. Here Easterby-Smith (1996) is thinking of the ritual of 'happy sheets', customer satisfaction questionnaires distributed at the end of the standard short course as a social convention and for developers to capitalise on the euphoria which happens when strangers have bonded during a week of shared experience, even if that was a week of shared misery. This implies another function of evaluation which we will examine later. Evaluation can serve the benefit, for some, of proving performance data for internal organisational politics.

Source: Adapted from Easterby-Smith, M. (1996) *Evaluation of Management Education, Training and Development*, Gower.

14.4 Models and frameworks for evaluating MD

A coherent model or theoretical framework is a useful tool for identifying and working out causal relationships in learning. It helps developers think holistically and to focus their attention on nodal points where intervention is needed.

Most of the evaluation models which exist are geared to general training and development. Very few are specific to MD. That does not mean that the generic models are irrelevant to considering MD processes, merely that MD is more open, more unstructured, far less event-based and less specific than training. There is an experimental, interactive and emergent quality to MD which inhibits standardised evaluation. All the same, adult learning processes do not undergo a magical transmutation merely because the participants are managers rather than employees and many of the same principles apply. If an organisation wished to be systematic in evaluating management learning as a whole, what models for organising the data collection are available?

Most developers believe that effective evaluation requires the collection of data at a number of levels. These are the classic evaluation models. They imply a step-by-step approach to evaluation in terms of a range of organisational processes, learning methods and activities. The Hamblin Model (1974), the Bramley Model (1999) and the Kirkpatrick Model (1958) are all of this kind. The composite model in the box below is a synthesis of the core ideas within these models, well known and well used by professional trainers as a framework organising logic and a justification for their work.

> ### A composite 'levels' model of evaluation
>
> It is difficult to be involved in the area of learning and development without becoming familiar with this model. It is the orthodox starting point for all attempts at elaborating evaluation practice. The model is based on the view that any learning event can (and should) be evaluated at a number of levels.
>
> *Level 1*: *The reaction level.* Here an attempt is made to tap the immediate reactions of learners to the content, methods and teaching of a learning event. What was the degree of satisfaction with the content, location, style and methods of learning? Did the participants feel they could apply much of what they had learnt to their work?
>
> *Level 2*: *The learning level.* At this level, the concern is with the amount and nature of the learning that has taken place. What has been the learning gain? Were the learning objectives fulfilled and did participants learn what was intended? What knowledge skills and attitude change can be demonstrated as a result of the learning experience?
>
> *Level 3*: *The behavioural level.* The focus here is on performance. Is there evidence that the job performance of the learner has improved because of development? Have learners transferred their knowledge and skill to the workplace? Is there evidence that the lessons of training have been absorbed and reflected upon? Have people noticed a difference in what the manager does and how s/he does it?
>
> *Level 4*: *The results level.* This is often subdivided into results at the departmental level and at the business performance level. What has been the value of the learning to the wider organisation? Has the investment paid off in terms of measurable performance results? Can some clear relationships be established between course objectives, development and performance? What was the impact on strategy and hard performance indicators such as financial results and productivity?
>
> Source: Kirkpatrick (1958); Hamblin (1974); Bramley (1999).

There are many variants of this 'hierarchical' or 'escalator' model of evaluation. Some theorists believe in a causal chain between the levels, so that the effects at lower levels have a consequence for those above (e.g. positive results at the reaction level will imply successful learning at other levels including the fulfilment of higher objectives). Others believe that the levels are hermetically sealed off from each other. But whatever the differences of emphasis between these theorists, all proponents of this approach believe that evaluation is complex and involves multiple data sources.

Not surprisingly, this orthodox approach has been subject to considerable criticism. Claims of natural links between the levels (e.g. Hamblin 1974) have been widely debunked as deterministic; no research has yet found any vertical chain of cause and effect. It is also suggested that 'evaluation' at some levels is hardly worthy of the name. For example, favourable reactions to a learning event merely indicate participant satisfaction; they do not necessarily mean that anything has been learned or that behaviour will change. Immediate post-course euphoria may have no relationship at all with organisational performance.

The 'multiple levels' model has also been criticised for taking the naive view that the purpose and process of doing evaluation is straightforward and objective. In the real world, there is always ambiguity and stakeholder politics involved which the model ignores, and its broad categories also ignore differences in organisational context and contingent and individual experience.

Critics further suggest that it is idealistic to believe that organisations will have the time, resources or inclination to undertake evaluation above level 3. In fact, it is particularly difficult in MD, even more than in training, to isolate the impact of development above the individual level or plausibly demonstrate consequences for organisational performance. As Leigh (1995) says, even with the most sophisticated methodology and systematic analysis, how could you effectively show that a short communications course, for example, although arguably vital for personal development at the micro-level, has any impact on the profit levels of the company?

Recent critics like Holton (2002) make the telling point that hierarchical evaluation by levels effectively disconnects individual and corporate performance. These models can appear to assume that the sum of individual performances adds up to the whole corporate performance. This misses the contribution of an OD element which acts as a catalyst making the whole greater than the parts. If the 'levels' model is to continue to influence professional practice, it will need to accommodate this insight. Holton proposes an alternative model (the Evaluation Research Measurement Model) which is claimed to be more holistic and incorporates a wider range of factors, for example, training design, participant motivation, learning differences and so on which are not included in earlier 'hierarchical' models.

Inevitably the 'multiple levels' model is at its weakest in evaluating the informal and collective social processes which constitute MD. However, it is a model which remains attractive to training professionals. It has stood the test of time and is an embodiment of the traditional training cycle. It also has a symbolic status in the folklore of training with which any developer seeking to introduce a more sensitive alternative will have to engage.

However, in recent years some evaluation frameworks have developed which are less concerned to evaluate a learning 'event' and far more concerned with considering 'process'. As such, they are arguably more suited to the open nature of MD in which learning through working is a seamless experience. Here we consider a few of the most cited frameworks in the literature.

The CAPIO model for evaluating MD

This is a well-known framework which has been proposed as a way of conceptualising the system of learning as a whole and systematically assessing the different elements which compose it. What are these elements?

Context. This category considers the circumstances which brought the programme into being. Evaluation along this axis provokes a broad range of questions. Why is the programme being funded and what expectations do the various stakeholders have of it? How accurately have the learning needs been assessed? How were the learning objectives set? How far did the designers take into account issues of culture and learning transfer? What did the programme mean for different organisational subcultures and who 'owned' it?

Administration. Focuses on the mechanisms by which the learning programme was established and how it ran. How were learners selected? What criteria underpinned nomination and selection? This will tell the evaluator a lot about what agenda the programme is really following, whatever the official definitions. Easterby-Smith suggests some typical logics for selection: 'my turn to go'; 'this person needs a reward'; 'this person is performing inadequately and this is their last chance'. Are these the best reasons? Are the right learners selected for the right reasons to meet the programme objectives?

Evaluation within this category will also examine the utility of the briefing, support and follow-up arrangements for the learning programme.

Process. The evaluation within this category focuses on the inputs to the programme and the meanings which the events and/or learning activities had for the participants involved.

So how well designed, planned and conducted was the development programme? Were the methods well chosen and combined? Was the use of resources both appropriate and cost-effective?

What were the feelings of the participants about the learning process? Did they feel motivated and engaged? What did they think they were learning and how were they learning?

Evaluation within this category is likely to involve qualitative methods which seek to understand the inter-subjective aspects of learning experience, for example, the perceptions of different factions, relationships between tutors and students, the mental constructs of learners as they make sense of their learning.

Inputs. These are the methods, techniques, the trainers and facilitators who contributed to the programme. This involves an assessment of the tangible resources, such as interactive technology, as well as the intangible, e.g. the intellectual capital, pedagogies and qualifications, skills, experience and character of the programme practitioners and managers.

Outcomes. Evaluation here tries to establish what actually happened as a result of the learning experience; what changes in knowledge, skills, attitudes and behaviour occurred. Can we say what objectives were met? Were there any unintended outcomes?

Easterby-Smith goes beyond the mere mechanical plotting of factors against categories to raise questions about the impact on learning on the overall organisational culture. He also emphasises the importance of feedback of measured outcomes to those responsible for providing inputs to the process and creating a dynamic interaction within the loop of objective setting, performance review and continual service development.

Source: Adapted from Easterby-Smith, M. (1996) *Evaluation of Management Education, Training and Development*, Gower.

Critics have applauded the CAPIO model for offering a framework to serve a variety of aims in conducting evaluation (e.g. see above: proving, controlling, learning, improving, etc.) (Stewart 1999). It also offers a holistic and contextualised approach which integrates internal and external factors and emphasises the link between individual and organisational needs in designing MD activities in the real world of the workplace. This is all useful and certainly allows a modelling of evaluation which goes well beyond the rigid gridiron of the 'levels' approach. It offers a comprehensive overview of the evaluation process, and its flexibility is attuned to the interactive nature of modern MD. However, the model has not escaped criticism. Although systematic, it is claimed that the Easterby-Smith model is not yet a 'systems model' in the true sense of that word. It is more a taxonomy than the representation of a process. The links between categories remain indistinct and feedback loops only sketchily defined. Woodall and Winstanley (1999) suggest that the model is still tied to evaluating structured learning events and the procedures of learning rather than the processes of learning themselves.

Woodall and Winstanley (1999) suggest an alternative 'Training for Impact' process model as more systemic and action-oriented. We do not have space to consider this here, but the interested reader is referred to Woodall and Winstanley's (1999) book and challenged to decide for himself/herself what the framework adds to the toolkit of evaluation. It may be that we still await a genuinely systemic model which captures the fluidity of experientially based MD through a nexus of iterative feedback and adjustment linkages.

A parallel strand of evaluation which we might consider, at least in passing, is that of *auditing* systems. Auditing of MD and evaluation of MD obviously merge together, but audit is usually based on accounting logic and concerned with strictly measurable outcomes for performance. Cost–benefit analysis (CBA), investment appraisal and other financially based tools are often used to measure the benefits of development. They are effective for comparing the direct costs of development inputs (e.g. training facilities, materials, time, trainer fees, etc.), and even the incidental and opportunity costs of development. They can also assess tangible outcomes which can be weighed as part of a financial calculation (e.g. in terms of criteria such as economy, efficiency and value added). This in itself is useful data for the development manager considering the comparative per capita costs of different programmes in terms of bottom-line results. However, even the most sophisticated auditing systems seem, at present, to be unable to capture the informal, subjective and often unexpected benefits of MD, 'factor out intervening variables' or isolate the precise link between cause and effect (Winterton and Winterton 1997). The Aladdin trick of conjuring the genie out of this MD bottle seems too much for this rationalistic tool.

Finally, a word about *strategic frameworks of evaluation*. Most evaluation is done at the operational level but the shift to a strategic role for MD has led to the search for analytical models and techniques which can evaluate the extent to which learning and development activities, such as MD, are having a strategic impact.

The Balanced Score Card is one of the methods used to build the strategic architecture of a company (Kaplan and Norton 1996; 2001). It is a tool for specifying the strategic learning needed and evaluating outcomes. In the model, learning is seen as one of four key clusters of factors making up the corporate strategy. Using the audit tools and inquiry approach of the score card, a high-level assessment can be made of learning and development in terms of strategic outcomes.

In a systematic way, key questions, such as those we considered in our chapter on strategy (Chapter 4) are considered. Is the top committed to MD? Is MD supplier-driven or client-led? Can we say that MD helps competitiveness? Does the culture and climate support MD or disable it? Does MD integrate with proactive planning? Does MD mesh with line managers' conceptions of MD priorities and learning needs? Processes of evaluation are set up which consider learning in relation to financial, customer and internal business and strategic perspectives. MD is audited according to the expectations of different specialised audience groups. From the evaluation, areas of concern can be flagged up which become strategic learning priorities to be addressed.

Strategic evaluation of this kind is often used in conjunction with benchmarking systems, for example, European Business Excellence Model (The Development Partnership 2001). This allows strategists to take a whole-systems view of the relationship between enablers (people, leadership, processes, etc.) and key results. Where are the leading gaps and how should they be addressed? Undertaking organisational self-evaluation against benchmarking criteria within the model also allows a clearer understanding of quality standards in areas like learning in comparison with other organisations.

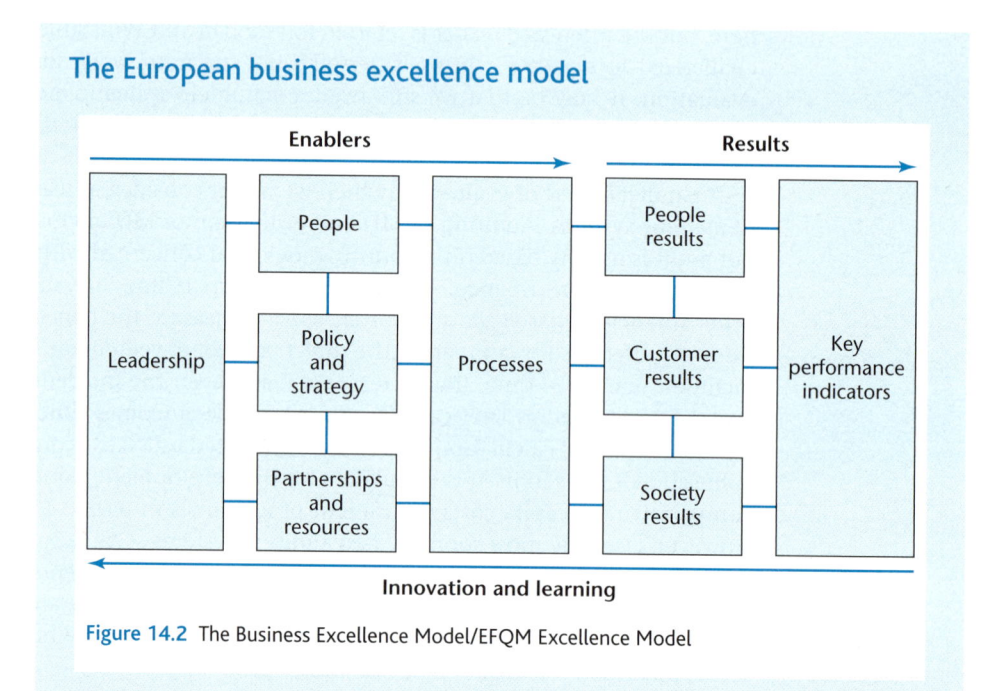

The European business excellence model

Figure 14.2 The Business Excellence Model/EFQM Excellence Model

Key to diagram

Leadership: How the organisation's leaders facilitate the vision.

People: How the organisation releases the knowledge and potential of its people.

Policy and Strategy: How the organisation implements its vision through a stakeholder strategy.

Partnerships and Resources: How the organisation plans and manages its external partnerships; internal resources in terms of its plan.

> *Processes*: How the organisation designs, manages and improves the procedures which add value.
>
> *People Results*: What the organisation is achieving with its people, for example, productivity, commitment, initiative and so on.
>
> *Customer Results*: What the organisation is achieving with customers, for example, loyalty, satisfaction, commendation.
>
> *Society Results*: What the organisation is achieving in relation to local, national, international society, for example, impact on community; ethics; environmental responsibility.
>
> *Key Performance Results*: What the organisation is achieving in relation to its planned performance, for example, measures like market share, margins, targets, performance in relation to competition.
>
> Source: The EFQM Excellence Model, European Foundation for Quality Management, 1999.

Although massively complex, not to say cumbersome, these systems offer the best hope of assessing the value of MD as a part of the business. Evaluation at this elevated level may help in making explicit 'cause and effect' relationships, asking 'what if' questions and disentangling the effects of MD from other business activities and monitoring impacts. This may show, in sharp relief, where the wheels are squeaking. However, in the end, the sophistication of the performance measures and the evaluative audit will be far less important than the depth and insightfulness of critical thinking and sensitivity to subtle factors such as quality, culture, motivation and diversity of experience, which are not easily captured by the metrics.

14.5 The special problems of evaluating MD

14.5.1 The criteria for evaluating MD

As we have suggested, there is a need to evaluate MD. Much of it is isolated, fragmented and piecemeal, separated from the everyday realities of managers' work and uncoupled from the strategic objectives of the business. It may also fail key tests for outcomes of management learning and development (see box below).

> **Key criteria for evaluating MD activity**
>
> This is an amalgam of the criteria suggested by commentators for evaluating MD outcomes.
>
> - *Economy*: have the costs of development been kept as low as possible?
> - *Utility*: has the intervention been useful to a critical audience group (sponsors, participants, higher managers, etc.)?

- *Efficiency*: did the intervention show a good relationship between the use of resource and the outcomes gained?
- *Propriety*: did the development meet standards of ethical acceptability?
- *Satisfaction*: did the development satisfy the subjective exopectations of the participants?
- *Financial objectives*: did the development achieve financial goals (e.g. higher levels of financial performance; productivity; cost savings, etc.)?
- *Effectiveness*: did the intervention have a significant impact? That may mean achieving learning objectives but also adding value in terms of skills, knowledge, attitudes and behaviour which may not have been anticipated but conduce to the greater good of the organisation as a whole. Was intervention effective in the longer term as well as the short term; for the individual as well as the organisation?
- *Standards*: did the development conform to an audit of standards (e.g. ISO 9002; Investors in People; professional validation standards, etc.)?

Source: Adapted from Woodall and Winstanley (1999); Thomson et al. (2001); Bramley (1999); Robson (1997).

The conceptual and methodological issues involved in evaluating MD are particularly pronounced. As we have seen, a lot of organisations do not evaluate MD; when they do, it is done in a piecemeal way – without enthusiasm and concerned more to satisfy immediate rather than longer-term outcomes. Certainly it is a rare organisation that attempts to evaluate MD as a component of an integrated HR system which is intended to drive real behavioural and cultural change and have a demonstrable effect on economic performance.

14.5.2 What are the special issues involved in evaluating MD?

There are five main ones that need to be considered.

The standard methodologies of evaluation are difficult to apply to MD. As many commentators suggest (e.g. Thomson et al. 2001; Bramley 1999; Mumford and Gold 2004), the higher up the occupational scale that development is targeted, the more difficult it is to evaluate its effectiveness. Soft skills such as those involved in developing managers are much more difficult to evaluate than hard skills. Many of the training evaluation tools which are available only really apply to measuring quite specific craft or operative skills in technical jobs which can be defined quite clearly.

Overall training evaluation is geared to structured training and educational *events*. It is task-specific, yet as Woodall and Winstanley (1999) make clear, MD is often informal, unplanned and process-based. How do you measure something as open, flowing and interwoven as a learning process? This is further complicated by the difficulty of defining what managers do and the nebulous nature of the skills involved. MD is typically concerned with guided experiential learning to improve qualities such as judgement, creativity, thinking, sense-making, self-awareness and so on. These are mercurial aspects of the self which are very difficult to measure. Always, there will be a lot of interpretation and most HRD departments would feel that they lack the skills and time to confront the methodological issues in constructing reliable measurement of the often subtle processes which are involved.

Similar issues of imprecision are involved in setting learning objectives for MD activities. Defining learning objectives for an MD programme is usually much more difficult than in training. Setting good clear objectives at the beginning of any learning event is advocated as good practice by many writers in HRD (e.g. Reid and Barrington 2000). In reality, the intentions of many MD processes are vague. To a degree, this may be a reflection of poor professional practice but also an expression of the intangible, often inter-subjective issues involved. Setting objectives and expected outcomes for a 'time management' or 'production planning' course is one thing, but defining objectives for a 'transactional analysis' workshop or a 'peer support' group is another, and far more difficult.

All the same, it is difficult for MD purists to escape the requirement of setting objectives. Unless there are objectives, even if slightly fuzzy like their subject matter, no measurement is possible and in the current business climate the programme is vulnerable to sceptical doubt about its value.

Another big issue in evaluating MD is how to link MD processes to organisational performance. There are real methodological problems involved in relating something as ill-defined as experiential development activity to a tight, hard 'bottom line'. Paradoxically, although the main justification for MD is that it contributes to a performance culture, it is difficult in practice to draw out the causal connections between investment in MD and improved organisational performance.

As Garavan et al. (1998) say, it is tempting to believe in a 'functional performance rationale', a linear connection between MD, improved managerial performance, higher corporate performance and better national performance, but does that link exist? Even if it can be demonstrated that the investment in development changed behaviour, was this the primary cause of a performance effect? As everyone knows, the effectiveness of managers can have nothing to do with MD, and the processes of unravelling one set of influences from another can be daunting. The imprecise nature of leadership development and the complexity of organisations make the precise delineation of causality to tangible organisational pay-off always elusive. Even in the most rigorous studies the fog of attribution remains.

A related problem is the issue of distinguishing between the direct and indirect effects of MD. As Thomson et al. (2001) demonstrate, an MD activity may have limited direct impact on financial performance or even knowledge and skills transfer to the workplace. However, if there has been improved staff morale, a better commitment to quality, greater flexibility or a more responsive management style – all intangible and indirect spin-offs – then it is arguable that the activity has been beneficial and worth doing. Given the importance of managers to the enterprise, it could be argued that anything which has even a small positive impact on their behaviour is a good investment. This is expressed well by Poulet (1997):

> Success is relative. You can go on a course and learn nothing but you meet people who challenge your thinking and you come back with new ideas . . . The litmus test of MD is whether it energises you.

There is also the issue that MD may take time to have an impact. People are not always aware of the relevance of what they have learnt at the time of learning it. That may be particularly true for MD interventions which aim to prepare people for the next level of responsibility. The time lag between completing a programme and then putting into practice some ideas which have an organisational impact can be considerable, but it should be 'factored in' to any evaluative study.

Finally, the evaluation of MD is often compromised by the context in which it is done. We will consider the politics of management evaluation a little later. However, here it is enough to say that the cultural context in which evaluation is done often does little to encourage those responsible for MD to overcome the very real methodological issues we have discussed. Developers (especially if outsourced) tend to be mainly concerned with delivery rather than higher-level outcomes. Development managers are often overstretched and have no time for evaluation which goes beyond the obvious and symbolic. Besides, line managers often lack the interest in reviewing benefits and have their own political agendas. Higher-management sponsors may be mainly concerned with high-profile attention-grabbing initiatives which confer on them a progressive and innovative aura. When you also add in the factor that MD in many organisations is a lot about chasing the 'flavour of the month' to seem forward-looking or to find instant solutions to intractable problems, it is obvious that the difficult task of evaluation is not always high on the corporate agenda. Indeed, it is easy to see that in many places, much of the time, evaluation can seem unfashionable and a poor use of available time and resources (Easterby-Smith 1996).

14.6 Design issues in the evaluation of MD

What emerges from the foregoing is that professional, systematic training models do not really apply to much of MD as we have defined and discussed it in this book. At best, they apply only to Mumford's (1993) Type 3 formal activities (Chapter 7). But, of course, this is just one element in MD; informal approaches imply a range of activities in learning, many of them ad hoc, unspecified and undefined. However, the modern reality is that business insists on evaluation. How then to design a system of evaluation appropriate to the special conditions of MD?

Writers on MD have responded to this challenge in various ways. At one end of the spectrum, some commentators, often American, call for a reassertion of methodological rigour and a scientific mindset to control the maddening fuzziness at the heart of MD activity. For example, Latham and Seijts (1998) call for 'more rigorous and systematic empirical studies of the extent to which MD programmes attain the objectives for which they have been designed'. Mabey (2002) asks for 'more evaluations which show the specific impact of MD in quantifiable terms'.

Commentators of this kind believe that too much evaluation is based on anecdotal evidence. The effectiveness of MD can be assessed more objectively if the right approach is taken. The following are among their many suggestions.

(a) Evaluation needs to be planned at the beginning of a learning programme so that it is integrated into the development process, not attached later as an afterthought. This increases the possibility of evaluation being taken seriously and conducted in a systematic fashion.

(b) To know if any programme has reached its objectives, even the most informal, logic requires an assessment of knowledge, skill, attitudes and so on *before and after* learning intervention. It is also important to do later follow-up to assess knowledge transfer and behavioural changes over time. Only in this way can learning gain be measured.

(c) Learning objectives need to be tightly defined and to show a clear line of sight with the diagnosis of performance gap and strategic priorities. It follows that evaluation has to be logically integrated with business and individual objectives identified through the performance management system (PMS). It also means that evaluation needs to consider the longer term as well as the short run and find ways of assessing higher-level impact.

(d) The criteria of evaluation should be concrete, measurable and objective wherever possible, for example, have costs been reduced? Have sales increased? Has managerial productivity increased? Can structured observation show the added value of MD in measurable terms? Do the indicators show that development has happened in areas which make a critical difference to the capability of the organisation to reach its strategic goals?

(e) The involvement of line management as a partner in evaluation at the earliest possible stage is essential if it is to be taken seriously and carried out aptly, coherently and with a commitment to make proper use of the results.

(f) Developers should manage a dialogue with all stakeholders to the learning process – managers, learners, facilitators and so on – so that there is agreement of the learning needs, processes and the form of evaluation. Through discussion, issues which are vague can be made explicit and a broad consensus emerges on the criteria of evaluation and appropriate measures.

(g) MD effectiveness should be reviewed in terms of integrated systems. Has MD been integrated with other HR systems and initiatives so that the behaviour which MD is intended to develop is reinforced by performance review, reward and recognition? It is claimed that with a clearly targeted evaluation, rigorous design and sophisticated measurement, the costs and benefits of MD can be quantitatively assessed.

'Constructionist' or 'interpretivist' critics (e.g. Guba and Lincoln 1994; see following section) will look coldly at this list. They are likely to see the search for rational procedures and functional performance criteria as unfeasible, narrow and naive. What is the point of making a fetish of objectivity and sophisticated method if intangible but essential issues like leadership, changes in style, emotional intelligence are not addressed because they are not easily measurable, and unintended outcomes which may be crucial are ignored?

Another tradition of evaluation emphasises 'fit for use' values of design which are seen as more appropriate to the essential nature of MD. This approach highlights the differences between MD and training. The work of managers is far less easy to define, and development objectives more difficult to prescribe, than for most other groups of workers. By implication the evaluation of MD must go much beyond the evaluation of courses to consider informal development processes which, by their very nature, are inter-subjective and interpretive (e.g. ALS, self-development, etc.). In these terms, trying to evaluate MD with methodologically pure instruments which miss the confusing human complexity will inevitably displace ends with means (Mumford and Gold 2004).

Legge (1984) believes that MD is a classic case of 'loose coupling'. However carefully the objectives are set and the plans implemented, there will be 'unintended consequences'. Intervening variables, which could not be anticipated, may intrude and shape the result. He suggests that 'functionalist formulae' for evaluating the effectiveness of MD programmes be replaced by a holistic evaluation process, integrated with the development process itself, which judges MD activity in terms of its context.

This is a theme taken up by other commentators. Bramley (1996) emphasises that managerial behaviour is only effective within a defined context – the job situation, organisational climate and design of work. This sets the frame for the learning process and the frame for evaluation. Have the management skills and behaviour for this context been disaggregated? Have the learning experiences needed for effectiveness been clearly identified? Is the work environment supportive of development? Is this a context that encourages experimentation with new ways of working? This implies an evaluation of MD within the context of a set of agendas and cultural relationships which may help or hinder individual managers (and 'management' as an organisational group) in becoming professionally effective.

An evaluative approach which concentrates on context and culture moves sharply away from neat technocratic, HRD-style prescriptions. Modern on-the-job MD is multiply woven and it is difficult to understand the relative impact of a mix of experiential activities. There will always be varied interpretations of how, what and why development improvements have happened. This leads some observers (e.g. Easterby-Smith 1996) to propose integrated and eclectic methodologies which seek to capture the perspectives of key stakeholders to a development initiative and link these to an appraisal of the balance of organisational forces within which the initiative was set.

Stakeholder evaluation, linked to extended 360-degree assessment, is also a theme taken up by Mumford and Gold (2004). They suggest an approach to evaluation in which evaluation takes the form of a a series of dialogues about expectations, progress and results of learning between important stakeholders. Performance and feedback data become an interpretive resource for stakeholders who ultimately come to a common agreement on the effectiveness of development as an element in strategy and the dynamics of change.

This leads on to the final turn, an evaluative design which merges with OD. 'Action evaluation' or 'process evaluation' (e.g. Marshall and Reason 1997) links the evaluation of development to the development of the organisation as a whole. Evaluation of MD becomes part of the cultural lifeblood of organisation. This model recognises the organisational complexity of stakeholders negotiating and renegotiating the goals and effectiveness of MD. This negotiation process *forms the culture* of the organisation and evaluation forms the participative process of transitory agreement on meaning and shared experience on which culture ultimately rests. The success or failure of an MD activity is no more or less than a consensus of perspective among the stakeholders involved.

14.7 Methodology and evaluation in MD

As the foregoing suggests, there is no one right way to do evaluation. A host of factors – cultural, instrumental, financial, operational and so on – will combine to define what is sensible in the circumstances. Ideological issues about what constitutes evidence and the rules of data collection will also have an influence on the evaluation design. This raises issues of research methodology. What model or philosophy of research will drive the evaluation? How are methods to be combined so that they yield the most revealing data? There is no ideal methodology; it is always a compromise.

The following are some of the choices which evaluators need to make.

14.7.1 What research paradigm should guide the evaluation?

The classic division is between *positivistic* schools of research which purport to be 'scientific' and 'objective' and the *naturalistic* research school which tends to be 'constructivist' and 'interpretive'. Here the reader is assumed to be relatively familiar with these distinctions and we will not replay the arguments for either paradigm (if you are not you may like to consult Robson 1997 or any other handbook of research methods in social science).

The nature of the data which is collected will be governed by the reason for the evaluation and the expectations of the sponsors. However, it will also be influenced by the general orientation of the evaluator. Does s/he believe that there are specific and tangible outcomes to learning activities, facts which can be identified and output data which can be measured? If so, this will predispose him or her to a very structured, scientific approach which attempts to operationalise all variables in strictly quantitative terms. The methods of choice are likely to be questionnaires, surveys based on attitude scales, structured interviews. Such techniques lend themselves to statistical analysis and presentation of results.

However, if the evaluator believes that management development is part of social process, s/he will adopt a more 'phenomenological', 'naturalistic' or 'anthropological' approach to research. Here s/he will be concerned to gather ethnographic data, especially the views of different stakeholders at different stages of the developmental experience. S/he will be interested to infer multiple perceptions. What are the expectations and judgements of managers about their learning experiences? What are the perspectives of the other parties to the learning process? Is it possible to find patterns in the meanings people give to things?

The philosophical differences between these two approaches are fundamental. As we saw in our discussion of research frameworks, one school sees evaluation as something 'pre-ordinate': methodologies can be specified in advance and discrete data collected using objective and externally verified tools of measurement. The other school sees evaluation as 'responsive' It is flexible; it develops in the process of conducting the evaluation and it seeks to bring out the multiple views of the experience held by all the stakeholders without valorising one perspective over others. Collaborative inquiry is part of this perspective. In its terms, evaluators are not in a privileged position of omniscience (as a 'managerialist' perspective might insist) and all voices of involved parties have an equal validity and an equal right to be considered seriously (see Easterby-Smith 1996 for a full examination of these different approaches).

Guba and Lincoln (1994, 1995) are particularly associated with 'post-positivistic' or 'constructionist' approaches which they call 'fourth generation evaluation'. They emphasise a form of evaluation which recognises its emergent and co-constructed nature, which values subjectivity over spurious objectivity, ambiguity over false clarity and an organisational not just an individual focus.

Some of the well-known commentators in this field (e.g. Stewart 1999) talk of the 'delusion of objectivity' and regret the stranglehold of positivistic philosophies, quantitative methods and 'realistic-functionalist' perspectives in the framework evaluation design that are dominant in this area (e.g. see Kirkpatrick (1958), Hamblin (1974), Bramley (1999), Harrison (2002) and commentary in the section above). However, there does seem to be movement towards more constructionist approaches which place an emphasis on multiple perspectives and a growing acceptance of qualitative methods. However, as we will see, there are political and cultural blocks to a full acceptance of the constructionist position. While academically acceptable, qualitative methodologies do not sit well with the managerialism which animates most organisations and is ideologically aligned to positivistic approaches. In the real world of the modern organisation, softer, perceptual data may not be acceptable to sponsors. It tends to be subordinated to hard impersonal data and cost-consciousness dictates fast and administratively convenient methods which favour structured methodologies.

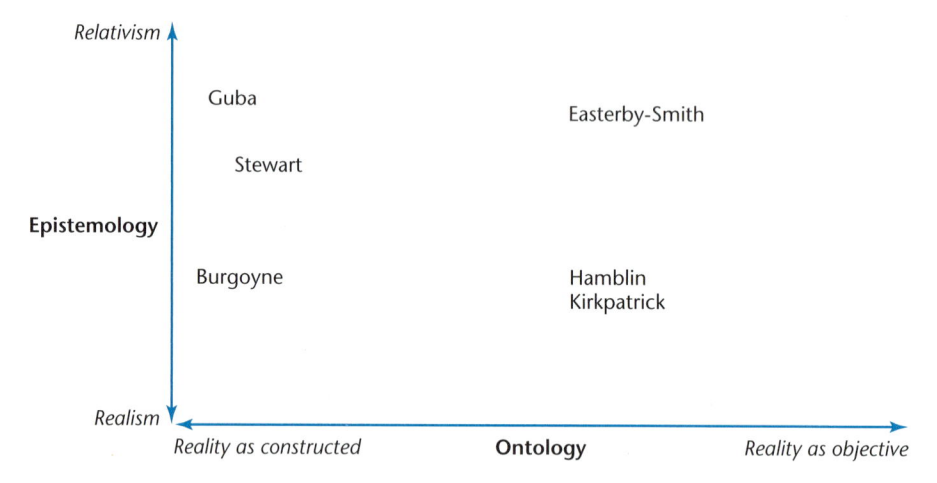

Figure 14.3 The theoretical roots of key models of evaluation

In practice, most progressive and ambitious evaluations will try to combine the strengths of both qualitative and quantitative methods. Part of the art of evaluation design is bringing together multiple methods so they are mutually supportive in terms of the overriding purpose of the evaluation and the values and expectations of key stakeholders. So, an evaluation programme might successfully synthesise data on the perceptions of participants (qualitative) with an assessment of the impact of a programme on performance (quantitative).

Summary of the differences between qualitative and quantitative evaluation

Qualitative approaches

- Concerned with understanding actors; own meanings and perspectives
- Close to the research situation being examined

- Values subjective/inter-subjective experience
- Inductive, that is, deriving patterns from immersion in the detail
- Provides holistic overview
- Concerned with processes
- Rich, vivid and textured findings
- Validated by research participants

Quantitative approaches

- Concerned with facts and causes
- Objectivist orientation
- External perspective
- Rigour and control are primary
- Verification through controlled measurement and replication
- Reliable, hard data
- Can generalise from the data

14.7.2 Validity or reliability?

An important choice for the evaluator is deciding on the weighting to be given in the choice and application of methods to the principles of *validity* and *reliability*. Both qualities are needed in an effective evaluative design but they pull in opposite directions. Validity tells us whether the interventions did or did not make any difference to the learning of those targeted by it. It allows meaningful inferences to be drawn from the data collected in relation to the evaluation criteria. Reliability demonstrates that the results are replicable: that is, if others were to conduct the same study they would reach similar conclusions (Robson 1997).

In terms of our previous discussion, positivistic methodologies, dominated by concepts of 'hard science', put most emphasis on 'reliability' which dictates a very systematic, quantitative inquiry process. But this can be at the cost of driving out validity. Results may be defensible in terms of rational process but they may tell us little of real substance about outcomes. Certainly a conservative methodology which valorises 'reliability' is likely to miss the experiences and perceptions of the participants themselves, a variable often vital to the success of learning. Equally, some of the more qualitative approaches (e.g. cooperative inquiry, narrative evaluation, ethnographic methods, etc.) which try to interpret how managers construct their understanding of the world are vulnerable on grounds of reliability. Effective methodological design seeks a dynamic compromise between these principles.

14.7.3 When to evaluate?

An important methodological choice is between a single evaluation or multiple evaluations of a learning experience. Is a single snapshot of outcomes needed or should it be more of a 'moving picture'? If the former, then simple monitoring procedures may be sufficient. If the latter, then longitudinal research might be preferred, although this will massively complicate the methodology involved (e.g. time-series analysis, balancing research samples over time, etc.).

At the level of an MD course, there is the question of whether the evaluation methodology should be *formative* as well as *summative*. Most evaluation is summative: it is concerned with measuring the final result. Does the learning achieve its objectives? Formative evaluation means evaluating development as it progresses. It promises valuable feedback to developers on how the programme is proceeding and allows opportunities for improvement as the course unfolds. Often formative evaluation involves informal talks and short group discussions with participants on how things are going. Bringing together these two strands of data – summative and formative – can provide good insight into the behavioural processes of any formalised MD programme as well as demonstrating its impact (Simmonds 2003).

However, as we know, MD is often more informal and complex than discrete courses, and evaluation may seek to assess the effect of multiple yet interwoven strands of activity. An important challenge for evaluation is to engage with the ambiguous nature of MD and measure changes as a result of development.

One approach here might be to take a series of measurements of shifts over time of understanding, knowledge, skills, attitudes and behaviours (UKSAB) and learner experience. For example, a skills and attitudes inventory before and after a learning programme (or a suite of programmes) might demonstrate the effects of learning intervention and tracking of development along a time line. Indeed, if the purpose of an evaluation is to discover how useful a learning experience has been in reaching agreed standards, then, in logic, before and after data might seem to be essential (Harrison 2002).

However, while it might seem unexceptionable to establish a fixed baseline for evaluation against which all activity can be judged, this is easier said than done in MD. Pre/post evaluation may be relatively straightforward where the learning involves a specific off-the-job training event cultivating practical skills and demonstrable outcome (e.g. the mastery and application at work of a new computer package). However, it is far more difficult where subtle social skills and higher-level cerebral functions, like strategic thinking and judgement, are involved (as on an executive development programme) and the learning experience is a blended combination of formal and informal over a considerable period of time (as with most progressive MD) (Gibb 2002).

14.7.4 How to isolate cause and effect?

Resolving this question will also involve methodological choice. As the foregoing suggests, disentangling variables in a blurred and complex area such as MD is notoriously problematic. It is always difficult to show an unequivocal link between MD, personal and organisational performance. Management effectiveness may have little or nothing to do with formal MD systems. There are so many intervening conditions that even distinguishing between influences in explaining a shift in behaviour is always problematic.

The most important issue here is: how convincing does the link have to be? As above, establishing a fixed benchmark measurement and then making periodic assessments over time will be suggestive, not conclusive. If a higher standard of proof is demanded by sponsors then a quasi-experimental design may be needed. This involves setting up a target group which receives development input and a control group which does not. In theory, any changes in behaviour can then be attributable to development rather than anything else.

Of course, in the real world there will be many practical and methodological problems:

- Sample sizes are likely to be small in the first place and over time there will be natural shrinkage so that comparisons between the groups become statistically unsound.

- It is often difficult in practice to match control and target groups in terms of key characteristics which are held to be important (seniority, roles, responsibilities, etc.), so the process of comparing like with like becomes suspect.

- It is often impossible in the complex conditions of the organisation to control the significant factors and keep work conditions, technology, management and so on constant between the two groups so that the influence of one significant variable – development – is examined.

The problems involved in using experimental methodologies may suggest a common experience in MD evaluation. Sophisticated methods may be to no avail if they fail to engage with the realties of organisation and the culture in which MD is embedded and from which it takes its meaning. This leads naturally to the next theme.

14.7.5 How thorough and deep should the evaluation methodology be?

Given the time and cost involved in undertaking evaluation, there is no point in being purist and doing a more sophisticated evaluation than the situation requires. The developer may opt for relatively simple methods which are quick and easy to administer or s/he may go for more elaborate measuring devices which are more cumbersome and time-consuming.

A major issue for the evaluator is deciding on the level of analysis which is needed. This will be led by the purpose of the evaluation. Determining the satisfaction of participants on a course will require simpler evaluation methodologies than a strategic impact study which tries to distinguish between the relative effectiveness of different strands of MD activity on organisational performance. What is needed is a structured approach for design of methodology in terms of evaluation purpose.

The 'multiple levels' model revisited

Earlier, we reviewed the Kirkpatrick, Hamblin etc. 'levels' model. We noted its limitations as a rather mechanistic framework for evaluating MD. All the same, it remains remarkably useful scaffolding for linking level of evaluation with appropriate methods.

The reaction level. Because the need here is for an assessment of participant satisfaction, the main instrument will be a questionnaire or structured interviews or group discussions. These techniques are often referred to derisively as 'happy sheets'. Reactions may be tinged with euphoria at the end of a course which evaporates on return to work.

This data will probably tell us little about the genuine feelings of participants or their learning gain, but may be all that the system requires at this stage. Requests for further development and the return of past trainees can be useful indicators that the learning experience was at least enjoyed by those who were part of it.

The learning level. This is the level at which an attempt may be made to assess learning gain. It may be the point at which tests of knowledge, skill, attitudes and behaviour may be used. If prior data has already been collected, return assessments will provide consistent data on learning gain at the end of a learning process. ALS reports, appraisal interviews, psychometrics, informal discussions and self reports may provide supplementary evidence of personal and professional growth during the reporting period.

In blended MD programmes there may be no obvious end point of learning, but the conclusion of a major component of a programme (e.g. a series of ALS meetings or a rotational assignment) may provide a natural pause to reflect on the nature and effectiveness of learning.

In choosing methods of measuring learning, the evaluator may want to distinguish between learning which has been of value to the organisation and that which is of most value to the individual (Harrison 2002).

The job behaviour level. Improvement in the job behaviour of managers, as defined by learning objectives and needs analysis, is often seen as the litmus test of learning intervention. Where the evaluation is formal, some follow-up a few months after the event/s may provide evidence of knowledge transfer and behavioural modification.

Mann and Robertson (1996) believe this is the vital level of assessing the value of a programme. Has learning been retained and has there been a noticeable change in behaviour? Often there is a time lag between development and the appearance of an improvement in performance. Follow-up will assess whether the manager has tried to enact change based on learning and whether the organisation has facilitated him/her. Mann and Robertson (1996) believe that what often emerges from follow-up is that specific knowledge may have faded but self-efficacy (or self-confidence in learning through doing) has grown if the manager has been allowed to make changes following the learning episode. Successful innovation emboldens the learner to build on change and become self-developing. The lesson here for organisations keen to maximise learning transfer is to give the learner an opportunity to gain a sense of mastery through supported quick wins at the end of a learning experience. This can be fundamental in developing active managers even when the details of learning have evaporated (Reid and Barrington 2000).

At this stage of evaluation there is a lot of scope for interpretive measures which focus on attitudes, values, beliefs and the sense people make of their behaviour. Observations of behavioural change are also useful. The 360-degree data gathered from bosses, colleagues and subordinates can be revealing. However, there are methodological problems. Changes in managerial behaviour where the changes are subtle (e.g. a more participative style of leading a team; more persuasive communication, etc.) may not always register with stakeholders at the conscious level, and observation is always bedevilled with subjectivity. When 360-degree observers are asked to report behavioural changes, it is not unusual for auto-suggestion (i.e. we see a problem now that you have raised it) to exaggerate any change which might have occurred (Easterby-Smith 1996).

The strategic results level. As we have seen, this is the most difficult level for credible evaluation because of the problems of disentangling influences and demonstrating cause and effect in linking learning with performance.

In terms of methods, strategic evaluation is likely to require carefully designed research strategies. If the purpose is establishing the cost-effectiveness of a programme, the methodology is likely to be heavily skewed to the collection of hard data (performance indicators such as profitability, revenue, productivity improvements, new business, customer satisfaction, etc.) within the organisation and benchmark data from comparable organisations.

Other strategic impact studies may favour more eclectic methodologies – statistical data balanced by softer OD information (e.g. learning and improvements in team cohesion and decision-making; organisational climate; creativity and the rates of innovation, etc.). An imaginative methodology for strategic evaluation might be behaviourally led. How do top managers construct their organisational world and, as coaches, are they enabling or disabling their line reports? Is the organisational context as a whole facilitating managers in creating a climate of continuous learning and innovation which results in holistic organisational improvement? If not, where are the strategic blocks? Strategic evaluation of learning becomes strategically driven OD (Thomson et al. 2001).

It is not surprising that few organisations attempt evaluation at this level. The conceptual and methodological problems in drawing clear 'line of sight' relationships are too great and the costs involved are seen to far outweigh the benefits (Harrison 2002).

An organisation which evaluates systematically at a number of levels builds a bigger, richer picture of its learning processes. Whole-systems evaluation loops back into reviewing the feasibility of the original learning strategy, the relevance of its objectives and diagnosis, the quality of the learning and the capability of the organisation to support desired change. Multilevelled evaluation gives a value to the learning as a whole and its impact on the organisation as a whole. To progress up the levels is to raise consciousness from a technocratic HRD focus to an OD focus – that developing the managerial workforce implies thoroughgoing development of the organisational context in which they learn.

Pause for thought

Evaluation may be your only defence

Consider this quotation from an incensed sceptic of MD in a top position in an American transnational which Ready and Conger (2003) include in a recent article on leadership development.

> We spend $120 million a year on this stuff and if it all went away tomorrow it wouldn't matter. Disconnected programmes sold by consultants to HRD managers and MD advisers who don't understand management, can mean that the line sees LD as a code for irrelevant courses, fashions and often slightly 'wacky' initiatives unlinked to the business.

Question
How would you set about designing an evaluation programme to convince this cynic that MD/LD is more than good intentions and adult entertainment?

Source: Ready, D. and Conger, J. (2003) 'Why leadership development efforts fail', *Sloan Management Review*, Spring 2003.

14.8 MD and the politics of evaluation

As we have seen, evaluation can never be merely technical. Despite all the sophisticated methods available, it is unlikely that measuring the acquisition of learning in a process as undefined as managing/leading will ever be achieved in ways which are transparent, objective and acceptable to all. As Easterby-Smith (1996) says, evaluation cannot easily be divorced from issues of power, politics, values and sectional interests. Emphasising the techno-rational aspects of evaluation design and methodology only gives an *impression* of objectivity. A pseudoscientific approach excludes important aspects of evaluation which are ever present – interpretive judgement, the claims of sectional interests and political game-playing.

As Doyle (2001, 2007) suggests, MD in any organisation is subject to conflicting definitions, viewpoints, philosophies and expectations of what it should be and do. Always, there is a range of stakeholders playing political games and fighting turf wars which mobilise and deploy rival rationales and agendas of MD.

Corporate HR may hold to an interpretation of MD as a force for collective learning, leadership and organisational transformation. Line managers may be more interested in MD as a cultural lubricant helping managers to adapt to downsizing, restructuring and the new lateral career pathways of the post-millennium organisation (Woodall and Winstanley 1999). Higher managers as a whole may push a form of MD which is corporatist and performance-led, but individual managers may see MD more as a vehicle for credentialism, promotion and careerism.

Interwoven with the purposive strategies will be emotion. Some will be frightened of MD because it is something new. Others will be concerned that MD may build the profiles of their juniors at the expense of their own security. Yet others will interpret MD as an irrelevance to their work, part of a 'tick box' process imposed from above or a menu to be sampled and cited as part of image-building (e.g. for the CV). A few will see the invitation to participate in an MD programme not as an opportunity but as a threat, an implication that they are officially defined as incompetent in their work and require remedial training.

Within the contested area defined by MD, many contradictory tensions are found and many debates which illuminate the rival rationales of MD. Around these divisions cluster sectional groups concerned to shape the policy agenda in MD. So, often we find competing philosophies of how managers learn, rival definitions of skill sets for the future and methods of development (e.g. *my* planned, integrated programme is *your* generic sheep-dipping), all with their own corporate champions. Whose will prevails in these organisational debates has as much to do with the locus of power and with the rhetoric of persuasion as with rational argumentation of the case for a model of development.

Through these debates, 'development' is brokered as a symbolic resource for conferring legitimacy, status and reward. Those responsible for MD need to decide where power lies and how to build the most credible alliance of interests which will underpin progressive MD strategy. But this is difficult. In the 'negotiated order' within which MD is located, power may be constantly shifting between key actors – clients, sponsors, managers, participants, providers. It may also be that formal authority and actual power are unaligned. The MD department may be formally charged with guardianship of the MD strategy but real control lies elsewhere. Perhaps the board is reluctant to abdicate control over the criteria for selecting and developing the next generation of managers. Some charismatic individuals may have strong views. Past declarations and promises may have created a culture of entitlement which cannot be ignored (Doyle 2001; Clarke 2003).

In these circumstances the MD director with responsibility, but without commensurate authority, needs all his or her political acumen to keep MD on a strategic path, despite the crosswinds of political pressure. It is the demonstrable capacity of MD professionals to navigate in these political waters, remaining true to authentic values, that will do more for raising the profile of MD as a strategic discipline respected in the counsels of power than any amount of special pleading for professional recognition. MD will be treated by the top management as the strategic force it should be if its senior practitioners show they have the political sophistication to navigate the choppy waters of the policy process.

Nowhere are these waters more turbulent and require more political skill in negotiating than in evaluation. Indeed, evaluation is often used as a weapon in the manoeuvrings between organisational groups. Evaluation is always political because it has the potential to expose 'performance failures' and for providing evidence to support 'spoiling arguments' to sink a rival's unwanted programme. Evaluations can be part of a game of 'finger pointing', 'blame attribution' and 'whitewash' (Stewart 1999).

A key issue for the astute player is to ask: who are the sponsors of the evaluation and who are the intended users? Are there secret agendas? Whose issues are being served? Whose wishes are likely to prevail in the conclusions which the evaluation reaches and the recommendations which are made? Evaluations can be commissioned by departments which may have no stake in the content of a programme (e.g. the Finance Department evaluates a development programme on economic criteria alone); sometimes they can be part of a larger campaign (a very senior manager wants to demonstrate that the development route has failed, so 'tougher action' is needed). Evaluations may also be prompted as 'apple polishing' exercises by those with ownership of the programme to demonstrate that the investment was successful (Stewart and McGoldrick 1998).

Because of the politics, evaluations are often carried out without enthusiasm or with glee at the opportunity they provide for point-scoring against an opponent. Responses may be biased by fear; results are talked up to get repeat business; findings are doctored a little to meet the expectations or play to the prejudices of the board. However, even when there is a measure of integrity and openness, the MD strategy watcher will be on guard. Is one of the unintended consequences of *not* conducting a formal evaluation of a learning programme you have implemented that critical audience groups (e.g. the board and powerful line managers) are now open to persuasion by stories and oral impressions fed to them by those they trust (but may not be favourably disposed to your agenda)? Is the criticism of your evaluation methodology really well-meaning technical feedback for the greater good of the organisation or an attempt to discredit the evaluation by casting doubt on the quality of its findings (Thomson et al. 2001)?

As Easterby-Smith (1996) pithily suggests, the political context of evaluation does not mean that all evaluation is a cynical exercise in manipulation and the technical aspects of evaluation are unimportant: merely that political awareness is essential to 'avoid being a pawn in someone else's game'. This is no more important than in appreciating the mindsets of the main stakeholders, their concepts of convincing evidence and how they are accustomed to receive and judge data. Evaluation has to chime with the prevailing culture to have impact. In this there would appear to be organisational wisdom.

Case study: The politics of evaluation in a blue-chip company

This is the digest of an internal report on the evaluation strategy of an important MD programme within a family-name British multinational company. Working with a business school, a suite of blended executive education programmes (informal/formal; face-to-face learning/e-learning, etc.) was designed for senior managers who needed to become more outward-facing in their focus as the strategy of the company shifted. Some of the inputs were led by the in-company MD department and others by the business school. At the end, the head of MD conducted an evaluation on the effectiveness of this programme.

A top manager later brought in to do a meta-evaluation (i.e. an evaluation of how the original evaluation was conducted) made the following points in his corporate report.

- Using an eclectic typology of reasons for doing an evaluation (*proving, improving, learning, controlling, promoting*) (see Easterby-Smith 1996 and Stewart 1999 and earlier discussion), the meta-evaluator surmised that the main purpose in doing the original evaluation seemed to have been to *prove* that the programme was of value. The meta-evaluator inferred that this was probably to appeal to top managers' expectations that the programme demonstrated that VFM had taken place.

- The dominance of this motive may satisfy the expectation of the ultimate resource holders that the programme was an economic investment and justify the use of budget in boardroom discussion with the accountants, but other values were in danger of being ignored or given lower priority than they merited. For example, one might expect that the programme would have been commissioned to serve an *improving* agenda, and that top management would have been interested in this, but the evaluative criteria seemed to gloss this area (or so it seemed to the meta-evaluator).

- The only other core value which appeared to be prominent was *promoting*. The original evaluators were the MD department, which had designed and commissioned the programme, and their university providers. To the meta-evaluator this seemed to fall far short of objective evaluation. Although insider evaluation should not be dismissed out of hand as biased, in this instance there seemed to be an implicit collusion of interests between interested parties. The university was obviously interested to maintain its reputation and ensure repeat business. The MD department wished to show its wisdom in its philosophy, design and choice of external provider and build its status. The evaluation report on the programme, jointly authored between local sponsors and external providers sought to confirm that the outcomes of the programme were as they had hoped them to be.

- The meta-evaluator also believed that the agendas of other legitimate stakeholders to the programme had been overlooked in the original evaluation. For example, no authentic attempt seemed to have been made by the evaluators to map the expectations of the participants, their colleagues, their work teams and their line managers, who may have wanted to emphasise *learning, improving* and *controlling* agendas.

- The meta-evaluator noted that the dominant values of the evaluation designers and their budget (just 1 per cent of the costs of the programme) dictated a quantitative, questionnaire-led approach to data gathering. Fixed-response categories were in danger of 'leading the witnesses'; the choice of questions seemed to emphasise the safer *administration* and *inputs* rather than *context* and *processes* aspects of the CAPIO model. The meta-evaluator concluded that this allowed data about effectiveness to be manipulated under the guise of pseudo-objectivity.

- Finally, it appeared that the evaluation design distanced itself from the hard test of strategic impact. While originally defining and justifying the programme in terms of 'its links to business needs and organisational goals', the evaluation assessed effectiveness by the less exacting measures of reaction, learning and behavioural transfer (Kirkpatrick 1958) using economic, efficiency and (heavily managed) participant response which ignored the perceptions of most stakeholders to the programme.

Given the heavily skewed criteria, design and methodologies used in this evaluation, applied by parties who were judge and jury in their own cause, it came as no surprise to the meta-evaluator to find that the programme was presented as a 'success'. However, as the meta-evaluator argued, the story might have been different if the evaluation had focused on strategic effect and on *learning* and *improving* as well as *proving*; if the approach had been more constructivist and qualitative rather than positivistic and quantitative; if it had been collaborative in involving a whole range of stakeholders and conducted with proper safeguards to ensure detachment and independence.

The evaluation had been designed to get the results which key parties wanted. Without controls, evaluation can easily become a weapon for self-serving political agendas, and in these manoeuvres the devil really is in the methodological detail.

Source: Confidential correspondence and conversation with senior managers.

14.9 Conclusion

Enormous sums are spent on management and leadership development every year but learning activities regularly go unevaluated or only superficially evaluated. However, the potential benefits of evaluation are considerable. There are many evaluation models and frameworks but evaluation can never be a mechanical or technical exercise. There are problems with the imprecise and unstructured nature of MD as a professional body of knowledge and approaches; there are equally intractable problems of contested evaluation philosophies, rival ideologies of methodological practice and the clashing perspectives and interests of stakeholders. Effective conduct of evaluation requires judicious balancing of these variables. In particular, it needs to be contextualised to recognise the strategic value of evaluation and ensure that it is embedded as a systemic part of the development process.

Review questions

1. How would you assess the balance of advantage between external evaluation of an MD programme by an outsider against internal evaluation by insiders?

2. How would you go about designing an evaluation of an emotional-intelligence programme which used a blend of informal and formal methods?

3 How far would you agree with the statement that organisations, as a rule, don't understand or value evaluation and as a result it is often done in a cursory way with superficial results?

4 How can evaluation of MD be used to support OD?

5 What steps would you take to ensure that evaluation of management learning is a continuous process and integrated in the design of learning rather than an add-on at the end of formal programmes?

6 What would you say to one of the stakeholders to development who tries to argue that an evaluative study is premature because insufficient time had elapsed to see behavioural change?

7 How would you design an evaluation of collective (as opposed to individual) leadership development?

Web links

For information on a new form of evaluation which is qualitative and context-sensitive, i.e. narrative evaluation, go to:
www.lingupenn.edu/-wlabov/home.html

A website which is also a noticeboard for all kinds of evaluation approaches and methods:
www.policy-evaluation.org/

The UK Evaluation Society has useful advice:
www.seval.ch/en/index.cfm

Recommendations for further reading

Those texts marked with an asterisk in the bibliography are recommended for further reading, especially the following:

Easterby-Smith, M. (1996) *Evaluation of Management Education, Training and Development.* Classic and much-cited work which covers the main theories and techniques.

Hannum, K. et al. (2007) *The Handbook of Leadership Development Evaluation*, Centre for Creative Leadership. Although a dauntingly large read and chapters are written quite densely, masses of useful information on evaluation strategies for the professional.

Read, C. and Kleiner, H. (1996) 'Which training methods are effective?' *Management Development Review*, Vol. 9, No. 2. Very much aimed at the practitioner, provides good appraisal of the effective of different techniques and approaches in management training.

Bibliography

Beardwell, J. and Claydon, T. (2007) *Human Resource Management*, Prentice Hall.

Beardwell, I. and Holden, L. (2001) *Human Resource Management*, Prentice Hall.

*Bramley, P. (1996) *Evaluating Training*, CIPD.

*Bramley, P. (1999) 'Evaluating effective management training', *Journal of European Industrial Training*, Vol. 23, No. 3, 1999.

Burgoyne, J. (2001) 'Tester of faith', *People Management*, 22 Feb.

Burgoyne, J. and Reynolds, M. (1997) *Management Learning*, Sage.

Burgoyne, J. and Singh, R. (1977) 'Evaluation of training and development', *Journal of European Industrial Training*, Vol. 1.

Clarke, N. (2003) 'The politics of training needs analysis', *Journal of Workplace Learning*, Vol. 15, No. 4.

Cummings, T. and Worley, C. (2001) *Organisational Development and Change*, Ch. 11, South Western College Publishing.

*Currie, G. (1994) 'Evaluation of management development: a case study', *Journal of Management Development*, Vol. 13, No. 3.

The Development Partnership (2001) Information pack on the Business Excellence Model; EFQM Excellence Model.

Doyle, M. (2001) 'Management development', in Beardwell, I. and Holden, L. (2001) *Human Resource Management*, Prentice Hall, and Beardwell, I. and Claydon, T. (2007) *Human Resource Development*, Prentice Hall.

Eadie, A. (1999) 'Banging the bongo', *The Telegraph*, 27 June.

*Easterby-Smith, M. (1996) *Evaluation of Management Education, Training and Development*, Gower.

Easterby-Smith, M. and Thorpe, R. (1997) 'Research traditions in management learning, in Burgoyne, J. and Reynolds, M. (1997) *Management Learning*, Sage.

Edwards, C. (1999) 'Evaluation and assessment', in Wilson, J. (ed.) *Human Resource Development* (1999) Kogan Page.

Findley, J. (2004) 'Evaluation is no white elephant', *People Management*, Vol. 10, No. 6, March.

Garavan, T., Barricle, B. et al. (1998) 'Management development: contemporary trends, issues and strategies', *Journal of European Industrial Training*, Vol. 23, No. 4.

Gibb, S. (2002) *Learning and Development*, Palgrave.

Guba, E. (1995) *Fourth Generation Evaluation*, Sage.

Guba, E. and Lincoln, Y. (1994) 'Competing paradigms in qualitative research', in Denzin, N. and Lincoln, Y. (1994) *Handbook of Qualitative Research*, Sage.

Hamblin, A. (1974) *Evaluation and Control of Training*, McGraw Hill.

Hannum, K. et al. (2007) *The Handbook of Leadership Development*, Centre for Creative Leadership, Jossey-Bass.

Harrison, R. (2002) *Learning and Development*, Chs. 17, 18, CIPD.

Holton, E. (2002) 'Theoretical assumptions underlying the performance paradigm of HRD', *Human Resource Development International*, Vol. 5, No. 2.

Industrial Society (1999) *Notes on Evaluation and Development*.

Jennings, D. (2002) 'Strategic management: an evaluation of the use of three learning methods', *Journal of Management Development*, Vol. 21, No. 9.

Kaplan, R. and Norton, D. (2001) *The Strategy Focused Organisation*, Harvard Business School Press.

Kaplan, R. and Norton, D. (1996) 'The balanced scorecard', *Harvard Business Review*, Jan.

Kirkpatrick, D. (1958) 'Techniques for evaluating training programmes', *Journal of the American Society of Training Directors*, Nov.

Latham, G. and Seijts, G. (1998) *Management Development*, Psychology Press.

Legge, K. (1984) *Evaluating Planned Organisational Change*, Academic Press.

Leigh, D. (1995) *A Practical Approach to Group Training*, Kogan Page.

Lewis, P. and Thornhill, A. (1994) 'The evaluation of training', *Journal of European Industrial Training*, Vol. 18, No. 8.

Lundy, O. and Cowling, A. (1996) *Strategic Human Resource Management*, Routledge.

Mabey, C. (2002) 'Mapping management development practice', *Journal of Management Studies*, Vol. 39, No. 8.

Mann, S. and Robertson, I. (1996) 'What should training evaluation evaluate?' *Journal of European Industrial Training*, Vol. 20, No. 9.

Mant, A. (1977) *The Rise and Fall of the British Manager*, Pan Business Books.

Marshall, J. and Reason, P. (1997) 'Collaborative and self-reflective forms of inquiry in management research', in Burgoyne, J. and Reynolds, P. (1997) *Management Learning*, Sage.

Megginson, D. and Banfield, P. (2000) *Human Resource Development*, Kogan Page.

Mullins, L. (2007) *Management and Organisational Behaviour*, Prentice Hall.

Mumford, A. (1993) *Management Development: Strategies in Action*, Chs. 5, 7, CIPD.

Mumford, A. and Gold, J. (2004) *Management Development: Strategies for Action*, Ch. 8, CIPD.

Paquet, B. et al. (1987) 'The bottom line', *Training and Development Journal*, Vol. 41, No. 5, May.

Poulet, R. (1997) 'Designing effective development programmes, *Journal of Management Development*, Vol. 16, No. 6.

Rae, L. (2001) *Develop Your Training Skills*, Kogan Page.

*Read C., and Kleiner, H. (1996) 'Which training methods are effective?' *Management Development Review*, Vol. 9, No. 2.

Ready, D. and Conger, J. (2003) 'Why leadership development efforts fail', *Sloan Management Review*, Spring.

Reid, M. and Barrington, H. (2000) *Training Interventions*, Ch. 10, CIPD.

Robson, P. (1997) *Real World Research*, Ch. 7, Blackwell.

Sadler-Smith, E. (2006) *Learning and Development for Managers*, Blackwell.

*Simmonds, D. (2003) *Designing and Delivering Training*, CIPD.

Staines, R. and Patrick, C. (2003) in Wilson, D. et al. (2003) *The Future of Learning for Work*, CIPD.

Stewart, J. (1999) *Employee Development Practice*, Chs. 10, 14, Prentice Hall.

Stewart, J. and McGoldrick, J. (1998) *Human Resource Development*, Ch. 10, Prentice Hall.

Thomson, A. et al. (2001) *Changing Patterns of Management Development*, Ch. 9, Blackwell.

Walton, J. (1999) *Strategic Human Resource Development*, Chs. 1, 18, Prentice Hall.

*Winterton, J. and Winteron, R. (1997) 'Does management development add value?' *British Journal of Management*, Vol. 8, June.

Woodall, J. and Winstanley, D. (1999) *Management Development: Strategy and Practice*, Ch. 2, Blackwell.

15 The future direction of management and leadership development

Learning outcomes

After studying this chapter you will be able to understand, analyse and explain:

- emergent challenges to management;
- the changing nature of managing;
- the future of management and managing;
- the turn to leadership and leadership development; 'new wine in old bottles' or a radical departure from past practice?
- alternative approaches to leadership development in the future;
- possible agendas and future directions for management;
- development and leadership development.

15.1 Introduction

In this last chapter an attempt is made to consider MD as a body of professional thinking and practice as a whole and how it may develop in the future. We look at trends in the context of MD including new global challenges to managers and the management process. Is management itself disappearing, and with it management development, while leadership and, by extension, leadership development is taking its place? Finally, we do some crystal-ball gazing to delineate some possible new directions for leadership/management development and the agendas which it may come to adopt.

15.2 The changing nature of management and the context of MD

In this section, we consider the emergent challenges which managers may be facing in the future, how management as a body of work and as a process may be transforming itself and how management skill sets may be shifting. All these themes will have important implications for future patterns of MD.

As a caveat to all that will be said in forthcoming sections, the reader should bear in mind that despite the claims of universalism, the cross-cultural differences in management are as important as cross-cutting similarities. Although it may be possible to identify some general trends which will impact on managers everywhere, the big-picture building which is attempted here mainly applies to Western management trends (in particular, Anglo-American management), and localised management could well stand apart or even contradict these tendencies.

15.2.1 The challenges facing management

The *economic, social and technological context* in which management is conducted is changing rapidly. Since the 1990s, organisations have been reinventing themselves as they struggle to cope with deregulated markets, intensified competition, pressures for higher productivity, quality improvement and more vocal shareholder demands for higher returns on investment and more control over management (Cooper 2005). Similar competitive pressures are set to open up the public sector to more commercial ways of working.

The *new institutional power of corporate stockholders* (e.g. pension fund managers, hedge fund managers) is likely to remain as an important influence in the corporate world in the years to come. This external pressure will mean that the downward focus on staff costs and short-term returns to investors and pension holders is set to continue, at least into the foreseeable future. That means that top commercial managers will have to give most of their energy and attention to winning the confidence of institutional investors, satisfying the demands of the financial community and building shareholder value. Doing financial deals, bolstering the share price and translating results into terms which investors understand will dominate the agendas of higher management (Batt 1996; Osterman 1996).

The skills needed in these activities set new criteria by which managers are assessed for promotion. Useem (1996) talks about the old career ladder being pulled up and another one lowered in its place. It also conditions managers' priorities in where they give their energy and attention. The focus in future is likely to be outwards, building relations with analysts, bankers and institutional shareholders, rather than inwards in terms of building the organisation, that is, developing culture and capabilities. The development of an external market focus may be essential for competitive advantage, but it is likely to be at the expense of top management understanding the pressures on other levels of managers or truly understanding the new change agendas or development needs which face them (Useem 1996; Cooper 2005).

Globalisation means that managers have to increasingly think beyond national borders to exploit larger and more complex markets, respond more sharply to volatile customer demands and handle greater diversity in their coordination of commercial activities. Global businesses face a new order of complexity, scale, unpredictability and pace of innovation. These factors will increasingly require managers who can remain strategic despite the pressures of the moment and can balance competing demands and act entrepreneurially in anticipation of market changes (Garavan et al. 1999).

The rate of *technological change*, already fast, is likely to further gather pace. Harnessing the power of new technologies and building knowledge management will be important themes in the future. Digitalisation means that the adaptation of technology to the business, and vice versa, will be constant. The new technology means that decisions about production systems, product problems and customer issues can be made in hours rather than weeks. Business forecasting can be far more accurate, product cycles shorter, monitoring of internal management operations easier (also less intrusive or heavy-handed from the top) and planning more flexible because the speed of data flows allows quick feedback, experimentation and sensitive adjustment of processes as the plan goes ahead (Heller 2003).

Technology is also radicalising the nature of organisation. In the last decades, new IT/expert systems have provided the means by which organisations can be de-bureaucratised. This is not the place to go into detail and the interested reader is referred to Sampson (1995), Osterman (1996), Berkley-Thomas (2003) and Heller (2003), among others, for a detailed analysis of the forces at work. However, the effect of developments in ICT (e.g. Business Process Re-engineering; Lean Production Systems; Just In Time systems; Total Quality Management, etc.) has been to remodel organisations. Smart technology – databases, web technology, microprocessors and electronic communications – linked to smart, creative people is increasingly seen as the framework for the knowledge-rich, continuously improving, leading-edge organisation of the future (Heller 2003).

Digitalisation can create an environment in which the best minds are brought together in flexible combinations to create new synergies. With the new technology, whole levels of management control can be removed and structures radically broken up so that they become more organic and adaptive. With ICT, responsibility for operational decision-making can be devolved while higher-level control is enhanced by making performance more transparent (Furnham 2000). The top management is freed to give more emphasis to strategy, functions can be outsourced and what remains in-house can be organised more flexibly around largely self-managing teams. Increasingly managers below the top are becoming involved in designing and coordinating horizontal networks of interaction and teams of multidisciplinary and multicultural workers through electronic technologies (Read and Anthony 1992; Handy 1986, 1990).

These tendencies are likely to become more pronounced as the IT-based hot-wired organisation becomes a reality. Virtual working will soon become commonplace and electronic technologies will provide the mechanism through which complex patterns of partnerships, joint ventures and strategic alliances will be coordinated and standards of performance monitored against quality criteria (e.g. Handy 1990). Managers are also likely to become digital managers facilitating multiple centres of expertise across a global network of activities, pulled together in temporary teams around projects. It will be the digital manager or the 'fusion manager', to use Heller's (2003) term, who will be mainly responsible for building and maintaining the architecture for creativity, removing barriers to the free flow of ideas, enhancing how people work together and creating a ferment in which new ideas emerge from a creative process (Furnham 2000).

Another way of putting this is that managers are in the front line of building the intellectual capital of the organisation by developing collaborative cultures or the *social capital of the organisation*. This is the essence of knowledge management – enriching work; building team cohesion and shaping the climate so that learning and reskilling become a way of life. Networks are built around shared values; people are empowered to think in new ways and ideas are nurtured as the lifeblood of a competitive organisation. In the conditions of the creative, synergistic organisation the management of the future is less about 'controlling', more about empowering people to be different, using progressive HRM and a positive psychological contract to harness the productivity of knowledge workers.

Organisations have woken up to the realisation that it is the intangible aspects of the organisation – good values, good talent, good learning process, good creativity and good motivation – which make the competitive difference and it is the soft nurturing aspects of management, in particular the ability to engender a reflex of learning as the main thrust to change, which may be the best hope for it to happen. Increasingly, it seems, management will be called on to provide the vision and cultural flexibility by which the spirit of the 'learning organisation', much heralded, long-awaited and much misunderstood, will eventually take concrete form as the dominant model of twenty-first century organisation.

Finally, let us say a word of two about the new social environment which is likely to face the managers of the future. Within the workplace, a major priority will be for managers to engage with greater *diversity*, with workforces diverse in terms of geography, race, religion, culture, gender, disability and job contract and creating cohesion out of the fragmentation without imposing homogeneity. The issues are compounded because integration has to be formed from virtual communities, globally dispersed, which may have fewer common points of reference than before (Hirsch and Carter 2002).

Particular issues of diversity will include: corporate adjustment to the feminisation of management as women become more prominent in the management workforce; accommodating an ageing workforce; providing ethnic minorities more opportunities for advancement and recognising the work expectations of the young. The demands of Generation Y/Z may be particularly significant here. This generation often expects involving and interesting work, development of transferable skills, flexible working arrangements which allow work/life balance, participative management and recognition of their talents with reward or they will leave. This counter-culture, which may soon become mainstream work culture, has the potential to radicalise how organisations work and redefine what managers do (Lawrence 2008).

Sensitivity will also be needed in handling the *environmental, social and ethical challenges* which, more and more, demand a management response. Managers are increasingly required by society to deal transparently and fairly with all stakeholders of the organisation – communities, employees, suppliers, customers and investors – as business partners. Increasingly, there will be pressure for the large company to think beyond bottom-line criteria to consider the impact of its behaviour on the wider world. This will include greater sensitivity to the external costs which organisations displace onto the societies in which they are based, growing community involvement in business decision-making and greater readiness to demand reparation for corporate injury.

In terms of the *physical environment*, the new expectations will mean responsible eco-management, mediating shareholder returns with enlightened green policies, balancing short-termism against sustainable development and the husbanding of natural resources for future generations. In terms of *social responsibility*, it will mean large organisations acting as corporate citizens with accountabilities to multiple stakeholders, behaving with ethical responsiveness and social justice in local communities and developing countries. In terms of *ethics and corporate governance*, it means principled behaviour with regard to human rights at work; transparency in accounting practices; more accountability in the conduct of corporate policy; senior executives who demonstrate more integrity, especially in dealings with local politicians.

While the new ethics may take some time to bite, public concerns about the exploitative, extractive and destabilising practices of multinationals and their retreat from protective HRM in recent years are unlikely to abate. The conduct of corporate management in the twenty-first century is likely to require far more complex judgement, involving longer-term considerations, social as well as economic criteria, clear moral values and political balancing of the demands of multiple constituencies (Garratt 1996; Mullins 2007).

> **Pause for thought**
>
> ### Whither management?
>
> Management is changing fast. As a busy manager, how should you focus your limited reserves of time and energy? The Chartered Management Institute (2007) reports that managers are increasingly placing concern for customers, concern for employee groups and concern to build an engaged culture of shared involvement as equal in priority to their traditional focus on shareholder returns. Looking to the future, managers believe the most important issues facing them will be managing change; customer satisfaction; effectiveness of IT; motivation of valued, core staff; managing diversity and the development of employee skills.
>
> **Questions**
> *What do you think are the main issues facing management? Are you geared up to these challenges?*

15.2.2 The changing nature of management

In responding to the impact of new trends and in anticipating those yet to come, management is changing. Management roles, style and the function of management may all be undergoing a period of rapid transition.

Up to the 1980s the number of managers as a proportion of the working population had increased annually in many Western countries. However, as we have seen, from the late 1980s onwards the flattening of organisations, new organic structures and business process re-engineering, among other factors, led to the removal of many management posts, especially those which were middle-level and specialist. For those managers who survived, their roles have changed substantially. Middle and lower level managers have more substantial jobs, with a broader range of responsibilities and far more intensified pressures on performance (Sampson 1995). On the upside, this means more scope and variety in what managers do; more challenge; more control over how the work is done and potentially more satisfaction from the results that are achieved. On the downside, there is more stress and pressure, less job security, and personal accountability (Hirsch and Carter 2002).

At the top, management seems to be transmuting into *strategic leadership*. This is partly because of the restructuring of capital and the greater demands of institutional investors, discussed above. Boards now give more emphasis to market analysis, corporate strategy and performance-monitoring than ever before (Useem 1996). Pathfinding and entrepreneurship, setting overall goals, ensuring objectives are achieved, selecting and grooming the next generation of top policy makers seem to be their main functions. Garratt (1996) applauds this shift away from operational management as a welcome reaffirmation of the role of the director as leader and conductor of the whole, shaper of the climate, not the problem solver and progress chaser on issues which could be dealt with further down.

The assertion of a leadership role by the top management has been accompanied by talk of disseminating power and empowerment of lower levels of management who are exhorted to take ownership of their destinies. However, the appearance of delegation can be misleading. Computerised financial systems can conceal where the real power lies. Many claim that decentralisation is more rhetoric than real, that the management of strategy and decision-making has been effectively centralised at board level through the new electronic networks and the transparency and control they allow of far-flung operations. It is responsibility which has been decentralised, not power (Useem 1996). The board no longer manages by decree but the participative language is misleading: it disguises a real augmentation of top-down control. Certainly the flamboyant behaviour, charismatic and directive leadership of some CEOs (e.g. Jack Welch of GEC) and the self-enriching behaviour of others (Geoff Schilling and Enron) might suggest the new self-confidence which the concentration of power brings. Some believe that trends suggest the fragmentation of management as a community, with new cleavages opening between top management and the rest (Grey 1999; Hirsch and Carter 2002).

Whatever the truth about shifts in the balance of real power between top managers and other levels, it seems that restructuring has redefined management roles at lower levels. For example, take the rise of strategic business units (SBUs), by which organisations are disaggregated into quasi-independent businesses run by general managers with considerable operational freedom to achieve organisational objectives. The switch from a functional to a corporate logic of organisation implies new roles for managers below the top. Divisional SBU directors are no longer functional specialists, but general managers with an extensive span of control, large budgets, coordinating diverse functions and accountable for big blocks of performance. In decentralised structures, management roles have become more complex and autonomous in the sense that managers in the middle are expected to control complete units of business and exhorted 'to act entrepreneurially', even if they work for a massive corporation (Thomson et al. 2001). Apologists claim that strategy-making and performance management are now shared between the top and the line. The growth of profit centres, output-focused units and cross-functional teams around brands and products is serving to broaden many senior/middle management jobs and confer responsibility for large blocks of work, making local managers responsible for innovation, improvement and performance. However, sceptics say that much of this freedom is an illusion. In the past, divisional heads had more de facto independence. The SBU director is told that s/he controls his/her destiny, but the real controllers are the constant computer printouts, monitoring statements and financial feedback and centralised targets laid down from HO (Batt 1996; Cooper 2005). Real control lies with the top: only responsibility has been devolved.

The rise of the SBUs is just one of the many forces transforming management below the board. Functionalist roles at the higher level are fast disappearing, and generalist management roles and general management skills are at a premium. Professionals are increasingly being forced into management activities, whether they are inclined to management or not. That applies as much to the doctor required to manage a budget or the engineer required to run an operations team.

Serial corporate restructuring has dramatically reduced the numbers of middle managers and transformed the roles of middle managers and will continue to do so. Many roles – in-house specialists in narrow roles, liaison officers, advisers, coordinators – have disappeared completely, either outsourced or automated. Modern IT means there is less need for roles engaged mainly in information-passing and maintaining order. The top can get the information it needs about vital performance through other channels (Worrall and Cooper 2001).

The old model of massed ranks of salaried 'corpocrats' in stratified levels seems to be over. Many of the old jobs were often very narrow, technical and administrative (Sampson 1995). Their replacement by larger, more involving managerial work which values judgement rather than obedience is surely to be welcomed. So too is the re-design of management work and the removal of unnecessary administration, by business process re-engineering and other processes, so that it becomes more proactive and creative. That said, middle managers often feel under siege from all sides, organisational processes re-engineered around them, their numbers cut, exhorted to be entrepreneurs, to introduce the 'learning organisation' and 'to do more with less' without the trust and loyalty of the top or the authority to do the job (Cooper 2005).

There seems to be no room any more for the 'solid corporate citizen', the middle manager of service, loyalty, experience and often wisdom (Sennett 1999). A different model of management seems to be emerging in which new elites are pushing aside the older 'organisation men', and management processes are becoming dispersed. Yet, many organisations now speak of the internal social distancing between levels of management and miss the linking role of the middle in interpreting the top's intentions to other groups and reporting back qualitative, cultural data about attitudes and feelings which no management information system can do (Sampson 1995). Perhaps organisations will swing back to re-establishing lost roles of the middle mangers in some new form, but for the time being the middle managers who remain are those with leadership ability and skills that go beyond passing data and controlling the numbers (Grey 1999; Talbot 1997).

It is a new breed of managers which is taking over. The future seems to lie with the specialist project managers who can move quickly and seamlessly from one process improvement team to another: people with the skill to adapt quickly to circumstances, build teams quickly and give them direction. It also lies with the mobile lone managers, intellectual and creative, who can act as catalysts for corporate renewal, helping organisations to think afresh about what they are and where they are going (Sampson 1995). Some of these will be internal consultants and troubleshooters for powerful managers at the top, moving from one assignment to the next. Others will be 'guns for hire', self-employed consultants finding work on the internet and through their own networks of contacts. Then there are the interim managers, often well qualified with MBAs and blue-chip experience who do not expect long-term careers with any organisation, but have a profile of skills and situational experience (e.g. set up, turnaround, dissolution, etc.) which an organisation requires at this specific point in its journey (Cole 1995).

Brave new world: brave new management

The senior management team of a large computer services company meet once a month on a Sunday at 7 a.m. Why the bizarre time? Because that is the only way for the ten worldwide managers scattered across the globe to 'meet' – electronically.

Virtual management. Increasingly managers and those who work for them are no longer in the same location. Gone are the days when managers can supervise the hour-to-hour work of their staff. In the virtual environment, managers now need to lead by focusing on the overarching processes shaping performance along with the results that staff must achieve. This can be done only if managers have a good sense of how to structure virtual projects, set appropriate goals and milestones, shape behaviour and develop metrics to analyse what progress is being made – through cyberspace.

Virtual projects often start with in-depth face-to-face meetings, but projects can then be managed by e-mail, by electronic discussion groups and by videoconferencing. Unfortunately, nothing substitutes for being there and critical phases of any project require physical proximity for trust and deeper mutual understanding.

Managing without authority. Complex products and services which span national boundaries are not easily monitored. Managers are needed who can work with and influence people who are not their subordinates: managers who can trust their reports to work well and gear their activities with others. Among the most important skills of the new manager are team coordination even if s/he is not in direct contact with the team, that is, skills of constructive persuasion; inspirational appeals; exchange of favours; coalition-building and informal consultation.

Shared leadership. Because more and more work is being done in cross-functional teams, leadership has to be shared between team members. To build shared leadership, managers must select team members who can perform well without strong direction from a superior. Team problem-solving is needed. That often means deferring critical decisions to the group and managers becoming facilitative, turning leadership over to capable subordinates or peers.

This is so contrary to traditional models of managing that a courageous and enlightened manager is needed who appreciates that his or her effectiveness is increased if s/he gives it away. Where working relationships are scattered across the globe, only shared leadership and empowerment can deliver results.

Extensive networks. An important part of getting work done in a complex and virtual organisation, without authority, is through networks. Managers need timely, well-woven networks of influential people who know people. Having timely and appropriate information allows the manager to lead without being in direct control.

Question:
Is the organisation you work for adapting 'virtual' forms of organising? Do they work?

Source: Adapted from Conger, J. and Lawler, J. (2005) 'People skills still rule in the virtual company', *Financial Times*, 26 August 2005.

Other developments may be transforming the roles of the ordinary managers of the modern organisation. Globalisation has required many to adapt to the demands of international roles, acting as team leaders of an international brand or innovative new product, coordinating disparate multidisciplinary and multicultural teams, a theme we discuss in Chapter 12. Outsourcing of support and institutional functions (e.g. IT, HRM, training, facilities, etc.) as part of a strategy of concentrating on core functions means that far more managers are involved in quality monitoring of services over which they have no control. Many managers have larger jobs, with higher performance targets, larger spans of control, more coordinating and quality-focused activities but less direct supervision. They also have less formal authority and must rely on influence. Increasingly, managers are losing the authority to allocate tasks, progress chase and reward or punish. Management prerogative is disappearing as management itself becomes shared with other roles – advisers, specialists, HRM, consultants, trainers and line workers themselves (Osterman 1996).

This brings us to the single most significant trend in management which may have radical implications for the future – the growth of team-based work in the modern networked organisation. The removal of functional 'chimneys' and the reduction of hierarchy in the typical organisation has gone hand in hand with the growth of self-managing teams around projects, quality management, productivity, innovation, product and service development. These are cross-disciplinary teams of knowledge workers and front-line staff, often interfacing electronically as well as face to face, undertaking many of the tasks traditionally associated with management. They are involved in the thinking, innovating, planning, implementing and monitoring work which managers have always done (Osterman 1996).

The role of the manager here is to share authority with team members, providing a supportive environment for creativity, stimulating learning, building energy, enabling synergies, motivating and encouraging, providing resources and political cover to teams of largely self-directing workers. This implies a model of management and managing which is far less directive and controlling than before. These teams can be relied upon to be largely self-policing and to regulate themselves. Increasingly well-educated professional employees and consultants do not need close supervision, and the nature of their work means that much of it will be virtual and conducted away from the workplace. Knowledge workers can be largely self-managing, led by performance criteria for the team which is well known by all participants. Individuals can be trusted to align their actions to the goals of the organisation, the targets of the project and the criteria of evaluation and reward (Sennett 1999; Harrison 2002).

As the economy shifts to tertiary knowledge-based work, it is likely that this pattern of activity will become increasingly common. Inevitably it raises questions about the future of management. Self-directing workers, semi-autonomous teams and partnerships for learning and creativity all imply a radical reappraisal of the management role, management style and skills (Mullins 2007). Yet, for the foreseeable future, there will be a continuing need for managers as coaches, coordinators, facilitators and change agents.

The change in emphasis from control to facilitation will require new skills profiles. The managers of the future will need soft skills of persuading, inspiring, recognising and releasing talent, creating a climate of continuous learning. They will have to be emotionally intelligent, sensitive, empathic and socially aware. They will need to understand learning styles and conditions for learning and know how to put people together to create new synergies. They will have to be great communicators, articulating shared values, evangelising the company vision, interpreting it for front-line teams (Salaman and Butler 1994). They will have to embrace the ambiguity of creativity and practise value-led management by reconciling cultural differences across boundaries in new projects and programmes. They will have to be skilled in integrating the activities of teams and units so that their activities are mutually supportive and geared to the organisation's strategy. Increasingly organisations seem to be resembling universities with cells of specialised and committed specialists rather than 'machine bureaucracies' and the professionals within them need sensitive and respectful handling ('light touch' leadership not 'command and control' management). (Gratton and Pearson 1994; Heller 2003).

These are the skills of the 'new manager' as network builder, team developer and masterly coordinator. However, s/he will also function as internal consultant, designing parts of the organisation to remove blocks to energy and unlock the potential of its members. Some of this may require the removal of administrative distractions from the creative activity of the teams and developing flexible roles and relationships which allow talent to shine. Finally, the new manager will have to be far more of a strategist and entrepreneur than ever before: sensing market trends and opportunities (DfEE 2000), being proactive in experimenting with good tries, building knowledge management systems to learn the lessons of experience, using judgement in shaping organisational activity for the future (Mumford and Gold 2004; Hirsch and Carter 2002).

Many managers in mid-career will see the philosophy of shared management (or 'distributed leadership' as we will see later) as a diminution of the management role and a reduction in management authority. Certainly much of the detailed controlling, directing, planning, budgeting, monitoring and evaluative work traditionally associated with managing will become absorbed by self-managing teams. The new model implies that far more people are taking on management tasks and doing bits of managing who do not have 'manager' in their job title. Empowerment of teams means the dispersal of the management functions (both to teams and to specialist units like quality management and HR). As the traditional management role becomes shared with others, then so too is traditional management prerogative and the authority which flows from it. Some would say that the scripts available to managers are now less elevated and the status of managers is being undermined (Worrall and Cooper 2001; Grey 1999). But is this really the emasculation of management? The management jobs which remain within restructured organisations are actually more demanding because they are much more ambiguously defined and broad-based. They also require the subtle interactive, social and persuasive skills which are at a premium; no longer can the manager rely merely on the force of his or her formal authority to do the complex enabling work which is now required (Hirsch and Carter 2002).

You're as good as your last deal

The life expectancy of Britain's top business leaders continues to drop. The average tenure of the FTSE 100 chief executives is now around 4.5 years (about half of the figure for USA or Asia). Deprived of the steadying influence of the long-stay chief executive, British companies are slaves to short-term market whims.

Today's CEOs are running scared. In a world where one slip can cost you your job, the temptation to play safe is obvious. So is the tendency to stress short-term wins, not long-term gains. CEOs are frightened of unsolicited takeovers, activist hedge funds, bad headlines and the share price.

Question
What effect do you think these conditions at the top will have for the conduct of management below the board and for values of development?

Source: Adapted from Roberts, D. (2007) 'Britain's disposable managers', *Sunday Telegraph*; shortened version reported in *The Week*, 9 June 2007.

15.2.3 So where is management going?

However, what of the future; where is management going? Some writers (Grey 1999; Mullins 2007) suggest that management as we know it is disappearing. It is being squeezed between increasingly empowered teams and the rise of technical jobs (like modern HRM) which take on specific aspects of the general management task. Increasingly the distinction between 'managers' and 'non-managers' is becoming blurred. Burgoyne and Reynolds (1997) suggest that a continuing trend towards empowerment, team control, self-development and the self-employed contractor might eventually lead to the disappearance of the concept of management. Grey (1999) suggests that with the rise of the 'networked organisation', virtual forms of working management and the increasing replacement of middle-level jobs with technology, management is in danger of being 'written out of the script'. If we are all managers now, management as a special set of tasks and activities ceases to be the preserve of any one group. However, the possible demise of management, as an occupation and as a vital part of the techno-structure of control, is compatible with the triumph of 'managerialism' as an ideology.

Grey (1999) speculates about a world in the not too distant future in which management values and definitions have become dispersed into a much wider range of human activities and social processes, both within the organisation and in society at large. Teams and individual knowledge workers have internalised the norms of self-control and self-management, rationality, efficiency and bottom line, defining their problems and acting in the spirit of the management code. Grey (1999) claims that this would be the ultimate triumph of management because it would become the dominant ideology of the age. Its discourses would become a hegemony, a new common sense of thinking and language by which all situations are judged.

Grey (1999) sees this as a dystopian future, partly because he perceives the spread of management perspectives as self-alienating (all of life becomes 'managed' not 'lived'), but also because it will be mystificatory. Even if everyone is defined as a self-manager in self-managing teams, organisational actors will not be equal in terms of power or reward. While capitalism remains, it is arguable that there will always be an elite of super managers – directors, specialists, troubleshooters, consultants – who retain real corporate power over strategy and performance and they will set the limits to the emergence of new social relations at work.

However, returning to the more limited concerns of this book, the dispersal of management will have implications for management development. Will self-managing teams and semi-autonomous, empowered professionals have an impact on the nature and scope of MD programmes? Will MD become something else, more an 'appreciation of management process' for the workers of the new knowledge economy? Tantalising questions indeed but, before we make that turn, we need to return to a theme raised in Chapter 1: is 'management' now 'managerial leadership' and, if so, how can that leadership be developed?

The managers of the past *v* the managers of the future

This is a diagrammatic representation of how the management role seems to be changing. As we discuss below, is management transmuting into leadership?

	Old management	New management
Role	Controller; director	Facilitator; team leader
		Developer; advocate
Leadership	Transactional	Transformational
Learning	Specialist/functional	Continuous/generalist
Influence	Formal authority	Knowledge/social skill
Orientation	Planning	Vision
Culture	Monocultural	Multi-cultural
Style	Managing machine	Visionary/managing cultures
Change	Compliance	Commitment
Values	Competitive	Cooperative
	Reactive	Proactive
	Individualist	Team-based

Question
Does a list like this help you understand changes in management or does it just reinforce crude stereotypes?

15.3 Leadership and leadership development

For the reasons we have briefly discussed above, particularly restructuring and the rise to prominence of high-performing teams, flattened organisations and wider spans of control, there are fewer management jobs overall and those that remain generally demand *leadership* skills.

As we argued in Chapter 1, this new shift to leadership does not mean that all previous professional knowledge and practice in management development is now redundant. Indeed, progressive MD has always attempted to build individual leadership skills outside the use of formal authority, and management/leadership development techniques overlap to such an extent that it is misleading to try to separate them out.

Indeed, it is difficult to see a corpus of professional knowledge which is exclusive to leadership development. That said, the priority now given to develop the leadership capabilities of managers is likely to change the nature of MD in the future. Indeed, because potential for leadership is now the *sine qua non* of acceptance into management, MD and LD are likely to become synonyms.

Here we consider some broad, general themes in leadership development.

15.3.1 Can leadership be taught?

How to develop leaders has long perplexed philosophers, learning theorists and practitioners alike. Are leaders born or made? If they are to be made, can leadership be taught or do people have to learn it for themselves?

In the literature there is no final resolution of these issues. Many people believe that leaders are born. They talk of 'natural leaders' (Jackson and Parry 2008), but it is difficult to find a consensus on the qualities of the natural leader. The 'laundry lists' of traits proposed are endlessly varied. Besides, studies of identical twins in Sweden (Avolio 2005) suggest that genetic inheritance only accounts for a proportion of leadership capability; how you use your potential is crucial. This is an ancient debate. Conger (1992) suggests that some personal qualities associated with leadership like self-confidence, intelligence, drive, extraversion, stamina and energy may be innate. Other qualities may be laid down quite early on. For example, Hunt (1991) talks of the force of circumstances which often means that the first-born in a large family takes on a leadership role on behalf of siblings. Family influences, parenting styles, early engagement in sports and taking the team captain role, class influences and going to the right school, can all combine to shape the development of leadership ability from a very young age.

> **Pause for thought**
>
> ### The origins of leadership
>
> 'Development of leadership ability is a very complex process. It may start at birth by inheriting the right genes that favour intelligence and physical stamina . . . Family influences and the influences of peers, education, sports and childhood experience influence the child's need for achievement, power and risk taking . . . Work experiences and mentors shape the raw leadership materials of early adulthood into actual leadership by providing essential knowledge and behavioural skills . . . Then you need opportunity and luck as final determinants in getting a chance to lead'.
>
> #### Question
> *How far do you agree with this statement?*
>
> Source: Adapted from Conger, J. (1992) *Learning to Lead*, Jossey-Bass, p. 33.

These are complex and inconclusive issues. Certainly sensing yourself to have leadership qualities and choosing to lead may emerge early on. However, it is also true that some leaders who peak early do not go on to take leadership positions in adult life, and others fail because they are unable to continuously learn and develop.

Becoming a leader is an uncertain process. It seems that some people have a head start, but there are plenty of late bloomers. Although the role of outstanding visionary leader may not be within the grasp of everyone and may be in part genetic, with the right attitude and conditions it seems that many more people can serve as adequate leaders than was ever thought possible. This is the justification for expending effort on developing leaders (Jackson and Parry 2008).

But this frustrating debate leads to another, equally inconclusive. Can leaders be taught? Again, the jury is still out on this. One perspective, the optimistic school, exemplified by Kouzes and Posner (1998), defines leadership as a set of behavioural skills, and like any skills they can be built on. To claim otherwise is to succumb to the mystique of leadership. While there is widespread agreement that leadership cannot be developed in the classroom, the optimists believe that a well-designed blending of the formal and the experiential can be effective. They say that leadership can be taught to people who already have a record of high achievement, are well motivated, have the intellectual equipment to think strategically, are emotionally intelligent and committed to learning.

A middle position in the debate (Grint 2001) takes the line that some aspects of leadership can be taught in quite systematic ways but other parts of leading can only be developed informally by the person himself or herself. So, appealing to Aristotle and his treatise on the selection and grooming of the guardians of the Greek city state, Grint suggests that leadership is an amalgam of skill, knowledge and wisdom. Formal and informal development programmes may build skill and knowledge, but wisdom requires the development of insight for which there are no rules.

The most pessimistic position denies the trainability of leadership. The process of learning how to lead is just too complex, too intuitive, too individualised and too unconscious to be a planned development. While some systematic processes might be possible as a stimulus to learning (e.g. supervised practice, mentoring feedback, discussion of success and failure, role modelling), it is contended here that by far the most important leadership lessons will only be learnt by individuals themselves reflecting on their stream of experience and making choices about future behaviour (Ready and Conger 2003). Putative leaders know this. They are committed to seeking out experiences from which they can grow. As we suggested in Chapter 7, they are constantly finding opportunities to lead and opportunities to gain wisdom from reflection on the processes of living. From this viewpoint, learning leadership is indistinguishable from the Socratic injunction to live an examined and reflective life, finding the learning in any situation and having the flexibility to adapt your behaviour from the lessons of everyday experience.

15.3.2 Models of leadership

Designing effective leadership programmes presumes a coherent philosophy or well worked out model of leadership. To develop a programme without a clear mental picture of the leadership you hope to promote is to attempt change without a vision or criteria to judge the outcome.

This is not the place to review the universe of literature on leadership. The interested reader is referred to Jackson and Parry (2008) or Yukl (2002). However, the prime movers of leadership development need to know the main debates in the leadership field and to critically appraise them in terms of the social context of their organisation.

Very briefly, the literature suggests that the trait or personality based approach is simplistic and unreliable as a rationale for selecting and developing leaders. In recent years, Burns (1978, 2003) has drawn the distinction between *transformational* and *transactional* leadership which has become the inspiration for thousands of competency frameworks, skills lists, psychometric tools (e.g. the Transformational Leadership Questionnaire) and development programmes which purport to measure the capacity of individuals for transformational behaviour. Concurrent with and overlapping this trend, the fashion has been to develop charismatic, visionary leaders or 'hero leaders' (e.g. Conger and Kanungo 1987; House et al. 1991; Kotter 1990) who can motivate their followers by heightening their sense of self-esteem, giving them confidence to achieve higher performance.

However, in the wake of a wave of corporate disasters brought on by 'charismatic leadership' we are in the period of reaction to these romanticised models of leading. Loud, proud leaders may know how to influence others but are they following a wise course for the future? Too often they exhibit hubris, narcissism and self-seeking acquistiveness. The new search is for *Level 5 leaders* (Collins 2001) who are more humble, more consensual, quietly empowering and politically sensitive. This same reaction to the excesses of charisma also accounts for the quest to find an ethical, socially responsible basis for business leadership. *Authentic leaders* who are true to a code of ethics, who operate with trust and integrity, now seem to be in demand (Gardner 1995). A new cry is for *servant leadership* (Greenleaf 1977), even *spiritual leadership* (Fry 2006). The new orthodoxy is that good leaders have a sense of higher purpose, build an emotional bond with those they lead and try to turn them into leaders themselves. Genuine transformative leadership is about working for the longer-term good of the organisation, leading by example rather than exhortation and building on the best in people. Like a good parent the leader learns from those s/he leads and does all s/he can to empower them to become independent decision makers in their own right.

Another important trend in the leadership field is the new recognition of culture as a defining influence on leadership behaviour. Within this perspective, leadership is defined as the 'management of meaning' (Bennis and Nanus 1985), aligning interpretations of situations with the understandings of followers. This discourse takes place within a cultural context (organisational and social values, coordinates of time, place and identity) which sets the terms of debate the leader must handle in achieving change. This is also the logic which defines the new model of international leadership, no longer privileging the globe-trotting troubleshooter with a toolkit of tried and tested 'universalist' solutions, but his/her nemesis, the cross-cultural leader who can rise above his/her own socialisation to become a creative facilitator of cross-national partnerships (Thomas and Inkson 2004).

Some strands of debate take thinking about leadership much deeper. In the West, the cult of the individual leader itself is under attack. The new focus is on how acceptable the leader is to the group and how far s/he reflects their values, norms and expectations. This is captured in the new concept of *distributed leadership* or *shared leadership* (Parry and Bryman 2006). Within this model, followers are no longer recipients of the leadership style of an individual but co-producers of the leadership process. This can take several forms. It is argued that the complexity of modern organisation makes it difficult for any one person to have the range of skills required to lead in all conditions. Distributed leadership recognises that in any management community there will be individuals who excel in inspirational communication, logistical planning, creative thinking, managing complex change and complex problem-solving. With distributed leadership, different people will take the lead at different times, as issues of the moment play to their strengths.

However, an even more radical model, which has been called *'dispersed leadership'* implicitly declares that leadership as a position is dead. Leadership is now a *collective process* in which all participate (Day et al. 2004; Raelin 2004). Leadership skills are inherent in everyone and can be drawn out where the systems are facilitative and empowerment is genuine. The challenge for the future is to develop leaders at all levels; all have a role to play in the flexible, ever changing ensemble of organisation. Whether this is a form of romanticism which takes the reaction to leader-centric models too far and underestimates the need for hierarchical power and direction, only time will tell.

The leadership models presented above (largely without criticism) obviously creates dilemmas for the thoughtful MD practitioner. Quite manifestly, they are contradictory: 'leader oriented' perspectives clash with 'follower centred' models; 'heroic leadership' philosophies are at odds with 'authentic leadership'; 'visionary leadership' with 'dispersed leadership'. However, what must be apparent is that choosing a theory, model or philosophy of leadership will shape the content of the leadership programme, its logic and the development techniques which will be selected. In the end there is no choice but to choose. Not to define a leadership programme or process in terms of a leadership model is to surrender it to incoherence and irrelevance. Besides, an explicit intellectual underpinning to LD also offers participants an opportunity to critically examine their own experience against the model and gives the spur to participants to develop that most useful of tools – a reasoned personal philosophy of how to lead.

To hell with great men (and women too) . . .

If history is, as Thomas Carlyle said, 'the doings of great men', then business must be the achievements of great CEOs. Our commercial and industrial processes unfold through the decisions ad mistakes of great executives. Or do they?

For Tolstoy, the 'doings' of 'great ones' were very much circumscribed by context and events. The great men whose activities were recounted were not the people who determined the course of events, but the people who happened to occupy positions of leadership when events occurred. They may appear to control but in the volatile conditions of modern business small groups of decision makers are swept along by forces they barely understand.

Leaders are like the bow wave surging ahead of the ship. The wave moves ahead of the ship but doesn't determine its direction. The leader is less the director than the vehicle of history.

Such perhaps is the condition of modern executives in charge of organisations and events that operate and change in ways outside their control. When they despair over the failure of a change management programme, they are frequently as distant from the reality of what is happening to customers as Napoleon was from events on the battlefield. If, as Tolstoy says, no one knows who controls the course of a battle and the general is as dependent on events as the lower orders (even if 'great ones' appear to be in control), then some humility is needed. The market may be more mysterious and more intractable than the best-laid plans can conceive.

The Tolstoyian picture is the antidote to so much modern thinking around the leader as heroic visionary and direction giver. How far can leaders really control the complexity of modern organisations in modern conditions? Returning to Tolstoy, Prince Andrei, after listening to the over-rationalised strategic presentations of staff officers, asks to return to the ranks. He realises that leaders depend on their followers for success. The success of a military action relies less on strategic plans than on the everyday culture of the organisation. How could a nineteenth-century Russian have understood modern leadership and business realities so well?

Source: Adapted from Berlin, I. (1979) *The Hedgehog and the Fox*, Penguin; Kay, J. (2005) 'War and peace: a business primer for our times', *Financial Times*, 30 August 2005; Berkeley-Thomas, A. (2003) *Controversies in Management*, Routledge.

15.3.3 Themes and trends in leadership development

Around the world, many hundreds of courses are run in colleges which purport to develop managers, usually senior managers, into leaders. 'Leadership development' is a 'totem' word and it is big business. Since the millennium the annual corporate budgetary growth in LD has been 10 per cent and may now stand at some $70 billion a year, although it is also true that this investment has been tailing off in recent years (Ready and Conger 2003). However, Buus (2005) has reported that half of the large European companies included in a survey had chosen not to increase their leadership budgets in the future. This may reflect macroeconomic issues, but also the growing belief within the big companies that too much may have been expected of leadership and leadership development. As Ready and Conger (2003) say:

> Publishing houses are shaking the trees in the hopes of finding the author of the next blockbuster leadership book, consultancy firms are searching for new models and CEOs have carefully honed speeches about developing the next generation of leaders at every level . . . Yet despite the eloquent statements and all the investment this has not produced a 'pipeline' of leaders in most organisations

A corrective to the endless hype around new models and techniques for developing leaders is surely the appreciation that leadership is ancient and probably timeless in its essentials. It is unlikely that some recent fad (e.g. Goleman et al's *Primal Leadership* (2002), Blanchard and Johnson's *The One Minute Leader* (1981) or Peters's *The Pursuit of Wow* (1994), all listed in the bibliography) will provide a touchstone for turning base metal into gold or even of finding the gold within existing base metal. It seems that seriously developing people in the subtle arts of leading requires time, patience and wisdom and it is not reducible to a few mantras and simple formulae.

In many organisations there is now extensive debate on the meaning and practical application of leadership development, i.e., how it interweaves with strategy formulation; the extent to which fixed competency models can capture the elusive qualities of leading; the degree to which leadership (and leadership development) should be seen as distributed throughout the organisation or concentrated on individuals of assessed potential; how to set clear objectives for LD and how to evaluate results.

One interesting development seems to be a move away from LD as a means of building specific attributes, skills and traits. Competency-based systems remain a key element in LD, but their limitations are increasingly apparent and there is a new shift to assess the 'whole person' as a potential leader (Hernez-Broome and Hughes 2005). There is also a new tendency to understand the interplay between individuals and their context. Jane in Accounts may have great talents but how do they meld with the subculture of her part of the organisation and is she right for leadership at this phase of the organisation's history? Part of this generic approach to identifying and developing leadership capabilities is the new emphasis given to emotional intelligence which we discussed in Chapter 2. There is a growing recognition that the transformational leadership and the team motivation and coordination required by new times involves more emotional awareness of the sensitivities of followers who cannot be dragooned into change against their will. The leader of tomorrow may need to understand the emotional realm of organising, to understand both the needs of followers and his or her own emotional needs and how these can be met (Goleman 1998).

Alongside the traditional management skills the twenty-first century leader needs qualities of self/other reflectiveness, the ability to persuade others of change by imaginatively entering their 'lived experienced' and arguing effectively in their terms. Managerial leaders have always required good social skills, but a new model of the leader may be emerging; the desirable qualities are those of empathy combined with toughness; good psychological adjustment and confidence; high levels of energy; ability to take on challenge without succumbing to stress. Integrity and an ethical orientation are also increasingly defined as essential to leadership (Fry 2003) Whether or not this is corporate propaganda, the public messages which organisations are sending about their selection and development criteria for future leaders seem to be shifting (Sinclair 2007).

The need to develop emotional competences and 'holistic' capabilities may partly account for the movement away from formal methods for developing leaders. The larger and more sophisticated providers seem to agree that leadership can't be taught in the classroom. The old pattern of sequential blocks of formal development provided for the middle manager as s/he moves into a senior, leadership, seems to have largely given way to a model of experientially based learning. At its best, formal development is integrated in a planned and blended system which emphasises learning as a continuous process rather than a series of one-off events. Development of the leadership skills which can be learnt in the classroom – presentation, decision-making, facilitation, interpersonal communication, emotional self-awareness – is interlinked with, and designed to reinforce, everyday learning in the workplace. Increasingly, leadership development is less about designing learning events and programmes, more about creating processes and experiences from which fledgling leaders can learn for themselves in a climate of support.

However, this is not to imply that 'high potential' employees are required to develop leadership skills by themselves. In progressive organisations a myriad of LD techniques are available – coaching, mentoring, action learning sets, drama workshops, T-groups, job rotation and so on; indeed, the whole range of techniques in MD, which we have discussed in other chapters, are relevant to leadership development.

There is a marked tendency for LD programmes to be diversified and for a range of methods to be used. This is valuable if it means that experiential techniques (e.g. stretch projects) outside formal institutions can be synthesised with reflection on the experience within the safe space of the development centre or university (Kouzes and Posner 1998). Multiple settings can encourage people to have the growth experience and then take time out to explain the behaviour and consider ways of conceptualising it.

In some organisations, the settings chosen to jolt the participant into awareness can be highly imaginative, for example, outdoor adventures such as white-water rafting or wilderness survival, working with the homeless or a spell in a monastery. All can be defended in terms of learning from the unfamiliar. However, as Kaagan (1998) suggests, there are a lot of grandiose gestures in LD; some of the exotic diversity is surely a form of 'edutainment' for elites and has a modish quality. Quite as much can be achieved by more modest interventions which blend settings and techniques to create the virtuous cycle of experience, feedback, thinking, reflecting and experimentation which is essential for leadership self-awareness. Creating the right, safe atmosphere in which to try things out and derive lessons through open dialogue with others are the conditions needed and they do not require exotic locations.

One technique which seems specifically relevant to LD is the new turn to a 'leaders developing leaders' approach. Part of the logic behind the shift to decentralisation and a flattened organisation is that the time of top management can be released to be more involved in talent spotting and grooming the next generation of organisational leaders (Cacioppe 1998a). Organisations as varied as GEC, HP, Intel, Shell and US Navy Seals draw on the leadership wisdom and experience of top managers to develop the next generation of leaders. This can take various forms: CEOs giving keynote addresses on LD programmes, higher management facilitating ALS and coaching promising talent. Meeting with those on the way up is said to give top leaders an opportunity to interpret the strategic plan to those charged with the task of implementing it, to share their philosophies of leadership and pass on their experience to the 'bright stars' of tomorrow (which Cacioppe (1998a) calls 'finding a teachable point of view') and identify the younger talent who will eventually replace them.

'Leaders developing leaders' seems to work when the people at the top are well regarded for their leadership abilities (not the norm in most organisations) and younger leaders are interested to hear from them. It also requires top leaders to have some teaching and facilitating skills so they can convey their experience and draw people out in thinking for themselves. Where successful, Mumford (1997) claims, this technique can have dramatic results. The lessons of experience handed down and the ideas generated in interaction have the credibility which comes from exposure to the current leadership and that can make the experience very memorable for aspiring leaders in the middle. The involvement of the top also helps younger leaders to better understand the challenges at the higher level, and top leaders to understand the work realities and the culture of those below them. It can stoke up the enthusiasm of senior people for leadership and management development and give them the personal satisfaction of helping others to learn vicariously through their experience. Sometimes real business issues are confronted in the encounters and performance is improved. The literature mainly reports success stories, but is it cynical to believe that for every engaging 'leader teacher' and resonant 'teachable moment', there are many other ego trips by executives whom the younger generation do not want to hear from?

Leadership development at IBM

We can develop our own ideas of what seems to work in LD by looking at the experience of others. Here are the espoused principles by which IBM conducts its leadership development.

- *Sharing ownership.* A common problem in designing LD is that key elements in management, for example, the board or business unit managers are not made accountable for making LD work. IBM has overcome this by promoting shared ownership. The board defines LD as a priority for all managers, and all managers are held accountable for identifying people with leadership potential and agreeing development plans. Line managers are not considered for senior executive positions unless they can demonstrate a track record of developing the talent within their sphere of responsibility. As an expression of the values of 'leaders developing leaders', managers are expected to coach upcoming leaders of potential, give them stretch assignments and monitor progress.

- *Invest in processes and not products.* A leadership competency framework derived from close observation of the skills and behaviours of exceptional leaders at IBM is used as the main instrument for distinguishing between fast-track leaders and mainstream managerial leaders. IBM attempts to target the best, who are given challenging assignments of high visibility, but also addresses the development needs of all managers.

- *Experiential learning.* Although formal courses are used from time to time, IBM believes that most learning to become a leader is through on-the-job experience. ALS and project teams are used to build experience, and facilitation ensures that review and reflection of the lessons takes place. Planned job rotation means that upcoming managers are deliberately exposed to a range of experience in which they can demonstrate leadership skills (e.g. a turnaround situation; initiating a start-up; managing cultural diversity; managing a cross-border partnership, etc.).

- *The investment in leadership development is long term.* In the past, IBM has paid the price of a quick-fix mentality, cutting the LD programme during a downturn only to lack the talent to take advantage of opportunities when market conditions changed. There is a guarantee to identify and groom talent at all levels and around the world regardless of prevailing economic conditions. Besides, the integration of LD into the organisational culture makes LD a deeply embedded and continuous presence in the company.

- *Commitment to evaluate.* While acknowledging the methodological problems of measurement, IBM is committed to evaluating the effectiveness of LD in terms of achieving business results. While resisting a fetish of evaluation in an area as vague as LD, establishing approximate ROI is considered politically essential if the top is not to tire of LD and revert to 'Darwinism and the passive waiting for leaders to emerge'. In a spirit of scepticism, management fashions have to prove themselves though evaluation before they are adopted wholesale.

Questions
What do you think of these principles? Do you believe they represent good practice in LD?

Source: Adapted from Ready and Conger (2003) 'Why leadership development efforts fail', *Sloan Management Review,* Spring 2003.

15.3.4 Leadership development as an experiential process

A widely held view among practitioners and developers alike is that the key lessons of becoming a successful managerial leader are best derived from experience. Assignments rather than programmes should be the centre point of leadership development. That said, relatively little is known about the range of experience needed for leadership, the type of experience needed at each stage of a career, how people learn from experience and why some learn and others do not (McCall et al. 1988; Cacioppe 1998a).

In Chapter 7 we considered experiential learning and MD in depth and we do not propose to revisit these debates even if they also have obvious relevance to leadership development. However, some general observations may be in order.

Because leadership is a real-world skill, it seems natural and appropriate that experience may be the best teacher in developing leaders. Many commentators (Kaagan 1998; Raelin 2004; Hernez-Broome and Hughes 2005) speak of the value of workplace-based or contextualised learning for leadership development. You learn leadership by doing it. In the process of dealing with real organisational issues, intending leaders gain self-insights from trying out skills, listening to feedback and reflecting on mistakes and triumphs. Experience provides the medium for learning with and from others (shared learning) and learning through self-reflection.

However, this is not to suggest that leaders will automatically learn from experience or even recognise that events unfold useful lessons for self-understanding and self-development. Learning from experience is very individual; people seem to vary greatly in experience; they often respond differently to the same experience and the lessons drawn by one will contradict those of another. What seems to be required is an attitude of mind which is continuously attuned to the learning opportunities presented by work experience and a capacity 'to reflect on the meaning of experience in the midst of action' (Sadler-Smith 2006).

'Reflection in action' requires moral and intellectual courage – facing up to discomforting ideas, being open to the candid questioning and feedback of others, reframing definitions and experimenting with new approaches. These in turn become the basis for reflection, discussion, thinking and elaboration in another cycle of interpretive thought, emotion and action.

Of course, being a genuinely 'reflective practitioner' in the arts of leadership is ultimately dependent on the qualities and potential of individuals (especially their conceptual skills and emotional sensitivity) and the organisation cannot control the lessons individuals derive from experience. However, the organisation can help by providing a supportive climate for experiential learning. The techniques involved are identical to those used in MD (e.g. stretch assignments; early responsibility; action learning; mentoring; learning partnerships, etc.) to which the reader is referred. There is no magical touchstone for developing the leader apart from the manager.

As may be obvious from the foregoing, leadership development is not easily planned. People learn to be leaders as part of a *life-long* process of iterative reflection (e.g. questioning assumptions, reframing, experimenting with new interpretations and behaviours, reflecting again). You are learning every time you encounter an unfamiliar problem and improvise a way of responding to a leadership challenge. The learning never stops. The common experience is surely that there is no sudden revelation of how to lead, no epiphanies. We learn disjointedly in fits and starts, often making the same mistakes again but getting better with each cycle, gradually refining concepts of what works and under which conditions (McCall 2004). Of course, some of us learn faster and have greater facility with the sense-making involved than others. These are the people who have the 'Nelson touch'. As Jones and Gosling (2005) suggest:

> Nelson was that rare combination, a diligent manager and an inspiring leader . . . Nelson was fastidious, taking great pains to ensure his ships and men were supplied with everything they needed. But he also had the ability to build confidence and arouse commitment . . . As one of his contemporaries, a fellow admiral, recalled, 'Nelson had the magic art of infusing the same spirit into others which inspired his own action' . . . He was also entirely self-taught from experience.

Even allowing for historical romanticisation and the distortions of sentamentalism, this a model of what can be achieved when natural talent is combined with reflective self-experience.

Learning leadership: the lessons of experience

In an excellent book on developing executives (to which the reader is referred), McCall et al. (1988) appeal to intending organisational leaders to take their own experience seriously as a guide to learning. They attempt to classify the common experiences by which people in management learn to become leaders. Here are some of them.

- *Trial by fire*: insights into self and process through facing significant problems in terms of scale and complexity; tackling interwoven issues with no clear solution; sudden leaps in responsibility; handling crisis situations.
- *Learning from others*: learning from different types of bosses (the good, the bad, the flawed); learning particularly from an exceptional, inspirational leader; sensitivity in dealing with diverse people; understanding others' perspectives; handling people over whom you have no authority; being responsive to different subcultures.
- *Coping with unfamiliar situations*: taking on issues where tried and tested solutions don't work; building a portfolio of dealing with a variety of leadership situations, for example turnarounds, start-ups, building growth; finding a way around despite 'false dawns', false friends', false trails'.
- *Learning from personal events*: becoming deeply aware of personal strengths and weaknesses; knowing how to compensate for weaknesses and build on strengths; developing an attitude of critical inquiry, constantly searching for the lessons of life experience.
- *Hardships*: showing resilience and true grit in rising above mistakes, setbacks, disappointments, failures; learning from the negative and moving on without becoming traumatised and losing confidence.

It is by recognising the opportunities for learning by experience that we become our own teachers.

Source: Adapted from McCall, M. et al. (1988), *The Lessons of Experience*, Lexington Books.

15.3.5 Leadership development as a collective process

The leadership development we have discussed so far is based on the belief that 'leadership can be put into people' (Raelin 2004). This is the traditional view, that the leadership of an organisation can be built by selecting the right people, tailoring individualised development programmes to their needs and then carefully deploying them as a valuable organisational resource for maximum impact (succession planning). This is reminiscent of heroic 'great man' concepts of leadership, that individuals with the right talents and orientations can take the organisation in new directions. Perhaps it also implies a logic of critical mass, that if enough individuals are developed as leaders, then they will form a catalyst for change which will transform the organisation as a whole. However, critics of this approach claim there is a fatal flaw in the argument. You can put leadership into people – through informal and formal development – but the people often have to accommodate themselves to an unreconstructed organisation (Risher and Stopper 2004). It could be career breaking to resist the embrace of the old culture, however dynamic the individual.

Recently, there has been a shift to 'putting leadership not into people but into the organisation itself' (Raelin 2004). This implies a different construction of leadership, leadership as a collective process rather than a defined position of authority or a personalised relationship of influence between an individual and a group. Raelin (2004) characterises this as moving from leadership which is 'upfront and followers in line' to leadership which is *leaderful*. By this he means that good leadership development aims to release the leadership potential of everyone. Here leadership is defined as building the organisational systems, structures and cultures which encourage people of all kinds and of all levels to initiate and lead on issues where they have real expertise and passionate interest. Leadership is not fixed in particular roles; people lead through their competency in the moment. The organisation in no longer directed by a few 'big brains', but many smaller brains within a learning community, collectively engaged in fashioning a creative future (Hernez Broome and Hughes 2005).

Day (2000) makes the distinction between 'leader development' (building the human capital of individuals) and 'leadership development' (building communities in which people are genuinely empowered and everyone participates in leadership as a process). A 'leaderful' philosophy blurs the distinction between leaders and followers. It implies a perception of leadership as 'co-produced', as involving 'distributed leadership functions' and shared responsibilities. Within this logic, leadership is a mutual social phenomenon in which many individuals have an influence. Leadership is designed into the organisational process; it supports the trend to new models of organisation, empowered workers and teams learning together to achieve higher levels of performance. To the extent that the role of the leader remains the identity of any individual, the role of the leader is that of facilitator acting to build integrated work communities and release the leadership potential of everyone. This means designing and developing processes and culture which support a 'community of learning' (Day 2000; Jackson and Parry 2008).

In these conditions leadership development loses its focus on identifying and grooming 'great ones' (Risher and Stopper 2004) for upper management positions. The new focus is on developing organisational processes which liberate people at all levels to think and behave more creatively. Leadership development becomes organisational development. It becomes less about developing 'high potential talent', more about building a context which supports collective leadership and enabling the means by which the capacity of all members of an organisation finds its greatest expression (Sinclair 2007; Raelin 2004).

While this democratisation of leadership is exciting, some caution may be needed in embracing leadership as an expression of the knowledge and skill of self-regulating learning communities. Are we in danger of debasing the term 'leadership' by suggesting that everyone is a temporary leader within the organisation? Is the new thinking going too far in debunking individualistic models of leadership? Is there a danger that this is a new and flawed phase of thinking about leadership?

Will the organisation of teams not still require a framework of formal leadership and, if so, is this leadership qualitatively different from team leadership? Is the leadership of a cluster of work teams the same in nature but only different in sophistication and complexity from executive leadership, or are levels of leadership qualitatively different? These are core questions for developers. Should we democratise leadership development for all levels of management and indeed for self-regulating teams or are we in danger of debasing the term 'leadership' (i.e. 'if everyone is someone, no one is anyone')? Or perhaps we need to be more discriminating in our conceptualisation of leadership (or leadership(s)) at micro-level and macro-level, requiring different but linked development processes. These are issues on which the practitioners of leadership development will need to have a view.

Leadership at different levels

Perhaps we can distinguish different levels of leadership which may involve different skills and styles of leading.

- *Leading and the self*: self leadership, for example, self learning; persuading, influencing, personal efficiency and organisation.
- *Leading a team*: knowing how to delegate, how to motivate, giving a sense of common purpose, project leadership.
- *Functional leader*: leading across boundaries; harmonising the work of a cluster of teams; showing professional leadership; political and social skills.
- *Divisional leader*: leading a senior team; taking responsibility for a significant block of corporate work of strategic importance to the organisation as a whole.
- *Strategic leader*: an even larger strategic role with responsibility of taking a large part of the organisation into the future; envisioning and strategic management, team building and troubleshooting.
- *Corporate leader:* the CEO/Chairman position, ultimately responsible for the organisation as a whole; leadership through envisioning, strategic problem-solving; handling the boundary between the organisation and its environment.

Question
Some might think the nature of the leadership role at these levels varies greatly. Others may see the skills involved in leading as constant although the complexity of the leadership challenge increases with seniority. Do you find the debates differentiating management from leadership and around 'leadership' as a unified or a diverse process illuminating or obfuscating?

Despite the explosion of thinking and writing about leadership in recent years, the last word on leadership will not be written for many years. As Marturano and Gosling (2008) wittily suggest, when talking about leadership and leadership development, 'we still don't have all the pieces out of the box and we don't even know what the end product should look like'. Although the world needs more and better managerial leaders, we don't yet know how to educate such people for their responsibilities. Little wonder then that our thinking on leadership development is like a weathercock blown hither and thither with each prevailing breeze of fashion.

How we develop our leaders: trends in leading and development in the West

	Traditional	Post-war	1980s–2000	Post-millennium
Concept of leadership	Leader directs	Leader persuades	Leader as charismatic figure	Leader as facilitator
Leadership style	Perogatives; command and control	Communicates and motivates	Inspires and builds new paths	Constructs mutual meanings with teams
Method of leadership development	Born to rule; learning from observation of peers	Formal and planned development	Self-awareness and self-development	'Self/other' interactions with teams

Table 15.1 Trends in leading and development in the West

To the extent that any tabulation like this is useful, the focus of leadership is moving from 'leading organisations' to 'leading within organisations'. Increasingly, the emphasis is on the relationship between leader and followers (e.g. 'distributed' or 'co-leadership') and development becomes interactive, processual and informal.

15.4 The future for management and leadership development

In this final section, we consider how the practice of MD may develop in new directions in the future. In considering this we will glance back at themes we have mentioned in the text and look forward to the challenges of the future. Futurology is a notoriously difficult undertaking doomed to ridicule by the passage of events, but not to attempt to predict the future is to be at its mercy. What follows is largely the views of the author, although aligned to the literature, which are offered tentatively and in a spirit of opening the debate rather than closing it down.

15.4.1 Future trends in MD/LD: the challenge of management change

As we have suggested, organisations are likely to continue to need managers, even if they assume new titles (team leaders, facilitators, coaches), to provide vision, gear the parts of the organisation into the whole, motivate and innovate. As Handy (1986) predicted in the 1980s with his 'shamrock organisation', fewer people are now engaged just to be managers but those that remain require more sophisticated skills. Many more people are combining bits of managing with practical work and they need the outlook and core skills of the professional manager.

The implication of these trends seems to be that MD/LD is in the process of fragmentation. At the higher end, there is increasing interest in finding advanced ways of developing the small groups of top managerial leaders who will now have far more strategic decision-making, OD and talent management responsibilities. At the lower end, MD/LD has a role in expanding basic managerial literacy among the large numbers of professionals, knowledge workers and technicians who now have supervisory and team-leading responsibilities, as well as giving teams of workers an appreciation of the ABCs of managing (including self-managing) (Woodall and Winstanley 1999).

This new bipolarity may partly explain the massive increase in the number of independent organisations providing basic skills training in management at one end and also the explosive growth in postgraduate/post-experience qualifications at the other. Even in the mid-1990s, 80 per cent (Beddowes 1994) of large companies were involved in MD/LD and there has been great expansion since then. Another consequence of the diffusion of management means that MD/LD is no longer the preserve of the larger organisations; it is being extended to new markets – smaller organisations, technical and support workers, professionals, the self-employed. The demographics are also changing – more women, minority ethnic groups, the disabled, who bring new concerns and priorities to which MD/LD is beginning to respond (i.e. programmes which respond to diversity and management; small businesses and management; ethics and management; women and management, even spirituality and management). This involves the search for ways to fit MD/LD into the lives of people with multiple organisational roles, of which management is only one (e.g. e-technology; flexible learning; guided experiential learning; blended learning, etc.) (Cooper 2005; Cole 1995).

As a consequence of the broadening base of management learning and development and the increasingly undifferentiated nature of its target population, MD/LD is losing its separate identity (Woodall and Winstanley 1999). This may be welcomed as progressive if it means that the traditional elitism associated with management education and development is breaking down. One sign of this is that organisations seem to be turning to more broad-funnelled development of employees in their early years, with fewer 'crown prince' graduate programmes; instead, they are giving natural leaders time to emerge before they are specially groomed for high office on 'talent management' schemes. For future managers, their initial contact with MD/LD may increasingly be as part of a general induction programme on 'organising skills' (communications; time management; work planning, etc.) which may be built on in time with more sophisticated approaches if the participant moves into a dedicated management position (Storey 1989).

This merging of MD/LD with HRD may be a good thing if it opens up development to talent wherever it is found in the organisation. However, a plethora of superficial catch-up courses and learning experiences presented under the badge of MD/LD that trivialise the complexities of managing, so reducing it to a set of buzzwords, formulae, slogans and simplistic models, may serve to undermine respect for management as the complex judgemental practice that it really is. A populist interpretation of MD/LD, which 'dumbs it down' for a mass audience, implying that management and leadership are easier activities than they really are, does not help the cause of building future generations of skilled managers (Brungardt 1996).

For managers at all levels the changes in managing suggest that the skills of the future which will be in greatest demand will be the soft skills: of team building, facilitation, influencing within flatter organisations, adaptability to a constant stream of change, getting higher performance without having direct control and pushing for high standards on specific projects while keeping an eye on the longer term. These themes seem to apply across the board in management from the highest to the lowest and suggest the outlines of a strategy of MD/LD (valuing the informal and experiential) to address them.

15.4.2 Future trends in MD/LD: institutional challenges

A strong priority for the future will be the need to provide a 'strong corporate architecture' for organising MD (Hirsch and Carter 2002). The importance of aligning MD/LD with corporate goals and business performance is likely to increasingly preoccupy the minds of higher management. As we have seen, part of the process of redefining the top management role as strategic and developmental is that it gives top managers space to focus on issues of talent selection/succession management and the use of MD as a strategic tool. This may be a potentially important development for MD, raising its status as a function, demonstrating learning as a central value in strategy and signalling that MD/LD is an integral part of the business plan, succession, performance and reward management (Thomson et al. 2001). When top managers take an interest in MD/LD, as the reports suggest they increasingly do, MD/LD planning features more strongly on the radar of SBU managers and are owned by them. This is good news for MD as a learning process which goes deep within an organisation and engages line manages as role models and creators of a genuine climate of learning.

However, building corporate architecture goes further. As we have seen, MD has often been accused of incoherence, with initiatives at different organisational levels shooting off in different directions with little strategic integration. Ironically, the widespread decentralisation of MD/LD in recent years has added to this sense of incoherence. So, it is argued, has the movement from formal to informal, from standardised courses to individualised, informal processes. We may now be seeing the beginnings of a reverse trend back to the centralisation of MD/LD in the search for a clear picture of what managers need to learn and clear frameworks to help them achieve these ends (Hirsch and Carter 2002). In this case, it will hopefully not mean a return to the rigid training regimes of the past and 'set-piece courses' for whole strata of managers ('the sheep-dip'), but it may involve the resurrection of core development programmes at transitional career points in management, retrospectively seen to have provided some institutional consistency in skill development and a stimulus to corporate culture building, now sadly missed (Cullen and Turnbull 2005).

Perhaps this presages a new rebalancing of MD/LD, a corrective to the recent emphasis on self-managed career development and learning. While personalised, tailored learning is here to stay, leaving learning to the individual delivers an uncertain result for the organisation in terms of its leadership pipeline and skills-profiling for developing the management stock. Perhaps we are witnessing a partial reaffirmation of the value of standardised development as a guarantee of common skill standards, but now more skilfully blended with individualised approaches within coherent, customised frameworks of development planning.

The search for coherence also signals the need for new commitment to MD/LD as a corporate activity, for example, systematically defining the MD implications of business plans at high levels of the organisation, interweaving MD into HR planning and HR systems and creating a new dynamic between top–down and bottom–up processes. In the institutional frameworks of the future, simple, concrete, regularly updated competency frameworks may steer audits of learning need from the top, mediated by elaborate multilevel dialogues between all stakeholders giving feedback from the bottom. Balancing the strengths of systematic assessment and the strengths of negotiation with the interests involved is now seen as providing the best fit for satisfying the expectations of the range of constituencies with a stake in MD/OD (Watson 1995).

These may prove to be important trends for the future agenda of MD/LD. Perhaps they signify a drawing back from overly complex and technocratic assessment techniques (e.g. comprehensive competency frameworks) to more flexible profiling which does not try to see further into the future than is realistically possible. A related trend is the dissatisfaction with PDPs as the cornerstone of assessment because they are seen as too job-specific, focus too much on the short term and are too subject to the bias of the appraiser. A richer mix of development tools may be emerging which attempt to map the changing skill needs for groups as well as individuals against a range of plausible corporate scenarios for the future (Hill 2004).

Balancing the needs of the business and the individual in integrated development programmes will probably become a major priority for the MD/LD of the future. MD/LD as a process of development 'done to' people seems past. The growing organisational consensus that the organisation and the individual have a shared responsibility for development will probably become a commonplace, but there will still be much room for debate about relative rights and obligations. In time, organisations may come to appreciate that the corollary of abandoning paternalism and requiring individuals to develop themselves could mean that less learning actually happens; there is more 'pretending to know' for political reasons and people choose an 'inappropriate' focus for their learning in organisational terms. The haphazard nature of individualised learning raises many problems for development planners and line managers which are unlikely to be resolved by exhortation to be self learning or implicit threat of being passed over or being sacked if they do not (in the end, can people be forced to develop and is it moral to require them to do so if the organisation has renounced responsibility for their careers or even their employment?) (Arnold 1997).

The amount of support which the organisation is prepared to give to individuals managing their development and who should bear the cost of this are set to be flashpoints of tension in the psychological contract of most managers and their employers in the future. For example, the shift to active self-managed, experiential learning should suggest the extension of techniques, such as professional leadership coaching, which have long been used in executive development, to other groups of managers of whom more is required. But the extent to which corporate expenditure on this highly personalised form of development, well regarded as a professional technique in learning to become a leader, can also be justified within constrained development budgets, is a matter for conjecture. How democratically the jam is spread will tell the organisationally saavy manager what the true values of the top may be, whatever its declarations (Watson 1995).

In the context of institutional frameworks, there are some observations to be made about career management. The fragmentation of career development into planned work experience for the elite 'pool' of high-potential leaders and a free market (internal and/or external) for all other managers, the pattern increasingly common in big companies, may come to be seen as threatening to trust and cohesion of management culture within these organisations. The 'officers and other ranks' feel to these arrangements can create resentment among those not chosen, especially if the criteria for selection are not made transparent or 'owned' and those who are in the chosen elite are not palpably high-level performers.

Moving away from progressive, planned career development creates other problems. It can greatly increase the influence of patronage and informal networks, with powerful sponsors well placed to advance the interests of their protégés. It also means that the development of the individual is left more to chance and the haphazard experience this brings than most organisations with a 'search for talent' rhetoric may care to acknowledge. While some might advocate this as an appropriate expression of a 'Darwinist struggle' in which the 'best and brightest' prevail, others, with some justification, may regard it as a very random way to give future leaders (even those destined for the more middling slopes) the balanced portfolio of talents they need. Then, there is a sense in which this logic flies in the face of the need to attract and 'grow your own' for all functions and levels ('developing pools of talent') at a time when people, especially young people, feel little sense of obligation to their employer and will move to where the best opportunities are available (Arnold 1997). It will be interesting to see if this is just a temporary phase in the history of career development with an eventual return to designated 'development jobs' planned assessment and review for the 'sergeants' as well as the 'captains' of future management.

A final theme concerning the institutional framework of MD/LD is that of accreditation and national regulatory systems. In UK, Handy's 1980s criticisms that MD/LD as a national system remain remains poorly coordinated, with no qualification in management as a licence to practise, remains true and presents government, employers and individual managers with a massive challenge for the future. While the Management Standards Centre, the Institute of Management and the European Foundation for Management Development (EFMD) are well respected as arbiters of good practice, employers seem reluctant to link their MD programmes to national systems of quality control and accreditation. Some of the objections are philosophical; the NVQ-benchmarked approach is based on universalistic principles in management which many regard as unrealistic. Other objections are more practical: the inflexibility and bureaucracy involved in gaining accreditation, and fear that supporting employees in becoming professionally qualified may lead to retention problems when the sponsored trainee qualifies.

Cost and perceived relevance of the qualifications to the practical work of everyday managing is linked to enduring scepticism that management is a profession which can be regulated and controlled by qualifications like other professions. This is a philosophical debate which we briefly reviewed in Chapter 9 and it remains unresolved. Certainly attempts to move management towards professional status have consistently failed in UK and other countries over the past ten years, and at present the

Mintzberg (2004b) view is firmly entrenched that management is more a social craft than a profession with abstract and universalistic knowledge. It is interesting in this regard that only a small minority of managers in UK belong to professional bodies in management (e.g. CIPD, Institute of Marketing, IOD, etc.). This may be partly explained by the typical career pattern by which the individual becomes qualified and skilled in a technician/technologist role (engineering, ICT, etc.) before moving into management. In UK, at least, the professional identification typically remains with the former technical role not the managerial one.

Debates about the professional regulation of management are unlikely to go away, but it is equally unlikely that there will be professional closure on common educational achievements as the condition for practice in the near future (whether in UK or in other major industrial countries). However, what may emerge is increasing experimentation with and formalisation of an apprenticeship model of MD/LD in which 'professional artistry' in management is developed through guided practice, the understudy gradually taking on increasingly responsible tasks and exercising more independent judgement under the watchful eye of a 'management master' (Mintzberg and Gosling 2006).

15.4.3 Future trends in MD: agenda and delivery challenges

In considering new directions for the practice of MD/LD, the distinction between educating managers in the academy and developing them in the workplace, while still valid, is becoming increasingly blurred as spheres of thought and action increasingly overlap.

Management education is reorganising itself and will continue to do so in the years ahead. Many business schools have moved away from education for management as a series of functional disciplines (e.g. finance, operations, statistics, etc.) and rigorous problem analysis and solving to helping prepare managerial leaders for the complex and ambiguous situations which will confront them within organisations. This means developing character not just building skills. As Mabey (2002) says, modern education is increasingly about developing the moral, ideological and political consciousness of the managers as well as 'competency'. Finding convincing ways of replicating leadership situations in the classroom and supporting guided reflective practice in the workplace will be a major theme for the future.

The new turn to building leadership with the emphasis on critical awareness, wisdom, meaning-making and the use of symbols may increasingly redefine management education as a liberal art which draws on insights from the humanities and uses techniques from the arts (drama, narrative construction and literary analysis) to help managers think critically and with self-awareness. Mangham (1990) looks forward to a time when management education will focus on managers as 'performers' who are helped to be aware of their 'scripts' and elaborate them for a wider range of organisational behaviour.

However, this liberal-humanist model will face countervailing forces which may be gathering in strength – demands for vocational relevance, the commercialisation of higher education, the growing pressure on organisations to evaluate development with strictly measurable indices and concerns in some quarters that the pendulum has swung too far towards generic development, away from hard functional skills (Syrett and Lammiman 1999; Winterton and Winterton 1997).

Debates about the content of the business school curriculum, the wisdom of teaching leadership to young people with little organisational experience and the relationship between impersonal knowledge and knowledge through insight are likely to be lively over the coming years. It may well be that the MBA is replaced by something new or at least becomes increasingly reserved for experienced managers already occupying leadership positions. We can also expect to see radical new arrangements by which universities attempt to build the reflective focus of the classroom into experiential learning at work through role modelling, mentors, peer groups, projects and 'learning communities' (Burgoyne and Reynolds 1997; Fox 1997).

Within the university sector we can expect changes in the form of delivery, that is, more flexibility around the working lives of managers; more customised programmes run with specific organisations (joint ventures, partnerships and consortia); more blending using new e-technology. The rise and rise of qualifications from business schools is likely to continue, although this may be in the face of increasing scepticism among employers of the value of sponsorship (more students will be self sponsoring) and the growth of corporate universities. We can also expect to see even more attempt to differentiate courses to niche markets (e.g. professionals in management; finance for non-financial managers, etc.). *Executive* education and development is likely to remain a source of work much sought after by universities, although the competition will become even more intense and the expectation of leading-edge thinking and expert facilitation will be high (Collin 1996; Hirsch and Carter 2002).

However, the main providers of this management education are likely to change. The geopolitical shift in the centre of gravity in business may well mean that the influence of elite American institutions like Harvard and Stanford, and with it the model they represent, will begin to wane and new stars will arrive in the East offering different models for developing management leaders. This should be a time of iconoclasm and dialogue and experimentation about the purpose of management education, what works and what does not (Broughton 2008).

Corporate trends in leadership development

Hoping to resolve integration problems left over from the merger of Price Waterhouse and Coopers and Lybrand in the late 1990s, PwC turned to the Duke Corporate Education arm of Fuqua School of Business at Duke University, California.

The idea was to take the partners – the leaders of the organisation – out of their daily environment and give them tasks in which they had no expertise or official authority to force them to work in executive teams.

The programme that was agreed was heavily reliant on 'experiential learning' projects. Partners had to learn how to coordinate closely with others, persuade through natural skills and build trust. They did this in tasks like preparing and repairing a Formula 1 motor car in an intensely competitive race and running a political campaign for a candidate as an analogy for a new product.

This is application-based learning customised to the organisation. It may also signal the beginning of a trend to corporate sponsors using educational programmes for OD purposes. This was about building leadership talent but it was also concerned with creating organisational improvement and strategic change through

> education rather than going to traditional consultancy. As the head of US audit PwC says, 'Here there's a transfer of the knowledge – as opposed to getting a "how to" from a consultant'.
>
> For PwC, education is more than teaching. 'It's seeing education as a way to execute strategy. It's about how you shift behaviour', says Mr Evans, a PwC partner in charge of learning and education. For Fuqua, it was a learning experience too – how to pull on their networks to source the facilitators with the right skills, for example, racing-car maintenance with an appreciation of management learning.
>
> Source: Adapted from Murray, S. (2003) 'Risky lessons from judo and fast cars', *Financial Times*, 11 August 2003.

Within organisations, it is likely that experiential learning and self-managed development will become further consolidated as the premier forms of development for management and leadership. This would be consistent with the continuing priority to build interpersonal, political and social skills of leading. Mainstreaming personal forms of development such as coaching and mentoring will ensure that their growth, already rapid, will massively increase. The use of project work and stretch assignments will probably become more sophisticated with better support and opportunities for guided reflection so that the lessons of experience are translated into new behaviours. Informal and facilitated group learning (e.g. ALS, team dynamics and leadership, etc.) will also remain strong priorities in most MD strategies (Hirsch and Carter 2002).

Management learning will become more flexible and tailored to individual need as learners become more experienced in reflective learning and in using the services for personal support available to them (e.g. becoming more sophisticated in handling the dialogues which are at the heart of mentoring). Organisations may also become more proficient in providing better information and advice for individuals to reflect on their careers and the informal learning they need to acquire. In time, organisations will also doubtless provide more flexible packages of services – bringing together custom-designed one-to-one counselling, designated jobs which incorporate development, supportive feedback (e.g. ACs/DCs), selective secondments, role swaps and projects and organisational space for discussion and reflection, closely adapted to the needs of the individual (Garavan et al. 1999).

To enunciate principles of flexibility and personalised learning are easier than putting them into effect. At the very minimum, designers may need to embrace Argyris's double loop learning model and the 'learning styles' models of Kolb/Honey, Mumford and so on at more than just the declaratory level. In the past, MD practitioners have paid lip-service to these models, ritualistically acknowledging research findings that learners learn in different ways while applying their own prescriptions. This leads to the larger issue that learning theory has been too often ignored or used rhetorically to justify *post hoc design* decisions made on pragmatic grounds. Coherent management learning in the future implies a coherent philosophy of learning giving it both logic and direction (Burgoyne and Reynolds 1997).

Another major issue in realising a model of personalised, experiential learning will be the commitment of line managers. Line managers have a crucial role to play in developing their staff and creating a learning climate at work. However, they often know little about learning theory and practice. They may also lack the skills and temperament to act in the coaching and career advisory roles which the new MD/LD requires. Developing the developers may be part of the solution here, but greater use of HRD in advisory/development roles (going far beyond traditional training input) and the judicious use of external providers, could equally feature (Harrison 2002).

While the development of leadership through experiential methods will remain dominant and formal methods may be downplayed in the future, their contribution will not disappear. Multiple methods of development are likely to persist but better blended so that experiential learning at work will be given conceptual meaning in the classroom and classroom lessons ideas will be explicitly integrated in action learning processes in the workplace. There is also the possibility that the pressure to show measurable results in MD may drive some organisations to turn back to more programmatic forms of learning, probably reinforced by e-learning packages. However, even if this does happen, management training will be different from the past. It is likely to be more targeted on groups with special needs and at key stages of career transition. It is likely to be planned in conjunction with on-the-job interventions and action planning. It is likely to be sharper, 'just in time' training to satisfy and learning needs which are regularly assessed. It is likely to be delivered in partnership between an internal MD/LD function concerned with the selection and quality control of providers and high-profile externals who can stimulate deep engagement. Well done, this may provide the structure and sounding board for those managers who are not natural or enthusiastic self learners, who need a social context to validate the lessons of experience (Hirsch and Carter 2002; Talbot 1997).

Finally, the future of MD/LD is likely to be both more inclusive and more collective. We have already mentioned the diffusion of MD in line with the restructuring of organisations. Customised, personal support for development is likely to become normal for anyone taking on responsibility and asked to do more, at any level. As this happens, the potential for MD to become a force for organisational learning becomes widely recognised. There is certainly a danger that the new focus on sensitive one-to-one development may displace the equally important development of learning in teams and groups, but there is also another emergent force which defines the social and cultural aspects of learning as crucial to organisational performance and perhaps that is stronger. It may be that over time MD becomes subsumed within OD (Warner Burke 1994). Development which addresses the social issues of leadership, ethics, social responsibility, political and moral justice, which brings together people to share knowledge and sharpen their critical consciousness has the potential for transformational change. Historians looking back may identify MD as the detonator which ignited an explosion in new ways of thinking about organisation, new ways of making organisations fit for the people they employ and new ways of making them accountable to the communities they serve.

15.5 Conclusion

At the beginning of the millennium the future for management and leadership development looks promising. Globalisation, restructuring and changing psychological contracts, among other factors, mean that managers have to work in situations of rapid change and complexity. The need for managers who are adaptable and multi-skilled for strategic competitiveness further reinforces the need for a form of MD which is relevant to the organisational realities of managers. Organisations everywhere are searching for MD/LD systems which help managers to learn frequently, quickly, relevantly and within the context of their practice. While informal learning may act as the preferred model for self-development and career resilience, this is not the whole story. Organisations increasingly recognise that they have a responsibility to build the learning climate which moves the organisation away from 'command and control', helps managers innovate within their roles and creates a strong psychological contract by growing all the talent, not just 'polishing the stars'. The future path seems to be for organisations to increasingly view MD as a business responsibility, shared between the organisation and the manager. Perhaps we are likely to see more organisations seeking to design their systems, structures and cultures so they are responsive to diverse learning and proactive in encouraging managers to be the continuous, lifelong learners which the innovative, improving organisation requires.

Review questions

1. What experiences in your working and social life have been important in assuming leadership positions?

2. How far have you modelled your own leadership style – at work or in a sports or social situation – on the observation of people who impress you?

3. Where do you stand in terms of the proposition that leading is doing the right thing and leadership is doing things right? How would you justify your views?

4. Do you agree that leadership is a thing apart which requires careful selection and development or can many more people take on leadership if the climate is right to do so?

5. Do you think that women lead in different ways to men? What evidence would you cite to support your view?

6. If you were designing a leadership programme would you want to select 'rising stars' early on and groom them for leadership or give all available talent common development experiences and hold off defining 'leaders' until a later stage in their careers? Explain your rationale.

7. Managing and leading is craftwork based on experience and guided reflection. How far do you agree with this statement?

Web links

For associations which are concerned with the study of leadership:
Academy of Management:
http://www.aomonline.org/

International Leadership Association:
http://www.ila-net.org/

For leadership research centres:
Centre for Leadership Studies (University of Exeter):
http://www.leadership-studies.com/

Centre for Public Leadership (University of Harvard):
http://www.ksg.harvard.edu/leadership/

Centre for Creative Leadership, California:
http://www.ccl.org

If you are interested in storytelling and leading try David Boje's website:
http://cbae.nmsu.edu/~dboje/

For a critical approach to management and leadership try:
http://www.ephemeraweb.org/

DVDs/Videos

Other People's Money (1993) Directed by N. Jewison, featuring Danny De Vito
A black comedy which gives context to the reshaping of management in recent times. The shareholder's debate in the last scene is particularly apposite.

Wall Street (1987) Directed by Oliver Stone, featuring Michael Douglas, Charlie Sheen
This is the other great Hollywood film which considers international finance and the implications for management. The scene which pitches the corporate raider against the 'corporacy' brings some of the themes in this chapter alive.

The Thomas Crown Affair (1968) Directed by N. Jewison, featuring Steve McQueen, Faye Dunaway
This author has always thought that there is something about *Thomas Crown's* (Steve McQueen's) style here which suggests that in real life he would be cut out for the highest levels of international corporate management. See if you agree. Do you like him?

Recommendations for further reading

Those texts marked with an asterisk in the bibliography are recommended for further reading, especially the following:

Cooper, C. (2005) *Management and Leadership into the 21st Century*. A collection of chapters by different contributors (practitioners and theorists), reflecting on how management/leadership are changing and how to select and develop people for tomorrow. Provokes new thinking.

Grey, C. (1999) 'We are all managers now: we always were. On the development and demise of management', *Journal of Management Studies,* Vol. 36, No. 5. A radical paper that suggests that management as a profession is disappearing and shared leadership may be taking its place.

McCall, M., Lombardo, M. and Morrison, A. (1988) *The Lessons of Experience.* An excellent account of how executives actually learn how to lead from reflecting on experience.

Bibliography

Anon. (1997) 'Looking ahead: implications of the present', *Harvard Business Review,* Sept.

Anon. (2002) *Principles of Leadership Development: Best Practice Guide for Organisations*, Council for Excellence in Management and Leadership.

Anon. (2003) 'Preparing tomorrow's leaders', *Development and Learning in Organisations,* Vol. 17, No 5.

Arnold, J. (1997) *Managing Careers into the 21st Century*, Paul Chapman Publishing.

Ashton, D., Easterby-Smith, M. and Irvine, C. (1975) *Management Development: Theory and Practice,* Bradford: MCB.

Avolio, B. (2005) *Leadership Development in Balance,* LEA.

Barham, K. and Oates, D. (1991) *The International Manager,* Economist Books.

*Barler, R. (1997) 'How can we train leaders if we do not know what leadership is?' *Human Relations,* Vol. 50.

Batt, R. (1996) 'From bureaucracy to enterprise? The changing jobs and careers of managers in telecommunications', in Osterman, P. (1996) *Broken Ladders,* OUP.

Beardwell, I., Holden, L. and Claydon, T. (2004) *Human Resource Management: A Contemporary Approach*, Ch. 9, Pearson.

*Beddowes, P. (1994) 'Re-inventing management development', *Journal of Management Development,* Vol. 13, No. 7.

Bennis, W. and Nanus, B. (1985) *Leaders: The Strategies for Taking Charge*, Harper and Row.

Berkeley-Thomas, A. (2003) *Controversies in Management: Issues, Debates and Answers*, Routledge.

Berlin, I. (1979) *The Hedgehog and the Fox,* Penguin.

Blanchard, K. and Johnson, S. (1981) *The One Minute Manager,* Blanchard Johnson.

Bridges, W. (1994) 'The end of the job', *Fortune,* 19 Sept.

*Broughton, P. (2008) 'Harvard loses its lustre', *Prospect,* Sept.

*Broussine, M., Grey, M. and Kirk, P. (1998) 'The best and the worst time for management development', *Journal of Management Development,* Vol. 17, No. 1.

Brungardt, C. (1996) 'The making of leaders: a review of research in leadership development and education', *The Journal of Leadership Studies,* Vol. 3, No. 3.

Burgoyne, J. and Reynolds, M. (1997) *Management Learning: Integrating Perspectives in Theory and Practice,* Introduction, Chs. 1, 3, 6, 9, Sage.

Burns, J. (1978) *Leadership,* Sage.

*Burns, J. (2003) *Transforming Leadership: A new Pursuit of Leadership,* Atlantic Monthly Press.

Buus, I. (2005) 'The evolution of leadership development: challenges and best practice', *Industrial and Commercial Training,* Vol. 37, No. 4.

*Cacioppe, R. (1998a) 'Leaders leading leaders: an effective way to enhance leadership development programmes', *Leadership and Organisation Development Journal,* Vol. 19, No. 4.

Cacioppe, R. (1998b) 'An integrated model and approach for the design of effective leadership development', *Leadership and Organisational Development Journal,* Vol. 19, No. 1.

Cole, K. (1995) 'Management development to the millennium', *Management Development Review,* Vol. 8, No. 3.

Collin, A (1996) 'The MBA: the potential for students to find their voice in Babel', in French, R. and Grey, C. *Re-thinking Management Education,* Sage.

Collins, J. (2001) 'Level 5 leadership: the triumph of humility and fierce resolve', *Harvard Business Review,* Vol. 79, No. 1.

Conger, J. (1989) *The Charismatic Leader: Beyond the Mystique of Exceptional Leadership*, Jossey-Bass.

*Conger, J. (1992) *Learning to Lead: The Art of Transforming Managers* into Leaders, Jossey-Bass.

Conger, J. and Kanungo, R. (1987) 'Towards a behavioural theory of charismatic leadership in organisational settings', *Academy of Management Review*, 12.

Conger, J. and Lawler, J. (2005) 'People skills still rule in the virtual company', *Financial Times,* 26 Aug.

*Cooper, C. (2005) *Leadership and Management in the 21st Century*, Oxford University Press.

Cullen, J. and Turnbull, S. (2005) 'A meta-review of management development literature', *Human Resource Development Review,* Vol. 4.

*Day, D. (2000) 'Leadership development: a review in context', *Leadership Quarterly,* Vol. 11, No. 4.

Day, D., Zaccaro, S. et al. (2004) 'Leader development for transforming organisations: growing leaders for tomorrow, *Book Review, Academy of Management Executive*.

Department for Education and Employment (2000) 'The future skill needs of managers', *Research Report No. 182,* Jan.

Fox, S. (1997) 'From management education and development to the study of management learning', in Burgoyne, J. and Reynolds, M. (1997) *Management Learning,* Sage.

*French, R. and Grey, C. (1996) *Rethinking Management Education*, Sage.

Fry, J. (2006) 'Towards a paradigm of spiritual leadership', *Leadership Quarterly,* Vol. 16, No. 5.

*Furnham, A. (2000) 'Work in 2020', *Journal of Managerial Psychology,* Vol. 15, No. 3.

Gardner, H. (1995) *Leading Minds,* Basic Books.

*Garavan, T., Barnicle, B. and O'Sulleabhain, F. (1999) 'Management development: contemporary trends, issues and strategies', *Journal of European Industrial Training,* Vol. 23, No. 4.

*Garratt, B. (1996) *The Fish Rots From the Top Down,* Harper Collins.

Goleman, D. (1998) 'What makes a leader?' *Harvard Business Review,* Vol. 76.

Goleman, D., Boyatzis, R. and McKee, A. (2002) *Primal Leadership,* Harvard Business School Press.

*Gratton, L. and Pearson, J. (1994) 'Empowering leaders: are they being developed?', in Mabey, C. and Iles, P. (1994) *Managing Learning,* Open University.

*Greenleaf, R. (1977) *Servant Leadership: A Journey into the Nature of Legitimate Power and Greatness,* Paulist Press.

Grey, C. (1999) 'We are all managers now: we always were. On development and demise of management', *Journal of Management Studies,* Vol. 36, No. 5.

*Grint, K. (2001) *The Arts of Leadership,* Oxford University Press.

Handy, C. (1986) *The Future of Work,* Basil Blackwell.

Handy, C. (1990) *The Age of Unreason,* Arrow.

Harrison, R. (2002) *Learning and Development,* Ch. 18, CIPD.

Heller, R. (2003) *The Fusion Manager,* Profile Books.

Hernez-Broome, G. and Hughes, R. (2005) 'Leadership development: past, present and future', *Human Resource Planning.*

Hill, L. (2004) 'New manager development in the 21st century', *Academy of Management Development,* Vol. 18, No. 3.

*Hirsh, W. and Carter, A. (2002) *New Directions in Management Development,* IES.

House, R., Spangler, W. et al. (1991) 'Personality and charisma in the US presidency: a psychological theory of leadership effectiveness', *Administrative Science Quarterly,* Vol. 36.

Hunt, J. (1991) *Leadership: A New Synthesis,* Sage.

*Jackson, B. and Parry, K. (2008) *A Very Short, Fairly Interesting and Cheap Book on Leadership,* Sage.

Jansen, P., Van der Velde, M. and Mui, W. (2001) 'A typology of management development', *Journal of Management Development,* Vol. 20, No. 2.

Jones, S. and Gosling, J. (2005) *Nelson's Way,* Nicholas Brealey Publishing.

Kaagan, S. (1998) 'Leadership development: the heart of the matter', *International Journal of Educational Management,* Vol. 12, No. 2.

Kay, J. (2005) 'War and peace: a business primer for our times', *Financial Times,* 30 Aug.

Klagge, J. (1997) 'Leadership development needs of today's organisational managers', *Leadership and Organisational Development Journal,* Vol. 18, No. 7.

*Kotter, J. (1990) *A force for change: how leadership differs from management,* Free Press.

Kouzes, J. and Posner, B. (1998) *Encouraging the Heart,* Jossey-Bass.

Kumer, R. and Usurier, J. (2004) 'Management education in a globalising world', in Grey, C. and Antonacopoulou, E. *Management Learning,* Sage.

Latham, G. and Sijts, G. (1998) *Management Development,* Psychology Press Ltd.

Lawrence, V. (2008) 'Unlocking the talent of younger managers', *Management Today,* July.

Mabey, C. (2002) 'Mapping management development practice', *Journal of Management Studies,* Vol. 39, No. 8.

Mangham, I. (1988) 'Managing the executive process', *Omega,* Vol. 16, No. 2.

Mangham, I. (1990) 'Managing as a performing art', *British Journal of Management,* Vol. 1.

*Marturano, A. and Gosling, J. (2008) *Leadership,* Routledge.

Mathews, J., Megginson, D. and Surtees, M. (2004) *Human Resource Development,* Ch. 10, Kogan Page.

*McCall, M. (2004) 'Leadership development through experience', *Academy of Management Executive,* Vol. 18, No. 3.

*McCall, M., Lombardo, M. and Morrison, A. (1988) *The Lessons of Experience,* Lexington Books.

Mintzberg, H. (2004a) 'Leadership and management development: an afterword', *Academy of Management Executive,* Vol. 18, No. 3.

Mintzberg, H. (2004b) 'Managers not MBAs: a hard look at the soft practice of managing', *Book Review, Academy of Management Executive,* Vol. 18, No. 4.

Mintzberg, H. and Gosling, J. (2006) 'Management education as if both matter', *Management Learning,* Vol. 37.

Mullins, L. (2007) *Management and Organisational Behaviour,* Prentice Hall.

Mumford, A. (1997) *Management Development: Strategies for Action* Ch. 2, CIPD.

Mumford, A. and Gold, J. (2004) *Management Development: Strategies for Action,* Ch. 12, CIPD.

Murray, S. (2003) 'Risky lessons from judo and fast cars', *Financial Times,* 11 Aug.

Osterman, P. (1996) *Broken Ladders: Management Careers in the New Economy,* Oxford University Press.

Parry, K. and Bryman, A. (2006) 'Leadership in organisations', in Clegg, S., Hardy, C. and Nord, W. (eds) *Handbook of Organisational Studies,* Sage.

Paauwe, J. and Williams, R. (2001) 'Seven key issues for management development', *Journal of Management Development,* Vol. 20, No. 2.

Peters, T. (1994) *In Pursuit of 'Wow': Every Person's Guide to Topsy Turvy Times*, Macmillan.

Pye, A. (2002) 'The changing nature of managerial work', conference paper at Judge Institute.

*Raelin, J. (2004) 'Don't bother putting leadership into people', *Academy of Management Executive*, Vol. 18, No. 3.

*Ready, D. and Conger, J. (2003) 'Why leadership development efforts fail', *Sloan Management Review*, Spring.

Reed, M. and Anthony, P. (1992) 'Professionalising management and managing professionalisation', *Journal of Management Studies*, Vol. 29, No. 5.

*Risher, H. and Stopper, W. (2004) 'Reflections on the state of leadership development', *Human Resource Planning*, Sept.

Roberts, D. (2007) 'Britain's disposable managers', *Sunday Telegraph*, shortened version reported in *The Week*, 9 June.

Sadler-Smith, E. (2006) *Learning and Development for Managers*, Blackwell.

Salaman, G. and Butler, J. (1994) 'Why managers won't learn', in Mabey, C. and Iles, P. *Managing Learning*, Open University.

Sampson, A. (1995) *Company Man*, Harper Collins.

Sennett, R. (1999) *The Corrosion of Character*, Routledge.

Sinclair, A. (2007) *Leadership for the Disillusioned*, Allen and Unwin.

Stewart, J. (1999) *Employee Development Practice*, Ch. 7, Prentice Hall.

Storey, J. (1989) 'Management development: a literature review and implications for future research. Part 1: conceptualisations and practices', *Personnel Review*, Vol. 18, No. 6.

Syrett, M. and Lammiman, J. (1999) *Management Development*, Economist Books.

Talbot, C. (1997) 'Paradoxes of management development – trends and tensions', *Career Development International*, Vol. 2, No. 3.

Thomas, D. and Inkson, K. (2004) *Cultural Intelligence: People Skills for Global Business*, Berrett-Koehler.

Thomson, A., Mabey, C. and Storey, J. (2001) *Changing Patterns of Management Development*, Chs. 1, 2, Blackwell.

Useem, M. (1996) 'Corporate restructuring and the restructured world of senior management', in Osterman, P. (1996) *Broken Ladders*, OUP.

Walton, J. (1999) *Strategic Human Resource Development*, Ch. 2, Prentice Hall.

Warner Burke, W. (1994) *Organisational Development*, Addison-Wesley.

Watson, J. (1995) *Management Development to The Millennium: The New Priorities*, Institute of Management.

Watson, T. (2002) 'Change and continuity and the need to be self critical in management studies', conference paper at Judge Institute.

Winterton, J. and Winterton, R. (1997) 'Does management development add value?' *British Journal of Management*, Vol. 8, Special Issue.

Woodall, J. and Winstanley, D. (1999) *Management Development: Strategy and Practice*, Ch. 1, Blackwell.

*Worrall, L. and Cooper, C. (2001) 'Management skills development: a perspective on current issues and setting the future agenda', *Leadership and Organisational Development Journal*, Vol. 22, No. 1.

Yukl, G. (2002) *Leadership in Organisations*, Prentice Hall.

Index

ABB 371
ability testing 127
academies (as classification of form) 303–4
Accenture 387
accommodator 155
accountabilities 85
accreditation 479–80
   see also MBAs
accrediting body for MBAs (AACSB) 353
acting up 203
action evaluation 436
action learning sets (ALS) 190–1, 194–5, 212–17, 287, 361, 420
action maze 246
action mindset 38
action research/survey feedback approaches 400–1
action reviews 191
active listening 197–8
activists 156, 246, 419–20
Adventure Training see outdoor management development
Africa 337, 359
ageing workforce 454
agendas 20
agricultural rationale 55
analysers 304
analytical ability 373
analytical mindset 38
andragogy 152–4, 194
Anglian Water Services plc (case study) 172, 284
anthropology 50
application-based learning 481–2
appraisal systems 120–4
appraisal themes 93
appreciative inquiry 397
Apprentice, The 201, 255
apprenticeship 344, 361, 480
aptitude tests 127
arena thesis 61
Ashbridge MBA 380
Ashridge 4F model 53–4
Ashton model 53

Asia 337, 359
assessment 308
assessment centres 131, 135, 305
assessment of development need and development planning 105–40
   appraisal systems 120–4
   development centres 131–6
   development system, management development as 106–7
   multi-rater feedback or 360-degree assessment 125–7
   performance management and review 107–9
   personal development plans 137–8
   psychometric testing 127–31
   see also competency frameworks
assignments 311, 381–3
assimilator 155
Association of Accountancy Technicians 267
Association of Business Schools 263
Association for Management Education and Development 263
Association of MBAs (AMBA) 262, 263
attachments 202–3
attention (as a skill) 144
audience participation 242
auditing 92–4, 317–20, 429
authentic leadership 465
autonomy 265

BA 79
   Lancaster MBA 278
   Young Professionals Programme 233
balance of power 456
Balanced Scorecard 172, 429–30
Balloon Game 134
Bank of England 324
banking model of learning 180
baseball teams (as classification of firm) 304
Bath School of Business 279
Bath University 288
BBC 311
   Bradford MBA 278
behavioural analysis 93
behavioural level (evaluation) 426

behavioural objectives 228
behaviourism 143–5
Belbin Team Roles Inventory 129
benchmarking systems 430
bi-sociation 40
Big Energy plc (case study) 88
BigCorp (case study) 153–4
BIM 260
Blake and Mouton Leadership Grid 129
blended learning 190–1, 334
bottom-up development 307
boundaries 171
boundaryless careers/organisations 300–1, 312, 321, 329, 382
BP 356
Bradford MBA 278
brainstorming 250
Bramley Model 425
British Civil Service 131–2, 134, 305, 356
BT 136, 356, 393
Buberian debate 244
Buckingham Independent Management Centre: AL-based MBA 286, 287
'buddy managers' 384
building a tower of cards game 246
business managers 376
business schools 280–6, 334, 352–3, 356, 380, 481
buzz groups 244

Cable and Wireless Company 285, 310
candle game 251
Canon 166
capabilities questionnaire 136
capability development 308
CAPIO model 427–9
career management and development 302–15
  activities 306–7
  breaking the mould 307–8
  career action centres 310–11, 313
  career counselling 310
  career positioning 308
  concept 302–3
  individually driven methods 312–13
  labour market importance 303–4
  necessity for 306–7
  organisationally driven methods 310–12
  policy debates 305
  shared responsibility 309–10
  Unilever (case study) 313–15
  workshops 310
career planning 347
careers, trends in 296–302
  conceptualisation 300–2
  job security, declining 297

nature of managerial work, changes in 297–8
'psychological contract', changing 300
skills, new 298–9
case studies as learning tool 244–5, 272
catch-up 234
cause and effect, isolation of 440–1
central clearing-house system 204
Central and Eastern Europe 337, 359–60
centralisation versus decentralisation 97–8
centralised hub 368
centres of excellence 388
Centro 370
ceremonial rationale 55
certificates 267–8
challenges facing management 452–5
change, orientation to 31
changing nature of management 455–60
charismatic leadership 465
Chartered Institute of Personnel Development 262
Chartered Institute of Public Finance Accountants 262
Chartered Management Institute 111, 455
China 152, 279, 360
climate of learning 169
clubs (as classification of firm) 304
coaching 195, 206–7, 374
cognitive learning 145–9
cognitive processes 163
cognitive psychology 49
coherence of management strategy 82–3
collaborative approach 337
collaborative cultures 453–4
collaborative inquiry 437
collaborative mindset 38
collaborative partnerships 359
collective data 318
collective learning 161, 164
collectivism 336, 346, 360, 362
communication skills 34
communities of practice 150, 165, 287, 371
compensation rationale 55
competency framework: standards of competency 268
competency frameworks 109–20, 265
  'areas of competency' 115
  core 114
  criticisms 117–20
  definition 109–11
  'dimensions of competency' 115–16
  emerging 112
  emotional 468
  functionalist-behaviourist model 112–13
  high performance 114
  inter-cultural 374
  inventors 116–17
  maintenance of competency 234

maturing 112
person-centred/social model 113–15, 116
Regional Health Authority (case study) 119–20
scientists 117
superior 114
technical 29–30
threshold 114
traditionalists 116
transitional 112
units 110–11
values 111–12
competitive advantage and learning 168
composite 'levels' model 426
concept of leadership 475
Confederation of British Industry 263
confidence-building 151
consistencies and processes of management 20
constructing a paper aeroplane game 246
constructionist approach 149–51, 435, 437, 438
'contact managers' 384
context (inputs) of organisational strategy 58
contextualisation 6
continuous professional and personal development 200–1, 268, 343, 348
controlling and evaluation 425, 446
convergence thesis 335
converger 155
coordinated federations 369
coordinators, cross-border 374
corporate clowning 252
corporate education *see* formal management: education
corporate governance 454–5
corporate leadership 474
corporate managers 376
corporate restructuring 457
corporate strategy 10, 374
corporate training 343
corporate universities 284–6, 352
corporate values and culture 6
cosmopolitanism 360–1
cost-effectiveness/benefit evaluation 422
Council for Excellence in Management and Leadership 261, 263
Council for University Management Schools 261
country managers 376
courses 224, 235
Courthaulds 79
Coverdale Training 213
Cranfield 276, 278
creative dialogue 250
creativity 2–3, 6, 39–40

exercises 250–2
tests 130
credentialism 361
credibility 82
critical incidents 244
interviewing 120
critical theory 64–7
cross-border coaches and coordinators 374
cross-cultural management development 13, 17, 334–65
Central and Eastern Europe 359–60
China 360
comparative approaches 360–2
developing countries 359
France 340–3
Germany 344–5
individualism versus collectivism 336
Japan 345–50
masculine versus feminine cultures 336–7
organisational conflict 336
power distance, high and low 337
sensitivity training 386–7
Seychelles Institute of Management (case study) 362–4
uncertainty avoidance, high and low 338–9
United Kingdom 354–8
United States 350–4
Crotonville *see* John F. Welch Leadership Centre
'crown prince' development programme 361
cultural assumptions 410
cultural issues 189, 420, 436, 465
cultures, collaborative 453–4
current situation, analysis of 89–90
cybernetics 145

Dana University 352
DBA 279–80
deadwood 319
Dearing Report on Higher Education 262
decentralisation 97–8, 100
decentralised federation model 369
deconstruction of texts 66
deductive thinkers 37
defenders 304
defensive routines 182–3
definitions 3–4
demographic data 318
design issues and evaluation 434–6
designer (leader as) 170
Deutsch Bank University (DBU) 285–6
developers 83
development centres 131–6, 310
BT 136
games and exercises 133–4

development needs 228
diagnostic skills 41
diagnostic tools 194
dialogic methods 244
digitalisation 453
diplomas 267–8
discovery learning 152
discussions 243–4
disjointed incrementalism 36
dispersed leadership 466
distance-learning 276–7
distributed leadership 465
divergent thinking 251
divergers 155
diversified talent spotting 361
diversity 6, 314, 454
divisional leadership 474
doing management 18–19, 27–8
donkeys (inept) 42
double loop learning 162, 187, 240, 482
double talk 40
dramaturgy 30–1, 248–50
DVDs as learning aids 242

e-learning 246–7
economic context of management 50, 452
education 335, 355–6, 361, 479–80
   interventions 406
   see also formal management:
      education; learning; management
      education (Med)
egg game 251
emotional competencies 468
Emotional Competency Inventory 130
emotions 34–6, 158, 444
empathy 33
empty chair technique 249
empty-stimuli tests 128
enabling objectives 228
enactment and behaviour modelling 144
encounter groups 404
energy flow model 164
engineering ideology 283
Enrico, R. 327
Enron 324, 327
environmental challenges 454
environmental legitimacy rationale 55
environmental scanning 89–90
epistemology 64
EQ workshops 212
Ericsson 204, 371
escalator models 426–7
espoused theories 52, 163
Esso 310

ethics 109–10, 265, 275, 290, 319, 454–5
ethnic minorities 454
ethnocentrism 13, 259, 368, 382
ethnographic stage 368–9
Europe 359
   MBAs 270, 275, 276, 281
European Business Excellence Model 430–1
European Foundation for Management
   Development 479
European Foundation for Quality
   Management Model 172
evaluation of management development 410,
   417–48, 470
   acting up 436
   assessment 422
   Balanced Score Card 429–30
   benefits 422–4
   Bramley Model 425
   CAPIO model 427–9
   cause and effect, isolation of 440–1
   classic models 425–6
   composite 'levels' model 426
   cost effectiveness/benefit 422
   criteria 431–2
   definition 421–2
   design issues 434–6
   European Business Excellence Model 430–1
   Evaluation Research Measurement Model 427
   failure to evaluate 419–21
   formative 422, 440
   fourth generation 437
   Hamblin Model 425
   hierarchical or escalator models 426–7
   Kirkpatrick Model 426
   multiple levels model 427, 439–40, 441–3
   political issues 444–7
   pre-ordinate 437
   process 422, 436
   purposes 424–5
   research paradigm 437–8
   responsive 437
   single 439–40
   special issues 432–4
   stakeholder 436
   strategic frameworks 429
   summative 422, 440
   systematic training cycle 419
   timing of evaluation 439–40
   Training for Impact process model 429
   types 422
   validity or reliability 439
Evaluation Research Measurement Model 427
excellence movement 168
Executive development 233–4

executive MBAs 352
exercises at development centres 133–4
expatriates and assignments 381–3
experiential learning 36, 151–9, 179–218, 222–4, 337, 379, 478, 481–3
   andragogy 152–4
   blocks to learning 189
   group learning 212–17
   humanistic learning 151–2
   IBM 470
   informal management development: incidental/accidental learning 184, 185–6
   integrated management development: opportunistic learning 184–5, 186–9
   leadership development 471–2
   learning cycle 154–7
   learning styles 156
   new responsibilities, learning from 202–5
   opportunities for learning 190–2
   rise of 180–2
   see also one-to-one learning; self-development
experimental programmes 286–7
explicit learning 186
external factors 90
externally run courses 224
Exxon Oil 217
Eysenck's Personality Questionnaire 129

facilitation skills 34
facilitator 402–3
family unhappiness 384
feedback 125–7, 153, 197–8, 212
feeling as interpersonal and social skill 33
feminisation of management 454
films as learning aids 242
finding the deadly chemical game 134
firewalking 252
fishbowl exercises 248
'fit for use' values of design 435
flexible development 305, 307
flexible forms of organisation 99–101
focused approach 54
formal leadership 26
formal learning 190, 191, 204, 231, 238
formal management: education 258–93, 379–80
   business schools 280–3
   certificates and diplomas 267–8
   corporate universities 284–6, 352
   Council for Excellence in Management and Leadership 263
   criticisms 260–2
   experimental programmes 286–7
   new agenda 287–91
   planned learning 185
   professionalisation debate 264–5
   specialist postgraduate qualifications 268–9
   undergraduate business degrees 266–7
   vocationalism 261–3
   see also Master's in business administration
formal management: training 221–56
   courses 233–40
   design stages 227–33
   'informal' versus 'formal' debate 222–4
   patterns 224–7
   see also off-the-job methods
formalised approach 54
formative evaluation 422
fortresses (as classification of firm) 304
Forum for Management Education 261
Foundation for Entrepreneurial Management 284
Foundation for Management Education 263
foxes (clever) 42
fragmentation of career development 53–4, 479
France 335, 337, 338, 339, 342, 351, 361
   corporate training 343
   cross-cultural management development 340–3
   École des Mines 340
   École National d'Administration (ENA) 340–1
   École Polytechnic 340
   grandes écoles 340–3
   HEC School of Management 274
   ISA business school 275
   universities 343
fully integrated model 54
functional leadership 474
functional managers 376
functional performance 54
functional-defensive rationale 55
functionalist models 62, 72
functionalist-behaviourist model 112–13
Fuqua School of Business, Duke University, California 481
future directions 451–85
   challenges facing management 452–5
   changing nature of management 455–60
   leadership and leadership development 462–75
      as collective process 473–5
      different levels 474
      experience, lessons of 472
      as experiential process 471–2
      IBM 470
      models 464–6
      origins 463

future directions (*continued*)
   themes and trends 467–9, 475
   management and leadership
      development 475–83
      agenda and delivery challenges 480–3
      challenge of management change 475–7
      corporate trends 481–2
      institutional challenges 477–80
   tenure 460–1

g factor 127
games 133–4, 245–6
gaps, analysis of 92–4
gaps, closure of 94–5
GE 379, 380–1, 388
GEC 172, 324, 469
general management skills 457
general strategic drivers 89
generalist management roles 456–7
Generation X and Y 300, 301, 454
geo-centric stage 369
Germany 335, 338, 339, 342, 352, 361
   apprenticeship 344
   arbiter 344
   corporate management development 344–5
   cross-cultural management
      development 344–5
   MBA 345
   polytechnic 344
   techniker 344–5
   university 344
Gestalt approach 147, 149
global citizenship and ethics course 275
global mindset (think global act local) 373, 375, 381
global stage 369
globalisation 452, 459
   see also international management development
GMAT test 270
'godfathers' 384
Goleman's Emotional Competency
   Inventory 130
good practice 19
Greece 342
group:
   exercises 133
   feedback 153
   learning 212–17
   reflection 194
   work and an MBA 272

habits of thought 162
Hamblin Model 425
'happy sheets' 441
Harvard Business School 65, 244, 274, 354

headship 24
Henley Management College/Centre 276, 278, 279–80, 285
'hero' leadership 465
Hersey and Blanchard Situational
   Leadership Matrix 129
heterarchies 371
hierarchical models 426–7
high performance competencies 114
holistic aspect of management 57–8, 73–4, 118, 147–9, 346, 436
Honda 166
Hone and Mumford and Kolb's Learning
   Styles Inventory 129
honesty with onself 198
horizontal integration 77
host country nationals (HCNs) 369
House Tree Person Test 130
HP 469
HSBC 204
humanistic learning 151–2
humanistic psychology 50

IBM 298–9
   leadership development 470
ICI 305, 356, 407
ideological issues 420
idiographic view 128
'image theatre' 249
IMD 274
imitative learning 144
impact/outcome and organisational strategy 59
Imperial College 276
imprecision 21
improving 425, 446, 447
in-house/internal courses 224, 235
in-tray exercises 134
incidental/accidental learning 184, 185–6
InCorp (case study) 100–1
individual career management 307
individual data 318
individual difference 6
individual learning 143–60, 161
   behaviourism and social learning 143–5
   cognitive learning 145–9
   constructionist and situated learning 149–51
   self 159–60
   see also experiential learning
individualism 336, 362
individually driven methods 312–13
inductive thinkers 37
informal leadership 26
informal learning 190, 204, 231
   see also experiential learning

informal management development 184, 185–6, 225
informal networks 479
informal on-the-job training 221
information and communication technology 453
Institute of Directors 260
Institute of Management 263, 479
institutional obstacles 61
institutional power of corporate stockholders 452
integrated management development:
    opportunistic learning 184–5, 186–9
  formalised management development: planned learning 185
integrated network 369
integration of management development with other organisational activities 81–2
Intel 469
intellectual ability 373
intellectual brokers 374
inter-cultural competency 374
inter-cultural mediators 374
inter-group meetings 404
interactive skills exercises 248
interim managers 457
internal consulting 204
internal factors 90
international leadership 465
international management development 367–90
  assignments and expatriates 381–3
  corporate education 379–80
  cross-cultural sensitivity training 386–7
  factors involved in choosing managers 375–6
  GE (case study) 380–1
  globalisation of business 368–70
  McKinsey's entrance programme 378
  and organisational learning 388
  preparation for foreign assignments 384
  prerequisites for managers abroad 373–5
  re-entry from a foreign assignment (repatriation) 385
  recruitment and development 378–9
  selection for foreign assignment 383–4
  strategic issues 377
  support during foreign assignments 384–5
  transnationals 371–3
International Master's Programme in Practising Management (IMPPM) 269, 287
international perspective 361
internationalism 314
interpersonal awareness 35
interpersonal orientation 32
interpersonal skills 33–4, 248
interpretive meaning 19
interpretivist approach 435, 437

interviews 133
intuitive thinkers 37
inventors 116–17
Investors in People 172, 262
Issam company (India) 80–1
Italy 337, 338, 342

Jaguar 79
Japan 202, 265, 335, 337, 338, 352, 358, 361
  cross-cultural management development 345–50
  Gerba-Shingiis 350
  Keio Daigalu Business School 349
  Ringi 346
job behaviour level 442
job rotation 203
job security, declining 297
John F. Welch Leadership Centre, Crotonville, New York 380–1, 388
Johnson Wax 309
joint responsibility 306–7, 309
judging as interpersonal and social skill 33

'keeping in touch' arrangements 385
Kirkpatrick Model 426
Kite Game 134
knowing how 7
knowing what 7
knowing why 7
knowledge 43, 464
  abstract 264
  facilitators 374
  management 166–7
  spiral of 167
  tacit 166–7
  technical 374

labour market importance 303–4
lambs (innocent) 42
Lancaster MBA 278
landing on the moon game 246
lateral thinking 250
leader development and leadership development, difference between 473
leaders developing leaders approach 469
leadership 171
  authentic 465
  concept 475
  corporate 474
  development 7, 10
  dispersed 466
  distributed 465
  divisional 474
  formal 26

leadership (*continued*)
  functional 474
  informal 26
  international 465
  and leadership development *see* future directions
  level 5 465
  and management, spheres of 22–7
  origins 463
  servant 465
  shared 458, 465–6
  spiritual 465
  strategic 455–6, 474
  style 475
learned incapacity 182
learner experience 440
learning 10, 86–8, 446, 447
  across boundaries 169
  agility 326, 327
  agreements 193
  application-based 481–2
  banking model 180
  blended 190–1, 334
  centres 352
  cognitive 145–9
  collective 161, 164
  contracts 193, 361
  cycle 154–7
  discovery 152
  distance-learning 276–7
  domains 229
  double loop 162, 187, 240, 482
  e-learning 246–7
  as empowerment 169
  and evaluation 425
  explicit 186
  formal 190, 191, 204, 231, 238
  group 212–17
  humanistic 151–2
  imitative 144
  incidental/accidental 184, 185–6
  informal 190, 204, 231
  interventions 406
  laboratory 403
  level 426, 442
  log 194
  management 62–3
  models 62, 162
  observational 144–5
  opportunistic 184–5, 186–9
  organisation 168–74
    Anglian Water Services plc (case study) 172
    characteristics 168–9
    critique 173–4
    in real life 171–2

  Senge's model 169–70
  person centred 152
  philosophy 230
  plan/strategy, detailed 230
  planned 185
  prospective 186, 188–9
  resource centres 310–11
  retrospective 186–8
  review 198–9
  shared 169
  single loop 162, 240
  situated 149–51
  social 143–5
  structured informal 184, 186–9
  student-centred 242
  styles 31, 482
  systematised 168
  tacit 186
  taxonomies of types of 229
  team 10, 170
  theory 50
  triple loop 162–3
  tutor-centred 242
  types of 228–30
  unstructured informal 184
  see also action learning sets; experiential learning; individual learning; knowledge; organisational learning
Learning and Skills Councils 262
Learning Styles Inventory 129
lectures 241–3
left brain thinking 37
Lehman Brothers 387
level 5 leadership 465
liberal-humanist model 480–1
life experience 205
lifelong learner skills 374
line managers 83, 482–3
linear careers 301
list game 251
listening, active 197–8
Lloyds TSB 326
localisation 100
London Business School 274, 278, 284, 356
  Consortium Programme 380
losing face 337
Lotus Notes 276
loyalty 346
Lucas 79

MA 359
McDonalds 284
  University 352

McGill: International Master's Programme for Participating Managers 286
McKinsey's entrance programme 378
macro-level analysis 5, 93
management by objectives (MBO) 108
Management Charter Group/Initiative *see* Management Standards Centre
management education (Med) 6, 7, 224–5, 289
management learning 7, 62–3
Management Standards Centre 110, 111, 112–13, 115, 261, 268, 479
management training 6, 7, 224–5, 260
Management Wheel Diagnostic Test 129
management without authority 458
Manchester business school 356
masculinity/femininity 336–7, 362
Master's in Business Administration (MBA) 259, 269–73, 274–80, 286, 334–5, 358–9, 481
   benefits of degree 270–1
   contents of 271–3
   corporate/company 278
   curriculum, changes in 274–5
   differentiation 275–6
   distance-learning 276–7
   ethics 275
   executive 279, 352
   France 343
   Germany 345
   Japan 349
   Mintzberg's views on 281–2
   nature of degree 269–70
   United States 352
   see also business schools
Matsushita 166
MBA *see* Master's in Business Administration
meaning of management 17–22
   doing management 18–19
   process of management 19–22
mental maps 163
mental models 170
mentoring 191, 194–5, 208–10, 211, 361, 384
method of leadership development 475
Michigan University 275
micro-level view 5
mind mapping 148, 251
Minnesota Multiphasic Personality Inventory 129
mirroring 412
mobile lone managers 457
models and theories 38–9, 48–68
   critical theory 64–7
   emergent paradigm of management learning 62–3
   nature and value of theory 49–52
   radical pluralistic models 61–2
   systems theory 56–60
   typologies 52–5
Monsanto 172
motivation 383
Motorola 79, 87, 94, 172, 284
multi-rater feedback 125–7
multidisciplinary conceptualisation 63
multinational stage 369
multiple levels model 427, 441–3
Myers Briggs Test 129

National Forum for Management Education 261
national regulatory systems 479–80
National Training Agency 261
National Training and Enterprise Councils 262
national/domestic stage 368
naturalistic schools of research (constructivist and interpretive) 437
nature of managerial work, changes in 297–8
Natwest 284
NEC 166
negotiated order 22
'Nelson touch' 472
Netherlands 338, 342
Network Ireland 206
networking 20, 212, 312, 369, 458, 479
New Academy of Business 288
'New Deal' 192, 307, 329
new management 462
New Master's in Business Administration: Judge Institute, Cambridge 286, 287
new responsibilities, learning from 202–5
NHS 393
   Leadership Development Programme 233
nine-dot problem 251
Nissan 87
nomothetic view 128
Norway 352
NVQ qualifications 110–11, 261, 479

objective factors 19
objective indicators 423
objective methods 93
objectives 85, 228
observational learning 144–5
observing 206
off-the-job methods 229, 241–55, 349
   case studies 244–5
   creativity exercises 250–2
   dialogic methods 244
   discussions 243–4

off-the-job methods (*continued*)
  drama 248–50
  e-learning 246–7
  formal 221, 224, 225, 226
  games and simulations 245–6
  interactive skills exercises 248
  lectures 241–3
  outdoor development 252–5
  pedagogies of teaching and facilitation 242–3
  personal growth workshops ('away days') 212
  Socratic method 245
Oki Electronic Industry Company 254
old management 462
on-the-job, company-specific training (OJT) 221, 229, 347–8
one-to-one learning 153, 205–11
  coaching 206–7
  mentoring 208–10, 211
  observing 206
  shadowing 206
  sponsoring 210–11
open programmes 235
'open systems' approach 56–7, 59, 74
Open University 276
opportunistic learning 184–5, 186–9
opportunities, recognition and use of for personal growth 196
OPQ test instrument 129
organisation *see* strategy and organisation
organisational conflict 336
organisational development 7, 10, 392–414
  action research/survey feedback approaches 400–1
  critique 410–13
  definitions 395–6
  education and learning interventions 406
  first generation 397
  historical background 396–7
  inter-group meetings 404
  power and politics 406–7
  process consultation 404–5
  qualities required 408
  relationship with management development 393
  roles, spectrum of 409
  second generation 397
  sensitivity training 403–4
  skills of practitioner 407–9
  strategic management and organisational design 405–6
  team building and team learning 401–3
  third-party facilitation 405
  as 'total system' change 394
organisational inheritance rationale 55

organisational learning and the learning organisation 7, 11, 160–5, 388
  cognitive processes 163
  communities that learn, organisations as 163–5
  learning process model 162–3
  organisational process 162–3
  practical techniques 166–7
organisational maturity 73
organisational patterns 21
Organisational Transformation Project 328
organisationally driven methods 310–12
organisationally led career management 306
outdoor management development (OMD) 252–5
outplacement (OP) 311–12
outsourcing 98–9
Outward Bound *see* outdoor management development
owls (wise) 42

pan-centric stage 370
panel discussions 244
parent country nationals (PCNs) 368
participative decision-making 337
partnerships 83–4, 306–7, 359, 361
patronage 479
pedagogies of teaching and facilitation 13, 242–3
peer appraisal/assessment 125, 312–13
peer support groups *see* personal group sessions
people orientation and skills 374
Pepsi 327
perceptive thinkers 37–8
performance appraisal 311
performance management and review 107–9
performance management systems 406
performance, short-term 305
person centred learning 152
person-centred/social model of competency 113–15
personal career planning 312
Personal Construct Analysis 130
personal construct theory (PCT) 146
personal development 268
personal development plans (PDPs) 137–8, 202, 312
personal group sessions 212
personal growth 313–14
personal mastery 170
personal qualities 374
personal values 31
Personality Questionnaire (Eysenck) 129
personality testing 127–8
phenomenological approach to research 437
philosophy of learning 230
philosophy of management 230
physical environment 454
Pizza Express 327
placement work 267
planned career management 305

planned, formalised developments 5
planned learning 185
planning *see* assessment of development need and development planning
PMS cycle 120
policies/processes 58, 84–6
political factors 21, 50, 158, 189, 421, 444–7
 and organisational development 406–7
political reinforcement rationale 55
political skills 40–2, 340
polycentric stage 369
polytechnics 344
portfolio 329
 approach 318
 workers 301–2
positivism 280
positivistic schools of research (scientific and objective) 437
post-positivistic approach to evaluation 437
power 406–7, 452, 456
 distance 337, 346, 360, 362
practical theorists 193
practice and behaviour modelling 144
practices/outputs and organisational strategy 58–9
pragmatists 156, 246, 354
presentations 133
pretend ignorance (Socratic irony) 245
Price Waterhouse Coopers 481–2
priorities 85
problem employees 319
process, being part of 21
process consultation 404–5
process evaluation 422, 436
process of management 19–22
processes, investment in 470
professional growth 313–14
professional practices 63
professionalisation debate 264–5
programme monitoring 422
projects 204–5
 and a Master's in Business Administration 272–3
promoting 446
prospective learning 186, 188–9
prospectors 304
protocol analysis 251
proving 424, 446, 447
Prudential 326
psychic defence rationale 55
psycho-drama 248–9
psychological contract 10, 300, 314
psychometric testing 127–31
 test instruments 129–30
psychotherapeutic techniques 404

qualitative approaches 438–9
qualities *see* skills and qualities of managers
quality assurance 422
quantitative approaches 439
question and answer method of inquiry (Socratic dialectic) 245

radical pluralistic models 61–2
radicalism 281, 283
'rank and yank' employees/A/B/C categories 324
rationality 283
re-entry from a foreign assignment (repatriation) 385
reaction level 426, 441–2
reactors 304
rebalancing stage 398
recruitment 347, 378–9
reflection in/on action 215
reflective mindset 38
reflective practice 52, 63, 192
reflective practitioner 193, 471–2
reflective stage (developing future scenarios) 90–2
reflectors 156, 246
Regional Health Authority (case study) 119–20
relational perspective 60
relevance of management strategy 82–3
reliability 439
repertory grid 120, 130
results level (evaluation) 426
retention and behaviour modelling 144
retrospective learning 186–8
revisionist thinking 26
rhetorical ability 340
right brain thinking 37
ritualism 425
Roffey Park 286, 287
role:
 modelling 153, 198
 negotiation 404
 -plays 134, 153, 248
 -reversal 248
 taking 33
roles, cluster of 19
Romania 342
Rorschach Test 130
routines 162
Royal Agricultural College, Cirencester 276
RSC: Directing Creativity 249
Russia 359

'sacred cows' 19
scientism 280
scientists 117
secondments 202–3
selection for foreign assignment 383–4
self 127–8, 150

self knowledge 35
self and leadership 474
self and learning 159–60, 171
self resilience 35
self-appraisal 123, 125
self-assessment 133, 312–13
self-awareness 30–3, 150, 193, 312
self-concept 193
self-confidence 151, 193
self-control 35
self-development 7, 10, 192–201, 312–13
   Apprentice, The 201
   continuous professional development cycle 200
   diagnosis of your own learning needs 195
   feedback: seeking out and attending to 197–8
   honesty with onself 198
   learning, review of 198–9
   opportunities, recognition and use of for personal growth 196
   organisation and 200–1
   organisation of your own learning 195–6
   philosophy and practices of 193–5
   role models, choice and observation of 198
   self-reflective managers 197
self-directed behaviours 152
self-efficacy 151
self-esteem 150
self-evaluation 422
self-experience 472
self-image 150–1
self-learning 151
self-making 30–1
self-managing 195–6, 482
self-motivation 35, 193
self-reflection 30, 194, 196, 197
self-worth 151
seminars 243
sense-making 34
sensitivity training 386–7, 403–4
servant leadership 465
Seychelles Institute of Management (case study) 362–4
shadowing 206, 361
shaping skills 41–2
shared leadership 458, 465–6
shared learning 169
shared ownership 470
shared responsibility 306–7, 309
shared visions 170
'sheep dip' procedures 235, 477
Shell 190–1, 305, 356, 371, 469
simulations 245–6
single loop learning 162, 240
situated learning 149–51
Situational Leadership Matrix 129

six 'thinking hats' (de Bono) 251
skills 43, 464
   clusters 29
   new 298–9
   organisational development practitioner 407–9
   see also skills and qualities of managers
skills and qualities of managers 27–43
   emotion, management of 34–6
   interpersonal and social skills 33–4
   political skills 40–2
   self-awareness 30–3
   sense-making 34
   technical competence 29–30
   thinking skills 36–40
   wisdom, managerial 42–3
SMART goals 137
smile as you drink yak soup game 134
social action approach 163
social capital 453–4
social challenges 454
social context of management 452
social learning 143–5
social psychology 50
social responsibility 454
social skills 33–4, 248
socialisation rationale 55
socio-drama 248
socio-technical data 93
sociology 50
Socrates and self-reflection 196
Socratic method 245
Spain 342
specialist areas 85–6
specialist postgraduate qualifications 268–9
specialist project managers 457
spiral careers 301
spiral of knowledge 167
spiritual leadership 465
sponsorship 210–11, 385
stakeholder evaluation 436
stars 318
statements of intent 86
status 82
steady state careers 301
steward (leader as) 170
storytelling 148–9, 194
strategic awareness 373
strategic business units 456
strategic concerns 10
strategic coupling 71
strategic issues 377
strategic leadership 455–6, 474
strategic management and organisational design 405–6

strategic results level 442–3
strategy and organisation 70–103
   centralisation versus decentralisation 97–8
   coherence and relevance 82–3
   credibility and status 82
   current situation, analysis of 89–90
   flexible forms of organisation 99–101
   gaps and auditing 92–4
   gaps, closure of 94–5
   integration of management development with other organisational activities 81–2
   learning 86–8
   obstacles to strategic management 74–8
   outsourcing 98–9
   partnerships 83–4
   policies 84–6
   reflective stage (developing future scenarios) 90–2
   theoretical modelling as strategic link 72–4
   top management support 79–81
Strathclyde School of Business 279
stretch assignments 204
structured informal learning (guided, opportunistic) 184, 186–9
student-centred learning 242
sub-processes 6
subjective factors 19
subjective methods 93
succession planning and management 315–29
   audit 317–20
   balance sheet 322–3
   talent management 323–9
   traditional forms 316–17
   trends 320–3
summative evaluation 422
support and challenge techniques 404
surface level processing 243
survey feedback approaches 400–1
Sweden 352
syndicates 244
systematic thinkers 37
systematised learning 168
systems theory 56–60, 73
systems thinking 170

T-group 403–4
tacit knowledge 166–7
tacit learning 186
tactical skills 41
tailor-made courses 352
talent management 323–9
talent spotting 204
task forces 204–5
tasks 204–5
teacher (leader as) 170

team 171, 474
team appraisal 123
team approach 313
team building and team learning 401–3
team initiated exercise 274
team learning 10, 170
team motivation and coordination 468
Team Roles Inventory (Belbin) 129
team-based work 459–60
team-building 412
technical competence 29–30
technical knowledge and skills 374
technicism 19, 283
technocratic tools 109–10
technological change 452–3
technological context of management 452
tenure 460–1
testing 133
Texas Instruments 87
Thematic Apperception Test 130
theoretical modelling as strategic link 72–4
theories *see* models and theories
'theories in use' 52, 163
theorists 156, 246
thinking skills 36–40
   creativity 39–40
   model building 38–9
   thinking styles 37–8
thinking styles 31
third country staff (TCNs) 369
third-party debriefing 405
third-party facilitation 405
third-party peacekeeping interventions 405
thoughtful reflection 290–1
3M 79, 94
360 degree feedback 93, 125–7, 337, 423, 436, 442
time-off agreements 385
tolerances questionnaire 136
top management 116
   support 79–81
top-down appraisal 125
total quality management 410, 412
traditionalists 116
training:
   corporate 343
   formal off-the-job 221, 224, 225, 226
   informal on-the-job 221
   management 6, 7, 224–5, 260
   off-the-job 349
   on-the-job, company-specific 229, 347–8
   sensitivity 386–7, 403–4
   see also formal management: training
Training for Impact process model 429

Transactional Analysis 404
transactional leadership 465
transformational leadership 465, 468
transitory careers 301
transnationals 369–70, 371–3
Treasury 324
trends in management development 181–2
triple loop learning (deutero-loop) 162–3
trouble-shooting commissions 204
tutor-centred learning 242
typologies 52–5

uncertainty avoidance/acceptance 338–9, 362
undergraduate business degrees 266–7
understanding, knowledge, skills,
    attitudes and behaviours (UKSAB) 440
unified model 74–5
Unilever 204, 313–15, 356, 377, 379, 384
unitarist model 61
United States 358, 359
  competency frameworks 113
  cross-cultural management development
    335, 350–4
  evaluation of management development 417
  international management 383
  management education (Med) 266
  Master's in Business Administration 270, 275,
    276, 282
  Navy Seals 469
  strategic management 75
universalistic set of principles 6

university sector 285–6, 343, 344, 481
  see also corporate universities
unstructured informal learning 184
upside down thinking 251
upward appraisal 125
upward communication 337

vacancy filling 308
validation 421–2
validity 439
values 85
vertical/horizontal slicing 401
vignettes as learning aid 244
Virgin Holidays 326
virtual management 458
visual aids 242
vocationalism 261–3
Vodafone 326

Wellcome Pharmaceuticals 310
Whitehall game 134
'whole person' 10
  capabilities 468
wisdom 42–3, 464
wordly mindset 38
work projects 311
work redesign 311
workhorses 319
written work 133

Xerox Learning Centre 352